155.4
Hug
catpb.

PAVING
PATHWAYS

Child and Adolescent Development

D0565784

LAUREL HUGHES

University of Portland

AMADOR COUNTY LIBRARY
530 SUTTER STREET
JACKSON, CA 95642

WADSWORTH

™

THOMSON LEARNING

Australia • Canada • Mexico • Singapore • Spain
United Kingdom • United States

WADSWORTH
THOMSON LEARNING

Psychology Publisher: Edith Beard Brady
Development Editor: Sherry Symington
Assistant Editor: Rebecca Heider
Editorial Assistant: Maritess Tse
Marketing Manager: Joanne Terhaar, Kandis Malter
Marketing Assistant: Megan Hansen
Project Manager, Editorial Production: Teri Hyde
Print/Media Buyer: Robert King
Permissions Editor: Joohee Lee
Production Service: Ruth Cottrell

Text Designer: Liz Harasymczuk
Photo Researcher: Roberta Broyer
Copy Editor: Kevin Gleason
Illustrator: G&S Typesetters, Inc.
Cover Designer: Liz Harasymczuk
Cover Image: Michele Westmorland/Stone
Cover Printer: R.R. Donnelley, Willard
Compositor: G&S Typesetters, Inc.
Printer: R.R. Donnelley, Willard

COPYRIGHT © 2002 Wadsworth Group. Wadsworth is an imprint of the Wadsworth Group, a division of Thomson Learning, Inc. Thomson Learning™ is a trademark used herein under license.

ALL RIGHTS RESERVED. No part of this work covered by the copyright hereon may be reproduced or used in any form or by any means—graphic, electronic, or mechanical, including photocopying, recording, taping, Web distribution, or information storage and retrieval systems—without the written permission of the publisher.

Printed in the United States of America
1 2 3 4 5 6 7 05 04 03 02 01

For permission to use material from this text, contact us by
Web: http://www.thomsonrights.com
Fax: 1-800-730-2215
Phone: 1-800-730-2214

ExamView® and *ExamView Pro®* are registered trademarks of FSCreations, Inc. Windows is a registered trademark of the Microsoft Corporation used herein under license. Macintosh and Power Macintosh are registered trademarks of Apple Computer, Inc. Used herein under license.

Library of Congress Cataloging-in-Publication Data
Hughes, Laurel
  Paving pathways : child and adolescent development / Laurel Hughes.
    p. cm.
  Includes bibliographical references and indexes.
  ISBN 0-534-34809-2
    1. Child psychology.   2. Child development.   3. Adolescent psychology.   4. Adolescence.
  I. Title.

BF721.H696 2001
155.4—dc21   2001045414

Wadsworth/Thomson Learning
10 Davis Drive
Belmont, CA 94002-3098
USA

For more information about our products, contact us:
Thomson Learning Academic Resource Center
1-800-423-0563
http://www.wadsworth.com

International Headquarters
Thomson Learning
International Division
290 Harbor Drive, 2nd Floor
Stamford, CT 06902-7477
USA

UK/Europe/Middle East/South Africa
Thomson Learning
Berkshire House
168-173 High Holborn
London WC1V 7AA
United Kingdom

Asia
Thomson Learning
60 Albert Street, #15-01
Albert Complex
Singapore 189969

Canada
Nelson Thomson Learning
1120 Birchmount Road
Toronto, Ontario M1K 5G4
Canada

For Frank, Ben, and Bridie

About the Author

Laurel Hughes is a licensed psychologist in Beaverton, Oregon, who has special interests in child development and personal growth and adjustment. She has published a textbook on personal growth and adjustment and books on parenting for the popular audience. In addition to raising Frank, Ben, and Bridie, her experiences with children include child therapy, foster parenting, teaching Sunday school, and parent helping at the local grade school. Most recently having taught at the University of Portland, she is now an "empty nester" and is taking a hiatus from university life to pursue writing and her interest in disaster mental health. As an assistant officer with the American Red Cross, she provides disaster mental health instruction for other mental health professionals and also helps meet mental health needs at disaster sites across the country.

Contents

PART 1 **BEGINNING POINTS**

Chapter 1   Beginning Points of Theory   1

The Birth of Developmental Psychology   3

Controversies and Cornerstones of Developmental Study   4

  Constancy versus Change   4

  Quantitative versus Qualitative Change   5

  Continuity versus Discontinuity   5

  Of Bent Twigs and Fallen Fruit: The Nature versus Nurture Controversy   6

  Developmentally Universal versus Culturally Relative   9

  Single Causes versus Multiple Causes   12

  Study Thoughts or Study Behaviors?   13

Physical Development (Chapters 5, 8, 11, and 14)   15

Cognitive Development (Chapters 6, 9, 12, and 15)   16

  Contributions of Jean Piaget   17

  The Sociocultural Approach of Lev Vygotsky   18

  The Information-Processing Approach   18

  Intelligence   19

  Learning Theories and Development   20

Social and Emotional Development (Chapters 7, 10, 13, and 16)   23

  Sigmund Freud's Theory of Psychosexual Development   24

  Erik Erikson's Theory of Psychosocial Development   25

Summary   26

Key Terms   28

Concept Review   28

Resources for Further Reading   30

Chapter 2   Studying Child Development   32

Scientific Method and Experimental Design   34

  Controlling for the Effects of History   36

  Promoting Generalizability   36

  Enhancing Objectivity   38

  Capitalizing on Standardization   39

  Avoiding Placebo Effects   39

  Accounting for Intervention Effects   40

  The Final Product   40

  Statistical Analysis   41

Measurement Issues in Studying Child Development   42
    Cross-Sectional Designs   44
    Longitudinal Designs   45
    Time-Lag Designs   45
    Sequential Designs   46
Additional Resources for Experimental Variables   47
Ethics and Studying Child Development   49
    Protection from Harm   50
    Informed Consent   51
    The Right to the Truth   52
    The Right to Privacy   52
Alternative Experimental Designs   52
    Correlational Designs   53
    Designs Measuring Single Participants   54
Reporting Research Findings   55
Conclusion   55
BOX 2.1 From Research to Application   56
Summary   58
Key Terms   59
Concept Review   59
Resources for Further Reading   61

Chapter 3   Biological Beginning Points   63
Evolutionary Beginnings   64
Genes and Genetics   66
Sex Cells   68
Chromosomal Anomalies and Development   70
    Down's Syndrome   70
    X and Y Chromosomes   71
Genetically Influenced Attributes and Conditions   72
    Physical Appearance   72
    Temperament   73
BOX 3.1 Tried . . . . : Children and shyness   76
BOX 3.2 . . . . and True: Helping children overcome shyness   77
    Intelligence   79
    Psychological Disorders   80
How Much Nature and How Much Nurture?   81
Genetic Engineering   82
Genetic Counseling   83
    Early Testing Procedures   85
    Paving Pathways: Reproductive Options   86
Summary   88
Key Terms   90
Concept Review   90
Resources for Further Reading   92

Chapter 4   Entering the World   94

Prenatal Stages of Development   95
  The Germinal Stage   96
  The Embryonic Stage   97
  The Fetal Stage   98
The Prenatal Environment   100
  Maternal Factors   100
  Teratogens   102
  The Father's Contributions   107
  Conclusion   108
The Birth Process   108
Paving Pathways: Birthing Alternatives   109
The Newborn   111
Neonate Complications   111
  Insufficient Oxygen   112
  Low Birth Weight   112
  Premature Birth   112
BOX 4.1 Tried . . . . : Newborn rooming-in and parenting adequacy   114
BOX 4.2 . . . . and True: Parenting readiness and parental education   115
  Paving Pathways: Early Bonding   116
Summary   117
Key Terms   119
Concept Review   119
Resources for Further Reading   121

PART 2   **INFANCY AND TODDLERHOOD**

Chapter 5   Infant and Toddler Physical Development   123

Body Growth   125
  Height and Weight   125
  Gender Differences   126
Brain Development   127
  Neurons   127
  Brain Structures   128
Conscious States   130
  Sudden Infant Death Syndrome   131
Infant Nutrition   131
  Paving Pathways: Breast or Bottle?   133
  Undernourishment   134
  Obesity   135
Motor Development   135
  Theories of Motor Development   135
  Gross Motor Skills   137
  Fine Motor Skills   137
  Bowel and Bladder Control   138

Sensory/Perceptual Development   139
    Vision   139
    Hearing   142
    Taste   142
    Smell   143
    Touch   143
BOX 5.1 Tried . . . . : Taste and calming fussy babies   144
BOX 5.2 . . . . and True: What to do when baby cries   145
    Integrating Sensory Information   146
    The Role of Infant Stimulation   146
    Paving Pathways: Providing a Stimulating Infant Environment   148
Possible Signs of Developmental Difficulties   150
Summary   151
Key Terms   153
Concept Review   153
Resources for Further Reading   155

Chapter 6   Infant and Toddler Cognitive Development   157
Piaget's Sensorimotor Intelligence   158
    Substage 1: Reflexes   159
    Substage 2: Primary Circular Reactions   160
    Substage 3: Secondary Circular Reactions   160
    Substage 4: Coordination of Secondary Circular Reactions   160
    Substage 5: Tertiary Circular Reactions   162
    Substage 6: Mental Representation   162
    Conclusion   163
Information-Processing   163
Evidence of Infant Learning   164
    Classical Conditioning   165
    Operant Conditioning   165
    Imitation   165
Intelligence   167
    Intelligence Testing   167
    Predicting Individual Differences   169
    Paving Pathways: Supporting Intellectual Growth   170
BOX 6.1 Tried . . . . : Early experience and brain development   172
BOX 6.2 . . . . and True: The optimal infant brain development environment   173
Language and Communication   174
    Theories of Language Development   174
    Acquiring Language   176
    Paving Pathways: Enhancing Language Development   178
Summary   179
Key Terms   181
Concept Review   181
Resources for Further Reading   183

Chapter 7   Infant and Toddler Social and Emotional Development   185

Early Personality Development   187
  Contributions of Sigmund Freud   187
  Erik Erikson and Psychosocial Development   188
Infant Attachment Theory   189
  Importance of Infant Attachment   189
BOX 7.1 Tried . . . . : Infant bonding and adjustment   190
BOX 7.2 . . . . and True: Infant feeding 191
  The Securely Attached Relationship   192
  Measuring Infant Attachment   193
  Fathers as Attachment Figures   194
  Attachments with Nonparental Caregivers   196
  Infant Day Care Influences   197
  Paving Pathways: Choosing Infant Day Care   198
  Separation Anxiety   200
  Conditions Influencing Attachment   200
  Outcome of Secure Attachment   201
Infant Emotions   201
  Infant Emotional States   202
  Infant Crying and Emotional Development   203
  Recognizing and Responding to Others' Emotions   204
Self-Conceptualization   205
  Separation-Individuation   205
  Transitional Objects   206
  Self-Concept   207
  Paving Pathways: Developing Infant Competence   207
  "Others" Concept   209
  Self-Control   210
Summary   210
Key Terms   212
Concept Review   212
Resources for Further Reading   214

PART 3   EARLY CHILDHOOD
Chapter 8   Early Childhood Physical Development   216

Body Growth and Change   218
Brain Development   219
  Hemispheric Specialization   219
  Handedness   220
  Perceptual Advances   221
  Paving Pathways: Supporting the Growing Brain   221
Motor Development   224
  Gross Motor Skills   224
  Fine Motor Skills   225
  Early Drawings   225

Early Childhood Health Needs   226
    Sleep   226
    Nutrition   228
    Eating Habits and Preschoolers   229
    Paving Pathways: Eating Safety   230
    Paving Pathways: Fostering Eating Compliance   231
    Paving Pathways: Encouraging Independent Healthy Eating Habits   232
Health Problems   233
    Illness   233
    Environmental Exposures   234
    Excessive Stress and/or Lack of Affection   235
BOX 8.1 Tried . . . . : **Preventing injury to preschoolers   236**
BOX 8.2 . . . . and True: **Child care provider safety tips   237**
    Accidents and Injuries   238
    Child Maltreatment   238
Summary   241
Key Terms   243
Concept Review   243
Resources for Further Reading   245

Chapter 9   Early Childhood Cognitive Development   246
Piaget's Preoperational Thought   248
    The Symbolic Function Substage   248
    The Intuitive Thought Substage   249
    Limitations of Preoperational Thought   249
Vygotsky's Sociocultural Theory   254
Information-Processing   255
    Attention   255
    Memory   256
BOX 9.1 Tried . . . . : **The effect of suggestions on children's memories   258**
BOX 9.2 . . . . and True: **Avoiding false reports from preschoolers   259**
    Theory of Mind   260
Intelligence   262
    Individual Differences in Intelligence   262
    Emotional Intelligence   265
    Paving Pathways: Evaluating Preschool/Day Care Programs   266
    Paving Pathways: Television as an Educational Tool 269
    Language Development   271
    Vocabulary   271
    Grammar   273
    Conversation   273
Summary   274
Key Terms   276
Concept Review   276
Resources for Further Reading   278

Chapter 10   Early Childhood Social and Emotional Development   280

Personality Development   281
  Psychodynamic Influences   281
  Gender Identity and Gender Roles   283
Relationships   285
  Birth Order   285
  Culture   289
  Relationship with Mother   289
  Relationship with Father   291
  Relationships with Peers   292
  Paving Pathways: Parenting Considerations   293
Emotions and the Young Child   300
Anger and Aggression   300
Childhood Fears   301
BOX 10.1 Tried . . . . : Modeling and aggressive behavior   302
BOX 10.2 . . . . and True: How to minimize the effects of aggressive role models   303
Moral Development   304
Self-Concept and Self-Esteem   306
  Paving Pathways: Raising a Child with a High "EQ"   307
Summary   309
Key Terms   311
Concept Review   311
Resources for Further Reading   313

PART 4   MIDDLE CHILDHOOD

Chapter 11   Middle Childhood Physical Development   315

Body Growth   316
Brain Growth   318
Motor Development   318
  Gender Differences   320
  Organized Play   320
  Rough-and-Tumble Play   321
BOX 11.1 Tried . . . . : Mastery versus performance motivational climates   322
BOX 11.2 . . . . and True: How to motivate an underachiever   323
  Paving Pathways: Physical Education   324
Middle Childhood and Health   326
  Nutrition   327
  Paving Pathways: Helping Obese Children   329
  Stress and Coping   331
  Television and Children's Health 334
  Paving Pathways: Reducing Time with the Television   335
Summary   336
Key Terms   337
Concept Review   338
Resources for Further Reading   339

Chapter 12   Middle Childhood Cognitive Development   341

Piaget's Concrete Operations   342
Information-Processing   344
    Attention   344
    Memory   345
Intelligence, Learning, and Special Needs   346
    Intelligence   346
    Learning and Achieving   348
    Children with Disabilities   352
BOX 12.1 Tried . . . . : Parents' behavior and development of a mastery achievement style   354
BOX 12.2 . . . . and True: Encouraging healthy achievement traits   355
    Intellectually Gifted Children   360
    Creatively Gifted Children   362
    Paving Pathways: Fostering Creative Intelligence 364
    Home Schooling   365
    Paving Pathways: Should I Home School My Child?   367
    Children and Computers   368
    Paving Pathways: Choosing Software for Children   371
    Paving Pathways: Structuring Children's Internet Use   372
Language   373
    Vocabulary   373
    Grammar   374
    Reading and Writing   374
    Bilingualism   374
Summary   376
Key Terms   377
Concept Review   378
Resources for Further Reading   380

Chapter 13   Middle Childhood Social and Emotional Development   382

Personality Development   383
    Psychodynamic Influences   384
    Culturally Based Skill Building   384
    Competence   386
Relationships   387
    Relationships with Parents   387
    Family Constellations   388
    Paving Pathways: Easing the Effects of Divorce on Children   390
    Relationships with Peers   392
    Child Sexual Abuse   392
    Paving Pathways: Preventing Sexual Abuse   393
Emotions and Middle Childhood   394
    Normal Emotionality   395
    Excessive Emotional States   395

BOX 13.1 Tried . . . . : Negative emotions and social status   396
BOX 13.2 . . . . and True: Cognitive therapy for school-age children   397
    Paving Pathways: Helping the Anxious Child   400
    Paving Pathways: Helping the Depressed Child   401
    Paving Pathways: Helping the Acting-Out Child   402
Moral Development   403
Self-Concept and Self-Esteem   406
    Self-Concept   407
    Self-Esteem   407
    Paving Pathways: Encouraging Good Self-Esteem   408
Summary   410
Key Terms   412
Concept Review   412
Resources for Further Reading   414

PART 5   ADOLESCENCE

Chapter 14   Adolescent Physical Development   416

Body Growth   418
    Puberty   419
    Effects of Puberty   420
Brain Growth   422
Motor Development   423
Risk-Taking Behavior   423
    Paving Pathways: Reducing Risk-Taking Behavior   424
Sexuality   425
    Sexual Attitudes and Behaviors   425
    Pregnancy   427
    Life as a Teenage Parent   429
    Paving Pathways: Arranging Home Lives of Teenage Parents   430
    Sexually Transmitted Diseases   431
BOX 14.1 Tried . . . . : Abstinence versus safer-sex HIV-risk interventions   432
BOX 14.2 . . . . and True: Factors likely to promote safer sex practices
    among adolescents   433
    Date Rape   434
    Paving Pathways: Preventing Date Rape   435
Health Issues   435
    Sleep   436
    Nutrition   436
    Eating Disorders   437
    Paving Pathways: Preventing Eating Disorders   440
    Smoking   440
    Drug Use and Abuse   441
    Paving Pathways: Treating and Preventing Drug Abuse   443
Summary   446
Key Terms   448
Concept Review   448
Resources for Further Reading   451

Chapter 15   Adolescent Cognitive Development   452

Piaget's Formal Operational Reasoning   453
  Hypothetical, Scientific, and Deductive Reasoning   454
  Paving Pathways: Fostering Formal Operations   456
  Egocentrism during Adolescence   456
  The Fleeting Nature of Formal Operational Reasoning   458
  Adolescent Decision-Making   460
  Paving Pathways: Teaching Decision-Making to Adolescents   461
Information-Processing   465
Learning During Adolescence   467
  Secondary Schools   468
  Individual Academic Abilities   469
  Parental Effects on Learning   473
BOX 15.1 Tried . . . . : Learning disabilities and adolescent suicide   474
BOX 15.2 . . . . and True: Supporting learning disabled adolescents   475
  Peer Effects on Learning   476
  Extracurricular Activities   477
  Part-Time Jobs   478
  Paving Pathways: Helping Adolescents Succeed Academically   480
Career Development   483
  Transitioning from School to Work   484
  Choosing a Career   486
Summary   487
Key Terms   489
Concept Review   489
Resources for Further Reading   491

Chapter 16   Adolescent Social and Emotional Development   493

Personality Development   494
  Psychodynamic Influences   495
  Erikson and the Search for Identity   495
  Gender and Identity Formation   498
  Ethnicity and Identity Formation   500
Relationships   500
  Relationships with Parents   501
  Paving Pathways: Parenting and Teenagers   503
  Relationships with Peers   505
Emotions   508
  Emotional Regulation   508
  Depression and Suicide   509
BOX 16.1 Tried . . . . : The relationship between negative events and unhappiness   510
BOX 16.2 . . . . and True: Helping adolescents manage stressful social situations   511

Development of Morals and Values   515
Juvenile Delinquency   516
 Development of Juvenile Delinquency   517
 Controversy Regarding Development of Juvenile Delinquency   518
 Paving Pathways: Preventing and Intervening in Juvenile Delinquency   520
Self-Esteem   522
Rites of Passage   523
 Characteristics of Rites of Passages   524
 Problems Evolving from the Absence of Rites of Passage   525
 New Passages   525
 Paving Pathways: Creating Rites of Passage   526
 Transitioning to Passages of Adulthood   527
Summary   527
Key Terms   530
Concept Review   530
Resources for Further Reading   533

Glossary   534
Name Index   541
Subject Index   550

Preface

Welcome to the renaissance! Western cultures are showing a renewed interest in our children as the new millennium begins, refocusing themselves on a reality that less complex societies may never have disregarded: Our children are our future. Understanding and nurturing their developmental needs not only enhances their progress from conception through adolescence, but also paves pathways for the progress of humankind. This textbook is offered in the spirit of those efforts heralding in an era of growing enlightenment.

One of the beacons illuminating the need for a change in course has been the growing body of child development research. Over the last couple of decades the number of studies investigating child development has multiplied exponentially. As with any massive scattering of informational bits and pieces, trying to make sense of it all is a major undertaking—even for the scientists who gather the data! The informed consumer of developmental research needs to know where all these findings are coming from: sound empirical evidence, individual biases, or simply folklore. And how are consumers to interpret scientific findings in the face of experimental idiosyncrasies, diverse theories offered in explanation, and both supportive and conflicting alternative findings? Most important, to truly make a difference in the progress of humankind, the consumer must also be able to find ways of applying seemingly detached, "ivory tower" findings to the real world.

This textbook is most concerned with meeting the needs of those who will interact with children—as parents, educators, child care workers, and health service providers. Rather than being organized around the needs of the future Ph.D., it considers that some readers may not yet have any background in psychology, or have had so little exposure to the basics that review of main concepts is essential. It provides an empirically solid, broad, eclectic background in developmental theory and research, but the lion's share of elaboration is assigned to applications. Critical analysis of research and theory is not ignored, but it appears mainly in a form that emphasizes its relevance to application—thus bringing it closer to home. This greater emphasis on fostering considerations of practical and emotional intelligence in a text is sometimes referred to as "dumbing down," but in view of today's broader understanding of what intelligence and knowledge are all about, such an approach is no more "dumbing down" than is emphasizing analytical intelligence at the cost of practical and emotional intelligence. Emphases, as always, are a function of the educational goals.

How might a textbook portray developmental research in a manner that facilitates retention and applicational goals? First, the material should emphasize and encourage its integration into the reader's general knowledge base, rather than be chewed then spewed over the course of a semester. Second, given that information representing a graduate degree in psychology has a half-life of only about ten years, readers need to be shown how to evaluate and integrate the new information they will inevitably be encountering for the rest of their lives. Finally, the reader needs to become acclimated to an orientation of prudently applying whatever developmental research seems to be telling us.

People are more likely to integrate and retain information if it is presented in a way that lets them relate to it personally. The writing style of this textbook thus aims to be personal. It tends to be conversational, occasionally taking license with shifts to first- and second-person narrative. I share examples of personal encounters with the phenomena I describe, and at times encourage readers to consider how material might be consistent with their own observations or experiences. When possible, the writing style attempts to mirror or anticipate the reader's thought processes; for example, paragraphs occasionally begin with questions likely to arise from the preceding material. Features aimed at increasing retention include introductory questions at the beginning of each chapter that reappear alongside relevant parts of the text, and chapter summaries and practice tests at the end of the chapters.

Because the reader is not likely to achieve personal organization and integration of material if the textbook presentation itself appears to be a disjointed collection of factoids, I made it my priority to create an integrated work. This is not an easy task for a chronologically oriented book, and is only made the more difficult by a field that is notorious for its diversity of theory. While I believe that organizing material by age level is the best means of integrating material and highlighting its practical applicability, such an organization requires visiting and revisiting specific theoretical concepts as they differentially pertain to specific age groups. Meeting this necessity creates unnatural breaks in discussion that can impede the reader's ability to create a cohesive, integrated mental picture. To address this challenge Chapter 1 introduces the main recurring theories and concepts, then describes the consistent order of presentation that subsequent chapters follow, representing in turn the physical, cognitive, and social and emotional developmental data for the successive age groups. To further encourage cohesiveness, recurring sections often begin by refreshing the reader's memory as to where we left off at the previous age level.

Rather than being splintered off into the side boxes and addenda characterizing textbooks of the previous millennium, issues of culture are incorporated directly into the main text where relevant, and so also are issues pertaining to gender. Readers typically do not treat side box material as if it is part of the whole, and in a book emphasizing integration and application, this topic is too important to be isolated as a curiosity. For those who wish to make maximum use of the cultural perspective, a margin graphic indicates where culture is mentioned.

Appearing throughout the text are two special features that have been developed with an eye to highlighting application:

▶ The Tried . . . . and True feature is designed to help readers understand how to read, evaluate, and apply research-oriented journal articles. Following a consistent outline that is introduced in Chapter 2, this feature first describes a specific study and then develops the practical applications that the study explicitly or implicitly endorses.

▶ Substantive applications of research findings are also highlighted by the "Paving Pathways" feature, which screens relevant presentations within the main text.

Students are more likely to actually read their textbook if they find it to be enjoyable. The writing style I selected hopefully not only meets this end but also helps students feel at home with developmental data, enough so that their knowledge bases and confidence levels encourage them to pave pathways on their own.

A package of supplemental materials has been developed for *Paving Pathways,* designed to meet the needs of students and instructors alike:

STUDENT RESOURCES

▶ Accompanying each copy of *Paving Pathways* is a **Practice Test Booklet** that contains quizzes of 10 multiple-choice questions per chapter. These quizzes are intended to help students review material and prepare for tests. Answers are listed in a key at the end so that students can check their work.

▶ The **Child and Adolescent Development CD-ROM** is a multimedia learning tool that uses video, simulations, quizzing, and the Internet to illustrate the connections between theory and practice.

▶ Students can access additional resources through the **Wadsworth Psychology Resource Center** at *http://psychology.wadsworth.com.* This Web site includes links to guide students to child development resources on the Web.

▶ A four-month subscription to **InfoTrac College Edition** is included with every new copy of the book, giving students access to the latest news and research articles online. Easily searchable by keywords, this resource will help students research topics for papers and give them exposure to the kinds of articles and abstracts that are characteristic of the profession.

INSTRUCTOR RESOURCES

▶ The comprehensive **Instructor's Manual**, written by Randall Osborne, is closely tied to the textbook, providing chapter outlines, lecture ideas, Info-Trac College Edition keywords, video recommendations, discussion questions, student activities, and transparency masters. New and veteran instructors alike will find this manual to be a rich teaching resource, filled with a variety of ideas for effective teaching of child development.

▶ The **Test Bank** contains 100 test items per chapter: 75 multiple-choice and 25 essay questions. Multiple-choice answers are marked and designated with the main text page number reference, level of difficulty, and the type of knowledge assessed. Essay questions have main text page number references where the answer can be found. The Test Bank questions are also available in electronic version through **ExamView** computerized testing. This CD-ROM allows instructors to create customized tests by selecting and modifying the test questions from the test bank, as well as inserting their own questions.

▶ The **Multimedia Manager for Developmental Psychology** is a CD-ROM containing Power Point lecture presentations specifically tied to the text. Lectures are illustrated with graphics from the text, as well as video clips.

▶ Three **CNN Today Videos** are available for Developmental Psychology. Each video includes approximately 45 minutes of segments from CNN news coverage of stories related to child development topics.

ACKNOWLEDGMENTS

At a recent Academy Awards presentation, one recipient spared the audience from substantial yawning by announcing that he would thank all those who contributed to his episode of success privately, rather than broadcasting individual appreciations. I had hoped to follow his lead, but so many people, many of whom I have never met or spoken with, have contributed to the completion of this project that I have resigned myself to the usual preface fare. I would of course like to thank my family—including all those rotating in and out of Hughes Emancipation West—for their ongoing support during the course of this project. I thank those who shared or helped me ferret out examples of the phenomena this book describes: Brynne and Annie Chamberlain; Aaron Hudson; Frank, Ben, Bridie, and Bill Hughes; and Joan McIlroy. I am especially indebted to my fellow disaster work colleagues, who steadfastly provided support and encouragement in spite of their bewilderment over why I would want to write textbooks—matched only by the bewilderment of my publishing colleagues over why I would purposely go to disaster areas.

I would like to thank Jim Brace-Thompson for giving this project its wings and scouting out its potential destinations, and Vicki Knight and Jim Strandberg for later support and direction. Ruth Cottrell deserves special thanks for going above and beyond the call of duty as we accommodated the various twists and turns emerging along the production path. Thanks also go, in alphabetical order, to other publishing colleagues who played a role in the final product: Edith Beard Brady, Bobbie Broyer, Kevin Gleason, Megan Hansen, Liz Harasymczuk, Rebecca Heider, Teri Hyde, Robert King, Leslie Krongold, Joohee Lee, Marc Linsenman, Tami Strang, Sherry Symington, and Maritess Tse. Thanks also to those who reviewed portions of the manuscript: Alice S.

Alexander, Old Dominion University; Martha Arterberry, Gettyburg College; Beth Barton, Coastal Carolina Community College; Ronda J. Carpenter, Roanoke College; Brad Caskey, University of Wisconsin—River Falls; Edward Dana, Chapman University; Sandra A. Enders, San Antonio College; JoAnn M. Farver, University of Southern California; Thomas Gerry, Columbia-Greene Community College; Lisa Grinde, Beloit College; Barbara Myers, Virginia Commonwealth University; Ethan Remmel, San Francisco State University; Julia Rux, Georgia Perimeter College; Debra Schwiesow, Creighton University; Valerie Sims, University of Central Florida; Carolyn Spies, Bloomfield College; Tracy Thorndike-Christ, Western Washington University; Robert M. Voytas, Kutztown University of Pennsylvania; Anne C. Watson, West Virginia University; and Guy Wylie, Western Nebraska Community College.

CHAPTER 1

Beginning Points of Theory

FOCUS QUESTIONS

▶ How did the concept of developmental psychology begin?

▶ What are the cornerstones of current child development theory?

▶ How are a child's characteristics likely to change over time?

▶ Is child development a continually flowing process, or does it jump from level to level?

▶ What roles do nature and nurture play in child development?

▶ How does a child's culture of origin affect development?

▶ How do relevant influences individually or in combination affect a child's developmental outcome?

▶ What do we investigate if we want to see evidence of child growth?

▶ What are the historical contributions to the fields of child physical, cognitive, and social and emotional development, and how do they continue to be relevant today?

OUTLINE

The Birth of Developmental Psychology
Controversies and Cornerstones of Developmental Study
    Constancy versus Change
    Quantitative versus Qualitative Change
    Continuity versus Discontinuity
    Of Bent Twigs and Fallen Fruit: The Nature versus Nurture
      Controversy
    Developmentally Universal versus Culturally Relative
    Single Causes versus Multiple Causes
    Study Thoughts or Study Behaviors?
Physical Development (Chapters 5, 8, 11, and 14)

Cognitive Development (Chapters 6, 9, 12, and 15)
    Contributions of Jean Piaget
    The Sociocultural Approach of Lev Vygotsky
    The Information-Processing Approach
    Intelligence
    Learning Theories and Development
Social and Emotional Development (Chapters 7, 10, 13, and 16)
    Sigmund Freud's Theory of Psychosexual Development
    Erik Erikson's Theory of Psychosocial Development

Willie and Suzie were playing "store" in their playhouse. Willie wanted their business to sell cars; Suzie wanted to sell pets. They could not come to an agreement. Finally, Willie said they should be selling cars because of psychology. Suzie thought about it for a while, then asked Willie, "What's psychology?"

Willie drew himself up proudly and said, "That's when you're right and it's too hard to 'splain."

Those of us who traverse the field of child psychology are occasionally inclined to agree with Willie. The terrain is vast and the vistas varied. The paths of understanding we pursue are lined with diverse and conflicting theories and philosophies. Yet when we stand back to appreciate the beauty as the testimonies of varying perspectives converge within a simple display of a child's novel commentary or newfound ability, the only words that seem to explain the experience may be, "It's just psychology!"

The field of developmental psychology constantly reestablishes itself as it explores the question, "Where did we come from?" As researchers channel their energies toward seeking out answers, the nature of the question is continually changing. No one perspective or theory has succeeded in explaining everything that makes us who we are. Many circumstances contribute to who we become, including our experiences, our physical makeup, the culture within which we were born, and even whether we spent our growing years in a small town or a big city.

The pursuit of understanding human development has taken a number of twists and turns as researchers zero in on phenomena that seem most likely to reveal answers. As a working definition, **developmental psychology** can be viewed as the study of how individuals change or remain the same over time, and how various factors relate to continuity and change. Childhood certainly provides the most evidence that we learn and change over time, yet we continue to learn and discover differences about ourselves during adulthood as well. Thus more pertinent questions might be, "Where are we coming from, and where are we heading?" The study of child development answers many questions about how individuals get started on their developmental adventures, as well as helping with predictions and understandings of the directions their current and future development might take. Most importantly, it provides guidance for what we can do—as parents, educators, child care professionals, and health service providers—to smooth out the terrain that children are likely to encounter.

How did the concept of developmental psychology begin?

THE BIRTH OF DEVELOPMENTAL PSYCHOLOGY

The concept of developmental psychology is relatively new. For many centuries, scientists believed that we existed as miniature adults from the moment of our creation. They thought the man's sperm or the woman's ovum contained a tiny, fully formed human figure that would simply expand in size between conception and adulthood. Because of this belief in **preformationism** children were thought to be essentially the same as adults, able to reason and learn tasks in the same manner as do adults. Philosophers ancient and modern, from Plato to

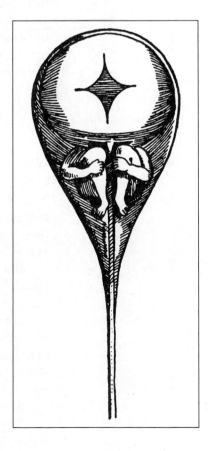

FIGURE 1.1

Preformationism. Early thinkers believed that we begin as tiny, completely formed figures within an egg or sperm, the only developmental change being an increase in size. Source, J. Needham, *A History of Embryology*, Second Edition. Copyright © 1959 Cambridge University Press. Reprinted with permission.

Descartes, proposed that even our ideas came prepackaged within our psyches, just waiting for a chance to emerge and be expressed.

The notion of preformationism fell from grace during the second half of the eighteenth century, when the newly introduced microscope failed to reveal any tiny human figures within sperm or ova. In addition, scientists were now able to observe that embryos pass through stages during which they show little if any resemblance to an adult human being. Scientists had little choice but to recognize children as developmentally different from adults—a recognition marking the birth of developmental psychology as a science.

CONTROVERSIES AND CORNERSTONES OF DEVELOPMENTAL STUDY

What are the cornerstones of current child development theory?

Acceptance of the idea that children are not fully developed at birth brought along a whole new set of questions. What will change, how will it change, when will it change, and what causes change? Many perspectives have emerged to influence how researchers answer these questions as they evaluate their developmental data. In fact, researchers' personal biases of perspective toward many philosophical dichotomies partly determine how they design their studies and interpret their findings in child research. These interpretations in turn determine how they go about applying their findings to childrearing practice and understanding each human's developmental beginnings. The following discussion introduces several dichotomies of perspective that we will revisit many times as we explore the field of child development.

Constancy versus Change

How are a child's characteristics likely to change over time?

If we are developmentally different at different ages, just how different are we? While our physical features may change as we grow, we also maintain a number of physical characteristics throughout our lives, such as our basic coloring and body build. Certain personality characteristics can also last a lifetime. When alumni attend their high school reunions they frequently run into individuals they have not seen in years, and make remarks such as "You're the same old Harry!" or "Jennifer hasn't changed a bit."

But just as Harry and Jennifer appear to have been left untouched by the ravages of time, there are others who change substantially between high school and later adulthood. The class loner may have evolved into a sophisticated social climber. The boy who spent much of his school career being sent to the principal's office may have become a principal himself. The former class president may not even attend the reunion because of a previous commitment at the state penitentiary. The students who underachieved during high school may have returned to higher education later in adulthood and achieved well enough to move on through graduate and professional schools.

The presence of both constancy and change is especially noticeable as we watch the rapid development characterizing infancy and childhood. Many parents comment that they see changes in their infants daily, and upon being reunited after a separation of a week or more may feel as if they are looking at a completely different child. Parents and educators alike are often amazed by changes in children's learning abilities as they progress through school. Yet in spite of ongoing, obvious changes, children still seem like the same people, having traits and mannerisms similar to those they may have demonstrated since birth.

Research often reflects the presence of both constancy and change. For example, toddlers demonstrate more and more evidence of being able to effortfully control their behavior as they approach age 3—an indication of change. Yet those children who have the greater ability for self-control as toddlers also have a greater ability as 3-year-olds—an indication of constancy (Kochanska et al., 2000). One of the tasks taken on by the study of child development is sorting out this apparent contradiction in observations (Brim & Kagan, 1980; Lerner & Tubman, 1989). Exactly which characteristics can be expected to change during the course of childhood and which characteristics will probably remain similar throughout the life span?

Quantitative versus Qualitative Change

What constitutes change? The advances we observe in children as they develop are both quantitative and qualitative. **Quantitative change** is numerically measurable change. It involves factors such as size, number, speed, and frequency of a particular ability or characteristic. For example, a child's specific musculature is present at birth, and these same muscles become larger and stronger as the child grows. **Qualitative change** involves modification of preexisting characteristics that are unrelated to quantity, such as the growth of immature reproductive structures into functional adult forms or the development of a more sophisticated reasoning strategy.

Often, both quantitative and qualitative factors apply to the changes we notice. For example, we typically observe that adolescents' memory capacity is greater than it had been during the elementary school years. Such improvement may occur because adolescents continue to use memory strategies learned in elementary school, but now apply them more often or can process them much more quickly. These are quantitative advancements. On the other hand the adolescent's advancing cognitive ability also results in the possibility of learning and applying entirely new, more advanced methods of memory enhancement than had been possible as a younger child. These represent qualitative change.

Continuity versus Discontinuity

Is child development a continually flowing process, or does it jump from level to level?

Do these quantitative and qualitative changes in children's abilities and characteristics occur in distinct steps or by continuous, gradual evolution? Many researchers believe development is a continuous process. They view change as occurring gradually and relatively seamlessly, like a river steadily flowing around, over, and within the obstacles defining its changing boundaries. Other researchers believe that development is discontinuous. From their perspective they note identifiable beginnings and endings to stages or qualitatively differing, age-related states during child development, similar to the abrupt changes in perspective a rock climber might enjoy when stopping to view the terrain from progressively higher plateaus (Case, 1992; Commons et al., 1998; Rutter, 1987).

Those who study physical development are especially likely to appreciate the perspective of discontinuity. There are definite beginning points for many forms of physical maturation, such as when an adolescent first has the ability to reproduce or when a child's coordination and muscle development have progressed sufficiently for the child to be able to pedal a tricycle. Some cognitive theorists such as Jean Piaget have noted beginnings and endings of certain types of reasoning as children develop, and have consequently formulated a "stage theory" approach to the study of child cognition. However, other cognitive theorists look more to changes in specific processes underlying reasoning abilities. Although children develop more advanced systems of information processing as they grow older, they do not necessarily stop using their earlier-developed skills. Thus cognitive skills can also be viewed as continuously expanding and becoming more refined, rather than shifting from one style to another.

Most developmental theorists agree that growth can be both continuous and discontinuous. But how they go about the science of studying their topic of inquiry will be affected by which of these perspectives they believe to be more important. Scientists emphasizing continuity will be more likely to study the actual process of growth, such as how children learn and the variables that promote learning. Those emphasizing discontinuity will be more likely to attempt to understand and look for new evidence of various developmental levels, or search for circumstances that promote or hinder the jump to the next level. Thus as scientists approach similar questions from these two differing angles, both perspectives contribute toward a fuller understanding of child development.

What roles do nature and nurture play in child development?

**Of Bent Twigs and Fallen Fruit:
The Nature versus Nurture Controversy**

"The apple doesn't fall very far from the tree."
"As the twig is bent, so grows the tree."

Which of these old adages has the inside track on child development? Is who we become predetermined by internally directed genetic influences, as the first saying implies? Or can children be molded into whatever we would like them to be, given the appropriate external influences? The musings that have occurred in response to these questions are collectively referred to as the **nature versus nurture** controversy (Ceci & Williams, 1999). This philosophical pendulum has swung wildly over the last century. Toward the end of the 1800s, as the field of developmental psychology began to take form, so also did considerations of its possible applications. Advice to parents centered largely on how to enhance children's physical growth, which was viewed as an isolated, naturally unfolding process unaffected by social or emotional issues. Similarly, education was designed to simply offer appropriate knowledge as the self-perpetuated process of learning occurred, an approach reflecting the eighteenth-century philosophy of Jean-Jacques Rousseau. Even as late as the 1930s, little if any emphasis was placed on the relationship between psychological growth and the environment or the role of parent-child relationships in child development (Goodenough, 1945).

Emphases changed as developmental theorists introduced environmentally based ingredients into the maturational formula. Sigmund Freud proposed that personality styles are determined by certain early-childhood experiences, and that mental illness develops in response to inadequate parenting (Freud, 1914/1959). Behaviorists such as John Watson reintroduced the seventeenth-century philosopher John Locke's concept of the mind as a **tabula rasa**, or "blank slate" (Watson, 1958). Locke had suggested that children's minds are voids, empty until filled in with influences from the environment—a proposition reflected by Watson's oft-quoted proposal:

> Give me a dozen healthy infants, well formed, and my own special world to bring them up in, and I'll guarantee to take any one at random and train him to become any type of specialist I might select— doctor, lawyer, artist, merchant chief, and yes, even beggar and thief—regardless of his talents, penchants, tendencies, abilities, vocations and race of his ancestors. (1958, p. 104)

Such sparks illuminating nurture more than nature were fanned into a major blaze during the post–World War II era. From a psychosociohistorical perspective, this is not surprising. Adults coming of age at this time had spent their developmental years experiencing conditions of considerable personal threat and loss, first due to the Great Depression and then as a product of war activity (Elder, 1974; 1998a). After being traumatized by an era during which sense of personal control over well-being had been so profoundly undermined, people would find any concept suggesting you could have absolute control over anything attractive indeed. Factor in society's postwar campaign to remove women from the workforce to make way for returning soldiers, as well as behaviorists and psychoanalysts encouraging parents to believe that dire consequences would follow if Mom were not monitoring and influencing her children's every move, and you create a whole generation of individuals convinced that nurture is the primary influence upon child development. Research over the next few decades reflected this bias, predominantly singling out various environmental factors—often culture-bound with Caucasian middle-class American goals— playing roles in child development (Parke et al., 1994a; Rosenthal, 1999). You will find notations of both cultural differences and cross-cultural similarities interspersed throughout this textbook (watch for the ◉ symbol in the margins).

Such research activity has revealed substantial evidence that experiences affect children's physical and psychological development, and future chapters will capitalize upon the fruits of these investigations. However, as occasionally will

This idealistic scene of a happy, affluent family characterized the dreams of many who had endured the hardships of the Great Depression and World War II. During subsequent years this cohort experience may have contributed toward research's overemphasis on the importance of nurture and child development.

Image Bank

be noted, the effects of such influences are, more often than not, relatively small (Harris, 1998; Rowe, 1994). In fact, a major review of studies investigating the influences of parenting on personality development concluded that these influences are extremely limited within this particular domain (Maccoby, 1992; Vreeke, 2000).

Freud's early proposals have taken a number of major beatings. Studies of child resiliency have found that vast numbers of children from extremely unfavorable family backgrounds nevertheless grow up to be well-adjusted (Freitas & Downey, 1998; Joseph, 1994; Schaffer, 2000; Ventegodt, 1999). Other lines of research have shown that in spite of the exalted position in which Freud had placed the role of the parent as a social determinant of child attributes and behaviors, peer influences have emerged as a major social contribution, at times becoming even more central than the influence of parents (Harris, 1995, 2000; Loehlin, 1992). Simultaneously, other research has demonstrated the substantial effects of nature (Harris, 1998; Rowe, 1994). Many forms of mental illness and other psychological conditions, although affected by environmental factors, are now known to have biological roots (see Chapter 3). In addition, current research suggests that substantial portions of our personality are actually initiated by inborn temperamental influences (Kagan, 1995). Once the genetic influences have been taken into account, full siblings who have grown up together often appear no more alike than individuals selected at random (Turkenheimer & Gottesman, 1991).

While a few hard-boiled behaviorists and psychoanalysts continue to support the bill of goods that had been sold to 1950s housewives, current developmentalists typically utilize a more balanced perspective of nature and nurture, often exploring how the two may intertwine (Collins et al., 2000; Lemery &

Like the saplings around him, this young man will experience some "bending" of his characteristics, depending upon the environmental influences he encounters. But just as the environment cannot reprogram these trees' relentless pursuit of sunlight, neither is nurture likely to override his many genetically determined traits.

How does a child's culture of origin affect development?

Goldsmith, 1999; Maccoby, 2000; Plomin, 1990; Rutter et al., 1999a). As an example, environmental factors and parenting practices can have differing effects on temperamentally different children. When my boys were young I occasionally used a form of "time-out" when they behaved inappropriately. My second son, Ben, was a boisterous outgoing young man who typically endeavored to place himself in the middle of everything. His time-out consisted of being isolated in his room for a brief period, which he experienced as absolute torture. On the other hand, Frank, my oldest son, was more of a loner and recluse. During Frank's time-out he would be briefly restricted from going to his room, which for him was equally aversive. Both strategies worked effectively as deterrents to undesired behavior.

I remember others raising a few eyebrows as they observed these practices, with some waving of the flag proclaiming that you must treat all children the same or else they will believe they are being treated unfairly. Frank and Ben, however, never questioned the differing consequences, perhaps even as youngsters recognizing that interacting effectively with others requires that we consider one another's individual differences. Our culture's historical preoccupation with the concept that the environment creates the child may very well have led to a tendency to sell our children short. As future chapters will illustrate, children's capacities for perception, information-processing, and learning—although at times qualitatively different from adult abilities—are nevertheless far greater, and occur earlier, than had ever been suspected by theorists favoring nurture.

So as you can see, the adage about the apple and the prediction regarding the twig both contain some truth about child development. Yes, as the twig is bent so grows the tree—but you'll never grow an elm from a sequoia.

Developmentally Universal versus Culturally Relative

In addition to the influences of biology and parenting, development is affected by the greater context within which a child develops (Kindermann & Valsiner, 1995). Even when parents adopt certain childrearing stances, the potential benefits of their interactions can be enhanced or undermined when others in the child's environment either help or hinder the process. In fact, the more that developmental settings are linked and supportive of one another, the greater is the potential for a child's development (Bronfenbrenner, 1979). Thus in addition to developmental factors shared by all children, some influences are unique to a child's individual setting.

Among such developmental microsystems, one of the most influential is a child's culture of origin. The effect of differing cultural experiences on child development first drew notable attention in the 1960s (Cole, 1996). Several factors contributed to this sudden interest. Research was revealing that environmental

FIGURE 1.2

Horizontal-vertical illusion. Both lines are the same length, but cross-culturally, individuals shown such a figure perceive the vertical line to be longer than the horizontal line, although physical environment can affect susceptibility to the illusion.

conditions could affect both the physical and functional development of sensation and perception (LeVay et al., 1980; Wiesel & Hubel, 1963). The horizontal and vertical lines in Figure 1.2 provide one interesting example of this phenomenon. Are these lines of equal or unequal length? Although most people see the vertical line as longer, they are of equal length. This tendency to misjudge lengths is due to the "horizontal-vertical illusion," and it occurs among individuals cross-culturally. However, the strength of susceptibility to the illusion varies depending upon the visual field within which specific individuals have been living. If they have spent their lives in forested areas or cities with many tall buildings, they have had substantial practice compensating for the illusion and therefore make less inaccurate judgments. On the other hand, those who have been living in rural areas or on the plains are more susceptible to the illusion (Segall et al., 1966).

Emphases on memory skills also differ among various cultures. The level of detail recalled and reproduced by members of less industrialized societies can put those of "more advanced" societies to shame (Cole, 1996). Examples are an Eskimo who can draw a vast complex coastline from memory, or a primitive herder who can recount seemingly indiscriminable details about individual cattle. Clearly, we develop cognitive skills and construct our realities based on what is personally meaningful, and what is meaningful varies with our physical and cultural environment (Miller, 1997; Valsiner, 1994; Vygotsky, 1934/1962).

As the study of cultural differences emerged, effects of this nature were observed in Western society among minority students as they attempted to succeed academically (Serpell & Hatano, 1997). They typically did not perform as

The children participating in this "Cherry Blossom" festival enjoy not only a pleasant event but also the benefits to be found in developing a sense of community, belongingness, and cultural identity.

Charles Kennard/Stock Boston

well as their majority counterparts, and they consistently received lower scores on tests of intelligence (Irvine & Berry, 1988; Jencks, 1998). Yet teachers intuitively recognized that these children were not unintelligent; they just weren't learning efficiently within an educational system designed for mainstream Caucasian-American children. Considerable research has accumulated as scientists and educators attempt to understand and accommodate to the varied ways of being, knowing, and learning represented by children of diverse cultures (Berry et al., 1992; Erickson, 1999; Segall et al., 1990).

One reason why the effects of culture are so pervasive is that part of a child's identity and ways of thinking are infused within the group of origin itself (Hong et al., 2000; Portes et al., 2000). Mental functioning can occur jointly among individuals, influencing how groups or dyads interact with the environment or one another (Bugental & Johnston, 2000; Hinsz et al., 1997; Smith, Murphy, et al., 1999). These learned processes differ with the individual culture employing them (Wertsch, 1991). We commonly observe ourselves and others "going along with the crowd" when if left to our own devices we might choose to behave differently. Exposure to such group influences in information-processing styles affects the development of a child's overall mental processing. While at times we tend to think of such group effects as being detrimental—citing such cautionary examples as the stampeding lemmings hurling themselves off a cliff—a well-developed sense of community is actually adaptive. A strong sense of community has been shown to serve as a source of resilience, especially during times of oppression and other hardships (Sonn & Fisher, 1998).

In 1998 only 65% of children in the United States were white non-Hispanic; 15% were African American, another 15% were Hispanic American, 4% were Asian American/Pacific Islander, and 1% were Native American/Alaska Native (Federal Interagency Forum on Child and Family Statistics, 1999). Given this expanding cultural diversity of the United States—which the populations of other Western nations are also undergoing—a child's cultural background is becoming increasingly more relevant to studies of childhood and adolescent development (McLoyd, 1998).

How do relevant influences individually or in combination affect a child's developmental outcome?

Single Causes versus Multiple Causes

Can some changes in children be explained by specific single causes, or are there always multiple causes? Life is much simpler if we can predict exactly what the outcome will be when a certain circumstance occurs. Developmental theorists are not immune to the attractiveness of this simplicity. Many theories have been proposed that rely on a single theme to explain why we turn out the way we do. Sigmund Freud focused on the role of emotions; Jean Piaget explored the effects of reasoning and other thought processes; and B. F. Skinner—even at the time of a speech he made two weeks before he died—expounded his bias that behavioral consequences were primary to development and that cognitive processes were inconsequential (Bales, 1990).

If you give a young boy a quarter every time he takes his dinner plate back to the kitchen, true to the foundations of behaviorism, he will most likely repeat that behavior. While on the surface this prediction regarding development of a responsible behavior sounds fairly simple and clear-cut, other less obvious factors also influence the potential outcome. We first might want to consider the boy's age. A 3-year-old might not yet understand the value of a quarter, and the average 13-year-old will probably not feel that a quarter's value makes carrying a plate worth the effort (if not viewing the whole proposition as downright insulting!). Also, what kind of relationship exists between the boy and his parents? Does he perceive his parents as consistent and trustworthy and therefore likely to continue providing quarters for repeat performances of the task? Within a greater context, does the boy's culture support continuation of the behavior, or does he live in a patriarchal society where the task would be considered "women's work"? Or, could it be that by the year 2050 a quarter will be of so little value that a child would be unlikely to pick one up off the street, let alone be motivated to pick up a plate in order to earn one?

Currently most developmentalists respect the multiplicity of factors and theories relevant to child development, and are moving toward more of a "developmental systems" perspective (Lerner, 1998; Meacham, 1999; Wachs, 1999). Urie Bronfenbrenner is a proponent of this perspective. His model of child development addresses all of the questions generated by the preceding plate-removal experiment: the interrelationships between individual developmental processes, the physical environment within which developmental processes proceed, cultural and social contexts, and continuities and changes that occur in a given culture over time. He refers to his model as a **bioecological model** of child development: "bio" because of the internal developmental programming and species limitations present at birth, and "ecological" because certain types of interactional support and environmental input contribute toward optimum development (Bronfenbrenner, 1977; Bronfenbrenner & Ceci, 1994).

As children advance, they arrive at numerous points of opportunity for new learning to occur, which will proceed according to the input they receive. Parents and children develop enduring interactions between one another called **proximal processes**. Examples include the way a parent soothes a fussy baby and how the baby responds, or whether a parent reading with a young child is accepting or intolerant of creative page-turning and other variants of adult reading habits. Proximal processes facilitate physical, cognitive, social, and emotional growth. As children progress to other developmental contexts such as child-child, teacher-child, and mentor-child settings, this interactional principle continues to apply (Bronfenbrenner & Morris, 1998).

The nature of research and experimental design is such that theorists are always teasing out the individual factors they prefer to study. Although seemingly single-minded, this practice actually contributes to the overall picture of child development by yielding an abundance of exact data for interpretation. Other studies are set up to consider multiple causes that act alone or interplay with one another to produce effects; and some may look at factors comparing multiple theories. Most typically we fit together multiple considerations by comparing and contrasting a number of individual research findings within the wealth of diverse information produced by empirical study—often leading us toward formulation of new testable hypotheses.

Study Thoughts or Study Behaviors?

What do we investigate if we want to see evidence of child growth?

Exactly what kind of data might we examine to best understand child development? Historically the focus of interest has progressed through varying phases. Early modern philosophers such as Locke and Rousseau examined children's cognitive changes and advances in how they reason or solve problems. They typically gathered their information by having children analyze their own thoughts and explain how they came to certain conclusions, a process called **introspection**. Later, Freud used a similar strategy, investigating child development by asking his adult patients to recall events, beliefs, and feelings from their childhoods. Thus much of the early research on child development focused on people's thought processes.

As might be expected from Watson's behavioral slant, he took issue with the focus on cognition (Rilling, 2000). He pointed out the shortcomings of gathering information through introspection, especially the difficulty of verifying the accuracy of study participants' reports. Only the participants have true awareness of their actual thoughts. The researcher thus collects data that can be riddled with inaccuracies produced by the influences of dishonesty, poor awareness of inner processing, and inept communication. Arguing that to be scientific, researchers need to study development in ways that are more easily and accurately measurable, Watson emphasized the study of behaviors rather than thought processes. Behaviors are directly observable and therefore can be more accurately and consistently measured and compared than can thought processes. In this manner he made a significant contribution to the refinement and expansion of the field of experimental psychology itself.

However, Watson appears to have gone overboard by discarding cognitive considerations as irrelevant. Under many circumstances we can consistently and accurately judge what sorts of thoughts or reasoning processes are going through others' minds by simply observing their behavioral responses to a situation, without having to ask them what their actual thoughts are. In fact, we are so accustomed to inferring the presence of certain reasoning processes that when we observe behaviors that do not match our predictions we are likely to do a double take! By applying the same experimental processes initially refined by behaviorists, we can study thought processes by observing, measuring, and comparing these types of cognitively driven responses. Investigations of cognitive process currently constitute the most prominent and fastest-growing area of research and publication within the field of child development; neuroscience research shows a modest increase in activity, and the number of studies of behavioral and psychodynamic influences has decreased (Robins et al., 1999).

However, all of these areas of focus merit examination. Children learn those behaviors that will eventually allow them to take care of themselves, and their choices of behavior are crucial for fitting in with the requirements of their society. We need to know what sorts of conditions help set such behaviors into place. And we can better understand the thinking that leads to the choice of a behavioral response if we can recognize the underlying cognitive processes. If learning or development alters these internal processes, a child's abilities and behaviors are likely to change. Observing and understanding these changes gives us clues about how we might improve a child's ability to learn, as well as support his or her natural development. Likewise, children's thought processes contribute to how they feel about themselves, which affects the development of their self-esteem and emotional well-being.

Thanks to miracles of modern technology, current study of psychological development reaches far beyond the behaviors and thought processes examined by earlier researchers. PET (positron-emission tomography) scans, CAT (computerized axial tomography) scans, and MRI (magnetic resonance imaging) readings provide information about the development of various brain structures at different ages (Nelson & Bloom, 1997). We have advanced techniques at our disposal for investigating the roles of genes, chemical processes in the nervous system, sensation and perceptual functioning, and other physical conditions that can affect psychological development (Greenough et al., 1987; Leavitt & Goldson, 1996; Plomin et al., 1990; Rutter et al., 1999a; Wahlsten, 1999). Thus studies of behavioral, cognitive, and biological factors all contribute to a fuller understanding of how children develop.

How do we go about studying such a massive field of investigation? This first, four-chapter section provides a basic foundation for investigating and understanding child development and discusses factors relevant to development up until the moment of birth. Following this introductory chapter, Chapter 2 describes how the scientific method is applied to developmental psychology, explaining how researchers gather data and draw their conclusions. Chapter 3 is devoted to the wide range of biological influences on child physical development, and Chapter 4 discusses the critical periods of pregnancy and childbirth.

The remaining four sections of the book are organized chronologically, covering in turn infancy and toddlerhood, early childhood, middle childhood, and adolescence. Within each section separate chapters present data collections describing physical development, cognitive development, and social and emotional development for that chronological stage. So closely are the three developmental focuses interrelated that assigning material to these three areas of emphasis is at times almost arbitrary. Nevertheless, this style of organization should allow you to more easily track specific aspects of development as children proceed along their developmental journeys.

The remainder of this chapter introduces the general topical organization of future chapters, as well as some of the major theories to be revisited as we delve into the study of the different age groups.

What are the historical contributions to the fields of child physical, cognitive, and social and emotional development, and how do they continue to be relevant today?

PHYSICAL DEVELOPMENT
(CHAPTERS 5, 8, 11, AND 14)

One of the earliest major contributors to the study of children's physical development was none other than Charles Darwin (Darwin, 1859; Gesell, 1948). He and others initiated the field of **ethology**, which investigates animal and human behavior within the context of evolution. Darwin's suggestion that our species evolves in ways that help us adapt to our environments implies that variations emerge and take primacy during phases of bodily development. Thus he helped establish the basic concept that human bodies actually do proceed through developmental change.

Another crucial factor that had not yet been established but we all now take for granted was the relationship between physical maturity and physical ability. G. E. Coghill (1929/1969) contributed to this effort by demonstrating the relationship between advances in nervous system functioning and potential behavioral development, a factor particularly relevant to understanding when and how children can begin to coordinate movements, crawl or walk, or be pottytrained. The role of brain and nervous system maturation in child development became a neglected topic after the cognitive explosion of the 1960s, but in the last decade has again begun enjoying increased respect as a fruitful field of scientific inquiry (Johnson, 1998; Robins et al., 1999).

Influenced by both Darwin and Coghill, Arnold Gesell systematically observed the orderly progression of motor development in infants and young children, and also gathered data regarding infant emotional expressiveness (Gesell, 1948; Thelen & Adolph, 1994). His observations supported the concept that a natural maturational process guides the progress of child development. During the last few decades, studies of physical development have expanded and focused more extensively on perception and sensation, especially in preverbal infants (Gibson, 1992). What can infants see, hear, or otherwise sense? How do they learn to discriminate between the varying characteristics of objects or individuals in their environments? What properties seem to help them with this task, or make certain characteristics more meaningful? As these questions were reformulated into scientific inquiry, researchers found that infants and young children do become progressively better able to discriminate meaningful properties of the environment. Most recently, theorists have begun to more extensively explore how environmental factors interact with the quality of a child's motor development and the timing of its maturation (Thelen, 1995).

The physical development chapters introduce this field of knowledge with a discussion of basic body growth—such factors as height and weight, and similarities and differences between the genders—as well as a discussion of brain development. The emergence of a child's increasingly advanced motor skills and perceptual abilities is then described. Following this backdrop are discussions of basic health needs that support and promote physical growth at various ages, and the health issues that can enhance or detract from a child's physical development. As in all sections of this textbook, certain areas will be covered more extensively in some chapters than in others as relevance varies from age to age. For example, factors affecting development of sensation and perception hold primacy during infancy, while the role of hormones is especially relevant to adolescent physical development. Other topics are germane to all ages, such as childhood nutrition. However, discussion within a particular topic also varies widely according to age group; within the topic of nutrition, for example, the breast-feeding versus bottle-feeding controversy applies to infancy whereas the impact of novel eating regimens arises during the exploratory, identity-seeking phase of adolescence.

COGNITIVE DEVELOPMENT (CHAPTERS 6, 9, 12, AND 15)

Philosophers were the first to investigate how our thought processes work (Wessells, 1982). René Descartes (1596–1650) formulated the theory that came to be known as **dualism**: namely that the mind and all its mental processes are separate from the physical body and its brain. Viewing internal mental processes as being separate opened up the possibility of placing them under greater individual scrutiny. In observing that some ideas, such as the concepts of God and infinity, seem to emerge independent of experience, Descartes promoted the beginnings of the "nature" side of the nature/nurture controversy. Continuing on this path of speculation, the philosopher Immanuel Kant (1724–1804) noted that concepts such as unity, space, time, causality, and organization of words and concepts into meaningful wholes also seem unlearned.

The beginnings of the "nurture" side of the story were not far behind. John Locke's theory that the mind began as a "blank slate" was taken up by nineteenth-century philosophers such as James Mill, John Stuart Mill, and Alexander Bain.

They proposed that all of a person's knowledge and beliefs are bound together by associations learned as a result of a person's life experiences. This emphasis on the connections between exposures to experiences and pieces of information collected from such exposures provided the foundation for much of current learning theory.

Chapters 6, 9, 12, and 15 begin with pieces of the "nature" story—Jean Piaget's stage theory of cognitive development, occasionally balanced with an alternative, sociocultural perspective introduced by Lev Vygotsky. In each of these chapters, this discussion is followed by contributions from studies of the information-processing approach, intelligence, language development, and learning theory. This next section provides a brief overview of basic concepts underlying each of these areas of inquiry.

Contributions of Jean Piaget

Jean Piaget was among the first to recognize that children use different reasoning strategies at different ages (Piaget, 1936/1974; Wadsworth, 1996). As a stage theorist he believed that children use one form of reasoning until physical development and an "Aha!" experience result in their ability to use a more advanced reasoning process. He proposed two mechanisms for incorporating new information: assimilation and accommodation. **Assimilation** is the process of accepting a novel piece of information without challenging existing perceptions. **Accommodation** is the process of altering already-accepted knowledge in ways that take into account newly assimilated information. As a 3-year-old my daughter Bridie illustrated these two concepts by referring to our laundry appliances as the "wetter and dryer." She had assimilated that the opposite of "dry" is "wet" but had not yet accommodated into her knowledge base that they are labeled according to their functions rather than their relationship with dampness.

As children assimilate and accommodate information, Piaget believed they develop **schemes** (Piaget, 1977). Schemes are organized collections of input that represent certain ways of thinking or strategies for behaviors. For example, an infant who knows how to make a mobile jiggle by shaking his or her legs and arms has developed a *behavioral scheme*. A 4-year-old who successfully copies an observed child's practice of putting a smiley face on a drawing of the sun has demonstrated learning of a *symbolic scheme*—the ability to internalize mental images or verbal codes that can be reproduced later. Older children demonstrate *cognitive operational schemes,* which involve the ability to mentally perform an action and realize the likely consequences without having to actually try it out.

Piaget believed that children's schematic capacities expanded in concordance with a naturally unfolding sequence of age-related improvements in cognitive ability. Parts 2 through 5 of this book correspond with the ages at which these improvements take place and elaborate upon the new stage of development. In recent years many of Piaget's conclusions about child cognitive development and children's abilities at different ages have been challenged. For the most part, research over the last couple of decades has suggested that Piaget underestimated young children's cognitive abilities (Karmiloff-Smith, 1992). Nevertheless, his concept of age-related cognitive growth has provided much of the impetus behind the study of child cognition.

The Sociocultural Approach of Lev Vygotsky

Lev Vygotsky differed from Piaget in looking more to how interactional processes contribute to children's development of higher mental functions (Daniels, 1996; Vygotsky, 1934/1962). He believed that children are born with certain basic mental functions, such as sensation, perception, attention, and memory, that prime them for learning. However, the extent to which they utilize and develop these basic functions depends on input from the environment. He proposed that development of most cognitive and language abilities is a function of a child's interactions with adults and more advanced peers. Children might indeed develop new skills in steps, but they do so as a result of the combination of readiness and guidance rather than as an independent, internally guided, unfolding plan (van der Veer, 1996).

Vygotsky was especially interested in what he called the **zone of proximal development**. The zone of proximal development represents the space between what a child can already do on his or her own and those skills that can readily be learned if the child receives appropriate guidance from others. In other words children learn most when presented with input that is consistent with whatever they are currently developmentally primed to receive. Since the guidance received will be tightly connected to what is most important in the teacher's and learner's environment, Vygotsky's theory effectively takes into account the role that cultural context plays in a child's cognitive development—hence its label, **sociocultural theory** (Furth, 1996; Kitchener, 1996). A child's future competence thus emerges in concert with the quality of cognitive tools mentors provide as they teach the child to function within their cultural arena (Arievitch & Stetsenko, 2000).

The Information-Processing Approach

The Piagetian influence dominated the field of child cognitive research until about 30 years ago (Palmer & Kimchi, 1986). In addition to Vygotsky, other cognitive theorists who gave Piagetian theory a closer inspection noted limitations. Their subsequent investigations led them to introduce the information-processing approach (McShane, 1991). Rather than focusing on overall developmental phases, they turned their attention to specific processes of receiving, storing, and retrieving information and performing mental actions upon it. As researchers have investigated these pieces of cognitive functioning, a variety of models interpreting how we process information have arisen.

Some investigators have adopted a "connectionist" perspective, viewing learning as a result of the quality of connectedness between pieces of information. Such developing networks of connections are believed to contribute to language acquisition, problem-solving, and concept formation (McClelland,

1995). Others, attracted by the seductiveness of the computer programming paradigm, have attempted to demonstrate that certain information-processing computational models represent how human cognitive "programming" occurs, although such attempts have revealed more differences than similarities between the information-processing abilities of machines and human brains (Klahr, 1992). Another approach concerns itself with "productions": What are the actual results—what practiced or novel cognitive processes are applied—as children encounter new input requiring cognitive action (Newell & Simon, 1972)? While no final verdict has yet been established regarding what represents the "true" model of human information-processing and how it develops, research based on each of these perspectives has contributed toward a greater understanding of child cognitive development.

Intelligence

What exactly is intelligence? There are perhaps as many definitions for intelligence as there are theorists investigating the field (MacKintosh, 1998). The trend of years past has been to define intelligence in terms of abilities measured by so-called IQ (intelligence quotient) tests, which appear to most consistently predict how well a person is likely to perform academically. Perhaps this consistency is to be expected—after all, the ability to achieve academically is certainly what enabled early theorists to become part of the academic milieu where the theories are built! Yet, even as intelligence first emerged as a major field of study, some theorists cautioned against overvaluing its importance (Terman, 1921). Until recently, those cautions appear to have been largely ignored.

Current studies of intelligence are more reflective of the recognition that there is more to being "smart" than cramming as many facts and analytical manipulations as possible into human mental functioning. Although such skills are at times important, building a happy life and finding other forms of success at living go beyond academic achievement. How often have movies and other products of Western cultures played up the stereotype of the genius who unfortunately lacks all common sense and is a miserable failure at developing a satisfying social life, or even marketing his or her superior intellectual abilities in the real world?

This commodity called intelligence actually involves a much broader range of skills than popular notions typically ascribe to it, and in fact a growing number of theorists describe it as being a collection of multiple intelligences (Friedman & Shore, 2000; Gardner, 1983, 1999; Guilford, 1967). Robert Sternberg emphasizes this more broadened view, and divides intelligence into three types (Sternberg, 1988). **Analytical intelligence** describes the traditionally recognized concepts of intelligence: the ability to achieve academically, solve problems, acquire and maintain knowledge, understand concrete and abstract concepts, and see the relationships between pieces of knowledge. **Creative intelligence** is the ability to produce original works or find novel solutions to problems, abilities that were hitherto considered talents in the arts rather than aspects of intelligence. **Practical intelligence** involves getting along in the real world: perceiving the social and emotional nuances necessary for success within one's own culture, applying knowledge in ways that are popularly called "common sense," and developing a comfortable niche in which to live one's life. Naturally, the developing child will have the greatest advantage if he or she is adept at using all three types of intelligence.

Another misleading concept is the belief that intelligence is a fixed characteristic. People often assume that we are born with a certain level of intelligence and that it remains stable throughout our lives. In reality, intelligence is more likely to vary over the life span. Intelligence is not just aptitude. It also reflects what a person has experienced and achieved thus far. As future chapters will describe in fuller detail, as an individual child's life exposures, opportunities, and degrees of effort vary, so also will the level of functioning of the child's intelligence.

Learning Theories and Development

What exactly is learning? Consider the following definition:

> Learning refers to the change in a subject's behavior or behavior potential to a given situation brought about by the subject's repeated experiences in that situation, provided that the behavior change cannot be explained on the basis of the subject's native response tendencies, maturation, or temporary states (such as fatigue, drunkenness, drives, and so on). (Bower & Hilgard, 1981, p. 11)

Simply stated, learning is the adoption of new behaviors and thinking patterns based on an individual's experiences. The sophistication and relative excellence of learning ability is in part inherited, ensuring that species members will be able to take in whatever information is necessary for their survival (Howard, 1997). For the better part of a century, much of learning theory and experimentation has focused on how learning occurs as a product of connections between stimulus-response pairs (Lipsett & Cantor, 1986; Postman, 1962; Sears et al., 1965; Thorndike, 1932). What kind of stimulus leads to what sort of response? Which additional conditions are likely to strengthen or weaken this connection—that is, act as the "mediators" of learning? Can thought processes act as mediators? And how might social consequences influence whether or not a connection is made between a stimulus and response? As experimentation began to provide answers to these questions, the fields of behaviorism and cognitive social-learning theory took form. These areas of scientific inquiry described learning processes that explained much about how and what children learn. We look at three such learning processes: classical conditioning, operant conditioning, and observational learning.

Classical Conditioning. The Russian physiologist Ivan Petrovich Pavlov is generally credited with being the first to recognize **classical conditioning** (Pavlov, 1928; Bower & Hilgard, 1981). Classical conditioning is believed to be responsible for many individualized feeling responses and other bodily related

Ivan Pavlov (with the white beard) encountered the basic principles of classical conditioning while investigating the salivation behaviors of dogs.

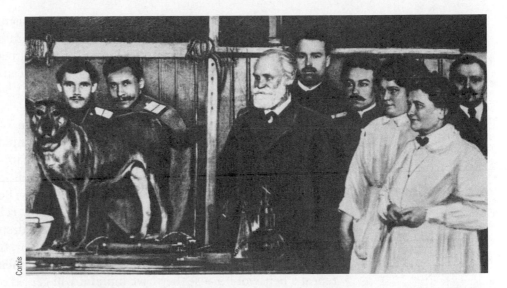

Corbis

reactions. Pavlov found that by pairing certain stimuli he could create responses that had not previously been present. In his experiments with dogs he used a bell to indicate that feeding was about to occur and then presented their food. The dogs salivated in the presence of the food. After several trials he found that all he needed to do was ring the bell and his dogs would start salivating, even though no food was present. He had discovered that if one stimulus (here, food) is paired with a second stimulus (the bell), the second stimulus will produce the same response (salivation) as the first stimulus.

Children's fears often develop by means of classical conditioning. An early well-known example of such learning is the case of "Albert and the White Rat" (Watson & Rayner, 1920). When 1-year-old Albert was presented with a white rat, he showed no signs of fear. When the experimenters began frightening him with a loud noise every time the rat was presented, Albert began to act fearful even when the rat was presented without the loud noise.

When my daughter Bridie was about a year old, a series of ear infections resulted in frequent trips to the doctor's office. Every time her white-jacketed physician got anywhere near her he poked and prodded right where it hurt. True to the tenets of classical conditioning, she eventually began whining or howling the minute he entered the exam room. However, the classical conditioning process did not end there. During this same time span I took her out of town to visit her grandparents, with whom she played happily all evening. The next morning her grandmother came into her play area wearing a white bathrobe. Bridie began acting apprehensive and did not want to go to her. Fortunately I figured out the connection, and Grandma's hurt feelings were assuaged by the discovery that simply changing clothes remedied Bridie's attitude. (The next time we visited the doctor's office I shared this story with my physician. Thinking back, I don't recall having seen him wearing a white jacket since that episode.)

The process of transferring classically conditioned learning to unrelated situations is called **stimulus generalization**. Watson and Rayner (1920) demonstrated a phenomenon similar to Bridie's fear of white cover-up apparel while working with little Albert. Within his circumstances Little Albert became fearful when presented with a stimulus having the rat's characteristics of being white and fuzzy, such as a wad of cotton or a Santa Claus mask. As you might well imagine, stimulus generalization can result in fearful reactions that are so far removed from the original scenarios that their roots can be almost impossible to uncover.

Operant Conditioning. The contemporary version of the early stimulus-response connectionist theories of learning was championed by B. F. Skinner (Skinner, 1938). His behavioral theory describes a familiar learning process, formally called **operant conditioning**. Operant conditioning shows how behaviors are learned through reinforcers and punishers (Bower & Hilgard, 1981; Dragoi & Staddon, 1999; Skinner, 1938). By definition, **reinforcers** are any consequences that can get us to repeat a behavior. If children feel rewarded by the praise they receive after performing a desired behavior, they are more likely to repeat the behavior. This is called **positive reinforcement**. Children may also repeat a behavior because they have found it will get rid of something unpleasant. An adolescent might sulkingly go clean up his room, not so much because he cares about its condition but because he knows that it will end the argument between him and Mom or Dad. This is called **negative reinforcement**. **Punishers** are consequences that result in a decrease in behavior. If a child's bike is taken away for a week after she rode it beyond agreed-upon boundaries, and from that point forward she sticks to the rules, taking her bike away has reduced the behavior of breaking bike-boundary rules and thus would be considered a punisher.

However, the effects of positive reinforcers, negative reinforcers, and punishers all have the potential to be undone by simply removing them from the scenario. This is called **extinction**. If a child no longer gets a treat every time he brings home an "A" paper, unless some other motivator is promoting that behavior the level of effort put into schoolwork may diminish to "pre-treat" levels.

Observational Learning.   Other forms of learning occur just from watching others. **Observational learning** explains how children learn new behaviors by watching role models and then copying their actions (Bandura, 1977; Miller & Dollard, 1941; Mischel, 1968). Albert Bandura, one of the most prominent observational learning theorists, extensively researched the relationship between modeling and aggression (Bandura, 1973). Children who watch aggressive behavior become more likely to perform similar acts of aggression themselves. However, if they see aggressive role models receive punishment for aggressive behavior, they are not so likely to copy them. This is called **vicarious punishment**. On the other hand, **vicarious reinforcement** occurs when children who see role models receiving rewards for aggressive behavior show a greater incidence of aggressive behavior. So, even if a child has not directly received a punisher or reinforcer, such observed consequences can still have an effect on his or her behavior by means of observational learning. Such learning occurs throughout childhood; indeed, it continues to apply to learning as adults.

SOCIAL AND EMOTIONAL DEVELOPMENT
(CHAPTERS 7, 10, 13, AND 16)

Scientific investigation of children's social and emotional development is actually a relatively new endeavor. Sigmund Freud was one of the first to hypothesize about what sorts of changes might occur during childhood and which factors could influence these changes. However, his theory grew mainly out of speculation, since it was based on his psychotherapy patients' recountings of childhood events. Not until the middle of the twentieth century did researchers of child development begin compiling the careful observations and comparisons characteristic of scientific study. Early research efforts looked at manifestations of infant anxiety or made note of emotional by-products occurring during experiments investigating perception and cognition (Gibson & Walk, 1960; Spitz, 1950). The importance of the style of attachment that occurs between infants or children and their parents also began to receive attention, although not with any scientific rigor until the 1970s (Ainsworth et al., 1978; Bowlby, 1958; Bretherton, 1994).

The last couple of decades have witnessed substantially greater interest in how children's experiences of emotions develop, how children learn rules of social interaction, and how the two are related (Campos & Stenberg, 1981; Tronick, 1989). Such investigations look not only to the emergence of specific emotions such as guilt, pride, and empathy, but also at how children of various ages understand emotions and learn to regulate emotional expressiveness and other social behaviors based on their understanding (Eisenberg, 1992; Zahn-Waxler & Kochanska, 1990). In this manner they not only learn the patterns of interaction that will shape their social lives, but also set up informal structures of interaction with the significant others who will further foster their social development (Field, 1991; Hartup & Rubin, 1986).

Over the last few decades, the important relationship between children's self-evaluations and their social and emotional competence has also received considerable attention (Coopersmith, 1967; Harter, 1982; Skinner, 1995). Although the earliest emphases on social and emotional development focused on children's relationships with their mothers, more current research has balanced the picture by revealing important aspects to their relationships with fathers, the family system, peers, the school milieu, and extended family networks (Parke & Ladd, 1992).

Personality theorists were among the first to attempt to investigate social and emotional development. The study of personality as a construct and how it relates to child development has achieved limited success because of the complexity of the subject. "Personality" is more of a popular term than a technical term, typically used to describe the more outstanding or typical aspects of an individual's abilities or displays of emotionality (Hall & Lindzey, 1978). With few exceptions, the aspects the describer chooses to highlight in a particular individual or when describing personality in general are entirely subjective, and the personality theorist is as prone to this subjectivity as the layperson. Thus personality theories vary widely in what sorts of traits, internal motivators, or other ingredients have been included in the soup. Not surprisingly, most personality theorists are less tied to tight research, are more speculative, and more loosely describe the nature of their beast than do other psychological theorists. In spite of their limitations, some of these early theories nevertheless opened the door to important developmental considerations.

The developmental stage theories of Sigmund Freud and Erik Erikson (both introduced briefly below) therefore open Chapters 7, 10, 13, and 16 and lead into sections exploring the substantial roles played by a child's relationships with others; the development of emotional experiencing, responding, and management; the field of moral development; the changing self-concept; and development of self-esteem.

Sigmund Freud's Theory of Psychosexual Development

Sigmund Freud formulated one of the earliest developmental theories of personality (Freud, 1914/1959). He described our inner processes as **psychosexual**, with the impetus for growth being fueled by "libidinal" drives stemming from sexual and aggressive impulses. He believed that how these impulses are managed during the earliest years of life is paramount to healthy personality development. He proposed that children pass through various psychosexual conflicts that emerge in a naturally unfolding, age-related sequence, and that personality develops according to how well children resolve these impulse-driven conflicts. As children proceed through the stages, three systems of the mind develop: the id, ego, and superego.

The **id** is made up of instincts and drives, such as self-preservation and sexual urges. The id is self-centered and unsocialized, and sends out impulses seeking gratification anywhere it can be found. Although the id's self-focus is adaptive from the perspective of self-preservation and species preservation (Freud appears to have been a Darwinist at heart!), if left unchecked its self-absorbed behaviors could be expected to get us into a lot of trouble. The counterbalance for the id, the **superego**, is made up of the societal values we adopt. It is divided into two parts: the conscience and the ego-ideal. The **conscience** represents our adopted moral values, and results in pangs of guilt feelings when we violate those values. The **ego-ideal** is what we aspire to be, and results in our feeling good about ourselves when we act consistently with this image.

The **ego** mediates between these two warring factions, the id and the superego, as they present themselves within the realities of everyday living. Conflict between the id and the superego creates anxiety. To help us cope with this anxiety we develop a number of **defense mechanisms**. Freud proposed that we learn to use defense mechanisms of increasing levels of sophistication at various ages (Cramer, 1997; Porcerelli et al., 1998). One of the earliest-appearing defense mechanisms is *denial*. When 3-year-old Emily is asked what happened to an obviously trashed doll house, she innocently replies "nothing"—an indication that she is coping with the conflict by denying that the problem exists.

Older children are capable of using defense mechanisms requiring greater reasoning skills, such as 8-year-old Tony calming himself with the *rationalization* that "I really didn't want to be on the softball team anyway." In addition to establishing emotional strategies for coping with anxiety, defense mechanisms play roles in defining an individual's personal style.

Erik Erikson's Theory of Psychosocial Development

Erik Erikson studied under Sigmund Freud and his daughter, Anna, who was also a psychoanalyst (Erikson, 1985). As his original educational background differed from Sigmund Freud's medical and biological foundation, he was not so convinced that child development centered solely on biologically based, psychosexually driven processes. He was also less focused on pathology and emotional defenses and more interested in healthy ego development. Drawing from his background and interest in art, culture, and other sociological aspects of humanity, he proposed that we pass through eight age-related **psychosocial** stages of development. He believed that at each of these stages we are predisposed to realize and then address certain inner conflicts, which ultimately result in specific adaptive and maladaptive outcomes.

For example, the infant's psychosocial task consists of determining whether his or her worldview will be guided by basic trust or mistrust. The infant begins by experiencing the conflict as a **crisis**—a turning point at which one route or the other must eventually be chosen. The route chosen depends largely on input the infant receives from his or her environment. While we naturally hope that the child will develop the capacity to trust others, Erikson points out that the child's perspective should also be sprinkled with the ability to engage in appropriate mistrust. Erikson believed the child's personality takes form as these influences of nature and nurture converge across the five psychosocial stages representing childhood.

While Erikson relied on his analysis of specific cases as a means of developing his theory, later, more scientific studies have given some support for his speculations. In one study, for example, when children of various ages were given pictures and asked to tell stories about them, the themes of their tales tended to reflect the crisis representing their most recent psychosocial stage (Ciaccio, 1971). Why is this so-called "scientific" study considered to be so much more valid and reliable than observing individual cases and making speculations? The next chapter clarifies how current study of child development goes about this business of empirical research—a practice that has challenged, tightened up, and built upon the beliefs of the earlier theorists.

► SUMMARY

The Birth of Developmental Psychology

In-depth formal study of development did not begin until after the invention of the microscope, when scientists discovered that we do not begin as fully formed miniatures and merely expand in size. The field of child development is made up of a collection of diverse theories and investigations of a variety of factors that can influence a child's developmental progression.

Controversies and Cornerstones of Developmental Study

Both constancy and change are observed during the development of a child's physical, emotional, and behavioral traits. Child development study aims to help determine what can be expected to change, when it will change, how and why it changes, and what is likely to remain constant. Change can be qualitative, quantitative, or both. Some development appears to occur in steps, while other development seems more continuously flowing.

The "nature versus nurture" controversy involves opposing beliefs regarding how much of a child's development is determined by an unfolding inner blueprint and how much is a result of environmental influences. During most of the twentieth century the influences of the behavioral and psychodynamic perspectives weighted popular belief toward an extreme "nurture" position. However, citing evidence from studies of parenting, child resiliency, temperament, and various biological influences, child developmentalists now encourage us to accept a more balanced perspective of how children become who they are.

While many developmental influences and outcomes are common to all children, some are mediated through a child's culture of origin. Children develop their ways of thinking and knowing based on what is relevant and meaningful, which varies among cultures. In the United States, children of diverse cultures may not do as well in classrooms that are organized around mainstream Western childhood experiences. In addition to individual developmental processes and culture, developmental systems approaches such as the bioecological model consider a child's specific environment, social contexts, and changes in society over time within an individual child's macro system of development.

The early study of child development explored thought processes revealed through introspection, which can be an unreliable source of data. The behaviorists turned attention toward measuring and evaluating objectively observable behaviors, which played a major role in tightening up research practices in psychology. New technologies have also allowed us to place the effects of biological processes and child development under greater direct scrutiny.

Physical Development (Chapters 5, 8, 11, and 14)

Early study of children's physical development was influenced by Darwin's theory of survival of the fittest, Coghill's demonstrations of maturation of nervous system structures, and Gesell's systematic observations of children's changing motor abilities. As the field has expanded, recent studies have emphasized progressions in infants' and young children's capacities for sensation and perception, as well as intricate relationships between environmental factors and development of motor skills.

Cognitive Development (Chapters 6, 9, 12, and 15)

The concepts underlying the study of cognitive development were formulated by philosophers. Descartes's and Kant's observations that thought processes appear to emerge naturally later gave rise to Piaget's stage theory of cognitive development. Piaget proposed that by means of assimilation and accommodation children develop progressively more advanced cognitive schemes in concert with naturally increasing capacities. In contrast, the information-processing approach ignores stages and instead explores how new individually distinct abilities emerge in the areas of memory, attending, concept-formation, comprehension, problem-solving, and language acquisition. The concept of intelligence originally focused on analytical intelligence, but now has expanded to encompass creative and practical intelligence as well.

Locke's belief that the infant mind is a "tabula rasa" and the beliefs of nineteenth-century associationist philosophers provided the foundation for much of current learning theory. Pavlov's and Watson and Rayner's studies of classical conditioning show how new stimulus-response chains can be learned and generalized. Skinner's operant conditioning has demonstrated how such consequences as reinforcers and punishers can alter an individual's behavioral repertoire. Bandura's observational learning studies show how watching role models and the consequences they receive for their behaviors can affect a child's choices of behavior.

Social and Emotional Development (Chapters 7, 10, 13, and 16)

Personality theorists initiated the study of children's social and emotional development. Freud believed that libidinally driven psychosexual stages of growth and the defense mechanisms adopted in response to these stages molded the development of three systems of the mind—the id, ego, and superego—creating personality characteristics in the process. Erikson's psychosocial stage theory focused on specific ego-related developmental tasks that Erikson thought occur at various ages and result in the formation of adaptive and maladaptive personality and behavioral traits. Over the last few decades research in the area of social and emotional development has placed greater emphasis on parent-child attachment, emergence and expression of emotions, emotional regulation, how children learn rules of social interaction, and development of self-esteem.

▶ KEY TERMS

accommodation
analytical intelligence
assimilation
bioecological model
classical conditioning
conscience
creative intelligence
crisis
defense mechanisms
developmental psychology
dualism
ego
ego-ideal

ethology
extinction
id
introspection
nature versus nurture
negative reinforcement
observational learning
operant conditioning
positive reinforcement
practical intelligence
preformationism
proximal processes
psychosexual development

psychosocial development
punishers
qualitative change
quantitative change
reinforcers
schemes
sociocultural theory
stimulus generalization
superego
tabula rasa
vicarious punishment
vicarious reinforcement
zone of proximal development

▶ CONCEPT REVIEW

1. Individuals change over time, and various factors affect these changes. Such factors are studied by the field of _____.

2. Scientists investigate child development from many perspectives. These perspectives are important to consider because they affect _____, as well as how scientists _____ their findings.

3. When a child becomes able to perform a familiar task more quickly or more frequently, this most likely represents _____ change. If the child becomes able to perform the task in a new manner, this represents _____ change.

4. Researchers who view developmental change as occurring gradually and seamlessly believe that child development is a _____ process. Those who view change as occurring in qualitatively differing stages believe that child development is a _____ process.

5. The debate surrounding how much of child development is the result of genetic as opposed to environmental influences is called the _____ controversy.

6. Since our cognitive and behavioral skills develop in concordance with what is meaningful within our personal environments, _____ and _____ are important factors to consider in the study of child development.

7. The developmental systems approach to the study of child development considers the interrelationships between _____, _____, _____, and _____.

8. Watson contributed to the study of both behavior and cognition by emphasizing the need for examining data that is _____.

9. The availability of PET scans, CAT scans, and technology for exploring genetic and chemical processes of the nervous system promote the study of the _____ factors affecting child development.

10. Two crucial assumptions directing the current study of child physical development are the concepts of _____ over time and the relationship between physical _____ and physical _____.

11. Piaget believed that children learn new _____, or ways of thinking or viewing the world, by means of two mechanisms: _____ is the process of accepting a new piece of information, and _____ is the process of altering old information in order to take new information into account.

12. Vygotsky believed that children are born with certain basic _____ that may develop differently based on _____. He proposed that children learn most effectively when offered guidance that is consistent with their current _____.

13. Rather than focus on thinking skills as developmental phases, the information-processing approach studies how information is _____, _____, and _____, as well as the _____ performed on information.

14. The study of intelligence traditionally focused on _____ intelligence. Currently, researchers also recognize and investigate the fields of _____ and _____ intelligence.

15. Learning that occurs because one stimulus is paired with a second stimulus in such a way that both stimuli produce the same response is called _____. Behaviors that increase or decrease in frequency as a result of the consequences they receive are the result of _____. Behaviors learned by children because they have seen role models perform them are examples of _____.

16. Sigmund Freud proposed that personality development occurs as children pass through _____ stages of development. He believed that children's personalities are shaped as they develop various _____ in response to conflicts between the instincts and

drives of the _____, the conscience and ego-ideal of the _____, and the daily realities dealt with by the _____.

17. Erik Erikson believed that children's personalities formed based on how they resolved specific _____ conflicts occurring at various ages.

1) developmental psychology; 2) what they study; interpret; 3) quantitative; qualitative; 4) continuous; discontinuous; 5) nature versus nurture; 6) physical environment; culture; 7) individual processes; the physical environment; cultural/social contexts; continuity and change over time; 8) easily and accurately measurable; 9) biological; 10) developmental change; maturity; ability; 11) schemes; assimilation; accommodation; 12) mental functions; environmental input; zone of proximal development; 13) received; stored; retrieved; mental actions; 14) analytical; creative; practical; 15) classical conditioning; operant conditioning; observational learning; 16) psychosexual; defense mechanisms; id; superego; ego; 17) psychosocial

RESOURCES FOR FURTHER READING

Ceci, S. J., & Williams, W. M. (Eds.) (1999). *The nature-nurture debate: The essential readings*. Oxford: Blackwell.

Cole, M. (1996). *Cultural psychology: A once and future discipline*. Cambridge, MA: Harvard University Press.

Daniels, H. (Ed.) (1996). *An introduction to Vygotsky*. New York: Routledge.

Erikson, E. (1985). *Childhood and society*. New York: W. W. Norton.

Harris, J. R. (1998). *The nurture assumption: Why children turn out the way they do*. New York: Free Press.

LeFrancois, G. (1995). *Theories of learning*, 3rd ed. Pacific Grove, CA: Brooks/Cole.

MacKintosh, N. J. (1998). *IQ and human intelligence*. New York: Oxford University Press.

McShane, J. (1991). *Cognitive development: An information-processing approach*. Cambridge, MA: Basil Blackwell.

Parke, R. D., Ornstein, P. A., Rieser, J. J., & Zahn-Waxler, C. (1994). *A century of developmental psychology*. Washington, DC: American Psychological Association.

Wadsworth, B. J. (1996). *Piaget's theory of cognitive and affective development*, 5th ed. New York: Longman.

INFOTRAC COLLEGE EDITION

For additional readings, explore InfoTrac College Edition, your online library. Go to http://www.infotrac-college.com/wadsworth and use the passcode that came on the card with your book. Try these search terms: nature and nurture

CHILD DEVELOPMENT CD-ROM

 Go to the Wadsworth Child Development CD-ROM for further study of the concepts in this chapter. The CD-ROM also includes quizzes and additional activities to expand your learning experience.

REFERENCES

For a list of references for this chapter, see the Wadsworth Psych Study Center Web site at: http://www.wadsworth.com/product/0534348092s

CHAPTER 2

Studying Child Development

FOCUS QUESTIONS

► What is scientific method?

► What benefits does scientific method offer over casually observing children?

► How does an experimental design refine observations?

► What measurement issues are particularly likely to interfere with accurate observation of child development?

► What sources do investigators of child development use to identify and measure variables of interest?

► How do research ethics apply to the study of children?

► What are child development researchers' alternatives when ethics prohibit a true experimental design?

OUTLINE

Scientific Method and Experimental Design
  Controlling for the Effects of History
  Promoting Generalizability
  Enhancing Objectivity
  Capitalizing on Standardization
  Avoiding Placebo Effects
  Accounting for Intervention Effects
  The Final Product
  Statistical Analysis
Measurement Issues in Studying Child Development
  Cross-Sectional Designs
  Longitudinal Designs
  Time-Lag Designs
  Sequential Designs

Additional Resources for Experimental Variables
Ethics and Studying Child Development
  Protection from Harm
  Informed Consent
  The Right to Truth
  The Right to Privacy
Alternative Experimental Designs
  Correlational Designs
  Designs Measuring Single Participants
Reporting Research Findings
Conclusion

Justin was having lunch at Sarah's house. He found a vegetable on his plate that he did not recognize. He poked it around for awhile, then wanting to be polite went ahead and took a bite, wrinkling up his face as he did so. Sarah observed his reaction.

"Don't worry," Sarah said. "The badder it tastes the gooder it is for you."

How do child development researchers go about developing and testing their beliefs? We all have our preferred ways of making sense of the world. We might speculate that Sarah's conclusion regarding food flavor and nutritional value was drawn from a life experience of parents encouraging her to eat less tasty foods by pointing out how good they are for her. The more she balked, perhaps the more enthusiasm her parents poured into their persuasions.

Sarah's error is common even among adults. We are all occasionally guilty of assuming that because two things occur together, one is causing or somehow related to the other. A stroll through any casino provides ample evidence of such assumptions, as patrons can be observed engaging in any number of superstitious behaviors that at some point in their gambling careers had "resulted" in winning ways. As upcoming discussion will reveal, assumptions of this nature can be and often are erroneous. While Sarah's errant conclusion was relatively harmless, at least in terms of how she applied it in her instructions for Justin, some faulty conclusions are not only misleading but also have the potential for causing harm.

For example, early in the twentieth century medical researchers performed autopsies on some children who had died of a condition under study. They discovered that the thymus glands of these children were larger than those of the child cadavers they had observed at the medical school and drew the conclusion that the particular condition was caused by overenlarged thymus glands. In hopes of reducing the incidence of the disorder, physicians began routinely administering radiation treatment as a means of shrinking the thymus glands of otherwise healthy children. Later scientists realized the true nature of the discrepancy in gland size: The thymus glands of the first set of children were not overenlarged; rather, those of the medical school cadavers—predominantly neglected and undernourished children from the slums—were in fact undersized. The practice of exposing children's thymus glands to radiation abruptly ended. But given the effects excessive radiation exposure can have on the body, who knows what kinds of unnecessary difficulties these individuals may have experienced later in life?

Consequently, scientists studying child development structure their research to maximize the certainty of their conclusions and minimize the risk of producing artifactual results—those caused by sloppy measurement or hasty assumptions. In addition to experimental concerns that plague all researchers, child development researchers face other constraints that can make accurate observation and interpretation especially difficult. This chapter reviews the basics of scientific measurement and looks at the problems of measuring human development and how scientists often work around those problems.

SCIENTIFIC METHOD AND EXPERIMENTAL DESIGN

What is scientific method?

The study of child development uses **scientific method**, sometimes referred to as "empiricism," as its means of measuring human processes (Giere & Richardson, 1996). Scientific method involves presuppositions, rules, and procedures that are respected by all those who use it. This consistency assures scientists that as they write up their findings they know they will be understood by those who read them—it's not unlike sharing a common second language. Likewise other scientists can design the same or similar research and be able to compare their findings to others' work, knowing that the similarities and differences they may find are not due to differences in gathering and measuring information.

What benefits does scientific method offer over casually observing children?

Even the results of legitimate scientific research, when presented by the media, are often misrepresented or misunderstood (Thompson & Nelson, 2001). What factors might you consider as you decide whether a new piece of information has merit? Let's say that Mary has read an article in the *National Intruder* stating that feeding children a regular diet of strawberries will result in improvements in their memory. She recalls that her son Tommy is sometimes for-

Hazel Hankin/Stock Boston

Do you believe everything you read in newspapers? How do you decide which news items to believe and which ones you're skeptical about?

getful, so she decides to feed him strawberries every morning. After a few weeks of this eating regimen she notices that Tommy does seem better able to remember things. She decides the improvement must be due to the strawberries.

Would you agree with Mary's conclusion? Users of scientific method would not yet be convinced, and in all likelihood would be quick to point out a multitude of alternative explanations that could account for Mary's observations. One of the main objectives of scientific method is to **control** the experimental situation so that other such possible explanations are less likely to be true. Scientists refer to all of the possible contributing factors as **variables**, so named because they may have the ability to vary, or alter, within the findings. The object of Mary's study, the memory benefit produced by consumption of strawberries, is called the **experimental variable**. All other effects on the observed improvement in memory—the potential spoilers—are called **extraneous variables**. The goal of scientific method is to create an experimental design that controls for the effects of extraneous variables and sets up the experimental variable so that its true effect will reveal itself as clearly as possible.

Scientists carry a variety of tricks up their sleeves as they set up experimentation to control for extraneous variables. Different methods are used to control for different types of variables, depending on the nature of the variable in question. The scientist essentially builds the experimental design by figuring out which extraneous variables might come into play, and setting up the experimental design in a way that minimizes or erases their effects.

Suppose we apply scientific method to Mary's experiment. Some of the necessary parts are already in place. Every experiment needs **participants**—representatives selected from the population under scrutiny. Tommy was the participant for Mary's experiment. We also need an independent variable and a dependent variable. The **independent variable** is the one that the scientists can assign or change as doing so satisfies their purposes. In our experiment, eating strawberries is the independent variable. The **dependent variable** is the one that "depends" on the independent variable, at least in terms of the aspirations of the experimental hypothesis. In our experiment, memory is the dependent variable. If there is indeed a relationship between the independent and dependent variables, the dependent variable will change along with the changes in the independent variable: We expect memory to improve if we introduce the independent variable of eating strawberries. If no relationship exists between the two, the dependent variable will remain the same; no memory improvement will be observed.

Next, let's evaluate our experiment for any potential extraneous variables we would like to control for.

*How does an
experimental design
refine observations?*

Controlling for the Effects of History

Could it be that Tommy's memory would have improved during that time period regardless of whether or not he had been eating strawberries? This is a concern about the effects of **history**. In an experimental design, history refers to anything happening in a participant's life between measurements that might also affect the results. What if right after Tommy started eating strawberries he also started playing a lot of memory-enhancement games on the school's computer? The additional practice at memorization certainly could have an effect on his overall memory.

A common experimental practice that offers some control over history is testing more than one person. While it could be true that memory-enhancement games gave Tommy an additional advantage, it is unlikely that a group of 100 children would all have begun playing memory-enhancement games during the same time period. So if the improvement really isn't due to strawberries, we would expect the effect of the memory practice to be canceled out by the performance of the other 99 participants, who did not play memory-enhancement games. The use of multiple participants also introduces the possibility that a few characters in the group would do something during the experimental time period that would impair their memory abilities, which would further balance the picture. Generally speaking, the greater the number of participants, the less likely we are to be misled by our results.

A form of history that is especially relevant to developmental study is the effect of **maturation**. Maturation refers to changes that could happen due to natural growth processes during the period of experimentation. Tommy's memory may have improved during those weeks simply because he was growing older. One strategy for ruling out the effects of maturation is to measure two groups: one group that does eat strawberries—called the **experimental group**, and another that does not—called the **control group**. Both groups are tested at the same time and their results are compared. If the experimental group and the control group get the same results, we might guess that any improvement appearing among the children was due to maturation rather than strawberries. If the experimental group shows greater improvement than the control group, then we might infer that the strawberries caused the improvement.

Promoting Generalizability

Studies of child development are typically performed for the purpose of providing data that can be used out in the real world. In other words, the data produced by experimental designs need to demonstrate adequate **generalizability**. How does Mary's study measure up in this respect? We might wonder if Tommy's improvement is due to something unusual about Tommy and not necessarily anybody else. What if, unknown to Mary and the rest of us, Tommy suffers from a mysterious strawberry sensitivity disorder that causes him to recover lost memory when exposed to strawberries? The improvement would still be a true improvement for Tommy, but the results might not be useful for other children. That is, in the language of scientists, we cannot generalize these results.

When scientists select participants, they want them to be true representatives of the population under study, which affords them some certainty that their results apply to the rest of that population. For example, trying out a new teaching method on participants selected only from a class of gifted children will tell us how successful the method is while working with gifted children, but we cannot say it will also be successful with mainstream students. A social skills training program that demonstrates dramatic successes among participants selected from a ward of schizophrenic individuals may not be successful with a mentally retarded population. We might find exciting differences in puzzle-assembly strategies among study participants selected from an Hispanic population, but would not necessarily be able to say that the same could be expected of Asian-American, African-American, Native-American, or Caucasian children (Laosa, 1990).

So when we choose participants for our study, we want to be sure a wide variety of children are represented. We can accomplish this by means of **random selection** procedures. We select participants as randomly as circumstances allow, such as by choosing every third child on an alphabetical listing, or whoever happens to be in the second grade at a particular school, or children of parents responding to a nationally published advertisement, and so on. A few biases will still remain, such as the possibility that second-graders at the particular school or parents who respond to such advertisements are exceptional in some way. Nevertheless, the more random your participant selection, the more you can generalize your results to the greater population.

In addition to selecting a truly representative sample of participants, we also need to make sure that the participants in the experimental group and those in the control group are essentially the same. Suppose Tommy's strawberry sensitivity disorder is actually a hereditary trait. If most of the children in the experimental group are cousins of Tommy's and the children in the control group are not, we might expect that the experimental group will show a greater improvement in memory than the control group. But again, since the experimental group is made up of children with a greater likelihood of having the unique disorder, such findings would not be generalizable.

We avoid this problem by randomly assigning participants to the two groups. When **random assignment** is used, all members of the pool of participants have an equal chance of being in either the experimental group or the control group. Thus it is not likely that the characteristics of one group will be so different from the other that the results will be affected. The process is similar to choosing sides for a softball game. We could have our participants number off one, two, one, two; we could throw all the names in a hat and draw them out as we assign them to each group; or we could even have a computer randomly assign our participants for us.

Enhancing Objectivity

Next we want to address the accuracy of our observations. What made Mary so sure she was seeing an improvement in Tommy's memory? This is a concern of **objectivity**. In other words, would we or anyone else have observed the same improvements? First we need to decide what to observe that will reflect improved memory. Was Tommy less likely to leave his coat at a friend's house? Was he doing better on multiple choice tests at school? Was he better at remembering when it was time to go home? Was he more skilled at remembering where the prizes were hidden on the "Concentration" game board? Was he better able to look up phone numbers and remember them long enough to dial the number? These questions reflect several types of memory, such as short-term versus long-term, recall versus recognition, or any combination of these.

We can simplify our experiment by choosing a specific memory task for all our participants to perform before and after the period of eating strawberries; we thus ensure that any performance differences between the two times of observation are not the result of looking at different types of memory being used in different circumstances. We decide to use a written test of memory. A paper and pencil task that anyone can look at and judge is much more reliable than depending upon our own chance observations of children's behavior.

Another reason we might question the accuracy of Mary's observations is the effect of **experimenter bias**, the phenomenon popularly summed up as "you find what you're looking for." Because Mary knew she was giving Tommy strawberries for the purpose of improving his memory, she was more likely to look for evidence of improved memory that she may not have been looking for before he started eating strawberries. Possibly Tommy was always pretty good at remembering where the prizes were hidden on the "Concentration" game board, but she had not started watching for this ability until after he had been eating strawberries. By virtue of the fact that she chose to perform the experiment we can assume that she was already somewhat invested in the validity of the hypothesis, and thus would be more likely to watch for instances when his memory was good rather than poor.

We can control for experimenter bias by performing the experiment "**blind**." When experimentation is blind, the person measuring the participants' progress does not know which ones are in the experimental group and which are in the control group. If we do not know who is getting strawberries during memory testing, we do not risk letting our expectations result in more generous test scores or other differential treatment for those whom we expect to show improvement. A number of strategies accomplish this end: We could bring in a technician to score the tests; we could score the tests ourselves, but disguise or cover the names so we do not know which group they represent; or we could have the technician keep track of who is in which group and we ourselves could score the tests blind.

Test materials such as these are typically standardized. Standardization results in every test-taker experiencing and responding to the same treatment, which makes comparison between individuals and groups more meaningful.

Capitalizing on Standardization

Now, what about the strawberries themselves? How do we know that it is the essence of strawberry that makes a difference, rather than other ingredients that might appear in the jam, fruit juice, toaster pastry, ice cream, or whatever other form Mary had chosen for Tommy? We can control for this type of extraneous variable by means of **standardization**. Experimental procedures need to follow a certain standard in order to ensure that all participants are having the same experience. Our using a specific task to measure memory is a form of standardization. Tests used for psychological assessment are usually standardized in and of themselves; that is, they require that certain procedures be used to administer the test in order to get valid results. Thus we could prescribe that all children be given plain fresh strawberries rather than processed ones. We would also need to make sure all of the children were eating the same amount. Left to their own devices they are likely to simply eat whatever amount appeals to them, and too small an amount may not produce the effect. Let's say we will give each child three ounces of berries every morning.

Avoiding Placebo Effects

Another consideration is the expectations of the participants themselves. Did Tommy know the strawberries were supposed to be helping his memory? If so, we need to be concerned about a possible **placebo effect**. When people believe a pill or treatment is going to help them in a certain way, oftentimes it will do so simply by the power of suggestion (Kirsch, 1999). In this manner, Tommy's beliefs could have had an impact on his performance of memory-related tasks.

Physicians and pharmacists have long been aware of the power of a placebo. For this reason studies on the effects of new drugs usually involve **placebo groups**. The members of a placebo group take some form of sugar pill instead of the real drug, but the participants themselves do not know whether they are in the placebo group or the experimental group: They are "blind" to whether or not they are getting the real treatment. If the scientists who are measuring improvement also do not know which participants are getting the real thing, the study is **double-blind**. Double-blind studies minimize the possibility that either the participants' or the experimenters' expectations will affect the final outcome. For our study we can create a placebo group by giving our control group apricots every morning (assuming, of course, that we are certain that apricots do not improve or disrupt memory).

Accounting for Intervention Effects

Another problem related to participant expectations is referred to as **intervention effects**. Even if all you do is measure study participants, measurement alone may affect them in a way that changes the results. For example, Tommy may have started trying harder to remember things since his mother had indicated how important it was to her. The memory pretest we have chosen may let the children know what sort of information we are interested in and they might become more aware of how well they remember things, perhaps enough for them to develop new memory-improvement strategies on their own. This could dilute the final results in both groups to the point of swallowing up a true experimental effect.

We can avoid this intervention effect by creating a little camouflage. By hiding the memory test among several paper-and-pencil tasks, we can keep the children guessing about the true nature of the study. So let's say we'll include three other tasks: several simple addition problems, a brief multiple-choice spelling test, and a questionnaire about hobby preferences.

Another intervention effect we would want to take into account is a possible **practice effect**. Having taken the pretest, the children may do better on the second try just because they have had some practice at it. To minimize this effect we will create two equivalent versions of our tasks, version "A" for pretesting and version "B" for posttesting.

The Final Product

So what have we finally created? Here is how Mary's original experiment looked:

Participants:	Procedure:
Tommy	Give strawberries, casually observe his memory

After controlling for concerns about history, maturation, generalizability, objectivity, standardization, placebo effects, and intervention effects, we have created the following experimental design:

Participants:	Procedure:
100 experimental participants	Test A—Strawberries—Test B
100 placebo participants	Test A—Apricots—Test B
Participants randomly selected and assigned to groups	Tests scored blind
	Amount and form of fruit standardized

What we have just created is called a **true experimental design**. The two ingredients that make it a true experimental design are random assignment of participants to the experimental and control groups and the ability of the experimenters to manipulate the independent variable (we can assign or not assign consumption of strawberries).

Our particular design is a simple pretest-posttest design, but as you might imagine, there are many other possibilities. A researcher might have more than one dependent variable, such as wanting to see the effect of strawberries on attention span in addition to memory. The researcher might want to conduct more than one trial, such as having more than one episode of diet change and measuring progress periodically over a long span of time. We might also want to match groups according to some extraneous variable that is known to have an effect, such as making sure that each group has an equal number of children with strawberry sensitivity disorder. The different possibilities for experimental designs are almost endless.

Statistical Analysis

Let's say we go ahead and perform our experiment. After collecting our data we look at the differences between the pretest and posttest scores for the two groups of children. How much more improved than the control group's do the strawberry group's scores need to be for us to conclude that the treatment was effective?

Scientific method answers this question with the use of statistics. There are two main categories of statistics: descriptive and inferential. **Descriptive statistics** describe data, such as the percentage of people who have blue eyes or the average age of children who go to Disneyland. **Inferential statistics** not only describe a collection of data but also show relationships between variables. Inferential statistics allow us to infer that as one variable changes, the other variable also will change. In our experiment we attempted to infer that if children eat strawberries, their memory will improve. In addition to describing and allowing for inferences, statistics can suggest that one variable causes another. Because a true experimental design controls for other variables that might cause changes in the dependent variable, the appropriate statistic can let us hypothesize that the independent variable is both related to and a cause of the dependent variable.

Although inferential statistics are useful, they rarely provide us with absolute facts. They only suggest the *probability* of something's being true. This likelihood can be high or low, depending on the numerical value of the statistic. Suppose we flip a coin ten times. Because the coin has a fifty-fifty chance of falling heads or tails, we might predict that it will most likely come up heads five times and tails five times. What if the coin comes up six times heads and four times tails? Would we then say the coin is crooked? Probably not, since a six-four outcome is pretty close to our expectations anyway. Since it could happen that way just by chance, we would dismiss the difference as not being meaningful. How about eight heads and two tails? We still wouldn't be too suspicious. Perhaps if the coin came up heads all ten times we would begin to wonder if there was something unusual about the coin. But even so, the chances of getting heads ten times in a row are not so far off that we would say for sure that the coin is crooked.

Inferential statistics are set up to tell us how far our results have to be from reasonable expectations before we can say they did not occur by chance. In other words, they tell us whether the differences measured between the experimental group and the control group are **statistically significant**. When statistics are reported, they include reference to how likely the results could have occurred by chance. Scientists use the following shorthand: $p < .05$, which translates as, the probability (p) is less than ($<$) 5% that the results came out the way they did due to chance. Or if you ran the experiment 100 times, fewer than 5 times out of 100 would you get a significant-looking result by accident rather than because of a true relationship between the two variables.

Less than 5 chances out of 100 is usually the lowest **level of significance** scientists accept as having any meaning. A level of significance such as $p < .01$ (less than 1 chance in 100 that it came out that way by accident) or $p < .001$ (less than 1 chance out of 1000 that the results are due to chance) makes the scientist's findings look even more believable.

Scientists choose the particular statistical equation that is best suited to their experimental design. The method by which they do this is beyond the purposes of this discussion; suffice it to say they apply an appropriate statistical equation and look at tables that will tell them whether the statistical results are significant. These tables are usually organized around the level of significance the scientist hopes to use and—not surprisingly—how many participants were in the experiment, since the greater the number of participants, the less likely are the results to be a product of chance.

Statistics are complicated and can be frustrating and downright maddening even for the most dedicated of scientists. What little is presented here is for the purpose of pointing out that statistics, as well as scientific method, do not produce absolute facts. They tell us only the probability that something might be true. And because it is just a probability, other important variables may be at play no matter how strong a certain scientific finding may appear.

So, if even all the controls we place on an experimental situation do not produce absolute facts, how much more unreliable, then, are the chance personal observations we casually gather throughout our lives! This description of experimental design and statistical analysis highlights the attitudes of humility and skepticism that must lie beneath the pursuit of science. Good scientists never believe they have all the answers. They continually question their results, and they fully expect and accept the fact that at times they will be proved wrong. Only by questioning and being willing to change our views are we able to learn of new probabilities.

What measurement issues are particularly likely to interfere with accurate observation of child development?

MEASUREMENT ISSUES IN STUDYING CHILD DEVELOPMENT

Research in child development repeatedly runs up against certain extraneous variables that are often unavoidable. Scientists at times base their choice of research design in part upon which of these particular extraneous variables they most wish to control for. The three main developmental variables they may wish to control for are age, cohort, and time of measurement.

The effect of age is clear enough. People of different ages can be expected to measure up differently because they are at different chronological stages of development. Such effects are in fact what scientists specifically look for in their studies. However, inherent difficulties make obtaining a pristine measure of age effects an elusive endeavor. Suppose you want to measure changes in feelings of dependency over childhood, and you begin by watching how toddlers demonstrate dependency with clinging behavior when they see the babysitter arrive. How do you remeasure dependency when these children have reached age thirteen? Watching for physical clinging or even the presence of a babysitter is no longer a relevant option. If you do find a means of measuring dependency at age thirteen, how do you know it represents the same construct represented by clinging during toddlerhood? Even treating different age groups the same, such as by asking them the same question, can produce different results not necessarily because of the effects of maturation but because one group understands the question differently than the other.

People born into the same era or socioeconomic class will have certain characteristics that they share in common and that differentiate them from those born at other times or into a different class. A **cohort** is a collection of persons who share some statistical factor, such as era of birth, that is of interest to scientists (Elder, 1998b). For example, individuals who grew up during the Depression are likely to handle money and view wastefulness differently than those who did not go through such a period of serious deprivation. A person who lived through World War II will have a different perspective of home, family, and the price of freedom than those who did not experience such a time. A person who came of age during the "rebellious sixties" will have a different attitude toward following the status quo or accepting the dictates of authority than a person from a less change-minded period. A person's cohort membership can have long-term effects that last indefinitely.

Time of measurement concerns refer to societal or cultural factors that are at work during the period of the study. For example, the general attitude toward President Clinton's administration was very positive at the conclusion of the conflict in Kosovo in spite of the impeachment proceedings that had recently been conducted. Individuals in Western culture have become more accepting of the idea of sex education in the schools since the arrival of the AIDS epidemic. Attitudes stemming from such concurrent social influences frequently have effects on how study participants perform.

Problems crop up in most forms of life-span research when more than one of these three variables affects the experimental situation, because more than one can potentially explain the results of the study. Say we were curious about the attitudes of 40-year-old adults toward elective abortion. In 1990 we gave a group of 40-year-olds a questionnaire and found that most of them were in favor of elective abortion. Is this finding the result of being 40 years old—the variable of age? Or is it due to the fact that in 1990 the attitude toward abortion was substantially more relaxed than in previous generations—the variable of

FIGURE 2.1

Measurement protocols for cross-sectional, longitudinal, and time-lag designs.

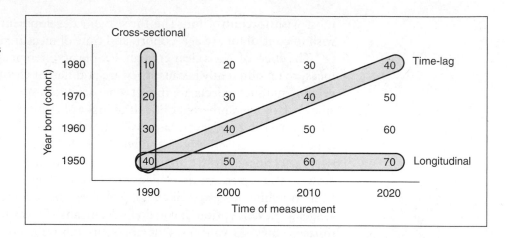

time of measurement? Or is it because someone who was 40 years old in 1990 would have come of age during the sixties, when the general attitude was to go against traditionally held beliefs—a cohort consideration?

When the effects of two or more variables cannot be separated from one another, scientists say the variables are **confounded**. In the above study we would say that age, cohort, and time of measurement are confounded. Certain types of experimental designs are used as means of controlling for one or more of these confounding variables. Figure 2.1 illustrates the measurement protocols of three such designs: cross-sectional, longitudinal, and time-lag.

Cross-Sectional Designs

The **cross-sectional design** measures a number of age groups at one point in time. Thus, as the label suggests, it looks at a cross-section of the general population at that moment. In our survey of attitudes toward abortion, a cross-sectional design might measure not only 40-year-olds, but also individuals who are 10, 20, and 30. Cross-sectional studies are often used because they are so economical. Everybody is tested at once, so the scientist can get it over with quickly and need not worry about people dropping out or moving away before all of the information has been gathered (not to mention worrying about getting a study published while it can still have an impact on tenure considerations!). Most studies of child development are in fact cross-sectional (Miller, 1997). The cross-sectional design shows the differences between age groups as well as the similarities.

However, since our abortion-attitude study participants are being measured at a single point in time, the results may reflect cultural values at the time of measurement rather than showing differences between the age groups. In addition, age and cohort are confounded: The differences that we find between the groups are as likely to be due to age differences as to the fact that each group comes from a different cohort.

Longitudinal Designs

Studies using a **longitudinal design** measure the same cohort more than once, typically over an extended period of time. Longitudinal studies are long-term studies, repeatedly measuring the researcher's variable of interest. We could perform a longitudinal study of attitudes toward elective abortion by taking people from one cohort and measuring their attitudes when they are ages 40, 50, 60, and 70. Repeatedly measuring the same cohort allows us a high degree of certainty that the differences found between the age groups are not a result of cohort differences. And if we are able to use the same participants—making a **within-subject** comparison—rather than measuring different participants at each decade—a **between-subject** comparison—our results become even more significant. Within-subject comparisons control for some of the interference that may spill into the variance from other individual differences when two different groups are compared.

Unfortunately, long-term studies have numerous disadvantages (Magnussen & Bergman, 1990). They are time-consuming, and we may not be able to see the results of our research for a very long time. They can be expensive, especially if someone must be hired for extended periods of time to keep track of people's whereabouts, past years' data, and other relevant materials. There is the problem of losing participants from within-subject studies because they have moved and cannot be found, have died, or just do not wish to be involved anymore—a problem known as **attrition**. If the same people are being tested and retested, intervention effects might skew the results; for example, experimental treatments might change their test-taking strategies or how they form their personal attitudes. Since we would be measuring only one cohort, we also would not know if our results could be generalized to any other cohort. And last, age and time of measurement are confounded. Any differences we might find from decade to decade could be due either to changing attitudes of the study participants as they age or to the changing cultural attitudes at the different times of measurement.

Time-Lag Designs

The **time-lag design** measures the same age group from many cohorts. For example, we could measure the attitudes of 40-year-olds who had been born in 1950, 1960, 1970, and 1980. Thus our actual measurements would take place in 1990, 2000, 2010, and 2020. Time-lag designs are useful for highlighting cohort changes. Since all study participants are the same age, differences seen between the groups can be attributed to cultural and other environmental changes rather than to the developmental changes going on in the individuals.

Highlighting cultural change is pretty much the only advantage of a time-lag design, and is the least used design. It is a long-term study, so we would not see our results for decades. Furthermore, cohort and time of measurement are

TABLE 2.1

Cross-sectional, longi-
tudinal, and time-lag
design benefits and
confounds.

Design	Unique Benefit	Confounded
Cross-sectional	Compares differences between age groups	Age and cohort
Longitudinal	Can illustrate changes in a single cohort or particular individuals over time	Age and time of measurement
Time-lag	Shows cohort differences	Cohort and time of measurement

confounded. Any differences found could be due either to cohort differences or to changing cultural values as the decades pass.

Sequential Designs

As you have probably suspected, scientists found a way to design an experiment that controls for age, cohort, and time of measurement. **Sequential designs** look like a combination of the cross-sectional, longitudinal, and time-lag designs. Typically scientists measure several different cohorts over several time periods. For example, people born in 1920 might have been measured in 1950, 1960, and 1970; another group of people, born in 1930, measured in 1960, 1970, and 1980; and yet another group, born in 1940, measured in 1970, 1980, and 1990 (see Figure 2.2).

Such strategies allow for a variety of inner comparisons that show the effects of age, cohort, and time of measurement, as well as maturation. The design appears to control for every conceivable confounding variable. But in spite of its seeming foolproof appearance, the sequential design has many practical disadvantages. As you have probably noticed, it is almost overwhelmingly complex. The researcher must round up a much larger number of participants than cross-sectional and longitudinal designs require. Since sequential designs are also longitudinal, they too are costly and seem to take forever.

These complex designs raise yet another problem during statistical analysis. Remember that statistics show significance in terms of the number of chances out of 100 that the significant-looking result could have come up by accident? This means that if you ran 100 statistical comparisons even when there were no real differences, you could count on at least a few producing significant-looking results due to chance. With these complex sequential designs you are making many internal comparisons, so you could expect something significant-looking to pop out regardless of whether it represents a true effect or chance.

This phenomenon is known as "**fishing error.**" The more times you throw in your line, the greater the likelihood that you will snag a significant-looking statistic. When evaluating large numbers of comparisons involving the same

FIGURE 2.2

Measurement protocol for a sequential design. Comparing this design to Figure 2.1, can you see how every sequential design also contains cross-sectional, longitudinal, and time-lag designs?

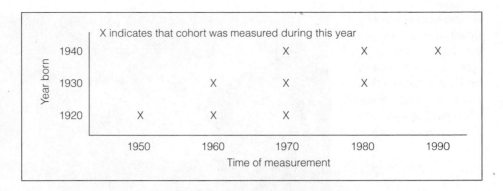

data, statisticians can use tables and procedures that tell them how much greater the value of their statistic must be in order to be considered significant. But these techniques invariably require a much higher statistical value before you can say your results are significant. So if there is a small true difference, you may end up assuming that your finding belongs in the discard pile when you really did have a winner.

What sources do investigators of child development use to identify and measure variables of interest?

ADDITIONAL RESOURCES FOR EXPERIMENTAL VARIABLES

Our strawberry study determined changes occurring in children's memory by using a test measuring mental performance, a common dependent variable in child research studies. Our abortion-attitude study could investigate the variations among the age groups with the aid of a survey, questionnaire, or structured interview (Krosnick, 1999). Survey, questionnaire, and structured interview methods are frequently employed as a means of gathering information about children from parents, teachers, health providers, and even other children.

Preverbal and partially verbal youngsters experience much that cannot be ascertained by the child's simply telling the researcher or the adult who is rating the child. Remember also that the self-report aspect of surveys, questionnaires, and interviews introduces considerable subjectivity into the data, both from how the participant self-observes and how the researchers or research instruments word the questions (Schwarz, 1999). For these reasons, observational studies have become increasingly popular (Irwin & Bushnell, 1980; Yarrow & Waxler, 1979). In **structured observational studies**, children are brought into laboratory settings where the researcher sets up an artificial environment especially conducive to revealing the effects of interest. In **naturalistic observational studies**, the researcher goes out into the field and observes how children behave while they are in familiar territory.

So, what do researchers observe? The answer to this question varies in complexity, depending upon the variable of interest. For example, in one recent

By means of observa-
tional studies using
one-way mirrors, re-
searchers can track and
evaluate behaviors that
often do not take place
when participants know
they are being watched.

Cary Wolinsky/Stock Boston

study the researchers wished to investigate the origins of joint visual attention
in infants (Corkum & Moore, 1998). Determining joint attention was a simple
matter of noting whether an infant turned its head in the same direction as the
experimenter's gaze. A more complex recent study wished to examine differences in interactive play behaviors between mothers of Down's syndrome children and mothers of more typically developing children (Roach et al., 1998).
What constitutes interactive play behavior? The researchers might begin by
watching everything going on between the mothers and their children and writing down as much as possible, creating **running narrative reports** as they do so.
After evaluating their reports they make note of play behaviors that seem particularly relevant to their interests and describe them as objectively as possible.
Here are some examples of these researchers' behaviors of interest (Roach et al.,
1998, pg. 80):

Child

Object play	Functional, exploratory, combinatorial, or symbolic play behavior with objects (for example, rolling the ball, talking on the phone, putting a driver in the car)
Vocalization	Any vocalization that carries communicative meaning or expresses joy or amusement

Mother

Demonstration	Demonstration of the properties of an object by performing some specified function (for example, stacking blocks, turning page of a book)
Vocal maintain	Vocalization in which the mother provides commentary, asks questions, laughs, or otherwise maintains the mother-child conversation (for example, "Where did the ball go?" "We have one of these." "Let's see what else we can find.")

Having chosen objectively defined behaviors such as these, researchers typically develop a coding system that allows the observer to simply check a box or add a tally when a relevant behavior is observed. In spite of careful definitions, however, observers, being human, will still introduce some subjectivity into their coding of behaviors. To guard against experimenter biases and other frailties of human observation, typically more than one observer codes the behavioral sample and the multiple codings are statistically compared for reliability. The greater access to videotaping in recent years has significantly increased the use of multiple coders to ensure the reliability of measurements.

The mother-child interactive play study gathered data by means of *time sampling*—the dyads were observed for a specific period of time during which occurrences of behaviors of interest were noted. When studies are more tightly focused on a specific behavior, the researchers will instead use *event sampling*, for which there is no fixed time limit. If researchers wished to investigate preschoolers' request-making behavior during free play, time sampling might be inappropriate: The target event might not even occur during a brief, fixed period of observation. For this study, the researchers might very well sit through an entire day's worth of free-play activity and engage in coding as request-making sporadically occurred.

To what extent do naturalistic observational studies such as these intrude into the lives of the preschoolers? Or for that matter, do their parents even want their children to be part of a research study? We next examine the system of ethics that protects children during developmental research.

ETHICS AND STUDYING CHILD DEVELOPMENT

How do research ethics apply to the study of children?

The 1960s witnessed some broad social changes in recognition of the role prejudicial attitudes play in society. One elementary school teacher in the Midwest believed that children's prejudicial attitudes could be reduced if they themselves had the experience of being the object of prejudice. She divided her class into two groups: those with blue eyes and those with brown eyes. Targeting one or the other group alternately for several days, she told the children in the targeted group that their eye color made them inferior. They were told they had to sit at the back of the class. Their responses in class were ridiculed, and when they made mistakes the teacher pointed out "that's just what you'd expect from a blue-eyed/brown-eyed person." They were restricted from recess, were made to be last in the lunch line, and were not allowed to use the playground equipment with the other children. At the end of the experiment, the children enthusiastically agreed that they would not prejudge people. However, by then most of the children also demonstrated evidence of psychological trauma, including tears and acting-out behaviors (*Eye of the Storm*, 1970).

What sorts of questions does this particular experiment bring to mind? When scientists study human participants, they must treat them according to certain ethical standards (American Psychological Association, 1990; Sales & Folkman, 2000). Individuals participating in experiments have rights, and researchers bear the responsibility of making sure that these rights are protected. Experimentation involving children is no exception, and actually introduces additional ethical dilemmas (American Psychological Association, 1968; Fisher & Tryon, 1990). As a safeguard against violating study participants' rights, researchers are currently required to have their proposed experiments evaluated by an institutional review board before implementing them (Chastain & Landrum, 1999). What might institutional review board members ask about the teacher's experiment on prejudice and children?

Protection from Harm

One of the first questions board members might ask no doubt addresses the trauma created for the children. Is it justifiable? Participants have the right to be protected from any physical and psychological harm that might occur during an experiment. If some discomfort cannot be avoided, the scientists evaluate whether the possible benefits of the study outweigh any possible adverse effects. If a participant is adversely affected, the scientist is then responsible for making sure that person gets whatever assistance is needed to overcome the effects (Fisher & Rosendahl, 1990).

Did the potential benefits of the prejudice experiment outweigh the trauma the children experienced? A goal of reducing prejudicial attitudes in society is certainly desirable. However, review board members would question whether the conditions needed to be as severe and as extensive as the teacher had created. They would want to evaluate the follow-up treatment that was offered to help the children counteract the effects of the trauma. They might also question her basic premise. Individuals often develop the rigid black-or-white reasoning style underlying prejudicial beliefs as a coping strategy after exposure to severe trauma. What evidence could the teacher provide that she would not be indirectly contributing to the underpinnings of prejudicial attitudes?

They might also be concerned about her proposed evidence of benefit (Danish, 1990; Lewis, 1990). Asking children if they will act prejudiced in the

Research ethics require that scientists obtain parents' informed consent before they use child participants in their studies.

St. Bartholomew's Hospital /SPL /Photo Researchers

future immediately after they have experienced unpleasant conditions due to prejudice is not likely to produce objective evidence of changed attitudes or behaviors. The review board would probably want to see an attempt to measure the predicted long-term effects of the experiment.

Informed Consent

The review board would also have concerns about **informed consent**. Participants should not be pressed into experiments against their will. When children are involved, both they and their parents must consent before they participate, and this consent must be "informed." In other words, they must be told as precisely as possible what is likely to happen to them in the course of the experiment, and of any short-term or long-term effects that might be encountered. Explanations must be such that both parents and children have a clear understanding. Furthermore, they must be told that they have the right to drop out of the experiment at any time they wish.

For the prejudice experiment, the review board would want to see evidence that the teacher had told both the parents and children what she wanted to do and had received their permission to proceed. They would also want to know what kind of classroom arrangements the teacher had made for students who were not participating or wanted to drop out of the experiment.

The Right to Truth

Participants have the right not to be lied to. When deception is a necessary component of an experiment, the scientist restores the participant's dignity at the conclusion of the experiment by revealing the deception, explaining its necessity, and making efforts to right any adverse effects of the deception. As it must with any form of potential psychological harm, an institutional review board will want to determine whether the deception is justified by necessity or can be eliminated by redesign of the experiment.

Deception of child study participants raises the concern of developmental level. While an adult may be able to understand the necessity of deception and shrug it off, children may process it a little differently. They are still developing their values and their rules for applying them. Given their often black-and-white thinking, instructing them that deception is okay under certain circumstances gives them an impression that "the ends justify the means" when it comes to personal integrity.

In the prejudice experiment, the teacher told the children that eye color makes people inferior or superior. The review board would want to know how she rectified this deception at the conclusion of the experiment and how she planned to take care of any possible developmental effects of the deception. They would also question whether deception was a necessary part of this experiment.

The Right to Privacy

How a participant performs in a study is considered confidential. Children especially have the right to protection of their identities in regard to both their participation and performance. Any information-gathering, write-ups, or other potentially public communications regarding a child development study must treat participants anonymously. For the prejudice study, the review board would want to know how the teacher planned to perform such an experiment in a public school without revealing which children are participating and what their treatment reactions are.

Clearly, many ethical issues would need to be addressed before an institutional review board would approve this teacher's experiment. While this particular study's questionable aspects are not difficult to recognize, a review board would be equally exacting for a much less toxic-looking project. The review system is concerned with protecting children's welfare above all else. Occasionally this concern may move researchers to abandon a study all together.

What are child development researchers' alternatives when ethics prohibit a true experimental design?

ALTERNATIVE EXPERIMENTAL DESIGNS

Rather than abandon a child study because it poses ethical dilemmas, researchers may choose to compromise the strength of their experimental designs. Suppose we wanted to scientifically measure the relationship between child abuse and aggressiveness in children. Remember that the essential elements of a true experimental design are random assignment of participants to groups and the ability to manipulate or assign the independent variable. For obvious practical and ethical reasons we cannot randomly assign participants to homes. Likewise we cannot ethically instruct one group of parents to be abusive and the others to be nonabusive. Thus we can only measure and compare aggressiveness in children from abusive and nonabusive homes as we identify them.

Correlational Designs

One of the more common, less intrusive forms of investigation is the **correlational study**. Correlational statistics indicate the degree to which one variable will change when another variable is also changing. A perfect correlation would be indicated by a statistical value of 1.00, but this is rarely if ever found. Usually a significant correlational statistic is much lower, around .30 or .40, depending on the number of participants. The nearer the correlational statistic approaches 1.00, the stronger the relationship. The statistic can be either positive or negative. A positive number indicates that the more that one variable occurs, the *more* the second variable occurs. A negative sign in front of the statistic indicates that the more that one variable occurs, the *less* the other occurs.

Our proposed child abuse study is a correlational study. Since we do not control which type of child goes into which sort of home, a positive correlation would not necessarily let us say that the abuse *causes* the aggressiveness, only that child abuse and aggressiveness in children tend to turn up together. This leaves the door open for alternative explanations. Perhaps aggressiveness is an inherited factor and the children are aggressive because they inherited it from their aggressive parents. Perhaps the causal relationship goes the other direction: Aggressive children produce abusive parents. Or maybe there is some third variable, such as living in crisis situations, that causes both abusiveness in parents and aggressiveness in children.

Although correlational studies do not show causation, they nevertheless have substantial utility. No matter what is causing aggressiveness in a child from an abusive home, a significant result still indicates that if a child is from such a home, he or she has a greater likelihood of being aggressive. On the basis of such a study, we could use knowledge of child abuse as a screening device when selecting children who would most likely benefit from an anger management program.

We can also use data-collection techniques to help get around some of the potential extraneous variables. The possibility that aggressiveness is inherited rather than trained in through abuse can be addressed through studies of identical twins. Since identical twins have identical genes, studies of twins raised separately are valuable. If one twin were raised in an abusive home and the other in a nonabusive home, we would be able to see the differences in the effect of training without worrying that inherited traits are muddying the waters. Twin studies and other methods of investigating the effects of shared and nonshared environments have been used many times to help sort out the effects of nature and nurture (Plomin et al., 1994; Rutter et al., 1999a; Wright, 1997). The question of whether aggressive children actually produce abusive parents could be examined by means of adoption studies. Does introducing an aggressive child into a previously nonabusive home result in abusive parenting, while introducing a nonaggressive child into the home does not?

Third variables such as living in a crisis situation can be tested separately. Let's say you discover a relationship between living in crisis situations and both parental and child aggressiveness. By devising methods that weight the abuse and aggressiveness measures differently for those families than for noncrisis families, you subtract the effect of being in a crisis situation from your final analysis of child abuse and child aggressiveness. Or, you might just leave identified crisis families out of your pool of participants. Does this sound complicated? It is! But it shows that even if you lack a true experimental design, scientific method enables you to develop procedures that control for most of the extraneous variables that you (or your skeptical fellow scientists) might think of.

But what if you can't think of a way to control for a certain variable? And what about other compromises to the integrity of an experimental design, such as needing to settle for nonrandomized groups or not being able to arrange for an appropriate control group (Cook & Campbell, 1979)? What do you do then? Probably nothing, at least insofar as you conduct your study as if there were no such limitations, but when interpreting your data you point out to your scientific audience which variables were not controlled for and speculate upon the implications this might have. Those who read your study can then judge for themselves whether the limitations were significant enough to invalidate your results, or perhaps they will think of a way to control for the shortcomings themselves.

Designs Measuring Single Participants

In spite of advances in scientific method over the last few decades, researchers still find value in gathering information by means of intensive observation of a single child. This is called the **case study method** (Blampied, 1999; Franklin et al., 1997; Hersen & Barlow, 1976). Such a study might examine trends in an individual child's academic success through elementary, middle, and high school. Another possibility would be to observe a child's social skills at one point in time and then compare them to social successes and failures later in life. Sometimes a scientist will intervene with little tests of sorts to help clarify what is going on within a particular child's development. For example, we might purposely put a child into a novel social situation and evaluate his or her social skills, then observe the child again a year or so later.

These "little tests" can evolve into **single-participant experimental designs**, during which a scientist notes the effects on an observed child when an experimental variable is introduced. In the previous example, a scientist might introduce the variable of a parent's presence in the novel situation and evaluate any observed differences in the child's socializing strategies. Then the scientist could try another new situation both with and without the parent, again observing any differences in the child's behaviors. Alternating trials of a control condition and an experimental condition in this manner produces what is known as an **ABAB design**.

The shortcoming of single-subject studies is that their results are difficult to generalize. We might find a true effect for one child, but is it a useful finding regarding other children? In the socialization experiment above we would need to be mindful that how a child reacts when a parent is in the room depends a lot on his or her past experiences with parents, a factor that varies considerably from child to child and would be likely to complicate interpretation of the results.

In spite of their limitations, studies centering on individual children still offer substantial utility in the study of child development. They often lead the way for more vigorous studies as observations lead to new hypotheses. Even Piaget began developing his original ideas on child cognitive development by systematically observing a single study participant—his daughter. He found similar patterns of cognitive advances as he observed his second and third children. When repeated individual case studies such as Piaget's reveal consistent findings, they begin to offer some of the empirical soundness of group experimentation (Kollins et al., 1999).

REPORTING RESEARCH FINDINGS

The vast majority of published research findings appear in the form of journal articles; some are reported in books. Scientists are careful to report their findings in an accurate, consistent, professionally accepted manner (Wilkinson et al., 1999). In doing so they provide adequate information for other researchers who wish to replicate the findings (Reese, 1999). Such consistencies also help those who interact with children apply research findings in their practice of applied developmental psychology (Pellegrini & Bjorklund, 1998; Rutter, 1998). The Tried. . . . and True box on pages 56–57 explains the format of a standard research-oriented journal article. Tried. . . . and True boxes appear in future chapters.

CONCLUSION

As you can see, measuring child development and interpreting findings is a complicated business. Rarely does a single study let a scientist make conclusive statements about a topic of study. The study of child development makes headway by fitting together many pieces of research in ways that both make sense and contribute toward benefit. It can be a difficult task but is certainly not an impossible one. This cycle of observation, experimentation, interpretation, application, and further observation also colors the study of child development with its exciting, ever-evolving nature.

BOX 2.1   From Research to Application

CHILD DEVELOPMENT SPECIALISTS ARE CAREFUL TO consider their research base before commenting on what to expect from children, counseling how to parent, assessing educational practices, and so forth. As you may have gathered from what you have read thus far, the study of child development is backed up by one complex research base. A current research tendency toward "metastudies" that evaluate numerous treatments or conditions at once adds even more confusion as developmentalists and casual observers alike attempt to make sense out of the data.

Psychology is actually both a science and an art. As a basic science, psychology uses scientific method to demonstrate principles of thoughts and behavior. As an applied science, psychology blossoms into an art when the practitioner takes into account both research and the unique situation at hand in order to create customized interventions and make predictions. The "Tried. . . . and True" boxes that appear throughout this textbook are designed to shed light on each: Where are all the data coming from, and how do child developmentalists go about applying interpreted results. The "Tried. . . ." sections describe the research—the basic science of psychology—in a form more easily digestible than you are likely to encounter in a standard journal article. In addition to summarizing concepts under investigation, these boxes will also most likely contribute toward your ability to mentally outline journal study articles as you examine them on your own.

Journal articles often become confusing for the neophyte because there seem to be three voices trying to make themselves heard at once. The general flow of articles becomes easier to understand once the different agendas of the various voices are sorted out. The trick to making sense of the clamor among the three is focusing on the right voice at the right time. There are three main voices in your average journal study article:

The Global Voice. This is the expansive voice, the voice of theory, the general body of knowledge involved, or perhaps the entire field of psychological inquiry.

The Specific Voice(s). Depending on the study, there are one or more specific voices. They represent the specific variables the study is attempting to explore.

The Experimental Voice. This is the cold-bloodedly objective voice. It is concerned with experimental design, statistics, and the other highly tailored manipulations of empiricism.

The configuration produced when you look at the voices' positions of importance within a standard journal article takes on an hour-glass shape, as Figure 2.3 shows. With the hourglass configuration as a structure, the Tried. . . . and True boxes will discuss the structures of selected journal study articles by answering questions like the following:

Introduction
- What are the relevant theories and applications behind this study?
- Which variable(s) is this study attempting to explore?
- What is the purpose of the study?

The Experiment
- Who are the study participants, and how are they selected?
- What treatments and/or methods of measurement are used?
- Are the results statistically significant?

Results and Discussion
- What has been added to our knowledge of the experimental variables?
- How do the new findings fit in with other studies and/or current theory or assumptions?

The corresponding sections, titled ". . . . and True," discuss how the findings derived from use of the scientific method fit in with the real world. Findings alone do not tell you what you should choose to do in any given situation. They tell you only the probability that a particular result is likely to occur if you follow a certain course of action. The consumers of scientific data have the re-

BOX 2.1   *continued*

sponsibility of considering the probabilities, interpreting them, and applying them as they see fit.

Perhaps we are interested in how a study explains a child behavior we have just observed. We might want to know how a child psychologist would interpret and apply the findings as he or she treats a particular client. A parent may judge the relevance of a study, deciding that it does not apply to a certain child's behavior because the child is so far removed from the population described by the study. Or, a particular child's sensitivities may lead to a parent's prediction that a research finding is especially relevant for the child. Perhaps a child development specialist puts together a customized program for a whole classroom of children that could incorporate the findings of more than one study into a practical plan. All of these are encompassed within the art of applied psychology.

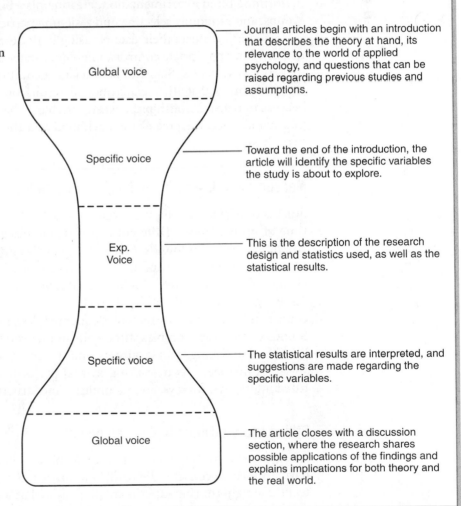

FIGURE 2.3

The configuration of voices within a journal study article.

Global voice — Journal articles begin with an introduction that describes the theory at hand, its relevance to the world of applied psychology, and questions that can be raised regarding previous studies and assumptions.

Specific voice — Toward the end of the introduction, the article will identify the specific variables the study is about to explore.

Exp. Voice — This is the description of the research design and statistics used, as well as the statistical results.

Specific voice — The statistical results are interpreted, and suggestions are made regarding the specific variables.

Global voice — The article closes with a discussion section, where the research shares possible applications of the findings and explains implications for both theory and the real world.

◢ *SUMMARY*

Scientific Method and Experimental Design

Scientific method is a process of studying human development that endeavors to create maximum objectivity of observation. It enhances objectivity by methodologically assigning variables under study and controlling for extraneous variables that potentially provide alternative explanations for experimental observations. Extraneous variables that may be controlled for during an experiment include history, maturation, concerns of standardization and generalizability, experimenter bias, placebo effects, intervention effects, and practice effects. Scientists control for these extraneous variables by such techniques as performing blind experimentation, creating placebo groups and other control groups, and randomly selecting and assigning participants.

Scientists evaluate their data by using both descriptive and inferential statistics. With appropriate controls, inferential statistics can also indicate causality between variables. Statistics help scientists evaluate their data by indicating the probability that their experimental results occur by chance rather than because of true relationships between variables. The greater the level of a statistic's significance, the greater the likelihood that the scientist has tested a valid hypothesis.

Measurement Issues in Studying Child Development

Studies of human development often confound the effects of age, cohort, and time of measurement. Different experimental designs are subject to different combinations of confounds. Cross-sectional designs may show differences between age groups but confound age and cohort. Longitudinal designs show changes of a cohort over time but confound age and time of measurement. Time-lag designs highlight the characteristics of a particular age but confound cohort and time of measurement. Sequential designs control for all three confounds but are very complex, time-consuming, and expensive and increase the likelihood of fishing error. Sources of measurement to be used as experimental variables include tests measuring mental performance questionnaires, structured interviews, surveys, and naturalistic and structured observations.

Ethics and Studying Child Development

All those who participate in experiments have rights, such as protection from harm, informed consent, the truth, and privacy. Scientists are required to protect these rights during experimentation, as well as to rectify any adverse effects participants may experience. To protect the rights of participants, scientists must have their experiments evaluated by an institutional review board before they can be conducted.

Alternative Experimental Designs

Occasionally research ethics require that the methodological integrity of an experimental design be compromised. Alternative experimental designs can be used, such as correlational studies, studies of nonrandomized groups, single case studies, and single-participant experimental designs. These studies are not as rigorous as true experimental designs, and their results must therefore be interpreted and applied with caution.

Reporting Research Findings

Scientists communicate their findings using a traditional format or structure. Journal articles typically include related theory, the experimental design itself, and discussion of the findings in ways that both allow the study to be replicated and also aid the reader's understanding of how findings might best be applied.

KEY TERMS

ABAB design
attrition
between-subjects design
blind experimentation
case study method
cohort
confounded variables
control
control group
correlational studies
cross-sectional experimental
   design
dependent variable
descriptive statistics
double-blind experimentation
experimental group
experimental variable

experimenter bias
extraneous variable
fishing error
generalizability
history
independent variable
inferential statistics
informed consent
intervention effects
level of significance
longitudinal experimental design
maturation
naturalistic observational study
objectivity
participants
placebo effect
placebo group

practice effects
random assignment
random selection
running narrative report
scientific method
sequential experimental design
single-participant experimental
   design
standardization
statistical significance
structured observational study
time-lag experimental design
time of measurement
true experimental design
variable
within-subject design

CONCEPT REVIEW

1. Scientific method is more accurate than casual observation because it
   _____ variables that can affect results or suggest alternative
   interpretations of a study's findings.

2. Experimental designs seek to maximize demonstration of the effects of
   _____ variables and minimize the effects of _____ variables.

3. Scientists can rule out the effects of history or maturation in their experimental data by including both _____ groups and _____ groups in their experimental design.

4. If experimental findings are so specific to the particular participants that they cannot be applied outside of the experimental situation, we say that the findings do not have adequate _____. Scientists can increase this aspect of a study's usefulness by means of _____ of participants representing the population under investigation.

5. A scientist's expectations can in turn affect his or her observations, resulting in _____. This can be controlled for by having the researchers gather data in a _____ manner.

6. Experimental designs investigating the effectiveness of new medications frequently include _____ in order to control for the phenomenon of participants' showing an effect simply because they believe the medication will work.

7. A true experimental design controls assignment of _____ to experimental and control groups and assignment or nonassignment of the _____.

8. _____ statistics describe data, while _____ statistics also show relationships between pieces of data.

9. If the differences measured between the performance of a control group and an experimental group are _____, we can say that the findings are likely to be due to the experimental manipulation rather than to chance.

10. Three factors that frequently confound one another and are especially relevant while studying human development are _____, _____, and _____.

11. An experimental design that measures a number of different ages at one point in time is called a _____ design, whereas a study that measures the same participants or cohort at several points in time is called a _____ design.

12. Designs that have the potential to control for age, cohort, and time of measurement are called _____ designs; however, the many measurements involved increase the likelihood that significant-looking findings actually occur due to chance, a phenomenon called _____.

13. Because children are not skilled at reporting thoughts and feelings, rather than using _____ or _____, child development researchers frequently use _____ as they gather data.

14. To protect child study participants' rights and well-being, researchers are usually required to have their studies approved in advance by a(n) _____ .

15. When a potential for harm is unavoidable within a research project, two important considerations regarding whether scientists should proceed include _____ and _____ .

16. A statistical design that shows how two variables are related but does not indicate which, if either, causes which is the _____ study.

17. A type of study that allows for intense, detailed investigation but can be limited in its generalizability is the _____ design.

18. The practice of reporting research findings in a consistent, objective manner contributes toward the possibility of studies being _____ .

1) controls; 2) experimental; extraneous; 3) control; experimental; 4) generalizability; random selection; 5) experimenter bias; "blind"; 6) placebo groups; 7) participants; independent variable; 8) Descriptive; inferential; 9) statistically significant; 10) age; cohort; time of measurement; 11) cross-sectional; longitudinal; 12) sequential; "fishing error"; 13) survey questionnaires; interviews; observational methods; 14) institutional review board; 15) the project's potential for benefit; means of compensating for harm; 16) correlational; 17) single-subject; 18) replicated

RESOURCES FOR FURTHER READING

Fisher, C. B., & Tryon, W. W. (Eds.) (1990). *Ethics in applied developmental psychology: Emerging issues in an emerging field.* Norwood, NJ: Ablex.

Miller, S. A. (1997). *Developmental research methods,* 2nd ed. Englewood Cliffs, NJ: Prentice-Hall.

Pellegrini, A. D., & Bjorklund, D. (1998). *Applied child study: A developmental approach,* 3rd ed. Hillsdale, NJ: Erlbaum.

Solso, R. L., & Johnson, H. H. (1994). *Experimental psychology: A case approach,* 5th ed. New York: HarperCollins.

INFOTRAC COLLEGE EDITION

For additional readings, explore InfoTrac College Edition, your online library. Go to http://www.infotrac-college.com/wadsworth and use the passcode that came on the card with your book. Try this search term: research ethics

CHILD DEVELOPMENT CD-ROM

 Go to the Wadsworth Child Development CD-ROM for further study of the concepts in this chapter. The CD-ROM also includes quizzes and additional activities to expand your learning experience.

REFERENCES

For a list of references for this chapter, see the Wadsworth Psych Study Center Web site at: http://www.wadsworth.com/product/0534348092s

CHAPTER 3

Biological Beginning Points

FOCUS QUESTIONS

▶ How far back can we trace our developmental beginnings?

▶ What mechanisms are at work as genes and genetic processes guide our development?

▶ How are sex cells formed?

▶ How can unusual chromosomal conditions affect human development?

▶ Which human characteristics appear to reflect genetic influences?

▶ How tightly is genetic programming tied to development?

▶ How close have we come to genetically engineering the perfect child?

▶ What is genetic counseling, and how can we benefit from it?

Evolutionary Beginnings	Intelligence
Genes and Genetics	Psychological Disorders
Sex Cells	**How Much Nature and How Much Nurture?**
Chromosomal Anomalies and Development	**Genetic Engineering**
Down's Syndrome	**Genetic Counseling**
X and Y Chromosomes	Early Testing Procedures
Genetically Influenced Attributes and Conditions	Paving Pathways: Reproductive Options
Physical Appearance	
Temperament	

Seventh-grade Todd had a crush on Bridgette, a classmate in his honors computer course. In the tradition of typical 12-year-old boys, this translated into looking for a way to give her a hard time. He decided to tease her about being one of the few girls in a male-dominated classroom.

"Hey, Bridgette," he said. "How come you dress up and look pretty like a girl but mess with computers like a boy? Don't you know about genes?"

"It's not so hard to understand," she replied, brushing off his attentions. "After all, I got half my genes from my mother and half from my father."

While mothers' and fathers' joint gene contributions do not function as Bridgette's quip might suggest, researchers are discovering more and more evidence of genetic influences in human development—physical, intellectual, and emotional. We begin the chapter by tracing the infinite course of evolutionary influences, the threads of development that connect each of us to the larger tapestry of life. We then narrow our focus to investigate the development of the individual: the role of genes, the basic biology of reproduction, and the twists and turns that development can take as the influences of nature and nurture intertwine.

How far back can we trace our developmental beginnings?

EVOLUTIONARY BEGINNINGS

Let's start at the very beginning—about 50,000 years ago—the era during which scientists estimate *Homo sapiens* emerged as a species. Charles Darwin pioneered the idea that human beings have not always been around in their current form (Darwin, 1859; Jones, 1999). He proposed the theory that all present-day species evolved from nonliving material and previous forms of life, bringing along with them only those ancestral characteristics that have either enhanced or not impaired survival of their species (Rose, 1998). He believed that as the demands of the environment have changed, so also have the collections of ancestral characteristics passed on to later generations.

Natural selection describes the process of change in a species over time: In the struggle for existence, individuals possessing favorable variations in inherited traits—variations that improve adaptation to the environment—are more likely to survive and reproduce than are those not inheriting the favorable variation. As the favorable variations accumulate over generations, descendants diverge from their ancestors. In other words, if a certain attribute is an asset to a species, such as having a long neck when all available vegetation is located in the treetops, longer-necked individuals are much more likely to survive than the shorter-necked; the latter die out, and those with longer necks mature and reproduce. A more timely example of how this could occur involves the AIDS epidemic. Unless some means is developed for containing it, the individuals most likely to mature and reproduce during this new millennium will be among that tiny percentage who appear to have a natural ability to fight off HIV (human immunodeficiency virus). In some African countries one-quarter of the population is infected, and numbers continue to increase. Natural selection may very well play a role where cultural traditions do not support safe practices.

Recently, investigators have been looking into the effects of cultural influences on natural selection (Durham et al., 1997). Cultures also evolve over time, with natural selection favoring the concepts, perceptions, values, rules, and principles most adaptive for the particular population (Tomasello, 1998). Cultural evolution and genetic evolution can affect one another, as happens, for example, when a society's mate-selection practices make certain culturally valued traits more likely to be passed on through reproduction, such as desired facial features.

A specific example of this "coevolution" involves tolerance for lactose, the sugar present in milk. Children the world over typically outgrow the ability to digest this sugar by adulthood, at which time consuming it may even leave them feeling ill. Yet as you are probably well aware, among some subpopulations, especially many of European and African descent, most adults tolerate lactose. This apparent modification of their gene pools has been traced to their historical reliance on dairy-based lifestyles, which would be expected to favor survival for those individuals who are lactose tolerant. Likewise, the ability of a population to digest lactose favors survival of the dairy industry in that culture (Durham, 1991)!

The theory of natural selection is well supported by studies such as the above, as well as by common sense. We can easily identify a variety of uniquely human characteristics that we would expect to have given us a certain edge in our species' survival, such as the influences of greater intelligence and the longer period of child-parent attachment until maturation. The role of natural selection will come up frequently during our exploration of child development in this textbook. Darwin's theory that life originated from nonliving material and less advanced life forms, however, is not so well supported. Having read Chapter 2, you may have already drawn such a conclusion: The hallmark of scientific method is controlled demonstration. The time factor alone prevents scientists from setting up an experiment that demonstrates the full process of evolution that Darwin proposed.

On the other hand, scientific method has excelled at revealing other aspects of our biological beginnings. The remainder of this chapter will take a look at genes, genetics, and other material related to the biology of reproduction.

GENES AND GENETICS

What mechanisms are at work as genes and genetic processes guide our development?

Our current understanding of genes and their effect on development originated with the work of Gregor Mendel, a nineteenth-century Austrian monk (Olby, 1985). His studies focused primarily on hereditary traits in peas and other plants. In concert with technological advancements, scientists have further investigated and identified a variety of physical structures and chemical processes responsible for some of Mendel's early observations (Gehring, 1998).

The story begins with individual cells. Most cells in the human body contain a nucleus. Within each nucleus we normally have 46 **chromosomes**. These chromosomes are made up of strings of **deoxyribonucleic acid**, better known as **DNA** (Plomin & Crabbe, 2000). **Genes**, which program our bodies to develop a certain way, are located on these strings of DNA, as Figure 3.1 shows. Genes not only control whether we grow into human beings or some other species but also direct development of the many unique variations in our features that allow us to tell one another apart (Ridley, 1999).

Chromosomes and their genes are organized in pairs. Since we generally have two genes for each gene site, we might have two differing genes for the same characteristic. For example, we might have one gene for blue eyes matched up with another gene for brown eyes. Genes often sort out these genetic conflicts by acting either dominant or recessive. A **dominant** gene is so named because it will "dominate" in determining how the person will look when paired with a less dominant gene. A **recessive** gene is one that "recedes" and allows the dominant gene to determine the person's characteristics. Those who study genetics use a type of shorthand to indicate dominance and recessiveness. An uppercase letter such as *T* identifies the dominant gene and a lowercase letter such as *t* identifies the recessive gene.

So our gene pairs for any given characteristic may consist of several different **genotypes**: We can have

▶ a *TT* pair, two dominant genes.
▶ a *tt* pair, two recessive genes.
▶ a *Tt* or *tT* pair, one dominant gene and one recessive gene.

When both genes are the same, as in *TT* and *tt* pairs, they are called **homogeneous**. When the two genes are different, as in *Tt* and *tT* genotypes, they are called **heterogeneous**.

An individual with the *tt* pairing of two recessive genes typically develops the recessive trait. If the gene for brown eyes is dominant and the gene for blue

FIGURE 3.1

DNA as it appears on a chromosome. DNA is made up of pairs of chemical bases. Here the strand of DNA is reproducing itself by splitting down the middle, then recreating the missing halves of the two new DNA strands by picking up the missing partner from substances surrounding the cell nucleus. Adapted with permission from E. Frankel, 1979, *DNA: The Ladder of Life,* New York: McGraw-Hill, p. 54.

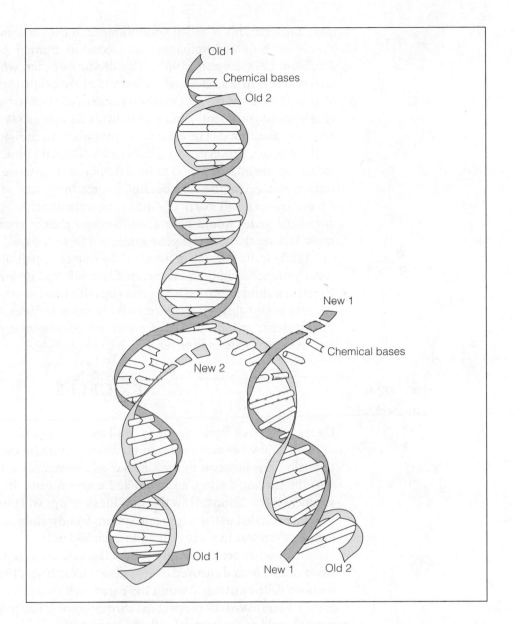

eyes is recessive, a person with two recessive genes for eye color will have blue eyes. You can be relatively certain that a blue-eyed person has two recessive genes for eye color.

However, you could not so easily predict the genotype of a person with brown eyes. The pairing could be *TT,* with two dominant genes, but it could also be *Tt* or *tT,* with the dominant brown gene having defeated the recessive blue gene in the battle of eye color. So when we describe how a gene pair actually expresses itself, we refer to it as its **phenotype**. *TT* and *Tt* genotypes thus have the same phenotype; in this case, the appearance of brown eyes.

Sometimes both genes express themselves. For example, a plant with one gene for white flowers and another gene for red flowers may actually produce pink flowers. This is called **codominance**. Sickle-cell anemia provides an example of how codominance can occur in human beings (Bloom, 1995; Durham, 1991; Serjeant, 1985). This deadly disorder, which occurs in individuals of black-African heritage, causes red blood cells to collapse into a sicklelike shape. Their effect on the circulatory system's ability to function is so profound that without treatment, almost all individuals with sickle-cell anemia die before reaching adulthood. The disorder occurs when an individual has inherited two of these genes. However, those individuals who have inherited only one gene for sickle-cell anemia are found to have significant resistance to malaria. Given this circumstance, that the gene became favored by natural selection is no surprise! In malaria-plagued parts of Africa, individuals with a heterogenous pair of sickle-cell genes would have a substantially greater chance of survival, while those lacking the recessive gene would not be so favored.

While traits that are determined by one gene pair are the easiest to study, most variance of human characteristics is affected by a number of gene pairs. Rarely is a child produced who grows up with traits identical to one or the other parent's personality, intelligence, or body characteristics. These traits are said to be **polygenic** in their inheritance patterns because many different genes work together to produce a final result.

How are sex cells formed?

SEX CELLS

Genes are passed from parent to child by means of sex cells. Women produce sex cells known as *ova* (**ovum** in the singular form), and men produce **sperm** (actually *spermatozoon* in the singular and *spermatozoa* in the plural form). A new life is created when an ovum and a sperm unite in the appropriate environmental conditions. How this new life develops will be determined largely by the genes carried in the ovum and sperm. So how does nature determine which genes will appear in these cells and which will not?

Our bodies are constantly producing new cells, replacing those that have worn out or been destroyed. New cells are usually created through a process of division called **mitosis**. Within the parent cell's nucleus, a new set of chromosomes is templated off the original chromosomes. The new set then breaks away from the old as the original cell divides in two, with each new cell having a full set of 46 chromosomes. Alternatively, sex cells are produced during the process of **meiosis**. During meiosis the parent's original chromosomal pair divides, with each sex cell that is produced containing half of each chromosomal pair. In this manner each parent contributes half of the genes necessary for production of an offspring. Figure 3.2 shows the similarities and differences between the processes of mitosis and meiosis (Bernard, 1990; Rieder, 1999).

A new life begins when an ovum and a sperm unite, a process called fertilization or **conception**. Within the newly formed **zygote**, the two half-sets of chromosomes from the two sex cells join together, matching up with their corresponding gene partners. Multiple births such as twins can occur from either

Step 1. Original parent cell (for illustrative purposes this cell contains but four chromosomes).

Step 3. The duplicate sets of chromosomes move to opposite ends of the parent cell, which then begins to divide.

Step 2. Each chromosome splits lengthwise, producing a duplicate.

Step 4. The cell completes its division, producing two daughter cells that have identical sets of chromosomes.

FIGURE 3.2A

Mitosis.

During the process of mitosis, cell division results in two identical daughter cells containing identical DNA.

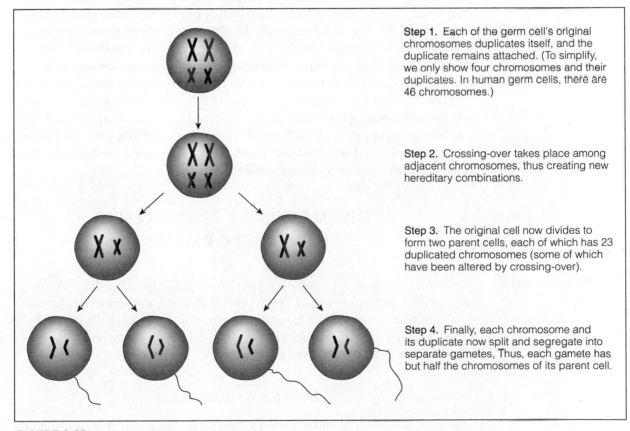

Step 1. Each of the germ cell's original chromosomes duplicates itself, and the duplicate remains attached. (To simplify, we only show four chromosomes and their duplicates. In human germ cells, there are 46 chromosomes.)

Step 2. Crossing-over takes place among adjacent chromosomes, thus creating new hereditary combinations.

Step 3. The original cell now divides to form two parent cells, each of which has 23 duplicated chromosomes (some of which have been altered by crossing-over).

Step 4. Finally, each chromosome and its duplicate now split and segregate into separate gametes, Thus, each gamete has but half the chromosomes of its parent cell.

FIGURE 3.2B

Meiosis.

The process of meiosis creates sex cells, each of which contains only half of the parent cell's DNA. When the two parents' sex cells are combined, the resulting cell will again contain a full complement of DNA, but will differ from both parent cells. Both from Shaffer: *Developmental Psychology.* Pacific Grove: Brooks/Cole, pp. 74–75.

one zygote or multiple zygotes. Sometimes a woman's ovaries will release more than one ovum. If two ova are released and fertilized at the same time the resulting twins would be **dizygotic**, having grown from two separate zygotes. Dizygotic twins do not share any more characteristics than they would share with any other full brother or sister, and are usually called "fraternal twins." Identical twins come from a single zygote and are therefore called **monozygotic**. Identical twins occur when a fertilized egg divides in two and the two new cells separate, each continuing on to develop into a separate person. Having come from the same zygote and therefore sharing the same chromosomes, these twins will be for the most part identical in their physical and even some psychologically based forms of development.

Some couples who have had difficulty conceiving have elected to use artificial methods of bringing sperm to egg, such as in vitro fertilization and embryo transfer (Stephenson & Wagner, 1994). Concerns have arisen regarding how children conceived in this manner might be affected developmentally or how these manipulations of nature might affect the parents' attitudes toward their child. Thus far most of these concerns appear to be unfounded. Children conceived in this way show no greater incidence of medical, physical, or cognitive developmental impairments (Levy-Shiff et al., 1998; van Balen, 1998). A study did find slightly poorer socioemotional development among boys and children of older parents, but it is not clear whether this is due to the procedures themselves or the parenting characteristics of those who turn to artificial methods for conception (Levy-Shiff et al., 1998). In fact, one study showed that mothers who conceived in this manner report more feelings of protectiveness toward the child and less satisfaction with family life than do mothers who conceived naturally (Hahn & DiPietro, 2001).

How can unusual chromosomal conditions affect human development?

CHROMOSOMAL ANOMALIES AND DEVELOPMENT

Sometimes events occur during these earliest beginnings of life that will drastically affect a person's eventual development. One such potential malfunction occurs during the process of meiosis when the chromosomal pairs do not split apart cleanly. The resulting sex cells might have damaged chromosomes, one chromosome too many, or even one too few.

Down's Syndrome

One such condition is called **Down's syndrome** (Cicchetti & Beeghly, 1990; Epstein, 1989). Individuals with Down's syndrome either inherit an extra chromosome—having 47 rather than 46—or one of the normal number of 46 is abnormally long. As genetic research has pinpointed this abnormality to chromosome 21, the condition is also sometimes referred to as trisomy-21 (Smith, 1985).

Individuals with Down's syndrome have faces that appear rounded and flattened-looking, almond-shaped eyes, and short and stocky physiques. They suffer from mental retardation, ranging from mild to very profound. However, the most significant features they share are impaired health functions, such as malformations of the heart and digestive system, hearing loss, and an inability to reproduce (Courchesne, 1988). Before the 1930s most children with Down's syndrome died of infections before reaching the age of ten. Thanks to improved health interventions, most individuals with Down's syndrome reach middle age, with 44% surviving to age 60 (Baird & Sadovnick, 1988).

X and Y Chromosomes

Other mishaps are related to the pair of chromosomes that determine gender—the X and Y chromosomes. During meiosis, the mother's sex cells normally end up with one X chromosome and the father's sex cells contain either an X or a Y chromosome. A person inheriting two X chromosomes will be genetically female, while a person inheriting an X and Y chromosome pair will be genetically male. Several conditions can develop as a result of faulty division or inherited characteristics of these X and Y chromosomes (McKinlay-Gardner & Sutherland, 1996; Schiari et al., 1988; Warbuton & Canki, 1991).

Supermale Syndrome. Some men are found to possess an XYY combination, a condition sometimes referred to as the **supermale syndrome**. They are usually exceptionally tall, have large teeth, and often have problems with excessive acne as teenagers but are otherwise physically and intellectually normal (Alvesalo, 1985; Ratcliffe et al., 1979; Voorhees et al., 1972). At one time they were believed to be mildly mentally retarded and overrepresented among criminal populations, but this perception was later proved false (Burns & Bottino, 1989; Hook, 1973).

Klinefelter's Syndrome. **Klinefelter's syndrome** occurs when a man has one or more extra X chromosomes (Bancroft et al., 1982). Men with this syndrome, like XYY individuals, also tend to be taller than usual. They have underdeveloped male features and fat distribution that is more similar to that of women and are usually sterile. About 20% are mentally retarded. They may additionally suffer from fragile X syndrome (described below), and are more susceptible than the general population to developing certain forms of cancer (Fryns & Van den Berghe, 1988; Harnden et al., 1971).

Mosaicism. **Mosaicism** is a condition that develops in women having one or more extra X chromosomes. These women tend to be mildly affected—often mentally retarded, socially withdrawn, and developmentally delayed. As with male individuals with extra X or Y chromosomes, they tend to be taller than usual. Their greatest intellectual deficit appears to involve verbal ability.

Turner's Syndrome. **Turner's syndrome** occurs when a woman has only one fully formed X chromosome (McCauley et al., 1987). Physically such women are short, have a shield-shaped chest, do not develop many of the female secondary sex characteristics, and are sterile. Early studies of their cognitive differences focused exclusively on difficulties with spatial relationships and organizing and constructing visual wholes, abilities required for puzzle solving (Shaffer, 1962). However, later studies have shown that their mild cognitive deficits are actually broader and more general in scope (Pennington et al., 1985; Waber, 1979).

Fragile X Syndrome. As researchers investigated the overrepresentation of males among the mentally retarded population, they discovered a specific mutation occurring on the gender-related chromosomes. **Fragile X syndrome** occurs because of a break located on a certain spot on one or both X chromosomes, which is typically inherited from the mother's gene pool. Since males do not have a second X chromosome to balance its effects, its presence affects more males than females. About 5% of the mentally retarded population has been found to carry this inherited mutation of the X chromosome, and as many as half of those institutionalized for mental retardation are carriers (Brown et al., 1987; Sherman, 1996). The carrier's degree of impairment can vary considerably, ranging anywhere between normal intelligence and profound retardation (Bennetto & Pennington, 1996).

The constellation of physical characteristics common among those with fragile X syndrome includes large, prominent ears; long, narrow face; prominent forehead; hyperextendable finger joints, or double jointedness; flat feet; and enlarged testicles (Hagerman, 1996). Their temperaments are often extremely shy or withdrawn, but paradoxically they also may be hyperactive or aggressive (Dorn et al., 1994; Freund et al., 1993). Recent evidence points to a relationship between fragile X syndrome and a portion of the autistic population (see Chapter 12) (Jenkins et al., 1992; Li et al., 1993).

Which human characteristics appear to reflect genetic influences?

GENETICALLY INFLUENCED ATTRIBUTES AND CONDITIONS

Most of our genetically transmitted material is identical to everybody else's. We have little difficulty determining whether or not someone is a member of the human species! The story of genetic influences becomes more interesting as we look at the areas in which we find individual differences and their apparent patterns of genetic inheritance.

Physical Appearance

The most obvious area of genetically transmitted differences is physical appearance. We often guess that people are related to one another as we observe shared traits such as height, body build, coloring, and facial features. Identical twins

The two girls on the left are identical, or monozygotic, twins; they share identical DNA. The boy and girl on the right are fraternal, or dizygotic, twins; they share the same amount of DNA as would any other full siblings.

provide the best example of physical characteristics that are the result of shared genetic resources (see the photographs).

Having accepted that family members look alike, we are usually more puzzled when they do not. Sometimes full siblings look little if at all like one another. This phenomenon is explained by the huge number of genetic combinations possible. When you consider the many genes that are involved in determining our development, and the millions of combinations that can occur when two parents each contribute a certain selection of half of their genes, perhaps more amazing is the fact that we look as much like our siblings as we do.

Temperament

Some human characteristics are assumed to have genetic origins because they appear when we are very young and remain stable over time. A possible genetic basis of **temperament** has been studied under this assumption. Temperament is the backbone supporting our personalities, influencing how we feel and determining the types of behavior that will feel comfortable to us. Parents of more than one child are often aware of their newborn infants' temperamental differences immediately after their birth, before the social environment has had much chance to affect their personalities. Some of the more commonly observed temperamental differences are level of inhibition, ability to adapt, activity level, irritability, and frequency of smiling (Kagan, 1989).

Studies comparing monozygotic and dizygotic twins suggest that traits related to temperament are about 40% heritable, while very little correlation is found between temperamental traits of children and their adoptive parents

(Heath et al., 1992; Loehlin, 1992). This finding appears to be consistent cross-culturally. For example, a comparison of Russian monozygotic and dizygotic twins found substantial effects related to heritability regarding extraversion, neuroticism, monotony avoidance, and impulsiveness but none related to environmental factors (Saudino et al., 1999). Some researchers have found that temperamental traits fall into five separate heritable patterns—labeling them as neuroticism, extraversion, openness to experience, agreeableness, and conscientiousness—and that each varies in its degree of heritability (Jang et al., 1998). Cross-cultural investigation has found that these personality patterns follow similar paths of development over the life span regardless of culture of origin (McCrae et al., 2000).

Physical evidence of temperamental differences is also beginning to emerge, which has the potential to enhance future research in temperament. For example, recent DNA research may have identified the actual location of genes suspected of influencing novelty-seeking behavior and neuroticism (Ebstein & Belmaker, 1997; Lesch et al., 1996). Differences in brain activity have been measured among young children of varying temperaments as well; one such measure shows less activity on the left side of the brain among children having an inhibited temperament (Fox et al., 1997).

Child Temperament Types. In an effort to better understand how such inherited roots of personality emerge in youngsters, a group of researchers tracked 133 individuals from infancy to young adulthood (Thomas & Chess, 1984). Following is a list of the temperamental dimensions they proposed. As you read them consider how their stability may or may not be true of you or of a child you have observed over time:

▶ *Activity level.* Are you usually on the go, or are you more laid back?
▶ *Rhythmicity.* Is your routine of sleeping, eating, and other bodily functions fairly regular, or do they tend to be somewhat unpredictable?
▶ *Distractibility.* Once you focus your attention, how easily can it be diverted elsewhere?
▶ *Persistence of attention span.* How long can you stay interested in an activity?
▶ *Threshold of responsiveness.* How strong does a stimulus from the environment need to be before you are likely to react to it?
▶ *Approach/withdrawal.* When presented with this new stimulus do you immediately adventurously explore it, or first pull back and consider it with caution?
▶ *Adaptability.* How long do you take to get used to changes in your environment, if ever?
▶ *Intensity of reaction.* When reacting to environmental stimuli, how strongly do you react: If someone tells a joke, are you more likely to give in to a subdued smile or break into a belly laugh?
▶ *Quality of mood.* What proportion of your moods would others describe as being friendly and happy or gloomy and unfriendly?

As researchers observed children they found that certain aspects of these temperamental behavioral characteristics seemed to cluster together. They named these clusters according to how well-adjusted the children were to their environment, evidenced largely by how easy they were to parent (Thomas & Chess, 1986). The **easy child**, which describes about 40% of children, is a delight to parent. The easy child is generally happy and friendly, has regular biological rhythms, and adapts easily to new environments and experiences. The **difficult child**, which describes about 10% of children, presents more of a parental challenge. These children are often irritable, are unpredictable in the timing of their biological needs, and react strongly and disagreeably to any changes in their environment. The **slow-to-warm-up child**, characterizing about 15% of children, is generally mild-mannered. Slow-to-warm-up children tend to be somewhat inactive, slow to react to changes in the environment, and slow to adjust to changes. Table 3.1 lists the characteristics of children who fall within these three clusters.

Evidence of such temperamental differences has been found even as children are still in the womb. Those who are more active as fetuses tend to be more difficult, unpredictable, and unadaptable as infants, while those with higher fetal heart rates are less difficult, more predictable, and less active as infants (DiPietro, Hodgson, Costigan, & Johnson, 1996; Kagan, 1995).

Shyness, Boldness, and Empathic Concern. A number of longitudinal studies have been initiated since the original set of findings suggesting the three cluster types. Most notable are those shepherded by Jerome Kagan in the investigation of shyness and boldness (Kagan et al., 1984, 1988). "Shy" children feel

TABLE 3.1

Patterns of child temperament

Easy Child	Difficult Child	Slow-to-Warm-Up Child
Regular eating and sleep patterns	Irregular eating and sleep patterns	Some regularity in eating and sleep patterns
Adapts easily to new situations	Slow to adapt to new situations	Cautious at first in new situations, but then adapts
Smiles at strangers	Fearful of strangers	Initially shy, then warms up to strangers
Frustrations create a little fuss, then are accepted	Frustrations produce tantrum behavior or withdrawal	Frustration results in some negative reaction, but with eventual recovery
Mood is generally positive, and of mild to moderate intensity	Mood more likely to be negative, intense, and frequent	Mildly intense moods, both positive and negative

Tried

BOX 3.1   Children and shyness

Kagan, J., Reznick, J. S., Snidman, N., Gibbons, J., & Johnson, M. O. (1988). Childhood derivations of inhibition and lack of inhibition to the unfamiliar. *Child Development, 59,* 1580–1589.

HOW CONSISTENTLY DO CHILDREN MAINTAIN AN INHIBited or uninhibited temperament as they grow older? Are there observable physiological markers that could explain their differing reaction styles? As a means of exploring these questions Jerome Kagan and his colleagues have been tracking two such groups of children, beginning at the age of 21 months. Creating a pool of participants began with telephone interviews with youngsters' mothers. If the mothers' descriptions were consistent with either of the two extremes, the children were brought in for laboratory observation. Inhibited or uninhibited temperaments were then determined by observing how long it took children to interact with unfamiliar adults, their avoidance of unfamiliar objects, how close they stayed to Mom, and absence of play or vocalizations.

Selecting the most extreme examples, the researchers developed two groups: 28 inhibited and 30 uninhibited children. At age 7 years the participants still available consisted of 22 inhibited and 19 uninhibited children; the researchers noted that some of the participants lost were the most extreme responders. The researchers hypothesized that the two groups of 7-year-olds would continue to demonstrate their reaction styles while interacting with unfamiliar adults and same-age peers. They also predicted that the two groups of children would have differing patterns of heart rate variability, as had been discovered when the participants had been observed at age 5.

The children were brought into a play area for a party. Their scheduled activity alternated between periods of free play and party games organized by two unfamiliar female adults. Observers who had no knowledge of the children's temperament histories noted how often they maintained a distance of more than an arm's length from any other child, or spoke with an adult or child. A month or so after the party the children's heart rates were measured as they performed a series of cogni-tive/affective tasks involving matching and picture arrangement. Researchers also noted how long it took children to respond to spontaneous examiner comments during the tasks.

Statistical analysis showed that as a group, the children identified as inhibited at age 21 months continued to demonstrate their temperament by maintaining more distance from others, engaging in less talk with others, and taking longer to respond to others' verbalizations than did the group of uninhibited children. Also, the inhibited children attained their highest heart rate earlier in the series of cognitive/affective tasks than did the uninhibited children and made more mistakes as the tasks progressed, as would be expected during a state of high arousal.

Collectively this evidence suggests that inhibited and uninhibited temperaments are generally stable over time. Furthermore, we might speculate that an inhibited temperament is fueled by a desire to avoid excessive stimulation due to inheritance of more sensitive arousal structures controlling heart rate and other autonomic responding. In other words, inhibited children may learn to hesitate or pull back because stimulating activity feels more arousing—uncomfortably so—than it does for uninhibited children.

When the children in each group were later examined individually, however, the researchers found that about 25% of the children who had been previously identified as uninhibited now behaved as inhibited, and 25% of the previously identified inhibited children now behaved as uninhibited. These findings deviate from the greater stability they had noted during previous measurements between 21 months and 7 years. They speculate that some uninhibited children may become inhibited due to traumatic life exposures, as is found in studies of child abuse and other childhood traumas. As for inhibited children losing their inhibitions, perhaps they develop strategies for dealing with their overreactive arousal wiring so that it does not prevent them from having an active social life.

... and True

BOX 3.2   Helping children overcome shyness

SOCIALLY, CHILDREN BORN WITH OVERREACTIVE arousal wiring are at a disadvantage. Not only are they less likely to initiate social interaction, but they also must deal with the fact that children are very good at recognizing which of their peers are easiest to emotionally stir up. Over time, youngsters can learn to appreciate the reward value of either literally or figuratively placing a "kick me" sign on an oversensitive child's back. In view of the impairment in critical thinking that Kagan's study found as the children became more aroused, they also find themselves behind the eight ball as they attempt to deal with spontaneously evolving predicaments. Since we do not yet have the technology to biologically repair overreactive neurological wiring, we can most help these children with their social lives by guiding them toward using effective coping strategies.

Because inhibited children's temperament appears to be at least in part biologically based, we first need to recognize that telling them not to be so sensitive is not going to work. Being so criticized is only likely to make them feel worse and impair their self-esteem. Instead we can jointly recognize their sensitivity and both accept and value it. We can point out the assets of being sensitive: its influence on the ability to be reflective, an increased capacity for appreciating the feelings of others, the greater ability to focus for long periods of time on tasks involving little stimulation.

Having so bolstered their ego strength, we can then help them develop ways of dealing with their sensitivity when it interferes with social functioning, such as when they are being teased. Systematic desensitization has been used successfully to remedy many forms of excessive anxiety, and can be used with sensitive children as well (Garber et al., 1987). Together, child and adult brainstorm a list of circumstances the child fears or has been teased about, and place them in order of least to most scary. Beginning with the least scary situation, the adult and child role play different ways of coping that serve the purpose of reducing anxiety. The child works

his or her way up the hierarchy as he or she feels less anxious while dealing with the easier situations.

For example, 8-year-old Bobby was often teased by his peers for having red hair. His mother, Joan, practiced with him as he learned several desensitizing coping strategies:

Self-instruction. Bobby rehearsed an internal monologue, telling himself that there really isn't anything wrong with having red hair. A lot of famous and talented people have red hair. Maybe the other kids are just jealous.

Relaxation techniques. Joan showed him how to breathe from the diaphragm. She helped him practice relaxing the muscles in his body so he could more easily recognize what relaxation feels like. She told him to think of times when he is more relaxed, so he could remind himself of that feeling while he is being teased.

Ignoring. Joan said the same taunts over and over, while Bobby practiced tuning them out. Joan warned him that they might try even harder to rile him at first, but that as they realized they couldn't upset him, they would eventually stop trying.

Derailment. Together they practiced things Bobby might say that might bring an end to the teasing:

"What is your motivation for saying that?"

"Sticks and stones may break my bones but words will never hurt me."

"You're just trying to make me upset. It's not going to work."

As Bobby practiced the coping techniques, he felt less and less anxious about this particular form of teasing. His mastery of this one target situation also bolstered his self-confidence, additionally inoculating him from the taunts of his peers.

Garber, S. W., Garber, M. D., & Spizman, R. F. (1987). *Good behavior: Over 1,000 sensible solutions to your child's problems, from birth to age twelve.* New York: Villard Books.

inhibited when placed in a strange situation, while "bold" children act as if they feel right at home in unusual circumstances. Studies of childrens' level of shyness or boldness have been found to be associated with how parents eventually choose to parent their children—evidence of nature actually directing nurture (Rubin et al., 1999)!

Tendencies toward shyness or boldness show some stability over the course of childhood, as well as into young adulthood (Caspi, 2000; Sanson et al., 1996). However, as elaborated upon in the Tried . . . . and True boxes on pages 76–77, shy children do not appear doomed to behave as introverts forever. Depending on environmental influences such as parental modeling and encouragement, many shy children become more outgoing as they grow older. Therefore, inherited predispositions are better viewed as tendencies, which children can potentially modify as they adapt to their environments (Goldsmith et al., 1997; Shiner, 2000; Thomas & Chess, 1986).

Twin studies have also examined possible genetic bases of the experience of empathy, or expressing **empathic concern** toward others. Children who are high in empathic concern recognize when others are distressed and show concern over their welfare. Even infants show evidence of empathic concern. Have you ever noticed how if one baby starts crying in a daycare nursery, a couple of others are likely to join in? One group of researchers measured levels of empathic concern shown by monozygotic and dizygotic twins under 2 years old (Zahn-Waxler et al., 1992). As with other genetically determined attributes, the monozygotic twins showed more similar responses than the dizygotic twins. This trait demonstrates stability, as preschoolers demonstrating such a trait continue to do so as adults (Eisenberg, Guthrie, Murphy, Shepard et al., 1999).

Side Benefits of the Study of Child Temperament. Studies of the biological basis of temperament have made indirect contributions to parenting; for one thing, they have reduced the feelings of guilt that parents inflict upon themselves over their children's development. The popularization of psychodynamic and behavioral beliefs encouraged parents to believe that their parenting is responsible for any desirable or undesirable traits their children might display. Thus parents at times have become overzealous, excessively strict or punitive, or overcontrolling as they attempt to shape an ideal child—or, on the flip side, have felt overwhelmed and given up. Either outcome actually causes more problems than it solves, as will be described more fully in Chapter 10, where parenting styles are discussed. Parenting and other environmental influences are indeed important but not to the extreme degrees that earlier child development theories had proposed.

Studies of child temperament also reinforce parents' intuitive recognition that they need to establish a "fit" with each individual child, creating a form of harmony in the environment that respects a child's inborn temperament. An outgoing child needs a parenting style providing much more structure and guidance to contain his or her explorations, while the more inhibited child needs more encouragement and protection during excessively stressful situations. Parents benefit from learning to become more accepting and comforting toward their difficult child, rather than taking the child's temperamental nature personally or becoming frustrated and detached in reaction to the child's demanding emotional needs.

Intelligence

Studies of intelligence indicate that heritability accounts for most of a child's intellectual potential (Plomin, 1990; Sternberg & Grigorenko, 1997). In decades past, researchers so firmly believed that the environment was the most influential factor in intellectual development that the governments of some countries, such as those in the Soviet Bloc, once prohibited scientists from even attempting to look for possible genetic origins (Grigorenko & Kornilova, 1997). Twin studies and adoption studies have demonstrated the polar opposite of such a perspective, as Table 3.2 shows. As you can see, the purely genetic influences represented by identical twins reared apart is quite strong, while the effect of the purely environmental influences shared by unrelated children in the same home is seemingly nonexistent (Scarr, 1997).

Yet, as the table also illustrates, there are small but significant differences between individuals sharing the same degree of genetic connection but not the same home environment. Such differences, however, tend to be greatest when we are young and diminish considerably as we proceed through adulthood, with genetic programming becoming more and more influential over time (Loehlin et al., 1997; McCartney et al., 1990). Some researchers explain this phenomenon as being a product of greater elasticity or receptiveness to environmental influences during the early years (Jensen, 1997). However, the

TABLE 3.2

Correlations of intelligence test scores between individuals sharing varying levels of genetic and environmental similarity. Adapted with permission from S. Scarr (1997) "Behavior-genetic and socialization theories of intelligence: Truce and reconciliation," in R. J. Sternberg & E. L. Grigorenko (Eds.), *Intelligence, heredity, and environment.* Copyright © 1997 Cambridge University Press.

Relationship	IQ Correlation
Identical twins (100% shared genetic influence)	
Reared together	.86
Reared apart	.76
Fraternal twins (50% shared genetic influence)	
Reared together	.55
Reared apart	.35
Biological siblings (50% shared genetic influence)	
Reared together	.47
Reared apart	.35
Adopted siblings (no shared genetic influence)	*.02*

specific traits of an environment that will result in a child's achieving higher IQ scores have yet to be reliably identified (Bouchard, 1993; Brand, 1993).

Psychological Disorders

Susceptibility to many psychological disorders has been found to run in families (Rutter et al., 1999b). Table 3.3 shows a partial list of these conditions, as they are found in the *Diagnostic and Statistical Manual—IV* of the American Psychiatric Association (American Psychiatric Association, 1994).

Sometimes researchers group together all the empirical studies they can find regarding a certain phenomenon and statistically analyze them for general trends. The resulting studies, called **meta-analyses**, are frequently used in studies of psychological conditions. One such condition is **schizophrenia**, a potentially disabling psychotic disorder. Meta-analysis of genetic and environmental influences shows concordance rates as high as .50 between identical twins suffering from schizophrenia and their birth mates; that is, among 50% of identical twin pairs studied, if one twin suffers from schizophrenia, the other will also. By contrast, concordance rates among parents and other siblings of schizophrenic individuals are .10 or less (Gottesman & Shields, 1972). These numbers suggest that heredity is a strong component of schizophrenia.

But what about the identical twins who did not develop the disorder? Aspects of the environment also affect the outcome. For example, children of

TABLE 3.3

Some psychological conditions with familial patterns

Anorexia nervosa	Obsessive-compulsive disorder
Antisocial personality disorder	Oppositional-defiant disorder (in children)
Attention deficit/hyperactivity disorder	Panic attacks
Autism	Pathological gambling
Bipolar disorder	Schizophrenia and schizotypal disorders
Bulimia nervosa	Separation anxiety disorder (in children)
Conduct disorder (in children)	Sleepwalking disorder
Depression and depressive disorders	Social phobias
Dissociative identity disorder (multiple personality)	Stuttering
Enuresis (bedwetting)	Substance addictions
Insomnia	Tic disorders
Mental retardation	

schizophrenic parents who are adopted out have a greater chance of developing schizophrenia if their adoptive homes have been rated as "disturbed" (Gottesman & Wolfgram, 1990). Recent studies indicate that schizophrenia follows a unique "neural diathesis-stress" pattern: Excessive stress activates a biologically based predisposition into a symptomatic stage, and the worsening symptoms in turn increase vulnerability to environmentally based stressors (Walker & Diforio, 1997). In this manner both nature and nurture play roles in determining whether or not a person will develop this disorder.

Some of the best and earliest evidence of the genetic basis of depressive disorders has been demonstrated by twin studies of **bipolar disorder**, also called *manic-depressive disorder* (American Psychiatric Association, 1994). This potentially psychotic disorder may involve severe depression alone, or more commonly alternates with periods of mania—unrealistic and delusional highs that often push sufferers toward destructive behaviors. The concordance rate among identical twins has been found to be as high as .79, while among fraternal twins it is closer to .20 (Bertelson, 1979). Thus, as with other psychological conditions, the concordance rates of identical twins show that heritability alone does not appear to result in a 100% likelihood of developing the disorder. Other factors such as the environment and life experiences appear also to be at work.

How tightly is genetic programming tied to development?

HOW MUCH NATURE AND HOW MUCH NURTURE?

These discussions of inherited traits illustrate evidence that both genes and environment play significant roles in a person's development. As you have probably suspected, development of some traits seems to be affected very little by environmental influences. **Canalization** refers to the tendency of some inherited characteristics to be so strongly prescribed that very few variations in developmental outcome are possible (Waddington, 1966). Examples include the age at which babies learn to crawl and walk and the onset of puberty. These and other canalized tendencies are described in future chapters.

On the other hand, the environment can affect even the most resilient of genetic programming (Gottlieb, 1991). One of the more fascinating examples of such an outcome emerged during ethological studies. Among many species, the young attach to their mothers at a very early age, a capacity clearly crucial to the little ones' survival. Yet the choice of whom the youngsters attach to can be tampered with. As Konrad Lorenz (1935; 1965) worked with baby geese, he found that hatchlings would **imprint** even onto an aging ethologist, following him around in single file much as they would have scampered after their biological mothers. Thus while some species' young may have a strongly canalized tendency to imprint, the programming determining the creature upon which they imprint appears to be much looser.

The breadth or narrowness of canalized outcome possibilities has been referred to as a genotype's **range of reaction** (Gottesman, 1963). An individual's

Nina Leen / Life Picture Service

The genetically programmed tendency for baby geese to imprint on and follow their mothers after hatching is apparently loosely canalized, resulting in their following Konrad Lorenz during this leisurely swim.

genotype may actually prescribe a range of potential outcomes. The eventual developmental outcome that emerges depends upon the specific individual's experiences with the environment. Rigidly canalized traits and behaviors have very narrow ranges of reaction, resulting in the commonalities shared among almost all members of a species, while some other traits demonstrate a fairly wide range of possibilities. As an example, members of the human species inherit one of many possible high, average, and low ranges for potential intellectual ability, but whether their IQ scoring establishes itself on a higher or lower end of their inherited range is affected largely by environmental influences (Bouchard, 1997; Turkheimer & Gottesman, 1991).

While this fact may suggest there are some areas of development in which we are doomed to become passive "products of our environments," genetic influences actually seem to give us a card or two up our sleeves for potentially greater self-determination. Children prefer and seek out environments that are compatible with their genetic predispositions (Scarr & McCartney, 1983). For example, a child genetically predisposed for higher intelligence will seek out the intellectually stimulating environment that may encourage development of even greater cognitive ability (Bouchard, 1997). A shy child is likely to choose solitary activity and quiet, low-key pursuits, while the extroverted child is more likely to place himself or herself in socially active situations. In so doing the shy child may encounter more experiences that are supportive of developing intellectual and analytical skills, perhaps leading to that child's one day becoming a scientist. The outgoing child's increased social experience may result in exposures that eventually shape the future politician who awards grants to the shy child scientist.

Our tendency to place ourselves in environments that feel the most comfortable for us has been called **niche-picking**, and explains in part why when identical twins separated at birth are reunited they find they share multiple common preferences, interests, and pastimes (Bouchard et al., 1990). Yet as niche-picking once more appears to give genetics some advantage over environment, we must also consider that any given child's choices are limited by the range of available environmental variables from which the child can choose (Gottlieb, 1991).

How close have we come to genetically engineering the perfect child?

GENETIC ENGINEERING

What if we attempt to stack the deck? The aim of **genetic engineering** is to introduce, enhance, or delete characteristics of an organism by genetic means. If you had been given a prebirth choice to alter your genetic makeup, would you have designated a preference for certain traits? Genetic engineers have already created a strain of fruit fly that learns ten times faster than those without the genetic manipulation (Aldous, 1995). If they found a way to perform a similar procedure on human beings, would you have wanted such an alteration performed? Some might say yes, indeed. However, others might begin to wonder about potential implications. Given such a fantastic memory, would they be stuck with remembering the unpleasantries of life that we are actually grateful for not remembering? Will they be able to effectively juggle their massively larger knowledge stores, or will the additional baggage interfere with being able to track day-to-day details? And if everybody made this same choice, only a small percentage would find jobs capable of providing sufficient intellectual challenge. Would you be willing to live a life of superior intellectual capacity yet be constrained by a relatively mundane job?

Genetic engineering among human beings is a highly controversial field (Gosden, 1999; Reiss & Straughan, 1996; Rothblatt, 1997). Currently the "gene therapy" practices used among human beings do not change the actual genetic makeup of an individual but rather utilize various genetic means of giving instructions to DNA that may be otherwise lacking, as in the case of gene therapy for cystic fibrosis (Friedmann, 1997; Watson, 1993). Animal experimentation, however, has successfully altered DNA to serve a variety of purposes, most often to promote faster or larger growth in livestock. Yet while in one case insertion of growth genes into pigs did result in a larger pig, the genetic manipulation also caused these pigs to be arthritic, partially blind, and prone to develop ulcers and caused impotence in the males (Gosden, 1999).

What sorts of correlates like these might we have encountered had we elected the learning-times-ten genetic manipulation? Since such a treatment does not yet exist, we cannot know. The inability to know the implications of genetic engineering's impact on the future raises a variety of concerns among scientists and philosophers alike. How likely will a genetically engineered organism fit in with naturally evolving species or gene pools for specific traits, given that it has been introduced outside of the adjustments having taken place over millions of years (Rifkin, 1985)? Could such alterations interfere with the natural, adaptive course of human evolution (Fox, 1990)? Who decides what constitutes "improvement" to a specific genetic makeup (Reiss & Straughan, 1996)? What if life as we know it changes in such a way that undesirable traits become desirable? And who has the right to introduce changes into a gene pool? Do individuals own their particular gene collection, or does our shared gene pool belong to the entire species (Rothblatt, 1997)? The proposal to find genetic means for ending genetically caused forms of human suffering is indeed attractive, but until questions such as these have firmer answers we have a long way to go before we can morally or ethically consider producing genetically engineered human beings (Czeizel, 1988; Holtzman, 1989).

What is genetic counseling, and how can we benefit from it?

GENETIC COUNSELING

Though genetically engineering the perfect baby is not currently feasible, parents still want to ensure the greatest possible likelihood of producing a happy, healthy child. The birth of a child with a serious disability has profound

TABLE 3.4

Some genetically determined developmental defects

Cystic fibrosis	A glandular disorder predominantly affecting the ability to breathe and digest food, often resulting in a shortened life span
Diabetes	Disruption of the ability to process sugar due to insufficient insulin; fatal if left untreated
Down's syndrome	Mild to severe mental retardation, characteristic facial deformities, and some medical complications involving cardiovascular and digestive systems
Hemophilia	Deficiency in the blood's ability to clot, resulting in excessive internal and external bleeding
Huntington disease	Degeneration of the central nervous system during adulthood, resulting in muscular coordination difficulties, mental impairment, and personality changes
Muscular dystrophy	A disease attacking muscle tissue, eventually resulting in difficulty with speech, walking, and other forms of voluntary movement
Phenylketonuria	Mental retardation due to metabolic dysfunctioning
Polycystic kidney disease	Enlarged kidneys, with cardiovascular and respiratory problems in infants; kidney failure in the adult form
Sickle-cell anemia	A blood disorder that impairs red cells' ability to process oxygen
Spina bifida	Spine and brain abnormalities originating during neural tube formation
Tay-Sachs disease	Excessive lipids in the nervous system, resulting in slowed mental and physical development; usually fatal by age 5

implications for the child, the child's family, and the community within which the child will live. While a number of parents are willing to accept and care for whatever child their genetic shufflings may determine, others prefer not to be so all encompassing in the dedication of their parental resources. They might question the quality of life a severely impaired child could expect, their own ability to cope, the effect of the child's disability and parental time consumption on siblings, and the potential drain on the community if the parents cannot care for the child. Table 3.4 lists a number of common genetically determined physical conditions that raise parental concerns (Wynbrandt & Ludman, 1991).

Now that we know that many forms of disabilities have genetic origins, couples can evaluate the risk of their producing children with such conditions. Through **genetic counseling**, couples are tested and consult with experts to evaluate this risk and decide whether or not to bear children (Baker et al., 1998;

Modell & Modell, 1992; Richards, 1998). Genetic counselors begin by taking an extensive family medical history. Do any of the couple's blood relatives have known genetically influenced conditions? Are there diseases or physical abnormalities prevalent within the family? What were the causes of death among the deceased? How common are miscarriages and stillbirths?

Early Testing Procedures

A number of tests are available for flagging possible genetic information (Decrespigny, 1996). The most elaborate examines the parents' karotypes. **Karotypes** are systematically arranged charts laying out the chromosomes found in tissue samples provided by each parent (see the illustration below). These charts can be examined for any abnormalities that have not been revealed by the parent's phenotype or family history. Since we know the location of some problematic genes, karotypes can help the counselor more precisely predict the probability that two particular parents would produce a child with a genetically influenced condition.

If the mother is already pregnant, the child can be tested directly for abnormalities. Gross malformations can be detected by the diagnostic technique called **ultrasound**, which uses sound waves to create a picture of the new life. About 7–8% of fetuses examined by ultrasound have some form of abnormality; but only about one-third of these fetal abnormalities are considered to be serious (Evans & Lampinen, 1998). Many malformed fetuses when karotyped are found to have underlying chromosomal anomalies (Campbell & Smith, 1984; Nicolaides et al., 1986). A physician might also explore for physical malformations using **fetoscopy**. This procedure allows the physician to place a tiny

Is this example of a karotype that of a man or a woman?

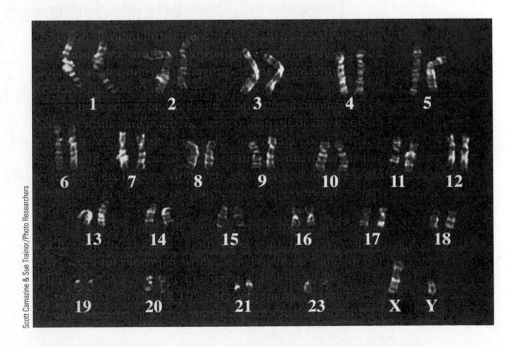

Scott Camazine & Sue Trainor/Photo Researchers

lens and lighting mechanism inside the uterus and actually view the child it-self—more accurate than ultrasound, but also presenting more risk to the well-being of the mother and child.

Ultrasound techniques are so simple and harmless that most pregnant women are now routinely examined. Some complain that from an economic perspective, the cumulative cost of routine screening is actually substantially higher than the cost of providing medical and societal support for congenitally disabled individuals (Waitzman & Romano, 1998). However, expectant mothers find the experience so reassuring and are so appreciative of the exciting opportunity for early bonding that health management organizations continue to provide the service for fear they will lose patients to systems that do perform routine screening (Buechler, 1998).

Amniocentesis is another procedure commonly used to examine the developing child (Rothman, 1994). The amniotic fluid surrounding the baby is extracted from the mother's womb by a large hollow needle penetrating the abdomen. The loose cells floating in the fluid are examined for possible genetic defects. The procedure is risky because of possible trauma to the womb or the baby. Clinicians find a 1% higher rate of miscarriage among low-risk pregnant women who go through the procedure (Tabor et al., 1986).

Even more risky than amniocentesis is a procedure called **chorionic villus sampling**. The procedure collects and examines the child's cells as does amniocentesis, but it can be performed earlier in the pregnancy. The cells are extracted from the tissue surrounding the baby, either by a needle through the mother's abdomen or by a vaginal catheter. Since this procedure is more invasive than amniocentesis and occurs during an even more vulnerable period of development, it has a greater likelihood of causing harm. A 3–4% increase in miscarriage is found among women who have the procedure, most often among women who are older or who have the procedure during the first 12 weeks of pregnancy (Cohen-Overbeek et al., 1990; Medical Research Council, 1991).

PAVING PATHWAYS ALONG BIOLOGICAL BEGINNING POINTS: REPRODUCTIVE OPTIONS

Suppose you were considering becoming a parent. Based on the preceding discussion, what sorts of decisions would you be facing?

Should I get genetic counseling? For certain, all potential parents benefit from knowing their genetic backgrounds, if only to calm their apprehensions. However, some of us are especially well-advised to receive genetic counseling:

▶ if you know you or your partner has a genetically influenced disorder or defect
▶ if you know of genetically influenced conditions in your family background
▶ if there has been a lot of intermarrying among extended family or within a small ethnic group
▶ if you have had difficulty conceiving

- if you have conceived before but always miscarry
- if you already have a child with a genetically influenced condition

Given the risks presented, should I go ahead and have a baby or adopt instead? This is a difficult decision. If you decide to take the risk, you will want to prepare for the worst-case scenario. Do you have the personal, financial, medical, and community resources to care for an afflicted child? Are you in a position to get the training necessary for dealing with a particular disability? Do you feel emotionally capable of dealing with the ongoing challenges and the stigma sometimes attached to having a disabled child? If the child needs to be institutionalized, can you cope? Are you willing to give up much of your lifestyle in order to deal with the demands of your child's disability?

On the other hand, adoption also has its drawbacks. With adoptees you may have difficulty knowing what you are going to get. The child may have been given up for adoption because the parents had genetically influenced emotional or physical problems that interfered with their ability to care for the child. Older children often become adoptees after tumultuous early lives with problematic parents. As might be expected, adopted children tend to be more likely to have emotional problems and learning difficulties than those who are not adopted (Verhulst, Althaus, & Versluis-Den Bieman, 1990).

However, both choices have benefits as well. Most of the genetic difficulties discovered among prospective parents present a relatively small risk. You may take the risk and have an unaffected child. Even if the child is affected, the rewards of raising and passing along your own flesh and blood may outweigh the exceptional difficulties you might experience. Likewise adoption agencies are very careful to screen both parents and adoptees in order to find suitable matches. The vast majority of children placed in adoptive homes do well even when they are previously known to have handicaps (Glidden & Pursley, 1989).

Should I risk procedures such as amniocentesis or chorionic villus sampling? The risk of harming the baby during these procedures is small, yet still should be considered. Chorionic villus sampling, for example, can be performed early enough for a less complex and safer abortion procedure to take place if the findings warrant. However, in addition to being linked to miscarriage, it appears also to have resulted in a few cases of birth defects (Seabrook, 1994).

This decision involves weighing the severity of the risks. If you are certain you wish to abort if there is a defect or the chance of a defect is high, the probabilities seem to favor having the procedure. Age is another consideration. The older the parents, the more likely they are to produce a genetically defective child, especially a child with Down's syndrome (Abroms & Bennett, 1981; Verp, Simpson, & Ober, 1993). Thus when the mother is over 35 or the father is over 45, the likelihood that the procedure will provide important genetic information increases.

Another consideration is the treatment options available for the potential disorder. The sooner you know about a problem, the sooner you can begin treating it. The detrimental effects of some disorders can be minimized while the child is still in the womb, such as hormone therapy for PKU (phenylketonuria) or X and Y chromosome deficiencies; in some cases such as hernias, surgeries can be performed in utero.

Should I abort the genetically defective child or prepare to care for a disabled child? This is an extremely difficult and painful decision for any parent to face. It is compounded by the need to choose quickly, while abortion is still an option. While every parent is going to have to draw his or her own conclusions, here are some factors you might want to consider should you ever find yourself in this position:

▶ Abortion itself is a hotly debated issue. Some view it as killing, while others do not view fetuses in early stages of life as having attained personhood. Where do you stand? Your views on this issue will affect how you feel after following through on your choice.

▶ All children deserve to be wanted. There is some evidence that children who are not wanted are not as physically or emotionally healthy as those who are wanted, effects that can even follow them into adulthood (David et al., 1988). How badly do you want this child? And if you do not want the child, what are the chances that the child can find a happy life elsewhere?

▶ Evidence of a genetic problem does not prescribe automatic doom. Many genetically influenced conditions vary drastically in the degree of impairment they produce. The child may be only mildly affected.

▶ What are your philosophical beliefs about passing along defective genetic material? Some people feel a social or moral obligation to consider the needs and resources of society itself when making such decisions.

▶ Even if your child has a defect, you can still develop a loving, rewarding relationship. Many parents report having experienced tremendous personal growth as they learn to relate to and care for their specially challenged children.

SUMMARY

Evolutionary Beginnings

The beginnings of human development are hypothesized to be tied to our evolutionary past. Physical and mental characteristics that are more adaptive are naturally selected for, since they have a greater chance of promoting maturation and reproduction. Cultural factors can affect which genes are likely to be passed on to the next generation.

Genes and Genetics

Genetic programming guides our development. Genes are organized as matched pairs located on chromosomes, which consist of strings of deoxyribonucleic acid (DNA) located within our cells' nuclei. Gene pairs, or genotypes, can be either homogenous or heterogenous. Individual genes can be dominant, recessive, or even codominant, which affects how a heterogenous pair will be expressed by the phenotype.

Sex Cells

Sex cells are produced through the process of meiosis, with each resulting sex cell containing only half of the parent's genes. Fertilization occurs as the man's sperm and the woman's ovum unite, creating a zygote with all 46 chromosomes. Twin births can be the result of one zygote—monozygotic or identical twins— or two zygotes—dizygotic or fraternal twins. Artificial means of uniting sperm and ovum, such as in vitro fertilization and embryo transplant, do not appear to interfere with normal development.

Chromosomal Anomalies and Development

Defects of the chromosomes themselves can result in certain developmental conditions, such as Down's syndrome. Other conditions can occur as a result of extra, missing, or defective X and Y chromosomes—the chromosomes responsible for determining gender. These conditions include the supermale syndrome, Klinefelter's syndrome, mosaicism, Turner's syndrome, and fragile X syndrome.

Genetically Influenced Attributes and Conditions

Human characteristics that have been shown to have a relationship with genetic influences include physical appearance, temperament, and intelligence, as well as some psychological disorders such as schizophrenia and bipolar disorder.

How Much Nature and How Much Nurture?

Some genetically determined traits are so strongly canalized (inflexible) that they vary little in their final developmental result regardless of environmental influences. Others have a wide range of reaction and therefore have more potential for reflecting the effects of the environment. Since we tend to place ourselves in environmental settings that feel most compatible with our temperaments and other genetically influenced proclivities, our inherited traits can affect which environmental exposures we receive.

Genetic Engineering

Due to the many philosophical, moral, and ethical issues yet to be sorted out, the use of genetic manipulations on human beings is currently limited to procedures that do not alter the heritable DNA.

Genetic Counseling

Genetic counseling helps prospective parents examine the possibility of their producing a child with a genetically transmitted condition. Counseling may utilize techniques such as karotyping, ultrasound, fetoscopy, amniocentesis, and chorionic villus sampling. Once the results are known, the genetic counselor can help the couple explore reproductive options such as adoption, abortion, or deciding to raise a child with a disability.

KEY TERMS

amniocentesis
bipolar disorder
canalization
chorionic villus sampling
chromosomes
codominance
conception
deoxyribonucleic acid (DNA)
difficult child
dizygotic twins
dominant genes
Down's syndrome
easy child
empathic concern
fetoscopy

fragile X syndrome
genes
genetic counseling
genetic engineering
genotype
heterogenous genes
homogenous genes
imprinting
karotype
Klinefelter's syndrome
meiosis
meta-analysis
mitosis
monozygotic twins
mosaicsim

natural selection
niche-picking
ovum
phenotype
polygenic
range of reaction
recessive genes
schizophrenia
slow-to-warm-up child
sperm
supermale syndrome
temperament
Turner's syndrome
ultrasound
zygote

CONCEPT REVIEW

1. The process by which specific ancestral traits are favored over others to be passed along because they are more likely to promote survival is called _____.

2. Gene pairs are located on corresponding pairs of _____, which are made up of strings of _____.

3. A member of a gene pair that overrides the instructions of its gene partner is called a _____ gene, while the gene whose instructions have been overridden is called a _____ gene.

4. A person's inherited heterogenous or homogenous gene pair for a specific trait is referred to as the person's _____; how the pairings express themselves within the person's physical characteristics is called the _____.

5. Sickle-cell anemia develops when a person inherits two genes for this disorder; if only one gene is inherited, the person develops resistance to malaria. This interaction between two members of a gene pair is an example of _____.

6. Normal cell reproduction passes on all 46 chromosomes to daughter cells during the process of _____; sex cells are produced with only half of the original 46 chromosomes during the process of _____.

7. When an ovum and sperm unite, establishing the new unique combination of 46 chromosomes, a _____ is formed.

8. Identical twins, who both have the same chromosomes, are called _____ twins; those who develop from separate collections of chromosomes are called _____ twins.

9. A genetic condition resulting in mental retardation that usually occurs when a person inherits an extra chromosome is called _____, or _____.

10. Klinefelter's syndrome, supermale syndrome, mosaicism, and Turner's syndrome are all examples of conditions that develop when there are extra or missing _____ chromosomes in a person's genetic makeup.

11. The backbone of our personalities, which appears to be about 40% heritable, is referred to as inborn _____.

12. Studies of shyness have shown that inborn temperament, though pervasive, can be modified some by _____ influences.

13. Studies of intelligence suggest that (more/less) of this trait is determined by heredity than by the environment.

14. Examples of psychological disorders that have been determined to have a heritable component include _____ and _____.

15. Expressions of a genetically determined trait can include numerous variations if the genotype has a wide _____.

16. The tendency for individuals to seek out environments that feel most compatible with their genetically influenced traits is called _____.

17. Thus far, _____ has been used in human beings only to correct errant DNA messages, rather than changing a person's actual genetic makeup.

18. An individual's specific gene sequences can be studied for abnormalities by separating and laying out the chromosomes on charts called

_____. Fetal genetic material can also be examined in this manner by collecting loose cells floating in the fluid surrounding the baby, a procedure called _____; or in tissue surrounding the baby, a procedure called _____.

19. Genetic counseling helps parents evaluate the _____ and _____ of prenatal testing or proceeding with future or current pregnancies.

1) natural selection; **2**) chromosomes; DNA; **3**) dominant; recessive; **4**) genotype; phenotype; **5**) codominance; **6**) mitosis; meiosis; **7**) zygote; **8**) monozygotic; dizygotic or fraternal; **9**) Down's syndrome; trisomy-21; **10**) X and Y; **11**) temperament; **12**) environmental; **13**) more; **14**) schizophrenia; bipolar disorder; **15**) range of reaction; **16**) niche-picking; **17**) genetic engineering; **18**) karotypes; amniocentesis; chorionic villus sampling; **19**) risks; benefits

RESOURCES FOR FURTHER READING

DeCrespigny, L. (1996). *Which tests for my unborn baby: Ultrasound and other prenatal tests.* New York: Oxford University Press.

Gehring, W. J. (1998). *Master control genes in development and evolution: The homeobox story.* New Haven, CT: Yale University Press.

Gosden, R. G. (1999). *Designing babies: The brave new world of reproductive technology.* New York: W. H. Freeman.

Olby, R. (1985). *Origins of Mendelism.* Chicago: University of Chicago Press.

Plomin, R., DeFries, J. C., McClearn, G. E., & Rutter, M. (1997). *Behavioral genetics,* 3rd ed. New York: W. H. Freeman.

Reiss, M. J., & Straughan, R. (1996). *Improving nature: The science and ethics of genetic engineering.* Cambridge: Cambridge University Press.

Rieder, C. L. (Ed.) (1999). *Mitosis and meiosis.* San Diego: Academic Press.

Rose, M. R. (1998). *Darwin's spectre: Evolutionary biology in the modern world.* Princeton, NJ: Princeton University Press.

Rothblatt, M. (1997). *Unzipped genes: Taking charge of babymaking in the new millennium.* Philadelphia: Temple University Press.

Zallen, D. T. (1997). *Does it run in the family? A consumer's guide to DNA testing for genetic disorders.* New Brunswick, NJ: Rutgers University Press.

INFOTRAC COLLEGE EDITION

For additional readings, explore InfoTrac College Edition, your online library. Go to http://www.infotrac-college.com/wadsworth and use the passcode that came on the card with your book. Try these search terms: child temperament, fetus-ultrasonic imaging, genes and behavior, genes and mental illness, genetic counseling, genetic engineering, human chromosomes, natural selection, sex chromosomes

CHILD DEVELOPMENT CD-ROM

 Go to the Wadsworth Child Development CD-ROM for further study of the concepts in this chapter. The CD-ROM also includes quizzes and additional activities to expand your learning experience.

REFERENCES

For a list of references for this chapter, see the Wadsworth Psych Study Center Web site at: http://www.wadsworth.com/product/0534348092s

CHAPTER 4

Entering the World

FOCUS QUESTIONS

► What happens during the germinal, embryonic, and fetal stages of prenatal growth?

► What maternal, environmental, and paternal factors are likely to influence prenatal development?

► What happens during the typical process of childbirth?

► What alternative birthing procedures are available?

► What are the characteristics of the newborn?

► How can birth complications affect a newborn?

► What role does bonding play in the life of a newborn?

	O U T L I N E	

Prenatal Stages of Growth
The Germinal Stage
The Embryonic Stage
The Fetal Stage
The Prenatal Environment
Maternal Factors
Teratogens
The Father's Contributions
Conclusion

The Birth Process
Paving Pathways: Birthing Alternatives
The Newborn
Neonate Complications
Insufficient Oxygen
Low Birth Weight
Premature Birth
Paving Pathways: Early Bonding

Mrs. Fredericks was showing her first-graders pictures of different baby animals. When she asked the class if there were any questions, Johnny raised his hand.

"Where did all those baby animals come from?" he asked. "And baby people, too. Where did I come from?"

Realizing that she was about to tread into dangerous territory, Mrs. Fredericks chose her response carefully.

"Both baby animals and baby people begin the same way," she explained. "We begin as an egg or a seed."

"Which one was I?" Johnny asked.

"It doesn't make any difference," said the teacher.

"Then how do you know if you're s'posed to be a bird or a flower?"

While Johnny's response revealed a childlike understanding of Mrs. Fredericks's explanation, he did touch upon one of the miracles of prenatal development. In addition to the question of how a simple zygote knows which organism to become, how do you explain the complex process by which cells begin separating, homing in toward specific locations, and forming the different structures within an organism? Researchers continue to explore and seek answers to this newly emerging field of the study of chromosomal programming and the mystery of reproduction.

What happens during the germinal, embryonic, and fetal stages of prenatal growth?

PRENATAL STAGES OF GROWTH

The previous chapter described how we begin with the unique DNA contributed by our two biological parents. A newly created DNA pattern directs prenatal development in three stages: the germinal, the embryonic, and the fetal stage (Aldred, 1997; Nilsson & Hamberger, 1990).

The Germinal Stage

The germinal stage lasts about two weeks. During the first week the fertilized egg, or zygote, travels down the fallopian tube from the ovary and implants onto the wall of the mother's uterus, which is referred to as the womb during pregnancy. By the time of **implantation**, one of the most amazing features of early development makes its entrance: the process of **differentiation**. Rather than continuing to divide into identical cells, individual cells begin to take on the characteristics of the structures they will eventually become. Furthermore, the differentiated cells know exactly where to place themselves, moving toward locations where they will eventually establish themselves and perform their function.

During the zygote's travel to the womb, these differentiating cells form a fluid-filled sphere called a **blastocyst**. The outer cells of the blastocyst will grow into a saclike structure called the **placenta**, which will be filled with **amniotic fluid**, and within which the developing life will remain until birth. The placenta serves as a transfer station, letting nutrients pass from the mother to the new life and allowing waste to pass back to the mother. This means of input and output will be facilitated by eventual formation of the **umbilical cord**, both attaching the baby to the placenta and providing an avenue for the mother and child's shared blood supply. The physical beginnings of the baby itself develop as a cluster forms on one side of the blastocyst, which is called the **embryonic disk**. Figure 4.1 shows the progress of the developing life by the end of the germinal stage.

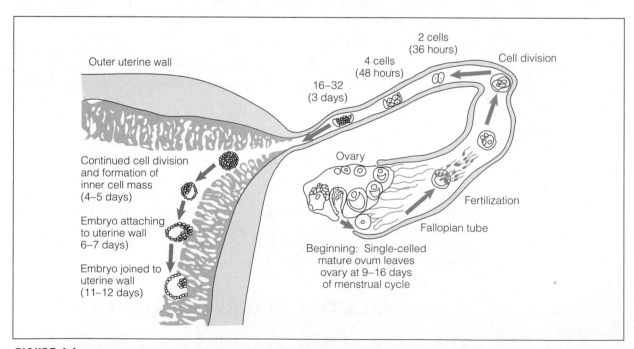

FIGURE 4.1

The location of the zygote at various stages in the early days after conception. Within two weeks an ovum can be fertilized, travel down the fallopian tube, and implant against the uterine wall, where it will remain and mature until childbirth. From Papalia, D. E., and Olds, S. W. (1990). *A child's world: Infancy through adolescence*, 5th ed., NY: McGraw-Hill, p. 95. Reprinted by permission.

Not all zygotes are viable. Occasionally the combination of genes they inherit is inadequate for promoting growth much beyond conception, or a sperm and an ovum may not join together successfully. Under these circumstances the zygote spontaneously aborts. Between 10 and 30% of all conceptions are spontaneously aborted within the first four weeks, so early in the reproductive process that usually the mother will not even know that she had been pregnant. Another 10 to 20% are lost between four and thirteen weeks (Lachelin, 1985). About half of these spontaneous abortions are known to occur because of chromosomal abnormalities (Alberman & Creasy, 1997). Occasionally a zygote may threaten the life of the mother herself by implanting somewhere other than within the womb, such as in the ovaries or fallopian tubes. Since the placement of these **ectopic pregnancies** makes them inviable, such fetuses must be surgically removed.

The Embryonic Stage

During the third through eighth weeks after conception, the new life is called the **embryo**. Its cells develop into three groups:

1. the **ectoderm**, an outer layer that will eventually develop into the nervous system, skin, and skin-based structures such as hair, nails, and sweat glands

2. the **mesoderm**, a middle layer that will become muscles and connective tissues, the skeleton, and the circulatory system

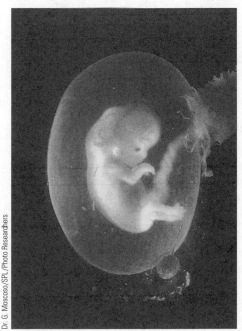

3. the **endoderm**, an inner layer that will form the various digestive organs, lungs, and other vital organs

By the end of the first month the mesoderm has developed a rudimentary heart, which is already pumping blood to the beginnings of other bodily structures. The cells of the ectoderm have folded over, creating a **neural tube** that will eventually become the spinal cord, with the top end swelling into a future brain (Martin, 1985; McConnell, 1995). The endoderm has differentiated into various inner structures that have already begun to look like the organs they will eventually become.

During the first month, most of the differentiation process involves inner structures. In fact, up until this point the human embryo does not look much different from those of other animal species. During the second month, more distinctive outer structures become recognizable. Arms, legs, hands, feet, then fingers and toes spread out from the developing embryo. The cartilagelike skeletal structure—which initially even includes a tail-like appendage—takes on the general proportions and shape of a human being. The nervous system becomes more sophisticated, and by the end of the embryonic stage the tiny embryo has begun to flutter within the womb and may even respond to touch. The new being is now about an inch long, weighs about one-thirtieth of an ounce, and is recognizable as a future human being.

This eight-week-old embryo has already developed some features that identify it as human.

Dr. G. Moscoso/SPL/Photo Researchers

The Fetal Stage

After the eighth week the embryo is called the **fetus**, and the period between now and the time of birth is the fetal stage. Common medical practice is to track the progress of a woman's pregnancy along three 3-month trimesters. The end of the first month of the fetal stage finishes out the first trimester. During this month the major organs complete their development and interconnect, the skeleton begins to harden into bone, and finer details such as fingernails, toenails, fingerprint patterns, buds of baby teeth, and eyelids appear. The muscles and nervous system become more functional as the fetus can now kick, blink, suck its thumb, form some facial expressions, and even make first attempts at breathing movements (de Vries, 1992; de Vries et al., 1985). The heartbeat becomes loud enough to be heard with a stethoscope. The genitals begin to form, and by using ultrasound techniques you can often tell whether the child will be a boy or a girl. Thus even though the fetus measures only about 3 in. long and weighs about three ounces, by the end of the first trimester it is amazingly highly formed.

The Second Trimester. From the fourth through the sixth months, the fetus increases in size tenfold. During the second trimester the mother begins feeling an occasional flutter or "thud" as the baby's body movements become increasingly vigorous. The fetus is most active during the fourth and fifth months, then slowly becomes less active during the rest of his or her stay in the womb (Patrick et al., 1982; Roodenburg et al., 1991; de Vries et al., 1985). The digestive and respiratory organs become more highly functioning, and the organs begin practicing the functions of digestion and breathing within the medium of the amniotic fluid. The heartbeat becomes much stronger and easier to detect with the stethoscope. The fetus begins growing hair, eyelashes, eyebrows, and adult tooth buds.

The brain matures more during this trimester than any other. By the end of the second trimester virtually all of the brain's neurons are set in place. Whereas the younger version of the brain did not give evidence of measurable electrical impulses, this more highly developed brain sends out waves recordable on an electroencephalograph (EEG), similar to those of infants living outside the womb (Parmelee & Sigman, 1983). Sensation will have developed to the point where a fetus can be stimulated by sounds, and may even try to shield its eyes from the light of a fetoscopy (Nilsson & Hamberger, 1990).

At some point between the twenty-second and twenty-sixth weeks after conception, the fetus reaches its **age of viability** (Moore, 1989). This means that the respiratory system and brain functions have matured sufficiently for the fetus to have at least a slight chance of surviving outside the womb. Attempting to sustain such survival, however, is an extremely risky business. Even with expert medical care, most infants born during this period do not survive. Weight appears to be the most important factor. After fetal weight reaches 2 lb, which is the usual weight at 26 weeks, its chances for survival become much better (Lin, 1989). By the end of the second trimester, the fetus is usually about 14 in. long and weighs about 2½ lb.

Trimester	Period	Weeks	Length and Weight	Major Events
First	Zygote	1		The one-celled zygote multiplies and forms a blastocyst.
	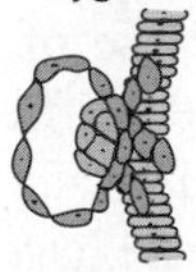	2		The blastocyst burrows into the uterine lining. Structures that feed and protect the developing organism begin to form—amnion, chorion, yolk sac, placenta, and umbilical cord.
	Embyro	3–4	1/4 inch	A primitive brain and spinal cord appear. Heart, muscles, backbone, ribs, and digestive tract begin to develop.
	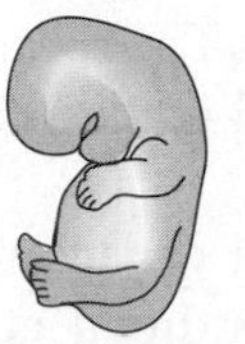	5–8	1 inch	Many external body structures (for example, face, arms, legs, toes, fingers) and internal organs form. The sense of touch begins to develop, and the baby can move.
	Fetus 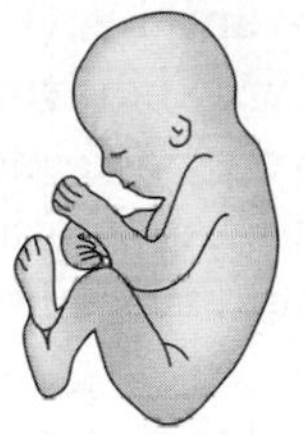	9–12	3 inches; less than one ounce	Rapid increase in size begins. Nervous system, organs, and muscles become organized and connected, and new behavioral capacities (kicking, thumb sucking, mouth opening, and rehearsal of breathing) appear. External genitals are well formed, and the fetus's sex is evident.
Second		13–24	12 inches; 1.8 pounds	The fetus continues to enlarge rapidly. In the middle of this period, fetal movements can be felt by the mother. Vernix and lanugo appear to keep the fetus's skin from chapping in the amniotic fluid. All of the neurons that will ever be produced in the brain are present by 24 weeks. Eyes are sensitive to light, and the baby reacts to sound.
Third		25–38	20 inches; 7.5 pounds	The fetus has a chance of survival if born around this time. Continued increase in size. Lungs gradually mature. Rapid brain development causes sensory and behavioral capacities to expand. In the middle of this period, a layer of fat is added under the skin. Antibodies are transmitted from mother to fetus to protect against disease. Most fetuses rotate into an upside-down position in preparation for birth.

FIGURE 4.2

The zygote, embryo, and fetus from conception to soon before birth. From Berk, L. E. (1993). *Infants, children, and adolescents.* Needham Heights, MA: Allyn & Bacon, p. 96. Reprinted by permission.

The Third Trimester. The last three months proceed with substantial prenatal fine-tuning as the fetus prepares for life outside the womb. Size greatly increases, as the fetus grows about 7 more inches and puts on about 5 more pounds. Much of this increase in weight represents development of a layer of body fat, which will not only help insulate body temperature after the baby is born but also serve as a store of nutrition while the baby waits for the mother's milk supply to catch up with the baby's level of need. The mother might notice that the fetus's movements have become more predictable or organized, falling into a personalized pattern of motor activity (Patrick et al., 1982; Romanini & Rizzo, 1995).

Fetal brain development also prepares for life on the outside. When researchers measure the brain's electrical impulses, heart beat patterns, and other fetal behaviors during the third trimester, they find that the fetus is beginning to show sleep and wake periods that are much the same as those of newborns (Groome et al., 1997; Muro et al 1996; Parmelee & Sigman, 1983). They respond to loud noises with sudden movements and changes in heart rate (Lecanuet et al., 1995; Schmidt et al., 1985). Observed changes in heart rate have indicated fetal preferences for music, as well as a preference for their mothers' voices over those of others (Lecanuet et al., 1992; Moon & Fifer, 1990). The species-specific behaviors for survival, such as the sucking reflex, are well established by now (Smotherman & Robinson, 1996).

During the last trimester fetuses even demonstrate a capacity for learning (Hepper, 1994; Robinson & Smotherman, 1995; Sandman et al., 1997; Smotherman & Robinson, 1996). For example changes in heart rate have been measured when one ongoing auditory stimulus is changed to another (Lecanuet et al., 1989). When pregnant mothers repeatedly read aloud a specific story during the last six weeks before childbirth, once their babies were born and heard the story being read on the outside, they responded more to its rendition than to presentation of unfamiliar rhetoric (DeCasper & Spence, 1986; DeCasper et al., 1994).

The viability of a prematurely born fetus during the third trimester will depend a lot on the development of the child's respiratory system (Manginello & Digeronimo, 1998). Even though the brain's respiratory center is functioning, the air sacs in the lungs may not have matured to the point of being able to adequately expand and contract or exchange oxygen and carbon monoxide. By the end of the eighth month of gestation, this tends not to be as much of a problem for premature infants.

What maternal, environmental, and paternal factors are likely to influence prenatal development?

THE PRENATAL ENVIRONMENT

No man (or woman) is an island, as the saying goes, not even while floating in amniotic isolation. Even though our biological programming is remarkably consistent as it directs our developmental beginnings, a number of environmental factors can also have substantial effects on its natural sequence.

Maternal Factors

The Mother's Age. What is the best age for a woman to have a baby? This is a tough question. In spite of the progress of feminism, the brunt of responsibility for child care still typically falls upon the woman. She will therefore consider not only health concerns but also how becoming a parent will affect her career and her personal and social life as well as what will be in the child's best interests. Some women prefer to become mothers at the onset of adulthood while others prefer to wait until they have achieved other life goals. This is a personal issue that only the woman and her co-parent can effectively evaluate.

However, research can give women some guidance regarding their likelihood of having a successful pregnancy. First there's the issue of becoming pregnant. Generally speaking, the older a woman is, the more difficulty she will have becoming pregnant. With other factors held equal, the chance of becoming pregnant is about 75% for women in their twenties, 62% for women between the ages of 30 and 35, and 54% for women over 35 (Schwartz & Mayaux, 1982).

The woman will also want to consider the effect of age on the likelihood of her having a healthy baby. Being at the younger or older ends of the age spectrum appears to have more potential for undesired effects on a baby's health. Very young mothers, such as those under 15, have a much higher incidence of stillborn births than do mothers of other ages (Leppert et al., 1986). Older mothers can also experience difficulties. Children born to older mothers show a higher incidence of Down's syndrome and other chromosomal mishaps than those born to younger mothers (see Chapter 3). A woman over 50 has as much as one chance in ten of producing such a child. Nevertheless, while some ages present higher risks of problem pregnancies than others, most women of any reproductive age produce healthy, normal babies provided they have received adequate prenatal care.

Nutrition. Since the baby receives all of its nourishment from its mother, the mother's eating habits are of paramount importance. Good nutrition during pregnancy is not that different from the usual nutritional guidelines: Eat a balanced diet and eat regularly. A mother should also figure on eating about 300 to 500 calories more than her usual daily intake and increase her consumption of foods high in protein. Making sure she gets enough folic acid—a nutrient commonly found in green leafy vegetables, liver, and some fruits—also appears to be especially important during the earliest stages of pregnancy (Keen et al., 1991; Ward et al., 1991). Some mothers worry that if they increase their eating they will put on too much extra weight. Normal maternal weight gain during pregnancy is actually around 25–30 lb. Keep in mind that a pregnant mother is putting on both the weight of the fetus itself and the weight of supportive structures such as the placenta, the amniotic fluid, strengthened muscles, and a storage of fat for sustaining future breast-feeding ability.

Understandably, poor nutrition can lead to prenatal difficulties. Malnutrition during pregnancy has been associated with low birth weight, premature and stillborn birth, infant mortality during the first year, and even newborn malformations (Jeans et al., 1955; Rosso, 1992; Stein et al., 1975). The effect on the developing brain is especially devastating. During the last trimester, prenatal malnutrition can limit the number of brain cells being produced to as low as 60% of what it ought to be (Winick et al., 1972). Newborns who were malnourished prenatally are often irritable and unresponsive to their caregivers, thus adding to infant's biological disadvantage the possibility of poor maternal attachment (Zeskind & Ramey, 1981). As such children grow older, their intelligence scores have shown deficits, including learning disabilities (Lozoff, 1989).

Good nutrition during pregnancy is thus so important that pregnant women are usually instructed to take vitamins and other dietary supplements.

As a society we now recognize the impact of prenatal malnutrition not only on these innocent fetal victims but also as the drain on social resources resulting from their impairments. Programs have been developed to serve disadvantaged pregnant women and their unborn children by providing them with dietary supplements. Doing so has in fact been found to improve the condition of their infants (Werner, 1979).

Exercise. In decades past, physicians were concerned that exercise workouts during pregnancy might be harmful to the baby. Subsequent studies indicated that this is not the case (Carpenter et al., 1988). As long as mothers are healthy, exert themselves only moderately, and do not excessively bounce or in other ways directly jolt the baby, exercise can actually be beneficial for the pregnancy. In fact, exercises that strengthen the back, thigh, and abdominal muscles may help the mother carry the fetus as it grows larger and may help in the process of childbirth itself (Artalmittelmark et al., 1991; Bing & Strickman, 1991).

Emotional State. Neuropsychological studies have shown that when we are distressed our bodies release a variety of hormones that prepare us for the "fight or flight" response. In a pregnant woman these hormones cause her body to tense up, reduce the amount of blood going to the womb, and can even pass directly through to the baby. Occasional emotional upsets do not appear to cause any long-term harm. However, on-going and/or severe emotional upset during pregnancy has been associated with such outcomes as miscarriage, premature birth, low birth weight, some physical defects, and oxygen deprivation during the birth process (Katz et al., 1991; Omer & Everly, 1988; Schneider et al., 1999). Negative emotionality and inhibited temperament among 5-year-olds have been associated with maternal stress during pregnancy, especially high stress during the first trimester (Martin et al., 1999). When monitoring the developmental progress of fetuses, researchers find less mature coupling of fetal heart rate and body movement responses among those whose mothers report being under considerable stress (DiPietro, Hodgson, Costigan, Hilton, & Johnson, 1996).

These outcomes suggest an indirect yet important relationship between a child's prenatal development and the mother's social support system. Women who have the support of spouses, friends, relatives, counselors, or other members of the community are less likely to experience such complications due to stress (Cohen, 1991; Norbeck & Tilden, 1983).

Teratogens

During a pregnancy both mother and fetus are commonly exposed to a number of foreign substances from their environment. Some of these substances when taken in by the mother's body can have a dramatic effect on the future of a developing fetus (Needleman & Bellinger, 1994). Such substances are called **teratogens**. Teratogens are agents that, when present during pregnancy, are likely to cause birth defects (Abel, 1987). The timing of exposure to a teratogen often

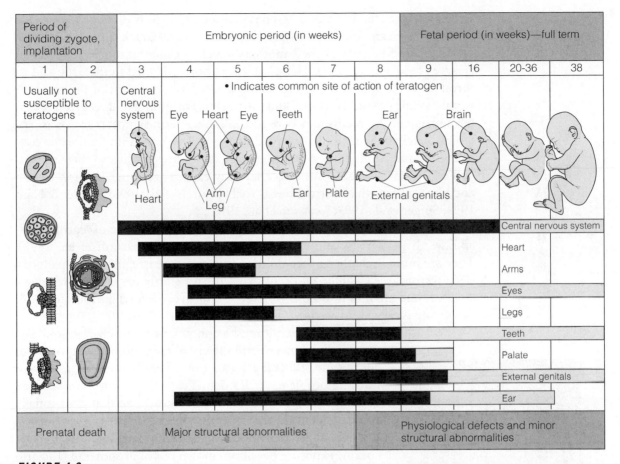

FIGURE 4.3

Fetal vulnerability during different stages of development. The dark bands represent critical time periods during which fetal characteristics are most vulnerable to developmental damage if exposed to teratogens. The light bands represent time periods during which damage still may occur but is less likely to. From K. L. Moore and T. V. N. Persaud (1993), *Before we are born: Essentials of embryology and birth defects,* 4th ed. Philadelphia: Saunders, p. 130.

makes a difference, because the fetal windows of vulnerability vary, as Figure 4.3 shows. The type of teratogen also affects the particular impairment that may develop.

Maternal Drug Use. In recent years considerable publicity has centered on what happens to a fetus when the mother takes drugs. One of the first major, well-publicized examples of such effects involved a prescription drug known as **thalidomide**. When expectant mothers were prescribed this drug during the 1950s and '60s, many of their babies were born with malformed or missing arms, legs, fingers, or internal organs. While what happened to the "thalidomide babies" was tragic, it did mark the beginning of more careful monitoring and testing of new prescription drugs for teratogenic effects. Unfortunately, as thalidomide has recently been discovered to be an effective treatment for leprosy, errant drug handling in some less developed countries is resulting in a new generation of infants who suffer the effects of prenatal exposure to thalidomide (Dobber, 1998).

Research of the 1980s and '90s has focused extensively on what happens to the fetus when an expectant mother uses illicit drugs. "Crack babies" have been so nicknamed because of their mothers' crack cocaine use during pregnancy (Harvey & Kosofsky, 1998). These babies are born addicted to the drug and go through withdrawal after leaving the drug-laced environment of the mother's womb. While physically painful and distressing, withdrawal is a relatively short-term problem. As infants they have shown longer-term symptoms such as irritability, excitability, and high-pitched crying that is almost impossible to console; or paradoxically they may be lethargic and unresponsive to their parents and other environmental stimuli. They may experience some sensory, motor, and physical growth abnormalities as well (Church et al., 1998; Schuler & Nair, 1999; Singer et al., 1999; Swanson et al., 1999).

As these children reach preschool age they show evidence of learning disabilities, hyperactivity, and attention span problems (Chasnoff et al., 1992). They are more likely than other children to experience irregular sleep patterns, sleep terrors (see Chapter 8), or an oversensitive startle response (Chiriboga, 1998). Some are found to be excessively impulsive, even when the quality of caregiving is taken into account (Bendersky & Lewis, 1998).

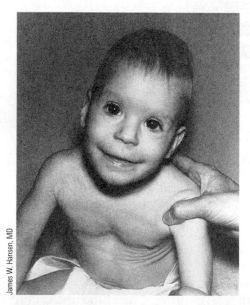

James W. Hansen, MD

This child is affected by fetal alcohol syndrome. Notice the widely spaced eyes, smaller head, and flattened-looking nose and upper lip—conditions frequently observed among those affected by this condition.

Because this population of children has only recently reached school age, the possible longer-term effects of their prenatal exposure to cocaine are still being sorted out. There is some indication of learning problems or IQ deficit, but these may be associated more specifically with the smaller head size that occasionally coincides with this syndrome (Chiriboga, 1998). Some suggest that the longer-term negative outcomes attributed to prenatal cocaine exposure have been blown out of proportion (Inciardi et al., 1997). When told that an infant is cocaine exposed, adults tend to rate the infant more negatively, an example of experimental bias that may also affect how researchers observe these children (Woods et al., 1998).

Almost all the commonly used street drugs have been shown to have some effect on the developing fetus. Research has shown newborn emotional difficulties and later verbal slowness and memory impairments when the pregnant mother uses marijuana (Fried & Watkinson, 1990). Mothers addicted to morphine, heroin, or codeine are more likely to miscarry, give birth prematurely, or give birth to a stillborn neonate (Schardein, 1985). Their newborns often show withdrawal symptoms such as irritability, tremors, convulsions, and vomiting. Even after reaching early childhood, some continue to show more emotional and intellectual difficulties than nonexposed children. (Householder et al., 1982).

Culturally accepted drug use can also become a teratogenic culprit. Alcohol use by expectant mothers, long suspected of affecting fetuses, was finally linked to a specific syndrome during the 1970s. Children born with **fetal alcohol syndrome (FAS)** have heads that are smaller than normal and may have less brain tissue than is normal or brain tissue that is not organized normally (Abel, 1998;

Clarren, 2000, Streissguth & Kanter, 1997). Often they are mentally retarded or learning disabled. Their facial features are characterized by widely spaced eyes, droopy eyelids, and flattened-looking noses. Heart defects and difficulties with fine motor control are also common. Some children with fetal alcohol syndrome show the entire spectrum of these symptoms, while others may have only a few.

Examining the specific characteristics of a mother's drinking habits does not necessarily reveal the likelihood or degree of impairment. While some mothers may drink daily and not have affected babies, others may drink very little and show the full effect (Hoyseth & Jones, 1989). This is in part explained by timing. Recent research has revealed that the most vulnerable point for the developing embryo is at about 20 days after conception. During this phase, activities crucial to brain and facial-feature development are occurring, which explains why children with "classic" FAS facial features are also often the ones most severely intellectually impaired (Clarren, 2000; Heyns, 1997). However, studies of alcohol consumption during both early and late stages of pregnancy show that the entire gestation period is vulnerable to teratogenic effects (Jacobson et al., 1993). Thus if a woman is even considering becoming pregnant, she is best advised to avoid alcohol use altogether.

Nicotine, the psychoactive substance found in tobacco, has also been found to be associated with fetal difficulties (Benowitz, 1998). Outcomes such as ectopic pregnancy, low birth weight, premature birth, and stillbirth all occur in higher incidences among mothers who smoke (Martin, 1992). Recent studies have shown an association between smoking during pregnancy and certain learning disabilities and behavioral problems (Day et al., 2000; Millberger et al., 1998). Unfortunately even though the public is now generally aware that smoking is potentially harmful to everyone, the addictive properties of nicotine are so profound that even the most dedicated and caring of mothers have difficulty giving it up.

Maternal Illness. One of the first diseases discovered to have teratogenic effects was **rubella**, popularly called "German measles." If a new life is exposed to the rubella virus very early in a pregnancy, the effects can be so severe that the mother miscarries. Fetuses that survive the viral assault are often born with defects such as deafness, blindness, heart malformations, and mental retardation. Exposure during the middle of the pregnancy can result in intellectual and emotional impairments (Samson, 1988). Fortunately, vaccinations for rubella are now available, and future mothers can be routinely vaccinated during their childhoods.

Toxoplasmosis is a minor parasitic infection that shows few if any symptoms in healthy adults. The parasite is found in raw meat, and cats also sometimes act as carriers and pass the parasite on by means of their feces. If a pregnant mother encounters the parasite it can cause problems such as miscarriage, premature birth, and birth defects involving the eyes and the brain (Ho-Yen & Joss, 1992). Pregnant mothers are therefore cautioned to eat only meat that has been well-cooked and to wash thoroughly after handling cats or changing their litter boxes.

Several sexually transmitted diseases can affect the developing fetus (Hitchcock et al., 1999). **AIDS (acquired immunodeficiency syndrome)** counts newborn infants as one of the fastest-growing populations of infection. Most mothers contract and pass on the human immunodeficiency virus (HIV) because of their own or the father's intravenous drug use. Even though newly developed drug therapies have been extending the lives of those who develop AIDS, beginning life as HIV-positive is still accompanied by an expectation of an agonizing early death sentence. **Syphilis** when present at birth can result in blindness and problems related to the central nervous system. Most states require women to be tested for syphilis during pregnancy so that measures can be taken to minimize its dangers. Newborns can also become infected by **herpes** as they pass through the birth canal, which frequently results in brain damage or even death. This outcome can be avoided by delivering the baby by cesarean section (described below) if a herpes outbreak is present at the time of delivery.

Environmental Hazards. A number of substances floating around in a pregnant woman's biosphere can have an effect on a developing fetus (Colborn et al., 1997; Paul, 1993). One of the first environmental hazards found to have teratogenic effects was atomic radiation. The unplanned field experiment that proved the case involved pregnant mothers in Japan who had been exposed to radiation from the two atomic bombs dropped in 1945. Most of the babies who were not miscarried were stillborn, or if they lived were physically defective or mentally retarded (Michel, 1989). More recently, babies prenatally exposed to the radiation from the accident at the Chernobyl nuclear power plant were found to have a higher number of developmental speech and language disorders, more emotional disorders, and lower intelligence test scores as young children (Kolominsky et al., 1999). Even the lower levels of exposure to radiation that occur during routine x-ray evaluations or treatments have been found to have a relationship with birth defects. Women who are either pregnant or planning to become pregnant are therefore cautioned to avoid medical x-ray exposure, as well as avoid any work environment that is likely to put them in frequent contact with radiation.

For a while there was a scare that pregnant mothers were receiving too much radiation from video display terminals. A preliminary study did show a higher incidence of miscarriages and birth defects among women who spent more than 20 hours a week in front of a video display terminal. However, the true cause of this finding may have been that these women were working during their pregnancies and thus experiencing more stress than the general population of pregnant women. Another study compared women in the same profession who either did or did not work with video display terminals. These two groups did not differ at all in number of miscarriages or other difficulties with pregnancy (Schnorr et al., 1991).

Mothers can be exposed to numerous harmful substances from the environment without being aware of their presence. For example, a mother may come into contact with excessive amounts of lead from old lead-based paints chipping off walls or lead settled from vehicle exhaust fumes of decades past, or she may be exposed to lead in her work environment. Children born to mothers so exposed continue to demonstrate a lower level of intellectual development even at the age of two (Bellinger et al., 1987).

Other industrially produced substances have also been identified as culprits. Chemicals called PCBs (polychlorinated biphenyls) were commonly used in industry up until the 1970s. When infants of mothers who had eaten fish from PCB-polluted Lake Michigan were evaluated, they tended to weigh less at birth and have smaller heads and to show some reactive and intellectual slowness as they grew older (Jacobson et al., 1985). In Japan during the 1950s an industrial plant released a great deal of mercury into a bay that provided the fish consumed by a number of pregnant women. Many of their babies were found to be brain damaged, often having difficulties with speech, coordination, and chewing and swallowing (Vorhees & Mollnow, 1987).

Some seemingly innocent environmental events can have an effect on the developing fetus. Mothers are now cautioned about using hot tubs. Since the fetus's head is essentially submerged under hot water, physicians are concerned that the excessive temperature could produce the same brain damage that would result from an excessively high fever. Under some circumstances simply having had a previous baby can prove detrimental. If a mother has a blood type that does not contain a protein called the **Rh factor** and the father's genes had passed on the protein to the first baby, the mother develops antibodies to destroy the substance. During a second pregnancy these antibodies attack the fetus's red blood cells, thus limiting the oxygen supply received by the child's developing organs. The end result can be miscarriage, stillbirth, mental retardation, and other serious impairments. Fortunately Rh negative mothers who have had an Rh positive baby can now be prevented from building up a store of such antibodies with an injection of RhoGam after they have given birth. Even if this injection was not given in advance, these mothers' subsequent children can often be saved with a blood transfusion either before or after birth (Queenan, 1994).

The Father's Contributions

If we survey the research of decades past we could easily assume that medical researchers saw no need to examine the role of the father in pregnancy outcome beyond his contribution of sperm. With the exception of conditions passed along by genes, identification of the father's contribution is a relatively new arena of interest. As the outcome studies begin to pile up, we are finding that fathers can and do play a significant role in the success of a pregnancy.

The previous discussion of a mother's emotional state is a good example. Now that we know that excessive stress can result in difficulties and that having a good support system increases the likelihood of success, a father's supportiveness during the mother's pregnancy takes on new meaning. In fact, one study found that when husbands behaved negatively toward the pregnancy, were nonsupportive, or were outright emotionally or physically abusive, the same complications that were attributable to stress were more likely to occur (Amaro et al., 1990).

We also saw the complications that can arise when a pregnant mother uses drugs or is exposed to other environmental hazards. Since a father's sperm supply is constantly replenishing itself, the interval during which paternal exposure to such hazards could affect the pregnancy is relatively small. However, sperm can be affected even during that brief period. Fathers whose employment requires them to be around unusually high levels of radiation appear more likely to have babies with chromosomal abnormalities (Schrag & Dixon, 1985). Those who are repeatedly exposed to electromagnetic fields on the job are found to be more likely to father children with nervous system tumors (Spitz & Johnson, 1985).

A father's smoking habits can also affect the developing fetus. Researchers are concerned about the effect of passive smoke on those in the environment, including fetuses. Newborns of fathers who smoked during the pregnancy are found to weigh less than those of fathers who did not (Rubin et al., 1986). In addition, fathers who use nicotine—as well as marijuana and alcohol—have been found to produce sperm showing a higher incidence of chromosomal and other abnormalities (Lester & Van Theil, 1977).

Conclusion

We have seen how biological mishaps, maternal experiences, environmental influences, and even paternal contributions can all have an effect on the developing child. Looking back at all of the potential difficulties, one might wonder how any of us managed to be born healthy and developmentally sound. Yet in spite of all the difficulties that can arise as nature runs its course, the vast majority of us are likely to produce normal, healthy children.

THE BIRTH PROCESS

What happens during the typical process of childbirth?

About 38 weeks after fertilization, the baby is full-term and ready to abandon the support and protection of the womb (Nilsson & Hamberger, 1990). Childbirth, or "labor," occurs in three stages. The first stage lasts around 12 hours, usually longer for new mothers and shorter for mothers with previous births. The mother begins experiencing a series of contractions in her abdominal area. As time passes, they become stronger, longer, and closer together as her uterus prepares to expel the fetus. These contractions stretch the cervix and lower uterus, and are excruciatingly painful for the mother. Researchers are still trying to figure out exactly what triggers the beginning of labor. Hypotheses include the size of the fetus, hormones released by the mother's genetic programming after nine months, hormones stimulated by fetal urine, or perhaps decreased blood flow to the uterus.

The second stage begins when the baby's head has begun to move through the cervix and birth canal. The mother begins feeling an urge to push, and during vigorous labor the abdominal muscles may even start pushing without the mother's voluntary control. The mother helps the birth process along by bearing down in concert with the contractions, as if she were trying to expel a bowel movement. At the end of the second stage, which usually lasts an hour or so, the baby emerges, still attached by the umbilical cord to the placenta inside the womb.

During the third stage, which lasts a few minutes, the contractions expel the placenta. The umbilical cord is then cut, marking the beginning of the child's physiological independence.

What alternative birthing procedures are available?

PAVING PATHWAYS FOR THE NEONATE: BIRTHING ALTERNATIVES

What is the birth process like for the newborn? Since we can't directly interview the baby, the topic is difficult to study. The brain's neurons are not sufficiently interconnected at the time of birth for the newborn to be able to hang on to the actual memory and report it once he or she has sufficient verbal ability. We do know that neonates experience stress by virtue of the high levels of stress hormones found in their bloodstreams after birth (Lagercrantz & Slotkin, 1986). This is not surprising. If we try putting ourselves in the place of the neonate we can imagine ourselves starting out in a warm, soft, cozy, wet environment. Then with little warning we are systematically shoved through a tight canal and unceremoniously dumped into an open, cold environment with relatively minimal physical support, and new survival requirements such as breathing air instead of amniotic fluid are foisted upon us. It has been speculated to be so distressing that childbirth experts have been seeking ways to make the process less stressful.

One such effort has been the movement back to natural childbirth. For several decades before this return, women in Western culture were separated from their husbands and most of their support system during labor, then put under anesthesia during the birth of the child. Such isolation results in stress for the mother, further compounding the neonate's independently produced stress. In addition most anesthesias used for pain management can pass through and sedate the neonate, a factor that can make his or her birth experience even more taxing.

The **Lamaze method** is a form of natural childbirth that teaches couples to work as a team during the birth process (Lamaze, 1958; Savage & Simkin, 1986). The parents are taught what to expect during the birth process so they will feel less of the stress that can arise from fear of the unknown. As an alternative to anesthesia, the mother learns breathing and relaxation exercises that will help her deal with the pain of delivery, and the father or support person learns how to coach her. The father or support person is typically present during the birth, providing the mother with much-needed emotional support for getting through the ordeal.

Another alternative birth process intended to relieve neonate stress is the **Leboyer method** (Berezin, 1980; Leboyer, 1975). Some believe that neonates need a softer, gentler birth environment than is found in the typical hospital delivery room. They suggest keeping the lights low, speaking in soft voices, and insulating the environment in such a way that instruments will not be so noisy. Placing the neonate on the mother's stomach immediately after birth and leaving the umbilical cord attached for a while gives the child a chance to adjust to the new surroundings. And since neonates are most familiar with warm and wet surroundings, proponents of this method recommend placing them in a tub of warm water immediately after birth to moderate adjustment to the outside world.

Occasionally circumstances arise such that either the mother cannot deliver through the birth canal or cannot attempt to do so without endangering herself or the fetus. The umbilical cord may be inextricably wrapped around the fetus's neck, or the baby may be in a **breech position** (feet or buttocks first rather than head first), which would complicate a normal delivery. Perhaps after an excessively long labor, the mother is too exhausted to push any longer. She may have a medical condition such as Rh incompatibility, herpes, or an illness that might affect the infant during a vaginal delivery. At some point the fetus may begin showing signs of distress, and its survival requires a quick delivery.

Under these circumstances, a surgical procedure called **cesarean delivery** is often performed, named for folklore suggesting that Julius Caesar was delivered in this manner (Churchill, 1997). A horizontal incision is made along the mother's lower abdomen, and the baby is removed from the womb through the surgical opening. It was once believed that after a woman had a cesarean delivery, all subsequent deliveries would also have to be cesarean (Kaufmann, 1996). Physicians were concerned that the scar tissue in the uterus might tear during a natural birth. However, such a rupture appears to be the exception rather than the rule, and if it does occur, it will heal with proper care and is not likely to endanger either mother or neonate (O'Sullivan et al., 1981). Concerns that cesarean deliveries affect quality of mother/infant relationships are also unfounded. No significant impact is observed when the dyads are measured four and twelve months postdelivery (Durik et al., 2000).

Unfortunately, cesarean deliveries are still overperformed in the United States, chiefly because obstetricians are concerned about liability should something go wrong. In view of the increased recovery time required after the surgery and the exceptional efforts needed to get the neonate breathing and responsive when "untimely ripped from his mother's womb," pregnant women are well-advised to assess their physicians' attitudes regarding cesarean delivery well before the delivery date. Such a discussion helps both physician and mother make well-informed decisions as they proceed through the process of childbirth (Kaufmann, 1996).

THE NEWBORN

What are the characteristics of the newborn?

Newborn infants, called **neonates** during their first month, have a number of common physical characteristics that make them look more like one another than their family members. Their skin is thin and dry, and they turn red and wrinkled-looking when they cry. Their heads seem top-heavy, with much forehead and little chin. Their skull area may seem bumpy or misshapen and their noses flattened—an outcome you might expect after having passed through the tight birth canal.

The newborn human infant has already developed many functions by the time of his or her birth that facilitate life outside the womb. Many of these basic abilities will be used throughout the infant's life, such as the ability to suck, swallow, cough, blink, breathe, and digest food. Dozens of reflexes are in place, and most of them will remain intact for a lifetime (O'Doherty, 1986). Some reflexes present at birth will be lost as the newborn leaves infancy. One of these is called the **rooting reflex**. If you touch the newborn's cheek, the baby will turn toward the sensation and make sucking motions. Another is the **Babinski reflex**. When the bottom of a baby's foot is stroked, the toes will fan out. Neonates also have a **grasping reflex**, closing their fingers tightly around any object that is touched against their palms. A fourth reflex is a type of startle response called the **Moro reflex**. If babies feel a sudden loss of support or are exposed to some other intense stimulus such as a loud noise they will arch their backs, throw back their heads, throw their arms out away from their bodies, then pull their arms tightly toward their chests. By the time an infant is a year old, these four reflexes are usually overridden by the increased voluntary control of more advanced brain functioning and are no longer observed.

Immediately following birth, babies are assessed for the presence of certain indicators of their ability to survive. The **Apgar scale** measures neonate heart rate, respiratory effort, reflex reactions, muscle tone, and color (Apgar, 1953). The baby is given a rating of 0, 1, or 2 for each of these indicators based on its strength. A neonate producing a total score of 7 or higher is considered to be in good physical condition. A score of 4, 5, or 6 suggests that the baby is having some adjustment difficulties and will probably need some special care, such as aid from an oxygen tent or spending some time in an isolette. A score of 3 or lower indicates that the infant is in serious distress and will need emergency medical attention in order to survive. Interestingly, one recent study showed that there is no relationship between ratings of the newborn's primitive reflexes and its subsequent motor development as an infant, highlighting the independence of these two forms of physical activity (Bartlett, 1997).

NEONATE COMPLICATIONS

How can birth complications affect a newborn?

Some conditions surrounding the birth itself can have an undesirable impact on the child. We look at three types of neonate complications: insufficient oxygen, low birth weight, and premature birth.

Insufficient Oxygen

During the birth process the child's mechanism for receiving oxygen shifts from the umbilical cord to the lungs. Problems can arise that interfere with either mechanism's capacity to function properly and thus deprive the child of oxygen (Haddad et al., 1993). The umbilical cord may become pinched or tangled and interfere with delivery of the oxygenated blood supply from the mother. Sedatives given to the mother during the birth process can be passed on to the infant, who may then only make sluggish efforts at trying out his or her lungs. **Anoxia** is the condition of having received insufficient oxygen during the birth process. Severe anoxia can have devastating effects on the newborn. Lack of oxygen to the brain for more than a few minutes can result in brain damage or even death (Maulik, 1998).

Low Birth Weight

Some neonates are born full-term but are notably smaller than the norm. When these babies weigh less than 5½ lb they are called small-for-date. Sometimes their condition can be traced to prenatal factors such as the maternal, paternal, and environmental factors described earlier, but on other occasions no explanation can be found. About 7.5% of infants are born with low birth weight. This percentage continues to be on the rise, due partly to increasing numbers of multiple births (Federal Interagency Forum on Child and Family Statistics, 1999).

Small-for-date infants are even more likely to have serious difficulties than those who are small because they are premature (Austin & Moawad, 1993). Some are actually malformed. Some will remain small in stature, never catching up with their cohort's size. The immune system may not be sufficiently effective and the infant becomes more vulnerable to infections. Small-for-date infants are more likely to suffer from brain damage, have learning disabilities or behavior problems, or show impaired intelligence. Their impairments are so pervasive that they also have a higher likelihood of perishing during the first year than do other infants.

Premature Birth

Preterm infants are those born more than 3 weeks earlier than the usual 38 weeks after conception and weighing less than 5½ lb (Manginello & Digeronimo, 1998). In addition to showing some of the difficulties experienced by small-for-date infants, they may suffer from conditions related to underdevelopment. **Respiratory distress syndrome**, also known as *hyaline membrane disease,* is common in infants born more than 6 weeks early (Nelson, 1985). Because the lungs are insufficiently developed the infant has difficulty keeping them from collapsing. Such infants are usually put on ventilators to help them breathe.

Other developmental difficulties result from the measures taken to keep the neonate alive. Preterm and some small-for-date infants are placed in isolettes. These small enclosed Plexiglas boxes are designed to meet the challenged

This tiny newborn is more likely to thrive with the added survival assistance of the isolette.

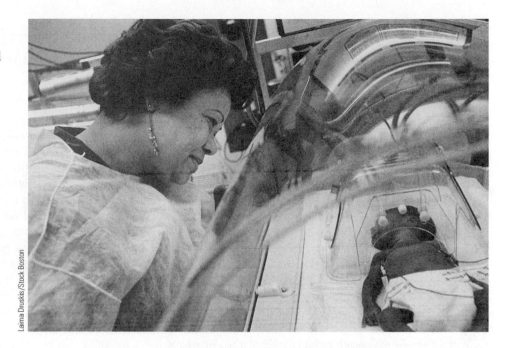

Laima Druskis/Stock Boston

neonate's survival needs. They are temperature-controlled, provide protection from bacteria and viruses, and facilitate the use of ventilators or feeding tubes.

While the isolette environment increases needy infants' chances of survival, it also isolates them from the physical stimulation an infant would normally receive. Being touched appears to be especially important to the developing newborn (McClure, 1989). The release of growth hormones appears to be related to the amount of physical stimulation an infant receives. Studies have shown that when preterm infants are massaged or otherwise physically stimulated while in their isolettes they gain weight faster, appear to be more alert, and at the end of the first year are more advanced in their mental and motor development than preterm infants who did not receive such treatment (Field, 1986). The restrictiveness of the isolette also interferes with the early parent-child attachment process that normally occurs between infant and caregiver. One study showed that when preterm infants finally went home, their parents spent less time holding, touching, and talking to their babies than did parents of full-term infants, thus providing less of the beneficial physical stimulation (Goldberg et al., 1980).

As the child grows older, premature birth continues to have implications for his or her cognitive and behavioral development. Prematurity has been associated with a lower than normal rate of development and other difficulties, especially when the child's birth weight is very low. School-age children who were born prematurely often lag behind their full-term cohorts in cognitive development and academic ability (Taylor et al., 1998). They are more likely to have behavioral problems such as oppositionalism and hyperactivity (Girouard et al., 1998; Halpern & Garcia-Coll, 2000; Taylor et al., 1998). As many as 75% of children born prematurely will at some point in their childhoods meet the

BOX 4.1   Newborn rooming-in and parenting adequacy

Tried

O'Conner, S., Vietze, P. M., Sherrod, K. B., Snadler, H. M., & Altemeier III, W. A. (1980). Reduced incidence of parenting inadequacy following rooming-in. *Pediatrics,* 66, 176–182.

MOTHER-INFANT BONDING IN HUMAN BEINGS APPEARS within an equal opportunity time window: It can happen during any period of the parent-child relationship. However, some studies have shown that prolonged postnatal separations, as often occur with premature babies, are associated with increased risk of child abuse or neglect. The researchers who conducted the above-named study looked at the impact of increased mother-infant contact the first few days following childbirth on the subsequent quality of parenting the children received.

The pool of participants consisted of babies born over a nine-month period at a hospital serving mainly low-income families. Infants and their mothers were selected for the study if they met the following criteria: normal pregnancy and labor, vaginal delivery, single birth, first child, infant birth weight of at least 5 lb, an Apgar score of at least 7, the infant remained healthy during the hospital stay, and the mother planned to keep the baby. The expectant mothers were not told the nature of the study other than that the researchers wanted to learn about what makes happy mother-infant relationships.

After giving birth, about half of the new mothers were placed in a setting where their newborns roomed-in with them. The control half experienced the usual hospital routine: Newborns stayed in the nursery and were brought to mother only during feeding time. Mothers were assigned to the rooming-in setting whenever space became available at the time of childbirth; if all rooming-in spaces were taken, the mothers were assigned to the control rooms. The nurses assigning the rooms and providing subsequent care were not told of the nature or expected outcomes of the study, and no differences were observed regarding how they interacted with either group.

When the children reached ages between 12 and 21 months, over 90% of both groups of participants were still available for evaluation—134 of the rooming-in children and 143 of the control children. At this time the researchers evaluated the adequacy of the mothers' parenting thus far. They found that the rooming-in mothers showed significantly fewer incidents of inadequate parenting than did the control group. Evidence included hospitalizations for such parental inadequacies as poor care during illness or failure to thrive due to insufficient feeding, referrals to child protective agencies, and having voluntarily or involuntarily given up the child to someone else to raise.

The authors suggest that the apparent success of rooming-in may be due in part to mother and infant venturing into a state of reciprocal adaptation at the outset. The infant is not misled by the artificiality of a hospital nursery, the mother is not lulled back into a without-child mind set through relative isolation from her newborn, and the two of them thus do not need to overcome any ambiguous early expectancies. Rooming-in appears to let them begin reinforcing each others' behaviors, attuning to one another immediately, and the mother's feeling successful before after-the-fact self-doubts have a chance to set in. Removing the baby immediately after birth and placing him or her in the care of professionals also may imply to a young mother that she is not competent to do the job herself, which may undermine her parenting self-confidence.

It is important to note, however, that over 90% of the mothers in the control group did not demonstrate any significant parenting inadequacy. Thus while rooming-in has some association with fewer problems related to mother-infant bonding, we cannot say that it is essential to the dyad's well-being.

BOX 4.2   Parenting readiness and prenatal education

... and True

NATURALLY, RECEIVING ADEQUATE PARENTING IS IN every child's best interests. The rooming-in study illustrates three important points: Parents must perceive their new role as a reality, mother-child relating and attunement is an interactive process, and the mother's self-confidence must be affirmed as she adjusts to her changing world. These outcomes can be maximized in many ways other than rooming-in after birth. Currently prepregnancy and prenatal education take a proactive approach in helping young adults prepare for the role of parenthood.

Parenting readiness. When is a person ready to become a parent? Helping young people become aware of the nature of parenthood may result in their putting off parenthood until they feel ready for the challenge. Below are some issues that are important for them to consider, framed as statements with which they can agree:

I like children.

I am becoming a parent by choice, rather than as a result of someone else's wishes or accidental pregnancy.

I am financially able to support a child.

I am willing to work within the time constraints of parenting, such as limiting time by myself or with my spouse, friends, or favorite pastimes.

I am ready for the intimacy, attachment, and personal vulnerability involved in a parent-child relationship.

I can handle a relationship that is almost entirely one-way, designed around my child's needs and wants rather than my own.

I am flexible and adaptable.

I do not fall apart over minor frustrations, failures, or the need to admit I'm wrong.

I have familiarized myself with parenting and child discipline techniques, and have developed a philosophy and plan that is consistent with those of my co-parent's.

My childrearing plan works in with my career pursuits.

I will view my child as a separate individual, with his or her own needs and preferences, rather than as an extension of me.

Prenatal education. Most expectant mothers are strongly encouraged to take classes during pregnancy that help them adjust to pregnancy, the birth process, and parenthood. Typical childbirth classes include the following:

- Explanations of human reproduction, what new mothers can expect about their bodies during pregnancy and childbirth, and how to cope.
- The nutritional needs of the expectant mother and the effect of nutrition on the developing fetus.
- The role of a companion during labor and birth.
- Options they may choose regarding birthing, such as natural childbirth, rooming-in, and home-style birth environments.
- Possible complications of childbirth and how they will be addressed.
- The social and psychological relationships within a family.
- What the newborn is like.
- How to care for a newborn, as well as an introduction to how to parent as the child grows older.

Studies of the benefits of childbirth classes have not yet empirically demonstrated their effectiveness in improving mother-infant attachment or parenting adequacy, mainly because outcome research designs have been inadequate (May & Mahlmeister, 1994). Nevertheless, we might speculate that taking such classes can help women feel empowered by having knowledge of the choices they can bring to bear, enhancing their self-esteem and possibly decreasing dissatisfaction with the birth process. Knowledge of the birth process itself and of what to expect from a newborn also helps remove some of the fears of the unknown. Any of these outcomes could help spare the mother the negative feelings toward a child that might otherwise arise from unpleasant associations classically conditioned to the process of pregnancy, childbirth, and becoming a parent.

May, K. A., & Mahlmeister, L. R. (1994). *Maternal and neonatal nursing: Family-centered care.* Philadelphia: J. B. Lippincott.

criteria for having a learning disability, attention deficit hyperactivity disorder, or language or neurological impairment, or will be referred for school-related problems (Cherkes-Julkowski, 1998). Perhaps as a consequence of any of these conditions, they have also been found more likely to become victims of child abuse (Starr, 1979).

What role does bonding play in the life of a newborn?

PAVING PATHWAYS FOR THE NEONATE: EARLY BONDING

If you walk by any hospital newborn viewing area you stand a good chance of seeing a parent peering through the window and staring at his or her newborn. You may feel tempted to stand and stare yourself. Even as newborns are strollered by on a sidewalk people often turn to catch a glimpse of these tiny beings. What makes newborn babies so fascinating? At this point we are not really sure. Perhaps it has something to do with their chubby rounded faces, softness, or sweet smell—characteristics that also apply to the other baby animals we seem to feel drawn to. New parents not only feel compelled to watch their babies but also tend to want to hold them, and upon doing so look into their babies' eyes, talk to them softly, and gently stroke them. This process of parents demonstrating initial attachment behaviors toward their new child has been called **bonding**.

Anne Rippy/Image Bank

This father and his infant are demonstrating bonding behavior. While bonding behavior is commonly seen among parents and newborns, bonding between parent and child can develop during any phase of childhood.

A couple of decades ago developmentalists became concerned about how the hospital childbirth practices of the day, which typically involved immediately whisking a newborn out of the birthing room and isolating it in a nursery, might interfere with bonding opportunities. They hypothesized that permanent damage could occur because of this perceived interference with early bonding. Alternative birthing situations were created, such as more homelike birthing rooms and infants rooming in with their mothers. However, research has not supported the initial hypothesis (Eyer, 1994; Goldberg, 1983). In fact, in one study, separation of mothers from their neonates was associated with an even higher level of maternal concern for infant well-being (Feldman, Weller, et al., 1999). There does not appear to be any critical period during which human infants bond with their parents. Parents appear to be able to develop feelings of caring, affection, and attachment toward a child during almost any point in their relationship. This is welcome news for adoptive parents, as well as for parents who are too exhausted after the birth process to immediately experience the full compliment of feelings related to bonding.

However, the emergence of the alternative birthing situations has provided parents with the opportunity to engage in more of the pleasurable bonding experiences possible during those first few days with their infant. Future chapters will elaborate upon the major role that attachment between parent and child plays in child development. Any practice that enhances early attachment is thus a welcome addition to child-birthing procedures.

SUMMARY

Prenatal Stages of Development

The germinal stage of prenatal development lasts about two weeks. After the egg is fertilized by the sperm, the resulting zygote travels down the fallopian tubes and implants itself as a blastocyst in the lining of the womb. By the end of the germinal stage the cells of the blastocyst have differentiated into several clusters: the placenta, the umbilical cord, and the embryonic disk—which will eventually become the baby. About half of all zygotes survive beyond this point, the others in some way not being viable.

During the embryonic stage, the cells of the embryo differentiate into the ectoderm, mesoderm, and endoderm—structures that eventually develop into specific collections of internal and external organs. At the end of the eighth week of gestation, the embryo is only an inch long but is recognizable as a future human being. The beginnings of most organs are in place, and the new life has begun moving and sensing.

The fetal stage consists of the last seven months of gestation. During the third month—marking the end of the first trimester—organs further develop and interconnect, and external details such as fingernails, teeth, eyelids, and genitals begin to appear. During the next three months—the second trimester—the mother can begin feeling the fetus move. Respiratory and digestive organs begin practicing their functions within the amniotic fluid. The brain's neurons are all set in place by the end of the second trimester, as the fetus reaches its age of viability. During the last three months—the third trimester—most growth involves the fetus's increase in size as it prepares for life outside the womb. The fetus develops a layer of body fat, and the brain begins showing electrical impulses, sleep-wake cycles, and learning capacities similar to those of newborns. By the end of the third trimester, the fetus weighs about 7½ lb and is about 21 in. long.

The Prenatal Environment

Maternal age, nutrition, exercise, and emotional state can all have an effect on a child's prenatal development. The presence of teratogens such as drugs, alcohol, nicotine, and some bacteria and viruses can result in serious long-term birth defects or even fetal death. Exposure to environmental hazards such as radiation and various metals and chemicals can also cause birth defects and fetal death. The father can negatively affect the child's prenatal development by contributing passive smoke, causing or alleviating maternal stress, and exposing his sperm to hazardous substances around the time of conception.

The Birth Process

Childbirth proceeds through three stages. First, the mother experiences abdominal contractions as the cervix and birth canal expand for the impending event, a process lasting an average of 12 hours. Second, the baby's head appears and the mother feels the urge to push along with the contractions, eventually expelling the baby through the birth canal. During the third stage, contractions expel the placenta and umbilical cord, and the umbilical cord is cut.

Paving Pathways: Birthing Alternatives

The Lamaze method of childbirth depends on breathing and relaxation techniques for dealing with the pain of labor and provides the support and encouragement of a partner, rather than isolating the mother and using anesthesias and sedatives. The Leboyer method rearranges the birthing situation so that it creates a less traumatic birth experience for the child, such as by keeping the environment dim and quiet, providing a warm transitional bath, and placing the baby on the mother's stomach immediately after birth. Because of various potentially hazardous medical conditions and complications, some fetuses are delivered by a surgical procedure called cesarean section.

The Newborn

Many neonate functions and reflexes are in place at the time of birth, including some infant-specific reflexes such as the rooting, Babinksi, grasping, and Moro reflexes. The Apgar scale measures infant responsiveness immediately after birth by assessing not only reflexes but also heart rate, respiratory effort, muscle tone, and color.

Neonate Complications

If neonates do not receive enough oxygen during the birth process, they become anoxic and can suffer brain damage or even death. Neonates that are small-for-date show a higher incidence of malformations, retarded growth, and inadequate immune systems, as well as later learning disabilities, behavior problems, and impaired intelligence. Preterm infants have some of these same difficulties and may also suffer from respiratory distress syndrome. Challenged infants are often provided with the mechanical supports of an isolette. However, this can interfere with the infant's receiving the growth benefits of early physical stimulation.

Paving Pathways: Early Bonding

Both mothers and fathers engage in bonding behaviors with their newborn infants, and there is no critical period during which bonding must occur. Interruptions with bonding during the early days are not found to cause any long-term developmental detriment for parent or child.

KEY TERMS

acquired immune deficiency
   syndrome (AIDS)
age of viability
amniotic fluid
anoxia
Apgar scale
Babinski reflex
blastocyst
bonding
breech position
cesarean delivery
differentiation
ectoderm

ectopic pregnancy
embryo
embryonic disk
endoderm
fetal alcohol syndrome (FAS)
fetus
grasping reflex
herpes
implantation
Lamaze method
Leboyer method
mesoderm
Moro reflex

neonate
neural tube
placenta
preterm infant
respiratory distress syndrome
Rh factor
rooting reflex
rubella
syphilis
teratogens
thalidomide
toxoplasmosis
umbilical cord

CONCEPT REVIEW

1. During the germinal stage of pregnancy, the beginnings of future body structures form through the process of cell _____. As the fluid-filled sphere called the _____ settles into the womb the outer cells form a nutrient/waste transfer organ called the _____, while an inner cluster of cells called the _____ forms the beginnings of the baby.

2. About half of all spontaneous abortions occur due to _____.

3. During the embryonic stage the cells of the embryo differentiate into layers: the _____ will become skin and nervous system structures, the _____ will become muscular, connective, skeletal, and circulatory structures, and the _____ will become the lungs and digestive organs.

4. During the _____ trimester of a pregnancy, a fetus is already responding to sensations, as well as showing EEG waves similar to those of brains of infants living outside the womb.

5. Between 22 and 26 weeks after conception, a fetus first stands a chance of surviving outside the womb, marking its _____.

6. During the third trimester, fetuses show evidence of behaviors that will continue after birth, such as _____, _____, and _____.

7. Very young mothers have a greater risk of experiencing _____ births, while older mothers have a greater risk of producing a child with _____.

8. Maternal malnutrition during pregnancy is especially detrimental to a fetus's developing _____.

9. Severe stress during pregnancy is associated with _____, _____, _____, _____, and _____.

10. Foreign substances present in a mother's body during pregnancy that are likely to cause birth defects are called _____.

11. Babies born addicted to cocaine show not only emotional difficulties but also _____ and _____ abnormalities; upon reaching preschool age they show a greater number of behavioral difficulties and _____.

12. A condition that can include smaller head size, unusual facial features, and mental retardation and that can occur even when a mother consumes very small amounts of alcohol is called _____.

13. Examples of viruses or illness during pregnancy that result in long-term effects on the developing fetus include _____, _____, and _____.

14. Examples of environmental exposures that can have detrimental effects on the developing fetus are the presence of _____, _____, _____, and _____.

15. The father can negatively affect development of a fetus by means of _____, _____, and _____.

16. A form of natural childbirth during which couples work as a team is called the _____ method; a birth procedure aimed at reducing neonate stress during birth by softening lights and noises and placing the infant in warm water following delivery is called the _____ method.

17. If a baby is delivered by means of _____, during which the child exits the womb through an incision in the mother's abdomen, the mother can/cannot deliver future babies vaginally.

18. The _____ scale assesses a newborn's physical viability after birth, including—among other aspects—the presence of the rooting, Babinski, grasping, and Moro _____.

19. Neonate birth complications that can have long-term detrimental effects include _____, _____, and _____.

20. The most common physical complication of premature birth is
_____; as premature babies grow older they show slowing or
abnormalities regarding _____ and _____
development.

21. Studies examining bonding activity between parent and child immediately
following birth indicate that having such an opportunity <u>is/is not</u> crucial for
developing healthy parent/child attachments.

1) differentiation; blastocyst; placenta; embryonic disk; 2) chromosomal abnormalities; 3) ectoderm; mesoderm; endoderm; 4) second; 5) age of viability; 6) sleep/wake patterns; learned auditory preferences; sucking; 7) stillborn; chromosomal abnormalities; 8) brain; 9) miscarriage; premature birth; low birth weight; physical defects; oxygen deprivation; 10) teratogens; 11) sensory; physical growth; learning disabilities; 12) fetal alcohol syndrome; 13) rubella, toxoplasmosis, sexually transmitted diseases; 14) radioactive materials; PCBs; mercury; lead; 15) lack of support of the mother; sperm damaged by environmental exposures; second-hand smoke; 16) Lamaze; Leboyer; 17) cesarean section; can; 18) Apgar; reflexes; 19) insufficient oxygen; low birth weight; premature birth; 20) respiratory distress syndrome; cognitive; behavioral; 21) is not

RESOURCES FOR FURTHER READING

Aldred, H. E. (Ed.) (1997). *Pregnancy and birth sourcebook: Basic information about planning for pregnancy, maternal health, fetal growth and development*, Vol. 31. Detroit: Omnigraphi.

Brazelton, T. B., & Cramer, B. G. (1990). *The earliest attachment: Parents, infants, and the drama of early attachment.* Reading, MA: Addison-Wesley.

Colborn, T., Dumanoski, J. D., & Myers, J. P. (1997). *Our stolen future: Are we threatening our fertility, intelligence, survival? A scientific detective story.* New York: NAL/Dutton.

Engle, B. (1998). *The parenthood decision: Discovering whether you are ready and willing to become a parent.* New York: Doubleday.

Gross, R. T., Spiker, D., & Haynes, C. W. (1997). *Helping low birth weight, premature babies: The Infant Health and Development Program.* Stanford, CA: Stanford University Press.

Needleman, H. L., & Bellinger, D. (Eds.) (1994). *Prenatal exposure to toxicants: Developmental consequences.* Baltimore: Johns Hopkins University Press.

Nilsson, L., & Hamberger, L. (1990). *A child is born.* New York: Delacorte.

Savage, B., & Simkin, D. (1986). *Preparation for birth: The complete guide to the Lamaze method.* New York: Ballantine Books.

Somer, E. (1995). *Nutrition for a healthy pregnancy: The complete guide to eating before, during and after your pregnancy.* New York: Henry Holt.

INFOTRAC COLLEGE EDITION

For additional readings, explore InfoTrac College Edition, your online library. Go to http://www.infotrac-college.com/wadsworth and use the passcode that came on the card with your book. Try these search terms: AIDS in pregnancy, Apgar score, childbirth, childbirth in middle age, childbirth—study and teaching, fetal alcohol syndrome, fetal anoxia, fetal diseases, fetal malnutrition, fetus—effect of alcohol on, fetus—effect of drugs on, fetus—psychological aspects, malnutrition in pregnancy, natural childbirth, prenatal influences, respiratory distress syndrome

CHILD DEVELOPMENT CD-ROM

Go to the Wadsworth Child Development CD-ROM for further study of the concepts in this chapter. The CD-ROM also includes quizzes and additional activities to expand your learning experience.

REFERENCES

For a list of references for this chapter, see the Wadsworth Psych Study Center Web site at: http://www.wadsworth.com/product/0534348092s

CHAPTER 5

Infant and Toddler Physical Development

FOCUS QUESTIONS

▶ How do a child's body size and bodily functioning change during the first two years?

▶ What changes occur in the infant brain as the child advances?

▶ In what ways do conscious states reflect the infant's physical development?

▶ What are the infant body's nutritional needs?

▶ How do infant motor skills progress?

▶ How does the infant sense and perceive the world?

▶ Why is stimulation so important to developing infants, and how can we create sufficiently stimulating environments for them?

OUTLINE

Body Growth
  Height and Weight
  Gender Differences
Brain Development
  Neurons
  Brain Structures
Conscious States
  Sudden Infant Death Syndrome
Infant Nutrition
  Paving Pathways: Breast or Bottle?
  Undernourishment
  Obesity
Motor Development
  Theories of Motor Development
  Gross Motor Skills

  Fine Motor Skills
  Bladder and Bowel Control
Sensory/Perceptual Development
  Vision
  Hearing
  Taste
  Smell
  Touch
  Integrating Sensory Information
  The Role of Infant Stimulation
  Paving Pathways: Providing a Stimulating Infant
    Environment
Possible Signs of Developmental Difficulties

Grandpa took 5-year-old Michael for his first visit to the zoo. He enjoyed observing Michael's wide-eyed wonder as they moved from display to display. Some of the animals were in Michael's picture books but there were others Michael had never seen before. As they were about to leave Michael stopped to look at a pictorial display of the many creatures he had seen.

"Well," Grandpa said, "what do you think of all these animals?"

After a brief period of critical analysis Michael replied, "I think the kangaroo and the elephant should change tails."

The seeming incongruity Michael observed between certain animals' tails and body sizes is not unlike the changing proportional differences we see in the growing child's levels of physical development during the first two years of life. The hallmark of these first two years of development is change. New parents are sometimes warned that their newborns are "only an infant for a moment." The quantity and quality of changes taking place during the first year or two are so dramatic that as parents review the photographs and videotapes of their child's earlier days, they are amazed that they represent the same child.

As new parents gaze in loving wonder at their tiny bundles of joy they often experience concern over whether their infant caregiving will optimize their potential. What can they do that will favorably influence their developmental progress? Actually, a good deal of an infant's rate of development is hereditary. Rates of growth and achievement of various milestones at all ages are more similar among individuals who are related to one another than among those who are unrelated (Tanner, 1990). Some infants may even reach milestones in an unusual order, such as learning to walk along furniture before figuring out how to crawl on all fours. Parents who worry about promoting early attainment of milestones of physical development are better assured that their babies' new talents will naturally emerge, as long as they are provided with a normal, healthy environment for growth.

A child's physical development progresses by means of a dynamic system of interconnections. It is determined not only by genetically programmed possibilities but also by perception, action, learning, motivation, and environmental constraints and freedoms (Thelen, 1997; Thelen & Smith, 1994). Each component of this dynamic system is both cause and product. For example, new capacities for coordination result in a child's attempting new tasks; successes at new tasks motivate the child to try activities that in turn "hardwire" proficiency of coordination. Thanks to this dynamic developmental system, infants themselves are active partners with their biological programming; they promote their own physical growth and find solutions for negotiating their physical world by means of exploration and experimentation.

BODY GROWTH

How do a child's body size and bodily functioning change during the first two years?

When we think about children's physical growth, increases in height and weight usually come to mind. While these are the most obvious markers of growth, the body is actually changing according to certain proportional and directional rules. For example, a 2-month-old fetus's body is about one-half head. By the time we reach adulthood our heads are about one-eighth of our actual height. This rule of development is called **cephalocaudal**: Body development begins at the head, and works its way downward. Figure 5.1 shows the changing proportions of head to body during childhood.

The figure also shows that the trunk of the body begins as substantially better developed early on and then proportionally becomes smaller as the child grows. This is the rule of **proximodistal** development: The early body is most highly developed at its center, and over time structural refinements work their way outward. For example, during prenatal development, the beginnings of internal organs have made an appearance long before fingers and toes have become evident. Muscular development during childhood is another good example of proximodistal development: The larger muscles of the trunk, arms, and legs develop sooner than the outer, smaller muscles of the hands, feet, fingers, and toes.

Height and Weight

The average North American newborn weighs in at about 7½ lb and measures about 20 in. long. After 6 months, weight will have at least doubled and by the first birthday will most likely have tripled. The child will grow in length during

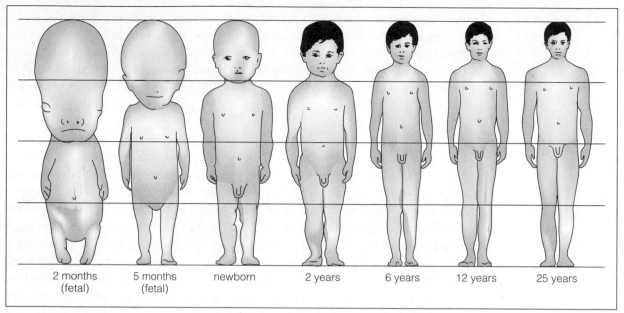

2 months (fetal)   5 months (fetal)   newborn   2 years   6 years   12 years   25 years

FIGURE 5.1

Changing body proportions during human development. As you examine these illustrations, how do they support the notion that development progresses according to proximodistal and cephalocaudal rules? From D. Shaffer (1999), *Developmental psychology*, 5th ed. Pacific Grove: Brooks/Cole, p. 154.

the first year at the rate of about 1 inch per month, finishing out at about one-and-a-half times the length at birth. At age one the average child weighs around 20 lb and is about 30 in. tall. During the second year, growth slows down to a rate that children typically follow until adolescence. The child puts on weight at a rate of about half a pound a month, and height increases about 2 or 3 in. a year. By the second birthday the child weighs around 28 to 30 lb, but has reached one-half of his or her adult height—somewhere between 32 and 35 in.

Gender Differences

The lore of teachers, parents, and others who work with children prophesies that "girls mature faster." Even during the first two years of life, differences in physical development between boys and girls have begun to appear. On average, baby boys are slightly larger than baby girls. However, the skeletal structure of girls is already stronger than that of boys at birth and will remain so throughout childhood. On the other hand, the more massive muscular development of the male may already be apparent by age two, as measured by little boys' and girls' muscle strength. In spite of such differences, we can observe—in such characteristics as activity level, responsiveness, and reaching maturational milestones—that boys and girls seem to make virtually identical progress in physical development during the first two years (Kolb & Whishaw, 1996).

*What changes occur
in the infant brain as
the child advances?*

BRAIN DEVELOPMENT

Before getting into the specifics of early brain development let's review the cellular make-up, basic structures, and functioning of the brain (Nolte, 1995; Pinel & Edwards, 1998; Spreen et al., 1995).

Neurons

The brain is made up of billions of nerve cells called **neurons**, as shown in Figure 5.2. They are supported and nourished by additional cells called *glia*. Messages are sent back and forth between the brain and the rest of the body by means of electrical impulses that are transferred from one neuron to another. When a neuron "fires," an electrical impulse begins at the dendrites and travels to the cell body, down the axon, and on to the terminal fibers. A fatty coating called the **myelin sheath** encapsulates individual neurons, which aids the speed

FIGURE 5.2

The anatomy of neurons. In a developing child, the nervous system advances as the myelin sheaths of neurons strengthen and the number of interconnections between neurons increases.

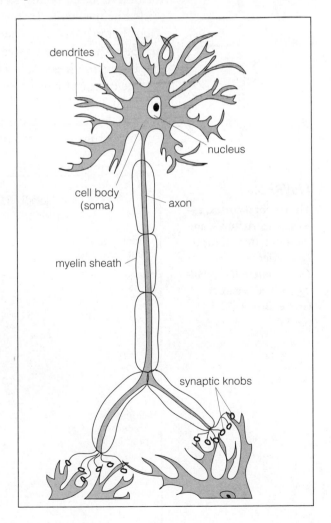

dendrites

nucleus

cell body
(soma)

axon

myelin sheath

synaptic knobs

and efficiency of the electrical impulse. Once the information reaches the ends of the terminal fibers, the information is chemically passed on to the next neuron at a juncture called the **synapse. Neurotransmitters** released from the synaptic junctures send specific messages to the dendrites of adjoining neurons, which then may fire themselves.

Brain Structures

The actual structures of the brain can be simplified by thinking of the brain as having two parts—outer structure and inner structures. The outer structure is the **cerebral cortex**, which is associated with thoughts, perceptions, knowledge, and voluntary control. It is divided up into four lobes, each being responsible for specific brain functions. Figure 5.3 shows the location and major functions of the four lobes of the brain.

The inner structures are associated more with involuntary processes and primitive, basic bodily functions. The brain itself is divided into two halves, called hemispheres. If you cut the brain down the middle between the left and right hemispheres the resulting cross-section would look something like Figure 5.4. The innermost structure, the **brainstem**, directs basic functions such as breathing and heart rate. The **cerebellum**, located behind the brain stem, is in charge of our physical coordination and refined motor movements. Some crucial structures lying just beneath the cerebral cortex are the thalamus and the hypothalamus. The **thalamus** is a relay station, sending information from sensory structures to the cerebral cortex. The **hypothalamus** is responsible for reg-

FIGURE 5.3

The cerebral cortex, associated structures, and their functions. From D. Shaffer (1999), *Developmental psychology*, 5th ed. Pacific Grove: Brooks/Cole, p. 159.

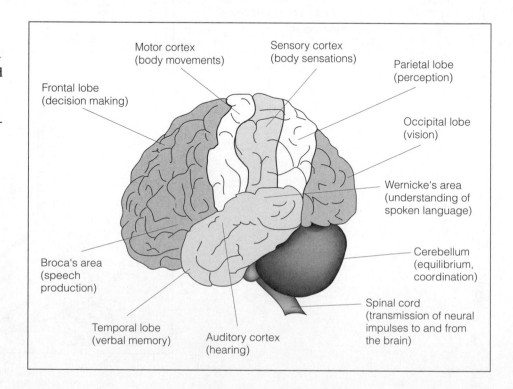

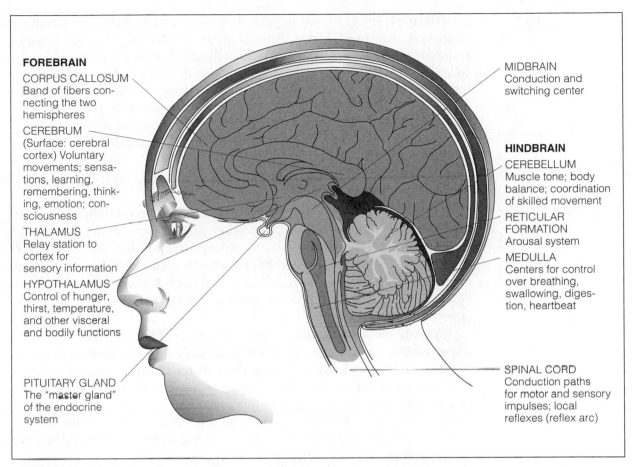

FOREBRAIN

CORPUS CALLOSUM
Band of fibers con-
necting the two
hemispheres

CEREBRUM
(Surface: cerebral
cortex) Voluntary
movements; sensa-
tions, learning,
remembering, think-
ing, emotion; con-
sciousness

THALAMUS
Relay station to
cortex for
sensory information

HYPOTHALAMUS
Control of hunger,
thirst, temperature,
and other visceral
and bodily functions

PITUITARY GLAND
The "master gland"
of the endocrine
system

MIDBRAIN
Conduction and
switching center

HINDBRAIN

CEREBELLUM
Muscle tone; body
balance; coordination
of skilled movement

RETICULAR
FORMATION
Arousal system

MEDULLA
Centers for control
over breathing,
swallowing, diges-
tion, heartbeat

SPINAL CORD
Conduction paths
for motor and sensory
impulses; local
reflexes (reflex arc)

FIGURE 5.4

Cross-section view of the brain and the important functions of main structures. Notice that the inner brain structures, which are the most well-developed at birth, are also the ones responsible for the most crucial survival functions of an organism. From Coon, D. (1992). *Introduction to psychology: Exploration and application,* 6th ed.
St Paul: West Publishing, p. 70.

ulating vital functions such as sleep, arousal, hunger, thirst, digestion, sexual
functioning, temperature, and emotions.

How well have these functions developed at the time of birth? On the cellular level, the infant brain is loaded with neurons, far more than the infant will
actually use. In fact, about half of them can be expected to die off during early
development. Over time unused neurons and meaningless synapses disintegrate
while those that are stimulated grow stronger and continue to interconnect
(Greenough & Black, 1992; Huttenlocher, 1994). The developmental level of
the neurons themselves is much lower than that of neurons in the adult brain.
The interconnections between neurons are more haphazard. The myelin sheath
is fairly well-developed around neurons supporting sensory relays, but those
contributing to motor control still have a long way to go.

During the first two years of life, the brain will grow in size from 25% of its
eventual adult weight to 75% of that weight. During the course of this **brain**

growth spurt, glia grow and increase in number and nourish and strengthen neurons at a rate much higher than will occur after the growth spurt. Synaptic connections continue to solidify, based on the child's early learning and experiences (Greenough & Black, 1992). The massive development occurring during these first two years explains why the child brain enjoys so much more **plasticity** than the adult brain. When an adult suffers permanent damage to the cerebral cortex, relatively little of its lost functions is recovered, since destroyed neurons do not replace themselves. However, a child who suffers a similar injury may recover some or all of a lost function, as the brain is still in the process of organizing and interconnecting neurons (Huttonlocher, 1994; Isaacson et al., 1995; Nelson & Bloom, 1997).

The first three years of life are thus especially important to brain development, particularly in regard to connections supporting emotional response. These neurons are especially sensitive to experience—they are "experience-expectant," so to speak. They may be permanently damaged if they are deprived of necessary stimulation. In deprived and abnormal childrearing situations, emotion-relevant dendrites, axons, synapses, and glia can simply wither away (Joseph, 1999).

At birth, the most highly developed structures of the brain are those most important for survival. Thus the brain stem, thalamus, and hypothalamus are in considerably good shape. The cerebral cortex, however, is still relatively primitive. Structures responsible for sensory and motor functions will be the first to mature. By the end of 6 months, voluntary motor control will have developed to the point where some of the inborn reflexes—such as the Babinski reflex and the grasping reflex—will be overpowered by the increased cerebral control and are no longer seen.

CONSCIOUS STATES

In what ways do conscious states reflect the infant's physical development?

The natural flow of infant consciousness appears to be a constant fluctuation between various levels of sleep and wakefulness. Like older children and adults, babies show states such as drowsiness, light sleep, and deep sleep as well as alert or highly agitated states (Berg & Berg, 1987). However, these states appear to be organized somewhat differently in babies. **REM (rapid eye movement) sleep**, the type of sleep during which we are typically dreaming, takes up about half of an infant's sleeping time but only one-fifth of an adult's (Carskadon & Dement, 1989).

Infants also spend significantly more time sleeping, usually about 16 hours a day, and in increments of around 3 hours. In Western culture, sleeping through the night is a skill that tends to be related to how an infant is handled. Babies usually are put down for the night in a separate, quiet room. Parents often choose to ignore indications of lighter sleep or slight wakefulness in hopes of encouraging the child to continue sleeping. Under these circumstances most infants eventually figure out that if it is still dark Mommy and Daddy will not respond, and comply with their parents' wishes that they go back to sleep. In other cultures, such as those in Asia and Africa, infants sleep with their mothers so they can be nursed whenever they show a desire. They also may be carried around on their mother's back all day, facilitating numerous catnaps as well. Under these circumstances infants may continue to sleep in 3-hour increments until they are almost a year old (Super & Harkness, 1982). By age one most babies are sleeping through the night, perhaps taking one or two naps during the day. By the time they are 2 years old they are still sleeping 12 to 13 hours a day.

Sudden Infant Death Syndrome

A tragic disorder of the infant sleep-wake cycle is **sudden infant death syndrome (SIDS)**, also known as "crib death" (Sears, 1995). At some point during a sleep period, usually at night, the infant simply stops breathing. While the exact cause of SIDS is still unknown, correlations have been found between SIDS and premature and low-birth-weight babies, those who had low Apgar scores at birth, and having a respiratory illness at the time of death (Buck et al., 1989; Cotton, 1990). Breast-fed babies seem less affected than bottle-fed babies (McKenna & Bernshaw, 1995). Infants of mothers who smoke show a higher incidence of this syndrome (DeFranza & Lew, 1995). Some attribute the deaths to having been placed face down on bedding that is too soft, resulting in infant suffocation (U. S. Consumer Product Safety Commission, 1999). In spite of such suspicions, one study actually found that babies who sleep with their mothers are less likely to fall victim than those who sleep in cribs, throwing a tragically ironic twist onto the term "crib death" (McKenna & Bernshaw, 1995).

What are the infant body's nutritional needs?

INFANT NUTRITION

Like any other living creature, infants require a diet containing a correct balance of nutrients that will ensure proper development. Immediately after birth, either breast milk or commercially prepared formula alone will be adequate, although typically physicians prescribe baby vitamin supplements as well.

Three of the more important nutrients babies need are fat, protein, and iron. Fat is needed for myelination of all those developing neurons (Dobbing, 1997). Human milk is higher in fat than that of other mammals, an excellent arrangement considering the developmental needs of our more advanced cerebral cortexes. An adequate level of protein must be ingested for healthy muscle development. Having iron-rich blood is also important, especially for brain development (Dobbing, 1990). The most common cause of anemia in childhood is iron-deficiency anemia in children under the age of three (McCoy & Votoubek, 1990). Plain cow's milk does not contain adequate iron for human infants (Sadowitz & Oski, 1983). Therefore bottle-fed babies are best provided with infant formulas that have been iron-fortified.

The earliest age at which most babies can switch to regular vitamin D enriched whole cow's milk is 6 months, and some pediatricians recommend waiting until 12 months. At 6 months infants are also ready to begin including some solid food in their diets. Often cereal is the first solid food offered, in part because it is usually iron-fortified. Bottle-fed babies may benefit from earlier introduction of solid food in order to supply nutrients they may not be getting.

However, 4 months is about the earliest that infants have any real nutritional success with solid foods because the **extrusion reflex** subsides at about this time. The extrusion reflex is one of many infant oral reflexes. If you touch or depress a newborn's tongue, the tongue will be forced outward. Just try sticking out your tongue and swallowing food from a spoon at the same time! Some mothers insist on trying solid foods at an earlier age for "educational" purposes, even though more food gets on the outside of the infant than inside. However, forcing the infant to wrestle with an uncontrollable reflex may actually be more of a lesson in frustration.

Over the second 6 months of life, infants can begin eating strained fruits and vegetables and eventually meat. By the end of the first year the baby should be eating a balanced diet of chopped table food (American Academy of Pediatrics Committee on Nutrition, 1986). Toddlers are best offered a wide variety of food flavors at this time because the older they get, the less receptive they tend to become toward new flavors (Birch, 1990). Remember, however, that the higher sensitivity of an infant's taste buds will cause some foods to be rejected as too strong-tasting. Therefore those preparing the youngster's meals should avoid overseasoning and not get pushy with foods that are inherently high in bitter, salty, or sour flavors. A toddler will be much more likely to appreciate an occasional sweet, high-fat snack such as a teething biscuit or a cookie, another appropriate addition to the toddler's diet.

The fat in the cookie that this youngster is happily munching will help aid myelination of the child's developing neurons.

Michael Dwyer/Stock Boston

> ## PAVING PATHWAYS ALONG INFANT PHYSICAL MILESTONES: BREAST OR BOTTLE?

The debate rages on regarding the choice to breast-feed or bottle-feed. The American Academy of Pediatrics (1982) advises that breast milk is the ideal infant food. It contains all the right vitamins, minerals, growth factors, and other nutrients—most likely including beneficial ones that we are not yet aware of. It contains antibodies, resulting in fewer infant illnesses and allergic reactions. Since it is more easily digested, infants' bodies both make better use of nutrients and have fewer gastrointestinal upsets. The sucking motions used in breast-feeding also appear to contribute toward straighter teeth (Labbock & Hendershot, 1987). While it is still too early to make any definitive claims, recent research has revealed a higher intelligence quotient among children who had been breast-fed as infants (Lucas et al., 1992). There are pragmatic advantages to breast-feeding as well. It is extremely economical, is readily available, needs no advance preparation, and is always the right temperature. Breast-feeding also has the advantage of increasing intimacy between mother and child (Eiger & Olds, 1999).

However, some women either should not or do not wish to breast-feed. A small percentage of mothers are unable to produce a sufficient supply of milk. Some mothers are taking medications or recreational drugs that could be passed on through breast milk and therefore are advised against breast-feeding. The mother may need to return to an employment situation that does not promote breast-feeding an infant, or perhaps she just finds the whole idea of breast-feeding to be aversive.

Bottle-feeding is a viable alternative for mothers who choose not to breast-feed. Formulas are available that contain all of the known necessary nutrients for the growing infant. It has a few advantages over breast-feeding as well. Dad can have the opportunity for the intimacy of feeding baby, as well as help out with night feedings so Mom can get more rest. Bottle-feeding also contributes toward the pragmatics of Mom and Dad getting away alone together for brief periods.

The disadvantages of bottle-feeding appear to be related to poor bottle-feeding practices. Especially in developing nations, women lacking education may overdilute formula to make it last longer and thus undernourish their babies, or may not dilute the formula and thus feed their babies toxically high levels of some nutrients. Unsanitary preparation practices or using tainted water can infect babies with various illnesses. Busy mothers may be tempted to leave baby propped up with a bottle, diminishing opportunities for building intimacy. There is also the problem that if babies take bottles to bed, their front teeth can rot from excessive exposure to sugar.

However, researchers who have examined the long-term health effects of bottle- and breast-feeding have found no significant differences in the effects of the two feeding regimens (Schmitt, 1970). Even the social/emotional benefits of breast feeding can be mimicked if the bottle-fed baby is held close during feedings in a position similar to that of breast-feeding. Children measured at elementary-school age showed no differences in levels of social adjustment based on feeding style (Fergusson et al., 1987). So, even if mothers do not or cannot follow the AAP recommendation to breast-feed, they can rest assured that their child's nutritional and emotional needs can be adequately met by bottle-feeding.

Undernourishment

The effect of undernourishment is most easily observed in developing nations, where severe malnutrition most often occurs. **Marasmus** is a condition seen when infants receive insufficient caloric intake. Infant body tissues waste away to little more than skin and bones. Other infants may have sufficient caloric intake but receive an insufficient amount of protein and develop a condition called **kwashiorkor**. Their bellies swell, they lose hair, they may become rashy, and behaviorally they become listless and irritable.

Marasmus and kwashiorkor are examples of extreme undernourishment. In Western society, milder forms are more common. Poverty is still alive and well in the United States, even though its presence and effects are less visible than in developing nations. Children born to impoverished families are understandably more likely to suffer from some form of undernourishment. One study showed that mildly malnourished infants at elementary school age were more anxious, less happy, and less active and socially involved than the other children (Barrett et al., 1982). Undernourishment may retard brain development and affect body size, at times resulting in long-term consequences for these unfortunate children (Tanner, 1990). Although historically we have blamed poverty for such tragic outcomes, some children who developed in this manner are suspected of having an exceedingly undemanding interactional style or low appetite as infants (Wright & Birks, 2000).

But why does undernourishment continue to occur among affluent families? The previous discussion suggests some scenarios, such as using cow's milk without the necessary supplements, or economizing by overdiluting infant formula. Another malady occurs when children develop an iron-deficient "milk anemia" because parents placed excessive dependence on the baby bottle during later infancy. An older baby who is habitually handed a bottle to soothe emotions, or temporarily calm appetite, or as a bedtime ritual may, as a result, not be interested in ingesting a complete range of nutrients at mealtime. The consequence is malnourishment.

The current cultural emphasis on reducing fat in the diet has also been a culprit. Limiting fat intake is a good idea for most adults, but babies need extra fat for both caloric purposes and myelination of neurons. The 1% milkfat or skim milk that may be healthiest for an adult does not provide enough fat for the developing infant. Babies need the fat content of whole milk during the first two years. Feeding babies low-fat or low-calorie diets has been found to lead to symptoms of undernourishment (Lifshitz et al., 1987).

Obesity

Some of the more endearing physical characteristics of babies are their plump little cheeks and round cuddly bodies. An adult exhibiting the same physical proportions as the average infant would be considered morbidly obese. Some parents are concerned that their chubby little cherubs may carry all this extra fat into their later lives. Their worries are unfounded. There is little if any correlation between infant weight and obesity in adulthood (Roche, 1981). Obesity has more to do with heredity than eating habits (Stunkard et al., 1986). Even the number of fat cells we have is probably inherited (Bogardus et al., 1986). The American Academy of Pediatrics Committee on Nutrition (1986) therefore insists that no child under the age of two should be put on a weight-loss diet. The most likely outcome of such a practice is malnutrition (Lifshitz et al., 1987).

So if babies indicate they are hungry, they probably really do need something to eat. Acknowledging the validity of infants' internal messages also avoids interference with the process of learning to listen to one's own body regarding eating behavior, an important skill for avoiding overeating later in life. Demand feeding therefore is recommended over scheduled feedings for young infants, as is maintaining some flexibility in scheduling meals and providing snacks for older infants.

How do infant motor skills progress?

MOTOR DEVELOPMENT

Immediately after birth, most of an infant's organized movement is restricted to reflexive responses related to bodily needs, such as sucking and others mentioned in the previous chapter. Beyond these reflexes, newborns do little more than wave their arms and legs around, using minimal voluntary control. Later the appearance of more advanced infant motor skills is especially delightful for parents as they appreciate this concrete sign of their little one's progress.

Theories of Motor Development

The development of infant motor skills and the approximate timing of their emergence were first painstakingly mapped out by theorists in the l930s and '40s (Gesell & Thompson, 1938; McGraw, 1943). One of the most oft-cited and influential studies of this period involved observations of the Hopi Indians (Dennis & Dennis, 1940). The Hopi often followed a practice of carrying their babies on their backs swaddled within a cradle board until they were a year old. The researchers discovered that in spite of this restriction, the swaddled babies learned to walk at the same time as did other babies. On the basis of such studies, developmentalists concluded that motor milestones depend entirely upon maturation, an unfolding biological program unaffected by the influences of the environment.

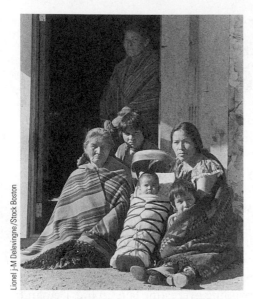

Although the baby shown in this portrait of a Navajo family will spend most of its first year wrapped in a cradle board, he or she will achieve motor milestones just as proficiently as infants from cultures who do not observe this practice.

This maturation perspective of motor development ruled more or less unquestioned for many years (Thelen, 1995). Its first challenge was made by a physiologist in the late 'sixties (Bernstein, 1967). He pointed out that physical motion can rarely depend upon physical ability alone. For example, as you reach above your head and open a cupboard door, your arm is fighting gravity. As you swing open the door your physical efforts adjust as you counteract any centrifugal force engendered by the swinging door. If you have a grocery item in that hand your effort would additionally take into account the weight and cumbrance of the item. Orchestration of the whole event will also be affected by ongoing motor efforts such as staying upright and balanced. Thus effective movement is actually contained by a continually changing force field rather than depending solely on the maturational level of a specific neural pathway. Likewise any number of varying neural pathways may find their way into the process of coordinating the same movement under different conditions.

As motor skills develop, infants must also coordinate efforts according to the supports and constraints of physics, weight, cumbrance, and balance. An interesting example of how changing environmental demands affect infant motor skills involves the infant **stepping reflex**. When newborns are held upright, "standing" on a supportive surface, they reflexively perform steplike movements. This reflex disappears after a few months. The maturational interpretation of this disappearance is that the more advanced functioning of the older infant's cerebral cortex overrides the reflex (McGraw, 1943).

However, other researchers have noted that the movement itself has not really disappeared (Thelen & Fisher, 1982). Infants lying on their backs might continue to make steplike motions during the play of kicking. The researchers also note that at age 2 or 3 months, normal fat buildup makes infants' legs considerably heavier. They hypothesized that this weight is the reason the reflex was no longer seen at this age. To test their hypothesis they placed these older infants in torso-high warm water, using its buoyancy to counteract the effect of the increased weight. The stepping reflex mysteriously reappeared. When weights were added to counteract the effect of buoyancy, the reflex disappeared again.

Over the last decade, considerably more research has accumulated in favor of the multicausal perspective of infant motor development (Lockman & Thelen, 1993). Throughout childhood, developing motor skills are affected not only by the maturation of the central nervous system but also by environmental supports or constraints, the body's muscular and skeletal development and the baby's resources of energy, and the specific demands of the task at hand. Thus every movement is unique, and every solution is fluid and flexible—or "softly assembled" as one set of theorists terms it (Kugler & Turvey, 1987). All of these factors play roles as infants approach and refine both gross and fine motor skills.

Lionel J-M Delevingne/Stock Boston

Gross Motor Skills

The first voluntary skills developed by the infant are **gross motor skills**, those involving the use, strength, and coordination of the larger muscles of the body (Bly, 1994). Gross motor skills increase according to a specific sequence, consistent with cephalocaudal and proximodistal patterns of development. The first evidence of expanding gross motor ability is the ability to lift and turn the head from side to side. Most newborns can do so at birth, but with varying degrees of success. In fact, experts now recommend putting down newborns on their backs rather than their stomachs so that any limitations in this skill do not result in suffocation (Sears, 1995). By the end of the first month, most infants have mastered adaptive head-raising and at 2 or 3 months have begun using their arms to push themselves up to get a better look around. The balancing act required for such a maneuver contributes to the emergence of the next organized skill: rolling over, which usually occurs between the fourth and fifth months. By the end of the sixth month, babies have learned how to push themselves up on all fours. While they are able to maintain a sitting position with some support as early as 3 or 4 months, they can sit without support by 7 or 8 months.

The next major set of gross motor skills to emerge are **locomotor skills**: skills involving movement from one place to another. Locomotion skills develop in concert with a child's everyday environmental exposures and physical experiences, body dimensions, and movement proficiency—as well as the active choices an individual child makes while exploring his or her environment (Adolph, 1997). Most infants have learned how to crawl by 8 months, and may figure out how to drag themselves forward with their arms before discovering the improved efficiency of propelling themselves on all fours. Next come the precursors of walking. By 10 months most infants can pull themselves to a stand and can maintain this upright position as long as they have something to hang onto for support. Over time they use surface contact less for mechanical purposes and more for orienting their bodies in space (Barela et al., 1999). First successes at walking usually occur as they move along the sides of furniture, a skill seen by the end of the first year. The ability to stand without support usually develops between 10 and 13 months, and by 14 months most infants have graduated to toddlerhood: They can walk about independently with ease.

While the sequencing of these gross motor milestones remains constant for almost all infants, there is a considerable band of variability regarding the actual age at which a child will develop each skill. Figure 5.5 shows this wide range between the early and late bloomers, all considered to be normal in their attainment of developmental milestones.

Fine Motor Skills

Fine motor skills are those using and coordinating smaller muscles, and are usually more complex than gross motor skills (Henderson & Pehoski, 1995). In concert with the rule of proximodistal development, these nonreflexive skills of

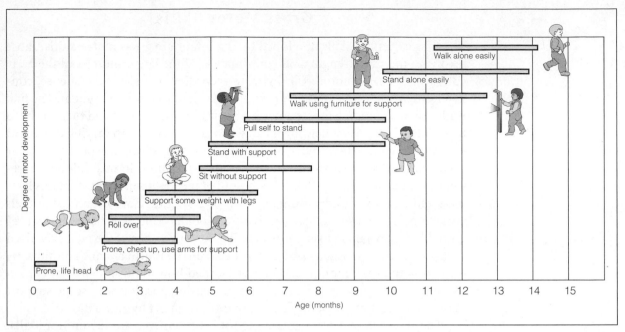

FIGURE 5.5

Gross motor skill developmental milestones. While infants and toddlers typically reach gross motor milestones according to this general progression, the band of time during which an individual child normally reaches a certain milestone is considerably wide. From Santrock, J. W. (1993). *Children,* 3rd ed., Madison, WI: Wm. C. Brown, p. 165. Reprinted by permission of McGraw-Hill Companies.

outer, finer muscles develop later than those of the more-centralized, larger muscles. Grasping behaviors using the finger muscles are the most easily observed examples of the progression of infant fine motor development. As you may recall, infants are born with a grasping reflex that is triggered by anything touching the palm of the infant's hand. By around 3 months, the infant has begun developing the **ulnar grasp**—voluntarily contracting all of the finger muscles so that the fingers slam against the palm. By the end of the first year, finer finger muscles have developed well enough for the child to pick up items with a **pincer grasp**—a movement restricted to the coordination of the thumb and forefinger.

Bladder and Bowel Control

The ability to voluntarily control waste elimination is a milestone eagerly anticipated by parents and others who must tend to diapers and other related cleanup duties. Mastering this relatively complex set of muscular skills requires a certain degree of both fine and gross motor development. Usually age 2 years is the earliest at which relevant muscles have developed sufficiently for parents to realistically consider toilet training. An infant's or toddler's waste elimination habits may develop a predictable pattern earlier than 2 years, and caregivers may become adept at predicting fruitful moments for placing an infant on a potty chair. However, these successes are evidence of caregivers' skills of observing naturally developing biological rhythms, rather than of early development of infant muscular control.

How does the infant sense and perceive the world?

SENSORY/PERCEPTUAL DEVELOPMENT

Given the many changes occurring in the infant brain and body, how does infant sensation and perception compare with adult sensation and perception? First let's define the two. **Sensation** is the actual physical reaction to a stimulus as it is taken in by the various sensory structures; specifically, the eyes, ears, nose, tongue, and skin. All of these structures are extensively interconnected with nervous system pathways by which sensed stimuli can be relayed to the brain. **Perception** is how the brain actually interprets the sensed stimulus. Thus quality of sensation depends chiefly on biology and level of physical development, while perceptual ability can be influenced chiefly by environmental exposures and learning. Following are discussions of five systems of sensing and perception: vision, hearing, smell, taste, and touch.

Vision

Vision is the most easily studied system of infant sensing and perception. We can infer how well an infant's visual sense is functioning by simply looking to see what the eyes are focused on. And thanks to infants' tendency to direct their gaze toward preferred stimuli, we can also infer that what they sense is actually being perceived and processed. Thus vision has been the most extensively studied of any of the infant's sensing abilities.

How much does the infant in fact see? I remember as a young child asking whether my newborn younger sibling's steady gaze in my direction meant that he was looking at me. An adult assured me that he did not yet make enough sense out of what was going on around him to be able to look at me, and that his brain was still "just so much nothing." This interpretation was consistent with what early developmental theorists once believed: that infant perception was no more than one big chaotic meaningless mess (James, 1890; Piaget, 1952).

We now know that infant visual sensation and perception are remarkably functional even during the first few days of life (Slater, 1992). At first visual acuity is very poor—somewhere between 20/200 and 20/600 (Haith, 1991). By age 6 months it will have progressed to 20/100 and by the end of the first year will be nearly as well developed as the adult's (Banks & Salapatek, 1983; Vitral-Durand et al., 1966). Even with poor visual acuity, infants are able to maintain a focus. At age 2 months they can both voluntarily change their focus and ignore distracting stimuli (Johnson & Tucker, 1993). They can track moving objects to an extremely limited extent at birth, but by age 3 months can follow a moving object as well as an adult can, a skill developed in part due to improvements in their ability to pay attention (Richards & Holley, 1999; von Hofsten & Rosander, 1997).

The newborn's peripheral vision appears to be poor (Tronick, 1972). Correspondingly, very young infants are more likely to focus on a single detail rather than scan a whole figure or gestalt, an observational strategy that typically emerges at around age 2 months (Salapatek, 1975). Infants can distinguish between colored and achromatic (black, white, or gray) stimuli at birth, and by age 5 months can distinguish between the main colors of the spectrum as well as do adults (Adams & Courage, 1998; Catherwood et al., 1989).

Early infant visual perception shows some sensitivity to certain rules about objects and their behavior, such as that objects move as bounded wholes, begin to move when acted upon, and continue to move unless obstructed (Bertenthal, 1996; Spelke et al., 1995). Beginning at around 3 to 4 months, infants will perceive two objects moving together, such as a head with a hat on it, as being the same object, just as do adults (Spelke et al., 1992). At age 4 months they may recognize that dropped objects will fall, and by age 6 months will show surprise if a dropped object appears to stop in midair (Needham & Baillargeon, 1993; Spelke et al., 1995). They notice changes in movement patterns, such as a mobile's change in direction of rotation (Laplante et al., 1996). Studies such as these certainly cast doubt upon the early Piagetian view of infant visual perception being "undifferentiated and chaotic" (Piaget, 1952)!

Development of these abilities in visual perception clearly require that the child's environment supply the relevant stimuli. Some visual exposures during infancy appear to be critical (Bornstein, 1989). For example, stereoscopic depth perception develops as practice with coordinating both eyes strengthens specific neuronal connections between the retina and the visual cortex. If one eye is weak or in some way impaired during this critical period of neuron sorting and strengthening, the relevant neurons and synapses find their way into the discard pile, and this particular source of depth perception may not develop at all (Greenough & Black, 1992).

Visual Preferences. Even very young infants have visual preferences. They seem more interested in colors than in achromatic presentations. They prefer contrast in their visual fields, choosing to look at patterns more than plain fields of color or brightness, even when they are as young as two days old (Fantz, 1963). They also show a preference for faces over other patterns, and gaze longer at female faces that adults would judge as attractive (Johnson et al., 1991; Rubenstein et al., 1999; Slater et al., 1998). Even brain activity differs when infants gaze at faces rather than inanimate objects (de Haan & Nelson, 1999). They attend longer to natural, active facial expressions than to still poses of certain expressions (D'Entremont & Muir, 1997; Johnson & Morton, 1991). Consistent with their tendency to focus on detail, newborns first seem most interested in the most obvious facial detail: the eyes. Infants as young as 4 days old have shown an ability to recognize their mothers' faces over others (Walton et al., 1992; 1997), apparently by focusing on the face/hair separation line and the outer contour of the mother's head (Pascalis et al., 1995). Between 2 and 4 months of age they expand their abilities to include more advanced scanning

Observing that the floor extends well below the glass plate before him, this young man is hesitant to venture further. Such "visual cliff" experimentation provided much of the earliest empirical evidence that infants perceive depth.

Science Source/Photo Researchers

such as focusing more on the mouth, the softer contours of the face, and other internal facial features (Johnson & Morton, 1991).

Depth Perception. Depth perception is the ability to perceive objects in the environment as being relatively near or far away. Infants appear to perceive depth at a very early age. The first investigations of infant depth perception involved a series of clever studies using a "visual cliff." A plate of glass was placed over a drop-off area. Infants old enough to crawl were encouraged by their mothers to come to them by crawling on the glass over the visual cliff. The infants were extremely hesitant to do so, suggesting that they perceived the possibility of falling should they comply (Gibson & Walk, 1960).

Some have suggested that these reactions were due to the infants' prior learning, such as earlier discoveries that proceeding beyond an edge may result in "going boom." However, in later studies, when prelocomotor 2- to 4-month-old infants were placed facedown over the dropped-off area of the visual cliff, their heart rates changed (Campos et al., 1970). Again the skeptical came up with alternative explanations, noting that infants were unlikely to encounter such a circumstance elsewhere and therefore were responding to the experimental situation as a novel stimulus. So researchers took a turn toward normal infant experience; they observed whether 3- to 6-week-old infants would react to an object slowly moved toward them in such a way as to indicate the depth cues of relative size and/or motion were functioning (Nanez, 1987). The infants reflexively blinked. Whether learned or innate, such behavior does appear to support the notion that even as infants, we have some ability to perceive and judge distances.

Hearing

Hearing capacity develops earlier than visual capacity. As you saw in the previous chapter, even fetuses still in the womb respond to sounds. At birth the inner and middle ear structures have already reached their adult size and shape (Aslin et al., 1983). Immediately after birth, however, infants' hearing is not as acute as adults' (Trehub et al., 1991); perhaps it is muffled by fluid not yet drained from various auditory passages. Within a few days infants' hearing significantly improves. Because of its more advanced sensory status, young infants tend to be more responsive to auditory stimuli than to visual stimuli (Lewkowicz, 1988). Presentation of an auditory stimulus such as "white noise" or the recording of a heart beat has in fact successfully distracted neonates from the pain of heel lancing and other invasive clinical procedures (Kawakami et al., 1996).

Much infant-hearing research has consisted of observing how infants' sucking patterns change in response to various stimuli. They seem to show the greatest interest in stimuli that are novel. Researchers have also observed infants' changing levels of interest by measuring changes in heart rate. Such studies have found that infants can distinguish between sounds, such as *a* and *i,* even when only a few days old (Clarkson & Berg, 1983). Newborns can also distinguish between a recording of their own crying and that of another infant (Dondi et al., 1999). Between 2 and 4 months they are as able as adults to distinguish changes in a melody's tempo (Baruch & Drake, 1997). By age 1 year their musical discriminative ability has progressed so well that they can distinguish between melodies that differ only slightly (Morrongiello, 1986).

Very young infants will also change their sucking patterns if they perceive that the production of a sound depends on whether they continue to suck or stop. By tracking such learning, researchers have been able to observe infant sound preferences. Even as early as 3 days old infants show a preference for their mother's voice over other voices (DeCasper & Fifer, 1980). They prefer soft sounds over harsh ones, such as those that are likely to produce the startle reflex, and also appear to enjoy music and dislike nonsensical noise (Butterfield & Siperstein, 1972).

Taste

Newborn infants not only distinguish between flavors but also show definite preferences. They prefer anything sweet-tasting over substances that are bitter, sour, salty, or neutral (Crook, 1978). Furthermore, they seem able to distinguish varying levels of sweetness: The sweeter the substance, the more enthusiastically will they suck (Haith, 1986). Sugar water even seems to put them in a better mood, appearing to have a soothing effect (Barr & Young 1999; Chiva, 1982). This concept is expanded upon in the Tried . . . . and True boxes on pages 144–145. Their sense of taste is actually more acute than that of the average adult (Cowart, 1981). If you have ever tasted baby food, you may have noticed its seemingly bland flavor. Nevertheless, babies seem to perceive enough of a flavor for it to hold their interest—especially if it is something inherently sweet!

Smell

I recall many episodes of soothing my own babies as they became fussy or attempting to rock them to sleep before bedtime, when success would escape me. As I became more and more exasperated with their squirming and squealing, Dad occasionally stepped in and took over. At times he would be rewarded by the gratification of having them miraculously simmer down after he had rocked them for seemingly only an instant. What was I doing wrong, I sometimes wondered. In later years as I reviewed research on infant sensation and perception I decided that my soothing behaviors were probably not the culprit.

Newborns have a well-developed sense of smell (Kawakami et al., 1997). Their facial expressions change accordingly when presented with pleasant or unpleasant odors (Steiner, 1979). They show recognition of familiar smells. Three-day-old infants are more likely to turn their heads toward the smell of their mother's amniotic fluid than toward some other mother's fluid (Marlier et al., 1998). Breast-fed babies show evidence of learning the specific smells of their mothers' underarms and breasts, and show a preference for those smells even as early as 1 week of age (Porter et al., 1992). This learning may explain why Dad sometimes seemed so much more proficient at getting baby to rock to sleep than Mom—all of those feeding-related smells can become a classically conditioned distraction. (But I still haven't mentioned this to Dad. . . .)

Touch

Of all our senses, touch is the most developed at birth, perhaps explaining why being touched and handled during the early days has such a beneficial effect on babies' subsequent development. In fact, all parts of our body are sensitive to touch well before we are born (Haith, 1986). As infants grow and learn, their perception of tactile stimulation advances. Well before the first year is over, infants can distinguish between objects by touch alone (Streri & Spelke, 1988).

In years past, newborn infants were believed to not yet be wired for the experience of pain. As newborns squealed and cried during heel lancing, circumcisions, and other bodily invasions, physicians would assure concerned parents that babies did not yet sense well enough to experience pain. This belief has now been refuted. The experience of pain in newborns has been evidenced by increases in crying, heart rates, blood pressure, facial expressions, and avoidant body movements (Anand & Hickey, 1987; Delevati & Bergamasco, 1999). Higher levels of cortisol, a substance released into the bloodstream during times of stress, have been found in baby boys after they have been circumcised (Gunnar et al., 1985). Babies given local anesthesia during circumcision

BOX 5.1   Taste and calming fussy babies

Tried......

Smith, B. A., & Blass, E. M. (1996). Taste-mediated calming in premature, preterm, and full-term human infants. *Developmental Psychology, 32,* 1084–1089.

HOSPITAL NURSERIES OFTEN GIVE SUGAR WATER TO fussy newborns. We know that babies can taste sweetness, and in fact show a preference for it over other flavors. But is it really the sweetness they find to be soothing? Or is it just the experience of fluid intake that calms the turmoil within?

Smith and Blass explored this issue by examining 36 healthy newborn infants: 18 preterm and 18 fullterm. The tests took place in a study room outside the hospital nursery. To ensure that other sensory stimulation was consistent among participants, the infants were tested while propped and supported with rolled-up blankets—a condition that also helped facilitate videorecording of the infants' facial expressions during the experimental procedures. Auditory stimulation was standardized by playing a recording of a Mozart string quartet.

The infants were examined immediately following routine diaper changing, a procedure that has a tendency to cause a state of arousal in otherwise contented babies. As they proceeded to squall, half of the babies in each group were given a 12% sucrose solution by means of a plastic syringe, administered at the rate of 0.1 ml per minute for 5 minutes. The other half of the babies were given plain sterile water at the same rate.

Fussiness was observed and measured during the 5-minute intervals preceding and following the procedures. Infants were scored as crying if the video recordings revealed both crying noises and crying faces during at least 50% of each 1-second time frame. Since the initial observers were familiar with the experiment, an experimenter who had no knowledge of the test conditions also rated the infants. The ratings between the observers produced a correlation of $r + .95$, a fair indication that experimenter bias was not a confounding factor in the ratings.

The researchers compared the amount of crying that had been measured before and after the experimental procedures. The newborns who received the sugar water cried significantly less than those who received plain water. The preterm and full-term newborns receiving sugar water reduced their crying by 63% and 85% respectively, while those who had received plain water reduced crying behavior by 36% and 33%. So it appears that while simply giving fluids gets some results, sweetness also plays a significant role in the calming effect.

So why do newborns find sugar water to be so soothing? Since other studies have found newborns to exhibit considerably less distress when given sugar water during painful procedures, Smith and Blass suggest that it has something to do with the release of opiatelike substances in the brain. These substances, such as endorphins, are natural pain-reducers. If you have ever been administered an opiatelike drug to manage pain, you probably noticed its added effect of producing calmer feelings. Thus sugar water may not only be the answer to calming routine newborn fussiness, but also might be considered as a relatively benign means of pain management during uncomfortable newborn evaluation procedures.

...and True

BOX 5.2   What to do when baby cries

USING SUGAR WATER TO SOOTHE A FUSSY BABY emerged as a parenting strategy long before it was studied empirically. The sounds and behavior of a distressed infant are extremely irritating, distressing for both caregivers and any others who cannot escape their sight and sound. Many strategies that have not been tested by scientists have demonstrated their effectiveness during the course of spontaneous field trials, their rates of success passed down through popular folklore.

So, other than using sugar water, how else might you soothe a fussy baby? A number of methods, both formally and informally tested, have emerged over the years (Eiger & Olds, 1999). First, make note of the importance of not taking a baby's crying personally. Newborns especially do a lot of crying. At first, most crying is related to hunger or some other form of discomfort. Later it more often expresses boredom, overstimulation, fatigue, or frustration. As they grow older, babies typically learn that cries of distress result in the appearance of a caregiver and use certain types of crying to communicate their desire for attention. However, most crying is not a demand, a criticism of the caregiver, or most certainly not an attempt to annoy the caregiver. Personalizing babies' crying in this manner only reduces caregiver motivation for meeting babies' needs.

Suppose you are taking care of 3-month-old Jenny. She starts fussing, and you note that she hasn't been fed for a while. You give her a bottle of formula, which she happily gulps down. Toward the end of the bottle she drifts off into contented drowsiness. However, 5 minutes later she is wide awake and fussing again. She doesn't want the remains of the formula, and her fussiness is escalating. What do you do?

First, check for anything that might be causing her discomfort. You already know she is not hungry. But since she has just eaten, she may have a bubble in her tummy that needs to come up. By holding her upright or facedown over your lap and gently massaging or patting her back you can encourage the bubble to rise into a burp. Or, perhaps a wet or soiled diaper needs to be changed. The lighting in Jenny's environment may be too bright. She may be too hot or too cold. The setting may be too noisy. She may be fatigued, and would prefer to be laid down to sleep. You check for all these possibilities, and none seem to be the culprit. Jenny is still upset.

Sometimes there simply isn't anything you can do, and you may need to comfort her as best you can until she gets herself over it. The following strategies may contribute toward helping her calm herself:

- Change the position in which you are holding her, since she may have other preferences.
- Rock her in a rocking chair—this mimics the motions she experienced while in the womb.
- Carry her upright and walk around the room, providing a change of scenery.
- Offer her a pacifier.
- Swaddle her snugly with receiving blankets—this gives some babies a sense of physical support and security.
- Give her a warm bath or massage.
- Sing or softly talk to her.
- Lie down and place her facedown on your chest and stomach, so she can experience your bodily warmth, softness, heartbeat, and breathing rhythms.
- Provide music or some other soothing background noise.
- Take her for a ride in the car or stroller.
- Put her down and let her cry for a little while—some infants precede sleep periods with a little crying.
- Let someone else hold her for a while, especially if you are beginning to feel frustrated or upset, which Jenny may be sensing.

Eiger, M. S., & Olds, S. W. (1999). *The complete book of breastfeeding,* 3rd ed. New York: Workman Press.

cry significantly less than those not given it (Stang et al., 1988). This is certainly evidence enough to support the practice of using pain-relieving techniques while performing painful procedures on newborns. The perpetuation of the original, erroneous belief also provides interesting evidence of how profound is our human tendency to ignore disconfirming data—especially when disconfirmation is potentially emotionally charged!

Integrating Sensory Information

When do infants recognize that the pretty yellow duck is the same toy that makes the squeaking sound? When do they figure out that the pacifier they see before them is the same object that provides comfort when placed in the mouth? These questions address **intermodal perception**—the ability to compare and coordinate information from multiple sensations and perceptions (Lewkowicz, 2000; Lickliter & Bahrick, 2000).

Infants show evidence of intermodal perception at an amazingly early age (Lewkowicz & Lickliter, 1994). One-month-olds have shown a preference for gazing at objects they had previously been sucking upon over those they had not tactilely sensed (Gibson & Walker, 1984). At age 4 months, as infant head turning becomes steadier and more dependable, infants have been presented with more than one film to watch and a sound track appropriate to only one of them. They chose to watch the film that matched the sound track (Spelke, 1979). Four-month-olds will turn their gaze toward facial images whose lip movements are consistent with presented verbalizations, demonstrating an early ability to "lip-read" (Kuhl & Meltzoff, 1984). When exposed to certain noises at 6 months, infants turn and look at the stimulus most likely to have produced the sound (Bahrick, 1983). At 7 months they will even be more likely to look toward a facial expression that matches the emotional tone of a vocal stimulus (Soken & Pick, 1999). Studies have suggested when information is introduced through multiple sense perceptions, infants learn more efficiently (Bahrick & Lickliter, 2000).

Some have argued that these findings are simply the result of learned associations rather than innate ability to integrate sensory information. However, one researcher attempted to teach infants inappropriate intersensory associations and was unable to do so (Bahrick, 1988). Given the early age at which infants begin coordinating such a wide variety of sensory information, we would not be out of line to suspect that the ability is present at birth. Scientists face the challenge of finding a way to test intermodal perception within the limitations of newborn motor and visual development.

Why is stimulation so important to developing infants, and how can we create sufficiently stimulating environments for them?

The Role of Infant Stimulation

Affection and stimulation are crucial ingredients for healthy infant development (Joseph, 1999). Infants need relevant input in order to encourage appropriate interconnections among and myelination of all those developing neurons. Studies examining the effects of enriched versus deprived environments for baby rats revealed that the adult brains of the enriched-environment rats were heavier, had more cell interconnections, and showed higher levels of neurochemical activity (Rosenzweig, 1984). Studies have also shown that deprivation of sensory input during infancy can result in permanent nonfunction of certain aspects of the senses, even after deprivation has been discontinued (Parmelee & Sigman, 1983). Language ability at age 2 years has been associated with the quality of stimulation in the child's home environment (Murray & Yingling, 2000).

During infancy, physical stimulation appears to be especially crucial. When human infants are frequently stroked or receive massage therapy, they show greater weight gain, spend more of their time awake and active, cry less, and achieve better scores on tests of infant development (Adderly & Gordon, 1999; Dieter & Emory, 1997; Scafidi & Field, 1996; Ottenbacher et al., 1987). Researchers have investigated the effect of reduced stimulation on human infant brains by measuring the EEG waves of infants of depressed and nondepressed mothers (Dawson et al., 1999; Field et al., 1996; Jones et al., 1998; 2000). As the graph in Figure 5.6 shows, measurements of those having depressed mothers indicate significantly less left hemispheric development; some suggest, however, that such differences could also be due to heredity, prenatal hormonal exposures, exposure to depressed behaviors and emotional expressiveness, or the stress of living with a depressed mother (Goodman & Gotlib, 1999). Fortunately, early intervention programs have demonstrated an ability to prevent

FIGURE 5.6

Left and right frontal lobe EEG power for infants with depressed and nondepressed mothers. Infants of depressed mothers appear to have less-balanced left and right frontal lobe activity than do infants with nondepressed mothers. Adapted from N. A. Jones, T. Field, N. A. Fox, and M. Davalos in "Newborns of mothers with depressive symptoms are physiologically less developed," *Infant Behavior and Development* 21, 537–54, copyright © 1998, with permission from Elsevier Science.

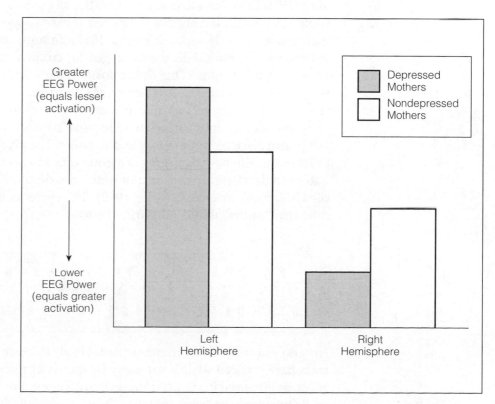

some of the cognitive deficits that have been associated with infants of depressed mothers (Cicchetti et al., 2000).

Nonorganic failure to thrive is the result of extreme neglect of the human infant's needs for stimulation and affection (hence the descriptive "nonorganic"; basic bodily needs are in fact met) (Boddy et al., 2000). The disorder occurs among infants who receive adequate physical and nutritional care but for any of a variety of reasons are deprived of environmental stimulation and affection from a primary caregiver. Some suggest that because of the constant stress and trauma such children often experience, the energies devoted to brain development are funneled disproportionately into the primitive structures that support a high state of alert, to the neglect of cortex development. These infants stop gaining weight, and may actually start losing weight. They often discontinue progression along expected infant motor milestones. Emotionally they show little if any attachment to their primary caregivers and a lack of interest in people in general. Physiologically they have been found to have abnormally low levels of growth hormone in their bodies (Gardner, 1972). Fortunately, sufficiently early home interventions or placement of such children in foster homes can cause restimulation of the growth hormone, and the children catch up with expected milestones (Drotar & Sturm, 1988; Hutcheson et al., 1997).

Yet other caregivers may be excessively enthusiastic in assisting their infants' physical development. One trendy practice of late has been putting infants through formal baby exercise programs. Actually, some cultures, such as those in the West Indies and Kenya, have traditionally used certain muscle-strengthening routines on infants that do indeed appear to speed attainment of some motor milestones (Hopkins & Westra, 1988). In some societies early motor development of certain skills is encouraged for cultural reasons; for example, in certain Ugandan cultures the child's position in society is affected by the age at which he or she is able to sit. However, the American Academy of Pediatrics advises against placing infants in formal exercise programs because putting more stress on bones, joints, and other supportive structures than their level of development can tolerate can easily lead to injury. The practice of teaching infants to swim can also have damaging consequences. Infants who swallow too much water can develop the syndrome of water intoxification, which sometimes results in seizures or comas (White, 1990). Thus parents are well advised to consider that "earlier" is not necessarily "better."

PAVING PATHWAYS ALONG INFANT PHYSICAL MILESTONES: PROVIDING A STIMULATING INFANT ENVIRONMENT

How do you create an environment that is likely to be stimulating to infants? Infants have revealed what is necessary by means of their demonstrated preferences, as discussed in the previous sections. They enjoy variety and novelty. Visually they prefer patterns, contrasts, faces—especially familiar ones, and bright colors. Auditorily they like the voice of their primary caregiver, soft sounds, and music, and dislike harsh sounds and chaotic noise. Their naturally emerging motor milestones illustrate how they enjoy reaching out and interacting with their environment, rather than sitting back as passive observers. Using these observations as a guide, parents and other caregivers can ensure their infants a stimulating environment by doing the following:

Engage infants with plenty of interpersonal contact. Newborns like to be held facing familiar caregivers, engage in eye contact, and listen to soft conversation. Being held close, cuddled, and rocked also provides pleasant stimulation. They enjoy spending time in the company of the rest of the family so long as the setting is not too chaotically noisy, as sometimes happens when there are numerous older siblings. At age 6 months they start appreciating games such as peek-a-boo and copying games such as making funny faces and sounds and pat-the-table. By the time they are a year old they will also employ copying behaviors as a caregiver stacks blocks or rolls a ball back and forth. They enjoy having books read to them, although the process may involve nontraditional page-turning, sudden beginnings, and abrupt endings. Conversation, even when it consists only of saying what you are doing or naming objects and events perceived by the baby, is appreciated throughout infancy. Singing songs and providing other exposures to music also appear to have beneficial effects for their brain development by building up neural circuitry that can later be filled (Huttenlocher, 1994).

Provide interesting playthings. Newborns can be offered visual stimuli such as mobiles and other toys. Remember that they like to look at objects or pictures offering contrast, patterns, faces, and colors. Brightly colored toys are preferred—yet at times a challenge to locate because toy manufacturers in Western cultures curiously tend to make toys for newborns in pastels. Music boxes are also usually a hit. Some infants like the sound of a ticking clock, perhaps because it reminds them of when they were still in the womb listening to mother's heartbeat.

By age 6 months they are ready for colorful toys suitable for grabbing, squeezing, and/or shaking, as well as toys that have moveable parts and make noises. They also enjoy fiddling with nontraditional "toys," such as tearing and crumpling up paper, banging together steel pans and utensils, and feeling different textures of varying scraps of fabric. As they begin eating table food, manipulating and squashing foods of different textures becomes a pastime of interest. By the time they are a year old they enjoy books with large, simple pictures (pragmatically washable cloth books are probably a better choice than those with paper pages).

Maximize exploration possibilities. While an infant is still in the prelocomotor stage, exploration will depend a lot on others' arranging the possibilities, such as placing toys and other interesting objects within the child's view. Make sure you place a toy close enough that the child can reach for it as coordination improves. As the baby becomes old enough to sit partially upright, using an infant seat will provide baby with a new perspective for visual exploration. Being placed upright can also accelerate muscle development in the neck, trunk, and legs (Thelen, 1986). Carrying babies around the room upright so they can look

Mobile infants learn more from freely exploring their natural environment than they can learn from exposure to educational toys.

at and touch new objects provides the prelocomotor infant additional opportunities for exploration and stimulation.

Once babies can move on their own, opportunities abound. Rather than being restricted to playpens, infants benefit more from free exploration of a baby-proofed home. What babies learn while exploring a natural environment is much more valuable than discoveries made by manipulating toys. The baby's environment should be as devoid of "no-no's" as possible. Babies given the unpleasant stimulation of continually being told "no" may tune people out.

Bath time is a great opportunity for exploring interesting sensations. Newborns experience the water's wetness, warmth, and trickling sounds, as well as the gentleness of the parent's touch. Older babies enjoy the exploration of splashing water, and later having a cup for pouring and floating experimentation. Before or after bath time babies also enjoy the novel stimulation of spending some time moving around while nude.

In recent decades many parents have let infants explore by routinely placing them in baby walkers. These do allow babies to maintain an upright position, move themselves around in a new way, and learn a few things about locomotion. Some parents use them as a type of babysitter, since they restrict the amount of mischief a baby can get into. However, baby walkers have not been found to help infants learn to walk any sooner, and they are also a significant cause of injuries as babies manage to tip them over or propel them down stairs and other drop-offs (Ridenour, 1982). In fact, one study found that infants who had been placed in walkers sat, crawled, and walked later than did other infants, as well as scored lower on measures of mental and motor development (Siegal & Burton, 1999). The use of baby walkers is thus currently discouraged.

Expose infants to alternative environments. Parents can expose their infants to numerous environments simply by keeping them with them during routine activity. Small infants can be carried around as the caregiver travels from one part of the house to another. They can come along for the ride as parents perform routine chores away from home. As infants grow older they benefit from visiting settings that offer additional novel exposures, such as the zoo or a shopping mall. Even spending a day at Grandma's is a new adventure. What may be mundane or boring to us nonetheless may be exciting new grist for the mill for the developing infant.

POSSIBLE SIGNS OF DEVELOPMENTAL DIFFICULTIES

Sometimes an infant does not respond to a healthy, stimulating environment because of unusual developmental or neurological conditions. Early assessment of such conditions and timely intervention increases an affected infant's chances of eventually catching up. Following is a list of warning signs parents should watch for that may indicate a need for professional evaluation (Healy, 1994):

▶ The infant almost always seems to be sleeping.

▶ The infant avoids eye contact, or seems uninterested in it.

▶ The infant frequently fails to respond to voices or other sounds.

▶ The infant's limb movements are markedly weaker or less active on one side of the body.

▶ Many or all of the milestones for motor development occur noticeably later than expected (keep in mind that premature babies' expected milestones are based on their full-term date, not their actual birthdate).

▶ The infant does not want to play pat-a-cake, peek-a-boo, bye-bye, and other forms of age-appropriate social responsiveness.

▶ The infant shows extreme sensitivity to physical stimuli such as noises, lights, and being touched.

SUMMARY

Body Growth

Early physical development progresses according to cephalocaudal and proximodistal rules. The average newborn weighs about 7½ lb and is about 20 in. long. By age 2 a child is typically one-half of his or her adult height and one-fourth to one-fifth of his or her adult weight.

Brain Development

Information travels back and forth to the brain and within the brain by means of neurons. Neurons are overabundant and disorganized at birth. During the brain growth spurt of the first two years, neurons interconnect, disconnect, become better myelinated, or even disintegrate depending on the infant's experiences. The inner structures of the brain responsible for survival functions are better developed at birth than is the cerebral cortex.

Conscious States

Infants experience the same states of arousal or sleepiness as do adults, but spend more time sleeping and more time in REM sleep. On tragic occasions infants may unexplainably stop breathing and expire during sleep periods (sudden infant death syndrome, or SIDS).

Infant Nutrition

Growing infants and toddlers need to receive a standard, recommended, age-appropriate set of nutrients. The most crucial nutrients appear to be iron, fat, and protein. Breast milk or fortified formulas are nutritionally adequate for the first 6 months, and babies fed by either method show no significant differences in physical and emotional well-being. Introduction of solid food begins at 6 months, and by 1 year, infants should be eating a balanced diet of chopped table food. Undernourishment can lead to such problems as iron-deficient anemia, malnutrition, kwashiorkor, and marasmus. Even mildly malnourished infants have demonstrated intellectual and emotional deficiencies after reaching grade school age. On the other hand, obesity during infancy does not appear to have much relationship with later obesity or other difficulties.

Motor Development

Infant motor development progresses as the central nervous system matures; opportunities for experiences and environmental supports and constraints encourage or discourage it. The first voluntary motor skills to develop are gross motor skills, followed by the fine motor skills as the child grows older. Infants tend to develop motor skills according to a predictable sequence and timetable; however, normal infants can vary considerably in the ages at which they reach these milestones.

Sensory/Perceptual Development

By age 1 year, infants' visual acuity is as good as the average adult's. At even earlier ages they can choose and maintain a focus, follow a moving object, distinguish colors, perceive the physical rules governing the behavior of viewed stimuli, and show preferences for visual stimuli such as bright colors, contrasts, and especially faces. Contrary to long-held beliefs stemming from "visual cliff" experiments, even infants as young as 3 weeks appear to perceive depth.

Infant hearing ability usually is as good as an adult's by the end of the first week, both in sensitivity to barely audible sounds and in the ability to distinguish subtle differences between sounds. Infants prefer soft sounds over harsh ones, music over nonsensical noise, and Mother's voice over other voices. Infants' ability to taste and smell are also well developed within the first few days of life. They prefer sweetness to salty, bitter, or sour flavors. The sense of touch is one of the best-developed at birth, and by age 1 year, infants can distinguish between objects by touch alone. Contrary to previously held notions, infants do indeed fully experience the sensation of pain. Intermodal perception has been seen in infants as young as 1 month, and as they grow older, their intermodal sensing even allows them to "lip-read."

Infants need an environment offering both affection and age-appropriate stimulation; nonorganic failure to thrive may occur when these ingredients are missing. The ideal environment is one that takes into account infant preferences: variety, novelty, stimuli representing the preferred sensory experiences, and active rather than passive involvement. Infants crave interpersonal contact and are especially appreciative of time with primary caregivers. The best environment is as unrestrictive as is safely possible; in other words, fit the environment to the child's developmental level, rather than try to fit the child to the environment.

Possible Signs of Developmental Difficulties

Early assessment and intervention can contribute toward a healthier future when unusual developmental and neurological conditions or symptoms appear.

KEY TERMS

brain growth spurt	intermodal perception	plasticity
brainstem	kwashiorkor	proximodistal
cephalocaudal	locomotor skills	REM (rapid eye movement) sleep
cerebellum	marasmus	sensation
cerebral cortex	myelin sheath	stepping reflex
depth perception	neurons	sudden infant death syndrome
extrusion reflex	neurotransmitters	(SIDS)
fine motor skills	nonorganic failure to thrive	synapse
gross motor skills	perception	thalamus
hypothalamus	pincer grasp	ulnar grasp

CONCEPT REVIEW

1. Those aspects of a child's development that begin with the head and work their way downward are evidence of the _____ rule of development; the tendency for the trunk to develop before the limbs supports the _____ rule of development.

2. By the time babies reach age 1, their weight has typically _____; by the time they reach age 2 they will have grown to _____ of their eventual adult height.

3. On average, baby boys have more _____ mass than do baby girls, while the _____ growth of baby girls tends to be more advanced than that of baby boys.

4. Neurons of infant brains are still developing many of the _____ that interconnect brain tissue, as well as still "greasing up" their _____, which speed up transmission of information.

5. During the _____ of the first 2 years, the infant brain grows from 25% to 75% of its eventual adult size. The massive development still occurring during these early years explains why a child's brain demonstrates so much more _____ after an injury than does an adult brain.

6. Healthy infant brain development is extremely dependent upon _____ from the environment.

7. Infants sleep for about _____ hours a day, and spend over twice as much of their sleep in a _____ pattern as do adults.

8. A fatal disorder of infancy during which the child stops breathing while sleeping is called _____.

9. To facilitate rapid growth and myelination of neurons, children under the age of 2 need more _____ in their diets than do adults.

10. Infants under the age of 4 months do not enjoy much success with spoon feeding because of the _____, but by the end of age _____, their feeding skills are so much more advanced that their recommended diet consists of chopped table food.

11. Most experts agree that nutritionally, _____-feeding is superior to _____-feeding infants; however, the two feeding methods are identical in terms of the child's eventual _____ development.

12. Severe malnutrition or undernourishment in children can result in extreme conditions such as _____ and _____. Yet even children from relatively advantaged backgrounds can suffer the effects of poor nutrition, such as a form of anemia that can develop when parents become overreliant on _____.

13. Obesity in infancy does/does not have a relationship with obesity later in life. The main determinant of obesity in older children and adults is _____.

14. The interrelationships observed between development of motor skills and physical ability, environmental supports and constraints, rules of physics, and the demands of the task at hand discount the _____ theory of motor development.

15. Potty-training involves using a complex set of muscular skills and requires sufficient _____ and _____ motor development, which is usually first in place at age _____.

16. Regarding a child's sensory and perceptual development, _____ is more closely tied to biological processes whereas environmental factors more greatly influence _____.

17. Studies of infant _____ show that, contrary to earlier beliefs, this sensory and perceptual ability is in a number of ways very similar to that of adults. The "visual cliff" experiments have been used to demonstrate the infant's capacity for _____.

18. The infant's ability to recognize mother's voice, distinguish changes in melodies, and process other auditory stimuli has been studied largely by observing changes in their _____.

19. The infant's sense of _____ is actually more sensitive than that of an adult.

20. Crying, heart rates, blood pressure, facial expressions, avoidant body movements, and measured levels of cortisol in the bloodstream all indicate that newborns do in fact experience _____.

21. The inability of researchers to teach infants to associate two sensory experiences that in fact do not go together suggests that infants are already developing their _____.

22. When infants receive insufficient stimulation, they may stop gaining weight, progressing along normal developmental milestones, or showing attachment behaviors. Such infants are suffering from _____, and often have a lower than normal level of _____ in their bloodstreams.

23. The environment that bests supports infants' physical development includes _____, _____, _____, and _____.

1) cephalocaudal; proximodistal; 2) tripled; one-half; 3) muscle; skeletal; 4) synapses; myelin sheaths; 5) brain growth spurt; plasticity; 6) stimulation; 7) sixteen; REM (rapid eye movement); 8) sudden infant death syndrome; 9) fat; 10) extrusion reflex; one; 11) breast; bottle; social/emotional; 12) marasmus, kwashiorkor; bottle-feeding; 13) does not; heredity; 14) maturational; 15) fine; gross; two; 16) sensation; perception; 17) vision; depth perception; 18) sucking patterns; 19) taste; 20) pain; 21) intermodal perception; 22) nonorganic failure to thrive; growth hormone; 23) interpersonal contact; interesting, age-appropriate playthings; opportunities for physical exploration; exposure to multiple environments

RESOURCES FOR FURTHER READING

Adderly, B. D., & Gordon, J. (1999). *Brighter baby: Boosting your child's intelligence, health and happiness through infant massage.* Chicago: Regnery Publishing.

Adolph, K. E. (1997). *Learning in the development of infant locomotion.* Chicago: University of Chicago Press.

Bly, L. (1994). *Motor skills acquisition in the first year: An illustrated guide to normal development.* Orlando, FL: Academic Press.

Eiger, M. S., & Olds, S. W. (1999). *The complete book of breastfeeding,* 3rd ed. New York: Workman Publishing.

Ezzo, G., & Bucknam, R. (1998). *On becoming baby wise: Learn how over 500,000 babies were trained to sleep through the night the natural way.* Sisters, OR: Multnomah Publishers.

Pinel, J. P., & Edwards, M. E. (1998). *A colorful introduction to the anatomy of the human brain: A brain and psychology coloring book.* Englewood Cliffs, NJ: Erlbaum.

Sears, W. (1995). *SIDS: A parents' guide to understanding and prevention sudden infant death syndrome,* Vol. 1. Boston: Little, Brown, & Co.

Snow, C. W. (1997). *Infant development.* Englewood Cliffs, NJ: Prentice-Hall.

Thelen, E., & Smith, L. B. (1994). *A dynamic systems approach to the development of cognition and action.* Cambridge, MA: MIT Press/Bradford Books.

INFOTRAC COLLEGE EDITION

For additional readings, explore InfoTrac College Edition, your online library. Go to http://www.infotrac-college.com/wadsworth and use the passcode that came on the card with your book. Try these search terms: breast-feeding, failure to thrive, infants—development, infants—food & nutrition, infants—growth, infants—physiological aspects, infants—weight, iron-deficiency anemia, perception in infants, toilet-training

CHILD DEVELOPMENT CD-ROM

Go to the Wadsworth Child Development CD-ROM for further study of the concepts in this chapter. The CD-ROM also includes quizzes and additional activities to expand your learning experience.

REFERENCES

For a list of references for this chapter, see the Wadsworth Psych Study Center Web site at: http://www.wadsworth.com/product/0534348092s

Infant and Toddler Cognitive Development

FOCUS QUESTIONS

► What is sensorimotor intelligence, and what role does it play in how babies learn?

► What do infants and toddlers remember?

► What types of learning and conditioning are observed in infants and toddlers?

► How do we measure infant intelligence, and can we forecast its future development?

► What can parents and caregivers do to enhance babies' intellectual development?

► How do nature and nurture interplay in early language development?

► How can parents and caregivers assist babies' language development?

OUTLINE

Piaget's Sensorimotor Intelligence
Substage 1: Reflexes
Substage 2: Primary Circular Reactions
Substage 3: Secondary Circular Reactions
Substage 4: Coordination of Secondary Circular Reactions
Substage 5: Tertiary Circular Reactions
Substage 6: Mental Representation
Conclusion
Information-Processing
Evidence of Infant Learning
Classical Conditioning
Operant Conditioning
Imitation

Intelligence
Intelligence Testing
Predicting Individual Differences
Paving Pathways: Supporting Intellectual Growth
Language and Communication
Theories of Language Development
Acquiring Language
Paving Pathways: Enhancing Language Development

Harold was giving 6-year-old Tammy a lesson in cooking hard-boiled eggs. He showed her how to put the eggs in the pan, add water until the eggs were covered, place them on the stove, and turn the heating element on high. They watched as the water heated and bubbles began to form on the bottom of the pan.

"Next," explained Harold, "the bubbles will come to the top of the water, and steam will rise up out of the pan. Then what do you think we do?"

"I know!" said Tammy. "Next, we hold the mail over the steam so we can find out what's inside!"

Infant and toddler cognitive growth follows the theme of a big scientific experiment of "let's see what happens next." Babies are amazingly competent and persistent as they explore their world and find ways of making sense out of their experiences. The natural emergence of cognitive exploration during the first 2 years of life is arguably one of the most documentable pieces of evidence that human intellect is advanced well beyond that of other creatures.

What is sensorimotor intelligence, and what role does it play in how babies learn?

PIAGET'S SENSORIMOTOR INTELLIGENCE

Infant and toddler learning is a venture of interaction between environment and self. Jean Piaget (1936/1974) painstakingly chronicled the progression of his own children's early cognitive development, all the while questioning whether babies had thoughts and ideas as adults and older children do. He noted that they appeared to amass a wealth of learning through the use of their senses and motor activity. Babies reach, squeeze, pound, throw, and shake their way into a perception of the world. While mapping his children's progress, Piaget named these first 2 years of cognitive development **sensorimotor intelligence**. As more recent research has implicated the substantial impact of stimulation on brain development (described in Chapter 5), Piaget's original observations of early learning seem to confirm that children naturally pursue the path that enhances appropriate growth.

Chapter 1 introduced the Piagetian concepts that children reason by using structures called schemes, add new information onto old schemes through assimilation, and create new schemes when new information so warrants by means of accommodation. **Equilibration** is another key learning concept that becomes especially apparent during infancy and toddlerhood. Equilibration describes the back-and-forth movement that occurs when a child solidly accepts a current scheme and is sorting out the confusion that follows when newer information and experiences just don't seem to add up.

For example, while waiting in an airport I observed a toddler watching in wide-eyed wonder as a jetliner taxied up to the gate. "Car!" she exclaimed, with much enthusiastic gesturing. "Plane," her mother countered, pointing as she did so (and probably suppressing a chuckle as well). Upon encountering this new information the child thus moved from a state of equilibrium to disequilibrium: she had previously categorized anything with wheels and moving along concrete within the scheme of "car," but here she was being presented with an example that seemed to disprove the mold. She will eventually develop more accurate internal representations of her collective observations, most likely by creating subcategorical schemes that account for the various "things that go." By this process, which Piaget called **organization**, she thus returns to a state of equilibrium. Throughout her childhood she will continue this process of equilibration, sorting out and interrelating old and new information and reorganizing schemes in ways that make sense for her particular level of development and personal idiosyncracies.

The characteristics of a child's cognitive level change substantially between birth and the conclusion of the 2-year period of sensorimotor development. So many changes occur in those 2 years that Piaget divided sensorimotor intelligence into six substages. The substages focus on **circular reactions**—the degree and quality of interplay between the child's actions and the environment. The role of physical development is thus especially relevant during the sensorimotor stage.

Substage 1: Reflexes

The first substage of sensorimotor activity, which covers the first month of life, is driven primarily by the biologically programmed reflexes discussed in Chapter 4. Although these reflexes are involuntary, the infant can acquire learning by observing how such reflexive actions interact with the environment. For example, the strength of the sucking reflex may result in an infant's latching on to an opportunely presented fist and enthusiastically persisting in sucking despite the lack of nourishment. In this manner, infants discover that putting fists in their mouths provides some comfort during emotional distress, and eventually choose to do so voluntarily once they have developed sufficient motor control.

Substage 2: Primary Circular Reactions

As their motor skills mature, infants are better able to respond to their perceptions of the environment. As they do so they first reveal that delightful self-absorbed joy of doing for the sake of doing that characterizes child-like experiencing. Between the ages of 1 and 4 months they provide early evidence that they interact with the world by means of **primary circular reactions**, repeating chance behaviors that appear to get a certain result. Alterations of behavior based on primary circular reactions center purely on effects to the self, such as the interesting sensations produced by gurgling noises or the pleasure of sucking on a fist.

Substage 3: Secondary Circular Reactions

Between the ages of 4 and 8 months, children become significantly more sophisticated in their motor skills. They are able to focus on a toy and grab it, bat at a mobile and make it turn, and shake a rattle and listen for the noise it makes. Thus during this third substage of **secondary circular reactions**, babies recognize that their behaviors can have certain effects on the environment. Shaking a rattle makes interesting noises; bouncing legs up and down can make a mobile jiggle and turn. They repeat minor-league experiments such as these in order to make interesting sights or sensations last longer. They also start to become aware that the environment is separate from themselves, as well as discovering that items previously perceived as part of the environment—such as their fists—actually come attached.

Substage 4: Coordination of Secondary Circular Reactions

Substage Four brings with it a variety of new and exciting changes and abilities. Between the ages of 8 and 12 months children begin more systematically organizing and applying their store of schemes. They illustrate such advances with the emergence of **goal-directed behavior**—purposeful actions that are coordinated in order to achieve certain objectives (McCarty et al., 1999; Piaget, 1953; Willatts, 1999). As an example, if you place a desired toy just out of a child's reach and then hide it under a cover, the child will coordinate three schemes: moving toward the object, pulling off the cover, then grasping the toy.

This example also illustrates the newly emerging scheme of **object permanence**. Since younger babies act as if an object no longer exists once it is hidden from view and do not even attempt to remove a cover, Piaget assumed that babies younger than 8 months could not function beyond the scheme of "out of

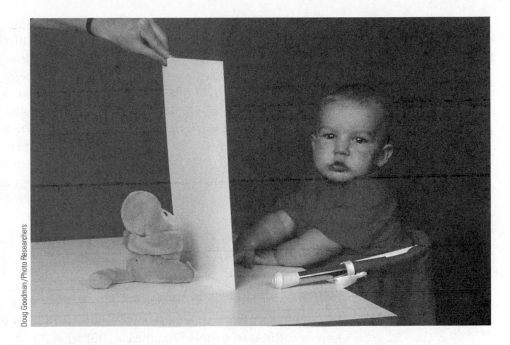

When the fuzzy toy is hidden from view, this infant reacts as if it no longer exists. Based on such observations Piaget hypothesized that young infants do not perceive object permanence.

Doug Goodman/Photo Researchers

sight, out of mind." He proposed that by age 8 months children realize that objects still exist even when they cannot see them. Their ability to imitate advances as well. They gradually come closer to imitating newly observed responses even if there has been a delay between observation and the opportunity for imitation. Such maneuvers have their limits, however. If an infant sees you hide a toy in one place and then hide it in a second place, the infant will continue to look for it in the first hiding place. Piaget called this phenomenon **AB search error**, and interpreted it as evidence that their ability to maintain the image of an object is still a little murky. However, cognitive psychologists suggest that failure at the AB search error task has more to do with the infant's limited capacity for tolerating delay before being required to recall new information, and thus is a product of underdeveloped memory processes (Bell & Fox, 1992; Marcovitch & Zelazo, 1999). How infants manage their spatial orientation may also contribute to this seemingly reasoning-based error (Schmuckler & Tsang-Tong, 2000).

Later research has questioned Piaget's interpretations of his observations in other ways as well (Mandler, 1998; Muller & Overon, 1998). Studies show that infants as young as 2½ months old demonstrate some knowledge of object permanence by showing greater interest in an unexpected presentation than an expected one (Baillargeon, 1987; Munakata et al., 1997; Wilcox et al., 1996). Another study showed that while in a darkened setting, 6-month-old infants will reach in the appropriate direction of a previously viewed object when they hear a corresponding auditory cue of its existence (Goubet & Clifton, 1998).

Actually, because successful demonstration of object permanence depends on a child's ability to coordinate schemes, Piaget's experimental design for observing this phenomenon in babies younger than 8 months is conceptually flawed. Piaget himself pointed out that children younger than 8 months do not yet coordinate schemes. Also, we might wonder if younger infants would not bother to try to remove a cover because of their notoriously short attention spans. Unable to see the toy, they may simply become distracted by more interesting stimuli and forget it is there. Piaget's assumptions regarding AB search error may also be based on flawed experimental design. Changing from one movement strategy to another takes significant motor coordination, perhaps more than an 8-month-old infant can muster. Thus failure to perform the task successfully may represent an insufficiently developed motor cortex rather than inadequate cognitive processing (Diamond, 1988). Others suggest that the error is due more to factors related to the infant body's orientation in space, memories of previous reaching activities, and the close connection between infant looking and reaching (Smith, Thelen, et al., 1999).

Substage 5: Tertiary Circular Reactions

Between 12 and 18 months, children begin experimenting more creatively with their circular reactions. They execute a variety of physical operations while interacting with the environment as they try to get a certain result or just to see what happens next. A child may have already discovered the pleasurable sensation of softness while touching the cat. But what sensations might also follow if the child strokes the cat? Makes scratching motions on her? Pokes her? Pulls her fur?

Such emerging strategies contribute to more successful problem-solving skills. The child will try multiple strategies in order to create a desired result and will be less likely to become stymied by phenomena such as AB search error. My niece, Annie, demonstrated her newly evolving creative problem-solving during this substage as she interacted with her older sister, Brynne. Beginning at a very early age, Annie took great pleasure in tormenting her older sibling. I observed her as she poked Brynne's foot, took her toys, stuck them in her mouth, knocked them over or moved them around in new and interesting ways, then stopped and looked up to see if her actions had resulted in the expected squealing and protests.

Substage 6: Mental Representation

During this span of development, the sensorimotor intelligence of babyhood and the mental operational ability of the young child converge. Between ages 18 and 24 months, a child begins showing the first signs of solving problems by thinking them out rather than relying solely on active experimentation. If an item has been placed out of reach, a child might stop and consider what pieces of furniture he or she might climb on in order to reach it. Thus the child has begun using mental symbols representing the environment that can be mentally manipulated as a means of solving problems. This new ability enhances not only problem-solving ability but also other skills using symbolic representation, such as the capacity for language development and the future fantasy of play and make-believe (Lyytinen et al., 1997; McCune, 1995; Walker-Andrews & Kahana-Kalman, 1999).

TABLE 6.1

A summary of
sensorimotor
substages

Age (months)	Substage	New Abilities
Birth–1	1: Reflexes	Some learning by observing results of reflexive movement
1–4	2: Primary circular reactions	Repeat chance behaviors related to basic need gratification
4–8	3: Secondary circular reactions	Repeat behaviors in attempt to manipulate interesting aspects of environment
8–12	4: Coordination of secondary circular reactions	Use goal-directed behavior by combining and organizing schemes; object permanence begins to emerge
12–18	5: Tertiary circular reactions	Apply multiple and novel schemes to same object or activity—the beginnings of problem-solving; object permanence firmly established; includes consideration of multiple hiding places
18–24	6: Mental representation	Problem-solving by thinking out possible solutions rather than acting them out

Conclusion

Given the dismantling of many of Piaget's main ideas about sensorimotor intelligence, researchers have been reconsidering how to conceptualize these early pieces of evidence of infant cognitive development. Some suggest that we start over and begin by distinguishing between representation of objects, permanence of objects, and identity of objects—discriminations not taken into account by Piaget (Gelman et al., 1999; Meltzoff & Moore, 1998). Although Piaget fell victim to a few experimentation blunders and premature conclusions, he did provide us with a clear and consistent sequencing of the sensorimotor skills observed during the first two years of life. His most important contribution was his emphasis on the interactive process between the infant and the environment. Infants do not simply absorb information as passive observers. Even at this early age they demonstrate our shared human characteristics of curiosity, experimentation, and persistence as they attempt to better understand their world, and continue to do so using better and more sophisticated systems as they mature.

What do infants and toddlers remember?

INFORMATION-PROCESSING

At what age do infants actually start collecting information and trying to make sense of it? As was mentioned earlier, theorists once assumed that the restricted quantity and quality of early infant behavior was evidence that not much activity occurs in a newborn brain. But as researchers have figured out clever ways of measuring infant cognition, the accumulating evidence has clearly shown that there is a lot more going on in the infant brain than we had thought (Meltzoff & Gopnick, 1997).

To process information, we first must be able to hang on to it long enough to sort it out and draw conclusions. Therefore we need a functioning memory store (Gathercole, 1998). Piaget's investigations of sensorimotor intelligence repeatedly demonstrated infants' ability to remember aspects of their experiences with the environment over the first 2 years. After all, their motivation for repeating their circular reactions is often based on the memory of an effect an action may have.

Infants show a capacity for memory at a very young age (Courage & Howe, 1998; Slater, 1995b). In one study, 6-week-old infants were presented with a person who repeatedly stuck his tongue out. When the infants were presented with the same person 24 hours later, he kept his lips closed. The infants stared longer at this individual than at others presented for the first time, and even started to push out their own tongues in his presence (Meltzoff & Moore, 1994). Two-and-a-half-year-olds have demonstrated that they retained memories acquired when they were as young as 6 months old (Rovee-Collier, 1993). On the other hand, when looking back on your own childhood, you have probably noticed that you have few if any memories of your first years of life. This phenomenon is called **infantile amnesia**. Investigations of early memories suggest that we generally have no conscious memories of events occurring before the age of 3 (Eacott & Crawley, 1998; Harley & Reese, 1999; Scheingold & Tenney, 1982).

If we have the capacity for remembering even as infants, why don't our memories of infancy survive into adulthood? In view of the massive development occurring in the infant brain, perhaps this failure isn't so surprising. As you recall from Chapter 5, we are born with more neurons than we will take with us into adulthood, and the numerous rearrangements of their interconnections most likely interferes with development of conscious long-term memories. Another possibility is that some of the brain structures responsible for maintaining long-term memories, such as the frontal lobes of the cerebral cortex and the hippocampus, are immature (Rosenzweig, 1996).

What types of learning and conditioning are observed in infants and toddlers?

EVIDENCE OF INFANT LEARNING

The most primitive form of human learning is demonstrated by the processes of **habituation** and **dishabituation**. When we first notice something new in the environment, we are likely to attend to it. Over time we get used to its presence and are less likely to pay attention to it or even consciously notice that it is there. Thus our brains have habituated to the novel stimulus. However, if something about the stimulus changes, we will once again take notice, thus having dishabituated our attentiveness.

Infants demonstrate the ability to habituate and dishabituate from the time of birth (Bornstein, 1985; Tarquinio et al., 1990). Researchers have presented neonates with repetitive stimuli such as certain sounds, touches, or visual materials and have discovered that infants both habituate and dishabituate to these stimuli. This tells us that the infant brain is capable of recognizing the familiar and is also likely to notice the unfamiliar. By observing these patterns of habituation and dishabituation, researchers have been able to investigate how infants process information. For example, such methodology has been used to show that infants as young as 3 or 4 months are beginning to cluster visual representations into broad categorizations such as four-legged creatures and non-four-legged creatures (Pauen, 2000; Quinn & Eimas, 1998; Quinn & Johnson, 1997). As they approach the end of their first year, their patterns of habituation and dishabituation demonstrate recognition of many categories of objects, including types of toys, food items, and furniture (Roberts, 1988; Younger, 1985).

Classical Conditioning

Studies of classical conditioning have also collected evidence of the infant's early learning ability. Watson and Rayner's study of "Albert and the White Rat," described in Chapter 1, is a good example of how a 1-year-old can be classically conditioned to produce a fear response. More recent research has shown that even infants much younger than little Albert have some capacity for learning through classical conditioning. Newborns have been classically conditioned to produce behaviors such as head-turning, blinking, sucking—essentially almost any response that is already part of their behavioral repertoire (Fitzgerald & Porges, 1971).

Operant Conditioning

Newborns also respond to operant conditioning. A study of 2-day-old infants showed that newborns could be taught to suck on a dry nipple in order to receive the reinforcer of pleasant music. When sucking on a dry nipple no longer produced music, they stopped sucking (Butterfield & Siperstein, 1972). Sensorimotor intelligence itself illustrates that operant conditioning is at work throughout the first 2 years: Babies interact with the environment in part because their efforts at seeing what kind of results they can produce are reinforced.

Imitation

Precursors of the elements described in Bandura's social learning theory are evident at the time of birth. The ability to imitate seems to come to us fairly easily. Infants only a few days old can learn to copy adult facial expressions such as sticking out the tongue or opening the mouth wide, as shown in the photograph on page 166 (Meltzoff & Moore, 1989). As children progress through their first 2 years, their ability to imitate improves. Between the ages of 1 month and

Infants are capable of imitating facial expressions at a remarkably early age.

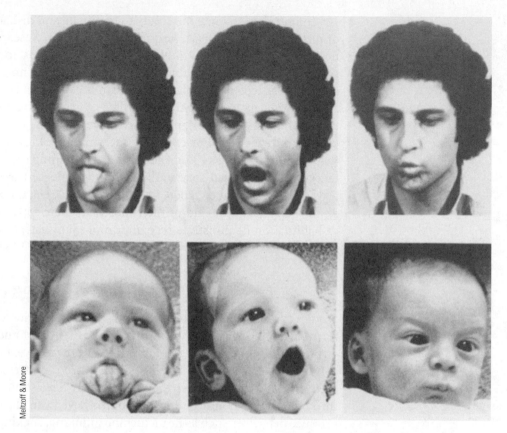

Meltzoff & Moore

8 months, infants will copy others' behaviors if the action is something they can already do, such as shaking a rattle or patting a table. By the time they are a year old, they have begun making their first attempts at imitating observed novel behaviors.

At this age they may even show some evidence of **deferred imitation**: the ability to repeat an observed behavior when some time has passed since they observed it. Piaget did not observe this ability in infants until they reached age 18 months to 2 years and concluded that deferred imitation did not develop until late toddlerhood. This conclusion appears to have been premature; later research has shown that infants as young as 9 months have at least some capacity for deferred imitation, such as shaking an object they had previously observed and heard rattling when shaken (Meltzoff, 1988).

By the end of the second year, toddlers are busily incorporating their imitative abilities into a number of organized schemes. When my oldest son, Frank, was almost 2 he developed a regular routine that was one of his versions of imitating and organizing observed behaviors. When his father came home from work he would often leave his shoes by the front door and throw his hat and tie on a nearby chair. If Frank were anywhere in the vicinity, within a few minutes we would hear him struggling to shuffle toward us, his tiny feet swimming in his father's shoes. As he rounded the corner from the front entry we would see that

L. Kolvoord/The Image Works

Even as early as age 2 children enjoy dressing up as same-gendered adults.

he was dealing with the additional handicaps of having a tie around his neck and dragging under his feet, as well as an over-sized hat continually slipping down over his eyes. Yet the apparent reward of looking like Daddy was enough for him to attempt to prevail over these encumbrances almost daily.

Another example of how infants discriminate and choose among observed actions they would like to copy involves recognition of intent. When adults model both intentional and accidental behaviors for 14- through 18-month-olds, the toddlers are twice as likely to copy the intentional actions as the ones the adults identify as being a "mistake" (Carpenter et al., 1998). What else might these amazing little beings be picking up from what they see around them? Studies such as these certainly make us wonder which aspects of our own behavior we might choose to moderate in their presence.

INTELLIGENCE

How do we measure infant intelligence, and can we forecast its future development?

How much of a child's future intelligence can be predicted during the first 2 years of life? Evidence of genetic influences on intelligence become more and more pronounced between the ages of 1 and 3 (Petrill et al., 1998). Yet life exposures, experiences, and personality idiosyncracies also contribute toward eventual level of intelligence, and the most influential predictor of intelligence level can differ from child to child according to how nurture and nature converge (Rowe et al., 1999). Let's take a closer look at how intelligence is measured and how it pertains to understanding infant intelligence.

Intelligence Testing

Analytical intelligence has received the lion's share of research attention and testing thus far (Sparrow & Davis, 2000). Intelligence testing of any sort first emerged when the French psychologist Alfred Binet was asked by the Parisian educational system to develop a method of identifying those students who would not be likely to benefit from regular classroom instruction. An adaptation of these early efforts, the Stanford-Binet Intelligence Scale, is currently one of the most widely used American intelligence tests (Terman & Merrill, 1973; Thorndike et al., 1986).

Intelligence tests are made up of various questions or tasks shown to have a relationship with academic performance and similar forms of success. The scoring reflects how the test-taker compares to other same-aged individuals who have taken the test. Because intelligence tests are standardized (see Chapter 2), the test developers analyze the scores of many individuals and create **norms**: the average scores achieved by test-takers at various ages. When a child takes an intelligence test, the achieved score is compared to the expected score for children of the same age. An **intelligence quotient (IQ)** is computed by taking the ratio of the child's actual chronological age to the mental age reflected by the test score and multiplying it by 100:

$$Intelligence\ Quotient = \frac{Mental\ Age}{Chronological\ Age} \times 100$$

The average IQ score is thus 100. If the mental age is higher than the chronological age, the child's IQ will be more than 100. If mental age is lower than chronological age, the IQ will be below 100. Almost all intelligence tests provide some way of converting their scores to reflect an average score of 100 for the sake of comparability. Determining scores in this manner effectively assesses how individual children compare with their peer group.

However, the standard deviations (see Chapter 2) surrounding these average scores vary from age to age. This throws a monkey wrench into any attempts to compare scores among children of varying age groups. Therefore the major intelligence tests such as Stanford-Binet and an assortment of tests by Wechsler no longer use the IQ scoring method described above. Instead they have converted their scoring systems to **standard scores**, for which raw scores have been transformed so as to have means and standard deviations that are consistent from age to age. Rather than performing a mathematical computation, the tester finds the final test score by using tables providing a **deviation intelligence quotient (DIQ)** based on the mathematical manipulations behind the creation of the standard scores. DIQs also work off of a mean of 100 and have standard deviations of 15 or 16. This consistency allows the tester to more accurately predict how a child is likely to perform in the future from current intelligence test scores.

Unfortunately, tests of this nature are useful only for older children. Obviously, babies are limited in their abilities to use language to express what they know, manipulate objects, or put the two together in ways that might reveal their more complex mental processes. Researchers therefore rely on other forms of testing for determining infant intelligence. The Bayley Scales of Infant Development (Bayley, 1969; Black et al., 1999b), the most widely used infant intelligence test, assess the abilities of infants between the ages of 2 months and 2½ years. By observing a large number of babies performing a variety of activities, the test designers developed three scales of infant intelligence: a mental scale reflecting memory, perception, learning, problem-solving, and vocalizations; a motor scale of abilities such as grasping, sitting, standing, or walking; and an infant behavior record that serves as a type of diary of infant personality style. Rather than producing a DIQ, the Bayley scales compute a **development quotient** using the ratio computational method and a mean of 100. A particular child's test performance thus can be compared to what is expected for that child's age group.

Predicting Individual Differences

The ability of developmental IQ tests to predict which infant will become the next Einstein is so limited that it approaches negligible. Since infant developmental scales do not have built-in standardized scores for older ages, they do not have a structure for suggesting future performance of whatever intellectual construct the scales are actually tapping. They also do not intercorrelate well with other measurements of intelligence as a child grows older (Lewis & McGurk, 1972). This is not unexpected: Many things occurring during a child's first 2 years can affect his or her intellectual future. Infant IQ tests are therefore most useful for their ability to flag problems early in a child's developmental history, such as deficits in neurological and emotional functioning or environmental inadequacies (Anastasi, 1976).

While this discussion appears to favor the notion of change rather than constancy in regard to human intellectual functioning, other indicators of intelligence suggest some stability between infancy and later childhood (Colombo, 1993). For example, the efficiency of the habituation-dishabituation response varies from person to person. Children measured for this ability as infants and administered standard IQ tests as preschoolers and preadolescents have shown considerable consistency in performance between the two measures (Rose et al., 1988; Rose & Feldman, 1997). A negative correlation has been found between the amount of time spent gazing at a visual stimulus as an infant and intelligence scores produced as an adolescent. The extensive gazing has been interpreted as evidence of needing a greater amount of time to figure out the stimulus, thus possibly providing a first indication of an information-processing style that spans the length of childhood (Sigman et al., 1997). Visual recognition memory at age 7 months has been demonstrated to correlate with IQ scores at age 11 years (Rose & Feldman, 1995).

Another study looking at the ability of a group of infants to distinguish between different patterns found that when the children were reassessed at age 3 or 4, their intelligence test scores correlated with this early ability (Miranda et al., 1977). One study found that the capacity of 3-month-old infants to distinguish between sounds correlated highly with their scores on standard intelligence tests at age 5 years (O'Connor et al., 1984). Yet another study showed that infants' reaction times, reflecting how they expected stimuli to behave, correlated with their intelligence test scores at preschool age (Dougherty & Haith, 1997). So if we continue to want to predict what we call "intelligence," perhaps studying individual cognitive processes as they occur within an infant's normal daily living would give us more useful knowledge than the artificial, statistically generated constructs represented by intelligence tests (Slater, 1995a).

What can parents and caregivers do to enhance babies' intellectual development?

PAVING PATHWAYS ALONG INFANT COGNITIVE MILESTONES: SUPPORTING INTELLECTUAL GROWTH

Clearly, receiving adequate one-on-one interaction with parents and caregivers affects babies' intellectual development. Recent studies of orphans living in poor-quality Romanian institutions have shown that even if adopted out at age 3, children with early one-on-one deprivation continue to demonstrate less-advanced cognitive development than those who had been adopted out at birth (Castle et al., 1999; O'Connor et al., 2000). Some overanxious parents have reacted to this knowledge by trying to create "superbabies," systematically drilling infants with material more manageable by older children (Meyerhoff, 1992). This trend has not necessarily addressed the best interests of infant cognitive development and in fact has the potential to do more harm than good (see the Tried . . . . and True boxes on pages 172–173).

So in what other ways can parents and caregivers assist an infant's cognitive growth? The key to applying infant cognitive development research is to remember Vygotsky's zone of proximal development, and foster the child's environmental influences in ways that support the next upcoming phase of learning potential. Some suggestions that seem to hold promise follow.

One method for identifying environmental influences likely to support intellectual growth is to examine the households where children seem to falter. One group of researchers developed a list of risk factors in such homes (Sameroff et al., 1993). The children in these homes had preschool IQ scores that were significantly lower than children from homes without the risk factors. Some of the conditions the parents had relatively little control over: the head of household was unemployed or low-skilled; the mother had not finished high school; the father was absent; or the family had been traumatized by stressful events, represented a minority group, or had three or more siblings in the home. Nevertheless, other factors suggested that parental growth in some areas might improve a child's lot. Interventions can adjust such variables as the mother's mental health, the rigidity of the parents' childrearing values, and the limited expression of positive feelings toward the child.

Measurements taken by research tools offer another potential source of information. One set of researchers developed an instrument for measuring a home's effectiveness at fostering a child's intellectual development (Caldwell & Bradley, 1984). The *Home Observation for Measurement of the Environment (HOME)* inventory contains six subscales that invite answers to the following questions:

► How responsive are parents, both verbally and emotionally, to the needs of the child?
► Do parents avoid restricting or punishing the child?

▶ What is the home environment like, and does activity structure allow for exposure to additional environments?

▶ Are play materials appropriate for the child's age?

▶ Do parents regularly interact with the child?

▶ Are daily stimulation opportunities varied?

Children whose early environments score higher on the HOME inventory are found to be more intellectually advanced as they grow older (Bradley et al., 1989). All of the factors on the HOME inventory are ones that we can choose to enhance. We can whole-heartedly involve ourselves in an infant's play and emotional and verbal life; we can reorganize any environment to be more infant-friendly; we can increase our expression of positive feelings and reduce punitiveness and unnecessary restrictions; and we can provide new and varied stimulation just by taking the infant along with us in our daily routine.

We might next ask, does eliminating risk factors make a difference for children? Apparently so. Studies find that the more a mother knows about child development at the time of infancy, the better the quality of the home environment, the fewer the child behavioral problems at age 12 months, and the higher the scores on intelligence tests at age 3 years (Benasich & Brooks-Gunn, 1996). Therefore child development centers focus on educating high-risk mothers of infants in the areas of childrearing, home management, nutrition, health, and related topics. At-risk homes receiving this kind of intervention have been found to produce preschoolers with higher intelligence test scores than those not receiving such help (Andrews et al., 1982).

So, a number of general principles and conditions appear to contribute to an ideal environment for promoting infant cognitive growth. But what about the critical instances of infant learning? What do you do when your toddler walks up to you with a new toy and presents an opportunity for teaching? A good rule of thumb for children of any age is to avoid doing those tasks that they are well able to do for themselves. Therefore the extent to which you assist a baby with any activity will differ according to the child's unique zone of proximal development. The sensorimotor style of infant and toddler learning provides a useful blueprint for creating lessons.

For example, suppose as a baby shower gift your child received a colorful ringed stack-toy. A 2-week-old infant will enjoy just having the toy placed in view or perhaps seeing it rocked or turned while he or she observes. At age 3 or 4 months the child will try to bat at it and perhaps move it as well, but will still need you to place it within reach. As gross motor control develops, you can guide the child's hand movements to show how the rings can be knocked off the peg. Then as fine motor control improves, you can demonstrate how the rings can be picked up and restacked, and perhaps directly guide the child's hand as well. A 2- or 3-year-old has developed enough cognitive organization to benefit from being shown how the rings can be restacked in an intended order.

Most of us would agree with the common sense of providing age-appropriate assistance. A 2-week-old infant is not going to benefit from being

BOX 6.1   Early experience and brain development

Tried.....

Radell, P. L., & Gottlieb, G. (1992). Developmental intersensory interference: Augmented prenatal sensory experience interferes with auditory learning in duck embryos. *Developmental Psychology, 28,* 795–803.

WHEN ETHICS PREVENT USING A TRUE EXPERIMENTAL design on human beings, scientists sometimes test their hypotheses on animals. Radell and Gottlieb wanted to study whether premature stimulation of child developmental processes can have a negative effect on the developing infant. Since the sensory abilities of birds and mammals mature in the same sequence, they decided to study the sensory development of baby ducks. A normally developing duckling will learn to prefer its mother's call after hatching, a characteristic clearly consistent with ensuring the survival of the species. Could the development of this crucial biological programming be led astray by tampering with the normal sensory input experienced during early development?

The participants for this study were mallard duck embryos due to hatch the following day. The eggshell surrounding their heads was removed to enhance sensory stimulation. The eggs were then placed on a gently rocking neonatal waterbed. Every 2.7 minutes the ducklings were additionally stimulated with a maternal duck call. There were several control groups: ducklings exposed to the duck call alone, to waterbed stimulation alone, to alternating conditions of waterbed stimulation and auditory stimulation, to a more natural level of motion stimulation accompanying the call, or to postnatal rather than prenatal stimulation.

About 6 hours after the ducklings in the experimental group were fully hatched they were exposed to two si-multaneous maternal duck calls: the one they had heard earlier and an unfamiliar call. They were judged as indicating a preference if they spent at least twice as much time in the vicinity of one of the two calls. The researchers found that the ducklings in the experimental condition were more likely to fail to learn their maternal call. The multiple control group ducklings developed the normal preference for the familiar call. While the statistical significance of the differences between the experimental group and the control groups were modest, the findings are consistent with those of other investigations regarding the effect of premature stimulation on baby ducks.

Interference with normal sensory stimulation during early development therefore seems to create a learning disability of sorts in ducklings. Researchers suggest that the deficit occurs because the overstimulated brain structures become overdeveloped and displace or interfere with development of the structures responsible for learning a maternal call preference.

Does this study add to our knowledge of the development of human babies' brains? As with any compromised experimental design, we must apply the findings of animal studies to the understanding of human functioning with caution. Nevertheless, we can probably safely speculate that normal human infant brain development may also respond to a normal, optimal sensory environment, rather than one with novel forced emphases. We might also consider that brain development, even as biologically well-programmed as it is, may be susceptible to the presence of extremely abnormal environmental input.

... and True

BOX 6.2   The optimal infant brain development environment

PARENTS ARE EAGER TO DO THE BEST FOR THEIR BABIES. One look at the sheer number of available books on parenting and childbirth tells us that there is a considerable market for any information of this sort. The specific topics discussed in parenting manuals typically reflect the values or societal emphases of the era. In recent years in various Western societies there has been a trend toward trying to beef up babies' intellectual development. One such strategy has consisted of trying to promote development of certain skills earlier than they normally develop, such as by presenting infants and toddlers with alphabet and word cards, drilling them with numbers and simple equations, and surrounding them with educational toys.

What can parents who are trying to enhance their children's intellectual development learn from the duckling study? Jane Healy (1994) is concerned that massive overemphases of any sort might actually hamper a child's brain development; if babies are overstimulated by advanced material, normal development of other important brain structures and learning abilities may be impaired.

Healy also expresses other concerns. For example, a child trying to accomplish the more advanced tasks may learn to use immature neural connections and develop a substandard processing habit that eventually interferes with the use of more appropriate neural networks. Pressure to perform in ways that are inconsistent with natural developmental processes can also lead to stress, and excessive stress can result in emotional difficulties and can interfere with development of cognitive skills.

In addition, these "advancement"-oriented activities are not congruent with what an infant or toddler needs for optimal intellectual development. As you saw in the discussion of sensorimotor intelligence, children learn most by being actively involved with the environment, not by sitting passively and being presented with stimulation. They also need activity that is relevant to their lives. Discovering that pushing a funny-looking button results in a beeping noise is not anywhere near as relevant to the infant's learning about the world as discovering the properties of gravity as the bored child tosses the educational toy out of the playpen. Healy likens this force-feeding of later-developing skills to racing a limousine down a goat path. You may actually reach your destination, but you won't like the condition of the limo once you do!

The duckling study also suggests the possibility of an optimal environment for the developing infant brain. Healy makes several suggestions for parents who want to ensure such an environment:

- Minimize the amount of time the child spends in a restricted environment, such as a crib or playpen. The child has the most opportunity for learning when turned loose in a baby-proofed home.
- Get down on the floor and join in the child's chosen activities. Babies spontaneously choose activity appropriate to their current window for learning.
- When talking to an infant or toddler, link your language to what the child is experiencing. Express such thoughts as "soft kitty," "big noisy truck," and "yummy pudding" *while* they are describing the child's current experience. Remember the importance of making sure the child is already focusing on the event.
- Present new toys or objects one at a time.
- Be patient with the child's delight in continually repeating the same activity. Neural networks take many repetitions before they will become firmly established.
- Provide playthings that will help the infant or toddler explore cause and effect. Some educational toys provide this experience, but remember the need for relevance: the experience of pounding a cardboard box with a wooden spoon provides more real-world learning than opening a little plastic door to see a picture of a kitty. Consider placing the child's playthings on an accessible shelf rather than in a toy box, so the child can more easily choose the toy that best fits his or her current interest.
- Whenever possible, reinforce and join in with early efforts at new challenges *as they spontaneously occur.* If your home has too many "no-no's," you may want to consider a little reorganization to make it an optimal learning environment.

Healy, J. M. (1994). *Your child's growing mind: A practical guide to brain development and learning from birth to adolescence,* 2nd ed. New York: Doubleday.

shown how to stack the toy, and a toddler will only become bored with being a passive bystander if you constantly fetch and manipulate toys in ways with which the child is already familiar. When parents fine-tune their assistance so that it acknowledges both the child's current interest and the next most useful step for their babies, their child's exploratory competence becomes more advanced (Belsky et al., 1980).

LANGUAGE AND COMMUNICATION

Few milestones are as exciting for parents as hearing baby's first word—especially if it is "mama" or "dada"! When infants begin to verbalize their thoughts, this new ability underscores their membership in our language-oriented human species.

How do nature and nurture interplay in early language development?

Theories of Language Development

Early theorists took extreme views regarding the origins of language development, each mirroring his or her stand on the nature versus nurture controversy. As was consistent with its explanations for the rest of human functioning, the behaviorist perspective examined the role of nurture in language development. Skinner believed that all language was learned through operant conditioning (Skinner, 1957). He noticed that as babies make random sounds, parents' reinforcement of a particular verbalization would result in repeated efforts. Or, parents might ignore certain utterances, and these would eventually become extinguished. Imitation also demonstrates its importance in the infant's acquisition of language. These processes are most evident as we consider a child's primary language. Children growing up in an Italian home certainly aren't likely to try to speak Chinese! They will speak Italian, or whatever other language is spoken in their presence.

On the other hand, Chomsky focused on the role of nature in language acquisition (Chomsky, 1957). He pointed out that grammar and other rules of language are too complicated to emerge solely on the basis of parental reinforcement. He suggested that we are all born with a **language acquisition device**, an innate grammatical method for putting language together once enough words have been learned to do so. After all, the languages of the world show remarkable consistencies in sentence structures and how words are used to represent such parts of speech as nouns, verbs, and so on. Furthermore, babies of all cultures seem to reach various milestones of language development at around the same time. How could such similarities exist without some form of biological predisposition?

Researchers now recognize that both views hold some validity and work hand in hand (Bloom, 1991; Werker & Tees, 1999). The interactionist perspective suggests that children have an innate capacity for language that is shaped by input from the environment and the child's interactive involvement with it

(Barnet & Barnet, 1998; Chapman, 2000; Karmiloff-Smith, 1995; McCune, 1995). Individual differences of both environment and innate capacity also influence language development. For example, inborn temperament can affect acquisition of language, as children inheriting a shy temperament can be slower to initiate speech (Paul & Kellogg, 1997). The importance of capacity for interaction with the environment is demonstrated by the finding that a child's ability to match the mother's gaze at 6 months correlates with future language development (Morales et al., 1998). And both influences are moderated by the quality of the child's attentional and memory processes as he or she learns to focus on appropriate referents while learning words (Samuelson & Smith, 1998).

An interesting language style seems to spontaneously emerge as parents react to an infant's or toddler's early vocalizations. Dubbed "**motherese**," it involves the use of exaggerated intonation and expressiveness. As the child grows older, parents use simplified words and very short sentences delivered in a melodic style with excessive enunciation. As if responding to some internal programming of their own, parents seem to limit expression choices to those that are one step ahead of the child's current expressive ability (Tamis-LeMonda et al., 1998). Infants and young children are in fact attracted to its melodic nature as they select the linguistic input to which they will attend, and show a general preference for motherese over normal adult conversational styles (Cooper & Aslin, 1994; Morgan, 1994; Pegg et al., 1992).

Language acquisition processes appear to work most effectively in childhood. If you have ever befriended non-English-speaking immigrants, you probably noticed that their children pick up the new tongue a lot faster than they do. Furthermore, the parents' English will no doubt be decorated with a foreign accent, while the children will have the accent of the locale in which they learned English. These observations, among others, have led researchers to believe that there is a critical period for language acquisition. Between birth and 4 months, infants are able to distinguish each of the 150 speech sounds used among all human languages (Kuhl, 1991). However, by about 10 months of age they are able to discriminate only those sounds that are present within their native tongue (Jusczyk et al., 1994).

Other evidence suggesting the existence of a critical period for language acquisition comes from children who have been rescued from near-wild conditions. One well-known example is the sad story of "Genie" (Curtiss, 1977). Genie suffered the misfortune of being born into an unfathomably abusive home environment. She spent her first 14 years of life locked in a back room, not only deprived of exposure to language but also beaten if she made any noise or attempts at language herself. After being rescued, she was the object of intensive rehabilitation efforts, including efforts at remedying her absence of language. Like other adult language-deprived individuals, she was able to learn only a simple vocabulary and compose primitive two- or three-word sentences, generally absent of syntax or grammar. In contrast, even normal 6-month-old infants are capable of recognizing certain hierarchical organizations of words, phrases, and clauses (Jusczyk, 2000). These observations suggest that a learning window present at a very young age may close its shutters by the time children reach adulthood.

Acquiring Language

Any new mother can tell you that her baby communicates—an ability especially effective during the wee hours of the morning (Adamson, 1996)! As her child grows older she will begin hearing the early beginnings of the development of language, the little goo's and gaa's that warm the cockles of a mother's heart. These first sounds, usually beginning at around age 2 months, are called **cooing**: The child establishes eye contact with the caregiver and makes a sing-song sound. Laughing and varying types of fussing also join the child's communication skills at this age.

By the time babies reach age 6 months they have used their well-developed oral musculature to practice a variety of new sounds, including squealing, spitting noises, and crooning. Between 6 and 10 months they typically make their first attempts at developing words by repeating certain single-consonant/single-vowel syllables, such as "da-da-da" or "ba-ba-ba." These verbalizations are called **babbling**, and are performed for the purpose of experimentation rather than to convey any meaning that might be attributed to the sounds produced, although intensity and duration my differ during times of stress (Davis et al., 2000). At this age they also begin using **preverbal gestures**—early communication tactics such as pointing at something they want, holding their arms out when they want to be picked up, or holding something up to show it to a caregiver.

Babies begin to comprehend that certain sounds have a certain meaning at around 10 to 12 months. They begin with a wide band of verbal sensitivities that

This infant cannot yet speak words, but he can communicate his thoughts by using preverbal gestures such as pointing.

Anne Rippy/Image Bank

they modify as their language ability tunes in to what is meaningful in their native tongue, providing the origins of their first words (Werker & Tees, 1999). Most languages have accommodated to infant babbling by attributing meaning to the sounds babies spontaneously produce, as in words like "mama" and "papa," thus making the job of beginning meaningful verbalization somewhat easier.

If you have studied a foreign language, you know that you understand a lot more of what you hear than is evidenced by your speaking ability. This human tendency, reflecting our **receptive language ability**, was present even when we were infants. Babies can understand and respond to verbalizations such as "no," "kitty," and "Daddy's home" before their first spoken words. Seventeen-month-old infants have even been shown to make the sophisticated distinction between "Big Bird is tickling Cookie Monster" and "Cookie Monster is tickling Big Bird," involving language utilization far beyond their expressive ability (Hirsh-Pasek et al., 1985). As they grow older, and probably throughout their lives, their receptive language ability will continue to be at least one step ahead of their speaking ability.

From age 1 year onward, babies slowly but surely shape their vocalizations to sound like those that will become part of their native tongue. When these single words are expressed as entire thoughts, as they often are, they are called **holophrases**. "Deuce" may mean "I want some juice;" pointing and saying "ball" may mean "the ball is under the couch." How often have parents shuddered in anticipation of what collection of information is being communicated by a toddler's simple utterance of "uh-oh!" At age 18 months most babies can say about fifty recognizable words.

European-American toddlers' vocabularies contain an overabundance of nouns, but this bias reflects the word usage of those around them. Toddlers speaking Mandarin Chinese tend, like their mothers, to use more verbs in their vocalizations than their English-speaking counterparts (Tardif et al., 1999). Likewise, Korean-speaking mothers interacting with their infants use a more balanced collection of verbs and nouns than do English-speaking mothers (Choi, 2000).

At age 21 months toddlers have usually begun putting words together in meaningful ways—simple two-word sentences, such as "juice gone" or "ball mine," that are called **telegraphic speech**. Like the language used in a telegraph, such verbalizations emphasize the meat of what a child is trying to communicate. As their capacity for language grows in leaps and bounds, 2-year-olds begin putting together three words or more and use fewer and fewer holophrases as they approach the preschool years.

The finer meanings of learned words follow after the actual acquisition of vocabulary. When a child first starts using the word "dog," he or she is likely to assign the same name to cows, guinea pigs, squirrels, or any other four-legged furry creature. This is called **overextension**. Many a mother has suffered the embarrassment of having her youngster point and say "da-da" at every man they pass in the grocery store. The breadth of meaning of a word may also at first be too narrow. A toddler may learn to ask for "juice" in reference to apple juice. If

Grandma tries to satisfy this child's request with grape juice, consumption may be replaced by experimentation with the properties of gravity. Limited meanings of this nature are called **underextension**, and possibly occur because the limited cognitive processing of the very young hampers their ability to make comparisons among like objects (Waxman & Klibanoff, 2000). Every new vocabulary word carries with it the need to establish boundaries of meaning, a process the child will continue to employ throughout childhood.

How can parents and caregivers assist babies' language development?

PAVING PATHWAYS ALONG INFANT COGNITIVE MILESTONES: ENHANCING LANGUAGE DEVELOPMENT

Language ability is based to a certain extent on inherited qualities. When adopted 1-year-olds' verbal abilities are compared to those of both their adoptive and biological parents, the correlation with their biological parents' is the stronger (Hardy-Brown & Plomin, 1985). Girls become somewhat more verbally advanced than boys at a fairly early age, and as they grow from infants to young women, neuroimaging demonstrates that the language-associated regions of their brains become proportionately larger than those of their male counterparts (Harasty et al., 1997; Jacklin & Maccoby, 1983). Parents' tendency to speak in motherese also seems to come naturally, requiring no special training or effort to promote their child's development of language. Mothers also seem to naturally suit their language-related gestures to their infant's current processing level, thus capitalizing on the child's zone of proximal development (Colas, 1999).

Whatever individual differences are rooted in heredity, there are specific methods that seem to enhance the natural process of language acquisition during infancy and toddlerhood. The simplest technique is to simply repeat back to the child whatever was said, perhaps making minor adjustments in pronunciation or sentence completion. If the child points and says "ki'," the parent can say "Yes, kitty!" Trying to get the toddler to say it back to you the "right" way, however, does not seem to promote language acquisition. If anything, it is more likely to frustrate the child and discourage future attempts at speaking (Leach, 1990). Most children will spontaneously clean up their language blunders by imitating what they hear repeated.

Another strategy for encouraging language acquisition is to create conversation out of the child's comments. If the child says "baby crying" the parent can respond with comments such as "Why is the baby crying?," "The baby is sad," or "The baby needs her bottle." Such responses are important for letting the child know that the message was successfully sent, as well as reinforcing the child's efforts with the delivery of a communicative response. Consistent with the philosophy of respecting a child's zone of proximal development, such responses are best digested if they are only one step ahead of the child's current language ability.

Even when babies' vocabularies are still extremely limited, their receptive language can be enhanced by describing objects or events to which they are attending. As toddlers learn to appreciate their parents' capacity for providing linguistic information, they begin using them as a sort of walking dictionary, pointing to various objects and asking "Dat?"

Healy (1994) offers a number of useful guidelines for fostering babies' communication skills:

▶ Babies best understand warm and loving interactions. Speaking in a friendly, personal tone of voice will increase the likelihood that the child associates a verbalization with something meaningful (Dixon & Smith, 2000).

▶ Much is communicated by eye contact. Most children naturally attempt to establish eye contact while speaking, and caregivers should also make a point of using eye contact as they speak to the child.

▶ Before attempting to communicate, caregivers should ascertain that they have the baby's attention such as by saying "Look here," "See this?" or simply establishing eye contact. Caregivers should keep in mind that the most effective of these language lessons will occur when language is connected with whatever the infant is already observing or doing.

▶ Older siblings are natural language teachers. Encouraging and supporting their interactional efforts can promote baby's speaking skills.

Above all, caregivers should remember that babies learn language within a social context. Simply exposing a child to language through television, radio, or recordings has an extremely limited effect on language development (Snow et al., 1976). The more individual time caregivers dedicate toward verbally interacting with children, the faster their language ability will develop (Tomasello et al., 1986). Here patience is especially a virtue: Going with the flow of their clumsy early attempts will help children much further along than will expressing personal frustrations, even if caregivers have to pretend to understand what babies are saying (Nelson, 1973). Certainly if most of what a child hears is angry admonishments to not do this or stay away from that, the child will not feel especially encouraged to tune into the world of communication. Language acquisition benefits most when it is a product of a friendly game between two actively engaged partners.

SUMMARY

Piaget's Sensorimotor Intelligence

Piaget called the first 2 years of cognitive development sensorimotor intelligence because so much of infant learning comes by way of sensory input and physical interaction with the environment. Over the course of six substages infants experiment with progressively more sophisticated forms of circular reactions, shaping their perceptions of the world and themselves as they do so. Piaget suggested that infants do not develop a sense of object permanence until age 8 or 9 months, but more recent research has supported the notion that much younger infants are capable of this cognitive skill.

Information-Processing

The information-processing perspective on infant cognitive development examines the individual mental processes involved in learning. Studies have shown that infants have a capacity for memory even as early as 6 weeks, and that 6-month-old infants' experiences have been retained as memories for as long as 2 years.

Evidence of Infant Learning

By watching patterns of habituation and dishabituation, classical conditioning, and operant conditioning, we can see that infants are capable of many forms of learning at birth. Their capacity for imitation has been demonstrated as they copy certain facial expressions when they are only a few days old, and at age 9 months they have even shown some capacity for deferred imitation. During the second year of life, toddlers incorporate more and more schemes and pieces of learning as they apply their understanding of the world to daily living.

Intelligence

Intelligence reflects both aptitude and achievement. Thus a child's varying life experiences, exposures, and degrees of effort expended can affect a child's intellectual functioning, and its level can be expected to vary over time. Standardized intelligence tests focus mainly on analytical intelligence, and are designed more for children of preschool age and above. Infant intelligence is more accurately measured using developmental scales, which are actually more useful for flagging possible problems than for predicting future IQs. Observing infants' habituation-dishabituation response efficiency, ability to distinguish between visual patterns or sounds, and reaction times based on expectations provides early prediction of intelligence.

While intelligence is in part hereditary, environmental influences also play a major role. Cognitive growth can be negatively affected by a number of unfortunate family-related conditions, but in many cases the effects can be reversed through parenting education, assistance, and counseling. The *Home Observation for Measurement of the Environment* is designed to assess positive-impact conditions in an infant's home. In addition to minimizing or maximizing factors revealed by this measure, caregivers can help infants learn by demonstrating new skills or challenging them as they reveal their interest of the moment, and by remembering to keep lessons age-appropriate.

Language and Communication

Skinner proposed that language is learned by means of reinforced or extinguished verbalizations—the nurture position; Chomsky proposed that language emerges because of an innate language acquisition device—the nature position. The interactionist perspective suggests that children have an innate ability for language that is shaped by interactions with the environment. A language style called "motherese" is a major reinforcer and attention-getter for infants as they develop their language skills. There may be critical periods for learning certain language skills, since children deprived of language stimulation beyond a certain age appear to lose the capacity to develop some language abilities as they grow older.

Early infant language consists of cooing, babbling, and preverbal gestures. Infants begin to ascribe meaning to their words at around 10 to 12 months and will begin to put words together meaningfully toward the end of the second year. Infants use holophrases and telegraphic speech as abbreviated versions of what they are attempting to communicate. Infants' receptive language ability exceeds their expressive language ability, as is also true for adults. As infants learn new words they will typically at first underextend or overextend the boundaries of word meanings.

Language ability also appears to be in part heritable. However, caregivers can encourage language development by reinforcing all efforts and providing feedback reflecting the next more advanced level of language ability. Warm and loving interactions, eye contact, being sure to have the child's attention during interactions, and treating language as a friendly, cooperative game are all techniques likely to encourage language acquisition.

KEY TERMS

AB search error
babbling
circular reaction
cooing
deferred imitation
development quotient
deviation intelligence quotient
  (DIQ)
dishabituation
equilibration

goal-directed behavior
habituation
holophrase
infantile amnesia
intelligence quotient (IQ)
language acquisition device
"motherese"
norms
object permanence
organization

overextension
preverbal gestures
primary circular reaction
receptive language ability
secondary circular reaction
sensorimotor intelligence
standard scores
telegraphic speech
underextension

CONCEPT REVIEW

1. Babies' practice of learning by means of moving about, interacting with the environment, and feeling what the world is like promotes development of their _____ intelligence.

2. Babies' early cognitive schemes are first disrupted then rebuilt during the processes of _____ and _____.

3. Babies' first exploratory interactions, _____, help them establish early schemes focusing predominantly on recreating personal sensations; between 4 and 8 months _____ help them learn how their actions affect the environment. By the end of the first year they are engaging in _____ behaviors that make use of multiple learned schemes.

4. While Piaget observed babies under age 8 months reacting as if they did not remember the existence of objects that were out of view, later studies of _____ suggest that such reactions occur because of infants' insufficiently developed _____ coordination and/or inability to coordinate _____.

5. By the end of the second year babies can solve problems by means of manipulating _____, rather than needing to try out potential solutions.

6. While infants demonstrate the capacity for forming memories at a very early age, we do not retain our infant memories, most likely because of the extensive _____ occurring during the infant years. This forgetting is called _____.

7. Newborns have demonstrated their amazingly early capacity for learning in studies observing patterns of _____ and _____, _____, _____, and _____.

8. Intelligence tests establish _____ representing the expected score for a child of a certain age. Current IQ tests establish an individual child's _____ by comparing his or her obtained test score to a _____ score.

9. Infant intelligence is measured by developmental tests such as the _____, which correlates well/poorly with the child's future intelligence test scores. Infant information-processing ability as demonstrated by studies of habituation and dishabituation, gazing patterns, reaction times, and distinguishing between patterns is a better/worse predictor of the child's future cognitive ability.

10. Infants who live in stimulating environments, as measured by the _____ inventory, have been found to be more intellectually advanced as they grow older.

11. In studies of risk factors, quality of maternal knowledge of child development has been associated with quality of _____, later child _____ problems, and _____ at age three.

12. Cognitive growth in infants is best encouraged by helping them learn to perform activities relevant to their _____.

13. Skinner believed language development occurs due to _____ influences, while Chomsky believed we are able to learn language because of our inborn _____. The _____ perspective of language development suggests that both processes play roles.

14. The tendency for adults and older children to speak to infants in a sing-song, simplified manner is called _____, which infants are <u>more/less</u> likely to attend to than to regular speech.

15. The fact that infants have the capacity to hear many sounds that adults cannot and then at age 1 become unable to hear the ones not regularly heard suggests that there is a _____ for learning language.

16. Early infant vocalizations such as _____ and _____ represent experimentation with making sounds; first attempts to use verbalizations for communication purposes occur at around age _____.

17. _____ are infant words that are actually intended to represent an entire thought; verbalizations representing early attempts to put two words together are called _____.

18. Infants' tendency to expand the meaning of a new word beyond its usual boundaries is called _____; their tendency to apply too restricted a meaning to a new word is called _____.

19. Jane Healy, a developmental neurologist, suggests that infant language development is best encouraged by means of _____ interactions, using _____ contact; gaining the infant's _____ before speaking, and providing opportunities for infants to interact with _____.

1) sensorimotor; 2) equilibration; organization; 3) primary circular reactions; secondary circular reactions; goal-directed; 4) object permanence; motor; schemes; 5) mental symbols; 6) brain growth; infantile amnesia; 7) habituation; dishabituation; classical conditioning; operant conditioning; imitation; 8) norms; deviation intelligence quotient (DIQ); standard; 9) Bayley Scales of Infant Development; poorly; better; 10) HOME; 11) home environment; behavioral; IQ scores; 12) zone of proximal development; 13) environmental; language acquisition device; interactionist; 14) "motherese"; more; 15) critical period 16) cooing; babbling; 10 to 12 months; 17) holophrases; telegraphic speech; 18) overextension; underextension; 19) warm and loving; eye; attention; older children

RESOURCES FOR FURTHER READING

Adamson, L. B. (1996). *Communication development during infancy.* Boulder, CO: Westview Press.

Barnet, A. B., & Barnet, R. J. (1998). *The youngest minds: Parenting and genes in the development of intellect and emotion.* New York: Simon & Schuster.

Black, M. M., Matula, K., & Black, M. M. (1999). *Essentials of Bayley Scales of Infant Development II Assessment.* New York: John Wiley & Sons.

Colombo, J. (1993). *Infant cognition: Predicting later intellectual functioning.* Thousand Oaks, CA: Sage.

Meltzoff, A. N., & Gopnik, A. (1997). *Words, thoughts, and theories.* Cambridge, MA: MIT Press.

Oppenheim, J. (1999). *The Oppenheim toy portfolio baby and toddler play book.* Oppenheim Toy Portfolio, Inc.

Simion, F., & Butterworth, G. (Eds.) (1998). *The development of sensory, motor, and cognitive capacities in early infancy: From perception to cognition.* Philadelphia: Taylor & Francis Inc.

INFOTRAC COLLEGE EDITION

For additional readings, explore InfoTrac College Edition, your online library. Go to http://www.infotrac-college.com/wadsworth and use the passcode that came on the card with your book. Try these search terms: cognition in infants, infant—education, infant—languages, intelligence and infants, intelligence tests, language acquisition, language and infants, learning and infants, memory in infants

CHILD DEVELOPMENT CD-ROM

Go to the Wadsworth Child Development CD-ROM for further study of the concepts in this chapter. The CD-ROM also includes quizzes and additional activities to expand your learning experience.

REFERENCES

For a list of references for this chapter, see the Wadsworth Psych Study Center Web site at: http://www.wadsworth.com/product/0534348092s

CHAPTER 7

Infant and Toddler Social and Emotional Development

FOCUS QUESTIONS

▶ How did early theorists' beliefs influence current notions of infant personality development?

▶ How does the quality of attachment between infant and caregiver influence a child's social and emotional development?

▶ What role does infant day care play in meeting the child's early social and emotional needs?

▶ When do infants begin demonstrating a capacity for emotions similar to those of adults and older children?

▶ What influences the emergence of and perceptions within an infant's self-concept?

▶ How can caregivers encourage development of an infant's sense of competence?

▶ How do infants perceive others?

OUTLINE

Early Personality Development
Contributions of Sigmund Freud
Erik Erikson and Psychosocial Development
Infant Attachment Theory
Importance of Infant Attachment
The Securely Attached Relationship
Measuring Infant Attachment
Fathers as Attachment Figures
Attachments with Nonparental Caregivers
Infant Day Care Influences
Paving Pathways: Choosing Infant Day Care
Separation Anxiety
Conditions Influencing Attachment
Outcome of Secure Attachment

Infant Emotions
Infant Emotional States
Infant Crying and Emotional Development
Recognizing and Responding to Others' Emotions
Self-Conceptualization
Separation-Individuation
Transitional Objects
Self-Concept
Paving Pathways: Developing Infant Competence
"Others" Concept
Self-Control

Four-year-old Brittany's parents had taken her on her first traveling vacation trip. One of the many new experiences she encountered during the adventure was eating her meals in restaurants. One evening after her parents had placed orders for their own meals, their server turned to Brittany and asked her what she would like for dinner.

"A peanut butter sandwich!" Brittany enthusiastically informed her.

"No," said Brittany's mother, "let's get her the child's chicken platter with . . ."

The server interrupted, asking Brittany, "And what would you like to drink with your peanut butter sandwich?"

"Milk," she said.

As the server turned and left they all stared after her, their mouths hanging open in disbelief.

"I know," said Brittany. "This one thinks I'm real!"

When do children begin perceiving themselves as separate, independently functioning, "real" human beings? As Brittany's reaction to her server's unique behavior implied, past experiences are at least one significant influence on how children view themselves. How much of a child's personality, emotional expressiveness, and social functioning are determined during infancy and toddlerhood? What specific mechanisms are involved, and what effect do they have on a child's eventual personal adjustment? The following discussion reflects past and current beliefs, and illuminates the important roles of attachments between infant and caregiver and parenting styles as infants separate and individuate into their unique selves.

EARLY PERSONALITY DEVELOPMENT

Chapter 3 describes inborn temperament as a major contributor to personality. This biologically based determinant of personal presentation is reflected even in the newborn's approach to life and becomes even more evident as the preschool years approach (Askan et al., 1999; Goldsmith et al., 1997). Twin studies and adoption studies of infants and toddlers have implicated heritability in such traits as motor activity level, inhibition versus extraversion, and persistence at a task (Braungart et al., 1992; Matheny, 1989; Saudino & Eaton, 1991). Even degree of "cuddliness" appears to be in part inherited, as baby girls are rated as cuddlier than baby boys even when raters are not aware of the infants' gender (Benenson et al., 1999). On the other hand, expression of positive affect and sociability appear to have a relationship with environmental factors (Goldsmith et al., 1997; 1999). Thus as with physical and cognitive development, the full complexity of a child's personality emerges and evolves in concert with varying life experiences.

Contributions of Sigmund Freud

How did early theorists' beliefs influence current notions of infant personality development?

The first attempt to conceptualize the underpinnings of infant personality development is generally credited to Sigmund Freud (Freud, 1914/1959). In the process of initiating the psychodynamic perspective of personality development, he placed substantial store in the idea that who we become depends largely upon experiences during early childhood. He believed that during the course of five innately driven psychosexual stages of development, certain internal needs or conflicts systematically came to the forefront. These needs were either successfully or unsuccessfully resolved at specific ages, with the outcome affecting a child's eventual personality. Two of his five proposed stages occur during infancy: the oral and the anal.

The **oral stage** lasts for the first year or so. Because at birth the oral musculature has achieved the most superior sensory and motor proficiency, infants depend on their mouths for much of their early activities. A good deal of their time is spent eating and sucking, and as they become more coordinated, they explore their world by trying to stick everything in their mouths.

Observing these infant behaviors, Freud proposed that during the first year the young infant's psychosexual needs are met through oral gratifications, which are largely controlled by others. If infants are provided adequate oral satisfaction, they proceed healthily to the next level of development. If, however, infants receive an inappropriate level of indulgence, Freud believed they do not sufficiently resolve the oral stage; as a consequence, he thought, they develop "fixations" that result in deficient personality traits. He believed, in short, that overindulged babies become self-indulgent adults who often are overtrusting, gullible, and overdependent, and that underindulged babies become critical, suspicious, and perhaps bitter adults.

The **anal stage** begins during the second year and may last as long as the end of the third year. At this age, in Western cultures, one of a child's most significant social events is becoming potty-trained. Struggling with a caregiver over the handling of waste elimination is one of the first occasions on which children are required to control a biological urge for the benefit of others. Freud believed that children whose parents were too pushy during potty-training would become adults who are stingy, stubborn, and preoccupied with orderliness and that children whose parents were not pushy enough would become adults who are passive, messy, and overly generous.

Erik Erikson and Psychosocial Development

Later psychodynamic theorists deemphasized the biological, psychosexual components of Freud's beliefs and focused more on the long-term effects of various infant/caregiver social need interactions. Erik Erikson proposed two stages of psychosocial development during infancy that mirror the timing of Freud's oral and anal stages (Erikson, 1985). Although Erikson also recognized the importance of feeding experiences during infancy he located their significance not in the amount of food but rather in how the child is handled during feeding. A caregiver may be attuned to the child's expression of oral need and feeding style and handle the child sensitively and lovingly, or, for any number of reasons, may miss or ignore the child's expressions of need. Erikson called this early phase of psychosocial development **basic trust versus mistrust**. Their experiences of caregivers either gratifying or not gratifying their basic needs will determine whether infants develop a trusting attitude toward others (sprinkled with a little normal distrust as they experience our human fallibility) or learn to not trust others and withdraw socially.

To the second stage, **autonomy versus shame and doubt**, Erikson assigned not only potty-training but also the many other representations of the toddler's management of individual impulses. At this age youngsters are typically moving about freely, interacting with other children, feeding themselves, and using language to express their needs and individuality. Every culture has its own set of standards for appropriate expression of self. The task of caregivers is to provide guidance and support that helps toddlers learn to comply with the expectations of the culture and still express their autonomy. Erikson proposed that children whose environments are under- or overcontrolling experience their early efforts of autonomy ambivalently and develop a sense of shame or doubt. The end result can be observed in their behavior: Children of mothers who enforce compliance either very little or by asserting a great deal of power show the greatest amount of defiance at age 2 (Donovan et al., 2000).

INFANT ATTACHMENT THEORY

How does the quality of attachment between infant and caregiver influence a child's social and emotional development?

Psychodynamically trained John Bowlby noticed how many of the early theories of infant personality development seemed to hinge on infants' relationships with mothers and eventually launched the study of mother-infant attachment (Bowlby, 1944; Bretherton, 1994; 1997). His early conceptualizations borrowed from psychodynamic and ethological theories. In his first proposals he adopted attachment processes that paralleled the ethological phenomena of imprinting and critical periods. He then merged these processes with the psychodynamic emphases that attachment occurs chiefly between an infant and a single caregiver and that learned personality styles are relatively permanent.

After spending many years engaging in systematic, sensitive studies of infant attachment, Bowlby concluded that his assumptions had been premature (Bowlby, 1988). His studies did not yield evidence of imprinting and critical periods for infant attachment behaviors, infants and young children typically develop attachment relationships with more than one adult (how could we have forgotten about Dad?), and personality styles observed during infancy are far from carved in granite (Cowan, 1997; Rutter, 1995). Bowlby joined the growing throng of child development theorists who have dismissed the psychodynamic theory of personality development as inadequate and/or contraindicated by systematic research (Emde, 1992; Zeanah et al., 1989).

The main thrust of Bowlby's theory of the importance of attachment between infant and caregiver, however, has been well supported by scientific investigation and is currently the generally accepted view of attachment during infancy (Dunn, 1993). Bowlby emphasized the importance of consistent caretaker responsiveness and sensitivity to children's individual differences during parent-infant relationship building. Effective attachment interactions determine not only how parents meet an infant's basic needs but also how they perform during learning experiences, discipline, and other parenting tasks.

Importance of Infant Attachment

What evidence supports the importance of early attachment? The possibility that mother-child attachment is based on biological need has been inferred from studies of infant monkeys, as highlighted in the Tried . . . . and True boxes on pages 190–191. We might also consider that since attachment between mother and infant of almost any species increases an infant's chances of survival, we may be looking at an adaptive trait that emerged through natural selection (Bowlby, 1988; Hinde, 1982).

Attachments and the activities of relating to attachment figures provide the primary arenas for healthy social and emotional development (Karen, 1998; Reis et al., 2000). Just as infants need physical and sensory stimulation for normal brain and body growth, so also do they need social stimulation for promoting social and emotional development. The significance of this need was

Tried

BOX 7.1   Infant bonding and adjustment

Harlow, H. F. (1958). The nature of love. *American Psychologist, 13,* 673–685.

WHY DO INFANTS BOND EMOTIONALLY WITH THEIR CAREgivers? Psychologists under the influence of the behavioral perspective proposed that love for one's parents is learned. Basic needs for relief from hunger, thirst, and pain or discomfort are most often met by the parent. From the behaviorist viewpoint, the pairing of need gratification and the presence of the parent would result in a conditioned preference for the need gratifier. However, if this phenomenon truly demonstrated behavioral principles at work, we would expect the bonding to extinguish as the child became more able to meet needs independently. In reality, we learn to love more deeply and more maturely as we grow older. Could it be that attachment to others is actually another basic need for human survival?

Harry Harlow's classic studies of baby rhesus monkeys explored this question regarding the nature of an infant's attachment to its mother. For his first landmark study he observed eight 2- to 3-day-old rhesus monkeys that had been separated from their mothers at birth. Each monkey's cage was outfitted with two surrogate mothers: a cloth mother and a wire mother. In half the cages a nipple for feeding was positioned in the middle of the wire mother, and in the other half the nipple was positioned on the cloth mother. The researchers observed how much time the baby monkeys spent with each mother.

From day one both groups of baby monkeys spent significantly more time on the cloth mother than the wire mother, regardless of which mother had been providing feedings. When the researchers tried putting fear-producing stimuli, such as a moving toy bear, in the cages, the infants clung to the cloth mother. As the monkeys grew older, the researchers tried placing some of them in a larger room filled with toys known to be pleasing to baby monkeys. Without the presence of the surrogate mother the babies showed fearful emotionality, with such behaviors as crouching, screaming, and rocking. When the cloth mother was introduced the babies would cling to it and behave less fearfully, while the presence of the wire mother did not reduce their emotionality. After a few exposures the baby monkeys accompanied by the cloth mother became braver, spending more and more time exploring their new surroundings, with occasional retreats to the cloth mother for reassurances.

What does this tell us about the emotional life of the infant? It suggests that even nonhuman primate infants require emotional sustenance, a need that apparently takes precedence over maintaining the availability of nutritional sustenance. The inner security that bolsters exploration of strange new worlds appears to require such a base of attachment. So profound is the need that children appear to actively seek it out through whatever means is provided, offering an explanation for why children exhibit attachment behaviors even when their parents are abusive.

revealed by studies during the 1940s that followed the development of human newborns raised in institutions. These babies were properly clothed and fed but were otherwise left alone in their cribs, receiving little if any interpersonal attention. By the time these infants approached age 1 year they had discontinued the usual infant attempts at social engagement such as crying, establishing eye contact, smiling, or vocalizing to caregivers (Spitz, 1945; 1965). Social and behavioral aloofness and other interpersonal difficulties followed these youngsters all the way into their adolescent years, especially if they remained institutionalized (Goldfarb, 1943).

... and True

BOX 7.2   Infant feeding

THE AFFECTIONAL NEEDS DEMONSTRATED BY HARLOW'S baby monkeys expand our understanding of the importance of infant feeding sessions. Nursing a baby not only meets nutritional needs but is also a major opportunity for providing frequent and intimate body contact. Such contact is crucial for the developing infant's need both for sensory stimulation and for attachment. What can a mother or caregiver do to maximize the emotional benefits of feeding sessions?

DO:

- Try to at least temporarily set aside current stressors and relax. Baby will sense your discomfort if you are feeling uptight.
- Change baby's diaper before the feeding, so the discomfort of being wet or soiled does not become a distraction. Check if baby is warm enough. Some babies like to be wrapped up in a blanket while they are fed.
- Hold the baby closely, comfortably resting his or her head on your arm and against your body. If you are breast-feeding, this position will be inevitable; if you are bottle feeding, mimic the breast-feeding position as closely as possible. Sticking a pillow or some other prop under your arm will help you support the baby without needing to tense up.
- Position the nipple so that the baby can easily reach it or release it. If you are breast-feeding, remember to make sure baby's nose is not pressed so closely against you that he or she has difficulty breathing.

- Look into baby's eyes, smile, speak softly, and gently stroke his or her skin. Some babies also like to be gently rocked while eating.
- Be sensitive and responsive to baby's feeding behaviors, just as you would apply interactional synchrony during other activity. Let baby determine when it is time to let up a bubble or finish the feeding session.

DON'T:

- Engage in other activities during feeding sessions. If you are caring for more than one child this may be difficult; but other activities such as reading, watching television, talking on the telephone, and low-key household chores can be set aside until later.
- Prop up a bottle with baby and leave. Obviously, such a practice eliminates opportunity for promoting attachment and security.
- Handle baby abruptly or impatiently during the feeding, or yell at the other children you may be caring for.
- Pull the nipple away prematurely. Babies are easily distracted and may briefly turn their heads away in order to check something out. Also, some babies enjoy mouthing the nipple for a little while before finishing or drifting off to sleep, even though they have clearly ceased sucking for nutritional purposes. If you are breast-feeding and your nipples get sore, try offering a pacifier at the end of the feeding.

So important do mental health professionals now consider infant-parent attachment to be that they identify certain attachment disorders of infancy as clinical diagnoses (American Psychiatric Association, 1994; World Health Organization, 1992). Numerous studies have revealed relationships between poor attachment during infancy and later personal difficulties during childhood and adulthood (Beckwith et al., 1999; Belsky & Cassidy, 1994; McCarthy & Taylor, 1999). Even as early as toddlerhood, a lower quality of social interaction with peers is observed among children who are insecurely attached (Kerns, 1994). This story does not end with childhood's end. Measures of mothers' own

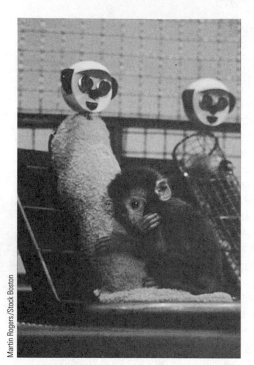

Martin Rogers/Stock Boston

Harlow drew conclusions about infant attachment by observing baby monkeys. This baby monkey is demonstrating its greater attachment to a soft terrycloth mother, even though the wire mother is the one that provides nourishment.

attachment insecurity during pregnancy have been found to predict subsequent insecure attachment with their infants, suggesting that mothers may have difficulty being part of a relationship they had never truly learned as children (Fonagy et al., 1994). Thus inadequate attachment not only affects the individual infant, but also may produce an ongoing legacy as insecure attachment patterns are transmitted intergenerationally (van IJzendoorn, 1995).

The Securely Attached Relationship

Exactly what constitutes a healthy attachment pattern? As with any interpersonal relationship, attachment is characterized by mutual liking and a desire of the parties to be with one another, and the way in which such attachments are experienced and played out by each dyad is likely to be different (Weinfield et al., 1999). Patterns of infant attachment behavior also differ cross-culturally, reflecting the norms of the particular society (Posada et al., 1995). For example, Anglo and Puerto Rican mothers have different socialization goals, with Anglo mothers oriented more toward individualism and Puerto Rican mothers oriented toward sociocentric goals. Thus Puerto Rican mothers spend more time structuring infant activity than do Anglo mothers (Harwood et al., 1999). Japanese mothers encourage more dependency during their interactions with their infants, aiming toward social development consistent with the cultural value of accomplishing goals as groups (Rothbaum et al., in press).

Mothers and their infants promote their unique attachment patterns by means of a back-and-forth communication style called **interactional synchrony** (Isabella & Belsky, 1991). As infants signal needs or otherwise attempt to communicate, their mothers respond accordingly, as a mother does by moving her head to half-way meet her infant's struggling gaze. Infants as young as 4 months demonstrate sensitivity to the timing and structure of social exchanges to which they have been exposed (Rochat et al., 1999).

Emotional states are especially fertile ground for demonstrating interactional synchrony, as when a mother speaks with a vocal intonation that mirrors the child's mood. The communication style called motherese (see Chapter 6) is a classic example of interactional synchrony during language acquisition. Parents even adjust their singing style when performing for their infants, mirroring infant preference for the features of the altered version (Trainor, 1996; Trehub et al., 1997). Likewise, infants respond differently to the varying characteristics of their mothers' renditions, becoming more outwardly focused during play-type songs and inwardly focused during lullabies (Rock et al., 1999).

These investments of maternal sensitivity contribute mightily toward the development of healthy infant attachment, and the payoffs begin early (De Wolff & van IJzendoorn, 1997; Thompson, 1997; van IJzendoorn et al., 2000; Volker et al., 1999). Even at age 4 months, greater interpersonal engagement and self-regulation are observed among infants whose mothers show greater emotional availability and quality of interactional synchrony (Kogan & Carter, 1996). Synchrony of emotional expressiveness at both 3 months and 9 months has been associated with the child's capacity for self-control at age 2 years—even when temperament, intelligence, and maternal style are taken into account (Feldman, Greenbaum, & Yirmiya, 1999). A longitudinal study showed an *inverse relationship* between healthy maternal responsiveness during infancy and disruptive behavior during middle childhood (Wakschlag & Hans, 1999). The success of this mutually responsive relationship during infancy also appears to have a relationship with development of conscience (Kochanska & Murray, 2000). Though mothers' and infants' needs will obviously conflict occasionally, these temporary asynchronies actually provide opportunities for working through frustrations and developing ways of coping and resolving conflicts (Biringin et al., 1997).

As interactional synchrony develops within the dyad, the mother becomes increasingly sensitive to her infant's individual peculiarities and preferences, eventually learning to anticipate them. Likewise the infant learns to anticipate that such needs will be met. Thus when the infant becomes capable of independent locomotion, the child who trusts the ongoing presence and sensitivity of the mother feels free to explore the environment, knowing that he or she can always return to mother and use her as a secure "base" (Bowlby, 1969; 1988; Waters & Cummings, 2000).

Measuring Infant Attachment

How can you tell if an infant is securely attached? The **Strange Situation** is an assessment technique measuring infant attachment quality between the ages of 1 and 2 years. A mother and infant are observed over a 20-minute period while in a playroom. As the infant plays and interacts with the mother, several events occur, such as a stranger entering the room and the mother leaving and returning. From observations of infants' reactions to the Strange Situation, researchers eventually identified four general types of attachment (Ainsworth et al., 1978; Main & Solomon, 1990):

Secure Attachment. Infants rated as experiencing **secure attachment** are comfortable exploring new surroundings, all the while using mother as a safe base to which they can return. They cry if their mothers leave and are not easily comforted by the stranger. When their mothers return, securely attached infants seek them out and are easily consoled.

Avoidant Attachment. The hallmark of **avoidant attachment** is indifference. Such infants are content to play independently in the new situation, but are no more responsive to their mothers and their comings and goings than they are to the stranger. The mother's return after the brief absence evokes little if any enthusiasm.

Resistant Attachment. Infants classified as experiencing **resistant attachment** are clingy, preferring closeness to the mother over exploring the playroom. They become extremely upset when their mothers leave and show continuing distress when they return, as evidenced by tantrum behaviors and an inability to be consoled.

Disorganized/Disoriented Attachment. Infants experiencing **disorganized/ disoriented attachment** react in ways that seem contradictory or confused. They may look blankly at mother after her return and not approach her, or exhibit crying periods that seem to occur for no apparent reason. This form of attachment is believed to be the most severely insecure.

Because much current research on infant attachment is based on the use of the Strange Situation, we are well advised to remember its limitations (Lamb et al., 1982). First, the technique picks up on only a certain collection of attachment-related behaviors. An infant may demonstrate attachment of greater or lesser quality in other circumstances. Second, the conclusions drawn by those using the technique depend upon the presupposition that separation has the same meaning for all infants, whereas the meaning of separation depends on the infant's personal experiences.

In this respect, cultural differences become a special concern. For example, infants in cultures that encourage independence during infancy, as is the case in Germany, may be mistakenly classified as avoidantly attached (Grossman et al., 1985). Japanese infants show a higher incidence of resistant attachment than U.S. infants. Japanese mothers so rarely leave infants with strangers that their infants might be expected to experience such an event as utter abandonment (Miyake et al., 1985). Furthermore, the goals of independence and self-expression that are so central to healthy infant development in Western cultures run counter to the goals of group dependence and self-restraint that are more adaptive for an infant who will eventually live in a Japanese culture (Rothbaum et al., in press). Thus a rating considered maladaptive in one culture may actually be desirable in another. Although cultural differences result in certain inaccuracies, the technique has nevertheless been extensively used cross-culturally because of the apparent validity and utility of the secure attachment classification (van IJzendoorn & Kroonenberg, 1988).

Fathers as Attachment Figures

I once overheard an exasperated father state, "If you want to speak with someone who knows absolutely everything there is to know about babies, just look for a first-time mother with an 11-month-old." No doubt he had been on the receiving end of an enthusiastic new mother's appreciation for the special pattern of interactional synchrony that had emerged between herself and her child. Note also that this mother is likely to find herself suddenly knowing considerably less if she has a second child!

The research emphasis placed on mother-infant relationships reflects the traditional primacy of mother-infant over father-infant attachment in industrialized societies. Nevertheless, fathers are not outcasts from the drama of infant attachment, and in the last few decades researchers have finally begun to investigate their roles and potential effects (Grych & Clark, 1999; Pleck & Pleck, 1997). From the very beginning, men are just as responsive as women to infant cues, and their frequent visits with their newborns while they are still hospitalized clearly attests to their emotional involvement (Frodi et al., 1978; Levy-Shiff et al., 1989). While talking to their infants they vary pitch and frequency range of vocalizations in proper motherese, perhaps even more so than mothers (Warren-Leubecker & Bohannon, 1984). And they match mothers in their anxiety over leaving their new little ones in the care of others (Deater-Deckard et al., 1994).

Though equally responsive and engaged with their infants, fathers interact with somewhat less sensitivity than do mothers; they are less inclined, for instance, to retrieve their crying infants (Donate-Bartfield & Passman, 1985; Heerman et al., 1994). Their verbal interactions tend to be less supportive and more negative—criticizing, disagreeing, or disapproving—although this difference from mothers diminishes as the children grow older (Leaper et al., 1998). Such differences between the two genders thus may reflect differences in opportunities for parenting experiences. Men who choose to participate more in infant caregiving show greater sensitivity and responsiveness than those who participate less (Levy-Shiff & Israelashvili, 1988). However, in most industrialized societies mothers continue to be responsible for most infant care needs, spending substantially more time with their infants than fathers do (Lamb, 1987; 1997). When fathers feel pressed into greater responsibility by the mother's full-time employment, they may also become less responsive and sensitive (Vandell et al., 1997).

Mothers and fathers differ in other ways in how they engage their infants. While mothers' behaviors tend to be more verbal, cuddling, and oriented toward expressing affection, fathers' interactions are more likely to be characterized by a task orientation and physically stimulating and unpredictable acts of play (Clarke-Stewart, 1978; Kornhaber & Marcos, 2000; Lamb et al., 1982; Teti et al., 1988). Mothers appear to be more effective than fathers when soothing a fussy baby, even as first-time parents (Kaitz et al., 2000). Perhaps these behavioral differences make infants more inclined to look to their mothers for comfort and security and to their fathers for a play partner (Clarke-Stewart, 1989; Lamb, 1977b). Interestingly, in some less-industrialized societies the tendency for infants to seek out fathers primarily as play partners is not observed; thus these interactional tendencies may be colored by cultural influences (Hewlett, 1990). Moreover, most researchers agree that the statistical differences found between mothers' and fathers' interactive behaviors represent a very small portion of the statistical variance, with such behaviors actually varying widely among individual parents of either gender (Lamb, 1997).

Boys especially seem to prefer their fathers as playmates (Clarke-Stewart, 1978; Lamb, 1977a). This may result from fathers' tendencies to spend more time with their infant sons than with their infant daughters, a tendency that intensifies during toddlerhood (Lamb, 1977a; Woollett et al., 1982). Some suggest that this favoritism in time investment emerges naturally without the effects of nurture as a manifestation of early gender identification and socialization processes (Bronstein, 1988).

The attachments infants feel toward their fathers are both evident and important. Infants protest when left by either parent and enthusiastically greet either when they return (Field et al., 1984). Infants with less interactive fathers begin protesting at an earlier age when left in nursery school than do those with highly interactive fathers. This seemingly paradoxical finding may indicate that infants receiving less attention are slower to develop the feelings of trust that would otherwise assure them of Daddy's eventual return (Spelke et al., 1973).

When the longer-term outcomes of mother-infant and father-infant attachments are compared, attachment with mother appears to be more predictive of future competencies. Mother-child interaction at age 1 was found to be associated with IQ at 30 months, while father-infant interactions showed no such relationship (Hunter et al., 1987; Tzuriel, 1999). Preschoolers' demonstrated confidence, conflict resolution ability, and absence of problem behaviors are linked more strongly to early attachments with mothers than with fathers (Suess et al., 1992; Youngblade & Belsky, 1992). Yet fathers can indirectly influence these outcomes: the better the relationship between the parents, especially regarding supportiveness and absence of mutual criticism, the more responsive the mother is to her infant (Cox et al., 1989; Pedersen et al., 1980).

Attachments with Nonparental Caregivers

Infants also develop attachments to consistently present caregivers who are not their parents, such as other family members or day care personnel (van IJzendoorn, Sagi, & Lambermon, 1992). The quality of these attachments appears to be independent of the quality of parent/infant attachments, perhaps reflecting infants' early capacity for adapting to any environment to which they are exposed over a long term (Goossens & van IJzendoorn, 1990; Howes & Hamilton, 1992a; 1992b). Day care settings in which two caregivers are assigned to the same infant have been observed. Some similarities between the attachment patterns developed by the two infant/caregiver dyads were noted, giving rise to two hypotheses: Both caregivers reacted to the same infant temperament or each caregiver observed the other and mutually adopted an interactional style that seemed to work for that child (Fox et al., 1991; Sagi et al., 1995).

A higher incidence of insecure attachment is observed among infant/nonparental caregiver pairings than among infant/parent dyads (Howes et al., 1992; van IJzendoorn, Goldberg, et al., 1992). More than one explanation is possible. Because caregivers typically look after several children, there is a greater delay between an infant's expression of a need and the meeting of the need, thus requiring more time for the secure attachment to form. Or there could have been measurement inadequacies: The infant simply had yet to develop any form of attachment with the particular caregiver (Sagi et al., 1995).

What role does infant day care play in meeting the child's early social and emotional needs?

Infant Day Care Influences

Bowlby's early prognostications regarding the importance of mother-infant attachments resulted in misguided applications. One was a fear that if time were not spent with an infant immediately following birth, bonding would not occur (see Chapter 4). The more unfortunate misapplication occurred when the World Health Organization (WHO) announced its belief that day care should be avoided because the child's separation from the mother is detrimental to child development (World Health Organization Expert Committee on Mental Health, 1951).

However, a review of human history suggests otherwise; WHO's policy statement was founded on a few misconceptions regarding infant needs. The practice of the mother staying at home with the children while the father goes out to work is actually an anomaly of industralized societies, which extend back in history no more than about 200 years (Pleck & Pleck, 1997; Zaretsky, 1976). Before industrialization, numerous family members commonly shared the responsibility of raising children (Werner, 1984). In many nonindustrialized cultures, work and the family unit still remain merged, with children closely relating to their extended family and helping out with the family's livelihood at an early age. If such an arrangement were detrimental to the well-being of an infant, we might expect the human race to have fallen apart before it ever got started!

A preponderance of empirical evidence has since assured us that day care in and of itself is not detrimental to the well-being of the developing infant (Clarke-Stewart, 1989; Harvey, 1999; Holcomb, 1998; Scarr & Eisenberg, 1993;

In many cultures children spend substantial time with extended family members rather than with parents, such as this youngster "helping" her grandmother work the fields.

George Bellerose/Stock Boston

Trnavsky, 1998). One study of day care infants, using the Strange Situation, initially raised a few eyebrows with its finding that a somewhat greater number of day care than non-day care infants were rated as ambivalently attached (Belsky, 1986). More recent studies do not support this finding, demonstrating that experiencing day care during the first year of life produces no differences in infant/parent attachment security (National Institute of Child Health and Human Development, 1997). As noted earlier, babies react to the Strange Situation on the basis of their personal experiences. Infants who are accustomed to and comfortable being left with other trustworthy caregivers are less likely to protest as robustly as infants who are not.

Some studies have shown more advanced social maturity, capacity for emotional regulation, and independence among children who spend time in day care, perhaps demonstrating the benefits to be reaped from multiple caregiver resources (Morales & Bridges, 1996; Scarr & Eisenberg, 1993). The increased financial resources resulting from maternal employment may also provide advantages that affect children's development positively (Harvey, 1999). However, in the overall developmental picture, day care placement has relatively little significance, as was demonstrated by its failure to mediate the family-related variables that affect child development; the strengths and weaknesses of family settings affect children consistently whether or not the children are in day care (Deater-Deckard et al., 1996; National Institute of Child Health and Human Development, 1998).

The caveat to the above, of course, is the quality of the care received. Just as an inadequately skilled mother might contribute toward insecure infant attachment, so also might an inadequate day care environment. An association has indeed been found between low-quality day care and poorer emotional, social, and intellectual development (Burchinal et al., 2000; Vandell et al., 1988). And unfortunately, quality of day care in the United States varies considerably more than in many other industrialized nations (Kammerman, 1991).

PAVING PATHWAYS ALONG INFANT SOCIAL AND EMOTIONAL MILESTONES: CHOOSING INFANT DAY CARE

Suppose you are the parent of an infant and are in need of a day care facility. Because U.S. infant day care facilities vary considerably in quality, you will need to do some homework before you are likely to choose a successful placement. What should you look for? There are three broad areas you would most want to evaluate: characteristics of the workers, the environment itself, and the facility's administrative practices (American Academy of Pediatrics, 1986; Berezin, 1990; National Association for the Education of Young Children, 1986; National Institute of Child Health and Human Development, 1996).

Child Care Workers

1. What is the ratio between the number of workers and the number of children? In an infant day care center, there should be a total of no more than 18 children with at least 1 worker for every 4 children. In a home day care setting, there should be a maximum total of 6 children with no more than 2 infants or toddlers.

2. Have workers received training in child care, safety, and first aid?

3. Are the same workers always assigned to the same infants? Minimal staff re-assignment and turnover is preferable.

4. Do the workers appear to like the children and to enjoy their work?

5. Are worker interactions with children warm, sensitive, and responsive, demonstrating characteristics consistent with interactional synchrony?

The Day Care Environment

1. Is the setting clean, baby-proofed, well-lighted, well-ventilated, and in compliance with local safety codes?

2. Is the environment large enough for the number of children and workers present? A rule of thumb is a minimum of 35 square feet of indoor space per child.

3. Are highchairs, cribs, and other appropriate infant care equipment present and in good repair?

4. Are separate areas designated for sleeping, eating, playing, diapering, and the like?

5. Is there a regular schedule for eating, sleeping, and other activities, flexibly applied when necessary?

6. Is the atmosphere typically relaxed and pleasant, rather than stressed or chaotic?

Administrative Practices

1. Is the facility licensed? It may also have attained other qualifications, such as being accredited by the National Association for Education of Young Children—an indicator of an especially high-quality program.

2. Do facility administrators confer regularly with parents, welcoming their questions and input regarding their child?

3. Are administrators' expectations regarding the needs, behavior, and development of infants consistent with what you have learned from these three chapters on infant and toddler development?

Separation Anxiety

Infants develop preferences for the caregivers who have served as consistent, trustworthy partners during the dance of interactional synchrony. In fact, at around age 6 months they begin showing signs of **separation anxiety**, becoming upset if their preferred caregiver leaves the room (Thompson & Limber, 1990). They also become significantly wary of any strangers in whose care they may be left (Sroufe, 1977). Infants with inhibited temperaments are especially susceptible to these reactions (Andersson et al., 1999). Provided that their primary caregivers are sufficiently consistent and predictable in their comings and goings, by 18 months most infants figure out that Mommy or Daddy will not be gone forever and their separation anxiety subsides. Infant separation and stranger anxiety can also be lessened by keeping as much of the familiar around as possible when parents must separate from them, such as arranging to have a sitter come to the child's home rather than leaving the child at a stranger's house (Sroufe et al., 1974).

Conditions Influencing Attachment

A number of factors help or hinder the attachment process. The first factor is the individual differences the caregiver and child bring to the dyad. In any relationship, some particular pairings click while others are more prone to clash — and mother-infant dyads are no exception. Dyad partners are more likely to develop a secure attachment if they bring with them the potential for a number of relating styles — as well as a little flexibility, which allows them to experiment and make adjustments as they seek a good fit (Hinde, 1983).

Infant or caregiver temperament can affect attachment (Fox et al., 1991; Seifer & Schiller, 1997). Infants inclined toward negative emotionality are more likely to develop attachment difficulties (Vaughn et al., 1992). If the mother just isn't comfortable with a lot of physical contact, her physical aloofness from her infant may result in impaired attachment, as also will a general lack of sensitivity (Belsky et al., 1984; De Wolff & van IJzendoorn, 1997; Goossens & van IJzendoorn, 1990). Mothers prone to depression may also struggle to provide consistent synchrony as they interact with their babies (Lyons-Ruth et al., 1990).

The second factor is the environment that surrounds the dyad. Stability appears to be an essential component for the development of secure attachment. First and foremost, infants need the presence and availability of a consistent caregiver for the times when they are distressed, hungry, tired, or facing some other challenging circumstance (Rutter, 1995). The temporary instability created by major life challenges within the family — such as moving or changes in employment or income — can at least temporarily alter the quality of attachment (Vaughn et al., 1989). Disruption of relationships such as through divorce and the breaking up of families can have a negative effect on attachment; the greater impact, however, appears to stem from the discordant relationships before and after the event rather than from the split itself (Cherlin et al.,

1991; Silverstein & Auerbach, 1999). Child abuse and neglect produce a considerably unstable attachment environment and appear to be the main precursors of the more serious disorganized/disoriented attachment style (Main & Solomon, 1990).

What can be done to ensure healthy caregiver/infant attachment? Although research suggests that parental sensitivity is one of the most important components, this finding, while robust, accounts for only a small portion of infant insecurity (De Wolff & van IJzendoorn, 1997; Goldsmith & Alansky, 1987; Pederson et al., 1998). How a parent views and experiences the attachment process itself can also play a role (Stern, 1995). Education and therapeutic interventions regarding either of these components encourage secure mother-infant attachment, although preventive work seems to be more effective than trying to remedy an already shaky attachment (van IJzendoorn et al., 1995).

Outcome of Secure Attachment

By age 2 years infants who have achieved secure attachment have also developed the beginnings of many positive emotional and cognitive traits. Their sense of confidence, self-worth, and personal mastery have been bolstered by the reassuring feedback received from their caregivers. They have also established some precursors of healthy intimate relationships; they are able to seek and receive care, give care to others, and experience emotional closeness. These end results of their attachment experience thus comprise one of many factors affecting their eventual personal adjustment as their emotional and social development proceed (Belsky & Cassidy, 1994).

When do infants begin demonstrating a capacity for emotions similar to adults and older children?

INFANT EMOTIONS

One of the most important cues guiding a caregiver's attachment behaviors is the infant's expression of emotions. Emotions themselves are entirely subjective: We can use labels to describe our inner state, but we experience emotions rather than think them. People often ask one another how they are feeling, expecting to hear a verbal account, which by definition preverbal infants cannot supply. Thus we depend largely on their behavior and facial cues and infer what they may be experiencing from knowledge of our own emotional functioning.

Emotional expression appears to be affected by both nature and nurture. Evidence of infant emotional states is present at birth: Few observers of infant squalling following the birth process will quibble with the inference that considerable distress is being expressed! Across cultures almost everyone seems to recognize certain facial expressions as representing certain emotions (Ekman & Friesen, 1972). Yet how we express our emotions or behave while experiencing them may differ from culture to culture, demonstrating the impact of nurture as well (Klineberg, 1938; Izard, 1991).

Infant Emotional States

Because inferences regarding infant emotional states can be so subjective, how do researchers go about studying them? One tool is the **Maximally Discriminative Facial Movement Coding System (MAX),** which systematically studies infants' facial expressions (Izard, 1982). By summing and categorizing various combinations of facial movements, the MAX provides researchers with the most objective indicator currently available for inferring infant emotional states. Studies using the MAX have revealed the beginnings of emotional expressions at various ages. Within the first few months, infants show evidence of interest, distress, disgust, and anger. The social smile occurs by age 3 or 4 months, becoming one of the major reinforcers of caregiver interactional synchrony. During the second year of life, emerging infant facial expressions are consistent with such experiences as sadness, fear, surprise, shame, and guilt (Izard, 1991). While infants around the world show these facial expressions, there appears to be some cultural or racial difference in degree of expression, such as Chinese infants being slightly less expressive than Japanese and European-American infants (Campos et al., 1998). Table 7.1 elaborates on the appearance of emotional expressiveness in infants.

As we look at these studies we must keep in mind that expressions are dependent upon the motor ability of an infant's facial musculature. Could it be that the full range of emotions is actually present at birth but the newborn simply is not yet able to produce the corresponding facial positioning? Also, most

TABLE 7.1

The appearance of certain infant emotions Adapted with permission from C. E. Izard (1991), *The psychology of emotions.* Copyright © 1991 Plenum Publishers.

Emotion	Age of First Appearance	Facial Characteristics
Interest	Present at birth	Slight raising or knitting of brows, gazing, lips pursed
Disgust	Present at birth	Upper lip raised, nose wrinkled, tongue sticks out
Joy	1 month	Smile, raising of cheeks, crescent-shaping of eyes
Anger	4–5 months	Severe frown (squared mouth in infant), brows go downward and inward, eyes narrow
Surprise	6–8 months	Lifted brows, rounded eyes, mouth oval
Sadness	6–8 months	Inner brows lifted, frown, chin pushed upward
Fear	Second year	Inner brows and eyelids lifted, corners of mouth retracted
Shame	Second year	Gaze averted, eyelids and face lowered

mothers have noticed that their infant's facial expressions can occur spontaneously or out of sync with what they are actually experiencing (Matias & Cohn, 1993). The most widely observed example of this phenomenon is the presocial smile, a reflexive newborn smile that has been interpreted as representing everything from misfiring neural networks during presleep states to having gas (Sroufe & Waters, 1976). Taking a look at other indicators of emotions such as vocalizations and body movements may eventually help clear up some of the ambiguity in our understanding of infants' emotional states.

Infant Crying and Emotional Development

Parents become most exasperatingly aware of their infant's emotional state during crying spells. The sound of a crying infant is adaptively irritating, insofar as it spurs caregivers into doing whatever satisfies the survival needs an infant's crying may represent. Unfortunately, it is equally irritating when all basic needs have been met and the infant remains inconsolable. The abundance of books describing methods for calming fussy babies that are eagerly purchased by parents of such infants illustrates the level of their frustration as they search for ways to make baby stop crying (e.g., Hill, 1999; Orenstein, 1998; Sears, 1990).

Is this path of endeavor what the crying baby needs? Yes and no. Infant crying represents many forms of infant need and internal experience (Boukydis & Lester, 1985). Among other things, crying is the infant's method of communicating distress. How caregivers react to the distress—literally giving the infant the proverbial "shoulder to cry on"—helps the infant and young child learn to self-soothe. Recent research on infant emotional development has examined this phenomenon on a neurobiological level (Goleman, 1995; Lewis & Ramsay, 1999). Such research suggests that calming practices can help the developing brain wire its emotional responding with rational responding, providing the physical structures that will facilitate future capacity for regulating emotions, even though soothing behaviors may not result in instant cessation of crying.

How do you feel when you are grieving or otherwise legitimately distressed and well-meaning people try to get you to "cheer up"? Crying is an adaptive stress-relieving technique. You probably recall from your own experiences that under circumstances such as these you often feel better after having a good cry. Infants are people too, and crying is one of the few stress-relieving techniques of which they can avail themselves. We might also consider whether distractions we introduce in our attempts to calm crying infants might also distract them from developing their self-soothing brain wiring. Thus from the standpoint of emotional development, calming techniques are less important for making a baby stop crying than for providing loving support as the infant works through the distress (Solter, 1999). Toddlers benefit from brief opportunities to regulate their emotions independently, reinforcing their newly forming self-regulatory skills by not having parents immediately jump in and rescue them from their emotions (Grolnick et al., 1998; Stifter et al., 1999).

As with other human characteristics, different babies spend different amounts of time crying. Do the ones who cry excessively have more problems

This mother's soothing behaviors will contribute to the child's eventual ability to self-soothe.

later on than those who cry less? In most cases, apparently not. Infants who cried a lot at age 6 weeks showed no differences from those who cried less, when measured at 15 months in the areas of temperament, behavior, and cognitive ability (St. James-Roberts et al., 1998). We might be concerned that if a baby is exceptionally fussy the situation can become so aversive for caregivers that parent/infant attachment is disrupted. Mothers who have babies who are colicky or cry excessively certainly feel less competent than other mothers, and also demonstrate more anxiety when separated from their infants (Stifter & Bono, 1998). However, the vast majority of these mother/infant dyads recover from their early trials and tribulations. When the infants reach age 18 months no significant differences are found in temperament, attachment style, or responsiveness between mother and child based on amount of early crying (Barr, 1998; Prudhomme-White et al, 2000; Stifter & Bono, 1998). So, as frustrated parents groan their way through seemingly unending infant crying spells, they can legitimately assure both themselves and their infants that "this, too, shall pass."

Recognizing and Responding to Others' Emotions

Newly mobile infants encounter huge volumes of novel exploratory material. As they examine every speck of dirt and find things to get into that mother may have forgotten even existed, they do not yet have the ability to verbally request mother's opinion when they find themselves in disturbingly ambiguous situations with unknown consequences. When my son Frank was passing through this creeping/crawling stage I recall an episode during which we were sitting in a large waiting area. As Frank struck out into virgin territory he left the main carpeted area and found himself traveling onto a rough, prickly, Astroturf-type surface. He picked up his hand and examined it, investigating what this novel sensation might have done to him. Upon finding no clear evidence of damage he turned and questioningly looked at me. "Prickly," I told him, using a pleasant tone and facial expression. He turned away and continued his trek across the Astroturf.

Infants are capable of obtaining information by reading others' emotional expressiveness. They show evidence of awareness of their mothers' emotions as early as 2 or 3 months of age, responding with bodily reactions and vocalizations that are consistent with the perceived emotion (Tronick, 1989). Like Frank in the above example, they use observations of others' emotional reactions during exploratory stages of early locomotion. If mother looks fearful or angry they understand that they might want to be cautious. If mother looks pleasantly interested or joyful they perceive her reaction as an "all systems go" for further explorations (Stenberg & Hagekull, 1997).

This infant and toddler tendency to look to others' responses as they figure out uncertain situations is called **social referencing** (Baldwin & Moses, 1996;

Feinman, 1992; Lieberman, 1993). Infants look not only to their mothers for such input but also to other trusted adults. By age 18 months they not only recognize such emotions but also gather information by observing what others are attending to as they express them (Repacholi, 1998). During their second year they include their toddler cohorts as resources for obtaining an emotional read on situations (Hornik & Gunnar, 1988). However, what I remember most about social referencing when my children were babies was actually a side-benefit. Their stopping, turning, and gazing at me frequently served as a reliable indicator that baby was thinking about getting into something!

What influences the emergence of and perceptions within an infant's self-concept?

SELF-CONCEPTUALIZATION

One of the most crucial aspects of anyone's development is the establishment of a well-functioning self-concept and good self-esteem. These provide the basis for our sense of security, self-control, stability, and individuality. Furthermore, how could we learn to like ourselves without first recognizing the existence of a unique, separate individual to be liked? The process of coming to know ourselves as separate, competent human beings begins in infancy.

By 18 months most infants recognize the reflection they see in a mirror as being themselves (Asendorpf et al., 1996; DesRosiers et al., 2000; Lewis et al., 1989). What process leads them to the conclusion that they are themselves, separate from the world around them? Allport believed that the beginnings of certain aspects of the infant's experience of separateness emerge in a specific sequence (Allport, 1961). Probably infants are first most aware of their **bodily self**, realizing that sensations such as hunger, softness, brightness, dampness, and so forth are in fact personal experiences. During the second year Allport suggests that a form of **self-identity** makes its first appearance, as infants sense the unchanging continuity of their selfhood within a past, present, and future.

Separation-Individuation

Margaret Mahler also believed that infants' early perceptions of selfhood occur in phases. She proposed that the infant sense of self begins as a merged state called **symbiosis**, with self and mother experienced as a single unit. Since the perceived self is thus actually a relationship, the success of the synchrony within the mother-child bond provides one of the first bases for the child's early inner security and self-confidence (Mahler et al., 1975).

As infants mature, the **separation-individuation** phase guides them toward a more independent self-perception (Mahler, 1994). The earliest differentiation occurs at age 4 or 5 months when they choose to focus on items of interest that do not involve Mom, perhaps even leaning away from her in order to do so. As their locomotor skills improve, they practice both separating from and reuniting with mother. All of the comings and goings provide opportunities for viewing mother from a variety of new perspectives, and continually reexpose them to the revelation that "I go, but Mommy is still over there."

At 18 months they become more aware of the scarier aspects of separateness. They may wander so far off that they cannot immediately get to mother, or they begin to recognize the potential for delay in receiving her comforting if they are apart. Such realizations often lead to the return of clingier behavior. This can be a major frustration for Mom, who in all likelihood had begun to enjoy the freedoms available when baby is content with exploring independently. With continued reassurances, however, the pendulum of infant independence eventually swings back toward a new and improved version of inner security.

Transitional Objects

As infants abandon the safety of mother and take off for their far horizons, they often become especially attached to a favorite soft cuddly object. This stuffed animal, blanket, or other toy accompanies them during their early adventures, acting as a **transitional object** between mother and their experience of independence (Grolnick & Barkin, 1993). Such objects may be dragged around for many years, as has been the case with Linus's "security blanket" in the *Peanuts* comic strip. Interestingly, children in cultures where the mother or other caregivers are constantly present do not seem to develop such attachments (Hong & Townes, 1976).

Most parents recognize and accept the role of transitional objects in their children's lives (Triebenbacher, 1997). However, some parents, observing the extreme tantrum that a child may throw when involuntarily separated from the transitional object, worry that this extreme attachment might be evidence of

Transitional objects such as this young man's teddy bear provide comfort when youngsters are separated from their caregivers.

James R. Holland/Stock Boston

emotional difficulties. Such fears are unfounded. The presence of transitional objects during infancy and childhood has not demonstrated evidence of later emotional or social harm. The children they accompany are every bit as well-adjusted as children who do not have such attachments (Passman, 1987). In fact, some evidence suggests that children who develop attachments to transitional objects experience healthier attachment with their mothers, although this finding is age-limited. Adolescents who continue to carry around their early transitional objects show a greater incidence of psychiatric problems or lower general well-being (Bachar et al., 1998).

Self-Concept

Recognition of separateness raises the issue of self-concept: Who or what am I? The earliest glimmer of self-concept begins at around 18 months as toddlers are beginning to categorize their world. They learn the difference between "good" and "bad," "boy" and "girl," and other such dichotomies, and apply them to both others and themselves (Stipek et al., 1990). Early self-classifications such as these appear to have an effect on how they believe they should behave. For example, soon after they recognize their gender they begin organizing their own activities according to their perceived gender expectations (Fagot & Leinbach, 1989). The appearance of emotions such as guilt, jealousy, and pride coincides with these classification skills, since such feelings are based in part on having an understanding of self- and other-evaluation (Kopp, 1982). As is the case with so many infant developmental issues, the fullness of an infant's self-concept appears to be related to the quality of attachment to mother: the more secure the attachment, the more solid the self-concept (Pipp et al., 1992).

How can caregivers encourage development of an infant's sense of competence?

> ### PAVING PATHWAYS ALONG INFANT EMOTIONAL AND SOCIAL MILESTONES: DEVELOPING INFANT COMPETENCE

Our inner sense of competence is a collection of skills, beliefs, emotions, and cognitive processes that assists us in our pursuit of successful social interactions and healthy emotional adjustment. Somewhere along the line, we decide to do things in certain ways because we believe in our methods and our ability to achieve. Competence also refers to actually getting successful results: do our chosen methods for living get us what we want?

Some children just naturally seem able to meet the challenge of whatever their life circumstances may place before them. Even when exposed to extremely high-risk situations, the **invulnerable child** seems able to elicit enough of what he or she needs from the environment for healthy social and emotional development to follow (Anthony & Cohler, 1987; Luther et al., 2000). The influences of nature and nurture within this developmental scenario are still being sorted out.

Some researchers believe that the first 3 years have a greater impact on a person's developing sense of competence than any other stage of life (White, 1990). At the end of toddlerhood, as children are getting ready to enter the preschool stage, what abilities are already observed that are likely indicators of developing competence? Competent children can recognize when a task has become too difficult for them, and when in need, know how to seek adult assistance in acceptable ways. They can get along with other children, can compete with them appropriately, and can express both caring and angry feelings in ways that are considered socially acceptable. They show pride in their accomplishments. They demonstrate the use of cognitive abilities necessary for success, such as language skills, maintaining a focus, noticing relevant details and discrepancies, and organizing themselves around goal-directed behavior (White et al., 1979).

Another angle for exploring competence is pursued by examining a child's early motivations for achievement. Why does a child even attempt to meet goals within the environment? Infants seem to do so purely for the joy of mastery. As children approach the age of 2 they look to others for affirmation as they proceed toward success or failure, and express pleasure when they receive approval. And as they near preschool age they begin using internalized performance standards, and experience pride or shame according to how close they approach their standards (Stipek et al., 1992).

Any parent would be delighted to have a child with a clear, positive sense of competence. Following are some suggestions of what parents and other caregivers can do during infancy and toddlerhood to help children develop healthy inner and outer competence.

▶ Babies need clear and consistent feedback about their discoveries and behaviors. Such feedback not only helps them judge their effectiveness but also contributes toward construction of their own future performance standards. Feedback regarding an event's "success" or "failure" needs to be appropriate for the child's developmental level, so that inner performance standards do not become unrealistically high or low.

▶ Any "labeling" of the child should be positive. The simplified language style of motherese makes comments such as "good boy" or "bad boy" very tempting. Such admonishments will indeed be understood. However, toddlers are in the process of developing categorizations for their world—including self-categorizations—and will behave according to their perceived personal descriptors. If a parent repeatedly says "bad girl," the parent has normalized "bad" or unsuccessful behavior as a part of the child's identity. Thus "badness" is what that parent will be likely to get. For obvious reasons, descriptors such as "stupid" and other forms of name-calling can have disastrous effects.

▶ Caregivers need to be available for spontaneous consultations as babies explore. This availability should be balanced; caregivers must be careful not to hover or unnecessarily anticipate requests. Otherwise babies will not have opportunities for practicing the skills of recognizing when they need assistance and getting the attention of a caregiver.

▶ Distractions and physical removal from a situation are the better interventions for when toddlers are having difficulty staying away from a "no-no." With baby's blossoming independence, the word "no" can actually increase a situation's intrinsic interest.

▶ When parents find themselves in a battle of wills, they should occasionally let the child win when the stakes are of little importance. Obedience is important, but so is modeling negotiation and respect for others' desires, as well as validating the child's sense of separateness.

▶ Parents sometimes need to keep in mind that it is all right if babies are cross with them. As long as they are not hitting, biting, or using other inappropriate expressions of anger, socially appropriate emotionalism can be reinforced with empathic comments such as "Tiffany mad." By acting angry or rejecting in return, parents can undermine the process.

▶ Infants benefit from the provision of plenty of opportunities for social relationships with peers, older children, and other adults.

▶ Babies need to be convinced that they are likeable. They gain little of value from parents' rejecting behaviors or acting disgusted with them because of their failures.

▶ Parents can provide the tools for building a sense of personal competence by using the techniques described in Chapter 6 for promoting development of cognitive skills.

▶ Babies are human beings and need to be treated with respect. They are sensitive to parents' moods. Thus during "foul weather" parents would best moderate their interactions with their infants just as they would while interacting with others in their lives.

"Others" Concept

How do infants perceive others?

Infants recognize others as separate at approximately the same time they develop self-awareness, usually at around age 18 months (Asendorpf et al., 1996). Over the last couple of decades, considerable research—as well as considerable controversy—has emerged regarding "other-awareness" in the formulation of the concept **theory of mind** (Flavell, 1999; Wellman, 1990). Theory of mind is a sort of personal folk psychology, or how we perceive one another's inner mental and emotional processes. Unless we have some sense of what makes others tick, their behaviors would seem chaotic and unpredictable, an outcome hypothesized as characterizing the perceptions of autistic individuals (Baron-Cohen et al., 1985).

When do children begin to perceive that others may have mental and emotional processes and begin to respond accordingly? Apparently they do so not long after they have begun to recognize their separateness. Eighteen-month-olds show recognition of intent when they observe adults attempt a task and fail, yet do not show such recognition while watching a mechanical device similarly fail (Meltzoff, 1995).

As was discussed earlier in the chapter, infants are capable of recognizing and reacting to the emotions of others. Even newborns act distressed when they hear the crying of other infants (Simner, 1971). However, at this early age, their response is more of a reaction to their own personal discomfort from being exposed to others' emotionality than it is an expression of empathy (Hoffman, 1993). By 18 months their recognition of others' inner experience is evidenced by their expressions of empathy. For example, when an experimenter "hurt" her leg and acted distressed, some youngsters offered comforting behaviors such as patting or giving a hug (Radke-Yarrow et al., 1983). Even if they do so as a reaction to their own distress over others' pain, they are still indicating some knowledge of others' inner experience and what is likely to "make it all better."

Self-Control

Having constructed some understanding of the difference between their identities and preferences and those of other individuals, youngsters begin to appreciate the fact that they may or may not choose to go along with the wishes of others. "No" and "mine" often become their favorite words as they reassure themselves of their developing identities by asserting their desires. Sometimes they seem to act oppositional just on principle, which has spawned the oft-heard label the "terrible two's."

In spite of the seeming contrariness of the age, by 18 months children do show some ability to adjust their behavior to accommodate the preferences of others (Kopp, 1982). They recognize a few of the rules of social acceptability for their environment, and will generally comply with them unless they conflict with impulses they would prefer to gratify. Self-regulation—the self-imposed delay of gratification of impulses to comply with rules or the needs of others—will arrive with the preschool years. Having greater verbal ability appears to increase compliance, perhaps because the child can more easily be distracted with alternative understandings of the situation at hand (Vaughn et al., 1984). And when parenting is sensitive, consistent, and reasonable, these "tiny tyrants" tend not to be quite so oppositional (Crockenberg & Litman, 1990).

SUMMARY

Early Personality Development

Early psychodynamic theorists believed that personality emerged through biologically programmed stages of development, with consequences for the adult personality that depended on how well conflicts in each stage were resolved. Freud proposed an oral and anal stage, while Erikson proposed the stages of basic trust versus mistrust and autonomy versus shame and doubt. While the psychodynamic theorists' treatment of personality development has not held up empirically, it did pave the way to the study of Bowlby's infant/caregiver attachment.

Infant Attachment Theory

The quality of a mother-infant attachment affects the child's social and emotional development. Quality of inadequate mother-infant attachment has been found to be associated with interpersonal problems with peers during toddlerhood, personal difficulties in later childhood or adulthood, and insecure attachment with one's own infants.

In secure infant/caregiver attachments, the two participants learn to respond to one another's signals using interactional synchrony. Caregivers thus learn to anticipate infant needs and preferences, and infants develop a preference for those adults who respond with this form of sensitivity. While the infant-mother attachment appears to be most important among infants in industrialized cultures, infants also develop significant attachments with fathers and other caregivers. In research settings, the Strange Situation technique has been used to measure infant attachment as secure, avoidant, resistant, or disorganized/disoriented. The secure attachment rating appears to be cross-culturally sound, while the resistant and avoidant classifications may not so readily apply to all cultures because infant-handling practices differ.

Factors influencing caregiver/infant attachment patterns include individual differences, such as temperament, breadth of available response capacity, and flexibility; and environmental influences such as stability and consistency. A parent's capacity for sensitivity toward the infant and the parent's feelings about attachment itself are relevant attributes that can be successfully enhanced through parenting interventions.

In spite of earlier beliefs to the contrary, using quality infant day care does not appear to impair infant/caregiver attachments. However, low-quality day care can have negative effects on social, emotional, and intellectual development; and quality of day care varies widely in the United States. Quality day care services are properly licensed and employ caring, consistent, and appropriately trained workers in a baby-friendly setting that is sufficiently large, safe, and well-organized.

Infant Emotions

Researchers have studied infant emotions by using the MAX (Maximally Discriminative Facial Movement Coding System), a system of coding facial musculature positioning as a means of inferring emotional states. Different emotional states are hypothesized to emerge at the ages at which corresponding facial expressions emerge. Infant crying represents many things, but those who cry excessively early in infancy show no deficits in attachment or other adjustment behaviors later in their development. Infants begin responding to others' emotions as early as 2 to 3 months of age. When in ambiguous situations, they use social referencing as a means of seeking out information from others by reading their emotional responses.

Self-Conceptualization

Infant perception of self is hypothesized to appear first as bodily sensing, then as a self-identity that is consistent from day to day. Mahler believed that infants at first merged as one with mother. Over the first 2 years, through the process of separation-individuation, they recognize more and more of their personal experience as separate as they practice independent activity using mother as a "base" to which they can return. At 18 months they begin identifying with categorizations such as "boy" or "girl." They also begin attributing separateness of function to others, as indicated by studies of theory of mind and early empathic responding. Oppositionalism may appear as a by-product of asserting their sensed separateness. However, by age two they are capable of enough self-control to comply with certain social expectations, as long as other immediate impulses do not conflict.

The toddlers' developing sense of competence is reflected in successful interpersonal and environmental interactions as well as apparent inner confidence and self-esteem. By age 2 they have developed some personal performance standards for their behavior and experience pride or shame according to how well they meet these standards. Parents can encourage infant competence by being sensitive, consistent, and available as well as by providing a variety of opportunities for social learning.

KEY TERMS

anal stage
autonomy versus shame and doubt
avoidant attachment
basic trust versus mistrust
bodily self
disorganized/disoriented attachment

interactional synchrony
invulnerable child
Maximally Discriminative Facial Movement Coding System (MAX)
oral stage
resistant attachment
secure attachment

self-identity
separation anxiety
separation-individuation
social referencing
Strange Situation
symbiosis
theory of mind
transitional object

CONCEPT REVIEW

1. Studies suggest that the roots of personal traits such as level of motor activity, inhibition versus extraversion, and persistence at a task are associated more with _____, while expression of affect and sociability are related more to _____.

2. Freud believed that during infancy personalities are shaped by the presence or lack of _____ gratification individuals received and that during the second year of life, the _____ stage, toddlers' personalities are affected by how parents handle potty-training.

3. Erikson described the psychosocial needs of early infancy as a time of developing healthy _____ versus _____ in caregivers and others; during the second year he believed that their mobile, exploratory nature provided personal lessons regarding _____ versus _____.

4. The aspects of Bowlby's early hypotheses regarding infant/parent attachments that continue to be supported are the importance of parent _____ and _____.

5. Early evidence that attachment during infancy affects social and emotional development came from observations of infants who had been _____.

6. The back and forth behavioral adjustments pursued by infant/caregiver dyads as they communicate with one another is called _____.

7. The Strange Situation is an assessment technique that designates the infant attachment patterns of _____, _____, _____, and _____ attachment.

8. Comparisons of mother/infant and father/infant dyads in Western cultures have found that _____ tend to be more sensitive and responsive to infant emotional needs, while _____ are more likely to be sought out by the infant as a play partner.

9. Studies of situations in which there are primary caregivers in addition to the parents suggests that attachments with parents does/does not affect quality of infants' attachments to the other caregivers.

10. While being placed in day care rather than being cared for by parents does not in and of itself affect healthy infant attachments, _____ of day care does make a difference.

11. At around 6 months of age it is not unusual for infants to begin reacting emotionally when parents attempt to leave them with alternative caregivers, thus demonstrating _____.

12. Quality of infant/parent attachment is affected most by parent and child _____, environmental _____, and parent _____.

13. Studies using the Maximally Discriminative Facial Coding System (MAX) have suggested that infants experience _____ within the first few months of life.

14. Studies of infant crying suggest that _____ an infant can assist in wiring the brain for rational responding and emotional regulation, and that babies who cry more often than others <u>do/do not</u> differ in temperament, behavior, cognitive ability, or attachment style when assessed as toddlers.

15. Infants use social referencing as a means of learning by observing others' _____.

16. Allport suggests that during the first year of life the infant's self-concept develops through his or her sense of _____, and that during the second year the infant begins forming a _____.

17. The infant/toddler sense of competence can be encouraged with interactions that facilitate or reinforce both inner feelings of _____, and _____ in the outer world.

18. Mahler suggests that the infant personality develops in response to how infants process their sense of _____. Infants may self-soothe the scary feelings associated with this sense by carrying around _____.

19. Studies of _____ indicate that even toddlers are able to perceive others' inner mental and emotional processes.

1) inborn temperament; environmental influences; **2**) oral; anal; **3**) basic trust; mistrust; autonomy; shame and doubt; **4**) responsiveness; sensitivity; **5**) institutionalized; **6**) interactional synchrony; **7**) secure; avoidant; resistant; disorganized/disoriented; **8**) mothers; fathers; **9**) does not; **10**) quality; **11**) separation anxiety; **12**) temperament; stability; sensitivity; **13**) emotions; **14**) calming; do not; **15**) emotional expressiveness; **16**) bodily self; self-identity; **17**) confidence; successes; **18**) separateness; transitional object; **19**) theory of mind

▶ *RESOURCES FOR FURTHER READING*

Brazelton, T. B., & Cramer, B. G. (1990). *The earliest relationship.* Reading, MA: Addison-Wesley.

Goldschmied, E., & Jackson, S. (1994). *People under three: Young children in daycare.* New York: Routledge.

Holcomb, B. (1998). *Not guilty! The good news about working mothers.* New York: Scribner.

Klaus, M. H., Kennell, J. H., & Klaus, P. H. (1995). *Bonding: Building the foundations of secure attachment and independence.* Reading, MA: Addison-Wesley.

Schore, A. N. (1994). *Affect regulation and the origin of the self: The neurobiology of emotional development.* Hillsdale, NJ: Erlbaum.

White, B. L. (1995). *The new first three years of life.* New York: Simon & Schuster.

INFOTRAC COLLEGE EDITION

For additional readings, explore InfoTrac College Edition, your online library. Go to http://www.infotrac-college.com/wadsworth and use the passcode that came on the card with your book. Try these search terms: crying in infants, emotions in infants, fathers and infants, infant attachment, infant day care, infants—psychology, infants—mental health, Strange Situation, toilet training, transitional object

CHILD DEVELOPMENT CD-ROM

Go to the Wadsworth Child Development CD-ROM for further study of the concepts in this chapter. The CD-ROM also includes quizzes and additional activities to expand your learning experience.

REFERENCES

For a list of references for this chapter, see the Wadsworth Psych Study Center Web site at: http://www.wadsworth.com/product/0534348092s

CHAPTER 8

Early Childhood Physical Development

FOCUS QUESTIONS

- ► What bodily changes occur as the preschool-age child grows and matures?

- ► What quantitative and qualitative changes take place in the young child's developing brain?

- ► What kinds of activities and pastimes are likely to foster the young child's developing brain?

- ► What new physical skills can be expected of preschoolers?

- ► What are the young child's health needs?

- ► What can parents do to help young children develop healthy eating habits?

- ► What sorts of conditions interfere with the preschooler's normal development?

OUTLINE

Body Growth and Change

Brain Development

Hemispheric Specialization

Handedness

Perceptual Advances

Paving Pathways: Supporting the Growing Brain

Motor Development

Gross Motor Skills

Fine Motor Skills

Early Drawings

Early Childhood Health Needs

Sleep

Nutrition

Eating Habits and Preschoolers

Paving Pathways: Eating Safety

Paving Pathways: Fostering Eating Compliance

Paving Pathways: Encouraging Independent, Healthy
Eating Habits

Health Problems

Illness

Environmental Exposures

Excessive Stress and/or Lack of Affection

Accidents and Injuries

Child Maltreatment

Six-year-old Darrell, who enjoys games and sports, is left-handed. He entered a beginning softball "T-ball" league, but for reasons other than his handedness, he just didn't seem to do well. His right-handed cohorts attributed his struggles to being a "leftie," making fun of how he stood on the "wrong" side of the plate. Their coach, Mr. Peterson, tried to discourage such commentary. However, Darrell's poor performance at bat continued to fuel taunting each time his team encountered a new team.

On Darrell's birthday Mr. Peterson decided to underscore the acceptability of left-handedness in sports by presenting Darrell with a left-handed player's baseball mitt.

"Wow, neat! Thanks, Mr. Peterson!" Darrell jubilantly exclaimed. "All I need now is a left-handed baseball bat!"

Ages 2 through 7 are often referred to as the play years. At least the activity generated by these little bundles of energy looks like play to us. However, for them play is serious business (Power, 2000). Almost every facet of their development is either enhanced by or depends upon being funneled through their spontaneous fun and games. Notice that children do not need to be taught how to play—it emerges naturally, as we might expect that any crucial element of human development would. As this chapter describes preschoolers' physical growth, you will recognize the many functions of play in a young child's world, whether in the form of free play or organized games such as "T-ball."

BODY GROWTH AND CHANGE

What bodily changes occur as the preschool-age child grows and matures?

The graphs in Figure 8.1 show the changes in weight and height of preschool-age boys and girls. Over the next several years they will grow about 2½ in. in height and gain around 6 lb each year. Their body shapes become more streamlined as they lose a lot of their baby fat. Girls continue to be a little smaller than boys and, as you can see from the wide range of normal measurements, there is still a lot of variability regarding a child's expected size during this early age span (Tanner, 1990).

The cephalocaudal and proximodistal rules of development discussed in Chapter 5 continue to apply. The head and trunk become less predominant as limbs and outer structures lengthen and become more sophisticated in their performance abilities. Other asynchronies in physical growth are less obvious. For example, during the first half of childhood the **lymph system**—which is responsible for assisting the immune system and processing nutrients—grows at a much higher rate than other body structures. Figure 8.2 shows the childhood growth curves for lymph, brain, reproductive organ, and general organ development.

FIGURE 8.1

Expected rates of height and weight growth during early childhood. From Berger, K. S., and Thompson, R. A. (1995). *The developing person through childhood and adolescence,* 4th ed. NY: Worth, p. 298, by permission.

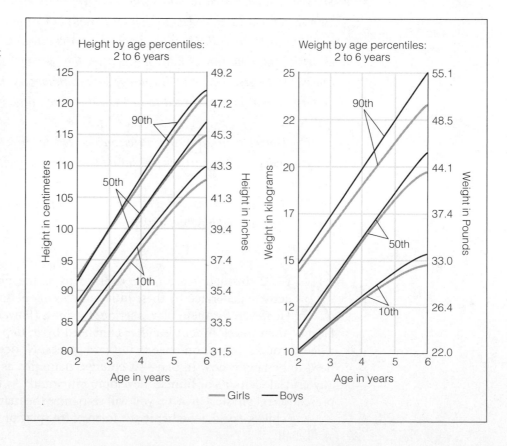

FIGURE 8.2

Organ system growth rates. During early childhood, the brain and lymphoid systems are developing the most rapidly. From *Growth at Adolescence,* 2nd ed., by J. M. Tanner, 1962. Oxford, England: Blackwell, by permission.

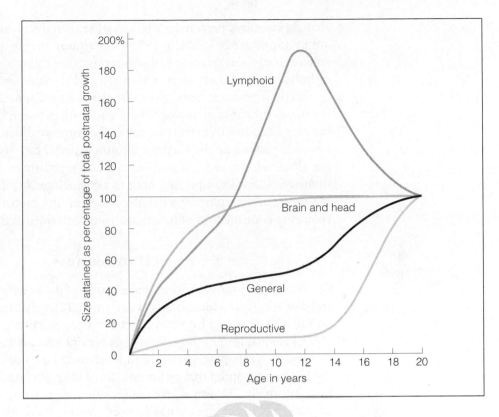

What quantitative and qualitative changes take place in the young child's developing brain?

BRAIN DEVELOPMENT

You can also note from Figure 8.2 that the preschooler's brain is continuing to grow at a speedier clip than the rest of the body. Brain size reaches about 90% of its eventual adult weight by the time the child is 5 years old (Lowrey, 1986).

Additional myelination and interconnections of neurons pave the way for development of more advanced motor and cognitive skills. Myelination of neurons is close to completion at around age 8, yet neurons involved in more sophisticated brain functions are still works in progress. For example, the neurons of the prefrontal cortex, which play a role in attending and short-term memory processing, do not reach full myelination until young adulthood (Jernigan et al., 1991).

Hemispheric Specialization

Chapter 5 described the brain's division into two hemispheres. While the two sides of the cerebral cortex may look identical, they actually specialize in different functions. For the average person, the left hemisphere is most responsible for language, detailed and analytical thinking, rational thought, and mathematical functions. The right hemisphere is more active in the areas of emotions, spatial reasoning, perceiving wholes rather than detail, and musical and artistic ability (Springer & Deutsch, 1985). On a more pragmatic level, the left hemisphere controls movement and sensations of the right side of the body, while the right hemisphere dominates movement and sensation on the left side.

To perform most tasks in our daily lives we use functions from both sides of the brain. Information is passed back and forth between the two hemispheres by means of a connective structure called the **corpus callosum**. At around age 4 the neurons making up the corpus callosum experience a growth spurt, enhancing the child's ability to learn and negotiate more complex cognitive and physical maneuvers. For example, learning to tie shoelaces involves both visual-spatial reasoning and employing a detailed series of fine motor manipulations, a task requiring coordination of functions from both sides of the brain.

Handedness

By about age 2 most children have shown a preference for using either their right or left hand. Handedness is determined largely by genetic influences, but also to a lesser extent by environment (Carter-Saltzman, 1980; Jones & Martin, 2000; Provins, 1997). About 90% of us are right-handed and the other 10% left-handed. In years past, parents and teachers tried to discourage dominance of the left hand, hoping that by forcing use of the right hand the child would function "normally." However, even in societies where using the left hand is considered a gross breach of cultural dictates, almost 2% of the population continues to function as predominantly left-handed (Hardyck & Petrinovich, 1977).

Numerous studies have explored possible differences between individuals with left- or right-hand dominance (Coren, 1993). Those who are left-handed are more likely to suffer from headaches, allergies, dyslexia, attention-deficit disorder, alcoholism, and stuttering (Geschwind & Galaburda, 1985). As a group, they have a shorter average life span than do right-handed individuals (Coren & Halpern, 1991). On the other hand (if you'll excuse the pun), lefties count among themselves a greater proportion of individuals obtaining the highest IQ and Scholastic Aptitude Test scores (Benbow, 1991; Bower, 1985). They also may demonstrate superior visual-spatial and creative abilities and find themselves naturally drawn to careers such as architecture, engineering, art, carpentry, and interior design (Healy, 1994).

However, only a small proportion of such individual differences is associated with handedness. For most, the significance of being left- or right-handed is more likely to be felt as children attempt to perform routine tasks in a society whose technology is designed for right-handed people, as was the case for Darrell in the chapter opening. Learning to write presents a greater challenge for left-handed children: a left-handed writer holding a writing utensil in the same manner as a right-handed person covers up what has just been written. Sensitive teachers will show left-handed children how to hold their pencils without covering their work, rather than let students struggle until a left-handed teacher coaches the technique.

Perceptual Advances

It is dusk. Seven-year-old Scott and 4-year-old Sandra both catch a glimpse of a deer moving quickly through the underbrush of their rural back yard. "It's a dog!" squeals Sandra.

"No, it isn't. It's a deer," Scott replies. "You know what a deer is!"

Yes, Sandra does know the difference between a deer and a dog. So why is Scott better at recognizing the animal than she is? Their different levels of **perceptual learning** play a major role. The ability to recognize the distinctive features identifying a figure is learned (Gibson, 1992). After more exposure to important cues—such as longer, more delicate legs and the bounding gait—Sandra will be better able to recognize the finer distinctions between a dog and a deer. Between the ages of 4 and 7, children's visual acuity improves substantially, resulting in greater ability to identify the finer distinctions between stimuli (Gibson et al., 1962; United States Department of Health, Education, and Welfare, 1977).

The ability to perceive minor differences between stimuli is especially relevant to a child's reading readiness. One of the endearing characteristics of preschoolers' early attempts at writing is their tendency to print letters backwards, as capitalized upon by the "ToysЯUs" toy store chain. Young children often confuse similar symbols, such as "d" and "b" or "p" and "q." By the time children begin addressing the more rigorous demands of elementary school, their discriminative ability will have advanced sufficiently to eliminate most errors of this sort.

During the early years, children tend to be far-sighted, since focusing on close stimuli requires significantly more eye muscle coordination and control than focusing on objects that are farther away. Another visual ability relevant for learning to read is that of sustaining a focus while following a line of small letters. Toward the end of the preschool years, the eye muscles have developed sufficiently for mastering these skills (Dhillon & Millar, 1994; Hifler & Sheffield, 1984; Vurpillot, 1968).

What kinds of activities and pastimes are likely to foster the young child's developing brain?

PAVING PATHWAYS ALONG EARLY CHILDHOOD PHYSICAL MILESTONES: SUPPORTING THE GROWING BRAIN

Figure 8.2 shows that brain growth during the preschool years progresses almost as rapidly as it did during infancy, and that it tapers off after the preschool years as does much of the brain's plasticity. Since much of this new development involves the creation and strengthening of interconnections between processes, environmental exposures and pastimes can play an especially important role in preschoolers' future physical and learning capacities.

Witness the case of "Charles," a precocious preschooler (Healy, 1994). Charles's parents were proud of his early interest in story-telling and proficiency at using computers. Since books and computer games were his preferred activities, they encouraged him by providing all the latest educational materials that capitalize on these interests. However, when he entered kindergarten he was miserable. He had a terrible time holding crayons or scissors and was clumsy in gym. He didn't like clay, paints, and other creative mediums because they seemed "messy." According to his teacher, he showed no ability to pretend or to use his imagination, and needed step-by-step instruction on how to proceed with any new task or unfamiliar plaything. He did not seem to know how to interact with the other children, who eventually started making fun of his awkwardness. Charles thus suffered not only from the effects of insufficient development of neuronal interconnections but from lack of interconnections with other children as well!

So what kind of play environment should we provide during this key stage of brain development? As Charles's experiences suggest, balanced, varied exposures are important for the growing brain and developing motor skills. Physical play, artistic play, analytical play, creative/imaginary play, and socially interactive play all use various interconnections among brain structures that will eventually be useful if not necessary for normal, day-to-day independent functioning.

Using more than one part of the brain at once is a skill that develops with time and practice (Healy, 1994). A wide variety of activities, especially those that reflect the child's day-to-day emerging interests, are more likely to meet the child's "bridge-building" needs than emphasizing the child's specialized interests or the parents'. Following are examples of activities for preschool-age children that require coordination of multiple brain functions:

Opportunities for group play contribute toward preschoolers' learning the interactional life skills necessary for cooperation and coordinating efforts with others.

Jonathan Nourok/PhotoEdit

► Physical activity using both gross motor skills and some analytical think-ing, as in games like tag, or even the spontaneous loosely organized physi-cal play we often see among preschool children. We may not be able to figure out what the structure of these "games" might be, and the children would not be able to tell us the rules if asked. Yet they seem to have enough grasp of the situation to play cooperatively—perhaps evidence of yet an-other way in which children naturally steer toward what they need for nor-mal development.

► Puzzles designed for preschool-age children. To assemble a puzzle, a child must combine the use of fine motor skills with the detailed analytical abil-ity of the left hemisphere and perception of the finished whole by the right hemisphere.

► Finger-painting, clay molding, and manipulation of other creative medi-ums. Even construction-type play in the sandbox can employ the combina-tion of functions involving tactile feedback, creative analysis, and physical manipulation.

► Asking children to describe what they are doing. Often as preschoolers play, you can hear them talking to themselves as they stack blocks, "drive" trucks, or rearrange figures in a doll house. This natural tendency spontaneously accomplishes the desired result: integration of verbal, analytical, and motor skills.

► Describe what *you* are doing as the preschooler is watching. Preschoolers benefit most from a narrative approach, devoted mostly to *what* is actually happening with occasional simplified explanations of *why*. Verbal, visual, and some analytical integration occurs: an important contribution toward reading readiness.

► Cooperative games such as ring-around-the-rosie, London Bridge is falling down, duck-duck-goose, and other speech- or song-narrated games that you yourself may recall from your early years. These games combine visual and verbal cues as well as coordination with various motor skills. And as group play, they have the added bonus of incorporating skills for social in-teraction into the venture.

► They benefit from assistance as they negotiate age-appropriate, real-life challenges requiring integration of brain functions, such as dressing them-selves, tying shoes, opening packages, negotiating an unusual stairway, or making their beds. They should be offered only as much help as they need to succeed; this can range from giving simple verbal instructions to actually modeling performance of the task. And patience is truly a virtue while men-toring preschoolers! If they continue to have difficulty performing the task, perhaps they are not ready. Integration of hemispheric functions continues even beyond puberty, and there will be plenty of additional opportunities for supporting children's brain growth.

*What new physical
skills can be expected
of preschoolers?*

MOTOR DEVELOPMENT

Gross Motor Skills

Most 3-year-olds can run, hop, and jump. Although their early productions of these movements are clumsy and limited, their efforts will become more solid and coordinated over the next few years. By age 4 they can climb and descend stairs, although they typically land both feet on each step. With practice and instruction most 5-year-olds can ride a tricycle, throw and catch a ball, and climb ladders. By the end of the preschool years, children are combining and incorporating their new gross motor abilities into formal games (Poest et al., 1990; Sutherland et al., 1988).

Boys and girls show slight differences in gross motor advances. Boys demonstrate some superiority in performance of basic actions involving the large muscles, such as running, jumping, and throwing. Girls often advance more quickly in activities requiring balance and coordination, such as jumping rope and hopscotch. As these differences in advancement become evident, the activity choices of boys and girls begin to diverge and the gap continues to widen, even though the gap between their physical capabilities remains unchanged until adolescence. This divergence in preferences has been generally accepted as being caused by our giving boys playthings such as footballs and baseballs and giving girls jump ropes and hula hoops (Thomas & French, 1985). But what about the role of positive reinforcement—the fact that we enjoy doing things that result in success? And what about the role of testosterone in encouraging more aggressive play activity?

The relationship between the presence of androgens during fetal development and male play behavior has been examined by looking at girls who have experienced congenital adrenal hyperplasia (New, 1985). In this condition female fetuses receive surges of androgens similar to those that male fetuses normally receive. When the affected girls are compared to those having had a normal female fetal experience, they are found to engage in more rough-housing, have a greater preference for male playmates and male activities, and show less interest in playing with dolls (Berenbaum, 1990; Berenbaum & Hines, 1992; Berenbaum & Snyder, 1995; Hines & Kaufman, 1994). Thus to understand the play behavior differences between the genders, we must take both biology and cultural experiences into account.

As their gross motor skills advance in the preschool years, can young children benefit from formal physical education programs? Activities such as tumbling, gymnastics, and free play in groups can certainly help keep children physically fit. And Darrell, our beginning softball enthusiast, might very well become more skilled at ball-throwing than other children if given adequate direct instruction and opportunities for practice. Other than these benefits, formal activity programs for preschool-age children do not appear to speed development of gross motor skills (Espanschade & Eckert, 1980). As they do during infancy, gross motor skills emerge naturally as children run, climb, hop, and jump in a relatively unrestricted, "preschooler-friendly" environment (Brehm & Tindell, 1991).

Fine Motor Skills

If you ask a 3-year-old to smile, his or her efforts may resemble a grimace, rather than the spontaneous smile of the limbic system. By the end of early childhood, the purposely produced smile will look more natural. This change reflects not only learning but also the increasing maturation of muscle and nervous system relays that coordinate movement of these smaller muscles.

Most advances in fine motor control are observed in hand and finger movements. Preschoolers become better skilled at using eating utensils. They learn to manipulate buttons, snaps, zippers, and the general cumbrance of clothing, eventually becoming able to dress themselves. Their opportunities for play expand as they can now successfully perform activities such as putting together puzzles, manipulating scissors and paper, stacking small blocks, and stringing beads (Frankenburg et al., 1992). Girls' fine motor skills tend to advance a little more quickly than those of boys (Thomas & French, 1985).

It is important to note, however, that fine motor advances rely upon more than maturation of certain small-muscle sensory and motor relays. They also involve learning that stems from eye-hand coordination, patience, and judgment. Consider also that the short, pudgy shape of preschoolers' hands and fingers is not particularly conducive to performing fine motor skills. In view of these additional elements, the progress children make during these early years is indeed impressive!

Early Drawings

Preschoolers take great pleasure in pushing a crayon around on paper. The increasing sophistication of their artwork as they pass through young childhood reflects not only improving fine motor skills but also advances in cognitive ability (Chappell & Steitz, 1993). In fact, clinicians are able to approximate the level of cognitive development by analyzing children's human figure drawings (Koppitz, 1968).

Early efforts begin with an impulsive "let's see how this turns out" application of drawing utensils. By the time children reach kindergarten, their drawings show much more planning (Allison, 1985). After analyzing many preschooler's artwork, Kellogg (1970) noted that improvements in their drawing strategies followed a predictable path regardless of culture, suggesting that brain maturation is the major player.

Two-year-olds typically scribble. While these random-looking markings may all look similarly chaotic to us, there are actually about 20 types of scribbles produced by 2-year-olds. By age 3, children draw shapes such as primitive geometric figures and soon afterward begin combining shapes. By age 4 or 5 they have begun drawing formal pictures intended to reflect reality, rather than

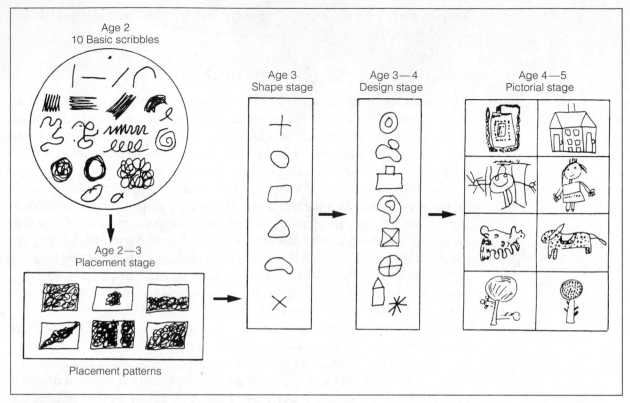

FIGURE 8.3

Examples of scribblings, shapes, designs, and early pictures likely to be produced at various ages during early childhood. From Santrock, J. W. (1993). *Children,* 3rd ed., Madison, WI: Wm. C. Brown, p. 253. Reprinted by permission of McGraw-Hill Companies.

abstract or experiential designs. Figure 8.3 shows this progression of children's artistic efforts.

Despite their increased effort at reflecting reality, older preschoolers still omit a number of significant details from their drawings. This is due in part to their not having attended to the pertinent details that differentiate and identify items, reflecting advances yet to occur in their perceptual development. When the attention of 6-year-olds is drawn to details relevant to an accurate depiction of an object, their drawings become more realistic (Sutton & Rose, 1998).

What are the young child's health needs?

EARLY CHILDHOOD HEALTH NEEDS

Sleep

With all of these new play and learning opportunities to tend to, young children need a lot of sleep (Webb & Bonnet, 1979). In addition to sleeping through the night, many young children continue to benefit from a nap or rest period during the day. Their sleep tends to be deeper than ours as well: You may have noticed how parents can pick up and move their sleeping preschoolers and not

Bedtime rituals such as bathing serve as a transition from awake-time to sleepy-time, increasing the likelihood of bedtime compliance.

Michael Weisbrot /Stock Boston

wake them. However, when it comes to achieving a sleep state after being put to bed, they tend to be less cooperative than they had been as toddlers. They now know that others are up doing interesting things, and their active imaginations let them envision scenes they would like to be part of. Overpermissive parents who have difficulty reinforcing bedtime not only create problems in the short run but also are more likely to find their children developing sleep disorders (Owens-Stively et al., 1997). Likewise preschoolers who do not get enough sleep are more likely to demonstrate behavior problems or be diagnosed with clinical emotional or behavioral conditions (Lavigne et al., 1999).

Patience and transitional rituals—such as an evening bath, pajamas, then story-time—can serve as wind-down strategies leading up to bedtime. When children have been especially prone to bedtime refusals and night wakenings, the approaches that seem to get the best results are ignoring protests and scheduled wakenings; parents may need education in these and other strategies (Mindell, 1999).

Sleep Disturbances. The brain's advances during the preschool years also produce a more sophisticated capacity for recognizing and imagining personal vulnerability. Several unpleasant sleep conditions first emerge during this stage of development (American Psychiatric Association, 1994; Ferber, 1985; Schaefer, 1995). Between the ages of 3 and 6, children typically experience their first **nightmare.** Scary dreams are common among preschool children, increase in frequency between the ages of 7 and 9, then decrease somewhat in frequency as children enter preadolescence (Muris et al., 2000). During a nightmare, preschoolers usually wake up crying, and when Mommy or Daddy comes in and comforts them they describe having been part of a scary story. Nightmares are especially scary for young children because they believe dreams are real. Over time they realize that dreams are not real, but for a while continue to perceive them as existing outside of themselves—as if they were watching a movie that others could see as well. By age 6 or 7, their perceptions of dreams become more similar to those of adults (Kohlberg, 1966).

A less common problem, **sleep terrors**, first occurs between the ages of 4 and 12. The child suddenly cries out, appears to be awake and intensely frightened or aroused, but is unresponsive to parents' efforts to comfort or awaken the child. After a few minutes the child will return to normal sleep, and upon awakening will have no memory of a bad dream or even the event itself.

As many as 30% of all children may experience an episode of **somnambulism**—better known as "sleepwalking," usually first occurring between the ages of 4 and 8. The child gets up while still asleep and walks around, perhaps performing routine activities such as putting on an article of clothing or going to the bathroom. As with sleep terrors, the child does not respond to conversation, is extremely difficult to awaken, and upon awakening will have no memory of getting up during the night.

While nightmares, night terrors, and sleepwalking episodes can be upsetting for parents, they do not represent a significant health problem for the child unless their frequency or severity is so great that it interferes with normal daily functioning. The main association found with children who experience nightmares, sleep terrors, and sleepwalking appears to be having family members who also have experienced such disturbances. When episodes are frequent, often there has been some form of trauma or stress in the child's life. Regardless, these sleep disturbances typically decrease in number or stop completely as the child passes through adolescence.

Bed-Wetting. After successful daytime potty-training, many parents still need to diaper their 2- or 3-year-old during the night. After all, getting up during a sleep period to go to the bathroom involves a more complicated collection of skills and personal prompts. Some children pick up the knack more quickly than others (Goin, 1998). Bed-wetting is fairly common up until the age of 5, and about 7% of boys and 3% of girls continue to wet the bed beyond that age. Hypotheses for continued bed-wetting abound, including stress, poor toilet training, and various physiological conditions (Butler, 1998). Also, many children who wet the bed often have biological relatives who had wet the bed as children. Like other sleep period difficulties, most bed-wetting ends as the child enters adolescence (American Psychiatric Association, 1994). When children are sufficiently mature, bed-wetting can be successfully treated by using a "urine alarm" that will go off when a small amount of urine has been released onto the bedding (Mellon & McGrath, 2000).

Nutrition

Parents usually notice a dramatic change in their children's eating habits as they enter the preschool years. They may eat substantially less than they did as toddlers. They become pickier about what they will eat. Serving foods according to certain rituals may become a requirement for avoiding rejection and/or tantrums. They begin showing a preference for oversweet and overfat junk foods. They may insist on having a certain food every day, then refuse to eat it for months. Some days they seem ravenous and other days they eat very little. Observations such as these often fuel parents' concerns that their preschoolers may not be receiving adequate nutrients for healthy growth. Fortunately, most of their worries are unfounded. The sudden fluctuations in appetite are normal, most likely a result of their slowing physical growth (Rozin, 1990).

What are the nutritional needs of the average preschooler? The general recommendation for the active young child's healthy development is roughly 1700 calories a day. However, young children vary greatly in their appetites, with some consuming two or three times as much as their same-age counterparts. Beyond the observation that boys tend to eat a little more than girls, specific explanations for this variability have yet to be established (Birch, 1991).

It is recommended that around 55% of all preschoolers' calories come from carbohydrates, 30% from fat, and 15% from protein. In spite of their picky eating habits, the diet of the average preschooler in the United States comes close to these caloric proportions, although a little higher in fat calories and lower in carbohydrates. One study suggested that African-American children tend to have a higher intake of fat calories, while Caucasian children may consume more complex carbohydrates (Kimm, 1990).

The nutritional deficiencies most often found in a preschooler's diet are shortages of iron, calcium, and vitamins A and C. Iron deficiencies early in childhood have been associated with lower scores in tests of mental and motor functioning among kindergarteners (Lozoff, 1991). As might be expected, nutritional deficiencies in general tend to occur most often among children from low-income families. Race and/or ethnicity do not appear to affect low-income preschoolers' intake of nutrients, at least when African-American, Hispanic, and Caucasian preschoolers are compared (Friedman, 1991).

Probably as a result of less favorable nutrition, by the end of early childhood, low-income children measure on average about an inch shorter than their middle-class cohorts (Goldstein, 1971). Typically, the diets of undernourished low-income children rely more heavily on fast foods and highly processed foods than do the diets of other low-income families; such foods are notoriously high in fat and sodium and low in recommended nutrients (Karp, 1984). However, not even children from advantaged backgrounds always receive proper nutrition. Only 24% of 2- to 5-year-olds are found to have a good diet—and unfortunately, this percentage decreases as they get older (Federal Interagency Forum on Child and Family Statistics, 1999). Multivitamin and mineral supplements for preschoolers can help guard against undernourishment (Mindell, 1992; Pipes & Trahms, 1993).

What can parents do to help young children develop healthy eating habits?

Eating Habits and Preschoolers

At one time researchers believed that young children given the opportunity to eat as they please would naturally select a balanced diet (Davis, 1938). This assumption stemmed from observations of circumstances where the only foods offered were those high in nutrition. Considering the abundance of junk food currently available to preschoolers of the 2000s, findings such as these cannot be directly applied. However, these early studies do suggest that if we consistently present young children with a variety of nutritious foods and limit the amount of available junk food, they will be likely to consume quantities that support their needs in spite of their unpredictable and idiosyncratic eating habits (Story & Brown, 1987).

The preschool years mark the beginning of children's independent eating habits. Their motor skills have sufficiently developed for self-feeding, not only at the dinner table but also by enabling them to gain access to stored foods and even to prepare simple meals such as sandwiches. Their early eating behaviors and choices appear to be determined largely by guidance from caregivers, environmental controls, what they see others eating, preferences, and appetite (Pipes & Trahms, 1993).

PAVING PATHWAYS ALONG EARLY CHILDHOOD PHYSICAL MILESTONES: EATING SAFETY

Safety is one of the first concerns for those monitoring preschoolers' eating habits. Given their easy distractibility and high energy level and the relatively new challenge of learning to effectively chew and swallow, their eating behavior can easily lead to choking. The foods most likely to fatally choke a preschooler are hot dogs, hard candy, nuts, and grapes. In general, anything that is firm and round is a likely candidate for becoming lodged in the windpipe. Softer foods like hot dogs or grapes can be cut into less hazardous-shaped pieces; however, pediatricians have suggested that caregivers restrict foods such as these from the diets of children under 5 (Duyff, 1995). The following strategies can also lessen the possibility of choking (Pipes & Trahms, 1993):

► Preschoolers require constant supervision while they are eating. Only a caregiver who is present and attentive can intervene with unsafe eating behaviors or assist a child who has begun to choke.
► Children should not be allowed to play or walk around while they are eating. They are not likely to be concentrating on chewing and swallowing if a game is afoot.
► They need reminders not to talk with food in their mouths.
► They should not be fed in the car, at least while it is moving. If a child begins to choke, the driver might not be able to safely pull over in time.
► Preschoolers should be offered well-cooked and other softer foods, which are more easily chewed and swallowed.
► If the child is being treated with rub-on medications for teething pain, remember that as the child swallows some of the substance, a little numbness may occur in throat muscles used for swallowing. If the medication was applied just before feeding, caregivers should observe the eating child all the more carefully.

PAVING PATHWAYS ALONG EARLY CHILDHOOD PHYSICAL MILESTONES: FOSTERING EATING COMPLIANCE

Once again everyone else has finished eating and 4-year-old Bobby is still just pushing food around on his plate. He is not ill, and no amount of coaxing seems to make any difference. Somewhere along the line most parents are likely to encounter such a scenario with their preschooler. They may also become exasperated—frustrated that their child is not complying with their wishes that he or she eat appropriately, and worried that the noncompliance may result in inadequate nutrition. They may apply substantial pressure as their preschoolers balk, urging them to eat more or eat more quickly. Preschoolers do in fact conform to such pressure, forcing themselves to eat more or at a faster rate than their bodies instruct them. However, some researchers associate this type of learning with later obesity (Drucker et al., 1999).

Young children are more likely to consume adequate amounts of nutritious foods if the foods are presented in ways that consider preschoolers' eating idiosyncrasies. Their individual appetites vary unpredictably, and occasionally picking over a meal rather than eating it is not likely to do harm. For proper nutrition, preschoolers need to eat more frequently than adults, somewhere between five and seven times a day. Those who eat less often than four times a day, as if adhering to the adult standard of three square meals, tend not to receive adequate nutrition (Frank, 1977). Thus if between-meal snacks include nutritious foods the nutrients skipped at mealtime may not be missed.

Preschoolers' eating rituals can actually become an ally. If they insist on sitting in "their place" at the table when they eat, by all means let them sit there. What harm is there in complying with their insistence that their food be served on a certain dish with specific eating utensils? If food must be cut a certain way or must not touch other foods on the plate before they will eat it, parents can simply use a little care when serving their food. Meals can be provided that are easier for the preschooler to consume: finger foods, prepared meats that are easier to chew, such as chicken or hamburger rather than roasts and steaks, and firmer foods cut into manageable morsels.

Another major frustration for parents is the preschooler's tendency to balk when new foods are presented. Considering the preschooler's increased independence and capacity for encountering potential consumables—including poisonous substances—this tendency is actually adaptive (Rozin, 1990). We also need to remember what was mentioned in Chapter 5: The young child's taste buds are more sensitive than ours. The bitter and sour flavors of foods we enjoy may be overpowering for younger, more sensitive palates.

Young children will eventually try new foods if they are presented repeatedly (Sullivan & Birch, 1990). Parents are more likely to meet with success if they begin by giving them small amounts and letting them request more if they so desire. Ignoring their balking behavior and praising them when they comply are successful behavioral strategies for addressing a variety of parenting dilemmas. A common overstepping of the bounds that caregivers commit while employing positive reinforcement during mealtime is telling the pre-schooler "if you eat your broccoli (or squash, spinach, and the like), you can have your favorite dessert." Doing so may get compliance in the here and now, but the long-term effect will be to reinforce the child's perception that dessert is the desirable part of the meal and vegetables are to be endured rather than enjoyed, thus actually increasing the child's preference for sweets (Birch et al., 1987).

PAVING PATHWAYS ALONG EARLY CHILDHOOD PHYSICAL MILESTONES: ENCOURAGING INDEPENDENT, HEALTHY EATING HABITS

The parent's ultimate goal is to help children develop healthy eating habits and apply them on their own, without the need for a parent's constant stream of behavioral maneuvers. Following are some suggestions for encouraging such an outcome (Kendrick et al., 1991; Satter, 1987):

► When possible, give preschoolers a choice of which nutritious food they would like to eat. They learn the difference between snack foods and meal-time foods through offers of options that reflect the differences.

► Present meals containing small, nutritionally balanced portions. Doing so repeatedly provides exposure to a model of the types of food that are best included in a balanced meal. Additional servings can be offered if the child wants more.

► Limit the availability of sweets. The occasional cookie or candy bar is not harmful and can actually be beneficial at times. Nevertheless, most sugary foods have limited nutritional value. Since sweetness is their preferred taste sensation, young children making choices at snack time are likely to overindulge if sweets are always an option. There has also been some indication that consumption of large quantities of sweets can be followed by certain behavioral problems in preschoolers. When preschoolers were given juice sweetened with sugar or artificial sweetener and observed an hour later for their ability to maintain attention to a task and inhibit inappropriate gross motor movements during free play, those who had consumed the sugar did not perform as well (Goldman et al., 1986).

► Avoid power struggles such as demanding that children try a certain food or "clean their plates." Pressuring children at mealtime tends to cause eating problems rather than solve them: Imagine how you would feel if you were constantly being forced to consume substances that were distasteful or overwhelming! Remember also that teaching children to eat when they are not hungry may create habits that can lead to obesity.

Developing healthy eating habits is more important for preschoolers than observing food-handling etiquette.

Elizabeth Crews/Stock Boston

▶ Make mealtime a pleasant and stress-free experience. Preschoolers should be included in conversations with adults and older children. Discussions involving conflict and other negative emotional material should be saved for some other time. Preschoolers' table manners should not be confronted unless a safety issue is involved. They will learn most table manners by observing caregivers and older siblings.

▶ Preschoolers imitate the eating habits they see around them. If they see their parents constantly eating junk food or engaging in compulsive or otherwise inappropriate eating regimens, they are likely to develop similar habits as they grow older, regardless of how parents have encouraged them to eat.

HEALTH PROBLEMS

Illness

What sorts of conditions interfere with the preschooler's normal development?

Children can be expected to contract a fair number of minor illnesses—the well-known childhood assortment of coughs, sniffles, and tummy aches. These illnesses usually run their course and after a few days the child is back to normal. However, major illnesses that keep children bedridden for long periods of time can affect their growth patterns, in part by lessening production of growth hormone (Tanner, 1990; Torosian, 1996). A child may stop growing temporarily as the body concentrates its resources into recovery efforts, and then experience a "catch-up" period later. If a child is moderately or severely undernourished, however, the catch-up period may not occur and effects of retarded growth will be permanent. Since undernourished children are more susceptible to disease, impoverished children are especially at risk for health-related growth impairments.

When I was young, all children were expected to contract the nonrecurring diseases mumps, measles, and rubella ("German measles"). In fact, because rubella in pregnant mothers leads to birth defects, we girls were often sent to spend time with playmates who had contracted the disease in hopes that early exposure would prevent us from getting it as adults. These diseases are now preventable through childhood immunizations. (Imagine my amusement when upon my return to school for doctoral training, bureaucracy required that I give proof of immunization for these diseases!) Diphtheria, whooping cough, and poliomyelitis—less frequently occurring yet potentially more serious diseases—can also be prevented with early inoculation.

Early childhood immunizations have dramatically decreased the incidence of these diseases in recent decades. However, the United States has more recently become somewhat lax in stressing the importance of childhood immunizations (Brody, J., 1993). Because of the effectiveness of prevention, few of us have been exposed to the gut-wrenching horror of watching children suffer death or permanent disability from these diseases, and yet we very well may have viewed rare but media-sensationalized instances of children suffering debilitating or fatal allergic reactions to immunizations (Murphy, 1997; Neustaedter, 1996). Such biased exposures are not conducive to helping parents, who do need to understand potential risks but also must weigh those risks against the demonstrated, substantial benefits of inoculating young children (Offit & Bell, 1998). Children of families living in poverty have been typically less likely to receive a complete series of vaccinations, but fortunately this tendency has been decreasing in recent years (Federal Interagency Forum on Child and Family Statistics, 1999).

Environmental Exposures

For most of the last century lead poisoning was considered the most prevalent and most serious environmentally caused disease of young children in the United States. Depending upon such factors as differences in individual tolerance and the quantity of lead accumulated in a child's system, the symptoms of lead poisoning can range from minor headaches to convulsions, coma, and early death. Lead poisoning has also been associated with later difficulties such as lower IQs, academic problems, hyperactivity, and antisocial or criminal behavior (Mendelsohn et al., 1999; Silbergeld, 1997). A recent longitudinal study showed a relationship between the level of lead in young children's teeth and poorer reading ability, poorer grades, or having dropped out of school when observed at age 18 (Fergusson et al., 1997).

Over the last few decades, lead has been removed from substances likely to find their way into a young child's environment, such as gasoline, house paints, and switching from soldered tin cans to aluminum cans. Thanks to these precautions, the quantity of lead found in blood levels in the United States has dramatically declined (Pirkle et al., 1994). However, lead poisoning still occurs in young children; the chief source is the old leaded paint lying beneath newer paint jobs often found on the walls of low-income inner-city housing and older fixer-upper homes. Babies and young children may ingest the lead by eating fallen paint chips or inhaling the contaminated dust floating in the play environment. Inner-city children may also be exposed to lead while playing in soil that has not yet been treated for contamination by settled leaded exhaust fumes of previous eras (Agency for Toxic Substance and Disease Registry, 1988). As a preventive measure the Centers for Disease Control currently recommend that every child be evaluated at least once for lead poisoning before reaching the age of 6 (Centers for Disease Control, 1988).

Second-hand smoke presents another environmental risk. The current flurry of research directed toward establishing its precise effects is painting a clear picture: this passive killer has a significant impact on young children's health (Aligne & Stoddard, 1997). Preschoolers who are regularly exposed to secondhand smoke show a higher incidence of serious respiratory illnesses, ear infections, and asthma attacks. A certain percentage of these children require hospitalization and/or surgeries for these conditions, and some eventually die from such ailments. If we also factor in the number of deaths and burn injuries to preschoolers from fires caused by cigarettes and related paraphernalia, others' smoking habits take a heavy toll indeed on the physical health of preschoolers.

Excessive Stress and/or Lack of Affection

Like infants who suffer from nonorganic failure to thrive, preschoolers may suffer stunted growth because of stressful family situations. Divorce, poverty, abusive relationships in the family, and other stressful living conditions can all affect a preschooler's physical development, even if only temporarily. In fact, recent research has shown that brain cells in the hippocampus actually die when the person suffers ongoing stress, a disastrous consequence for a hippocampus that has not completely developed (McEwen, 1995).

Emotionally detached primary caregivers may be so preoccupied, aloof, or generally uninvolved with their preschoolers that the missing affection alone affects their children's growth patterns. This severe condition is called **deprivation dwarfism**. Afflicted children do not gain the weight and height expected for their age group, and their skeletal growth tends to be especially retarded. Deprived children tend to be cognitively and emotionally dull and disengaged from what is going on around them. As might be expected, this has an impact on their quality of play, further impairing normal development (Kreppner et al., 1999). Laboratory analysis of children with deprivation dwarfism has found that their bodies have slowed or stopped production of growth hormone, the substance normally released from the pituitary gland that promotes body growth during child development. Fortunately, when these children are placed in more loving and stimulating environments, the levels of growth hormone in their bodies and their growth patterns return to normal (Gardner, 1972; Money, 1992).

Tried......

BOX 8.1   Preventing injury to preschoolers

Ulione, M. S. (1997). Health promotion and injury prevention in a child development center. *Journal of Pediatric Nursing, 12,* 148–156.

A MAJOR CHALLENGE FOR PROFESSIONAL CHILD CARE providers is keeping their busy and active groups of youngsters safe from accidents and injuries. This is a particular concern for toddlers and preschoolers, whose yet-to-be refined gross motor skills and sense of balance can result in a significant number of self-caused injuries. State health regulations advise and enforce some safety standards, such as having adequate space and staff-child ratios. However, following state regulations alone does not address many elements of injury prevention. What other measures might child care centers take as they attempt to ensure the safety of their charges?

Margaret Smith Ulione proposed that providing child care workers with a nurse-directed health promotion program could reduce the number of accidental injuries. A pretest-posttest design tracked the injury history of 29 day care children ages 6 weeks to 5 years. A registered nurse evaluated the child participants' incidences of injury once a week for 4 weeks. An injury was defined as any physical mark on the body, such as a bruise, cut, or scrape. The registered nurse also asked questions regarding how the injuries occurred and evaluated the children for illness.

The child care workers were then given 12 hours of health and safety training, of which 5 hours centered on prevention of child and staff injuries. The registered nurse next performed a second series of evaluations, again once a week for 4 weeks. Statistics revealed significantly fewer accidental injuries after the presentation of the health promotion program: 17 injuries were recorded before the program and only 9 after.

There are several limitations to this study. The number of participants is small, increasing the likelihood that the significant-looking results actually occurred by chance. The registered nurse who examined the children appears to have been aware of the nature of the study, which raises the possibility of experimenter bias. Likewise, since the nurse examined only the children participating in the study, the staff would have little difficulty figuring out which children were of interest and thus might have been treating them differently. The author herself points out that generalization of these findings to other groups would be premature, as this particular effort was actually a pilot study preceding a future, larger-scale examination of the health promotion program.

Given all of these limitations, how applicable is such a study? Although studies of training directed at reducing accidental injury risk in day care centers are still few in number, a number of studies demonstrate the effectiveness of similar interventions directed at illness prevention. Therefore we can make the assumption that child care workers are not only trainable in health-related matters but also can successfully apply what they learn to actual practice.

Pilot studies such as these also point toward a method of accomplishing a goal in the absence of any alternative methods. And the process of devising injury measurement instruments and identifying how injuries occurred brings to the surface contributing factors that otherwise might not be so apparent but that, once identified, can be corrected. Thus at least a partial direction is provided for child care providers who wish to address child safety before the definitive study finds its way into the literature.

... and True

BOX 8.2   Child care provider safety tips

WHILE PREPARING THE STUDY JUST DISCUSSED, THE RE-searchers both combed the literature for factors associated with accidental injuries and observed a few more factors for themselves. Based on their efforts, here are some child care provider safety tips for preventing two of the most common sources of accidental injuries in child care centers: falls and playground activity (Ulione & Dooling, 1997):

Reducing the Number of Falls

- Provide adequate supervision, so that personnel can prevent children from getting into dangerous situations.
- When spills of slippery substances occur, clean the floor immediately and limit access to the area until the floor has dried.
- Do not put furniture or other objects under windows in a manner that gives a child easy access to the window.
- Provide handrails on stairways that match the level of the child's grip. Stairways should be well-lit and children should be regularly cautioned to go slowly while using the stairway.
- In high-traffic areas do not place scatter rugs or allow debris, toys, or other items that children might trip over. Provide a semi-enclosed area for toys that tend to scatter, such as blocks.
- Secure any furniture that could fall or be pulled over.
- Graduate children from crib use when the crib sides are at the child's nipple level. Keep crib toys at a minimum so they do not become make-shift stepping stools.

- Model safe behaviors yourself. As with other behaviors, preschoolers are highly likely to copy their caregivers' safety practices.

Preventing the Risk of Playground Injuries

- All areas of the playground should be observable at all times.
- Closely monitor children on the playground at all times.
- Secure climbing equipment and swings in concrete footings that extend at least 6 in. into the ground.
- Ground cover should be soft—lawn, sand, or bark-dust—rather than concrete or asphalt.
- Provide playground equipment designed specifically for the preschooler's body shape, size, strength, and level of coordination.
- Do not introduce children to new playground equipment just before lunch. Because their blood-sugar is low just before lunchtime, late morning is the time of day preschoolers are most likely to be injured.
- Check the playground every day for new hazards such as trash, loose or wobbly equipment, sharp or protruding surfaces on play equipment, or inadequate surfacing.
- Regularly instruct children regarding safe play practices, both on the playground and indoors.

Ulione, M. S., & Dooling, M. (1997). Preschool injuries in child care centers: Nursing strategies for prevention. *Journal of Pediatric Health Care, 11,* 111–116.

Accidents and Injuries

Accidents are the number-one cause of childhood death in the United States (United States Bureau of the Census, 1994). The greatest number of such deaths are attributed to car accidents. Other causes include fires, drowning, poisoning, falls, suffocation, and choking—and preschoolers are the most likely of any age group to fall victim to this latter assortment of tragedies. Some preschoolers are more likely than others to become accident victims: males, those with a crabby or oppositional temperament, and those with low socioeconomic status (Matheny, 1987; Schwebel & Plumert, 1999). Interestingly, mothers observing their children on playgrounds were found to be more likely to intervene in situations posing the risk of injury when the child was female, even though boys are more frequently injured (Morrongiello & Dawber, 2000).

Parents have the greatest power for preventing injury. Most states require that vehicular passengers under the age of 5 be restrained in age-appropriate car seats, and compliance does appear to reduce the number of child deaths in car accidents. Because deployed airbags pose a threat to little people, car seats should be placed in the back seat rather than the front. Parents can install smoke detectors and practice family drills and educate their children regarding other major risks as well. Most other causes of injury or death in young children can be prevented by providing attentive adult supervision. However, this is easier said than done. Not even the most conscientious parent can be there at just the right moment all the time. Thus the best strategy for caregivers as they develop supervisory habits is to remain aware of any potential hazards in an environment and weigh them against each child's idiosyncrasies and behavioral history. The Tried . . . . and True boxes on pages 236–237 take a closer look at practicing child safety to reduce the risk of accidents and injuries to preschoolers.

Preschoolers are capable of understanding the concept of danger, but they need help in learning to identify the salient aspects of a dangerous situation (Hill et al., 2000). Formal educational programs have successfully assisted preschoolers in this endeavor by addressing some specific risky situations they may encounter (Ampofo-Boateng et al., 1993; Thomson et al., 1992). For example, one of the most important skills children learn is how to safely cross a road. Very few 5-year-olds can consider all the relevant variables without receiving specific instruction. Such instruction, however, considerably improves their ability to choose a safe route. Instruction makes preschoolers aware of objects or situations that obstruct their view of the road, teaches them to recognize the characteristics of intersections that make them especially complex and dangerous, and gives them an appreciation for the variety of dangers of wandering into or crossing a road (Thomson, 1997).

Child Maltreatment

Child abuse is the infliction of psychological, physical, or sexual harm on a child by an adult. **Child neglect** involves a caregiver's failure to meet a child's basic needs for physical or emotional survival. While our culture views child maltreatment as horrifying, it unfortunately has become more and more common. In the United States almost three million cases of child maltreatment are reported each year—and those are only the detected cases (McCurdy & Daro, 1994).

Incidence of child abuse varies among cultures. Among less violent societies, the core cultural rituals and traditions including parenting practices are more likely to enforce cooperative, harmonious beliefs and to devalue individual achievement and assertion of power because of their emphases on competitiveness and aggression (Bonta, 1997). Those cultures that value children highly, involve multiple caregivers, have minimal behavioral expectations of very young children, and frown upon violence in general are the ones that show the lowest incidence of child abuse (Korbin, 1994). Considering how distracted our busily industrialized nation is and Western cultural emphases on independence, personal control, personal competence, and power, little wonder that we struggle!

Causes of Child Maltreatment. Why parents abuse their children has been a topic of considerable study over the past couple of decades. While we

The behavior of this young girl demonstrates two effects of corporal punishment: modeling after the behavior she has observed and acting out her anger over the way she has been treated by behaving aggressively herself.

David Strickler/The Image Works

once speculated that anyone who would abuse a child must be mentally disturbed, this generally does not seem to be the case (Zigler & Hall, 1989). Child abuse is more often reported in homes where there are significant stressors, such as poverty, unemployment, substance abuse, frequent moves, dysfunctional or broken marriages, and overcrowded or chaotic households. Parents in such homes may take out their frustrations on the children or are just too burnt-out to parent effectively (Wolfe, 1985; Wolfner & Gelles, 1993). Children with difficult temperaments appear more likely to be emotionally neglected but not physically abused or neglected (Harrington et al., 1998).

There is also some indication that abusive parents may simply not know how to parent or what to realistically expect of young children (Reid et al., 1982). They may be excessively invested in controlling their child's behavior and view their child as "bad" when disobedient or otherwise not yielding to their efforts at control (Bugental et al., 1989). Often, abusive parents were abused by their own parents. They commonly choose an overcontrolling and punitive parenting style—the style with which they themselves were most likely raised—rather than one using reasoning and encouragement (van IJzendoorn, 1992).

Effects of Child Maltreatment. The effects of maltreatment on the developing child are substantial. The most severe possible consequence is child fatality, which occurs in 1 in every 1000 reported instances. While many abused children suffer physical injuries, their more common experience is an ongoing pattern of neglect of and assault on their emotional well-being (McCurdy & Daro,

1994). They endure ridicule, name-calling, put-downs, unreasonable demands or criticism, or are perhaps even out-and-out terrorized by those who are supposed to be caring for them.

One consequence of child maltreatment is the deprivation dwarfism discussed earlier. More commonly these children have problems developing relationships with peers and teachers, difficulty performing academically, and deficits in cognitive ability (Malinosky-Rummell & Hansen, 1993; Money, 1992). Their self-esteem is typically poor, and they often look sad and dejected. They tend to view themselves as "bad" people—why else would they deserve such treatment? Suicidal and self-destructive behavior are not unusual among abused children. Exposure to abuse and other forms of violence may disrupt a child's ability to perform common developmental tasks, resulting in the many difficulties that can follow an abused child throughout his or her lifetime (Margolin & Gordis, 2000).

Abused children's neurological functioning deviates from that observed among children who are not abused, especially in the area of perceptual motor development (Green, 1988). While head trauma would be an expected cause, a disproportionate number of neurological deficiencies are also found in abused children who have not suffered such injuries (Glaser, 2000; Martin, 1974). One study found central nervous system deficiencies among 52% of abused children, 38% of neglected children, and 14% of normal children (Green, 1981). Some speculate that absence of the healthy parent-child attachment and interaction that are so crucial to healthy brain development may play a role (see Chapter 7). Some children may have had neurological problems before the abuse started, and may in fact have provoked abuse by their hyperactivity and other difficult-to-manage behaviors (Sandgrund et al., 1974).

Interventions for Child Maltreatment. Most abusive parents do not truly wish to cause harm to their children. On some level they realize they are out of control but do not know what to do about it. Other abusive parents honestly believe that striking children is "for their own good" (Miller, 1983). Such parents can be helped through parenting education and crisis counseling (Stevenson, 1999). Parenting programs have even been effective for certain American minority groups among which the practice of striking children has become culturally ingrained (Alvy, 1994).

Unfortunately, for some families no amount of intervention can stop the abuse or neglect: the caregivers or the home situation are simply too inadequate (Crittenden, 1992). In these circumstances the only viable solution is foster placement. While foster care has come under a lot of criticism in recent years, it is preferable to leaving a child in danger of severe physical or emotional injury. Placements tend to be most successful when 1) the child is still very young, 2) serious behavioral or emotional problems are not yet present, 3) the birth parents have minimal involvement, 4) the family and foster child have been carefully matched, and 5) foster parents receive professional preparation and guidance (Scholte, 1997).

Even foster children in successful placements show more emotional and behavioral difficulties than children in the general population. Nevertheless, they tend to fare better than children left in abusive homes of origin (Minty, 1999; Widom, 1991). Single placements are associated with fewer emotional and behavioral problems than a series of home placements (Goerge et al., 1992; Marcus, 1991). The usual decline in foster children's academic performance immediately following placement can be mediated by continued enrollment in their old school (Ayasse, 1995).

Hillary Rodham Clinton (1995) is no doubt most quoted for her observation that "it takes a village to raise a child." Successful prevention of child abuse acknowledges the spirit of this observation. Formal education in the areas of child development and parenting effectiveness can begin as early as high school. Social service agencies can offer ongoing parenting support such as crisis counseling, classes, and child care for low-income families, as well as help parents address such problems as poverty, unemployment, and other social stressors that can lead to child abuse. More and more businesses and industries now offer on-site child care facilities and sick-leave policies that are "family friendly." Grassroots organizations such as Parents Anonymous provide peer support for at-risk parents as they struggle with the frustrations of childrearing.

However, the most important element in any plan for reducing child abuse may be a reevaluation of the cultural biases that fuel its likelihood: the acceptance of violence as a problem-solving strategy, as portrayed by media violence; the continuing belief among many that physical punishment is an appropriate childrearing strategy; and a societal resource distribution style that undervalues the importance of providing quality child care (Zigler & Hall, 1989).

SUMMARY

Body Growth and Change

Preschoolers grow about 2½ in. and gain about 6 lb each year, becoming more streamlined in appearance and less top-heavy. The nervous and lymph systems continue to grow faster than the other organs.

Brain Development

Brain size increases to 90% of its eventual adult weight. Hemispheric differences such as handedness become evident and the corpus callosum experiences a growth spurt, enabling combined cognitive and physical tasks to be better coordinated. As perceptual abilities mature, preschoolers become significantly better able to distinguish the finer differences among stimuli. Although they begin as somewhat farsighted and relatively inefficient at coordinating eye muscles, toward the end of the preschool years their visual abilities have advanced well enough for them to begin learning to read.

Motor Development

Coordination of abilities controlled by more than one part of the brain is learned. Attempting to create a "child prodigy" by organizing a child's activity around a single interest can work against normal preschooler brain development. Parents and child-care workers can help children enhance brain development by making sure they take part in a variety of activities, especially those that involve combinations of physical and cognitive functions of the brain.

Preschoolers learn and master a number of new gross motor skills, such as climbing stairs, riding tricycles, running, jumping, and hopping. Boys tend to be slightly more advanced at basic gross motor skills, while girls more quickly develop skills involving balance and coordination. Fitness programs for preschoolers are good exercise but generally do not hasten motor development. Fine motor improvements in their hands and fingers enable them to dress themselves and to manipulate objects such as scissors, puzzle pieces, and other small toys. They begin to express themselves through drawings, and the standard sequencing in which the sophistication of their drawings improves suggests that brain maturation plays the major role.

Early Childhood Health Needs

Preschoolers still need a lot of sleep, and sleep more deeply than do adults and older children. Their active imaginations now contribute to production of both dreams and nightmares. Sleep terrors and somnambulism may also occur. Bedwetting is common up through age 5, and is not all that uncommon as an occasional occurrence up until adolescence. Most children will have recovered from such difficulties as they enter adolescence. Preschoolers' eating habits can become very picky. Sudden increases and decreases in appetite or changes of food preference are normal and harmless. Nutritional difficulties such as iron deficiency can have long-term cognitive effects and are more commonly seen in low-income families.

As preschoolers learn to self-feed, safe eating habits need to be encouraged, such as sitting while eating and not talking while chewing, and caregivers need to limit availability of foods that can be choked on. Preschoolers can receive proper nutrition despite their picky eating habits if they are offered nutritious snacks between meals, their eating "rituals" are complied with, and they are given interesting finger foods. Since forcing young children to try new foods causes more problems than it solves, new foods are best introduced through repeated presentations of small amounts on their plate. Eventually the new foods will become familiar enough for the child to feel comfortable with trying them.

Health Problems

Colds, flu, and other minor illness are common among preschoolers. Some childhood illnesses, such as measles, mumps, and polio are preventable with vaccines. Environmentally caused health problems such as lead poisoning and secondhand smoke can significantly affect a child's physical health. So also can emotional causes such as excessive and ongoing family stress and/or absence of affection. Accidents are the major cause of death in young children. Child maltreatment often leaves physical, cognitive, and emotional scars, but can be prevented through parental education and community support efforts.

KEY TERMS

child abuse	deprivation dwarfism	perceptual learning
child neglect	lymph system	sleep terrors
corpus callosum	nightmare	somnambulism

CONCEPT REVIEW

1. Preschoolers' physical growth patterns are centered most conspicuously on the development of their _____, as well as a speedier rate of development of the _____ system.

2. By the time a child is 5 years old, his or her brain is _____% of its eventual adult size. A growth spurt experienced by the _____ aids the preschooler's ability to perform tasks requiring coordination of the two cerebral hemispheres.

3. About _____ out of ten children are left-handed; however, in spite of a few slight differences in physical and achievement-related characteristics, the main difficulty they encounter is _____.

4. Preschoolers' perceptual learning advances as they are repeatedly exposed to relevant perceptual _____.

5. The types of exposures and experiences important to early brain development are those that are _____ and require using _____.

6. Preschool-age motor skills requiring the use of _____ tend to progress more quickly in boys, while girls tend to progress more quickly in activities involving _____ and _____.

7. Advances in fine motor skills are due not only to maturation of _____ but also to _____. These advances can be observed in children's early drawings: 2-year-olds mainly _____, 3-year-olds can draw primitive _____, and 4- and 5-year-olds can organize drawings that are intended to represent _____.

8. The preschooler's less cooperative stance toward bedtime can be moderated by the use of _____. Sleep disturbances such as _____,

_____ and _____ commonly make their first appearances during the preschool years.

9. Parents often notice that their preschoolers' eating habits are much more _____ than they had been as toddlers. The most potentially significant nutritional deficiency of this age is insufficient _____, resulting in lower scores in tests of _____ and _____ abilities.

10. Preschoolers' eating safety is threatened by _____, which can be avoided by offering foods that are _____ and through greater parental _____.

11. Eating compliance can be encouraged when parents go along with their child's _____, and repeatedly _____ rather than _____ new foods.

12. Children who suffer through long periods of illness may experience stunted growth due to lessened production of _____. Fortunately, many of the more common potentially serious childhood illnesses are preventable by _____.

13. Historically the most common environmental contaminant affecting preschoolers, found to cause both mental deficiencies and serious health problems, is _____; more currently the environmental hazard of _____ has been linked to a higher incidence of upper respiratory diseases in preschoolers.

14. Studies of deprivation dwarfism have demonstrated that levels of growth hormone can be affected by the amount of _____ and _____ received by preschoolers.

15. The primary causes of death of preschool-age children are _____-related.

16. Potential causes of child maltreatment include family _____, child _____, and deficiencies in _____. Although many children have died from maltreatment, the more common permanent effects are related to _____ well-being.

17. Interventions that have improved the lot of maltreated children are _____ and _____.

1) limbs; lymph; 2) 90; corpus callosum; 3) one; living in a right-handed world; 4) cues; 5) varied; interconnections between brain structures; 6) muscles; balance; coordination; 7) sensory and motor relays; learning; scribble; shapes; reality; 8) transitional rituals; nightmares; night terrors; somnambulism (sleep-walking); 9) picky; iron; mental; motor; 10) choking; chopped smaller; supervision; 11) eating rituals; offer; force; 12) growth hormone; inoculations; 13) lead poisoning; secondhand smoke; 14) affection; stimulation; 15) accident; 16) stress, temperament; parenting knowledge; emotional; 17) parent education; foster placement

RESOURCES FOR FURTHER READING

Coren, S. (1992). *The left-hander syndrome: The causes and consequences of left-handedness.* New York: Vintage.

Ferber, R. (1985). *Solve your child's sleep problems.* New York: Simon & Schuster.

Gardner, H. (1980). *Artful scribbles: The significance of children's drawings.* New York: Basic Books.

Healy, J. (1994). *Your child's growing mind: A practical guide to brain development and learning from birth to adolescence.* New York: Doubleday.

Jenest, V. (1997). *Food for little fingers.* New York: St. Martin's Press.

Melton, G. B., & Barry, F. D. (1994). *Protecting children from abuse and neglect: Foundations for a new national strategy.* New York: Guilford Press.

Miller, A. (1983). *For your own good: Hidden cruelty in child-rearing and the roots of violence.* New York: Farrar, Straus & Giroux.

Pipes, P. L., & Trahms, C. M. (1993). *Nutrition in infancy and childhood,* 5th ed. St. Louis, MO: Mosby.

Stone, L., Stone, L., & Levy, L. (1996). *The safe and sound child: Keeping your child safe inside and outside the home.* Glenview, IL: GoodYearBooks.

INFOTRAC COLLEGE EDITION

For additional readings, explore InfoTrac College Edition, your online library. Go to http://www.infotrac-college.com/wadsworth and use the passcode that came on the card with your book. Try these search terms: accidental injury and children, bedtime rituals, bed-wetting, brain development and early childhood, child abuse, child neglect, childhood immunizations, children's drawings, early childhood education—activity programs, eating habits and early childhood, handedness, motor development and early childhood, nightmares and children, nutrition and preschoolers, secondhand smoke and children

CHILD DEVELOPMENT CD-ROM

Go to the Wadsworth Child Development CD-ROM for further study of the concepts in this chapter. The CD-ROM also includes quizzes and additional activities to expand your learning experience.

REFERENCES

For a list of references for this chapter, see the Wadsworth Psych Study Center Web site at: http://www.wadsworth.com/product/0534348092s

CHAPTER 9

Early Childhood Cognitive Development

FOCUS QUESTIONS

▶ What is preoperational thought, and how do we see evidence of it in the young child's thinking processes?

▶ What limitations can we expect to observe as the young child reasons?

▶ How do interactions with mentors affect what a young child learns?

▶ How effective are the preschooler's attending, memory, and perspective-taking functions?

▶ What affects development of the young child's intellectual ability?

▶ What is emotional intelligence?

▶ What kind of day care/preschool program best serves the needs of the young child's developing cognitive skills?

▶ What positive roles can television play in a young child's intellectual development?

▶ What kinds of advances occur in the preschooler's language ability?

OUTLINE

Piaget's Preoperational Thought
The Symbolic Function Substage
The Intuitive Thought Substage
Limitations of Preoperational Thought
Vygotsky's Sociocultural Theory
Information-Processing
Attention
Memory
Theory of Mind

Intelligence
Individual Differences in Intelligence
Emotional Intelligence
Paving Pathways: Evaluating Preschool/Day Care Programs
Paving Pathways: Television as an Educational Tool
Language Development
Vocabulary
Grammar
Conversation

A colleague once shared with me a description of how to handle difficult teacher-child situations. He had heard a speaker suggest that power struggles could be broken up if the teacher did something bizarre and out of character. As an example he described a situation where the entire class was doing assignments except for one problem student who was whooping it up in the back of the room. The teacher knelt next to the student, looked him in the eye, and asked "Want to buy a dead duck?" The student was bewildered for a few moments, then eventually focused himself onto his work.

I thought this tale was hilarious and I was certain that my 8-year-old son, Ben, would also enjoy it. I told him the whole story barely containing my laughter, and gave in to a tear-spangled guffaw when I got to the part about the dead duck. As I dabbed the moisture from my eyes I noticed that Ben was just standing there, his hands in his pockets and watching me intently.

"Well?" I asked. "Didn't you think that was funny?"

"So how much was the duck?"

Ben did not follow the humor in this story because he was tracking it along a single theme: the sale of a dead duck. In order to understand the joke he would need to additionally consider the second theme: the teacher's motive of trying to confuse the student long enough for the student to forget his antics and do his work. When I shared this story with Ben again at age 11 he easily saw the humor in it, as well as the humor in his original reaction as an 8-year-old.

During the preschool years a child's information processing and language skills advance by leaps and bounds. Parents observing such progress can easily begin expecting too much of their young children's cognitive abilities. However, missing pieces, such as the one ignored during Ben's processing of the dead duck story, are even more notable in preschoolers. For the young child, reasoning and drawing conclusions are not unlike trying to assemble a puzzle when you have only a few of the pieces—and then attempting to proclaim what you think the whole might be! As Piaget assessed preschooler cognitive ability, most of his research focused on the holes left behind as children assemble their short-handed cognitive puzzles.

What is preoperational thought, and how do we see evidence of it in the young child's thinking processes?

PIAGET'S PREOPERATIONAL THOUGHT

Piaget based his conceptualizations of preschoolers' thinking styles on his observations of their reasoning limitations rather than noting how preschoolers may have advanced since infancy and toddlerhood (Wadsworth, 1996). In spite of its limitations the stage of **preoperational thought**, occurring between the ages of 2 and 7, introduces more systematic use of mental representations as children create an understanding of the world around them. As the term "preoperational" implies, Piaget believed that preschool-age children are not yet able to apply more sophisticated mental operations such as logic as they develop these understandings (Piaget & Inhelder, 1966/1969). He divided the stage of preoperational thought into two substages: symbolic function and intuitive thought.

The Symbolic Function Substage

As we left off the discussion of sensorimotor development in Chapter 6, we noted that preschoolers who are completing the first cognitive stage are graduating toward the use of mental representations. Between the ages of 2 and 4, during the **symbolic function substage**, preschoolers not only expand their mental representation strategies but also begin using a variety of signs and symbols intended to represent aspects of their environment. Piaget defines a **sign** as a mental representation that more or less fits in with consensual reality, or the common perception of its meaning. Signs are the basis of interpersonal communication. Language is an agreed-upon collection of signs consisting of verbal representations of objects, thoughts, and ideas. Numbers are signs used to represent quantity and are so commonly accepted that one way or another, individuals who speak different languages are able to communicate quantity. Piaget defines a **symbol** as a more personalized mental representation than a sign. Sensory experiences, such as what it feels like to play in the bathtub or run through the tall grass, are symbols retained and retrieved as memories but vary some from person to person.

Make-believe play is a commonly observed example of children using symbolic functions. The frequency of make-believe play increases dramatically during the preschool years (Piaget, 1946/1962; 1990). A coffee-can lid with some blocks on it becomes a chicken dinner; throwing a blanket over the family dog turns him into a ghost; donning a makeshift cape turns the child into a superhero. Digressing from culture's previous beliefs, Piaget proposed that preschoolers' play is not only "for fun" but is also a means of practicing new schemes.

Just as play has proven to be an important component of preschoolers' physical development, so also does it appear to contribute significantly to a child's cognitive development. Children who spend more time in make-believe play score higher on tests of language and cognition (Fisher, 1992; Lillard, 1993). Preschoolers in fact seem to prefer such play, as they bring in a greater number of children, show greater personal involvement and cooperation, and draw out such games over a longer period of time than they do when participating in games that do not involve make-believe play (Connolly et al., 1988). Imaginary friends become common at this age, but they tend to accompany the only child and first-borns more than younger siblings (Gleason et al., 2000).

The Intuitive Thought Substage

One of the remarkable characteristics that sets human beings apart from other species emerges during the second half of the preoperational thought stage. Between the ages of 4 and 7 children begin looking for reasons why things happen the way they do. These "eternal why's of the child" can be quite challenging as adults attempt to provide explanations:

"Why do butterflies have two wings?"
"How does water get you wet?"
"Why don't things fall on the ceiling?"
"Why did you get to be the Mommy instead of the Daddy?"

A friend of mine was walking the buffet line at a social event when a young girl asked her to identify which of the cookies were peanut butter cookies. After my friend pointed them out the girl picked one up and said "This one looks like it has more peanut butter in it than that one." Sampling her selection, she announced "yes, I was right, it does," and happily trotted back to her table.

The knowledge base that preschoolers build is not founded on valid systems of logic or scientific reasoning, but rather on the child's simple acceptance of what he or she has been told and on disconnected bits and pieces of personal observations. Having noted numerous examples of preschool-age reasoning similar to the peanut butter cookie enthusiast's, Piaget labeled this period the **intuitive thought substage**. What the child "knows" stems from intuitive sensing and blind belief rather than logical thinking.

What limitations can we expect to observe as the young child reasons?

Limitations of Preoperational Thought

As Piaget explored preschoolers' cognitive abilities, he was fascinated by the novel reasoning processes—or observed lack thereof—they applied toward solving problems. While later research has confirmed similar limitations, the following discussion makes clear that they are not quite as drastic as Piaget proposed (Gelman et al., 1999).

Centration. Many of the following limitations are a product of the use of **centration**, the tendency to consider only one variable and exclude consideration of any other relevant information (Piaget, 1947/1973). This characteristic of young children's reasoning is most dramatically illustrated by Piaget's experiments with **conservation**. Conservation is the recognition that changing the shape or configuration of an object or collection of objects does not affect the actual size or quantity. If you have access to the services of a preschool-age child you can easily replicate his basic findings. Present the child with two glasses containing equal amounts of water and ascertain from the child that they are indeed equal. Then pour one glass of water into a wide flat bowl and ask the child which has the most water in it now. The child will either say the bowl has the greater amount because it is wider or that the glass has the greater amount because it is taller. The child is not likely to conserve quantity because he or she will center on the single variable of width or height, dimensions that are indeed different for the two presentations of liquid. Table 9.1 shows several conservation problems and typical preschooler responses. Notice that the responses are perception bound: The judgments are based on the greater size of a single feature of the second presentation, with no consideration that nothing has been added or subtracted from the initial presentation.

Two other limitations contribute to preschoolers' reasoning errors during conservation tasks: **irreversibility** and **perception-bound thought**. The child has difficulty thinking back to the beginning of a series of steps, thus treating them as irreversible (Piaget & Inhelder, 1966/1969). Once a transformation has taken place the results are treated as a permanent state. Daddy can be amateurishly dressed up as Santa and have his young child completely convinced that he or she has encountered the original yuletide elf. Preschoolers' reasoning thus tends to be *perception bound:* What exists is what they currently observe—in this case, Santa—no matter that the same person was Daddy a few moments earlier (DeVries, 1969; Flavell et al., 1983). Likewise, the two quantities of water in the conservation task are judged as different because they appear different at the time of observation, and the earlier perception of their having been equal amounts is not considered.

Although preschoolers consistently commit such errors, the cause may simply be that they have not been exposed to the more appropriate reasoning strategy, rather than that they lack the maturity to use it. Other researchers have walked children through the conservation task, explaining that the amount of water is still the same even though it looks different. When these preschoolers were later presented with other conservation tasks they made fewer errors (Field, 1987). Thus they appear able to employ such reasoning, but resort to centration and perception-bound thought when they have not yet learned more successful strategies.

Type of conservation	Initial presentation	Manipulation	Preoperational child's answer
Number	Two identical rows of objects are shown to the child, who agrees they have the same number.	One row is lengthened and the child is asked whether one row now has more objects.	Yes, the longer row.
Matter	Two identical balls of clay are shown to the child. The child agrees that they are equal.	The experimenter changes the shape of one of the balls and asks the child whether they still contain equal amount of clay.	No, the longer one has more.
Length	Two sticks are aligned in front of the child. The child agrees that they are the same length.	The experimenter moves one stick to the right, then ask the child if they are equal in length.	No, the one on the top is longer.
Volume	Two balls are placed in two identical glasses with an equal amount of water. The child sees the balls displace equal amounts of water.	The experimenter changes the shape of one of the balls and asks the child if it still will displace the same amount of water.	No, the longer one on the right displaces more.
Area	Two identical sheets of cardboard have wooden blocks placed on them in identical positions. The child agrees that the same amount of space is left on each piece of cardboard.	The experimenter scatters the blocks on one piece of cardboard and then asks the child if one of the cardboard pieces has more space covered.	Yes, the one on the right has more space covered up.

TABLE 9.1

Examples of conservation tasks, and a young child's typical responses. From Santrock, J. W. (1993). *Children,* 3rd ed., Madison, WI: Wm. C. Brown, p. 280. Reprinted by permission of McGraw-Hill Companies.

Egocentrism. In the movie *Jerry Maguire* a preschool-age child is conversing with Jerry, his mother's boyfriend, when Jerry inadvertently utters a profanity. The child looks shocked and points out Jerry's error. When Jerry appears concerned the child assures him not to worry, saying "I won't tell." The child has apparently assumed that like himself, Jerry has a Mommy somewhere who would punish him if he said a bad word. This is an example of **egocentrism**, the tendency of young children to center on their own personal experience and thus assume that others' experiences of the world are identical to theirs.

Another example of egocentrism is **animistic thinking** (Piaget, 1926/1963). Preschoolers often attribute lifelike existence to inanimate objects. Teddy Bear must also have covers over him or he will get cold. In preschoolers' drawings the sun often has a smiling face. Once, after an ice storm, my son Frank, who was 3 or 4 at the time, noted the coating of ice over the local flora with his comment, "the trees are crying."

In his original studies of egocentrism Piaget used a "perspective-taking" task. He presented children with a model of a mountain scene arranged on a table (see Figure 9.1) and had them observe the scene from a number of angles. He then positioned the children on one side of the model and placed a doll on the opposite side. Children were shown a group of photos and asked to select the picture representing what the doll could see. They typically chose a picture

FIGURE 9.1

Piaget's perspective-taking task. Piaget found that preoperational children observing a mountain range such as the one in this illustration had difficulty determining the doll's visual perspective, often deciding that it was the same as their own. When later studies used environmental scenarios more familiar to preschoolers than mountain ranges they had less difficulty with the task. From Berk, L. E. (1993). *Infants, Children, and Adolescents.* Needham Heights, MA: Allyn & Bacon, p. 314, by permission.

showing their own perspective of the scene. Piaget concluded that this error was evidence of preschoolers' inability to consider perspectives other than their own (Piaget & Inhelder, 1948/1969).

However, subsequent research has suggested otherwise. When presented with objects and scenarios that are more familiar to them than mountain ranges, preschoolers are much more successful at identifying the correct perspective (Borke, 1975). Thus they appear able to take the perspective of others but may simply resort to their well-worn centration strategy when the task becomes too difficult.

Difficulty with Hierarchal Classification. Preoperational children have difficulty considering classes and subclasses. Suppose you gave a preschooler a number of square blocks, most of them red but a few blue ones as well. If you ask whether there are more red blocks or more blue blocks, the child will probably answer correctly. If, however, you ask if there are more square blocks or more red blocks, the child will most likely report that there are more red ones. This error is a product of the preschooler's difficulty grasping such concepts as that color is a subclass of the collection of blocks, all of which are square.

Transductive Reasoning. The most strategically important concept that is missing from preschoolers' logical processes is the existence of general rules. For example, when we use **inductive reasoning**, we create general, abstract rules on the basis of multiple observations of particulars:

> Pansies, roses, zinnias, marigolds, and daisies all grow better when watered and fertilized. We can therefore assume flowers in general grow better when appropriately watered and fertilized.

To use **deductive reasoning**, we apply general rules to specific examples:

> Flowers grow better when appropriately watered and fertilized. Carnations are flowers. Therefore carnations should grow better if given water and fertilizer.

Rather than considering such rules, preschoolers use **transductive reasoning**: they relate concepts by simply going from specific to specific (Piaget, 1946/1962):

> I smelled this flower a lot. It's dead now. I smelled it too much.

Deductive reasoning requires considerable factual knowledge and familiarity with formal rules and models for mental processing, resources of which the developing preschooler is still in short supply (Johnson-Laird, 1999). By omitting relevant general concepts—such as the fact that all flowers will eventually wither away—preschoolers often attribute cause-and-effect between simultaneous events when none actually exists. As they approach the concrete operational stage, their growing store of knowledge and blossoming abilities to access long-term memories and apply general rules reduce the number of errors of this nature (Janveau-Brennan & Markovits, 1999).

VYGOTSKY'S SOCIOCULTURAL THEORY

How do interactions with mentors affect what a young child learns?

As the preceding discussion of preoperational reasoning showed, when the cognitive limitations that Piaget ascribed to preschoolers are reexamined, it turns out that with appropriate instruction they can learn and apply reasoning strategies that Piaget would not have believed possible. Lev Vygotsky would not have been so surprised. As you saw in Chapter 1, Vygotsky suggested that children's cognitive development progresses not as an innately driven, unfolding collection of specific cognitive skills, but instead emerges as a series of potentials for learning. As each new potential emerges, the child can incorporate it into new reasoning strategies only if opportunities for learning are presented within the so-called zone of proximal development (Vygotsky, 1934/1962).

Since timely guidance from influential others will mold these precursors into socially relevant reasoning strategies, the healthy development of children's cognitive abilities requires that a mentor be available—be it a parent, caregiver, sibling, or teacher. What do mentors do that capitalizes upon a child's zone of proximal development? First, they enlist and maintain the child's interest and attention for the task at hand, perhaps structuring an actual opportunity for learning. They explain the task in terms that fit the particular child's level of language, intellect, and understanding. They may model successful performance of the task themselves. As the child attempts a task, the mentor coaches the child through the steps, pointing out errors along the way, suggesting solutions for errors, and providing encouragement when frustrations arise (Burt & Perlis, 1999; Rogoff, 1990). What mentors actually coach children to do is, of course, culture-bound: They introduce and reinforce those behaviors and thought processes that are likely to contribute to successful living within the mentor's (and most likely the child's) culture, and choose those goals and tasks that they see as having utility within the particular child's society (Furth, 1996; Kitchener, 1996).

This child's mentor is teaching plant-handling techniques that are consistent with their culture. Notice how their practices differ from those being taught to the child on page 197.

If you observe young children as they address tasks on their own, you may note evidence of their past experiences with mentors. They will verbally coach themselves! Piaget called this self-talk **egocentric speech**, believing that it actually represented the preoperational child's self-oriented focus; the child was simply babbling on in a self-centered manner, not considering that the monologue might not be comprehensible to others. Vygotsky, however, argued that this **private speech** is actually internalized instructions from mentors serving the purpose of enhancing task performance, rather than communicating with others. As the child grows older, such self-instruction will become silent—not because of fading egocentrism, as Piaget would see it, but because it has become incorporated into the child's inner voice. Research on the private speech of young children has generally supported Vygotsky's view over Piaget's (Berk, 1992).

How effective are the preschooler's attending, memory, and perspective-taking functions?

INFORMATION-PROCESSING

The preceding discussion described a number of the reasoning strategies that young children learn and apply as they draw conclusions. The information-processing approach addresses the development of problem-solving strategies through a "nuts and bolts of learning" standpoint—the elements that underlie the picking up of a new strategy. During the preschool years children process information at ever greater speeds, independent of whatever inaccuracies or errors may be involved (Kail, 1991; Miller & Vernon, 1997). This next section will take a look at the roles of preschooler attention, memory, and theory of mind.

Attention

We might say that preschoolers do not have a problem with paying attention—they pay attention to everything! This is precisely the developmental predicament observed in young children. They have difficulty focusing on a single target, and even when they do so are easily distracted by whatever else their sensing abilities encounter. Thus while problem-solving they tend to focus on those stimulus characteristics that stand out for them, such as entertainment value, attractiveness, or curiosity-inducing ability, rather than on what might be relevant to solving the problem at hand (Flavell et al., 1993; Paris & Lindauer, 1982; Ruff & Rothbart, 2000).

Between the ages of 2 and 6, and especially between 2 and 4, the ability of children to sustain an attentional focus improves significantly (Ruff et al., 1998; Sarid & Breznitz, 1997). Cultural influences can affect how children learn to focus their attention; for example, Guatemalan Mayan caregiver-child dyads are more likely to track two events simultaneously whereas Caucasian-American dyads are more likely to focus on one event at a time (Chavajay & Rogoff, 1999).

The popular television program *Sesame Street* takes the preschooler's limited attention span into account (Anderson & Levin, 1976; Lorch et al., 1979). The program presents numerous brief vignettes rather than prolonged story telling; each presentation has a single focus so that the child will not be distracted by multiple agendas; and the quick succession of one vignette after another ensures that a child who does become distracted from the show will be drawn back by the novelty of the next vignette.

Although children's **selective attention**—the ability to shut out irrelevant stimuli and focus only on what is relevant—improves as they grow older (Flavell et al., 1993; Maccoby, 1967; McKay, 1994), it nevertheless remains elusive even at the conclusion of the preschool years; young children require considerable direction from others before they attend to what is most relevant

(Woody-Ramsey & Miller, 1988). Their relative inefficiency is due in part to the time and mental processing they require in order to identify which stimuli are truly relevant and should be attended to (Ridderinkhof et al., 1997).

Memory

As was discussed in Chapter 6, even very young infants show evidence of a functioning memory capacity. However, the quality and potential utility of an infant's memory are very different from a young child's. What improvements occur during the preschool years? The answer requires that we examine both the short-term and long-term properties of memory.

Short-Term Memory. **Short-term memory**, sometimes called immediate memory, is the process of maintaining a memory for less than half a minute (Best, 1998; Coltheart, 1999). An extremely common instance of short-term memory use is looking up and dialing a phone number. After dialing the number, unless we continue to mentally rehearse it or were already familiar with it, we probably won't recall it by the end of the phone conversation. Although a 3-year-old has short-term memory it is not yet sufficiently developed to hang on to a 7-digit phone number. A child given such a series of numbers can typically repeat only 1 or 2 digits. However, the amount of information young children can hold in short-term memory increases substantially during the preschool stage of development. By age 7 the child's short-term recall is likely to be able to produce around 5 digits—still not a complete phone number but remarkable progress (Dempster, 1981).

Long-Term Memory. Perhaps you would like to remember a particular phone number longer than half a minute. You then would be likely to transfer it to your **long-term memory**, a more permanent form of information storage where contents can endure for a lifetime (Best, 1998; Bourne & Healy, 1995; Brainerd et al., 1992). We accomplish such a feat by deepening the level of processing we use as we commit the phone number to memory (Craik & Lockhart, 1972). We might mentally rehearse the number, and after brief periods practice retrieving it from memory. We might connect its sequencing to our established general knowledge, noting its similarity to familiar numbers, or idiosyncratic patterns in the number, or even the physical sequencing of keys or the beeps we hear as we punch in the numbers on a touch-tone phone. Increasing the number of retrieval cues in this manner improves our ability to reaccess long-term memories when we need them.

Most preschool-age children can commit their home phone numbers to long-term memory—an absolute must for their safety given the relative ease with which young children can become inadvertently separated from their caregivers. However, there are qualitative differences between how the young child and older child or adult will master the task. The young child will need significantly more rehearsal and encouragement before succeeding. The child is also likely to recollect the number as a nonsensical collection of run-together syllables, perhaps enthusiastically delivered—"fivefivefiveohfoursixtwo"—further illustration of how the limited meaning a stimulus may have for the preschooler necessitates greater expenditure of effort before information can be committed to memory.

Preschoolers' long-term memory inadequacies stem in part from their not yet having learned how to remember. Rehearsing information in order to retain it is a skill that is learned, as also is determining which pieces of information are important enough to commit to memory. Young children also have a much smaller general knowledge base from which to create additional retrieval cues. Their smaller vocabularies limit the number of words that may be used to enhance storage and retrieval of information (Myers & Perlmutter, 1978). Much of the improvement in their memory over the rest of their childhood will come from advances in their storage mechanisms (Howe & O'Sullivan, 1997). Thus preschoolers are more likely to remember new information when they receive it in familiar storage formats such as songs or games, rather than in lecture style (Reese, 1999).

Examination of long-term memory raises the question of whether a memory is retrieved by recognition or recall. Think back to when you have taken short-answer or short-essay tests. On occasion you may have read a question you thought you ought to be able to answer, but you could not retrieve the necessary information. Later, while you are discussing the test with your classmates, the correct answer is revealed, and you say, "Of course! I knew that. Why didn't I remember it during the test?" The reason you did not recall the known information is that recognizing familiar material is a much easier form of memory retrieval than is recall, during which you must come up with your own retrieval cues. Chances are, if the question had been multiple-choice you would have answered correctly!

Young children also show this difference in ability at recognition and recall memory, but to a much greater degree than adults because the earlier-mentioned limitations affect their ability to create their own retrieval cues (Baker-Ward et al., 1993). As might be expected, they recall much more efficiently when the information is important to them—such as the location of hidden goodies (Wellman, 1988). If you ask a young child, "Can you tell me about your trip to DisneyWorld?" the child will most likely recite several aspects of the visit that were especially important from a child's perspective—and very dissimilar and incomplete compared to what the accompanying adult might answer. However, if the adult uses directed recall strategies such as asking, "What do you remember about Goofy?" the additional cue typically yields more recalled information (Hamond & Fivush, 1991). Thus it appears that young children have the capacity to recall but may need some cueing before they will produce what is relevant from an adult perspective.

False Memories. Cueing children as a means of tapping into additional recall memories can become a double-edged sword. Memory itself is not a template. Researchers have long understood that each retrieved memory is actually a recreation molded from stored bits and pieces (Bartlett, 1932; Lynn & McConkey,

BOX 9.1   The effect of suggestions on children's memories

Tried ......

Leichtman, M. D., & Ceci, S. J. (1995). The effects of stereotypes and suggestions on preschoolers' reports. *Developmental Psychology, 31*, 568–578.

HOW SOLID IS THE MEMORY OF PRESCHOOLERS? DO they recall events as adults do or do exposures to new information change their recall? Leichtman and Ceci explored this question with the assistance of "Sam Stone" and two groups of preschoolers. The children, ranging in age from 3 to 6 years, were situated in their preschool classrooms. There were 49 children in the experimental group and 47 children in the control group. Both groups were visited by Sam Stone, a stranger. He arrived during story-telling time and was introduced to the children. Sam commented that he knew the story they were reading and that it was one of his favorites. He continued to stroll around the perimeter of the classroom, then after a couple of minutes waved good-bye and left.

After the visit both groups of children were interviewed once a week for four weeks regarding their observations of Sam Stone. The control group was asked to report what they remembered about his visit. The interviewers did not make any additional comments about the nature of his visit or his behavior. The interviewers for the experimental group, however, probed for additional information. The probes contained misleading suggestions making reference to Sam Stone's getting a teddy bear dirty or ripping a book while he had been there. For example, a child might have been asked "When Sam Stone got that bear dirty, did he do it on purpose or by accident?"

Ten weeks after Sam Stone's visit all of the children were questioned by a new set of interviewers. They were first asked to give a free narrative of what they remembered about Sam Stone's visit. All of the children were then probed for additional information, first being asked if they had heard anything about a ripped book or a dirty teddy bear, then asked if they themselves had seen anything of this nature.

Children in the control group did not report any false allegations during the free narrative. When asked if they had heard something, a few of the very youngest children said they had, and a couple said they had actually seen the damage being done. A couple of the older children also said they had heard about the events but pointed out they hadn't seen them themselves. On the other hand, about 20% of the children in the experimental group reported false allegations during the free narrative. Almost 50% recalled having heard about the events and about 25% said they had actually seen them occur. When interviewers countersuggested to these children that they had not actually seen the events, about 10% continued to insist that they really had witnessed them. Age also appeared to play a role, in that younger children in the experimental group were significantly more likely to report false allegations and stick to their stories during countersuggestion than were older ones.

Why are preschoolers—especially the younger ones—so susceptible to recalling fictions as fact? Part of the answer is socially determined. Children are accustomed to looking to adults for reality checks. When an adult says or implies that something is so, young children are likely to mistrust or discount their own experience of the event and accept the adult's view. From a cognitive perspective, the researchers speculate that the suggestions produce actual mental images, which then fall into the memory pool and become undiscernible from true memory images.

As a follow-up the researchers decided to examine whether or not professional clinical interviewers would be able to tell whether the preschoolers' reporting was accurate or confabulated. During the course of various conferences, 119 researcher and clinician attendees were asked to observe videotapes of the participants' final interviews. They were unable to distinguish between accurate reporting and repetition of information only hinted at during the experimental condition. Thus not only are memory distortions likely to occur when preschoolers are repeatedly probed with leading questions, but are also likely to go undetected by those who hear the young children's reports.

...... and True

BOX 9.2   Avoiding false reports from preschoolers

SUPPOSE A 4-YEAR-OLD GIRL REVEALS THAT SHE HAS been sexually abused. As the event is fully brought to light, she will most likely be questioned by the person she informed, her parents, a child therapist, social service workers, and so on. She is likely to be interviewed between 4 and 11 times by forensic interviewers alone. Since a young child cannot be expected to spontaneously produce an adequate narrative summary of the experience, cueing of some sort will most certainly be necessary. Yet as Leichtman and Ceci's and similar studies illustrate, the manner in which such cueing is performed has the capacity to alter memories—essentially, to destroy the evidence.

Interviewers can take several measures that may reduce the likelihood of contaminating a young child's memory. Clearly interviewers should avoid implying facts not yet shared by the child as they question the child. Limiting the number of times a child is interviewed is also prudent: the greater the number of interviews, the greater the likelihood of creating false memories. Videotaping interviews can help contain their number as well as provide a permanent record of any interviewer's questioning having the potential to contaminate the child's memory. Spontaneous statements should be given more weight than those provided in answer to interviewer probes. The interviewer should also avoid appearing invested in any one position, since young children are likely to say whatever they think will please adults.

Sattler (1998) offers additional useful tips that can help interviewers judge reporting accuracy while attempting to tap into the memories of young children:

- The more often an event occurred and the longer the period of exposure to the child, the more reliable the child's memory.
- Young children remember events more accurately if they actually participated in them rather than passively observed them.

- Children under the age of 5 are significantly less efficient at encoding and retrieving memories than are older preschoolers. In general, the memory of a young child fades faster than that of an adult.
- Preschoolers are capable of giving coherent and detailed accounts of past events after long delays. However, they often embellish or modify information as they pull together their recollections. Thus from recounting to recounting, their stories can be highly inconsistent. Facts reported consistently are thus the ones most likely to be true.
- Complex, highly detailed events are much more difficult for preschoolers to encode into memory than are simple events.
- Young children of the same age can vary greatly in intellectual and language abilities. While interviewing be sure to at least informally assess the child's current level of cognitive functioning. Children respond to questions in accordance with what *they* understand the interviewer to be asking. Examine whether questions have been framed in a manner consistent with the particular child's level of cognitive development.
- Young children often assume that adults already know everything. They may leave out certain details because they feel certain the adult must already be aware of them. Interviewers can encourage fuller reporting by adopting a presentation style similar to that of the final interviewer during the saga of Sam Stone, who reminded the children that "I wasn't there that day. Can you tell me what happened?"

Sattler, J. M. (1998). *Clinical and forensic interviewing of children and families: Guidelines for the mental health, education, pediatric, and child maltreatment fields.* San Diego: Jerome M. Sattler, Publisher, Inc.

Mark C. Burnett/Photo Researchers

Because children are so susceptible to developing false memories, interviewers must use special care not to ask leading questions.

1998). These representational snippings swirl together as one big pool of memories, which can and do interfere with one another as we dip in to retrieve relevant information (Greene, 1992). Thus our memories easily become distorted, and fictions can arise from facts as we misattribute retrieved pieces of memory to inaccurate original sources (Loftus et al., 1995).

When subjected to repeated interviewing and retrieval-cue guidance, young children appear to be especially susceptible to forming false memories (Bruck & Ceci, 1999; Ceci, 1995). Just as their selective attention is impaired by their limited ability to tune out the irrelevant, so also are inappropriate memory cues difficult for them to inhibit, especially if the cues are highly salient (Carlson et al., 1998). The Tried . . . . and True boxes on pages 258–259 describe the factors that seem to play a role in creating distorted memory as well as how child interviewers can minimize the possibility of tainting or misevaluating a young child's memory retrievals.

Theory of Mind

If three accountants are conversing at a cocktail party and a psychologist joins them, you then have three accountants and a psychologist. If three psychologists are conversing and an accountant joins them, you then have four psychologists. Regardless of professional background, everyone has a personalized view of the human mind and why people do what they do—perceptions drawn largely from experiences and exposures within an individual's culture of origin (Flavell, 1999; Lillard, 1998; Wellman, 1998). In Chapter 7 we saw how, even as early as toddlerhood, we are putting two and two together to come up with a theory of mind.

During the preschool years, children accelerate development of their understanding of what others think (Astington, 1993). Rather than going from no theory of mind to one consistent with adult perspectives, their theories appear to go through various transformations during successive stages of development. One of the most consequential shifts occurs at around age 4 years (Astington & Gopnick, 1991). The average 3-year-old already understands the difference between things and thoughts—that is, between actual viewed stimuli and mental representations of things one might see. The child knows that there is a relationship between what people want and what they do, and between what they see and what they know. What is remarkable about the 3-year-old's theory of mind is that it conceptualizes the relationships between thoughts and actual reality as direct connections. In other words, if 3-year-old Tanya knows that her brother Austin wants a toy and she knows the toy is lying under the bed, she assumes that Austin will go directly to where the toy is located.

However, as Tanya observes Austin's efforts she will notice that he does not immediately look in the toy's actual location. At first she will ignore data that challenge her 3-year-old theory of mind and will be unable to explain to herself why Austin looked in the wrong place (Wimmer & Mayringer, 1998). Over time she will start taking note of other discrepancies and tack on ad-hoc hypotheses to her original supposition. And if somebody asks Tanya why Austin looked in the toy box instead of under the bed, in retrospect she might even be able to come up with the explanation that he thought the toy was there. However, if she is again asked to predict where Austin will look for a hidden object, her response will reflect the belief that he will know exactly where to look.

As the data piles up against Tanya's 3-year-old theory of mind, the addendums and exceptions make it too complicated to be useful. At around age 4 she will develop a theory that takes more of the relevant data into account: People do indeed look for things because of an internal desire to find them, but they search where they believe the objects to be. Tanya's leap in understanding will be that others' mental processes are only *representations* of how they perceive the world to be, rather than how the world actually is (Gopnik & Wellman, 1994). By age 6 she will have developed the corresponding ability to take the perspective of another's mental representations (Pillow & Mask, 1998). How these perspectives shape up will of course depend upon the theory of mind endorsed by her culture (Flavell, 1999).

Advances in theory of mind coincide with preschoolers' development of a greater working memory within which to hang on to and process such a construct (Gordon & Olson, 1998). They appear to advance more quickly if their mothers talk about others' thoughts and feelings, thus providing them with pieces of knowledge necessary for development of a more accurate theory of mind (Brown et al., 1996). Boys' theory of mind tends to be more heavily represented by knowledge of what a person's thoughts might be, while girls' theory of mind contains a heavier representation of what a person might be feeling (Dunn et al., 2000). A positive correlation has been found between sophistication of theory of mind and number of siblings, probably because in larger families children have a greater number of exposures to thought-behavior relationships and contrasting perspectives (Perner et al., 1994).

The appearance of this more advanced theory of mind contributes significantly to preschoolers' abilities to problem-solve in social situations (Astington, 1993). Accurate knowledge of how others feel, think, or perceive is an important component for empathic responding, altruism, and behaving in ways that will make others happy. Between the ages of 4 and 5, advances seen in theory of mind appear to coincide with children's advances in taking the emotional perspective of others as well as in developing positive social skills (Watson et al., 1999; Hughes & Dunn, 1998). Deficits in development of theory of mind have been associated with development of conduct disorders, perhaps indicating that children showing this association have not developed the emotional perspective-taking that would otherwise inhibit such behavior (Happe & Frith, 1996). However, on the downside of having a more sophisticated theory of mind, knowing that people can perceive inaccurately also marks the beginning of the child's ability to effectively practice deceit or manipulate situations in order to meet purely selfish needs (Polak & Harris, 1999). By age 5 the normal preschooler is likely to be experimenting with any or all of these less desirable practices.

Nevertheless, recognizing others' mental representations is a crucial piece of a young child's early development. Indeed, that recognition enhances the learning process itself. Children choose to imitate procedures parents, caregivers, and teachers model because they understand that these mentors are envisioning specific outcomes which the children themselves would like to produce.

What affects development of the young child's intellectual ability?

INTELLIGENCE

Levels of preschooler intelligence have been studied primarily in terms of analytical intelligence—typically those skills that are likely to lead to academic success. The two main tests used for examining the intelligence of young children are the Wechsler Preschool and Primary Scale of Intelligence (WPPSI) (Wechsler, 1989) and the Stanford-Binet Intelligence Scale (Thorndike et al., 1986) (see Chapter 6 for a review of how IQ scores are computed and interpreted). The WPPSI, one in a series of Wechsler intelligence tests, is designed for ages 4 to 6½. Eleven subtests are administered, providing verbal and performance-related intelligence scores as well as an overall intelligence score. The Stanford-Binet is used for children ages 2 through 18. It too consists of a series of subtests, though focused predominantly on verbal and reasoning skills. Rather than producing IQ scores, it assesses level of development of specific abilities. Although all intelligence tests are limited in their ability to accurately assess intelligence of children from diverse cultures, the Stanford-Binet is touted as being more "culture-fair" than the Wechsler tests.

As you may recall from Chapter 6, tests developed to measure infant and toddler intelligence do not correlate very well with later indicators of intelligence. However, the preschool years bring motor skills and verbal ability that allow children to perform tasks more similar to those assessed in intelligence tests for older children and adults. Thus scores obtained from intelligence tests given during the preschool years tend to correlate well with academic performance in later years (Siegler & Richards, 1982).

Individual Differences in Intelligence

What affects preschooler intelligence? As we have seen in previous chapters, hereditary influences and environmental health variables both play important roles. One apparent hereditary influence is gender. Even as preschoolers, boys begin to outperform girls on tasks involving spatial ability, such as mentally rotating figures or negotiating maze puzzles (Levine et al., 1999). However, conditions within a child's social interactional environment seem to be especially important at this age. The disproportional growth of the brain during the preschooler years as compared to later in childhood signals the importance of quality learning experiences during these early years.

Home Environment. The quality of the home environment continues to dictate a portion of the young child's progress (Molfese et al., 1997). One of the most significant predictors of high intelligence scores on the Stanford-Binet is the parent's ability to provide a learning environment that is user-friendly for preschoolers (Stevens & Bakeman, 1985). Such parents provide age-appropriate books as well as toys that let preschoolers develop their emerging conceptual frameworks. They are also actively involved with their children's day-to-day spontaneous lessons in learning. They converse with their children, read to them, provide structure and discipline without becoming excessively punitive, offer suggestions regarding how to accomplish desired ends rather than commanding or doing things for them, and create an atmosphere that is friendly and positive. Even as early as age 4, children in verbally active families show higher IQ scores than those families that are less verbal with their youngsters (Hart & Risley, 1995). Secure mother-child attachment during infancy has also been associated with higher IQs in preschoolers (Crandell & Hobson, 1999).

Birth Order. First-borns and only children, on average, tend to perform better on IQ tests than do those who come later in the birth order (Ernst & Angst, 1983; Zajonc, 1976). This finding reflects the important role that interaction with others plays in a child's cognitive development. The fewer children there are to tend to, the more attention parents have available to direct their way (Evans et al., 1999). Thus first-borns and only children typically receive significantly more attention than do children who are born later. Younger children also spend significantly more time with siblings, whose cognitive development is not as sophisticated as that of adults.

However, as we look at the relationship between intelligence and birth order we must also consider that parents with lower IQ scores tend to have larger families. Therefore the lower IQ scores of children who have siblings could be due to in part to inherited factors, and studies of this nature typically compare one-child versus several-children families. Under these circumstances we can expect to find higher IQ scores among first-borns regardless of any true effect of birth order, since the one-child families are more likely to have parents with higher IQ scores (Rodgers et al., 2000).

Day Care and Preschool. Since approximately two-thirds of preschool-age children in America have mothers who work outside the home, the typical young child spends a significant amount of time in settings other than being at home with Mom (Children's Defense Fund, 1996). Traditionally, the term *day care* has referred to meeting basic physical and supervisory needs of children, while *preschool* has focused on providing some form of education in a group setting. Currently most day care centers and preschools tend to do some of each.

As they do during infancy and toddlerhood, day care/preschool experiences appear to have an effect on a young child's intellectual development. Poor-quality day care, as is found in settings that provide child warehousing and little more, has been associated with children's scoring lower on measures of cognitive skills (Howes, 1988). But preschool enrollment has also been associated with definite cognitive gains, such as when settings are staffed by trained child care professionals, have a low child-to-staff ratio, provide a play space conducive to creative and constructive play, and use a curriculum focusing more on cognitive development and less on just controlling children's behavior (Beardslee & Richmond, 1992).

Certainly stay-at-home parents can provide these same benefits during early childhood if they are sufficiently dedicated, competent, and creative in finding ways to bring their children into groups with other same-age children (Elkind, 1988). However, not all parents are gifted with such abilities and personal resources. And some parents may be so overwhelmed by challenging living circumstances that their children, even before they reach preschool age, are identified by social service agencies as being "at risk" for poor academic achievement.

Project Head Start. During the early 1960s, the newly declared "war on poverty" introduced an educational program for preschoolers called Project Head Start (Mills, 1998). The goal of the program was to provide educational and environmental benefits for preschoolers from at-risk homes, in hopes of negating the intellectual deficits observed in children whose homes were not conducive to healthy cognitive development. Early outcome studies did show an initial IQ advantage in at-risk children who had been involved with Project Head Start activities. However, the improved IQ scores tended to deteriorate and revert to the original baseline after a few years of grade school, leaving researchers wondering whether the program was really providing any benefit (Gray & Klaus, 1970).

Fortunately, some researchers looked at other variables of personal success besides IQ scores. As the Project Head Start children continued through their academic careers they were found to be less likely to drop out, be placed in special education, or be held back a grade. They were also more likely to meet the basic educational requirements of their school systems. Both the children and their mothers showed higher levels of optimism about achievement and pride in the children's academic successes (Galper et al., 1997). These students had higher aspirations for their future than did those who had not received the Project Head Start advantage (Lazar & Darlington, 1982). Young adults who had been in similar preschool programs have also shown success indicators: They have more stable family lives, complete more years of higher education, and have greater earning capacities, as well as being less likely to have a criminal record or seek social assistance services (Schweinhart & Weikart, 1993). Findings such as these assist program developers as they revise the original vision, maximizing these programs' influence on children's academic and social successes (Ellsworth & Ames, 1998; Zigler, 1995).

Thus it appears that the potential benefit of preschool compensatory education is not necessarily production of higher IQ scores, but rather enhancement of those aspects of intelligence needed for real-world successes. On the other hand, intervention that begins earlier than preschool may indeed produce longer-lasting IQ score improvements. When newborns from at-risk homes are placed in full-time compensatory education programs, they continue to show higher IQ scores, as well as enhanced scores on other measures of academic achievement, even at the age of 12 (Campbell & Ramey, 1994; Campbell et al., 2001).

What is emotional intelligence?

Emotional Intelligence

If the Project Head Start participants did show superior abilities to make intelligent real-world choices and succeed, why weren't these successes reflected by higher IQ scores? What the researchers had stumbled across was an element of intelligence that functions somewhat separately from what has been traditionally measured by psychometrics (Mehrabian, 2000). Currently dubbed **emotional intelligence**, this aptitude reflects skills related more to practical than to analytical intelligence (Salovey & Mayer, 1989).

Western society's changing attitudes toward the various kinds of intelligence and their relative importance to success is reflected by the popular *Star Trek* series (Goleman, 1995). Back in the '60s, when analytical intelligence was valued above all other forms, Mr. Spock was the cult hero. His superior logic was rarely impeded by emotions, which he viewed as an unnecessary and irrelevant encumbrance. Much of the humor in the series centered on how he used his cool logic to perform one-upmanship over the emotional Dr. McCoy. The '90s, however, introduced Mr. Data—an android incapable of experiencing emotions. His bumbling, ongoing quest consisted of attempts to interact appropriately among human beings without the benefit of emotional intelligence. The strikingly different collection of humorous predicaments that resulted accurately reflected our culture's attitudinal changes regarding what is valuable and necessary for successful human functioning.

On a more scientific level, we can observe the effects of overvaluing analytical intelligence and undervaluing emotional intelligence by examining changes

These two classic characters were popular in their respective eras because they centered on each cohort's intellectual emphases: Mr. Spock's cool logic reflecting the 1960s emphasis on analytical intelligence and Mr. Data's pursuit of experiencing and understanding emotions reflecting the 1990s emphasis on emotional intelligence.

in children over the last 30 years (Shapiro, 1997). Intelligence scores on average have gone up perhaps as much as 20 points—raising some questions about their actual utility for predicting normality versus superiority or inferiority (Herrnstein & Murray, 1994; Neisser, 1998). Yet the emotional functioning of children seems to be deteriorating, in terms of both the increasing seriousness of child-produced social ills and the greater incidence of depression during childhood (Children's Defense Fund, 1996; Seligman, 1995).

So just what is it we might observe in children as potential indicators of their emotional intelligence? Following is a list of characteristics likely to be present in an emotionally intelligent child (Salovey & Mayer, 1989).

▶ *Has awareness of his or her own feelings.* The emotionally intelligent child recognizes feeling states and can identify them as they occur.
▶ *Is able to manage feelings.* When feeling glum, angry, or frightened, the emotionally intelligent child can self-soothe.
▶ *Can self-motivate.* When contrary impulses and emotional states arise, the child can stifle these nonproductive feelings and effectively focus on the task at hand.
▶ *Recognizes the emotions of others.* Not only does the emotionally intelligent child accurately perceive and interpret the emotions of others, but also has the ability to identify with their emotional states and feel compassion for them—the roots of basic empathy.
▶ *Knows how to relate to others.* Upon recognizing and managing his or her own emotions and empathizing with the positions of others, the child develops the social competencies necessary for popularity, leadership ability, and overall interpersonal effectiveness—crucial elements for succeeding in a social world.

Clearly, the presence or absence of such skills is most notable when children's social and emotional lives are examined. Thus we will revisit the topic of preschoolers' emotional intelligence in the following chapter.

What kind of day care/preschool program best serves the needs of the young child's developing cognitive skills?

PAVING PATHWAYS ALONG EARLY CHILDHOOD COGNITIVE MILESTONES: EVALUATING PRESCHOOL/ DAY CARE PROGRAMS

What should we look for in a preschool/day care setting to ensure that it supports healthy cognitive development? The questions we ask are similar to those we use when evaluating an infant/toddler program. What is the physical setting like? What are the staff like? What are the administrative policies? These elements were reviewed in greater detail at the conclusion of Chapter 7.

As is the case with infant day care, a solid relationship has been demonstrated between preschool child care quality and cognitive and socioemotional outcome (Peisner-Feinberg & Burchinal, 1997). High-quality programs pique preschoolers' interest in learning and participation in the classroom, while poor-quality programs result in higher levels of anger and defiance (Hausfather et al., 1997). About 48% of young children are enrolled in preschool, a percentage that represents a continuing increase among children from all backgrounds but especially among African-American children and those living in poverty (Federal Interagency Forum on Child and Family Statistics, 1999).

The new quality-control issue under consideration by anyone who cares about child development—parents, educators, researchers, etc.—as children reach preschool age is the educational component. What sort of curriculum is appropriate for young children? Because the number of children who later perform at substandard academic levels has increased, many educators are introducing "reading, writing, and 'rithmetic" in preschool, believing that earlier is better. This may not be the case. Early gains achieved in these skills do not necessarily persist into later grades, and the children may not do as well as those who had more relaxed preschool experiences (Marcon, 1999; Miller & Bizzel, 1983). In fact, children who spend a lot of time in unstructured play with friends show higher incidences of literate language and more advanced reading ability and thought processes than those who have the simple acquaintanceships that are more likely to characterize overstructured preschool environments (Bornstein & O'Reilley, 1993; Pellgrini et al., 1998). Worldwide, societies in which children show the highest levels of academic achievement have preschools that do not emphasize academics at all. Japan is an example. How do Japanese preschool educators design their programs (Lewis, 1995)?

▶ *They focus on the whole child.* The preschool program looks at the child's complete needs: the need to play, to make friends and learn how to successfully interact with both adults and other children, and to use their developing skills to accomplish desired ends and create things of beauty. This goal is fostered by structuring the majority of the child's time around free play.

▶ *They emphasize prosocial values.* Prosocial goals such as kindness, cooperation, responsibility, and persistence are reflected in daily lessons, and are frequently spoken of explicitly.

▶ *They build a supportive community in the classroom.* They create learning opportunities that encourage the development of close, trusting relationships among students and between students and teachers. Toward meeting this end, they typically keep an entire group of students and teachers together for all activities—even lunch—for 2 years!

▶ *They use methods of discipline that promote personal commitment to values.* Rather than depending on external controls such as authority figures delivering rewards and punishments, they build the child's ability to self-manage. The *children* are held responsible for quieting their classmates during lessons, leading class meetings, making class rules, and solving problems that arise. The educators have learned that tolerance for chaotic preschool classroom behavior as children learn to self-manage pays off later in greater self-control in the classroom and an ability to self-focus and self-motivate during the educational process.

▶ *They focus lessons on thinking, problem solving, and discussion.* The key curriculum focus of Japanese preschool education is cooperation. Lapses in cooperation are treasured as teaching opportunities for encouraging the use of cognitive skills.

▶ *They tap into the child's natural emotional reactions and interests.* Rather than isolating preschoolers' cognitive functioning with various worksheets, lessons engage children's *feelings* about topics. What will spark a preschooler's personal interest, grip the child's emotions, and create shared emotional experiencing with classmates? This type of learning is active, interpersonally complex, and process-oriented.

▶ *They create opportunity for reflection.* Teachers regularly stop and have children self-evaluate their progress. What did I do well? How did we work well together? What goal can I make for myself to do better next time? What did I enjoy most? Did I do anything to help others?

As you have probably surmised, these teaching practices address much more than the preschooler's academic needs. They address the child's developmental needs as well—the basics of thinking, feeling, and interacting with others. Perhaps these emphases explain the lower incidence of school dropouts, juvenile delinquency, and self-destructive behavior than is found in other industrialized countries (United States Study of Education in Japan, 1987).

To what extent have American preschools incorporated such practices into their curricula? The **Montessori method** reflects one of the earliest attempts to teach the whole child (Wentworth, 1999). It centers mainly on the immediate learning needs of an individual child, thus addressing each child's unique emerging zones of proximal development. The program is designed to present graduated sequences of learning in language, motor, and sensory skills. An additional aim of the method is to teach and encourage such values as cooperation, self-control, responsibility, and considering the needs of the group. Other preschools' curricula have also incorporated goals similar to those of Japanese preschools, not because they see them succeeding in Japan but because they are dictated by the research on young children's developmental needs (Lewis, 1995). Yet a number of preschools still overemphasize the "three R's" of education during the preschool years.

So given the current variety of emphases among preschool programs, parents can watch for the following indicators that a curriculum is likely to produce a positive preschool experience for their child:

▶ ample opportunities to interact with adults
▶ lots of supervised free play time, during which adults offer lessons of life as situations arise
▶ stimulation of the senses through exposure to music, art, and tactile media such as finger paints, clay, sand, and water
▶ discipline based more on explaining values than delivering rewards and punishments

▶ group discussion periods
▶ more emphasis on collaborative learning—such as choosing and working toward group goals, and less on practices that foster competition between students—such as "student of the day" designations
▶ limited emphasis on academics
▶ controlled and limited access to television

What positive roles can television play in a young child's intellectual development?

PAVING PATHWAYS ALONG EARLY CHILDHOOD COGNITIVE MILESTONES: TELEVISION AS AN EDUCATIONAL TOOL

Considering all the controversy regarding the role of television in a young child's life, how can television viewing be structured as a positive influence in a young child's cognitive development? The practice of letting preschoolers indiscriminately watch television has long been criticized. Critics note the effects of advertising, as well as the effect of viewing repeated portrayals of violence and stereotypes—topics to be revisited in later chapters. There is also the problem that excessive television viewing takes away time a child might spend pursuing active play, book reading, and social interaction—crucial elements for the healthy development of a young child (Huston et al., 1999; Singer & Singer, 1990).

However, television viewing also offers the advantage of exposing children to learning experiences that they might not encounter in their own living environments, as well as encouraging mental skills that reading and writing do not (Anderson, 1998; Greenfield, 1984). Children spend the most time watching educational television when they are 3 or 4 (Huston et al., 1990). The task at hand is to decide upon how much and what type of television might actually be beneficial for the preschool child, as we also factor in the developmental needs and abilities of the age level.

First, how does television teach? For us to learn anything from a media presentation, it must have the capacity to become integrated with our existing modes of thinking and feeling. Once we have incorporated the new material with established themes and schemes, we develop a personal understanding of and ability to use the new information. While viewing our own favorite media presentations we engage in processes such as separating the main idea from esoteric trivia, attending to sequencing and integration of events, and relating characters' feelings and motives to those with which we are personally familiar (Wright & Huston, 1984).

Given these processes and the limitations of the preschooler's cognitive processing abilities, what characteristics should we look for in media presentations for this age group? Consider the basic stages of information processing. First, a stimulus must capture the child's sensing and perceiving—not a difficult task for a compelling visual and auditory device that occupies the living area's most prominent position in most American homes. Next, the child must attend to the stimulus, in some way encode and store the information, and then be able to retrieve what has been learned during applications to the real world (Pezdek, 1985). We saw, for example, how a program like *Sesame Street* accommodates the preschooler's information-processing ability, with its difficulty in harnessing indiscriminate attention, by showing a rapid stream of brief, constantly changing vignettes (Zill et al., 1994). Such teaching has been found to meet some academic goals, such as learning letters, numbers, and vocabulary (Rice et al., 1990).

However, some point out that the applicability of information incorporated in this manner is as disjointed as its presentation style. Relevant here are the issues of information storage and retrieval. Committing learning to memory takes time, as we mentally rehearse new information and connect it with previously established memories and establish retrieval cues. Quick-paced programming does not give children the chance to either mentally rehearse or connect new learning with relevant personal experiences. A comparison of different styles of children's television programming showed that learning from those

Bob Daemmrich/Stock Boston

By joining her preschoolers as they watch television, this mother can generate a discussion about how programming might be consistent with the value system she wants them to adopt.

that were slower-paced and contained simple, flowing story lines seemed to contribute to more elaborate make-believe play (Tower et al., 1979). So while bits and pieces of rote learning necessary for success in the world of academia may benefit from *Sesame Street*-style presentation, psychosocial learning may better be incorporated through simple story telling.

The most effective lessons learned from television, however, may not necessarily be those resulting from loading a preschooler-focused video into the tape player and leaving children to incorporate what they may. Since we can reasonably expect them to be bombarded with media presentations for the rest of their lives, they need assistance in becoming wise television viewers (King et al., 1981). How much of what they see is real, or at least amenable to integration with their own experiencing? How much consists of manufactured irrelevancies to reality, with only entertainment value, if that?

Parents cannot always have absolute control over children's television viewing, but they can play an active role in enhancing the educational value of what children see (Traverso, 1998). One of the most effective lessons parents can provide is simply to comment aloud about what they are watching, thus helping their children evaluate input. As they discuss program content with their children, parents can reinforce their own beliefs and perspectives of personal and social behavior. This practice also helps children with sequencing, understanding cause and effect, and personally integrating the new material. Another advantage is that it points out to children that whatever is served up on television does not need to be swallowed whole. We (at least hopefully!) evaluate what we watch rather than accept everything we see as fact. During the course of channel-surfing, parents can simultaneously model the fact that they do not indiscriminately watch everything and explain why they make each of their rejections. They can even model the lesson of putting the pastime of television-viewing itself into perspective. Its potential teachings are best incorporated when limited in quantity, as well as balanced with other intellectual, physical, social, and real-world pursuits.

In spite of all the practices and safeguards we might enforce for children's television viewing, remember that many factors affect its actual impact on a child. Any presentation contains numerous subtle and obvious messages regarding personal and social learning. And different children can be expected to incorporate these messages according to their varying personalities, cognitive abilities, and personal experiences. So just as with other life events, we can never be entirely certain what psychosocial impact any given presentation will have on an individual child (Berry, 1988).

What kinds of advances occur in the preschooler's language ability?

LANGUAGE DEVELOPMENT

One of the most exciting consequences of children turning 3 is that we have a greater ability to figure out who they really are. The preschoolers' true personalities reveal themselves as they become more able to verbally express their inner workings. In fact, children develop more language skills during the preschool years than during any other stage of their development.

Twin studies have indicated that their proficiency at learning the spoken language and their early demonstration of reading ability are substantially influenced by heredity, at least by half (Bishop et al., 1995; Hohnen & Stevenson, 1999). When twins from shared and nonshared environments are compared, environmental factors are indeed found to be relevant to quality of language development, but to a lesser extent than apparent inborn ability (Hohnen & Stevenson, 1999; Olson et al., 1994). Also, girls continue to advance in language skills more quickly than boys in the areas of vocabulary, length of utterance, and general language ability (Roberts et al., 1999). Yet the environment plays a major role in how quickly language develops. Both the number and sophistication of words to which a child is exposed affect early vocabulary (Weizman & Snow, 2001). When mothers are encouraged to spend more time in narrative conversation, and taught how to ask open-ended questions, improvements in their preschooler's language ability are observed even a year later (Peterson et al., 1999).

Vocabulary

Preschoolers soak up new words at lightning speed. While at age 2 they usually use only about 200 words, over the next 5 years they may learn as many as 20 new words a day (Jones et al., 1991). They accomplish this feat by a process called **fast mapping** (Fenson et al., 1994; Golinkoff et al., 1992; Locke

1690/1975). Researchers hypothesize that children's early language abilities are organized with the use of an internal set of categorizations or a sort of language grid. Upon hearing a word for the first time, the child hangs it on the language grid according to its interconnectedness with words the child already knows.

Thus preschoolers more easily learn words within categories already heavily represented within their grid—such as animals, colors, snack foods, and other categories of interest to the average preschooler. Concrete words such as nouns, which commonly describe objects highly evident in the preschooler's world—are also easier for the child to incorporate (Gentner, 1982). Words that represent abstractions such as "fair" or "contentment" or that involve new grid categories are more difficult to incorporate. However, when parents or teachers provide contexts for new words that fall outside the child's mainstream experience, more possibilities for grid placement are suggested, thus increasing the likelihood that the new words will be woven into the fabric of the child's language ability. While at times annoying, complying with preschoolers' penchant for having the same story read over and over actually improves both their expressive and receptive vocabulary, as repeated exposures help them sort out and solidify the meanings of new words (Senechal, 1997). The more stimulating and responsive the home environment, the more advanced the child's language development will become (Roberts et al., 1999).

While the process of fast mapping helps children quickly incorporate new words, they understand their meanings very superficially. Nouns representing classes at first refer to prototypical examples, such as "bird" referring to a sparrow but not an ostrich. Atypical examples are built upon the initial concept as the child becomes more knowledgeable, with items of slightly dissimilar shape being first to be incorporated (Meints et al., 1999; Poulin-Dubois et al., 1999). They may use newly adopted words in other ways that do not accurately reflect their nature. Once as I dropped off my 5-year-old son Frank at a friend's house I reminded him to behave. He responded by pointing out "I *am* being 'have'!" The preschooler's understanding of new words is also extremely literal. As I watched my 4-year-old nephew Aaron play with block "buildings" and a fire engine, he repeatedly made growling noises as he rammed the fire engine into the block structures. When I asked Aaron what the truck was doing, he replied "He's fighting fires."

Preschoolers' efforts at expressing themselves through their limited vocabularies often reveal significant creative effort. When unable to come up with the right word, they may create metaphors in order to explain their thoughts (Winner, 1988). For example, when my son Ben was a preschooler he informed me that he had an earache by stating "There's fire in my ear." Preschoolers also may transform or combine words in unique ways, such as calling a hole-punch the "hole-er" or referring to a waiter as the "food man" (Clark & Hecht, 1982). The fact that they can make such combinations and transformations points out that in addition to memorizing words, they have also picked up some rules about word management.

Grammar

As they apply certain rules of word management, preschoolers also learn rules regarding how words are modified or combined in the process of putting together sentences—better known as grammar. They learn to add "s" to account for plurality and "no" or "not" as a modifier when desiring to negate a concept. They comprehend the concept of past tense and accordingly learn to add "-ed" to verbs. They learn how to add "-ing" to describe a verb's ongoing state, or even to create a verb out of a noun. They construct sentences of increasing complexity in a subject-verb-object manner, at least in most languages of European origin. This does not necessarily imply that the order of emerging language skills is culture-bound. Children speaking diverse languages appear to acquire grammatical rules within the same age range, in spite of the vast differences among the world's systems of grammar. Apparently the brains of preschoolers are programmed to learn rules of language during this particular stage of development (Slobin, 1985).

One of preschoolers' stumbling blocks during grammar acquisition is their potential for **overregularization** of language (Maratsos, 2000; Marcus et al., 1992). As they learn new grammatical rules, they occasionally overapply them. For example, as a 3-year-old a child may have memorized an irregular verb construct such as "I went to school" while describing the day's events. After picking up the rule of adding "-ed" to transform a regular verb to past tense, a 4-year-old child might say, "I go-ed to school"—seemingly a step backward in language development. Errors of this nature are actually fewer in number than they may seem to the anxious parent, and eventually discontinue as the child bolsters his or her grammatical rule systems with relevant addendums (Tager-Flusberg, 1989).

Conversation

The primary purpose of language is to provide a means of communicating with others. The preschooler's third collection of developing rules of language is called **pragmatics**—how do you use language appropriately within a social context? How do you alter your language behaviors in order to produce the desired effect?

While preschoolers probably would not be able to tell you the actual rules they are using, they do show evidence of having acquired a number of the rules of pragmatics. They know that they take turns speaking in conversations, and that they can get a response from someone by phrasing statements in the form of questions (Garvey, 1975). They increase eye contact as a means of sustaining their conversational partner's attention (Podrouzek & Furrow, 1988). They alter their language style to "motherese" when speaking with toddlers, and change their speaking styles in ways that reflect the status of roles they have taken on during make-believe play (Anderson, 1984; Shatz & Gelman, 1973).

The conversational difficulty that preschoolers continue to stumble over reflects aspects of egocentrism and limitations within their current theory of mind. When expressing themselves, they may not include enough information for their conversational partner to understand the message (Beal, 1988). For example, a preschooler might tell his mother "I want a shirt like Donny's," not taking into account that Mom has never seen the shirt in question, or may have seen Donny wearing many different shirts. As parents respond to preschooler comments in ways that help draw out additional specific information—such as asking "What does the shirt look like?" rather than simply commenting "Oh, really?"—young children become more linguistically competent, as well as better joined with their social world (Snow, 1984).

SUMMARY

Piaget's Preoperational Thought

The preoperational thought of 2- through 7-year-olds develops the use of mental representations. During the symbolic function substage, preschoolers use both signs and symbols as means of mentally storing their experiences. Language and make-believe play are examples of symbolic functions. During the intuitive thought substage, children begin looking for reasons why things happen. However, they tend to indiscriminately accept the answers they receive or invent on faith and as isolated facts.

Preoperational reasoning lacks many aspects of adult reasoning. Preschoolers are limited by centration, as seen in reasoning errors during conservation tasks. Their thinking is also characterized by irreversibility of process, perception-bound thought, egocentrism, animistic thinking, and difficulty with hierarchical classifications. Logic-based reasoning, both inductive and deductive, is typically absent from their thinking processes.

Vygotsky's Sociocultural Theory

Vygotsky suggests that new reasoning skills and other more advanced abilities are actually coached into children by mentors as each child enters the appropriate zone of proximal development.

Information Processing

Preschoolers have short attention spans, are easily distracted, and tend to organize their focus on factors with interest value rather than pragmatic value. Their short-term memory is limited early on, but by the end of the preschool years its capacity is almost as large as an adult's. Their long-term memory storage and retrieval are limited by their lack of practice at remembering, not knowing what is important to commit to memory, and having a smaller pool of general knowledge and language networks to supply retrieval cues. The discrepancy between their recognition memory and recall memory is greater than that of adults. Cueing children improves recall, but repeated cues can summon inaccuracies that have the potential to create false memories. Around age 4 the child's theory of mind begins recognizing thoughts as only personal representations of events, thus having the potential to be inaccurate.

Intelligence

Preschoolers' intelligence test scores begin to approximate their long-term IQ scores. Home environment, birth order, and preschool/day care experiences account for individual differences in addition to heredity. Intervention programs such as Project Head Start have been shown to have an impact on both analytic and practical intelligence of at-risk preschoolers. Researchers have only recently begun to systematically examine emotional intelligence, which predicts a child's ability to transform knowledge into success in the social world.

Preschool/day care settings need to be further evaluated for their educational components. Introducing advanced academic skills early does not appear to have lasting effects. Successful curricula focus less on academics and more on each child's developmental needs, prosocial values, the classroom as a community, discipline that relates to personal commitment to values, opportunities for discussion and problem-solving, and time for personal self-evaluation.

Indiscriminant television viewing is not appropriate for young children. Nevertheless, television does provide benefits such as exposure to learning experiences children might not otherwise encounter, as well as encouragement of mental skills not addressed by the "3 R's." Educational programs for preschoolers should be presented in ways that hold their attention and use scenarios with which they can personally identify. Young children also benefit from television viewing as a family experience, provided parents discuss why certain shows are or are not watched, what is real versus pretend, and how TV characters' behavior does or does not fit the family's values.

Language Development

Language skills advance more during the preschool years than at any other stage of development. Through fast mapping they learn as many as 20 new words a day, and are more efficient at learning words of familiar categories such as animals or snack foods. They learn a number of the basic rules of grammar involving word order and word transformations. They also learn the rules of conversation, although their conversational skills are limited in part by their immature theories of mind.

KEY TERMS

animistic thinking
centration
conservation
deductive reasoning
egocentric speech
egocentrism
emotional intelligence
fast mapping

inductive reasoning
intuitive thought substage
irreversibility
long-term memory
Montessori method
overregularization
perception-bound thought
pragmatics

preoperational thought
private speech
selective attention
short-term memory
sign
symbol
symbolic function substage
transductive reasoning

CONCEPT REVIEW

1. Jean Piaget's observations of reasoning abilities during the preschool years, the period of _____, focused mainly on young children's reasoning _____.

2. The use of language and numbers coincides with development of cognitive representations called _____, while the developmental appearance of _____ is reflected by children's make-believe play.

3. Preschooler reasoning errors such as _____, _____, and _____ contribute toward their difficulties with _____ as they observe changes in a stimulus shape or configuration.

4. When preschoolers attribute lifelike existence to inanimate objects, which is called _____, they are demonstrating their _____ experience of their world.

5. Preschoolers are more effective in taking the perspectives of others if the stimuli involved with the reasoning task are _____.

6. The _____ reasoning of the older child or adult takes into account general rules learned from previous learning or experiences, while the _____ reasoning of the preschooler relates concepts according to how they may present themselves together in time and space.

7. Vygotsky pointed out that regardless of a child's cognitive developmental potential, active interactions with a _____ play a very significant role in what the preschooler will learn.

8. Piaget believed that preschoolers talk to themselves because of their _____, while Vygotsky believed that such

_____ actually plays a role in their organizing and improving task performance.

9. Preschoolers' ability to pay attention is limited because it is highly _____ and focuses primarily on whatever _____; their selective attention is in part limited by lack of knowledge regarding what is most _____.

10. Learning retrieval strategies and acquiring a greater knowledge base, a greater vocabulary, and more advanced storage mechanisms eventually contribute to preschoolers' development of better-functioning _____.

11. Young children are especially prone to developing false memories because they have not learned to inhibit inappropriate memory _____.

12. Preschoolers' theory of mind reflects more accurate evaluation of others' thoughts once they realize that thoughts are _____ rather than _____.

13. Scores on tests of preschool-age intelligence are more consistent with later measures of intelligence than are infant tests because of the preschooler's more advanced _____ and _____.

14. In addition to the contributions of heredity and environmental health factors to individual differences in preschooler intelligence, _____ and quality of _____ and _____ also appear to play roles.

15. While Project Head Start children did not maintain any initial improvements in _____, their early involvement in the program has been associated with later measures of _____ and _____ success.

16. Emotionally intelligent children achieve their real-world successes because they are more likely to recognize and manage their _____, as well as recognize and appropriately react to those of others.

17. Children attending preschool programs that focus on the "three R's" <u>do/ do not</u> maintain any early gains over other preschoolers' demonstrations of literacy. Preschool programs such as the _____ focus more on social learning and the individual child's _____.

18. Educational television for preschoolers is most useful if it is designed around their short _____ and the material presented is easily _____ in memory and _____ during opportunities for application. Parents' involvement during TV watching is especially useful for young children because they can help their preschoolers _____ what they are watching.

19. Fast mapping increases preschoolers' vocabulary by means of
_____ and _____ new words; however, they
make many errors while using newly learned words because their understanding of them is _____.

20. Though preschoolers' language skills advance substantially, their attempts
at communication are at times inadequate because of their developmental
_____ and their insufficiently advanced _____.

1) preoperational thought; limitations; **2)** signs; symbols; **3)** centration; irreversibility; perception-bound thought; conservation; **4)** animistic thinking; egocentric; **5)** familiar; **6)** deductive; transductive; **7)** mentor; **8)** egocentrism; private speech; **9)** distractible; stands out; relevant; **10)** long-term memory; **11)** cues; **12)** representations; reality; **13)** motor skills; verbal ability; **14)** birth order; home environment; preschool experiences; **15)** IQ scores; academic; social; **16)** feelings; **17)** do not; Montessori method; developmental needs; **18)** attention spans; stored; retrievable; evaluate; **19)** categorizing; incorporating; superficial; **20)** egocentrism; theory of mind

RESOURCES FOR FURTHER READING

Astington, J. W. (1993). *The child's discovery of the mind.* Cambridge, MA: Harvard University Press.

Berry, G. L., & Asamen, J. K. (1993). *Children & television: Images in a changing sociocultural world.* Newbury Park, CA: Sage Publications.

Calkins, L. (1997). *Raising life-long learners: A parent's guide.* Reading, MA: Addison-Wesley.

Gelman, S., Scholnick, E. K., Miller, P. H., & Nelson, K. (1999). *Conceptual development: Piaget's legacy.* Hillsdale, NJ: Erlbaum

Gettman, D. (1987). *Basic Montessori: Learning activities for under-fives.* New York: St. Martins Press.

Goleman, D. (1995). *Emotional intelligence: Why it can matter more than IQ.* New York: Bantam.

Herrnstein, R. J., & Murray, C. (1994). *The bell curve: Intelligence and class structure in American life.* New York: Free Press.

Hohmann, M., & Weikart, D. P. (1995). *Educating young children: Active learning practices for preschool and child care programs.* Ypsilanti, MI: High/Scope Press.

Schacter, D. L. (Ed.) (1995). *Memory distortion: How minds, brains, and societies reconstruct the past.* Cambridge, MA: Harvard University Press.

Traverso, D. K. (1998). *TV time: 150 fun family activities that turn your television into a learning tool.* New York: Avon Books.

INFOTRAC COLLEGE EDITION

For additional readings, explore InfoTrac College Edition, your online library. Go to http://www.infotrac-college.com/wadsworth and use the passcode that came on the card with your book. Try these search terms: cognition in children, early childhood and education, educational television and young children, emotional intelligence, language acquisition and young children, make-believe play, memory in children, mentoring and children, Montessori method, preoperational thought, private speech and children, Project Head Start

CHILD DEVELOPMENT CD-ROM

Go to the Wadsworth Child Development CD-ROM for further study of the concepts in this chapter. The CD-ROM also includes quizzes and additional activities to expand your learning experience.

REFERENCES

For a list of references for this chapter, see the Wadsworth Psych Study Center Web site at: http://www.wadsworth.com/product/0534348092s

CHAPTER 10

Early Childhood Social and Emotional Development

FOCUS QUESTIONS

- ► Which factors contribute to the development of a preschooler's personality?

- ► Why do preschoolers adopt gender stereotypical roles and behaviors?

- ► What effect does birth order have on the developing personality?

- ► What roles do relationships with family, peers, and cultural milieu play in the emotional and social adjustment of young children?

- ► Which parenting style is most likely to result in a well-adjusted child?

- ► How do preschoolers experience and manage emotions?

- ► What affects a child's moral growth?

- ► How do preschoolers view themselves?

- ► How can we foster a child's emotional intelligence?

OUTLINE

Personality Development
  Psychodynamic Influences
  Gender Identity and Gender Roles
Relationships
  Birth Order
  Culture
  Relationship with Mother
  Relationship with Father
  Relationships with Peers
  Paving Pathways: Parenting Considerations

Emotions and the Young Child
  Anger and Aggression
  Childhood Fears
Moral Development
Self-Concept and Self-Esteem
  Paving Pathways: Raising a Child with a High "EQ"

"Mommy, Daddy, watch me. Watch me. Watch this. Keep watching. No, wait. . . . All right. Now watch me. Watch me, Daddy. Mommy, you're not watching. Watch me. Keep watching. . . ."

What parent hasn't endured this torture? We nonetheless force ourselves to observe our preschoolers as they demonstrate their newly discovered "competencies." Perhaps some built-in parental programming cues us that how we respond to and validate our preschoolers' efforts can have far-reaching effects. The advancing physical and cognitive abilities of preschoolers thrust them more fully into social and emotional realms. How they learn to manage the new challenges they encounter will depend largely on interactions with significant others, especially with parents.

Which factors contribute to the development of a preschooler's personality?

PERSONALITY DEVELOPMENT

Temperament continues to contribute to the individual differences observed among young children's personalities. This is especially true for extreme traits parents might have observed: The crabby baby becomes the irritable preschooler; the easygoing baby is exuberant and boisterous as a young child (Lemery et al., 1999; Novosad & Thoman, 1999). Of course, the overwhelming number of environmental influences encountered by young children will also play a major role in their social and emotional adjustment.

Psychodynamic Influences

I once heard a speaker comment that you can judge the degree of a man's greatness by how long people continue to poke fun at his mistakes (Sapolsky, 1995). Freud's view of personality development during early childhood has persisted in

Jill Fineberg/Photo Researchers

Young children develop their gender identity by identifying with their same-gendered parent or another same-gendered person, such as this young man identifying with his older brother's behavior.

providing material for such stature-raising comedy routines for almost a century, especially his conceptualizations regarding the preschool years.

Freudian psychosexual theory proposed that ages 2 through 6 could be described as a **phallic stage** (Freud, 1901/ 1965). He believed that children of this age group were especially interested in their genitals and the gender differences they represent, and subsequently developed an interest in sexually possessing their opposite-gender parent. Recognizing the inappropriateness of such a union, the child begins experiencing a sense of conscience or moral guilt. The child also experiences a troubling sense of rivalry with his or her same-gender parent and fear of being abandoned should the child's longings be revealed.

Freud proposed that boys resolve the external and internal conflicts produced by this desire by proceeding through the **Oedipus complex**. They perceive themselves as being in competition with their fathers for their mother's affection, but recognize that their fathers are bigger and more powerful than they are. In reaction to this realization they develop **castration anxiety**, fearing that their fathers will retaliate by physically castrating them. They resolve the fear through **identification** with the father, incorporating the father's male characteristics into their own personality. In this manner boys can be both more accepting of their "rivals" and identify with their male gender.

Carl Jung (1917/1966) proposed an equivalent process for girls that he called the **Electra complex**, a stage characterized by **penis envy**. He believed that girls abruptly realize that they do not possess a penis and blame their mothers for not having provided one. They endeavor to win over their fathers' affections as means of vicariously owning a penis. They eventually resolve their envy and blaming attitudes by identifying with their mothers' gender and coming to accept their mutual misfortune of having been born female.

If this is the first time you have heard the full, uncut origins of popularized terms such as "penis envy" and "Oedipus complex," you may be suppressing the same chuckle as an entertained populace for decades. Yet if you replace the genital terminology with words related to having power, Freud's and Jung's proposals do not seem so far-fetched (Horney, 1951). We all feel safer when we sense that we have control over our lives, and we find control by looking to sources of power. In Freud's and other patriarchal societies, overt power tends to be held by men. Within such cultures boys strive for power by becoming rivals of other men. Likewise most girls recognize that their options might have been more expansive had they been born male, which can be interpreted as a form of envy.

Nevertheless, even most ego psychologists no longer accept these more sexually charged aspects of the psychodynamic perspective of early childhood personality development (Blos, 1987; Kupfersmid, 1995). Theorists disagree about the validity of Freud's attempts to smelt the ore of his investigations into a theory of childhood psychodynamics. Nevertheless, he opened important veins of research for others to mine. Erikson, for one, contributed to the understanding of personality influences by expanding upon Freud's speculations of the young child's development of a sense of conscience.

Specifically, Erikson (1985) saw the preschool years as a time of **initiative versus guilt.** As with physical and cognitive development, the young child's personality is in part molded through active play. Preschoolers become more aware that they can initiate their own behavior and make independent decisions. As they explore their world of play, some choices work out and others do not. How adults react to young children's successes and failures significantly affects their experiences of guilt feelings. Rewarding successful choices provides them with a blueprint for how to assert their wills in socially acceptable ways, while punishing unacceptable choices facilitates development of the guilt feelings likely to inhibit such choices in the future. However, if caregivers are either over- or undercritical, the path toward successful assertion is less evident to them, and the resulting failures cause children to become inhibited by excessive guilt feelings. As a result, they may become timid or inhibited in their approach to the world in general.

Gender Identity and Gender Roles

Why do preschoolers adopt gender stereotypical roles and behaviors?

Another facet of Freud's conceptualizations of early childhood that has withstood the test of time is his emphasis on establishment of gender identity. **Gender identity** on the most basic level is recognition of one's gender assignment. By age 3, almost all children identify themselves as either a "boy" or a "girl" (Pogrebin, 1980; Thompson, 1975). **Gender stability**—the realization that one's gender assignment will not change with age, and **gender constancy**—recognition that modification of behavior or dress will not change one's gender assignment—do not appear until around age 5 (Marcus & Overton, 1978). Meanwhile 3- to 5-year-olds believe that you can become a member of the opposite gender by dressing as one, or that you can choose whether or not you grow up to be a "mommy" or a "daddy."

Gender-role beliefs are constructed by a much more complex blending of nature and nurture. **Gender roles** are the behavioral expectations cultures develop regarding what we should be like as men or women. In Western cultures masculinity is usually assigned such attributes as independence, aggressiveness, being a hard worker and good provider, nonemotionality, strength, and athletic ability. Femininity is typically assigned characteristics such as passivity, sensitivity, nurturance, emotional expressiveness, dependence, fragility, and vulnerability (Bem, 1981).

So how do children arrive at their own conclusions about gender roles? The previous chapter described how the young child's cognitive processes are busily conceptualizing and categorizing any information sponged up from the environment. Preschoolers organize concepts such as differences in race, gender, and other regularly observed physical characteristics into easily discernable stereotypes (Hirschfeld, 1996; Levy et al., 1998). In this manner, young children develop **gender schema**—organized sets of beliefs about the role requirements of being a boy or girl, man or woman (Bem, 1981; Smith, 1985).

Play that is consistent with a child's respective gender stereotype is very popular during young childhood.

Erika Stone/Photo Researchers

Upon recognizing that boys and girls are different, they then concentrate on whatever accentuates those differences. Which toy is each gender likely to play with, and how do the genders dress? Which jobs are held by women and which by men? Which games or behaviors seem appropriate for girls and which are meant for boys? Their concrete interpretations and dichotomy arrangements result in especially rigid gender stereotypes during the preschool years, even in cultures with more liberated attitudes such as Sweden (Goldman & Goldman, 1983).

According to **gender schema theory,** young children transform their gender-role observations into stereotypes by means of both cognitive-developmental and socialization processes. On the cognitive level, they apply their observed differences to the extreme—just as they would during any other information classification task. As they make additional observations of male and female behavior, **confirmation bias** takes hold: They make note of whatever fits their accepted gender schema and forget whatever does not fit in. They then use characteristics of their perceived stereotypes as guidelines for their own behavior and gender identity. They become more likely to approach "gender-consistent" toys and activities, thereby increasing proficiency within stereotypical gender-role behavior and minimizing familiarity with attributes of the opposite-gender stereotype. In fact, in a recognition task, both boys and girls demonstrated greater memory for the presence of toys that were consistent with their gender's stereotype (Cherney & Ryalls, 1999). The end result of these tendencies is further accentuation of differences between the genders (Martin & Halverson, 1981).

Since children's observed differences are environmentally driven, their social world supplies the characteristics they incorporate into their gender stereotypes (Beal, 1993; Yelland, 1998). Adults provide much of such input. They react to boys and girls differently according to how experiences with children have affected their expectations. Parents dress the genders differently, and people typically give children "boy" or "girl" toys long before they are old enough to indicate a preference. When my son Frank was born, my 15-year-old brother gave him a football as a gift. Obviously, a newborn cannot make much use of sports equipment. Given the apparent gender stereotyping at work here (which in fact undergoes a resurgence of rigidity during the teen years), it is highly unlikely that my brother would have thought to purchase a football had Frank turned out to be a Shawna.

Preschool children also intensify minor biological differences by choosing to interact more frequently with same-gender playmates. The level of physically aggressive play that little boys find appealing—and that is supported by their more advanced large muscle development—can be too intense for little girls to enjoy. The advanced verbal ability of the girls gives them superiority during cooperative ventures such as making polite requests or using the art of persuasion—socialization skills that may not yet seem relevant to little boys. Thus the two genders self-segregate, choosing playmates with the most comfortable play style and reinforcing one another for their gender-stereotyped behavior (Maccoby, 1990; 1998).

A boy or girl who tries to act differently than the accepted gender stereotype is likely to be ridiculed or even ostracized by peers (Fagot, 1977). One example of how preschoolers adjust to perceived gender norms involves power assertion during conflict. Little girls in conflict with their female cohorts use power assertion as much as do little boys. Yet when in conflict with little boys they resort to less assertive reaction styles, a tendency that appears in little girls as young as 3 years of age (Sims et al., 1998).

In recent years feminist efforts have sought to minimize socialization effects that intensify behavioral differences (and belief systems) observed between the genders; more dolls, for example, have been pushed toward boys than hitherto and more toy trucks toward girls. But given preschoolers' practices of rigid categorization—including their definitions of what is supposed to be a "girl" or "boy" toy or behavior—can we really expect such interventions to have much of an effect? Perhaps we would be more practical to look at why we object to gender stereotyping in the first place. For the most part, adherence to stereotypes tends to limit an individual's opportunities and is therefore seen as an impediment to individual rights. Within Western and many other patriarchal cultures, the primary gender limitations involve women's access to power and low tolerance for men who take on nurturing roles. The feminist movement has addressed issues of equality longer than issues of limits imposed on men's behavior; thus more attention has been given to girls' developmental needs.

The most relevant limitation young girls are at risk of imposing upon themselves is the absence of a sense of agency—the belief that you can act on your own behalf rather than wait for someone else to cooperate, make decisions, or gratify needs for you. One attempt at incorporating a sense of agency into young children's stereotypical expectations of girls has been made through storybooks. Rather than depicting a Cinderella or Sleeping Beauty waiting around to be rescued by Prince Charming, feminist storybooks depict role reversals, such as by showing women rescuing men. This role reversal alone is not enough to change a stereotypical expectation: Children typically view such a scenario as a boy acting like a girl or a girl acting like a boy. But if the heroine's sense of agency is explained, such as by indicating how she made her choices and acted in her best interests, some children may recognize the feminist message.

In one study, young children were asked to retell what they had heard in such stories. Some did indeed include perceptions of the heroine's empowerment. Interestingly, though, these particular children came from families in which the mother worked outside the home and the father participated in household duties. This suggests that there must also be exposure to a model of personal choices outside of gender stereotypes before the message of such stories is likely to be perceived (Davies, 1989). Children with fathers who play a more nurturing role in the home or with employed mothers who have a positive attitude toward their work have been found to express less gender stereotyping of adult roles (Baruch & Barnett, 1986; Carson, 1984). When preschoolers are exposed to examples of adults choosing careers outside the stereotypes and are additionally provided with explanations that personal interests and abilities are most important when choosing life courses, they are less likely to limit themselves with gender-biased views (Bigler & Liben, 1990).

RELATIONSHIPS

Gender expectations and characteristics are but one example of the many arenas in which early relationships influence young child personality development. We now take a look at the possible effects of birth order, culture, parents, and relationships with peers.

What effect does birth order have on the developing personality?

Birth Order

Imagine you are a couple's first-born child. You enter the scene as the object of the excitement, wonder, and adoration of first-time parents. You become the center of their universe. They are fascinated with your every toe wiggle and are dependably attentive to every perceived need. They take you along with them as they go about their lives, introducing you to a number of other attentive adults and explaining points of interest in the world around you.

Now imagine that you are a second-born child. As you come onto the scene, you find it already inhabited by another being who is dependent on the same caregivers for time and attention. They seem to like you but are at times a little slow to meet your needs. They are more likely to leave you behind as they go about their business. You also need to contend with this other being who is bigger, smarter, and stronger than you are and has few qualms about asserting these advanced abilities when it so suits him or her (Sulloway, 1996).

The arrival of a new sibling is a common experience for preschoolers. How might the different early experiences of first-borns and later-borns influence

Birth order will result in this older brother's early experiences differing from those experienced by his tiny younger sibling.

Heila Hammid/Photo Researchers

personality development? Meta-analysis of the many studies of personality and birth order shows minor yet significant relationships between being first-born or later-born and a child's social and emotional functioning (Ernst & Angst, 1983; Harris, 1998; Wallace, 1999). Frank Sulloway (1996) gives an overview of these tendencies, speculating upon how birth order effects measure up in terms of five basic personality dimensions (Digman, 1990; McCrae & Costa, 1990).

Extraversion versus Introversion. Is a child outgoing, sociable, and self-confident or more shy and sensitive? Since they are bigger, stronger, and smarter than younger siblings, first-borns are typically more successful at getting their way in conflicts with younger siblings. They also have had the experience of being the center of attention in their parents' lives. These factors contribute to feelings of self-assurance and encourage assertiveness in first-born children. Later-borns find themselves being dominated by older siblings' developmental superiority. Their own efforts to defend themselves often prove futile, and they learn to depend on parents to come to their rescue. Thus later-borns are more likely to be nonassertive or dependent than their first-born siblings (Stewart, 1992).

Agreeable versus Antagonistic. Older siblings experience the reward that their developmental superiority gives them in enabling them to dominate younger siblings. But as a consequence they have little or no experience of the need to set aside their own interests or to consider the needs or desires of others. Later-borns often find themselves in a submissive position. Through practice they are more likely to experience the reward of using persuasion and other social skills to gain cooperation. Thus later-borns become more likely to develop a peer-oriented, empathic, and altruistic orientation while first-borns become more accustomed to asserting their will and/or ordering others around, often being drawn toward leadership positions (Sutton-Smith & Rosenberg, 1970).

Conscientiousness. To what extent do first-borns and later-borns internalize the values and standards set forth by parents? Because of their strong early identification with parents, first-borns generally trust and understand their parents precepts and behavioral requirements, more or less accept their authority, and in fact come to value authority as a construct. When the younger competition arrives, older children also find they can retain favor with parents by assisting with later-borns and taking on some parent-guided responsibility. Because of these experiences, first-borns have a greater investment in the wishes, standards, and values of parents, thus becoming more conscientious than later-borns. Their greater acceptance of achievement-related values may contribute to first-borns' modest academic superiority and their excelling at other intellectual endeavors as well (Baskett, 1984).

Emotional Stability. First-borns' experience of suddenly having to give up the exclusive attention of their parents is emotionally trying. Later-borns, accustomed to sharing parents from the beginning, do not suffer this trauma of loss. Even if the family continues to grow, later-borns do not experience as sharp a disruption as first-borns. First-borns also experience the anxiety that comes with the responsibility imposed by themselves or others as the oldest child. Thus first-borns tend to be more emotionally intense than later-borns. The Biblical story of envious Cain eliminating his favored brother Abel provides a very early illustration of how first-borns can be more jealous and vengeful than later-borns (Koch, 1955)!

Openness to New Experiences. How adventurous, unconventional, or rebellious are first-borns and later-borns? Given their stronger identification with parents and experiences with responsibility, first-borns tend to be more conservative. It is notable that over the centuries first-born scientists have been more likely to dismiss the radically new ideas and findings that later-born scientists have been more willing to consider or accept. Experiencing less identification with the status quo presented by parents, later-borns more easily adopt new ideas and take risks. In addition, their greater ability to empathize with the "underdogs" makes them more inclined to support and work toward social change (Bragg & Allen, 1970; Stewart, 1992).

What if there are no later-borns? Suppose the first-born is an only child. Will he or she be the spoiled, self-centered brat portrayed by the stereotypes? A recent study of only children in Korea showed that while they were equally popular and sociable with other children, they also measured higher on a "brattiness" scale, even though the mothering they received was not any more attentive or overprotective (Doh & Falbo, 1999). Nevertheless, most only children exhibit characteristics similar to those of first-borns. And since they do not spend a lot of their time with easily dominated younger siblings, they are more likely to learn their social skills by interacting with peers. This leveling of the playing field necessitates development of more appropriate social skills. They also enjoy the developmental advantage of not having to share the valuable resource of parental attention. In general, only children tend to enjoy good relationships with peers and adults, have high self-esteem, and show some superiority at achievement and intellectually related pursuits (Falbo & Polit, 1986; Wallace, 1999).

What roles do relationships with family, peers, and cultural milieu play in the emotional and social adjustment of young children?

Culture

Different cultures prescribe different relationships among a society's members. As preschoolers strike out into increasingly larger arenas of social interaction, those they meet there directly or indirectly draw their attention to those aspects of the environment relevant to social success within their particular culture. They are taught social rules, develop an understanding of the structure of their world, and learn to react appropriately and consistently with what they have learned (Cole, 1996; Gelman, 1990).

The number and type of relationships contributing to a young child's emotional and social development also vary according to culture. At first glance, families in some minority ethnic groups, such as African Americans and Hispanic Americans, appear to be working at a disadvantage. These families are more likely to have a single, unmarried parent dealing with a greater number of children while having fewer financial resources and less education than Caucasian-American families (Edelman, 1987).

However, cultural differences themselves may make up for the lowered quality of individual attention one might expect a child to receive while living under these conditions. African-American and Hispanic-American families are more likely to engage large, extended-family networks in the childrearing process, actually increasing the number of significant relationships in a child's life (Wilson, 1989). Thus in various cultural milieus, the child may receive as much attention as a Caucasian-American child, but from a wider variety of caregivers.

While children of all cultures appear to play by means of pretending, endeavoring to involve others, and incorporating objects in the environment into play activity, play relationships differ from culture to culture. Do they play more with caregivers or other children? How much of play activity is social or solitary? Who initiates play, the child or caregiver? What are the play themes? Cultural differences in play relationships affect a child's learning and the extent to which caregivers use play activity as a means of teaching important social lessons. For example, Chinese caregivers are more likely to use the play arena for teaching appropriate conduct than is the case for Irish caregivers (Haight et al., 1999).

Relationship with Mother

Young children continue to thrive by means of healthy attachment to a primary caregiver who in most homes continues to be the mother. A strong sense of selfhood and feelings of competence are more likely to occur in children who experience a secure child-mother attachment during the preschool years

(Verschueren et al., 1996). Attachment strength is associated with development of a healthy understanding of emotions, especially negative ones (Laible & Thompson, 1998). Secure attachment with mother has also been associated with less anger and aggression in preschool, more secure attachment with the preschool teacher, and greater popularity with peers (DeMulder et al., 2000; Moss et al., 1996). Mothers of preschoolers who are securely attached owe much of their success to their ability to judge their child's level of competence and give appropriate instruction, as well as using less negative and more positive feedback (Meins, 1997). Preschoolers who feel neglected or rejected suffer from multiple styles of social withdrawal, including social isolation, sadness and depression, and lack of sociability (Harrist et al., 1997).

The fact that most preschoolers' mothers now have employment outside the home has raised concerns over whether preschoolers can still get the attention and adult-driven life exposures they need for healthy emotional and social development. Yet research reviewed in Chapter 7 pointed out that even infants can spend their weekdays with alternative caregivers and not show detrimental effects. How can this be?

To fully examine this puzzle we need to take a look at the differences between homes of the new millennium and homes of previous eras. Before modernization simplified the jobs of housekeeping and running a household, mothers spent significantly more time on those tasks, and they were also likely to have a larger number of children than today. Both of these elements limited the amount of time mothers could devote to one-on-one interaction with their children. Thus working outside the home has not necessarily reduced the amount of time mothers have for their children; it has simply changed what mothers do while they are not available.

We might also keep in mind that problems may arise if the stay-at-home mom has invested all of her interests, energies, identity, and self-esteem issues into her children. As is true of many qualitative versus quantitative issues, more is not necessarily better: Children can process only so much parenting. If over-invested mothers continually search for additional ways to provide input for their children, they risk becoming overcritical or overcorrective, resulting in their children developing feelings of self-doubt and anxiety. Constant streams of parenting interventions also have the potential to interfere with a child's ability to develop autonomous functioning.

Although working outside the home certainly limits a mother's flexibility in deciding when to interact with her child, mothers who use day care are found to spend just as much actual individual time with their children as those who do not (Ahnert et al., 2000). Also, an important factor in parenting is what mothers do or have to offer when they interact with their children. Working mothers bring with them the broader range of emotions, skills, and social experiencing that comes with the territory. And stay-at-home mothers can enhance what they have to offer by embellishing their lives with interests other than childrearing. The fuller the life exposures a child has access to, the better prepared the child will be for one day dealing with the real world on his or her own (Hoffman, 1989; Holcomb, 1998).

Relationship with Father

While most fathers are not highly involved with the care of their preschoolers, the amount and style of care they do provide varies widely, both among individuals and among cultures (Hewlett, 1990). While mothers' play activity tends to emphasize affiliation, fathers' play style tends to emphasize assertion (Leaper, 2000). Their interactions with their youngsters tend to be more physical and action-oriented than the mother's are, and they become special playmates during the preschool years (MacDonald & Parke, 1986; Siegal, 1987). Their rough-and-tumble interactions introduce manageable levels of apprehension and risk-taking, providing opportunities for the preschooler to practice emotional management in a social context. Yet fathers and mothers tend to treat preschoolers similarly when they engage in teaching and disciplinary behaviors (Hart et al., 1992; Wordon et al., 1987).

Relationships with fathers seem to have more of an impact on little boys than on little girls, perhaps because fathers provide a role model for being male. Meta-analyses have implicated fathers' behaviors as a major force in preschooler gender-role development, because they are more likely to encourage playing with gender-typed toys and engage in more physical play with boys than with girls (Siegal, 1987). The degree of difference between fathers' and mothers' gender-typing behaviors is actually relatively modest (Leaper, 2000; Lytton & Romney, 1991). Yet, however slight this difference may be, it is especially forceful for preschoolers because such feedback occurs at a time when they are especially sensitive to establishing their gender-role identity (Fagot & Hagan, 1991).

Interactions with fathers affect other aspects of the preschooler's social realm as well. The father's negative reactions and conflictual father-child interaction have been associated with negative interactions between preschoolers and their peers (Youngblade & Belsky, 1992). Overall, mothers' responsiveness appears to be a greater predictor than fathers' regarding preschoolers' prosocial development (Pratt et al., 1992; Volling & Belsky, 1992). The impact of preschooler relationships with mothers appears to be long-lasting: Adults who were interviewed about their early relationships with parents demonstrated associations between satisfaction with their mothers and higher self-esteem, less anxiety and depression, and higher satisfaction with peer relationships; no such association was found regarding their relationships with their fathers (Hojat, 1998). On the other hand, children seem to struggle more with math-type skills when there is no father in the home, suggesting that fathers' greater contribution may involve the presence of a cognitive style that is unique to men (Radin, 1981). A study of African-American dyads showed that when fathers were satisfied with parenting, were contributing financially to the family, and were nurturing with their 3-year-olds, their children showed more advanced cognitive and language skills even when maternal factors were controlled for (Black, Dubowitz, & Starr,1999a).

Given the newness of the investigation of the relation of fathers' roles to outcomes, the extent to which these differences are socially or biologically determined is still unclear. As the roles of mothers and fathers continue to shift in

Western cultures, studies focus more on non-Western cultures, and as additional longitudinal data emerges, new research will hopefully add further understanding of the unique role of fathers during the preschool years (De Angelis, 1996; Lewis, 1997).

Relationships with Peers

During the preschool years children develop their first true friendships. These friendships are organized largely around self-interest, such as the desire to find someone who likes to play the same games, and are thus less stable than friendships formed later in childhood (Furman, 1982). Early childhood friendships are typically organized in dyads rather than broader social networks, and center on having opportunities for play and shared activities (Cairns et al., 1988). These relationships provide the earliest opportunities for learning and practicing social and emotional skills in the real world. While preschoolers are with their peers, everybody is on relatively equal footing. Rather than having a parent or adult direct or correct the flow of play, children must figure out for themselves how to join in, cooperate, gain cooperation, and solve problems as they arise. Thus healthy development of the preschooler's social and emotional skills relies heavily on having substantial access to groups of children and on being accepted into both group and individual friendships and acquaintanceships. Well-run preschool programs or even supervised regular play groups provide opportunities for developing these important social competencies (Zaslow, 1991).

The significance of early peer friendships is not to be underestimated. In one study the behaviors of preschoolers facing separation from long-term classmates who were graduating to another school program were observed. As the impending separation loomed before them, these children exhibited increases in fussiness, activity level, and negative commentaries, as well as increases in health and self-care problems, as Figure 10.1 shows (Field, 1984). Thus in spite of their limited nature, early peer friendships appear to be yet one more important strand woven through the web of attachment relationships supporting the young child's social and emotional life (Field, 1996).

Some children are easily accepted into peer groups, and even rise to the status of being an especially popular playmate. Other children may be ignored, picked on, or ostracized by their peers (Mendelson et al., 1994). Why do some children gain acceptance and others do not? As researchers examine the family patterns of both popular and unpopular children, they find evidence suggesting that the ability to gain peer acceptance is at least in part related to social conditions experienced at home. Children whose parents' style of discipline is characterized by reasoning and explaining tend to be more cooperative and less aggressive in their play styles, and thus more easily gain acceptance by their peers. Those whose parents apply punitive and coercive disciplinary measures tend to be less socially competent and less likely to gain peer acceptance (Hart et al., 1992). If a mother's attitudes and behaviors toward a child are accepting rather than rejecting, the child is more likely to experience acceptance by peers

FIGURE 10.1

Behavioral problems observed among young children following peer loss. These early friendships appear to be important attachment relationships for young children. Adapted with permission from T. Field, "Attachment and Separation in Young Children," *Annual Review of Psychology,* Vol. 46, © 1996 by Annual Reviews www.annualreviews.org

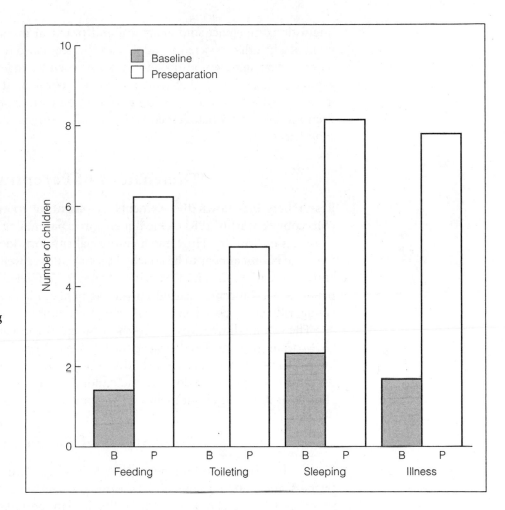

(MacKinnon-Lewis et al., 1997). Secure attachment to mother is an especially important precursor to the capacity for enjoying and cooperating with peers (Park & Waters, 1989). Having sibling playmates who are cooperative and friendly, rather than aggressive and nonsupportive, is also associated with fitting in well (Stormshak et al., 1996).

Which parenting style is most likely to result in a well-adjusted child?

PAVING PATHWAYS ALONG EARLY CHILDHOOD SOCIAL AND EMOTIONAL MILESTONES: PARENTING CONSIDERATIONS

As the importance of early childhood experience in future social and emotional adjustment has come to light, many research projects have been designed to examine the effect of parenting on a young child's development. The previous two chapters touched upon many of them. Parenting style affects a preschooler's linguistic competence and analytical and practical intelligence. The development of a healthy conscience and good self-esteem also relates to feedback from parents. Managing emotions and impulses such as anger and aggression, engaging in altruistic acts, behaving in a socially competent manner and thus being accepted by peers all show some connection with the type of parenting children receive. Just what elements of parenting consistently appear to make a difference?

Dimensions of Parenting

Researchers boil down the elements of parenting to two main dimensions (Maccoby & Martin, 1983). One dimension is parental warmth versus parental aloofness or hostility. How much emotional support does the parent provide? Does the parent appear to be attached to the child, as well as being in tune with and responsive to the child's specific developmental needs? How often does the parent express affection, caring, encouragement, and praise, as opposed to punishing, ridiculing, criticizing, or ignoring the child?

The second dimension reflects the amount of control, structure, and guidance parents provide. Do they keep track of what their children are doing? What kind of limits do they place on children's behavior? Do they enforce those limits? And how much freedom do the children retain when making behavioral choices or decisions about their lives in general?

Four Styles of Parenting

Figure 10.2 shows the four possible styles of high and low parental supportiveness and parental control. The three most extensively studied parenting styles used on preschoolers are the authoritarian, permissive, and authoritative (Baumrind, 1967). Later research has also taken a closer look at the effect of uninvolved or rejecting parenting on young children (Maccoby & Martin, 1983).

From what you have learned thus far, which of the styles on this chart do you think you would be most likely to observe in the homes of well-adjusted

FIGURE 10.2

Relationship of parenting dimensions to four parenting styles.

		Structure and Guidance	
		Low	High
Warmth and Supportiveness	High	Permissive	Authoritative
	Low	Uninvolved	Authoritarian

children? If you picked the authoritative style, you are correct. **Authoritative parenting** provides both support and guidance. Authoritative parents provide rules and expect them to be followed, but are more likely to enforce them with reasoning and explanations rather than coercion and punishers. In addition, the parents involve children in the rule-setting process, and may even change the rules in response to the children's feedback. Consistent with the practice of not doing things for children that they have become able to do for themselves, they allow children to make as many decisions for themselves as they are developmentally able. They use encouragement and praise and limit criticisms, and when they do administer punishment are more likely to arrange something that "fits the crime" rather than follow a pattern of generic punitive measures such as yelling, grounding, or spanking. The power-sharing and reciprocity of respect characterizing this parent-child relationship transfers into the child's inner feelings of competence and worth, as well as teaching social skills that will lead to successful interacting with peers (Russell et al., 1998).

Table 10.1 shows how an authoritative parent might react to various child-rearing situations. The table also illustrates how other parents using the authoritarian and permissive styles might react. Note how decision making, discipline, and instruction differ dramatically according to which style of parenting is used. **Permissive parenting** is long on affection and supportiveness but short on guidance and structure; parents may provide rules but enforce them either inconsistently or not at all. Children of permissive parents are allowed to take the reigns of decision-making long before they are developmentally equipped to make sound choices. Thus these children typically get whatever they want, are underchallenged, and are not given the opportunity to learn to be responsible.

Some parents are overly permissive because they do not know what to do, or perhaps lack confidence in their ability to effectively intervene in their child's behavior. The permissiveness found in **uninvolved parenting** could reflect active rejection of the child, but appears to be most strongly associated with parental depression (Radke-Yarrow et al., 1985). These parents may be so overwhelmed by life circumstances that providing either structure and guidance or affection and emotional support can feel beyond their reach. The impact of uninvolved parenting on a child's socialization skills is evident as early as age 3 in the child's significantly impaired ability to interact appropriately with others (Miller et al., 1993).

Other permissive parents honestly believe that children need absence of structure in order for their true selves to naturally emerge. The proof, however, is in the outcomes found when their children are observed. Preschoolers of permissive parents show more immaturity, disobedience, impulsiveness, dependency on adults, and underachievement than those raised with an authoritative style of parenting (Baumrind, 1971). Children need opportunities to learn how to balance their needs, desires, and impulses with relevant social demands and constraints since one day they will be living independently in a structured social world. Children of permissive parents are not given the opportunity to tackle such challenges.

TABLE 10.1

Examples of the authoritative, authoritarian, and permissive parenting styles.

Parenting Opportunity	Authoritative Style
Jason brings home a flyer from school announcing sign-ups for beginning band.	Jason and his parents discuss the expense, time commitment, and other considerations involved. Jason decides he would like to give it a try. He commits to staying in the band for 1 year. He also agrees to practice at least 20 minutes 5 days a week. He is having trouble deciding which instrument he wants to play, so they discuss the pros and cons of various instruments with the school band director. Jason decides he would like to play the trombone. He and his parents examine a number of trombones, and Jason picks one he likes from among those that are within the agreed-upon price range. Jason finds he enjoys band, and at the end of the agreed-upon year decides to play for a second year.
Three-year-old Amy is busily emptying her sister Ginny's toy box, gleefully and indiscriminately tossing toys behind her. Toys are scattered everywhere, and Ginny comes running to her mother to complain.	Mother kneels down next to Amy. She gently puts her arm around her shoulder, partially restricting her physical activity. Using a tone of voice reflecting frightened concern, she explains to Amy that someone or something might get hurt. She then uses a sad tone of voice, pointing out how Ginny would feel if a toy were broken, as well as what Mother will miss out on if she has to clean up the mess. She points out that in the past Amy has been a good helper, and asks Amy what she thinks could be done to make things better. Amy sticks her finger in her mouth and looks thoughtful. She picks up a nearby toy, puts it in the box, and expectantly looks up at Mother. Mother smiles and says "Yes, I knew you were a good helper," and offers additional praise as both Amy and Ginny put toys back in the box.
Seven-year-old Jonathon wants to help bake the cookies.	Father reads out each ingredient and tells Jonathon where to find it. He shows Jonathon how to measure the first cup of flour, filling the cup, then leveling it with a spatula. He lets Jonathon do the second cup, and praises him for his effort. As Jonathon experiences some difficulty stirring the stiff dough, Father shows him how to do a creaming motion by holding the spoon with him and guiding his hand. When Jonathon drops spoonsful of dough that seem too large, Father says, "Let's make them this size, so we can be sure they will cook all the way through," continuing to model the appropriate size as they both place dough on the sheet. Jonathon alters some of his cookies so they match Father's. After baking they have cookies and milk together. Father tells Jonathon what a good student he is, and thanks him for helping.

Authoritarian Style

Jason's parents see the flyer and decide that Jason should play a musical instrument. They tell him he will play the violin because his older sister played it and they still have the instrument. They tell him he will practice an hour every day, and that he will continue to play the violin until he finishes grade school. Jason is not so sure he wants to play an instrument, but he knows he will get in big trouble if he does not follow his parents' orders, so he half-heartedly complies. When his parents criticize his slow progress, he assures them he is doing his best.

Mother yells at Amy to knock it off. When she doesn't get immediate compliance, she stomps into the playroom and swats Amy on the behind, yelling at her and telling her she is a "bad girl." She orders Amy to start picking up the toys and set up the row of books that had been knocked over. Sobbing, Amy picks up toys and unsuccessfully struggles with getting the books to stand between the bookends, resulting in additional angry admonishments. Eventually Mother places the books back in order, all the while expressing disgust over Amy's lack of coordination.

Father gets out the ingredients and tells Jonathon to measure the flour. He spills over the sides of the measuring cup, and Father angrily says "Watch what you're doing!" As Jonathon tries to stir the stiff dough, Father tells him he's not doing it right and eventually takes over the task. As they drop dough onto the baking sheet, Father provides critical analyses of various attempts as too big, too small, or somehow misshapened. Frustrated, Jonathon lets Father finish baking the cookies.

Permissive Style

Jason tells his parents he would like to play the saxophone because it is the instrument he saw President Clinton play. His parents take him to the music store and let him pick out the one he likes, which turns out to be somewhat expensive. After taking lessons for a couple of months the difficulty of the instrument and the tediousness of practice result in his losing interest, and he drops out. The saxophone finds its way to the back of the closet, as his parents continue to make payments on it.

Mother asks if Amy would please stop. Looking up at Mother and smiling, Amy continues to pick up toys and throw them around the room. Mother continues to plead. Amy ignores her. Finally, Mother tells Ginny that she will help her pick up later on. Ginny balks at the idea of helping. After the children are in bed, Mother cleans up the mess herself.

Father gets out the ingredients and tells Jonathon to get two cups of flour. Jonathon plays in the flour canister for a while as Father waits, then dumps in two heaping cupsful. As the dough is extra stiff, Jonathon adds a few original liquid ingredients as a means of making it easier to stir, against his father's recommendations. While baking the cookies emit a nontraditional aroma. Not wanting to hurt Jonathon's feelings, Father tries one and says they are delicious, hiding a grimace as he does so. The next day they go without dessert in their lunch boxes.

However, the importance of providing structure and guidance is not so great that it merits becoming the only relevant factor in childrearing. **Authoritarian parenting** sacrifices supportiveness as it maximizes control. The parents make the rules and expect absolute obedience with no room for flexibility or re-examination of the rules, and if the rules are broken, punishment will follow. They make nearly all decisions for their child. Their interactions with the child are characterized more by corrections, orders, and criticisms than by encouragement, praise, reasoning, and explaining. The vast majority of the undesirable parenting outcomes described in this book tend to occur in concert with authoritarian practices, including less-sophisticated cognitive and social skills, lower levels of self-confidence and self-esteem, and less internalization of moral values and standards (Heller et al., 1996). There is some indication that the lack of warmth characterizing authoritarian parenting may have a genetic component (Losoya et al., 1997). However, the verbal punitiveness and corporal punishment associated with the authoritarian parenting style appear to be the most consistent predictor of preschooler behavioral problems, regardless of the presence or absence of nurturing behavior (Brenner & Fox, 1998; Jacobsen, 1998).

Of course, we must also consider that the directionality of these correlational studies may be opposite of such an assumption: that is, parents of temperamentally difficult children may feel constrained to resort to authoritarian childrearing techniques. However, when the parents in such families receive parent effectiveness training, the gains observed in their children suggest that parenting plays at least a partial role in the unfortunate correlates of authoritarian parenting (Alvy, 1994; Cunningham et al., 1995). A recent longitudinal study revealed both sides of this association's bidirectional nature (Eisenberg et al., 1997). Parental punitiveness is associated with more problem behaviors down the line, yet problematic child behavior and the frustrations parents experience appear to lead to an increased used of authoritarian tactics.

While describing the authoritarian style of parenting in my classroom, I have observed students from diverse cultures as they listen with their mouths hanging open in disbelief, occasionally bursting into fits of laughter. Other cultures have long recognized the common sense that affection, warmth, reasoning, and explaining are the hallmarks of effective parenting and that using violence and coercion as disciplinary measures has destructive effects. Acceptance of this reality by the mainstream within Western cultures is only now emerging, in the face of empirical data contradicting the authoritarian folklore that has permeated past Western practices.

Pitfalls of Punishment

A particularly troublesome parenting practice that is most frequently observed among authoritarian parents is reliance on punishment as a disciplinary intervention. When parents punish their children their intention is that the punished child will discontinue an undesired behavior in order to avoid being punished again. Avoidance of pain and discomfort is indeed a powerful motivator, but perhaps too powerful. Having a primary motivation of avoiding punishment can be expected to produce behavioral changes that reflect avoidance of receiving the punisher, but not necessarily correction of the faulty behavior.

Suppose Sandra is not doing her homework, so you take away her Sony PlayStation whenever she procrastinates. She may in fact avoid the unpleasantness of losing her favorite pastime by getting her homework done, but she may also adopt many other behaviors in her attempts to avoid punishment:

► She might lie, convincing you that her homework is already done when it is not.
► She might copy someone else's homework and pass it off as her own.
► She could endeavor to use the PlayStation at her friend's house instead.
► She could use the PlayStation when you are not at home.
► She could sneak into the classroom during recess and try to steal or alter the teacher's records.
► She might ease the boredom by finding alternative forms of stimulation, such as ill-advised risk taking, getting involved in a street gang, taking drugs, shoplifting, becoming sexually active, and so on.

Creation of unwanted avoidance behaviors is not the only drawback of reliance on punishers. On the most basic disciplinary level, punishers fall short because they do not tell a child what the desired behavior is. All the child learns is what is not wanted, and that he or she will be punished when the behavior occurs. And any changes that occur due to punishment can be expected to last only as long as the possibility of punishment is perceived. Unless some other motivator exists, the changed behavior will extinguish once the punisher is removed. Yet the classically conditioned feelings associating the parent's presence with the painful experience of punishment may last a lifetime.

A child can become even further confused if the parent insists on explaining, "I do this because I love you," or hugs the child after the spanking. The parent's expectation in this scenario is so far afield from what the child is experiencing emotionally that the child's options are to live in the anxiety of the cognitive dissonance, learn to ignore his or her inner experience, or link the experiences of affection and violence (not a pretty picture as such children begin having romantic and sexual relationships). In general, parents' use of spanking has been clearly associated with preschoolers' aggressively and physically retaliating when another child is perceived as having wronged them—an example of modeling at work (Strassberg et al., 1994).

As children grow older and their cognitive abilities expand, they realize that the presence of a punisher is not "an offer they can't refuse." They have a choice: They can do what you want and avoid the punisher, or they can simply endure the punisher and thus still have their own way. The use of punishment also models the use of coercion during conflict rather than discussion, reasoning, and negotiating, which can stunt development of healthy conflict-resolution skills.

And as the mention of moral development earlier in the chapter indicated, extrinsic manipulations interfere with the development of intrinsic motivations—the mechanisms that will guide a child's behavior when others are not around. Without a solid internal sense of right and wrong a child will simply look to external guidelines, such as what everyone else is doing or suggesting, when making behavioral choices. The most undesirable and unfortunate outcome of reliance on punishers, however, is their tendency to turn parenting interventions into child abuse.

How do preschoolers experience and manage emotions?

EMOTIONS AND THE YOUNG CHILD

As their cognitive skills become more sophisticated, preschoolers soon experience and express more complex, socially based emotions (Lagattuta et al., 1997). They learn to read the social implications of others' and their own behaviors and become familiar with emotions such as pride, shame, guilt, envy, and embarrassment. They begin to recognize the correlates of emotions, the cause and effect relationships that are at work when, say, Buddy becomes angry because he can't find his favorite toy (Russell, 1990).

At first they interpret all causes as external—if they see Sharon becoming upset while struggling with the snaps on her doll's dress, they are likely to say the doll is making Sharon upset. The more sophisticated theory of mind of the 4- or 5-year-old considers possible internal causes as well, such as that Sharon is actually frustrated with herself for not being able to snap the dress on her own (Gross & Ballif, 1991).

Preschoolers' first spontaneous efforts at coping with their emotions tend not to be particularly socially appropriate. If a playmate tries to take away a toy they very well may deal with their anger by pushing, yelling, hitting, or throwing tantrums. As adults and older children show them more appropriate approaches, such as asking the offender to stop or seeking intervention by a caregiver, they become better able to cope with emotions as they socially interact (Eisenberg et al., 1994; Garner & Power, 1996). Parents also teach their children how to manage emotions by modeling their own successful or unsuccessful strategies (Eisenberg et al., 1992). Children show evidence of better emotional control when regularly provided with opportunities to discuss the stress in their lives and how it affects them emotionally (Reynolds et al., 2000). Children who have learned to self-regulate their emotions tend to be less impulsive, better focused, better liked by peers, more socially competent, and more likely to engage in prosocial behavior (Durkin, 1995; Eisenberg et al., 1994; Fabes et al., 1999). The fruits of emotion-based learning during the preschool years are far-reaching, predicting some aspects of healthy adjustment even as children become young adults (Cramer & Block, 1998).

Anger and Aggression

Learning socially acceptable ways of managing anger is an especially important component of emotional self-regulation. The young child's usual impulse to react with aggression no doubt emerges as a throwback to the self-protective role played by arousal-driven behaviors (Tavris, 1982). Left unmodified, however, such impulses are likely to lead to a host of social and emotional difficulties.

Young children aggress for varying reasons. **Instrumental aggression** occurs when a child is trying to attain a goal or meet a certain end, such as pushing someone off the swing set so the aggressor can use it. **Hostile aggression** occurs solely for the purpose of hurting someone, often as retaliation for an act that has angered the aggressor. Hostile aggression tends to increase during the preschool years while incidences of instrumental aggression decrease (Shantz, 1987). These changes occur in concert with the child's advances in cognition, language, and emotional understanding (Maccoby, 1980). As preschoolers grow older, they have less need for instrumental aggression because they can get what they want through other forms of communication and negotiation. Hostile aggression may increase because they can now recognize or suspect hostile intent in others and they understand the impact their aggressive behavior is likely to have on others.

Little boys tend to be more aggressive than little girls—possibly due in part to higher levels of testosterone, though some believe testosterone's role may be exaggerated (Caplan & Caplan, 1998). Parents may exacerbate minor hormonally based influences by reacting differently toward displays of aggression according to the gender of the child (Lytton & Romney, 1991). Boys' aggressive behavior tends to be tolerated more than girls', as parents figure that "boys will be boys." Also, girls are more likely to be disciplined with verbal admonishments while boys are more likely to be spanked or commanded to comply—interventions that do not promote internal controls, as will be discussed further in the upcoming section on moral development.

Hostile aggression tends to persist among children of either gender when their parents discipline by threats and spanking, as is typical of the authoritarian style of parenting (Strassberg et al., 1994). There is also a solid relationship between viewing violent television programs and behaving aggressively (Singer & Singer, 1986). Both of these circumstances contain the element of modeling, thus teaching aggression by example. The Tried . . . . and True boxes on pages 302–303 take a closer look at how young children who observe aggressive models later display aggression.

Childhood Fears

Fear tends to be one of the more distressing emotions for preschoolers (Dupont, 1983). They are now able to recognize how small and vulnerable they are. Their powerful imaginations can dream up all sorts of possible threats, not to mention fear of the unknown, and they do not yet fully understand real versus pretend. Fear of the dark, animals, doctors, thunderstorms, and other loud noises is common. Girls have a tendency to express more fearfulness than boys, but it is not clear whether girls are innately more cautious or responding to fostering of dependency by caregivers.

In any event, these common fears typically disappear as the child grows older. Meanwhile preschoolers take comfort from reassurances by their caregivers

BOX 10.1   Modeling and aggressive behavior

Tried

Bandura, A. (1965). Influence of models' reinforcement contingencies on the acquisition of imitative responses. *Journal of Personality and Social Psychology, 1,* 589–595.

YOUNG CHILDREN LEARN A HEFTY PERCENTAGE OF THEIR social behaviors by watching others, including their aggressive behavior. Aggression appears to contain some natural, adaptive components insofar as it emerges in almost all infants, toddlers, and young children. Yet how a child eventually uses aggression or chooses to inhibit aggressive impulses is shaped by what falls within the child's cultural norms. What processes mediate such learning?

In the classic study named above, Albert Bandura examined the effects of exposure to aggressive models on preschoolers' learning of aggressive behavior. The 66 child participants ranged in age from 3½ to 6 years old. They were randomly assigned to 3 groups, with both genders equally represented and distributed.

All of the children were individually shown a five-minute film of a man becoming angry with a "Bobo doll"—an adult-size inflatable punching toy. The model displayed unique forms of aggression toward the doll, chosen because such behaviors had not been observed among the spontaneous choices of preschoolers in previous studies using the Bobo doll. For example, the model laid it on its side, sat on it, and punched it in the nose while remarking "Pow, right in the nose, boom, boom;" or hit it while it was standing and saying "Sockeroo . . . stay down." Following the standard film presentation, one group of children watched an additional clip, during which the model was rewarded with treats and praise for having beaten up on the Bobo doll. A second group was shown a clip of the model being punished—swatted with a rolled-up magazine and admonished never to do such a thing again. The third group was not shown any form of reinforcement clip.

Immediately following the "TV show" the children were allowed to play alone in an experimental room containing a number of toys, including a Bobo doll. During the children's 10 minutes of free play, observers behind a one-way mirror made note of any aggressive acts mimicking the behavior of the model; the observers did not know what exposure group any of the children were assigned to. Consistent with similar studies of the effects of observing an aggressive model, a certain number of children from all groups imitated the model's behavior. Boys in general were significantly more likely to copy the aggressive behaviors than were girls. However, the number of aggressive imitations varied according to the consequences the children had observed. Those who had seen the model punished were much less likely to copy his behaviors than were those who observed the reward or saw no consequence.

Did the different consequences change what the children had learned, or just how they had chosen to behave themselves? As a follow-up the researchers offered rewards to the children if they could show the researchers what the model had done. Children of all three groups were able to demonstrate more of the behaviors than they had actually performed during the 10-minute session, with the boys slightly but significantly outperforming the girls.

This study highlights vicarious reinforcement and vicarious punishment at work, phenomena that are not restricted to the behavioral choices of preschoolers. We all learn new behaviors by watching those around us, yet we do not need to be directly punished or reinforced before our behavioral choices will be affected. Seeing a drinking driver pulled over by police and then dredged through the legal system certainly discourages a number of people from engaging in such a dangerous practice. Children therefore benefit from childrearing strategies that not only teach them appropriate management of aggression but also help them process the consequences of the spontaneous behaviors they may observe around them.

BOX 10.2   How to minimize the effects of aggressive role models

. . . . and True

THE BAD NEWS IS THAT CHILDREN ARE LIKELY TO STORE away observed aggressive acts as potential choices for future behavior, regardless of whether they use them immediately. The good news is that their choice to use or not use the learned behavior can be mediated. If imitation is perceived to have reward value, the behavior is more likely to be produced. If imitation is perceived to make punishment likely, the behavior becomes less attractive. Being aware of these variables, what can parents do as they endeavor to decrease their preschoolers' aggressive behavior?

Limit exposure to aggressive models. What sorts of aggressive models are apparent in a particular child's environment? Television programs, a major culprit, can be monitored for violent content. However, since children most closely identify with their parents, the most influential models for aggressive behavior are the parents themselves. How parents interact with one another provides one of the more salient models for how to manage conflict and angry feelings. Certain types of parenting also have aggressive components that can be modeled. Spanking teaches that if others do things you do not like, you hit them. Parenting styles characterized by commanding, criticizing, and being inflexible also model interpersonal strategies that would be considered aggressive in most social contexts.

Maximize punitive consequences for aggressive behavior. Appropriate levels of guilt feelings can be extremely effective as self-punishers. The practice of induction—pointing out how the child's actions make the other person feel—promotes the empathy that fosters a sense of conscience. When a preschooler has become worked up to a point beyond the ability to reason, "time-out" is an effective strategy. Temporary withdrawal of adult approval—remembering to associate the disapproval with the child's *behavior* rather than with the child also makes future acts of aggression less tempting.

Minimize the reward potential of aggressive behavior. If Tony pushes Jimmy off the slide so he can use it, restrict Tony from using the slide. Remember also that some children act out to gain attention. If a child tries this in the form of minor transgressions, the parent might try ignoring the aggressive acts. When intervention is necessary, a time-out will both act as punitive and minimize the attention the child may be seeking. When children see superheroes or other TV characters using aggression to get their way, parents can point out that it is just a TV show and generate a discussion of how markedly different the consequences would be in the real world.

Maximize the reward value of nonaggressive alternatives. Praising children for socially appropriate management of anger and aggression increases the likelihood that they will use such techniques in the future. They benefit from being instructed in effective alternatives to aggression, such as conflict resolution and problem-solving. In doing so they gain the reward values of managing the discomfort of their anger, attaining a working solution, and meeting the approval of those around them.

when irrational fears arise. Sometimes strategies for alleviating fears benefit from taking a creative slant. I recall one mother describing her child's fearing monsters in his room once the lights were turned out. She took an old, empty aerosol can and replaced the label with one that said "Monster Spray" and let her son spray the room every night before retiring. His fears abruptly ended. By designing her intervention around the child's reality rather than adult reality, she had relieved herself and her child of a significant bedtime stressor.

What affects a child's moral growth?

MORAL DEVELOPMENT

The preschooler's increased sophistication at recognizing and responding to the feelings of others makes a major contribution toward development of the child's moral reasoning and behavior. In fact, morals are shaped more during the preschool years than at any other stage of development (Mussen & Eisenberg-Berg, 1977). A longitudinal study showed that the progress preschoolers had made in developing prosocial behavior was associated with measures of prosocial dispositions when they became adults (Eisenberg, Guthrie, et al., 1999).

Preschoolers' cognitive advances allow for greater understanding of rules and motivations, and their increased interaction with others influences development of their sense of conscience. How is a particular act right or wrong? What rules or conventions are internalized that will eventually guide the child's behavior? How do the feelings produced by the conscience actually interrelate with choices of behavior, such as feeling guilty after a moral transgression? Child temperament appears to influence the rate of advancement. Those children who at toddlerhood had exhibited an introverted temperament or the ability to inhibit their behavior through effortful self-control appear to have a better-developed conscience by the end of the preschool years than their peers (Kochanska et al., 1997).

Piaget noted that preschoolers perceive newly learned social rules as absolute and unchangeable (Piaget, 1932/1965). They also tend to judge how "good" or "bad" a behavior is according to the consequences of the act, rather than the actor's intentions (Arsenio, 1988; Smetana, 1985; Zelazo et al., 1996). If one child breaks a tray full of cups while trying to help Mommy and another child breaks one cup while trying to steal a cookie, the average preschooler will say that the child who broke many cups was the naughtiest. Furthermore, preschoolers believe that punishment will automatically follow after a rule is broken, as if the two are inevitably intertwined. As children mature to school age, they learn that rules are actually created and enforced by people, and that moral judgments address a person's intent rather than the actual behavior.

In spite of these changing understandings, the lessons experienced during the learning process remain effective. Moral behavior continues because the child has learned to self-reward with feelings of pride, empathy, and good self-esteem if he or she has complied with his or her own internalized rules for moral behavior and to self-chastise with feelings of guilt and shame if not. Thus influences encouraging moral growth are those that help the child learn social rules and conventions, emphasize the child's inner experiencing during critical instances of moral learning, and encourage self-control. The more solid is the child's attachment to caregivers, the more willingly will the child internalize caregivers' values (Bretherton et al., 1997; Cohn, 1990).

The social learning perspective points out that internalized rules are typically absorbed from the environment. Children need to see social rules in practice around them, especially as modeled by their parents and other significant peers and caregivers. Observing a model behaving morally has been found to increase a child's moral behavior (Mills & Grusec, 1989). Reasoning and explanations play powerful roles in prosocial development as well (Smetana, 1997). However, mothers' explanations and reasoning during the preschool years typically are more likely to reflect concerns over self-care and physical safety than social conventions (Gralinski & Kopp, 1993). Often these explanations come in the form of commands; perhaps this explains why preschoolers' understanding of social conventions tends to lag behind understanding of basic right and wrong (Smetana, 1995).

Explanations of why a certain behavior is considered moral or immoral are especially likely to enhance the child's learning if they employ **induction**—the practice of pointing out to the child how his or her behavior affects others (Hoffman, 1988). The adult can increase the effectiveness of the explanations by using the tone of voice that mimics the expected emotion of individuals affected by the child's behavior. Another effective moral training technique is called **attribution of prosocial characteristics**. When a child performs an altruistic or otherwise empathic act, the parent attributes the behavior to inherent characteristics of the child: "You must be one of those people who like to help," or "So you're a patient person." Children believe in the labels we give them, and

Telling the comforter in this picture that she is a caring person because of her empathetic behavior is likely to promote future incidents of caring and empathetic behavior.

Carroll Seghers/Photo Researchers

interventions of this nature increase the likelihood of similar behavior in the future (Grusec, 1982).

Environmental influences can also work against moral development. Murky presentations of rules or the absence of rules as well as conditions encouraging an external rather than internal personal focus diminish the likelihood that a healthy conscience will be established. This scenario occurs most often when a child's parents use the authoritarian disciplinary style that relies heavily upon threats, demands absolute unquestioning obedience, imposes punishments such as spanking and withdrawal of love, and uses physical force to make the child comply. These measures do not effectively teach the rules underlying an appropriate behavior. They also promote an external focus, encouraging the child to pay attention to coercive measures in the environment rather than internal feelings and beliefs about right and wrong. Children raised in this manner experience lower levels of guilt, shame, and other conscience-related feelings and have poor impulse control. Their self-esteem also appears to flounder, which impairs their ability to pat themselves on the back when they do behave in concert with their internalized values (Zahn-Waxler et al., 1990). The home environment that best fosters development of moral reasoning is characterized by the family warmth, involvement, and support of authoritative parents (Walker & Taylor, 1991).

SELF-CONCEPT AND SELF-ESTEEM

How do preschoolers view themselves?

Older infants and toddlers recognize themselves in a mirror, have a sense of what is part of their body and what is not, and understand that their selfhood is continuous. Preschoolers' more complex cognitive processing builds upon this earlier version of self-concept, but is still largely concrete. Typically, preschoolers begin defining their personal uniqueness on the basis of their roles and behaviors: "I am a girl, I go to school at Busy Bees, I jump rope, I have a baby sister, and I drank my milk all gone" (DesRosiers et al., 2000; Harter, 1988). They are also inclined to describe themselves according to specific physical characteristics, such as having brown hair or blue eyes (Broughton, 1978). As adults give them choices in some realms and not others, they learn to differentiate which aspects of their lives are in fact separate and personal (Killen & Smetana, 1999). As they approach school age, they still do not describe themselves in terms of actual personality traits, since such abstractions are still beyond their cognitive processing ability. However, they do share concrete descriptions of inner observations of self: "I like practicing my letters," for example, indicates recognition of an achievement orientation (Miller & Aloise, 1989).

As the self-concept becomes more complex, issues of self-esteem emerge in the developing child. **Self-esteem** represents self-judgment. If you essentially like yourself, are proud of your good points but recognize your bad points, and are optimistic about your ability to self-improve and perform effectively in the future, you have good self-esteem. If you don't like what you see in yourself, focus more on your inadequacies than on your strengths, and have doubts about how well you might perform in the future, you have low self-esteem.

Preschoolers typically start out with unrealistically high self-esteem. They overrate their ability to accomplish almost any task, even in the face of resounding failure (Stipek et al., 1992). Given their need for persistence while addressing the many new tasks they tackle during these early years, their overenthusiastic optimism is actually a motivational asset! At around age 5 or 6, they start comparing their abilities to those of their peers as a means of judging how they are measuring up (Ruble et al., 1994).

The most influential environmental input, however, comes from parents (Coopersmith, 1967). Parents of children with high self-esteem usually have high self-esteem themselves. Their parenting style is likely to be warm, loving, and supportive. Their style of discipline is likely to make more use of rewards than punishment. They provide clear and consistent rules and explain the rules, thus indicating the route by which children can travel and expect to succeed. In other words, children learn to think well of themselves because their parents' behavior implies that they should indeed be thought well of. Good self-esteem in a preschooler is associated with social and emotional competence during middle childhood (Verschueren et al., 2001).

How can we foster a child's emotional intelligence?

> **PAVING PATHWAYS ALONG EARLY CHILDHOOD SOCIAL AND EMOTIONAL MILESTONES: RAISING A CHILD WITH A HIGH "EQ" (EMOTIONAL QUOTIENT)**

The previous chapter described emotional intelligence, a form of intelligence based not on how much knowledge a person tucks away but rather the person's ability to apply knowledge during the course of day-to-day living. The emotionally intelligent child is aware of his or her feelings, is able to effectively cope with them and express them appropriately, can self-motivate in the face of contradictory impulses and emotional states, recognizes emotions in others, and is able to relate to others in a socially competent manner.

Lawrence Shapiro points out that while a child's inborn temperament affects how much ease the child will experience in developing emotional intelligence, interactions with others are the major influence (Shapiro, 1997). Children with oversensitive temperaments will have a harder time of it. However, even these children when carefully guided can learn to overcome the emotional whirlwinds produced by their challenged neurocircuitry (Kagan, 1995).

When parenting is done with emotional intelligence in mind, the most critical ingredient is the time the child spends with others: with the parent, with other significant adults, and with both individual and group child friendships. Emotional intelligence is taught by means of experiences, exposures, examples, and explanations. Suppose you were trying to increase a particular child's emotional intelligence, what we could call his or her emotional quotient (EQ). How might you go about it? Following are some suggestions for coaching the child.

Encourage the child's emerging sense of empathy. In the section on moral development we saw that the child's ability to empathize with others helps guide moral behavior. While the language and thinking parts of the brain are also involved, the emotional part of the brain will experience the pride and sense of belonging that come from altruistic and caring behavior, thus reinforcing and shaping the child's conscience and behavior.

Endeavor to see that children experience appropriate levels of shame and guilt. Explaining how their actions run contrary to their values helps develop appropriate guilt; chastising them over every moral or practical error creates overzealousness and destructive guilt feelings. Appropriate guilt feelings act as a stopper when emotional impulses start to flow; nonexistent or excessive guilt feelings may not.

Encourage realistic and optimistic thinking. First teach the value of honesty—through reasoning, explanations, and by your own behavior. Then model how you are honest with yourself, describing your feelings as they occur and admitting shortcomings when you make mistakes. You can also share the concept of optimism by verbalizing how you handle your own frustrations and personal shortcomings: "One mistake doesn't make me a bad person. I'll do better next time." "Just because so-and-so isn't coming over doesn't mean nobody would like to. I have lots of friends." "This isn't any fun right now. But it will be over soon." Shape the self-talk that naturally emerges during the preschool years through displays of positive and realistic statements the child can use during times of trial. Make up or read stories about children who illustrate realistic and optimistic thinking, appropriate problem-solving, and self-rewarding self-talk for efforts made.

Encourage appropriate expression of emotions. Both model and explain the appropriate ways of expressing feelings in the child's culture. Show children how to listen actively so they will understand the emotions they see in others, as well as recognize how others are reacting to them. Which facial expressions go with which feelings? What does a particular tone of voice mean? What other nonverbal communications might indicate a person's feelings, such as their body posture or movements? Also teach and model conflict-resolution skills such as negotiation, compromise, or seeking mediation so they will have means of moderating emotions when difficulties with others arise.

Teach children to view goals, obstacles, and difficulties as challenges to approach and problems to be solved. Rather than letting them catastrophize or solving their problems for them, provide them with a problem-solving framework and let them fill in the blanks. Coach them as they generate a list of possible courses of action, evaluate the pros and cons of each possibility, then decide which one seems to have the most advantages and fewest disadvantages. Explain the concept of time management and describe how they can both monitor their time and evaluate how well they are using it as they work toward personal goals.

Bolster their basic social skills. Teach and model good manners. Coach their conversational skills, such as deciding how and when to share personal information, ask questions of others, and express interest in and acceptance of others. Cultivate their sense of humor, a trait that is not only highly valued by others but also serves as one of our most effective coping strategies. Explain the difference between hostile, put-down humor and nonhostile humor and the effects these two styles of humor have on others. While parents' time is crucial for instructional purposes, remember that children also need substantial opportunity for practicing social skills with a diverse assortment of friends and acquaintances, both one-on-one and in groups.

As is the case with other forms of teaching, the teacher often learns along with the student. Generating strategies for coaching emotional intelligence requires closer examination of our own skills and abilities, as well as how we ourselves might hone our emotional approach to life. Thus by helping children work on their emotional intelligence, we may very well raise our own EQs!

SUMMARY

Personality Development

Inborn temperament continues to make itself known during young childhood. Freud was first to identify the preschool years as a significant window for development of a sense of conscience and gender identity. Erikson elaborated upon the development of a conscience, pointing out how early childhood experiences contribute to longer-term feelings of initiative or guilt. Gender schema theory suggests that both cognitive level of development and social processes are at work during preschoolers' identification and stereotyping of gender roles. Biological gender influences, differential treatment of boys and girls by adults, and peer behaviors can all influence adherence to perceived gender roles. Exposure to alternative gender role models can help diminish gender stereotyping among preschoolers.

Relationships

The personalities of first-born and later-born children are influenced by differing life experiences associated to birth order. First-borns are more likely to hold leadership positions, as well as be assertive, conscientious, antagonistic, emotionally intense, and conservative in both values and behaviors. Later-borns are more likely to take up social causes, as well as be dependent, empathic, peer-oriented, altruistic, adventuresome, willing to take risks, and likely to consider new ideas.

Culture may affect who actually spends time with a child, rather than how much quality attention the child actually receives. Working mothers do not necessarily spend less time with their preschoolers than those of the stay-at-home generations, and in fact may expose their children to a broader range of social and emotional experiencing. Involvement with fathers appears to play a role in emotional management and development of math skills. Relationships with peers provide substantial social and emotional training and practice. Young children are more likely to achieve peer acceptance if parents use authoritative rather than authoritarian parenting and have an accepting rather than rejecting attitude toward their child.

Parenting styles are characterized by various combinations of two dimensions: supportiveness and structure. The authoritative style of parenting provides both of these elements. It is characterized by warm, loving interactions that reinforce consistently presented rules with explaining, reasoning, encouragement, and praise; simultaneously allowing the child as much control and decision making as is appropriate to the child's developmental level. The authoritarian style—depending on absolute control and not moderated by supportiveness—is characterized by demands, criticisms, punishment, and expectations of blind obedience. The permissive style provides much warmth but little guidance, and the uninvolved style provides little of either. Children of authoritative parents are the most likely to be well-adjusted, showing higher levels of self-esteem, moral development, acceptance by peers, and academic achievement.

Emotions and the Young Child

Preschoolers begin experiencing in themselves and recognizing in others more complex, socially based emotions such as pride, shame, guilt, envy, and embarrassment as well as the correlates of emotions, both internal and external influences. They also begin learning how to regulate emotions and express them appropriately. Anger is first expressed through aggression. Boys still tend to be more aggressive than girls. Aggressive behavior can be altered by increasing verbal skills, direct instruction, observation of aggressive models, consequences of aggressive behavior, and parents' style of discipline. New childhood fears appear during the preschool years, but tend to disappear as children grow older.

Moral Development

Moral development can be influenced more during the preschool years than at any other stage of development. At first, preschoolers see moral rules as absolute, applying to the consequences of the act, and inevitably intertwined with punishment. Later they see that rules are changeable, punishment is other-related, and apply more to intent than to consequences. Moral norms can be internalized more effectively through induction, having the child observe altruistic models, and pointing out prosocial characteristics. Internalization is discouraged by inconsistent rule reinforcement and reliance on controlling children with commands, threats, and punishers.

Self-Concept and Self-Esteem

Preschoolers' self-concepts are at first based on their roles and behaviors, then progress toward recognizing that aspects of their inner character are constant. Their self-esteem at first overestimates their abilities, then is shaped by feedback from the environment. Children who develop good self-esteem tend to have parents who also have good self-esteem, provide clear and consistent rules, and use a parenting style that is warm, loving, and supportive rather than critical and punitive.

Paving Pathways: Raising a Child with a High "EQ"

The development of a child's emotional intelligence is influenced largely by interactions with others. Emotional intelligence can be promoted by encouraging the child's sense of empathy, appropriate shame and guilt, realistic and optimistic thinking, and appropriate expression of emotions. Emotional intelligence also benefits from modeling of and regular instruction in appropriate social skills, as well as having the child be taught to view goals, obstacles, and difficulties as challenges to be approached or problems to be solved.

KEY TERMS

attribution of prosocial
   characteristics
authoritarian parenting
authoritative parenting
castration anxiety
confirmation bias
Electra complex
gender constancy

gender identity
gender roles
gender schema
gender schema theory
gender stability
hostile aggression
identification
induction

initiative versus guilt
instrumental aggression
Oedipus complex
penis envy
permissive parenting
phallic stage
self-esteem
uninvolved parenting

CONCEPT REVIEW

1. Freud believed that preschoolers progress through a _____ stage, and in the process of recognizing and dealing with their sex assignment develop their senses of _____ and _____.

2. Erikson believed that during an _____ versus _____ stage preschoolers learn appropriate levels of social assertion by means of _____.

3. At age _____ preschoolers realize that their gender will not change with age, but not until age _____ do they realize that gender cannot be modified by dress or behavior.

4. Preschoolers' rigid gender role stereotypes begin with conceptualizations called _____, which are accentuated by young children's tendency to perceive extreme _____ and reinforced by playmates as they self-_____. They may be less gender-biased when parents expose them to less stereotypical _____.

5. Studies have shown some minor yet significant associations between birth order and the personality dimensions of _____, _____, _____, _____, and _____. Only children tend to exhibit characteristics similar to _____.

6. Children of differing ethnic groups appear to receive a _____ amount of familial attention as those of the mainstream of Western cultures, but differ regarding the familial _____ of that attention.

7. While working mothers have more _____ opportunities for the timing of their interactions with their preschoolers, the children benefit from what working mothers can share from their additional _____ .

8. The rough-and-tumble of fathers' play with preschoolers appears to provide them with opportunities to practice _____ . _____ appear to engage in more gender-typing behaviors than the other parent, by means of more _____ with boys than girls and being more inclined to offer gender-typed _____ .

9. The earliest friendships, occurring during the preschool years, tend to be less stable than those of older children because they evolve mainly out of _____ . Play group peers are important in the life of the preschooler's life not only as partners for practicing _____ and _____ competencies but also in their capacity as _____ relationships.

10. The parenting style associated with the most well-adjusted children— _____ parenting—is high in providing both support and guidance; _____ parenting offers support but insufficient guidance, while _____ parents provide guidance but insufficient support.

11. Punishers do not necessarily cause children to change their behavior because punishers motivate _____ behaviors and do not necessarily teach _____ behaviors.

12. Young preschoolers first view emotions as caused by _____ events, while older preschoolers begin to realize that emotions occur due to _____ events. Emotional regulation is learned largely by means of _____ .

13. Early childhood aggression begins as instrumental aggression, which occurs as a means of _____ ; later preschoolers employ hostile aggression, which is motivated by the desire to _____ . Greater levels of hostile aggression are associated with the _____ parenting style and other forms of aggressive _____ .

14. Young children are especially susceptible to excessive fears because they do not yet fully understand the differences between _____ and _____ .

15. Young children tend to view the "rightness" or "wrongness" of a behavior according to its _____ rather than its _____ .

Solid _____ and _____ facilitate the young child's eventual internalization of social rules and moral values.

16. The authoritative parenting style is most effective in teaching morals because this style _____ moral behaviors, makes use of _____ and _____, and provides the _____ that motivates children to want to emulate their parents and their values.

17. The self-concept of the preschooler is based largely on _____ factors, rather than _____ observations. Their self-esteem is at first unrealistically _____; later it tends to be drawn from comparisons with _____ and what they believe their _____ think of them.

18. Parenting strategies that best encourage emotional intelligence occur in the context of _____. Such strategies encourage the child's sense of _____, appropriate levels of _____ and _____, thinking that is both _____ and _____, appropriate expression of _____, and an attitude of viewing life difficulties as _____ or _____; as well as bolstering basic _____ skills.

1) phallic; conscience; gender identity; 2) initiative; guilt; feedback from parents; 3) three; five; 4) gender schema; classifications; segregate; role behaviors; 5) extraversion versus introversion; agreeable versus antagonistic; conscientiousness; emotional stability; openness to new experiences; first-borns; 6) similar; source; 7) restricted; life exposures; 8) emotional management; Fathers; physical play; toys; 9) self-interest; social; emotional; attachment; 10) authoritative; permissive; authoritarian; 11) avoidance; desired; 12) external; internal; observing others; 13) goal attainment; hurt someone; authoritarian; modeling; 14) real; pretend; 15) consequences; intent; attachment relationships; observing role models; 16) models; reasoning; explanations; warmth/supportiveness; 17) concrete; inner; high; peers; parents; 18) relationships; empathy; shame; guilt; realistic; optimistic; emotions; challenges; problem-solving; social

RESOURCES FOR FURTHER READING

Bandura, A. (1973). *Aggression: A social learning analysis.* Englewood Cliffs, NJ: Prentice-Hall.

Block, D. (1993). *Positive self-talk for children: Teaching self-esteem through affirmations.* New York: Bantam Books.

Brood, L. P., & Butterworth, N. T. (1991). *The playgroup handbook: The complete practical guide to organizing a home play group.* New York: St. Martin's Press.

Coopersmith, S. (1967). *The antecedents of self-esteem.* New York: Freeman.

Greenberg, M. T., Cicchetti, D., & Cummings, M. E. (1990). *Attachment in the preschool years: Theory, research, and intervention.* Chicago: University of Chicago Press.

Nelsen, J., Erwin, C., & Duffy, R. (1993). *Positive discipline for preschoolers.* Rocklin, CA: Prima Publishing.

Piaget, J., & others (1997). *The moral judgment of the child.* New York: Free Press Paperbacks.

Shapiro, L. E. (1997). *How to raise a child with a high EQ: A parents' guide to emotional intelligence.* New York: HarperCollins.

Slade, A., & Wolf, D. P. (Eds.) (1994). *Children at play: Clinical and developmental approaches to meaning and representation.* New York: Oxford University Press.

Wallace, M. (1999). *Birth order blues: How parents can help their children meet the challenges of birth order,* Vol. 1. New York: Henry Holt & Co.

INFOTRAC COLLEGE EDITION

For additional readings, explore InfoTrac College Edition, your online library. Go to http://www.infotrac-college.com/wadsworth and use the passcode that came on the card with your book. Try these search terms: early education—social aspects, working mothers, discipline of children, emotions and young children, fear in children, gender identity and early childhood, gender identity and preschoolers, gender stereotypes and children, moral development and children, self-concept and children, self-esteem and young children

CHILD DEVELOPMENT CD-ROM

Go to the Wadsworth Child Development CD-ROM for further study of the concepts in this chapter. The CD-ROM also includes quizzes and additional activities to expand your learning experience.

REFERENCES

For a list of references for this chapter, see the Wadsworth Psych Study Center Web site at: http://www.wadsworth.com/product/0534348092s

CHAPTER 11

Middle Childhood Physical Development

FOCUS QUESTIONS

- ► What advances in physical and motor development occur during middle childhood?

- ► What qualitative changes occur in the school-age child's style of play?

- ► How can physical education instructors help address the needs of children who are so diverse in maturity level?

- ► What is the health status of today's school-age children?

- ► What kinds of nutritional challenges emerge during the growing independence of middle childhood?

- ► What roles do stress and coping play during the school-age years?

- ► How can television viewing affect children's physical well-being?

Body Growth	**Middle Childhood and Health**
Brain Growth	Nutrition
Motor Development	Paving Pathways: Helping Obese Children
Gender Differences	Stress and Coping
Organized Play	Television and Children's Health
Rough-and-Tumble Play	Paving Pathways: Reducing Time with Television
Paving Pathways: Physical Education	

OUTLINE

Mrs. Martin was entertaining some important socialite friends whom she wished to impress. Just as she was serving tea and coffee she heard her 8-year-old daughter, Heather, clomping down the staircase in a most undignified manner.

"Heather," she called, "let's see if you can do that with a little less noise. Go back to the top of the stairs and try again."

Heather dutifully ran to the top of the stairs, then after a few moments quietly entered the room in which Mrs. Martin and her friends were visiting.

"That was very quiet, Heather!" said one of the visitors. "What did you do differently that made you sound so ladylike?"

"It was easy," she proudly replied. "This time I slid down the banister."

Ready, set, go! Middle childhood brings with it an explosion of new possibilities. More advanced physical ability, increasing exposure to the nuances and responsibilities of being a member of society, and improved powers of observation and reasoning all whet the school-age child's appetite for trying new physical skills. Given the lower incidence of death and disease during this stage of development, the absence of physical immaturities that restrict young childhood, and the not-yet-experienced hormonal uproar faced at adolescence, middle childhood tends to be a comparatively smooth and carefree phase of living.

BODY GROWTH

What advances in physical and motor development occur during middle childhood?

School-age children continue to grow about 2–3 in. and gain about 5 lb each year. While children's structural features during infancy and early childhood tend to be relatively similar, by middle childhood changes are taking place that emphasize their individual uniqueness. Between the ages of 6 and 12 their generally rounded look diminishes as fat levels decrease and skeletal and muscular

During the preschool years children are relatively similar in size and shape. By the end of middle childhood children vary dramatically in size and shape.

Elyse Lewin /Image Bank

David De Lossy/Image Bank

structures mature. Lung capacity increases, contributing to their physical endurance. While earlier developmental energies had focused on internal functions and structures, now outer structures become more refined, resulting in proportionally shorter trunks and longer limbs. The specifics of these added dimensions vary according to both hereditary and environmental influences; when compared with a group of preschoolers, the typical group of fifth graders contains an assembly of individuals looking remarkably dissimilar from one another.

Some variance among growth patterns can be traced to individual differences. African-American children measure as slightly larger than Caucasian-American children (Rauh et al., 1967). Gender differences abound (Tanner, 1990). At around age 10 girls surpass boys in average height and weight, as Figure 11.1 shows. Girls' skeletal development also forges ahead, gaining as much as two years' maturation beyond their male counterparts. Often **menarche**—the onset of menstruation—coincides with the girls' growth spurt. Boys continue to be stronger than girls as a function of their greater overall number of muscle cells.

FIGURE 11.1

Growth rates of boys and girls during middle childhood. From Berger, K. S., and Thompson, R. A., (1995). *The Developing Person through Childhood and Adolescence,* 4th ed. NY: Worth, p. 413, by permission.

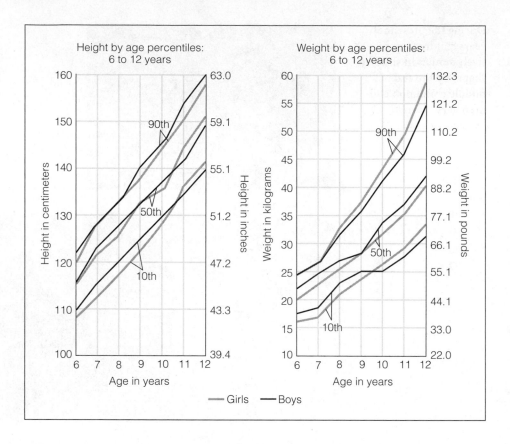

BRAIN GROWTH

While the brain is developing at the same rate as it did during earlier years, the school-age child's brain is nonetheless continuing to make significant advances. Existing functions continue to strengthen with increasing numbers of synapses. Many neurons that have not yet become myelinated do so during these years. Those relays affecting attention span continue to remain a little thin on myelination, thus contributing to the occasional squirming in chairs, talking out, giggles, and slips in attention typically observed in elementary school classrooms (Tanner, 1990).

MOTOR DEVELOPMENT

The advances in brain and structural maturation set the stage for an encore performance of rapid increases and improvements in physical abilities. Children become stronger and faster, more flexible and agile, and have greater endurance. Reaction time improves (Southard, 1985). Coordination of perceptual and motor abilities also develops significantly during middle childhood. For ex-

FIGURE 11.2

A comparison of children's handwriting at various ages. As children's handwriting advances, their letters become smaller and more uniform and errors such as reversals (Bridget), indiscriminate use of capitals (Dresden and Anthony), and letter dropping (Terri "Kirkhop") become less likely. From Santrock, J. W. (1993). *Children*, 3rd ed. Madison, WI: Wm. C. Brown, p. 365, by permission.

ample, an 11-year-old is much better than a 6-year-old at using visual information to throw a ball more accurately (Bard et al., 1985). The typical 11-year-old's ability to anticipate when and where a moving ball, person, or other object will end up and then react effectively is as good as an adult's (Haywood, 1980). Opportunities for activity are especially important at this age, helping children continue to become stronger, faster, and more coordinated. Observations of school-age children on the playground or even the extraneous physical behaviors interrupting their walk home from school suggest they intuitively know the value of activity for their developing physical abilities.

If you compare the handwriting of a 7-year-old to an 11-year-old's, the improvements in fine motor ability evidenced are dramatic, as Figure 11.2 shows. The older child's writing is clearer, smaller, and more uniform. Eye-hand coordination improves, as does manual dexterity. In fact, by age 12 a child's manual dexterity is as good as an adult's, allowing for quality performance of skills such as playing musical instruments, as well as manipulating tools and utensils such as a screwdriver or a needle and thread (Cratty, 1986).

Gender Differences

During middle childhood, girls are typically somewhat better than boys at fine motor skills and at gross motor skills involving precision and coordination such as hopscotch and jump rope. Boys continue to excel at larger-muscle skills, outperforming girls at running, throwing, catching, and kicking—providing one explanation for why boys are more often seen playing ball games during recess (Crum & Eckert, 1985). Because of physical developmental differences and social influences that encourage dichotomies of "male" or "female" pastimes, the differences between boys' and girls' choices of physical activities continue to widen (Eccles & Harold, 1991). In spite of the differences, school-age boys and girls are still sufficiently similar in structural, perceptual, and motor development to be able to play together in most sports (American Academy of Pediatrics Committee on Pediatric Aspects of Sports, 1981).

What qualitative changes occur in the school-age child's style of play?

Organized Play

The loosely organized play of the preschooler gives way to greater, more detailed organization during middle childhood. Children's games now have more explicit rules, and the various participants are typically assigned specific roles. They often play games that have been passed down from generation to generation, such as mainstream Western culture's kick-the-can, red light/green light, and freeze tag; but they are also likely to make up new games of their own. The flexibility of such games gives children opportunities to try out new roles, creative ideas, and emerging physical skills without suffering the consequences for failure that might occur if similarly applied in the real world. Their boisterous nature also requires physical activity, an important component of healthy physical and motor development. Cognitive development benefits as well, as they create and conform with the constructs of organized play (Bornstein & O'Reilley, 1993).

During these years, children begin devoting more time to adult-organized games such as football, soccer, tennis, and basketball. Being competitive, these games are yet another step away from the laid-back, free-for-all play of young childhood. In some circumstances, these activities cease to be play. Play is defined as activity that is fun, has no extrinsic purpose, occurs by choice, involves active participation, and involves principles related to living in general (Garvey, 1990).

Compare these requirements to what frequently happens in Little League baseball games! Alternative agendas such as competition, needing to show up whether or not you feel like playing that day, trying to please parents and avoid the wrath of the coach, and a tendency to emphasize performance over having fun deteriorate the play value of such activities, not to mention increasing the likelihood of frustration and anxiety for those participants who are less skilled (Horn, 1987).

Adult-organized sports do offer the advantages of helping children develop specific skills, manage feelings of competitiveness, and experience being part of a team effort, even if they do not truly qualify as play. Involvement in extra-curricular activities in general can also promote the development of social skills (Eder & Parker, 1987). There is also some evidence that extracurricular activities may keep children from dropping out of school, and may more positively engage them with the school environment (Mahoney & Cairns, 1997; Nettles, 1991).

Participation in competitive extracurricular sports becomes a problem only if it replaces the less rigid, more natural play that contributes to healthy child development or destroys the sense of play that we all need for good personal adjustment, even as adults (Groos, 1908). The "Tried . . . and True" boxes on pages 322–323 elaborate upon the effect parents and other adults can have on children's involvement with organized sports.

Rough-and-Tumble Play

When I was about 9, one of my favorite playmates was a boy in my fourth-grade class. We goofed around on the playground together and occasionally visited one another's homes. One day as we and his male playmates were gallivanting about the neighborhood, another boy took the liberty of chasing me down and pinning me against the grass in a wrestling hold. At first I put up some resistance. Upon recognizing his greater size and strength, I eventually let myself go limp and let him hold me down. Making a few token gestures at struggling to get up, I looked up at him with an expression of ". . . and your point?" After a few moments of established physical superiority he began looking bewildered and let me go, the thought finally having dawned upon him that I was in fact a *girl*.

What I had experienced was an attempt at **rough-and-tumble play**, play that may look like aggression but is actually pursued in fun. It involves chasing, wrestling, mild "punching," and other behaviors that, if anger were present, would be interpreted as fighting (Eibl-Eibesfeldt, 1989). Rough-and-tumble play occurs among many species. If you have ever cared for a litter of puppies or kittens, you have most likely observed their playful wrestling first hand. This style of play is believed to emerge as a result of our species' early survival needs, preparing us to be able to defend ourselves or chase down prey. The activity itself contributes to children's developing of coordination of physical and cognitive skills (Pelligrini & Smith, 1998). An important social component of rough-and-tumble play is its role in establishing a **dominance hierarchy**, a social organizational strategy that determines ahead of time who will have the last word (Pettit et al., 1990). Once established, a dominance hierarchy actually reduces the amount of hostile aggression observed in a group (Fine, 1980).

Children typically do not have much trouble telling the difference between rough-and-tumble play and aggressive fighting, although children with learning disabilities at times may struggle at making such distinctions (Costabile et al., 1991; Nabuzoka & Smith, 1999). It differs from true fighting in that no real conflict is involved. It is good-natured, frequently involving laughter and a friendly facial expression, with victim and aggressor occasionally trading roles.

BOX 11.1   Mastery versus performance motivational climates

Treasure, D. (1997). Perceptions of the motivational climate and elementary school children's cognitive and affective response. *Journal of Sport and Exercise Psychology,* 19, 278–290.

WHAT MOTIVATES CHILDREN TO GET INVOLVED IN PHYSI-cal activities? What contributes to their development of a complementary attitude—having faith in their own physical ability, or believing that their efforts will bring them success? What makes children enjoy their physical education classes? Darren Treasure examined these questions by looking at the roles played by mastery and performance orientations in physical education classes. A mastery orientation centers learning experiences on each individual student's developing skill level, maximizing activity that will help the child improve. By contrast, a performance orientation focuses more on winning or how a child compares to other students and their skill levels. How do these two motivational climates affect student attitudes?

This study involved 233 students ranging between 10 and 12 years of age, about half male and half female. During their regular physical education classes the students filled out a questionnaire in which the items were arranged so that students responded to 5-point *Likert*-type scales. Rather than forcing responses such as "true" or "not true" and "agree" or "disagree," *Likert* scales let the responder indicate varying degrees of agreement or disagreement, thus not losing variance data by examining responders' strength of belief. This questionnaire included items representing the four domains in question:

Mastery and performance orientations. Participants used the five-point scale to indicate their level of agreement or disagreement to mastery items such as "In physical education, the teacher makes sure I understand," and performance items such as "In physical education, I feel good when I outperform other students."

Causes of success. Given choices ranging from "not at all" to "a lot," participants indicated the extent to which they believed certain variables contributed to success. Half of these items reflected the role of ability—"stick to skills they are really good at," and half reflected the role of effort—"work really hard."

Perceived ability. Participants used a four-point scale ranging from "very true" to "not true" to respond to items such as "I am very good at P.E." and "I am one of the worst in P.E."

Attitude toward activity. Participants responded to the question, "How much do you like physical education?" using a five-point scale ranging from "not at all" to "a lot."

The participants' scores on the cause of success, perceived ability, and attitude toward activity portions of the test were compared to scores representing the participants' perception of their classes' mastery and performance emphases. The results showed that in a climate perceived as having a high mastery/moderate performance orientation, students were most likely to believe that their effort will result in success, have confidence in personal ability to perform, and have a positive attitude toward physical education. Perception of a low mastery/high performance orientation was associated with focusing on ability rather than effort, less confidence in personal ability, and a negative attitude toward physical education.

Western culture is largely made up of competitive societies. Part of becoming a member of such a society is becoming comfortable with competition, and a good deal of a child's early experiences with competition can be found in the realm of physical activity. Yet the findings of this study suggest that parents and educators clearly need to balance competitiveness with a heftier emphasis on personal encouragement if children are to maintain interest in physical activity.

Tried

... and True

BOX 11.2   How to motivate an underachiever

A CHILD'S INTEREST AND INVOLVEMENT IN PHYSICAL ACtivity holds importance not only for immediate developmental needs but also for the process of setting a healthy pattern for the child's adult lifestyle choices. The Treasure study suggests that encouraging interest in physical activity requires a greater emphasis on personal skill mastery than overall performance. What can parents, teachers, coaches, and other influential adults do to encourage a continuing interest in physical activity?

Stanley Greenspan (1993) describes a variety of factors that help determine whether a child develops a mastery orientation. Let's examine some of these factors by taking a look at Charlie, an energetic 8-year-old who participates in a soccer league. He is a bright student and a good athlete but is also known as being a bit of a "free spirit." While on the playing field he sometimes follows the flow of the game and contributes appropriately but most of the time seems lost and overwhelmed. His teammates are becoming frustrated with his disengaged playing style. Coach Jackson decides to make a special effort to help Charlie stay engaged.

First, Coach Jackson takes a look at what influences he has had on the situation so far. He realizes that he has been guilty of stereotyping. Having seen Charlie's limited skills and participation he has subconsciously labeled him "not likely to go very far." His low expectations of Charlie have had the effect of a self-fulfilling prophecy, and he has been less active coaching Charlie. He decides he will counteract this tendency and pursue more active involvement with Charlie.

Second, he watches Charlie play with an eye to his strengths. He observes that Charlie really does have athletic ability; he is able to run fast and demonstrates physical strength as he tangles with other players. Coach Jackson decides he will help Charlie develop these positives.

Third, he considers the simple, focused skills that make up the game of soccer. He also considers what Charlie's own aspirations might be. He asks Charlie what he would most like to be able to do on the soccer field. Charlie says he wants to be able to "kick the ball far." As this is consistent with his apparent physical strength, Coach Jackson sets up a regular routine in which Charlie practices only kicking the ball far and straight. Together they establish a personal performance goal of kicking the ball at least eight times in each half. His mother gives him a gold star each time he accomplishes this personal goal, and after receiving four gold stars he earns an ice cream cone.

Since Charlie now thinks mainly of kicking the ball, he does not become overwhelmed by such thoughts as where he should be on the field for offense or defense, and he does not track the other team's strategies or worry about which part of his foot he should use to kick the ball. Instead he keeps up with the action because it is the only way he can get close enough to the ball to kick it. He picks up a lot of strategies through active learning, discovering and implementing previously confusing techniques simply because they go along with getting in position to kick the ball. The incentives of gold stars and ice cream cones are much easier for him to relate to than the goal of looking forward to being a great soccer player in high school. Over time, he becomes a regular dynamo on the soccer field, actively engaged with his team rather than merely hanging around on the fringe.

Greenspan, S. I. (1993) *Playground politics: Understanding the emotional life of your school-age child.* Reading, MA: Addison-Wesley.

Unlike truly aggressive children, those who engage in rough-and-tumble play are more likely to be socially competent as well as popular with their peers (Garvey, 1976). And, as my "adversary" during my own middle childhood experience eventually realized, rough-and-tumble play is an activity much more commonly pursued among boys than girls (DiPietro, 1981; Pelligrini & Smith, 1998).

How can physical education instructors help address the needs of children who are so diverse in maturity level?

PAVING PATHWAYS ALONG MIDDLE CHILDHOOD PHYSICAL MILESTONES: PHYSICAL EDUCATION

Alexandra is one of those children we might call a "late bloomer." She is the smallest, least physically mature child among all of her same-age classmates. As such, she has learned to dread her physical education class. Why? Because when compared with her peers' agility, strength, balance, and flexibility she comes up short. The inferior status of her motor skills is accentuated every time she dribbles a basketball, runs across a soccer field, or swings a baseball bat. Adding insult to injury, when her classmates choose up sides for sports, she is always chosen last. Upon reaching the age of 12, she experiences a growth spurt and catches up with most of her peers. However, the damage has already been done. She views herself as physically inept, and feelings of inefficacy have spilled over into her general self-concept. She has also learned to focus more on sedentary activities less likely to result in failure, and has an aversion to physical activity in general.

Children are more likely to choose physical activity as a pastime if they perceive themselves as physically competent or skilled at sports (Biddle & Goudas, 1996). Their overall perception of themselves also plays a role. **Self-efficacy** is an individual's belief that his or her attempt at a certain behavior is likely to have the desired outcome (Bandura, 1977). Children who have a high degree of self-efficacy are more likely to engage in physical activity than those experiencing low self-efficacy (Trost et al., 1996). Of course, children also frequently choose active pastimes simply because they enjoy engaging in them (Stucky-Ropp & DiLorenzo, 1993).

Unfortunately, as we think back to our own elementary school days and other groups of children we have observed, most of us can recall someone in Alexandra's evolving predicament. Her physical immaturity and physical education experiences thoroughly discouraged her from appreciating active pastimes. The presence of an Alexandra among any group of children is a given: Normal physical development during middle childhood encompasses so huge a range of variance that there will always be children who stand out as either the most or least skilled.

Numerous studies have shown that elementary school programs can affect the level of physical activity children choose. Physical education programs that include not only moderate to vigorous physical activity but also efforts toward encouraging children's sense of self-efficacy are especially likely to succeed (United States Department of Health and Human Services, 1996). So what can physical education teachers do that might minimize frustration for the less physically mature child, yet not underchallenge or otherwise short-change those of average or advanced maturity (Dieden, 1995)?

Managing competition. One strategy teachers might consider is changing the nature of competition during physical education activities. Team sports are inherently competitive, and in fact help the child learn to channel aggressive and competitive energies into socially appropriate arenas. However, children also benefit from competition with the self: "Can my next try be better than my last?" "Am I better at this than I was before?" Rather than noting the number of baskets made, running speed, or distances students can throw a ball, the chart on the classroom wall might record how much *better* each student is performing since the beginning of the year. Since improvement values do not necessarily favor the most highly skilled, the early bloomers who might otherwise run the risk of becoming complacent are also presented with a healthy challenge (Nicholls, 1989).

The competitiveness of sports can lead to losing the joy of simply playing. When children become overinvolved with or overfocused on how they themselves are performing, they do not persist as long or challenge themselves as greatly as those who are focused more on being part of the joint task at hand (Solman, 1996). Opportunities for free play should continue to be offered as they allow children to freely experience without necessarily evaluating themselves competitively. In addition, a physical education teacher can introduce organized noncompetitive play activity such as nature hikes, dance, and cooperative games such as having the entire group work together to keep a giant inflated ball from touching the gym floor.

Another piece of fall-out from the competitiveness of amateur sports in the United States is the tendency to allow only the most skilled to play. Tryouts often determine who is good enough to be on "the" team, and anyone not meeting the mark is rejected. In other countries, such as Australia, everybody who wants to participate can do so. Tryouts simply determine skill level; different "leagues" are created to allow competition between teams having similar levels of ability. When possible, school sports programs might also consider offering such breadth of participation.

Choosing sides creatively. There are many ways of dividing children into teams that do not repeatedly leave the lesser skilled conspicuously standing out as the unwanted. Teachers can divide students into groups on the basis of birthday months, clothing colors, alphabetical considerations, numbering off, or drawing from a deck of playing cards. Choosing up sides can become a game in itself, such as a "freeze game" in which the children run around the gym, stop at the sound of a whistle, then are placed on sides in combinations of two quadrants of the "freeze" placements.

During some physical education activities, teachers are concerned that skill levels be equally distributed so that one team does not "cream" the other. On these occasions, they can create teams of equivalent skill level by using a technique scientists often use when they must ensure that a certain variable is equally represented in both the control group and the experimental group. In **matched designs**, researchers first assess participants regarding the variable in question. For example, to study the effectiveness of a new reading program, they must consider the level of intelligence of the participants. They pair all the participants on the basis of their performance on intelligence measures: the two highest scorers, the two next-highest scorers, and so on. Then by flipping a coin or using some other randomizing procedure, they assign one member of each pair to one of the two groups. By thus ensuring that the more advanced students are not overrepresented in the experimental group, researchers can avoid minimal or nonsignificant outcomes that may obscure the fact that the new reading program is especially helpful for students scoring lower on measures of intelligence.

Teachers can also use matched designs to preselect groups. Most teachers can informally assess students' levels of physical ability just by noting their physical maturation and observing their playground activity. Assessment is even easier if the school's physical education program regularly assesses students' abilities, perhaps providing numeric values by which children could be matched into pairs. Then, like the scientist, the teacher need only randomly assign divided pairs and announce the resulting teams—and the students never need know how the teams were selected.

MIDDLE CHILDHOOD AND HEALTH

What is the health status of today's school-age children?

At some point during the school-age years most children suffer from an acute illness such as a viral infection, bronchitis, or strep throat (Starfield et al., 1984). Yet in spite of the importance placed on maintaining good health in the United States, especially for children, not all sick children will receive adequate treatment (Institute of Medicine, 1993). In the wake of the transition toward managed health care, low-income families have become dramatically underserved. Only the most severely economically depressed families qualify for government-assisted health care. Considering that one out of four children in the United States lives in poverty, and that children from low-income families face a greater likelihood of suffering illness, a huge sector of contemporary children does not receive adequate health care. Because of their parents' financial straits, these children frequently receive needed medical care—even when they are in poor or only fair health—only after their condition has reached emergency-room severity.

Such families are also very unlikely to have access to preventive measures such as education in nutrition and basic child care. Statistical trends in health service delivery and socioeconomic status reflect this unfortunate circumstance: low-income children receive a greater share of acute care services, while higher-income children receive more of the preventive services that can keep them healthy (Roghmann & Pless, 1993). Health care providers and health service communities in general have their work cut out for them as they seek ways of getting services to those who need them while negotiating the evolving environment of health care delivery systems.

Two major factors play significant preventive roles in health management during middle childhood: nutrition and stress management. And television viewing habits can also affect children's physical well-being.

What kinds of nutritional challenges emerge during the growing independence of middle childhood?

Nutrition

When my children were young I occasionally helped out as a parent volunteer at their elementary school. On these days I would typically try the school cafeteria's hot lunch. One day as I shuffled down the food line I was served a corn dog, Tater Tots, milk, and a gelatin dessert with a few pieces of something resembling canned fruit floating in it. Contemplating the nutritional content of the meal, I asked the server how vegetables were represented. "Ketchup," she replied, as she cheerfully plopped a small paper container of the condiment on my tray.

Nutritional Challenges of Middle Childhood. The notion of nutrition I had encountered in the school cafeteria encapsulates a dilemma facing those of us who attempt to encourage good eating habits in school-age children. During middle childhood, children develop eating patterns and food preferences that will likely follow them into adulthood. Typically these preferences are the same as their parents', but additional influences and opportunities also affect their eating habits (Pipes & Trahms, 1993). Their greater access than when they were younger to money, grocery stores, and fast food outlets allows them to make more independent eating choices, which are not always the most healthy ones. They spend more and more of their time unsupervised, during which time they often snack as they please.

School lunches containing lower levels of fat, salt, and sugar and a healthy representation of fruits, vegetables, and whole-grain carbohydrates often find their way into the cafeteria garbage can. Limited menu choices also affect consumption: When the choice is "take it or leave it," a good percentage of any number of children will choose to leave it. A relatively new wrinkle is competition between a real lunch and the food-vending machines that have popped up in many elementary schools to enhance revenues.

Since school-age children eat less frequently than they had as preschoolers, they have fewer opportunities for ingesting necessary nutrients. Yet they require more: a balanced diet of about 2400 calories every day (Williams & Caliendo, 1984). A number of the impediments to good nutrition that had haunted them when they were preschoolers may continue, such as living in a low-income household, poor parental eating habits or knowledge of nutrition, or rigid or limited food regimens that have become reinforced by parents who either push or never offer disliked foods. Chronic undernourishment during childhood can lead to permanent damage, which often first appears during middle childhood; their physical and motor development will have fallen behind that of their

A daily ritual of having dinner together as a family enables these parents to both provide a current standard of nutrition and establish some healthy long-term eating habits for their children.

Bob Daemmrich/Stock Boston

better-nourished peers, and they show lower intelligence and impaired attending ability (Lozoff, 1989).

Encouraging Good Nutrition.   On the bright side, the school-age child is able to comprehend that there is a connection between proper nutrition and positive health and growth. Good nutrition can be taught in a number of ways (Pipes & Trahms, 1993). At home, children benefit from being actively involved in meal planning. Parents can monitor and model consumption of three square meals a day—especially breakfast, one of the most important meals, yet one that children may begin choosing to skip at this age (Conner, 1984; Morgan et al., 1986). Eating meals together as a family goes a long way toward modeling healthy eating habits, as well as making sure a nutritious, balanced meal is served.

Some school lunch programs also have begun to include students in school meal planning. More food is actually consumed when the menu offers choices and when the popular meal choices such as tacos and hamburgers and the ingredients in the salad bar are sources of proper nutrition. In addition to having a hot lunch program, some schools emphasize the importance of eating breakfast by offering school breakfast programs. Replacing the cookies, chips, and candies in the school vending machines with fruits, nuts, seeds, and granola bars also helps provide a model of healthy snack choices.

Obesity.   Amidst the growth spurts, most children's body proportions at some point take on shapes or sizes that would be considered somewhat overweight or underweight. But if their bodies exceed the expected weight for their age, gender, and body build by 20%, they fit the definition of **obese**. Over 20% of school-age children could be defined as obese, and this number appears to be increasing (Gortmaker et al., 1987). If children are relatively recent emigrants from a developing nation, the "thrifty genes" that helped their ancestors get by on less can contribute toward obesity and hypertension as they consume the high-fat, high-sodium diet of Western societies (Sapolsky, 1997).

Being the "fat kid" is not only physically unhealthy but can also be emotionally devastating. Since children typically identify one another according to their most notable characteristics, a child's weight may end up defining his or her social identity even when other children are not being intentionally cruel. And even children who have been taught about the medical causes of obesity tend to shun an obese child (Bell & Morgan, 2000). Given Western culture's current overemphasis on excessive thinness, many people—often including the obese child—judge the obesity as evidence of some form of inferiority. Obese children are thus more likely to experience low self-esteem and depression and to be unpopular with peers (Mendelson et al., 1996; Pierce & Wardle, 1997; Strauss et al., 1985). The extra weight also slows a child down, limiting or impairing the child's attempts to join in with other children's activities. Unlike the chubby infant or toddler, the obese preschool or school-aged child is also more likely to be obese as an adult (Zack et al., 1979).

While there is a temptation to infer that all obese children simply eat too much, the story is much more complex. Elements related to both nature and nurture, cognitive and behavioral influences, and physical and emotional factors all have been associated with childhood obesity. Table 11.1 lists many of the conditions that may contribute.

PAVING PATHWAYS ALONG MIDDLE CHILDHOOD PHYSICAL MILESTONES: HELPING OBESE CHILDREN

Many obese children (not to mention adults!) are moved to try various dieting aids for which advertising makes claims of dramatic success rates. Often these involve "crash" diets such as protein-sparing modified-fast diet drinks. Many of these so-called "crash" diets involve eating regimens or diet drinks supplying limited nutrients, or appetite suppressants. If these crash diets work at all for a particular person, their success rate for long-term weight loss is extremely limited, and they can even make matters worse: The body adapts to severely reduced caloric intake by slowing its use of calories; when the dieter resumes a more normal caloric intake, the body begins to gain weight (Wing, 1992). For children, crash diets are especially ill-advised because they are unlikely to provide the quota of calories and nutrients that normal development requires.

Weight-management programs for children take into account the factors that lead to obesity, many of which are related to the home environment. Any

TABLE 11.1

Some factors associated
with childhood obesity

Heredity	The number of fat cells and the rate at which children burn calories is in part genetically determined (Bouchard, 1994).
Physiological Problems	Some hormonal and metabolic conditions result in obesity (Lowry, 1986).
Cues for Eating	Obese children are more likely to use external eating cues such as sight, smell, taste, and time of day rather than internal cues such as feelings of hunger (Constanzo & Woody, 1979).
Activity Level	Children who are less active are more likely to become obese (Goran & Poehlman, 1992).
Family Eating Habits	Children are likely to develop poor eating habits that can lead to obesity if they observe poor parental eating habits (Kendrick et al., 1991).
	Parents who reward children with food or provide it as means of solace are more likely to have obese children (Bruch, 1970).
	Overabundance of foods containing simple sugars (candies, desserts, etc.) in the family diet can produce increases in appetite and overeating (Rodin et al, 1985).
Socioeconomic Status	Children from low-income families begin as less obese than those from high-income families, but by adolescence this tendency has reversed (Garn et al., 1981).
Traumatic Events	Chaotic and/or nonsupportive family environments are associated with childhood obesity (Christoffel & Forsythe, 1989).
	Childhood obesity has been associated with prolonged or permanent separation from mothers (Kahn, 1970).
Television Viewing	A predictive relationship has been established between amount of time spent watching television and future obesity (Kolata, 1986).

weight-management plan for a child must therefore be aimed at the entire family. When parents are not a part of the treatment program, children tend not to maintain their weight loss (Epstein et al., 1987). Reluctant parents who decide to let their obese children figure out their own solutions after they are grown may want to consider that early intervention is much more likely to result in ongoing success than waiting until adulthood, when habits have become ingrained (Epstein et al., 1990).

Effective weight management for obese children aims toward changes in overall lifestyle. Parents are educated about good nutrition and are given guidance and support as they improve their family's eating habits. They are advised to reduce availability of sweets and refrain from using food as a reward, and they are assisted with brainstorming more opportunities for physical activity. Being active as a natural part of one's daily habits tends to be more effective than introducing brief artificial aerobic stints (Epstein & Wing, 1987). A positive reinforcement schedule rewards the child as he or she attains jointly set goals of losing weight and maintaining weight loss. It also increases feelings of confidence and self-esteem, providing concrete evidence of success in an area where the child may have given up hope. However, the most profound reward tends to be pride in the weight loss itself. Multicomponent behavioral treatment programs such as these have demonstrated superiority over programs that provide education only (Jelalian & Saelens, 1999).

What roles do stress and coping play during the school-age years?

Stress and Coping

During the school-age years, children begin feeling some pressures similar to those that adults feel. At school they encounter the pressure to perform. Add in the factor of competition and its pressures as they try out for sports teams, positions in musical groups, and other coveted but limited opportunities. Making friends and fitting in with the peer group are sources of anxiety, as is learning how to deal with the class bully. As children increase their understanding of their environment, they become more aware of the implications of what they observe, and new stresses can emerge from old stressors, such as worries about potential threats posed by ongoing difficulties at home or dangers in the neighborhood. What effect does such stress have on the physical well-being of children?

Stress. **Stress** can be defined as the internal condition we experience when we are confronted by any factor that makes us feel pressured to act. As we react to stress, our bodies go through a process identified as the **general adaptation syndrome** (Selye, 1976). Hormones, especially **epinephrine**, signal the brain and body that a threat is afoot and prepare us to do battle. We experience increases in heart rate, blood pressure, blood sugar level, rate of respiration, and speed of message transmission through the nervous system. As we deal with the source of stress, we use up these hormones and their levels return to normal. However, if the source of stress continues, so also do the surging of hormones and the corresponding physiological responses.

Unfortunately, our bodies cannot endure this routine indefinitely. In the short run, we become exhausted and no longer able to effectively deal with stress. In the long run, such prolonged increases in heart rate and blood pressure are associated with heart disease (Krantz et al., 1988). Furthermore, depleted hormone supplies and other metabolic changes that occur during periods of continued stress eventually interfere with the functioning of the immune system, diminishing the ability to fight off disease. Research has revealed that behavior, emotions, the brain, and the effectiveness of the immune system are tightly related (Cohen & Herbert, 1996; Maier et al., 1994; Salovey et al., 2000).

Researchers examining the effects of stress on children find that the presence of significant life stressors correlates both with incidences of child illness and the number of contacts parents make with medical facilities (Roghmann & Haggerty, 1993). The long-term effects of excessive stress during childhood has not been sufficiently studied, but the presence of high blood pressure and hypertension during childhood has been associated with the beginning of an ongoing pattern of cardiovascular overreactivity (Murphy, 1992).

The Type A Behavior Pattern. Substantial research has focused on a specific form of achievement-related stress that has been dubbed the **type A behavior pattern**. The condition was originally called the "coronary-prone personality" because adults who experience this form of stress are more likely to develop heart disease (Friedman & Rosenman, 1974). These individuals are highly competitive and achievement oriented. Yet the health risk emerges from the fact that they base their self-esteem on these accomplishments and from the experience of "free-floating hostility"—contributing toward the sufferer's blowing up over every obstacle to goal attainment. The frequent emotional outbursts and the rush to bolster floundering self-esteem with as many achievements as possible stimulate surges of hormones that slowly wear away at the functioning of the cardiovascular system, not to mention the sufferer's emotional well-being (Friedman & Ulmer, 1984).

Researchers have also examined type A behavior in children. As early as age 3 children may begin showing the tell-tale signs, including higher levels of aggression, impatience, and restlessness (Corrigan & Moskowitz, 1983). Type A children push themselves excessively hard to excel, constantly compare themselves and their performance to that of their peers, and focus more on the competitive aspects of childhood pastimes than on simply enjoying them (Matthews & Volkin, 1981). The end result of this self-imposed stress is a greater likelihood of illness, cardiovascular symptoms, and sleep disturbances (Thoreson et al., 1985).

There is some evidence that type A children are more likely to have type A parents, suggesting that—as is true of most learned behaviors—modeling plays a role in the development of the behavior pattern (Forgays, 1996; Weidner et al., 1988). Yet studies have also implicated contributions by inherited traits (Ewart, 1994); children who have irritable, oversensitive temperaments may be especially susceptible to type A traits. Nevertheless, factors such as an authoritarian parenting style and/or lack of a positive affiliation with parents are believed to play a more significant role (Woodall & Matthews, 1989). The extent to which type A behavior patterns developed during childhood continue into adulthood is not yet clear (Steinberg, 1986).

Helping Children Cope with Stress. Physical activity is by far one of the best methods for coping with stress, since it enables the body to use up those excess energizing hormones. Numerous studies have demonstrated a relationship between children's blood pressure and how often they exercise (Alpert & Wilmore, 1994). Most children generate physical activity with ease, but under stressful circumstances may need some encouragement. Like adults, children vary in the types of defense mechanisms they may choose: *regression,* during which children act less mature than they really are; *acting out,* which usually involves misbehaving or tantrums; or *withdrawal,* hiding out in their rooms or in front of the TV and avoiding interaction with others. Encouraging physical activity guides children toward a healthier, more adaptive alternative.

Children tend to become better copers as they mature. By the end of middle childhood, they are considerably better than when they were preschoolers at using coping skills focused on managing emotions. They also have the capacity to consider or be trained in such problem-focused coping skills as generating multiple solutions to problems and identifying the sequence of steps necessary for reaching a solution (Compas et al., 1992). Children tend to cope more successfully if their parents are good copers and they have a strong relationship with their parents, especially with their mothers (Kliewer et al., 1996).

Children also appear to be better copers when they have a **stress buffer** in their lives—a social support providing a perceived safety net that they know they can fall back on in times of need There is some suggestion, however, that stress buffers are more effective with girls than with boys (Cohen & Park, 1992; Llabre & Hadi, 1997). Still, this is an indication that even during middle childhood a strong positive attachment with a caregiver continues to contribute toward the growing child's well-being.

A variety of the cognitive-behavioral coping skills used by adults are also effective when training children to manage stress; these include relaxation techniques and biofeedback, positive self-statements, imagery, attention distraction, and behavioral rehearsal. Setting up reward systems for using the new coping strategies is also effective. When children are trained in the use of combinations of such coping strategies as a prelude to aversive dental and medical procedures, the strength of the positive results has been impressive (Dahlquist, 1992).

Because a parent and a disaster worker are acting as "stress buffers" for this girl, she will be less likely to experience short- or long-term emotional consequences from the trauma of her disaster experience.

American Red Cross

How can television viewing affect children's physical well-being?

Television and Children's Health

Children watch more television per day during the elementary school years than they do during any other stage of childhood (Collins, 1984). What effect does all this television viewing have on them? Most research regarding the controversy surrounding television and children has looked at its effect on social development, especially concerning aggression. Less studied are the indirect effects that excessive television viewing can have on physical health.

Activity Level. Obviously, children cannot simultaneously watch television and engage in meaningful physical activity. Physical activity is necessary for normal development of both physical structures and motor skills. A child who spends many hours in front of the television is less likely to be getting the exercise he or she needs.

Brain Development. We do not know the exact effect that prolonged television viewing may have on brain development, but we do know that repeated exposure to any stimulus is highly likely to have neurological consequences, especially during the years when the brain is still experiencing considerable plasticity. Children's extensive close-up television viewing can contribute to **myopia**—better known as near-sightedness. The same can be said of any activity that requires exceedingly long periods of focusing on near stimuli, including reading or artwork (Angle & Wissmann, 1980). However, rarely do you see a child spending the same amount of time on these activities as the average child devotes to watching television.

Risk-Taking Behaviors. Television has another potential indirect impact upon health through its depictions of various forms of risk-taking (Tinsley, 1992). The abuse of drugs and alcohol, reckless driving, stunts such as ill-advised climbing and jumping, and impulsive unsafe sexual practices are not only presented but also downright glamorized. Furthermore, the very likely health consequences that such risky behaviors have in real life are rarely shown. How often have you seen James Bond-types get into drinking-and-driving accidents or receive DUIs, test positively for sexually transmitted diseases, or suffer permanent disabilities because of physical stunts? Seeing such models for behavior without vicarious punishment or dire consequences, children may imitate them and suffer drastic health effects. Linking displays of high-risk behaviors to examples of their more realistic consequences can actually have a beneficial impact. Children who watched safety education videotapes showing a dangerous activity, the injurious result, and then a safer alternative behavior were found to be less likely to engage in the risky behavior (Potts & Swisher, 1998).

Eating Behaviors. By far the most extensively studied physical health consequence of television viewing involves eating behaviors. Since television viewing is a sedentary activity, viewers often eat just to be doing something rather than to satisfy hunger. Indeed, television often models that very behavior—eating for purposes other than satisfying hunger—yet rarely shows the expected consequences—such as an obese or malnourished child (Palumbo & Dietz, 1985).

The vast majority of foods advertised during children's programming are not particularly healthy, and are typically high in fat and sugar. Commercials for these foods do succeed in influencing children's snack preferences (Carruth et al., 1991). These commercials also tend to highlight such food attributes as sweetness or being "chocolatey" or "creamy" as if these are the most important attributes the child should consider. There is some concern that excessively focusing children's attention on this narrow band of food characteristics may interfere with normal exploration of the interesting and potentially enjoyable attributes of healthier foods, such as the crispness of a piece of celery or the leathery, chewy feel of a dried apricot (Gussow, 1972).

Consider also that as children fall into a mesmerized state in front of the television set, their metabolism slows, slowing in turn their burning of the calories they consume (Klesges, 1993). Combine inactivity with high-calorie, high-fat eating habits, and it's little wonder that children who watch a lot of television tend to become obese (Kolata, 1986). Even if such children do not suffer from obesity, inappropriate eating habits can interfere with consumption of the nutrients necessary for healthy development.

PAVING PATHWAYS ALONG MIDDLE CHILDHOOD PHYSICAL MILESTONES: REDUCING TIME WITH TELEVISION

The concept of limiting the amount of time children spend in front of the television is nothing new. But limits are frequently difficult to enforce because watching television is often a "default activity" (Murphy & Tucker, 1996). Children who are told they've had the TV on long enough often complain, "but I don't have anything else to do!" Taking away television time leaves a gap in a child's day. Ensuring that children with newly set limits will change their habits requires that something else fill the void.

Regular trips to the library and investment in board games and crafts materials are ways to make sure that other leisure activities are readily available. During middle childhood, however, physical activities are among the most important pastimes to encourage. Parents have influence over many of the factors determining whether or not a child will pursue physical activity (Hogan, 2001):

▶ Do children need to be encouraged to increase the amount of time they spend outside ?
▶ Do they have the equipment necessary for outdoor activities?
▶ During bad weather, do they have access to gym facilities?
▶ Are there activity programs they can be signed up for?
▶ Do they have friendships with active children that can be encouraged?

▶ Do the parents support the concept of being physically active and/or model it themselves?

▶ Do they provide guidance and instruction necessary for skilled physical activities?

Once again, success comes not from a quick fix but through parents investing their time, attention, and resources in their children's ongoing developmental needs.

▶ SUMMARY

Body Growth

School-age children grow about 2–3 in. and gain about 5 lb each year. Skeletal and muscular growth makes increasingly obvious each child's individual uniqueness in body appearance. Girls may progress to be as much as 2 years ahead of boys in physical maturity, but boys' greater number of muscle cells maintains their superiority in overall strength.

Brain Growth

Brain growth slows significantly, consisting mainly of increases in numbers of synapses and improved myelination of neurons.

Motor Development

Children become stronger and faster, as well as more coordinated, agile, and flexible. They show improvements in endurance, reaction time, and ability to coordinate perceptual and motor skills. In spite of differences in physical abilities and activity choices, the genders are still sufficiently similar that boys and girls can play together in sports. Comparing handwriting samples of children at the beginning and end of middle childhood gives evidence of improvement in fine motor skills.

Play activity becomes more organized and complex. Children spend more time participating in adult-organized games such as Little League. While such games are useful for teaching management of competition, skill development, and team effort, they should not take the place of the more natural forms of play that contribute to overall physical, motor, and social development. For example, rough-and-tumble play allows children to practice some physical skills as well as learn the roles and rules of dominance and submission in a friendly, good-natured manner.

Physical education programs can take control of some factors in order to encourage ongoing enjoyment of physical activity. Instructors can manage the negative aspects of competition by including noncompetitive group activities and emphasizing personal improvement rather than interpersonal comparison.

Considering the huge diversity of size and skill level among children close in age during this stage, teams are better chosen through creative means rather than having children choose up sides. In this manner the less maturely developed children are not discouraged by being unchosen, and those of greater maturity are not encouraged to rest on their laurels.

Middle Childhood and Health

Children are likely to contract at least one serious illness during the school-age years. Currently, in the United States, children from higher-income families are more likely to receive adequate illness and preventive health care than those from low-income families. Proper nutrition becomes more challenging as children encounter a greater number of temptations while developing more independent eating habits. Chronic undernourishment can lead to impairments in physical and motor development, intelligence, and attending ability. Better nutrition can be encouraged through both child and parental education. Obesity during childhood affects both physical and emotional well-being. Successful treatment of childhood obesity requires intervention in the entire family's lifestyle.

Excessive stress and/or lack of coping skills during childhood can lead to illness by stimulating production of excess hormones and impairing the immune system. An angry, unhealthy achievement style known as the type A behavior pattern can also lead to illness, as well as to cardiovascular problems and sleep disturbances. Children become better copers as they mature, becoming better able to use problem-solving and cognitive-behavioral strategies for managing emotions. Physical activity is especially helpful for reducing stress. Having a stress buffer relationship reduces the impact of traumatic and stressful events.

In addition to its psychosocial effects, television viewing can have indirect effects on physical health. Television viewing involves long periods of inactivity, as well as viewing habits that can contribute to myopia. Television programming often models highly risky behavior but without showing that it risks physical well-being in the real world. Television encourages unhealthy eating habits: viewers eat for something to do, and television itself models ill-advised eating practices and advertises unhealthy foods. Limiting children's television time is more likely to be successful when caregivers make alternative activities readily available and encourage their use.

KEY TERMS

dominance hierarchy	menarche	self-efficacy
epinephrine	myopia	stress
general adaptation syndrome	obese	stress buffer
matched designs	rough-and-tumble play	type A behavior pattern

CONCEPT REVIEW

1. School-age children grow about _____ inches and gain about _____ pounds each year.

2. As school-age children mature, their rounded look gives way to proportionally _____ trunks and _____ limbs, with girls developing their _____ structures earlier and boys continuing to maintain a greater _____ mass.

3. Attending ability continues to be a challenge while school-age children await more sufficient _____ of neurons. Complex integrated activities become more possible due to advances in _____ between perceptual and motor skills.

4. In addition to benefiting physical and cognitive development, play and games allow children to try out new _____ and _____ efforts. Adult-organized games can defeat the purposes of play by overemphasizing _____ .

5. A play style engaged in more by boys than girls, _____ play, not only helps develop integration of motor and cognitive skills but also contributes toward social development in the form of establishing children's _____ hierarchies.

6. Children experiencing low _____ in their physical abilities are less likely to choose to engage in physical activity; physical education teachers can minimize their reluctance by reducing the emphasis on _____ and focusing more on _____ .

7. While children benefit from _____ health efforts, low-income children often receive most of their health care only when they are _____ .

8. School-age children can develop poor eating habits because they are more _____ than when they were younger. Poor nutrition can lead to less advanced _____ and _____ development, lower _____ , and impaired _____ ability.

9. Better nutrition can be encouraged by means of _____ , more frequent _____ meals, and allowing children greater involvement in _____ .

10. Obese children, who weigh at least _____ percent above their expected weight, may as a result suffer from low _____ , _____ mood, and lack of _____ among peers.

11. Successful weight management programs for children typically involve the _____, addressing the family's eating _____ and levels of _____, as well as arranging for _____ that support rather than hinder healthy eating habits.

12. Children who experience excessive stress may become ill because ongoing stress can compromise the efficiency of their _____ systems.

13. Some children develop the physical symptoms of stress because of the Type A behavior pattern, which is fueled by excessive _____ and free-floating _____. Parents play roles in the existence of this behavioral pattern by means of _____ parenting and/or _____ contributions that may temperamentally predispose a child for such a pattern.

14. Children benefit from being encouraged to use _____ as a means of managing stress. They will become better copers as they _____, especially if their parents are _____ or if someone in their lives plays the role of a _____.

15. Television-viewing can affect children's health because it often reduces _____ level, may contribute to _____, presents _____ unrealistically, and can encourage unhealthy _____ habits. Parents can more easily limit their children's television-viewing time if they actively provide and model _____.

1) two or three; five; 2) shorter; longer; skeletal; muscle; 3) myelination; coordination; 4) social roles; creative; competition; 5) rough-and-tumble; dominance; 6) self-efficacy; competition; performing the task; 7) preventive; very ill; 8) independent; physical; motor; intelligence; attending; 9) education; family; meal planning; 10) twenty; self-esteem; depressed; popularity; 11) home environment; habits; activity; reinforcement contingencies; 12) immune; 13) competitiveness; hostility; authoritarian; genetic; 14) physical activity; mature; good copers; stress buffer; 15) activity; myopia; risk-taking; eating; alternative pastimes

RESOURCES FOR FURTHER READING

Cheung, L. W. Y., & Richmond, J. B. (Eds.) (1995). *Child health, nutrition, & physical activity.* Champaign, IL: Human Kinetics.

Dieden, B. (1995). *Games to keep kids moving: P.E. activities to promote total participation, self-esteem, and fun for grades 3–8.* West Nyack, NY: Center for Applied Research in Education.

Dlugokinski, E. L., & Allen, S. F. (1997). *Empowering children to cope with difficulty and build muscles for mental health.* Washington, DC: Accelerated Development.

Heller, R. F., & Heller, R. F. (1997). *Carbohydrate addicted kids: Help your child or teen break free of junk food and sugar cravings—for life!* New York: HarperCollins.

LaGreca, A. M., Siegel, L. J., Wallander, J. L., & Walker, C. E. (1992). *Stress and coping in child health.* New York: Guilford Press.

Murphy, J., & Tucker, K. (1996). *Stay tuned: Raising media-savvy kids in the age of the channel-surfing couch potato.* New York: Doubleday.

Pipes, P. L., & Trahms, C. M. (1993). *Nutrition in infancy and childhood,* 5th ed. St. Louis, MO: Mosby.

INFOTRAC COLLEGE EDITION

For additional readings, explore InfoTrac College Edition, your online library. Go to http://www.infotrac-college.com/wadsworth and use the passcode that came on the card with your book. Try these search terms: athletics and children, coping behavior and children, low-income children and health, obesity and children, rough-and-tumble play, self-efficacy and children, stress in children, stress buffers and children, television and children's health

CHILD DEVELOPMENT CD-ROM

Go to the Wadsworth Child Development CD-ROM for further study of the concepts in this chapter. The CD-ROM also includes quizzes and additional activities to expand your learning experience.

REFERENCES

For a list of references for this chapter, see the Wadsworth Psych Study Center Web site at: http://www.wadsworth.com/product/0534348092s

CHAPTER 12

Middle Childhood Cognitive Development

FOCUS QUESTIONS

▶ What is concrete operational ability, and how does it affect children's reasoning?

▶ What changes in information processing take place during middle childhood?

▶ What roles can intelligence tests play in a child's education?

▶ How do teachers, peers, parents, cultural influences, and children's individual characteristics affect learning and achievement?

▶ How can developmental and learning disabilities affect achievement, and how can a child's potential be maximized in spite of their effects?

▶ What are the needs of the intellectually and creatively gifted, and how can these needs be met?

▶ What factors might parents look at as they consider home schooling their children?

▶ What are the pluses and minuses of the computer age for children?

▶ How does language ability change during middle childhood, and what language issues arise for bilingual children?

OUTLINE	

Piaget's Concrete Operations	Home Schooling
Information Processing	Paving Pathways: Should I Home School My Child?
Attention	Children and Computers
Memory	Paving Pathways: Choosing Software for Children
Intelligence, Learning, and Special Needs	Paving Pathways: Structuring Children's Internet Use
Intelligence	**Language**
Learning and Achieving	Vocabulary
Children with Disabilities	Grammar
Intellectually Gifted Children	Reading and Writing
Creatively Gifted Children	Bilingualism
Paving Pathways: Fostering Creative Intelligence	

Donny loved the excitement of being in a third-grade classroom. Unfortunately, because of his excessive interest in what his neighbors were doing and his enjoyment in showing them the space-war art decorating his papers, he rarely finished his assignments on time. He was often sent home with his work still uncompleted after all his classmates had finished theirs.

Exasperated with trying to help Donny deal with yet another stack of work sheets, his father exclaimed, "Look, Donny. Who in your class seems be having the most trouble getting organized?"

"I don't know, Dad," said Donny, not catching his meaning.

"Well, let me put it this way. When all of the other students are reading their books and writing on their work sheets, who is just sitting there looking around and not accomplishing a thing?"

"Oh, that's the teacher!"

The main highlight of cognitive advances during middle childhood is organization. School-age children develop more advanced cognitive frameworks upon which they hang massive amounts of new information. Interconnections between the many informational "sound bites" they encounter are promoted by new reasoning strategies and an ever-increasing knowledge base, which ultimately help children sculpt a more advanced world view.

What is concrete operational ability, and how does it affect children's reasoning?

PIAGET'S CONCRETE OPERATIONS

Chapter 9 described Piaget's conclusion that preschoolers' cognitive processes are characterized most by the absence of important reasoning abilities. During the middle childhood phase of **concrete operations** Piaget observes children as moving from the world of "can't"s to "can"s (Piaget, 1936/1974). They can now perform mental operations on pieces of information and draw correct conclusions (Piaget, 1981). These new abilities contribute toward increased organization of and flexibility in thinking. The child's new perception of **reversibility**, the understanding that alterations can be reversed and materials returned to their previous form, allows the child to conserve. The child is also capable of **decentration**—shifting mental processing away from one manner of grouping objects and exploring alternative relationships between objects. Being able to break down groups of items into sets and subsets of hierarchal classifications, the child discovers new learning possibilities and develops a richer understanding of the world than was possible as a preschooler. All of these new abilities demonstrate the shift away from the dominance of perception over reasoning that is seen in preoperational thinking (Gelman et al., 1999; Wadsworth, 1996).

As the term *concrete* implies, however, the reasoning processes of concrete operational children are limited to those that can be made up of concrete representations. Take, for example, the logic-based skill of **transitive inference**, shown in Figure 12.1. Preschoolers can make judgments about relative size if they can observe the actual items (Piaget, 1952). However, if you tell concrete operational children that Mary is taller than Susan and Susan is taller than Jane, they can intuit that Mary is taller than Jane without having the three girls standing before them. They accomplish this task by mentally imaging the three girls

FIGURE 12.1

These children are told that Mary is bigger than Sandra and Sandra is bigger than Jessica. When then asked who is larger, Mary or Jessica, younger children solve the problem by comparing mental images of the three girls' sizes. School-age children are more likely to solve the problem by using rules of logic.

and comparing them. They are also aware that observation, guessing, and mental processes such as making inferences all yield knowledge that can be held with different levels of certainty (Pillow et al., 2000).

Children vary considerably in how quickly they develop concrete operational reasoning strategies. Vygotsky would reinforce the recognition that children not only need the relevant cognitive ability but also must be exposed to opportunities for developing the various strategies. For example, learning the skills behind seriation and transitive inference involves more than trial and error. Children try out a number of strategies and eventually advance over time after encountering the appropriate exposures and opportunities (Artman & Cahan, 1993; Southard & Pasnak, 1997). Children who do not receive formal schooling or come from cultures that have less use for such strategies tend to learn them much later (Rogoff, 1990). Heredity also appears to play a role, perhaps explaining why children who achieve high IQ scores tend to develop these reasoning processes at an earlier age (Flavell, 1982).

What concrete operational children still lack is the skill or ability to make judgments that involve abstract representations: in the case of transitive inference, that if A > B, and B > C, then A > C. Their scientific reasoning is also limited in its capacity for creating and testing hypotheses, since hypotheses are abstractions of positing what might be rather than what actually is. When presented with a hypothesis for testing, they are more likely to try one or two possible solutions to the problem and then give up, rather than exhausting all the possibilities available. Yet in spite of the abstractness of logic, children as young as 8 have begun to recognize that logic is more important than the concrete content of an argument (Morris, 2000).

INFORMATION-PROCESSING

What changes in information processing take place during middle school?

Early in middle childhood, the preschooler's piecemeal information-processing methods begin to be replaced by methods of making interconnections. Thanks to stage-related cognitive advances, the child more effectively integrates new knowledge with what he or she already knows, threading the pieces together according to the rules of mental operations. Likewise, the child's current knowledge influences his or her likely choice of new information to process and integrate. The relationship is interactive; the child's sensitivity toward or desire for certain knowledge motivates him or her to develop the skills necessary for absorbing it. Thus the child slowly builds the knowledge base that will accompany him or her throughout the learning years (Chi & Ceci, 1987).

Attention

Ability to pay attention improves dramatically during middle childhood, in part because more neurons are myelinated. Some improvements emerge as the child's personal experiences and growing knowledge base indicate to the child what needs to be attended to and what should be ignored (Strutt et al., 1975).

Suppose 6-year-old Freddie is trying to build his first kite. The task is big and exciting. He enjoys handling the sample model his father has provided. Numerous crayons and colorful markers have been supplied for decorating purposes. The wooden sticks make neat snapping noises when slapped against the table. Freddie's father provides considerable direction and redirection for Freddie as his kite-building efforts are repeatedly derailed by all of these fascinating but irrelevant stimuli. At age 11, Freddie knows what he needs to do in order to succeed at building a kite and he focuses his attention exclusively on the necessary tasks. He is also better able than he was at 6 to shift his attention when necessary, such as temporarily focusing back on adjusting the skeleton to better fit the shape of the paper (Flavell et al., 1993).

The school-age child's selective attention becomes increasingly better controlled, more sensitive to the social context within which stimuli are presented, and better able to take in the distinctive or relevant characteristics of new information (Howe et al., 2000). As always, children are most likely to attend when the relevant stimuli are clear and comprehensible. If teachers or parents are ambiguous or tentative regarding the need to perform a task or in some other manner appear powerless as they provide instruction, children not only attend more poorly but also perform more poorly on mentally demanding tasks (Bugental et al., 1999).

Memory

As children accommodate all the new information coming their way, they begin employing memory strategies (Kail, 1990). One of the earliest-appearing strategies is the technique of **rehearsal**. Either by hit-or-miss or through observed demonstrations, children eventually discover that repeating information to themselves will increase the likelihood that it will stick (Flavell et al., 1966). As middle childhood progresses, they make greater and more effective use of rehearsal as a memory strategy (Flavell et al., 1993).

Now that their concrete operational ability supports various ways of classifying items, children also begin using **categorization** as a means of memorizing lists or multiple pieces of information. They organize like information together and memorize it as a single chunk, such as a collection of commands for getting into their favorite computer program. Early in middle childhood, children can be taught to create and memorize clusters of words by semantic categories, perhaps grouping birds, mammals, and reptiles likely to appear on a science quiz (Best, 1993; Hock et al., 1998; Pierce & Lange, 2000). By the end of middle childhood they may spontaneously use such strategies, but categorization is a skill much more likely to be used regularly by adolescents and adults (Hasselhorn, 1992).

Given children's greater ability to use mental pictures as they reason in middle childhood, they may begin using various forms of **imagery** (McDaniel & Pressley, 1987). Once as a parent helper I worked with a student who had used such a strategy during test preparation. He had been trying to remember that the midwestern United States is a "farming heartland" by imagining a big heart sitting in the middle of a map of the United States. When presented with the relevant test question he successfully reproduced the mental image. However, the answer he wrote had something to do with the origins of Valentine's Day. As this student approaches adolescence he will most likely create more effectively complex mental images—such as amending his earlier image by placing the infamous heart on the seat of a tractor (Pressley et al., 1987).

School-age children also make more use of their short-term memory, and thus also their working memory. While 7-year-olds are relatively constrained in their ability to work out problems in their heads, by age 11 children are much better at manipulating pieces of mental computations regardless of their competence in arithmetic (Adams & Hitch, 1997). Associations have been found between advances in school-age children's working memory and both reading comprehension and length of written works (Swanson & Berninger, 1996).

What roles can intelligence tests play in a child's education?

INTELLIGENCE, LEARNING, AND SPECIAL NEEDS

Think back to a typical year of the course work you pursued during high school. You no doubt signed up for about six classes per term focused on relatively narrow topics—a schedule including such choices as geometry, biology, Spanish, English literature, volleyball, and photography. Now think back a little further and recall what you studied during a typical year of elementary school. You will most likely realize that you covered a greater breadth of topics in elementary school. For example, geometry was only one of the many areas of math you explored. Each year you learned bits and pieces of many sciences rather than zeroing in on a single field. You were engaged in a number of sports and physical activities, dabbled in a variety of artistic mediums, were introduced to backgrounds and unique aspects of many different parts of the world, and read or were read to from books covering any number of topics.

The middle childhood years are an important introductory phase of lifelong learning. School-age children are exposed to more previously unfamiliar fields of knowledge than they are likely to encounter for the rest of their lives, not only in their formal education but also in the process of learning the rules of their culture and society.

Intelligence

The issue of a child's intelligence and IQ scores becomes most relevant as children enter the school years. After all, IQ tests were originally designed for the purpose of predicting success in academia. The entering elementary school student's IQ score tends to correlate more closely with scores in later childhood, adolescence, and adulthood than do scores from infancy and the preschool years (Sameroff et al., 1993).

Testing. School-age children are frequently measured using group-administered IQ tests as educators track their students' academic progress and emerging abilities. Individually administered tests, however, more specifically address the needs of the individual student. The **Wechsler Intelligence Scale for Children-III (WISC-III)** is one of the most widely used IQ tests for the school-age group (Kaufman, 1994; Kaufman & Lichtenberger, 1999). Similar to the WPPSI (see Chapter 9), the WISC-III provides a verbal score, a performance score, and a full-scale score derived from a combination of the two subtests (Wechsler, 1991). High scores on tests such as these are often used for determining placement in programs for intellectually gifted children.

When unique difficulties appear to be interfering with a student's ability to learn, comparison of the verbal and performance scores can offer clues. Here's how it works. The verbal subtest measures the child's capacity for verbal comprehension, verbal ability as applied to problem-solving, and the knowledge base the child has acquired thus far. The performance subtest measures skills related to perception and motor ability, such as putting together puzzles, replicating block designs and coding patterns, and solving other problems requiring mechanical reasoning and recognition of spatial relationships. If the verbal score is significantly higher than the performance score, the student could either have a deficiency of perception or motor ability or could perhaps be striving to achieve beyond his or her current aptitude. If the performance score is significantly higher than the verbal score, often something is interfering with the educational process. Substandard learning can reflect learning disabilities, the distraction of an emotional trauma, ineffective instruction, the child's not having been exposed to the level or amount of formal education expected for the age group, or any combination of these causes.

A more recently developed IQ test used to assess a student's individual needs is the **Kaufman Assessment Battery for Children (K-ABC)** (Kaufman & Kaufman, 1983). Based on research employing the information-processing perspective of cognitive development, the K-ABC is designed to uncover the cognitive processes leading to correct or incorrect responses. Since successful intervention is typically designed to address such issues, the K-ABC has enjoyed some popularity because of its relevance and specific utility.

 IQ Tests and Culture. Most early IQ tests were designed to be taken by Caucasian, middle-class Americans. Because the norms of performance were therefore based on a specific culture, they may not be predictive of the true abilities of test-takers belonging to other cultures (Miller-Jones, 1989; Samuda et al., 1998). Let's take a look at some of the difficulties that may arise as educators attempt to test Nicolas, a 9-year-old growing up in a lower-income, predominantly African-American neighborhood in Los Angeles.

The dialect of English spoken in Nicolas's neighborhood differs from the traditional English used by his teachers. During the course of his education he has learned to speak traditional English but not as proficiently as his Caucasian-American classmates, who are also exposed to traditional English at home. Since

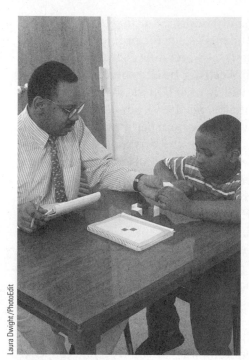

Standard intelligence tests may not accurately predict intelligence for children of diverse cultures, since cultural differences in interactional styles and information-processing practices at times run contrary to the conditions under which such tests were normed. Thus testers must take special care when administering and interpreting such tests with children of diverse cultures.

IQ test items are typically presented and scored on the basis of traditional English, he is at a disadvantage in his level of understanding and richness of response. His cultural experiences with language and conversation in general also tend to differ, more focused on personal experiencing, storytelling, and interpersonal exchanges than drilling or probing for "right" answers (Flannagan, 1996; Heath, 1983; Portes et al., 2000). The basic presuppositions he uses as he communicates and reasons are also representative of his home culture, not necessarily those of the culture the standardized tests draw from to measure ability (Greenfield, 1997). The differences in patterns of African-American and Caucasian-American information-processing do not appear to be differences in overall ability (Reynolds et al., 1998).

A number of IQ tasks involve toys such as puzzles, blocks, mazes, and other items familiar to most children but less so to low-income children such as Nicolas. Since intelligence scales measure both aptitude and related achievement levels, his minimal opportunities for practicing these skills can be expected to affect his performance on the corresponding subtests (Sternberg, 1988). A cultural emphasis on group cooperation as primary over individual competitiveness, as well as a deemphasis on hurrying through tasks as quickly as possible, will be likely to unfairly decrease Nicolas's scores on timed items (Anastasi, 1988).

Because of these and other factors, children of diverse cultures typically score lower on standardized intelligence tests than do Caucasian, middle-class American children (Anastasi, 1988). Yet Nicolas is about to be tested for inclusion in a talented and gifted program. What can be done to remedy his predicament? At one time, some researchers implied that nothing could be done, that the intellectual gene pools of races other than Caucasian are in fact deficient (Jensen, 1980). However, when studies have controlled for environmental influences and other related considerations, no consistent pattern of inferiority or superiority among the races has been supported (Plomin, 1990). Furthermore, the gap in achievement levels between Caucasian-American and African-American children in recent years has closed considerably (Neisser, 1998). Could this happen if the cause was genetic?

Aware of the cultural variables that can affect IQ test performance, Nicolas's test-giver decides to administer the K-ABC rather than the WISC-III. Because of its greater flexibility in administration, the test-giver knows he will have room to work in the more casual interaction and encouragement style familiar to Nicholas. The K-ABC has in fact been found to cut the typical discrepancies between African-American and Caucasian-American children in half (Kaufman et al., 1985; Samuda et al., 1998).

How do teachers, peers, parents, cultural influences, and children's individual characteristics affect learning and achievement?

Learning and Achieving

During elementary school, children begin learning numerous important skills that provide the foundation for later learning. Reading and writing, mathematics, and a solid knowledge base of how the world works are necessary not only for continuing education but also for just getting by in a literate, complex society. What factors affect how well a student takes advantage of the crucial skill-training offered during formal education?

Traditional versus Open Schooling. For many generations the traditional school environment was characterized by a teacher positioned at the front of the classroom and providing instruction to children who sat quietly for extended periods of time as they listened or worked independently on their assignments. After Piaget theorized that children learn by means of self-structured exploration, educators sought ways of loosening up the traditional rigid classroom protocol. The resulting **open classroom** concept required less passive learning and offered more opportunities for hands-on experience; students were seen as active agents in their own education. Open classrooms gave students the freedom not only to move around the room and speak freely but also to choose from a variety of learning activities at stations set up for their benefit.

Although students in open classrooms did show benefits in the areas of independent working ability and tolerance for diversity of solutions and perspectives, performance on basics such as reading, writing, and math suffered (Hedges et al., 1981). As might be expected, open classroom students spent more time developing aptitudes and pursuing tasks they found interesting, rather than addressing the ones requiring practice, memorization, and drilling. Currently most teachers use strategies from both traditional and open classroom structures, getting "back to basics" but still allowing opportunities to pursue independent learning.

Student Attributes. What attributes can we see in the students themselves that appear to promote behaviors that lead to achievement? Researchers have long recognized that some children are simply more oriented toward achievement than others (McClelland et al., 1953). Their desire to succeed and their success are evidence of having a high **need for achievement**. These children truly wish to accomplish their goals and/or do well, and will expend substantial effort in their attempts to make things happen for them. Personal confidence in their academic abilities fuels this effort (Greene & Miller, 1996).

Another factor that differentiates achieving and nonachieving children is the source of their motivational drive (Covington, 2000; Gould, 1978). Children who achieve tend to be intrinsically motivated, investing themselves in activity because of personal interest or internal reward mechanisms such as the joy of seeing a job well done. Those who are extrinsically motivated are more likely to achieve only enough to obtain an external reward or to relieve such pressures as demands and threats of retribution if homework is not completed. In fact, in some circumstances offering concrete rewards, such as payment for good grades, can actually undermine intrinsic motivation and thus reduce achieving behavior, especially once the rewards are no longer evident (Deci et al., 1999; Lepper et al., 1973; 1999).

High achievers appear to evaluate their successes and failures by a method of attribution that differs from that of lower achievers (Henderson & Dweck, 1990). Instead of attributing their failures to personal inner inability, children with a **mastery orientation** attribute failure to having something yet to learn about how a task can be mastered. Children with a **helpless orientation** are more likely to attribute their failures inwardly, as evidenced by comments of hopelessness such as "I'm just not any good at this" (Stipek & Gralinski, 1996). They might also simply say "I don't know" when asked why they succeeded or failed, attributing causality to unknown factors rather than hypothesizing how they can use their experience to improve future performance. Across cultures, girls tend to be more likely to devalue their talents and attribute their successes to luck, which is believed to be a form of conformance to gender stereotyping (Stetsenko et al., 2000). This information-processing style has also been associated with having parents who experience this form of external locus of control (Morton, 1997). Surveys have revealed that teachers in fact perceive low achievers as extrinsically oriented, which unfortunately implies a belief that their students' successes or failures are due to a lack of personal ability or effort (Sweet et al., 1998).

Teachers.   Why do teacher biases matter? An example will show why. A radio commentator recently shared a story about a fourth-grade teacher, whom I will call Mrs. Marsen, and her least-favorite student, whom I will call Bobby. Bobby was sullen and disruptive in the classroom, produced failing work, and often had problems on the playground. While doing a routine review of grade reports from previous years, Mrs. Marsen noted that during the first and second grade he had been considered a star pupil. His downward spiraling appeared to parallel the progression of his mother's terminal illness.

Following this discovery, Mrs. Marsen tried to be encouraging and positive with Bobby. At Christmas, while the students were giving gifts he presented her with a partially full bottle of perfume wrapped in rumpled brown paper. The other students snickered, but she thanked him and dabbed a little of the scent on her wrists. He told her, "Now you smell just like my Mom."

As she walked by during the spelling test, Mrs. Marsen noticed that Bobby showed a little more effort and "spark" than he had during previous tests. She decided to make a point of wearing the perfume on test days. She noticed an immediate improvement in his test scores, and by the end of the year his performance level had soared. As Bobby graduated from the fourth grade he wrote her a note, telling her she was his "best teacher ever." Several years later she received an announcement of his graduation from high school. Enclosed was a letter updating her on his triumphs and rough spots over the last several years, as well as reminding her she was still his favorite teacher. She received similar notes when he graduated from college, and then from medical school. One day she received an invitation to his wedding. It included a personal note mentioning that his father was also now deceased and that Bobby had no close family remaining. Would she be willing to sit in the pew reserved for parents of the groom? She tearfully accepted his offer.

Many of us can recall particular teachers who made a difference in our lives, both academically and personally. What do the Mrs. Marsens of the world do that has such long-term effects? Meta-analysis of studies examining relationships between teacher behaviors and student progress has revealed the phenomenon called the **self-fulfilling prophecy** (Harris & Rosenthal, 1985; Smith, Jussim, et al., 1999). School children are aware of teachers' expectations of them and tend to perform at a level consistent with those expectations, especially by the end of the elementary school years (Weinstein et al., 1987). Grouping children according to ability appears to produce a similar effect, tending to widen the gap between the superior and inferior achievers (Slavin, 1987). In other words, teachers who enhance student performance appear to engage in practices that demonstrate confidence in each individual child's ability to succeed (Reeve et al., 1999).

Peers. Affiliation with high- or low-achieving peers also influences a child's achievement level, perhaps even more so than family relationships (Steinberg et al., 1996). Group learning experiences are important, as a learning group itself can become the teacher (Schmuck & Schmuck, 1997). Children working together often provide one another with the missing pieces they need to fill in the blanks within their particular zones of proximal development (Rogoff, 1990). Working together in groups as they address problems allows them to absorb the knowledge and problem-solving strategies demonstrated by their classmates. Group exercises providing such opportunities have in fact been found to increase scores on standardized achievement tests (Klein, 1988).

Culture. Differing cultural values and goals influence how different societies educate their children. As a result, children of diverse cultures achieve differently. The most extensive comparisons have been made between Asian and American students (Stevenson et al., 1986; Stevenson & Lee, 1990). Japanese, Korean, and Chinese students all academically outperform students educated in the United States. By examining their educational practices we can see why. Asian cultures place a higher value on education. In Japan, for example, students spend 240, rather than 176 days a year in school. They attend 5½ days a week rather than only 5. They spend more time doing homework than the typical U.S. student. Much more of their class time is spent on academic topics, and they spend more time participating in group learning activities than working individually. Furthermore, Japanese teachers are better trained, better paid, held in higher esteem, and provided with more elaborate educational resources than are teachers in the United States.

One of the biggest and most significant differences between Asian and U.S. students concerns the influence of their parents. Communities and their individual cultural values and practices affect parents' beliefs about education, as well as their aspirations for their children (Wentzel, 1998). Many parents in the United States view education of their children as the responsibility of teachers and school districts, while Asian parents see themselves as primarily responsible and teachers serving as guides or facilitators. When surveyed about their children's academic lives, parents in the United States report less direct involvement with their children's education, lower standards for acceptable achievement levels, inaccurately high estimations of their children's actual performance, a greater perception that achievement level is related to ability rather than hard work, and less overall emphasis on the importance of doing well in school.

Parents. As the cultural comparison suggests, parents can have a tremendous impact on a child's achievement levels. Achieving children typically have parents who are actively interested and invested in their children's academic lives (Booth & Dunn, 1996). They use an authoritative parenting style, rather than authoritarian or permissive (Steinberg et al., 1992). Similar to effective teachers, they demonstrate confidence in their children—setting high but attainable standards and developing warm, supportive relationships with them (Hess & Holloway, 1984). They focus more on learning goals and less on superior performance or personal superiority (Ablard & Parker, 1997; Mueller & Dweck, 1998). The presence of a father in the home is associated with better school performance, provided the father's parenting style exercises both personal control and interpersonal warmth. This effect appears to be stronger among girls and African-American children than among boys and Caucasian-American children (Coley, 1998).

It is not difficult to see how these parental practices can help children develop the traits of healthy achievers—the presence of a high need for achievement, intrinsic motivation, and a mastery orientation. The Tried . . . . and True boxes on pages 354–355 elaborate on the relationship between parents and healthy achievement styles.

Children with Disabilities

How can developmental and learning disabilities affect achievement, and how can a child's potential be maximized in spite of their effects?

Developmental and learning disabilities become most relevant as children enter and progress through grade school. As students must master progressively more sophisticated material and meet higher levels of behavioral demand, disabilities or learning impairments that previously had gone unnoticed may eventually be revealed to their full extent. Fortunately, early intervention can help affected students overcome many aspects of their disabilities and lead full, happy lives (Ramey & Ramey, 1998).

Mental Retardation. Previous chapters described how a number of conditions during pregnancy and early childhood can result in mental retardation. As Table 12.1 shows, the possible degree of impairment and the expected living

TABLE 12.1

Degree of severity of mental retardation. Reprinted with permission from the *Diagnostic and Statistical Manual of Mental Disorders,* Fourth Edition. Copyright © 1994 American Psychiatric Association.

Mild Mental Retardation IQ: 50–70 Proportion: 85%

At first these children may appear to be developing normally, but by school age their slowness at learning becomes evident. They can usually acquire academic abilities up to about sixth-grade level and can learn appropriate social and communication skills. As adults they are able to hold semiskilled jobs and function on their own, as long as they have supports and resources for guidance in unusual circumstances.

Moderate Mental Retardation IQ: 35–50 Proportion: 10%

These individuals can be educated up to about the second-grade level. They can learn communication and simple vocational skills and can perform basic self-care. Limitations in their social skills may cause some interference in peer relationships, especially during adolescence. Because of their need for supervision, they usually live in group homes or with families and may find employment in sheltered workshops.

Severe Mental Retardation IQ: 20–50 Proportion: 3–4%

As young children, the severely retarded are notably unable to acquire language skills. With training, they can develop some basic language ability as well as take care of their personal hygiene. They are capable of learning to sight-read some "survival" words such as *stop, men,* and *women.* As adults they may be able to perform other simple tasks when provided with much supervision and guidance. They most often live in group homes or in family settings.

Profound Mental Retardation IQ: 0–20 Proportion: 1–2%

Those who are profoundly mentally retarded typically suffer from diagnosed neurological conditions accounting for the impairment. During childhood their sensorimotor ability is considerably impaired. With extensive one-on-one attention they may be capable of learning a few communication skills, how to move around independently, and some basic self-care. They most commonly live with families or in institutions, although some are capable of living in very sheltered group home settings.

patterns for affected individuals varies widely. Although most children suffering from mental retardation are educable, they may not be able to learn in the typical classroom at the same pace as unaffected children.

Thanks to Public Law 94–142 (1975), its amendments, and subsequent related rulings regarding the education of individuals with disabilities, schools are required to develop individualized education programs (IEPs) for children who are identified as having handicaps affecting their ability to learn (Haller, 1999; Hardman et al., 1999; Kelman & Lester, 1997). These children usually spend at least part of their day in a separate classroom or accompanied by a tutor, providing them with the extra attention they need for learning to occur. They spend the remainder of their day mainstreamed into the regular classroom. The philosophy behind **mainstreaming** is that it not only accustoms handicapped children to interacting in a normal social setting, but also provides

Hokada, A., & Fincham, F. D. (1995). Origins of children's help-less and mastery achievement patterns in the family. *Journal of Educational Psychology, 87,* 375–385.

Tried

BOX 12.1   Parents' behavior and development of a mastery achievement style

WHY DO SOME CHILDREN RISE TO A DIFFICULT CHAL-lenge and others pull back and give up? Hokada and Fin-cham investigated the role that parents play in the de-velopment these two very different achieving styles: the mastery and helpless orientations (see page 350).

First, to acquire a good-size sample of mastery- and helpless-oriented achievers, the researchers evaluated a large number of third-graders using two measures. One was an attribution scale on which each of ten items described a situation in which a child failed at a task. Participants were asked to indicate which of two expla-nations seemed most responsible for the child's failure: external causes or insufficient personal effort. Next, the participants were asked to solve a series of 12 mazes. The first two mazes were solvable, the following eight were unsolvable, and the last two were solvable. By com-paring how long participants spent on the last two mazes as opposed to the first two, researchers obtained a behavioral indicator of effort and discouragement af-ter failure.

The researchers identified 21 students who scored high in either the mastery or helpless achievement style, about half the total being assigned to each group and with a nearly equal number of boys and girls in each group. With their mothers present, the identified partici-pants were given problem-solving tasks to complete, such as arranging blocks, unscrambling anagrams, and the like. Two observers who were unaware of the partici-pants' achievement styles rated statements made by each mother as her child worked, using such coding cat-egories as task or child-ability attributions and quitting versus persevering. They also rated child behaviors such

as requesting help, expressing negative feelings, and verbalizing an emphasis on performance or ability. The ratings of the two observers were similar enough for the researchers to accept the accuracy of the codings.

When they compared the mothers' behaviors with their children's achieving styles they found significant differences between codings for the two groups. When participants with a helpless orientation expressed nega-tive feelings, their mothers were more likely to respond with negative emotionality of their own. These mothers were also less likely to offer suggestions when help was requested. Mothers of mastery-oriented learners were more likely to respond to statements of self-doubt with reassurances of ability, and when their children ex-pressed performance concerns they were more likely to redirect them toward learning goals. Mothers of help-less-oriented learners tended to respond to statements of self-doubt with suggestions that they quit, and when concerns over meeting performance goals arose were more likely to make comments reinforcing such an emphasis.

This is a relatively small study, as is often the case when individual participants are intensively examined, but its findings are consistent with those of other stud-ies examining parenting interactions and achieving styles. We see a clear relationship between achievement orientation and the type of feedback children receive from parents. The study does not determine whether the parent's behavior creates the child's orientation or whether the child's orientation elicits certain types of parental behavior. However, we do know that regardless of the particular realm in which they occur, parental commentaries tend to become part of the internal conversations that follow children long after parents are gone.

BOX 12.2   Encouraging healthy achievement traits

... and True

WHAT CAN PARENTS DO TO FAVOR DEVELOPMENT OF A mastery orientation? The Hokada and Fincham study offers some clues regarding the principles involved. Parents of mastery-oriented children are more likely to emphasize the intrinsic elements of achieving, such as expanding personal learning, persevering, and maintaining a positive attitude. They appear to do so by providing feedback and encouragement throughout the learning process, and by deemphasizing anxieties over performance level.

Dorothy Rich (1988) organizes healthy achievement traits on the basis of ten basic competencies. Mastering these competencies is not only likely to carry children through their academic achievement lives but also will bolster their efforts as they approach general lessons in living. The competencies can also serve as lesson goals to consider as parents formulate individual pieces of feedback meant to train their children for success. The following list provides examples of what a parent might do to encourage development of these "inner engines" of learning.

- *Confidence.* They encourage their children to believe in themselves and their ability to achieve. As a child shares a joke or some other witticism the parent might point out the inner strength supporting the accomplishment: "You have such a good sense of humor."
- *Motivation.* They endeavor to facilitate their child's motivation to succeed. Useful feedback includes sharing their own excitement about tasks, pointing out potential outcomes, and creating opportunities to succeed.
- *Effort.* They direct their child's attention toward the joy of simply putting out a good effort regardless of the outcome, and join with the child in the experience.

- *Responsibility.* They provide direct instruction regarding the importance of being responsible, promote the skills and behaviors necessary, and make sure they delegate plenty of age-appropriate independent responsibilities so their child has opportunities to practice.
- *Initiative.* They support trying out new things. When a new task becomes too big or overwhelming, they help their child break it down into smaller, more manageable parts or otherwise make it "do-able."
- *Perseverance.* They enforce sticking to tasks when they are important or when a commitment has been made. On the other hand, to protect their child from inadvertent failure, they help the child consider potential commitments and what they might entail before the child makes the commitment.
- *Caring.* They promote good communication and empathic recognition of how others feel and think. They especially emphasize communicating caring for their child, which provides a model for both the child's self-esteem and how to relate to others.
- *Teamwork.* They provide opportunities for practicing the give and take of cooperative group activity as well as demonstrate such skills themselves by the manner in which they interact with children.
- *Common sense.* They point out cause and effect of behaviors, and assist children as they make decisions and exercise their judgment.
- *Problem-solving.* They show children how to define a problem, generate and evaluate potential solutions, select a solution, and develop a plan of follow-through.

Rich, D. (1988). *MegaSkills: How families can help children succeed in school and beyond.* Boston: Houghton Mifflin.

regular classroom children with the opportunity to get to know them as individuals, thus destigmatizing their disabilities.

Mainstreaming children with learning-related disabilities has demonstrated benefits for all concerned (Lederer, 2000; Power-deFur & Orelove, 1997). In response to having a disabled student in their classroom, teachers find themselves using more collaboration with other educators, expanding the breadth of their professional development activities, and becoming more flexible and creative in their teaching approaches toward all of their students. Classmates demonstrate greater acceptance of disabled students in their school, and as a product of their own efforts to effectively interact with disabled students show a greater interest in learning themselves. Lower-achieving students learn more due to the review, practice, clarity, and feedback designed around the disabled students' needs. The disabled students themselves become more independent, learn skills and behaviors that are modeled or reinforced by their classmates, and show improvements in their standardized test scores. The school district itself saves money, since mainstreaming requires fewer special-education resources.

In view of all the benefits of mainstreaming, administrators have toyed with the idea of **full inclusion**. Why not do away with resource rooms and put all disabled children in the regular classroom? Learning specialists quickly point out that full inclusion is ill-advised (Kauffman & Hallahan, 1995). For example, any child who is more than mildly mentally retarded would have an extremely difficult time managing the basics of regular classroom behavior, let alone receive educational benefit. Teachers would spend so much time with such students' needs that other students would be short-changed. A number of conditions require more attention than can be provided in a regular classroom setting; among them are autism and attention deficit hyperactivity disorder (ADHD), and other learning-disabled conditions.

Autism. **Autism** might best be described as a severe impairment of social and emotional connectedness (American Psychiatric Association, 1994; Hobson, 1995). It appears to affect boys more than girls, at a ratio of diagnosed cases as high as five to one (American Psychiatric Association, 1994). Autistic individuals often score in the retarded range on intelligence tests and most of them are also classified as mentally retarded. The reason why they are not necessarily classified as retarded when they receive such scores is because their deficiencies do not follow across the board. In fact, autistic individuals may be extremely limited in some areas yet amazingly well-skilled in others. The movie *Rain Man* portrayed an **autistic savant**, Raymond, who was able to perform astounding feats of tracking, counting, and remembering quantities of toothpicks, playing cards, and the like. However, his lack of common-sense judgment misled him into believing he could walk to a K-Mart located hundreds of miles away.

Raymond also demonstrated the social and emotional pitfalls of the disorder. He showed little interest in relating to others socially, and even when he did he could not pick up on social cues or select socially appropriate responses. Normally emotions operate with a sort of "dimmer switch" allowing us to moderate the level of emotion we experience and express. Autistic individuals' emotions operate as if they are controlled by an "on/off switch." Either they demonstrate no emotionality at all, or if something disturbs them they become extremely agitated and upset, and often are inconsolable until the source of the disturbance is removed. Extreme sensitivity to bright lights, loud noises, and tactile stimulation are common as well.

Self/world/others boundaries also seem murky for the autistic individual (Klin et al., 1992). As was mentioned in Chapter 7, autistic individuals appear to lack any form of theory of mind. They seem to adapt to their missing internal structures by creating external structures that bolster some sense of selfhood. They have ritualistic ways of organizing objects in their private environment, repeating behaviors, and scheduling their time; and often talk to themselves as they reinforce or contain their inner process.

Autism appears to be at least partly genetic in origin, although birth complications increase its likelihood (Rutter, 2000; Sanua, 1984). Early in their development, autistic children often show little interest in their caregivers and are slow to learn to talk (Dahlgren & Gillberg, 1989). As they grow older they do not form friendships with peers—indeed, perhaps not even realizing they exist as separate individuals—and are content to play by themselves. They usually have extremely restricted interests, perhaps spending many hours studying a simple behavior such as spinning an ash tray or memorizing statistics on baseball cards. Development of their gross and fine motor skills is often delayed, and they may move in odd ways—rocking, spinning, swaying, or walking on tiptoe.

The educational needs of autistic children clearly exceed what the regular classroom can provide (Carr, 1993). While high-functioning autistic children do show benefit from partial mainstreaming, they also need speech therapy and separate instruction guiding them toward appropriate social interaction and management of emotion. Their delayed motor skills may require extra attention or just the passage of time before they can write effectively or successfully participate in physical education activities with their same-age classmates. As a group autistic children vary so widely in what they can and cannot do that many different approaches must be employed to successfully treat and educate them; yet most important for all approaches is active teamwork among parents, educators, and health care professionals (Howlin, 1998; Rogers, 1998). With early intervention, the less severely affected autistic individuals can develop the social, behavioral, and cognitive skills necessary for leading a relatively normal life (McEachin et al., 1993).

Attention Deficit Hyperactivity Disorder.   Let's return to the story of Donny, introduced in the chapter opening. His teacher, Mr. Anderson, is concerned about him. Donny is almost continuously squirming in his seat, talking to or poking at his neighbors, fidgeting with the contents of his very messy desk, or just staring out the window. His talking out and other behaviors disrupt Mr. Anderson's instruction and disturb other children. Donny seems plenty bright but performs relatively poorly on his graded lessons. In his disorganization he frequently loses his homework assignments or even forgets about them all together, further impeding his educational progress.

It was long assumed that children like Donny were demonstrating simple behavioral problems that disciplinary measures would correct. When teachers and parents found that discipline alone would not make a significant difference, these children were labeled "bad 'uns." Combine such a label with the sort of feedback the student is likely to get from frustrated parents and teachers and there is a high risk that a self-fulfilling prophecy will take its toll (Wender, 1987).

We now recognize that this problematic behavioral pattern is often driven by a neurological condition currently called **attention deficit hyperactivity disorder (ADHD)** (American Psychiatric Association, 1994; Barkley, 1990; 1996). The term *hyperactivity* has been variously included in or omitted from the term for this condition because not all children with attention deficits are hyperactive. Most individuals who have the disorder are both male and hyperactive. Because female sufferers more typically experience attention deficits alone and do not behave disruptively, their condition often goes unrecognized and untreated (Arnold, 1996; Ratey et al., 1995). This is especially unfortunate in view of the fact that ADHD girls are as much as two to three times more likely than ADHD boys to develop conduct disorder, alcoholism, or antisocial personality (Cohen, 1996; Eronsen et al., 1996).

ADHD is relatively common, afflicting as much as 5% of school-age children (American Psychiatric Association, 1994). Usually the problem does not become evident until such children enter school, where they must be able to sit in a seat and pay attention for prolonged periods. At first their behavior may be attributed to immaturity, since their easy distractibility, impulsiveness, and constant motor activity mimics that of the preschooler. But even when disciplinary and behavioral interventions do succeed in helping them learn to keep their impulsiveness under wraps, they continue to have difficulty concentrating at appropriate moments, shifting attention toward or away from stimuli, or organizing their work. For many children attentional difficulties will continue into adulthood (Kelly & Ramundo, 1995).

Where does this disorder come from? The causes appear to be many. Studies comparing identical and fraternal twins and prevalence comparisons among near and distant relatives suggest that ADHD is in part genetically determined (Faraone et al., 1993; Gilles et al., 1992; LeCouteur et al., 1996). Chapter 4 described other factors that can contribute toward development of attention deficits; these include poor prenatal nutrition, prenatal exposure to street drugs, and lead poisoning. At one time, some health service providers proposed that food additives and/or excessive sugar caused ADHD (Feingold, 1975; Smith, 1975). The diets they proposed for ADHD children enjoyed considerable popularity until controlled studies failed to back them up with consistency (Henker & Whalen, 1989).

ADHD children experience some relief from a number of their symptoms by means of prescription medications, especially certain stimulants and antidepressants (Aman et al., 1998). However, drug therapy alone usually does not get all symptoms under control (Barkley, 1990; Pelham et al., 1998, 2000). Training ADHD children to control impulses and learn socialized behavior requires that they receive immediate, frequently occurring, firmer consequences. ADHD children often require one-on-one time in the resource room to help them stay focused long enough to complete their assignments. They benefit from learning to anticipate problems that may occur because of their disability and to manage those aspects of the environment that can work against them, such as by making sure they are seated in a part of the classroom having fewer distractions. Learning techniques such as self-talk can help them shift and focus their attention as they problem-solve or work their way toward a desired goal (Kendall & Braswell, 1993):

"I need to listen now so I hear the instructions."
"The teacher said to do X, Y, then Z."
"You did X, now you need to do Y."
"Don't pay attention to the dog outside."
"Keep going. You're doing fine."

ADHD children are at risk of adopting the belief that having ADHD, taking medications, seeing a therapist, and the like make them some kind of freak or mental case. One way of normalizing the problem is explaining that just as some children need to wear glasses to improve their sight, others need "glasses" for paying attention. As an adult with ADHD, while at times I find my symptoms annoying, I do not view them as inevitably handicapping. Because on more than one occasion I have run into other writers—some quite prolific—who confess to living with the disorder, I suspect that the tenacity and creative diversity characteristic of ADHD in all likelihood contributes to the ability to address massive tasks. Others have made similar observations (Weiss, 1997). Currently I think of ADHD less as a disorder and more as an attentional condition. Conveying such an attitude to ADHD children may provide them with encouragement as they adjust to their own symptoms (but just try getting an HMO to pay for treating a mere "condition"!).

Learning Disabilities. A wide variety of information-processing peculiarities can cause children to be diagnosed as having **learning disabilities**. These children are of normal or above-average intelligence, have received adequate schooling, have no apparent developmental disorder, and yet have significant difficulties with certain learning areas (Reid, 1988). For example, **dyslexia** is a reading disorder that causes children to distort, substitute, or omit words or letters as they examine written language. These difficulties interfere not only with attempts to read the written word but also with development of a working knowledge of phonics and other reading-related competencies (Snowling et al., 1996). Math-impaired children lack the linguistic, fact retrieval, perceptual, attending, and/or basic arithmetic skills necessary for performing calculations (Alarcon et al., 1997; Bryant et al., 2000; Geary et al., 2000; Jordan & Montani, 1997). Children with a disorder of written expression have difficulty transferring the organization they exhibit in their speech onto paper.

Early recognition and intervention is especially effective in helping children with learning disorders (American Psychiatric Association, 1994). These children do well in a regular classroom as long as they also receive interventions that either remedy their particular disabilities or show them how to get around them.

What are the needs of the intellectually and creatively gifted, and how can these needs be met?

Intellectually Gifted Children

Intellectually gifted children are qualitatively different from other children. Their abilities allow them to analyze problems and intuit solutions in ways that are unlike those of other children at the same developmental level. They maintain and manipulate a more complex memory store in the area(s) within which they are gifted. They show a "rage to master," becoming absorbed within their domain and setting up new challenges as a means of keeping the "rage" going, without needing encouragement from others (Winner, 1996). Their intellectual prowess and interests tend to zero them into specific domains, as they are more likely to excel at a particular ability than perform at a superior level in all academic areas (Wilkinson, 1993). Some indirect evidence suggests that some of these characteristics may be due to atypical brain organization, especially in terms of enhanced right-hemisphere activity (Winner, 2000).

Intellectually gifted children also differ socially and emotionally. They are more likely to keep to themselves and become solitary and introverted as they (like all children) direct their energies toward what they find entertaining and rewarding: in their case, the self-stimulation going on within their own minds (Csikszentmihalyi et al., 1993; Gallagher, 1990). They also tend to be independent and nonconformist (Silverman, 1993a). When they develop good self-esteem it may be based on their intellectual abilities rather than who they are as a person (Gross, 1993). Unfortunately, extremely intellectually gifted children demonstrate a greater incidence of social and emotional problems; perhaps their isolation and self-focus having interfered with socializing processes during the developmental years (Janos & Robinson, 1985).

Special classes for gifted children emerged in U.S. schools in the late 1950s in reaction to the Soviet Union's having been first to get a man into outer space (Tannenbaum, 1993). Unrecognized by policy makers was the fact that intellectual giftedness during childhood is not a predictor of eminence during adulthood (Richert, 1997). Charles Darwin, who made some of the most dramatic and influential scientific contributions of the nineteenth century, belonged to the class of "late bloomers" whose gifts were not evident during childhood (Simonton, 1994). Conversely, there are famous cases like William James Sidis, a genius at math who graduated from Harvard at age 15, then dropped out of the math world (Montour, 1977). Ted Kaczynski, better known as the "Unabomber," is a more current, scarier example of how a gifted individual might choose to use his or her abilities. The actual movers and shakers of the world appear to be characterized more by well-directed personal drive, creativity, and aptitude for both working with and questioning the status quo—factors represented within the domains of creative and emotional intelligence (Gardner, 1993; Sternberg, 1996; Winner, 2000).

Over the years, the focus has shifted away from the notion of cultivating bright children as a national resource and instead examines the unique needs of the children themselves. Most programs are aimed at their need for a sufficiently challenging curriculum. In the regular classroom gifted children often become bored and inattentive, and therefore are increasingly likely to drop out (Gross, 1993; Westberg et al., 1993). They also need opportunities to meet equally gifted children with whom they can connect both intellectually and socially (Benbow & Lubinski, 1997). Most children selected for talented and gifted programs are placed in "pullout" programs, in which they meet together as a group for several hours a week (Riley, 1993).

The most widely used pullout program is the schoolwide enrichment model (SEM), which offers both development of thinking skills and opportunities for children to focus on their domains of interest (Renzulli & Reis, 1991, 1997). Participants in a pullout program can also enjoy the side benefits that their gifts are emphasized and they accordingly achieve a higher status among their peers (Cohen et al., 1994). Nevertheless, SEMs by themselves have limited success at keeping children interested in academic achievement (Winner, 1996). Although participants do show modest gains in achievement scores, the greatest gains appear to occur when the SEM curriculum is infused into the regular curriculum, which has shown the additional benefit of improving the performance of regular classroom students, and even those classified as mentally retarded (Robinson et al., 2000; Vaughn et al., 1991).

In view of these findings, some professionals suggest that the best way to meet the needs of intellectually gifted children is to raise standards and more extensively challenge all students (Winner, 1997). Parents can augment their intellectually gifted child's particular domain of giftedness by pursuing such options as enrollment in summer and weekend programs and setting up mentorships (Benbow & Lubinski, 1997; Gardner, 1993).

Most of the outcome research appears to focus on the effect of programs on various achievement variables. What most parents want for their children is that they have happy lives—an outcome not guaranteed by excelling within an intellectual domain, especially given the social and emotional difficulties that can develop in intellectually gifted children. Some researchers minimize this factor, pointing out the many survey studies suggesting that the behavior of the gifted is often more socialized than other children's. We should expect this outcome because it reflects their relative ease at deciphering and figuring out how to work within rules, social or otherwise.

However, these studies reflect neither the gifted child's feelings of loneliness nor the inner conflict percolating between wanting to follow personal interests yet also wanting to fit in with others (Silverman, 1993b). Nor do they consider the emotional fallout from the fact that their higher levels of cognitive development expose young gifted children to emotion-laden dilemmas before they have achieved the level of emotional development and acquired the life experience needed to effectively deal with them (Clark, 1992; Ellsworth, 1999). And although gifted children themselves say they would prefer to be doing things with others, the isolation that results from their obsession with inner stimulation detracts from engaging in the social interactions necessary for normal child development (Csikszentmihalyi et al., 1993). The unique social and emotional needs of the gifted child are typically underserved and clearly need further attention before they can truly be met (Silverman, 1993c).

Creatively Gifted Children

In Chapter 6 it was pointed out that we are endowed not only with analytic intelligence but also with a certain level of creative intelligence. A child receiving high IQ scores may also be creatively gifted; however, a child receiving average IQ scores may be as creatively gifted or more so than the high IQ scorer. A child with high IQ scores may even be exceptionally uncreative. How do we differentiate between the two talents? One way is to look at them as two different forms of thinking (Guilford, 1967). Intelligence tests typically measure **convergent thinking**. Data are presented and if analyzed appropriately will zero into the one correct answer. **Divergent thinking**, which is more characteristic of creativity, involves expanding the range of possibilities for solving the same problem. Creatively gifted children thus may begin producing masterworks before they have even begun to acquire the massive knowledge necessary for the convergent thinking typical of analytical giftedness (Hays, 1989).

Other differences can be found by examining creativity itself, focusing on factors of personality and disposition that contribute to creative endeavor (Perkins, 1984; Simonton, 2000). Creative works require an extensive amount of mental mobility and being appreciative of and comfortable with contradictions and opposing perspectives. In fact, creative individuals typically excel at ferreting out unique problems. Analytical works often allow less flexibility because the material almost by definition is organized around objective, nonexperiential facts. Aesthetics and appreciation of beauty are important aspects of creativity, tapping into the insights available by subjective experiencing as new possibilities emerge. Creative intelligence demonstrates a willingness to take risks and to take license with the traditional in order to uncover new realms. The pursuits of analytical intelligence typically focus on finding the one right answer to a problem and thus may avoid ventures into thinking styles that have a higher likelihood of failing to produce that answer.

One of the greatest differences between analytical and creative intelligence is how the two are motivated. Creativity is motivated by the human spirit, the desire to produce something beautiful or unique for its own sake. Some suggest that creativity is a way we use symbolism to explore our inner experience, attaching our spiritual selves with our physical existence as we find meaning in living (Holbrook, 1994). Of course, the exercise of analytical intelligence can also be internally motivated, pursued by the desire to experience the joy or satisfaction of solving a problem or finding that one right answer. However, the analytical effort has some form of extrinsic motivator more often than does the creative effort: pleasing a teacher or employer, looking "smart," getting a good grade, or earning a paycheck. Creative effort typically does not succeed by

Opportunities to apply creative intelligence are just as important to developing children's personal aptitudes as are learning activities that focus on analytical intelligence.

Bonnie Kamin/PhotoEdit

means of extrinsic motivators alone. I was once told by an editor that even textbook writing does not produce successful works if the primary motivator is making money! Rewarding children's creativity appears to be effective only if the rewards are limited to especially creative efforts and they are relatively modest so as not to interfere with the more crucial intrinsic motivators (Eisenberger et al., 1998; Schwartz, 1990).

Exceptionally creative children are often more difficult to identify for gifted programs than are the intellectually gifted. Usually schools use IQ scores and similar measures as a means for determining who qualifies, but because these are not necessarily relevant to identifying creative giftedness, creatively gifted children are often underserved (Runco, 1993: Sternberg & Lubart, 1993). Schools are also much better at creating programs that foster intellectual giftedness than creative genius. By necessity, schools focus on imparting a set curriculum containing the facts and analytical processes of a basic education. It is relatively straightforward to expand the scope of such a curriculum for those who are capable of incorporating a greater amount or a higher level of intellectual skill. But being highly individual and nonstandard by nature, creativity is much more difficult to address by modifying a regular curriculum.

Another wrinkle involves the characteristics of highly creative children themselves. As nonconformists they tend to focus on esoteric complexities and contradictions rather than pursuing an intended lesson result (Wallach, 1985). Teachers may experience creative children's efforts toward developing their gifts as thorns in their teachers' sides rather than something to be appreciated and nurtured. The passive learning and rote memorization characteristic of traditional education may actually derail students' creative effort (Hubbard, 1996). Japanese educational practices focus on memorization of massive amounts of information, arguably imparting more formal knowledge to Japanese children than children in any other culture receive. Nevertheless, Japan has the fewest Nobel Prize recipients per capita of any similarly developed country.

> ### PAVING PATHWAYS ALONG MIDDLE CHILDHOOD COGNITIVE DEVELOPMENT: FOSTERING CREATIVE INTELLIGENCE

Opportunities to apply creativity are beneficial to all children (Friedman & Shore, 2000). Inclusion of such opportunities in the curriculum has a greater association with academic achievement than does using traditional memorization/critical thinking techniques alone (Sternberg et al., 1998). Suppose you were a teacher. How would you foster and expand opportunities for creativity, not just for the gifted but for the benefit of all students? Following are some suggestions (Hubbard, 1996; Piirto, 1998):

▶ Both children and curricula require structure in the classroom, but students also need freedom to explore possibilities. Both structure and freedom can be introduced by using strategies of "flexible predictability." Build regular activities into the daily or weekly schedule that allow students a certain degree of independence. For example, try scheduling 15 minutes of free writing every Friday at 10:00 A.M. During this time the student can write something new, add to something written the week before, edit or rewrite previous works, or research a future project. When students—especially creative ones—expect to have such opportunities, they may make note throughout the week of ideas they would like to play with during their free writing time.

▶ Provide access to the tools of creativity. Offer a wide range of work settings—some where students can work alone, others where groups of students can work together, and other areas where a student may even choose to sit on the floor to read or think. Fill bookcases, computers, and arts and crafts bins with a variety of materials capable of sparking the imagination. Make arrangements for students to have opportunities to work with a variety of learners and teachers, especially with those who share common interests.

▶ Destigmatize the "oddness" of looking at things from unique perspectives, even when it involves making mistakes and appropriate risk-taking. What doesn't work teaches us at least as much as getting things right the first time. Rather than simply announcing that a student's response is "wrong," enthusiastically share the benefit of the discovery. This technique is also useful when bored creative students are acting out. For example, if during class discussion a child replies that camels live in trees, lead the discussion into an investigation of the environmental, anatomical, and other reasons why camels do not live in trees; or, set up an art project requiring students to depict what a camel would have to do in order to be able to live in a tree.

► Allow opportunities for letting the mind wander. Daydreaming expands creativity. Before successful writers even pick up a pen they spend a tremendous amount of time just sitting and thinking (Rico, 1983). Some teachers chastise students who stare off into space after completing their work, telling them to "find something to do" and not waste their time. From an existential perspective, there is no such thing as wasted time. We reap benefit from every moment of existence regardless of how we have spent it. Encouraging children to measure the value of their time expenditure solely in terms of product outcome and accomplishments teaches them a thinking style more characteristic of depression, an impediment to healthy and happy achieving lives.

What factors might parents look at as they consider home schooling their children?

Home Schooling

Some parents are displeased with the educational processes offered by organized school systems. They witness students exhibiting values other than the ones they are trying to teach, engaging in behaviors such as fighting, using bad language, using drugs, taking part in gang activity, and the like. They may be uncomfortable with the amount of time traditionally schooled children spend with instructional influences other than those of family, or may themselves not wish to be apart from their children during the day. They may suspect that their child's education will not be tailored to his or her individual needs. Sometimes students struggle and fail and parents believe it is the school's fault. In reaction to any or all of these circumstances, home schooling is currently the educational option chosen for almost a million children in the United States (Murray, 1996).

Parent Demographics. In general, parents who choose to home school their children have attended or graduated from college, earn an average income, and are highly invested and involved in their children's education. They tend to fall into one of two general groups (Van Galen, 1991). The largest group consists of Christian or Mormon parents, who generally tie in their educational choices closely with their religious ideology. The second, smaller group consists of parents who believe that schools in particular and society in general do not necessarily do a good job of educating. They place a higher value on independence and individuality than on the needs of their society, and see parents as the individual child's most natural teacher.

The two groups differ in their reactions to attempts to regulate home schooling (Van Galen, 1991). The religiously oriented group may perceive such attempts as an attack on the sanctity of the family or on their religion; some fear persecution for their choice to home school. The second group may also disdain such attempts, but tend to shrug them off as one more illustration of society's excessive bureaucracy. Home schooling advocates point out that both paranoia over and indifference to regulation can become problematic. Their legal experts encourage parents to simply become more aware of the local laws, statutes, and regulations regarding home schooling, not only to protect their rights but also to avoid difficulties that are easily prevented (Farris, 1990).

Student Academic and Social Competency. A number of studies have evaluated the differences between children who are being home schooled and those who attend traditional schools (Ray & Wartes, 1991). Academically, home-schooled children as a group perform as well as if not better than those receiving traditional education. This finding could be predicted on the basis of the typical home-schooling parents' higher educational level and greater involvement in their children's education; thus their children would be likely to perform as well even in a conventional school (Richman, 1991). So while the data do not necessarily support that home schooling is superior, neither do they justify the belief that it harms academic achievement.

Socially, home-schooled children also appear to be as well-adjusted as other children (Ray & Wartes, 1991). The only reported exceptions appear to be lower rates of involvement in organized sports, performing groups, summer camps, and the like and higher rates of complaints about feelings of social isolation (de Winter et al., 1999). The true test of how well home-schooled children are prepared for life will occur after they have become adults. Because home schooling is a relatively recent phenomenon in contemporary culture, the much-needed outcome studies of its effects have yet to emerge.

Controversy over Home Schooling. Psychologists are less concerned with home-schooled children's academic achievement scores than they are about the potential effects of their being shielded from certain social experiences and exposures during the developmental years (Murray, 1996). Home-schooled children are less likely to be exposed to diverse cultures and ethnic backgrounds. They are more likely to encounter only their parents' philosophies of life, and thus have little chance to evaluate the wealth of alternative possibilities while shaping views that will work for them. Especially at risk are children whose parents' world views are extremely narrow or maladaptive. Home-schooled children also get substantially less independent practice at evaluating and rejecting questionable or harmful aspects of society. They will surely one day encounter these social factors, but perhaps only after receptiveness to learning has passed its peak and parental guidance is no longer as available or effective. Lack of opportunities for a variety of meaningful social experiences in childhood has been linked with future psychosocial and behavioral problems (de Winter et al., 1999).

The group nature of a school setting helps children learn social skills they will need in order to get along in society, such as being on time, being accountable without benefit of individualized monitoring, waiting their turn, sharing textbooks, respecting others' views and needs, and controlling impulsive behaviors such as jumping out of their seats or shouting out answers. Many teamwork and leadership skills are learned by means of the group activity style typical of traditional education (Schmuck & Schmuck, 1997; Verba, 1998). Cooperative group learning activities often show better results than the direct-instruction method typical of home schooling (Manion & Alexander, 1997; McInerney et al., 1997).

Problems can arise if home-schooled children return to traditional schools, not only because of classroom behaviors they may not have learned but also because parents and school authorities may dispute appropriate grade level placement. Home-schooled children also may have difficulty getting into institutions of higher learning. Even if academically well-trained, they lack some of the traditional documentation schools typically use for evaluating appropriateness for admission. Inexperience with newer technologies and other school-system resources can also put children at a disadvantage if they enter modern classrooms midstream in their education.

Other critics of home schooling attack the concept from the perspective of social responsibility (Franzosa, 1991). They argue that the practice is based on certain premises that are not empirically grounded: that parents alone are always capable of judging what is best for a particular child and have the resources to provide it; and that self-sufficiency, individuality, and the needs and desires of one person are more important than the needs of a society. The school system is one of the primary playing fields for molding and enforcing a society's morals, determining what young citizens are taught, how it is taught, and what is learned (Dornbusch et al., 1996). By not being involved with the school system, home-schooling parents deny their important input into a society from which they reap benefits. Social advocacy, group solidarity, and other outcomes of life-long social striving are features of social interaction that develop out of a sense of responsibility to the whole; they are learned by experience during development, but not in the one-on-one learning environment derived from a self-oriented focus.

PAVING PATHWAYS ALONG MIDDLE CHILDHOOD COGNITIVE MILESTONES: SHOULD I HOME SCHOOL MY CHILD?

Acknowledging the potential drawbacks of home schooling, advocates suggest that parents examine the following factors as they consider the option for their children (Wade, 1991).

▶ Successful home schooling requires that one parent stay at home full-time. The role of primary caregiver is one full-time job; taking on the role of educator is a second one. Adding on a third job spreads the teacher/parent role far too thin to be truly effective.

▶ Home schooling requires a high degree of commitment and organization. Lesson planning often requires more homework for the teacher than for the student. Arranging to meet the child's social learning needs through group activities and field trips to hear alternative speakers takes an enormous amount of research and practical juggling.

▶ The teacher/parent must have adequate reading and math abilities and a solid general knowledge base, and must be able to understand and learn new material long enough to impart it to the student. The teacher/parent must also be willing to teach a full curriculum and present a wide breadth of philosophies and ideas, including areas that he or she finds uninteresting, "irrelevant," or contrary to his or her own perspective.

▶ Discipline problems and personality conflicts between parent and child result in tense relationships. If such tensions tend to be the rule rather than the exception, the childrearing conflict is likely to spill into the educational environment, which the home-schooled child will see as one more battleground. As the child reacts to educational efforts accordingly, the teacher/parent's motivation to do a good job will wane as well. Under these circumstances both child and parent are likely to benefit from pursuing an educational alternative.

▶ If a child has a learning disability or other special education needs, the teacher/parent must have regular access to relevant consultants and specialists. *Public Law 94–142* does require that public schools give all handicapped children access to such services regardless of where they receive the bulk of their schooling. However, those attending public schools typically are first in line for such limited resources as speech therapists, child development specialists, physical and occupational therapists, and school psychologists. Unless parents can afford to pay such professionals on their own, the disabled child who is home schooled may not reach his or her full potential.

▶ The degree of personal dedication needed for successful home schooling requires that parents examine their motivations for wanting to do so. Specifically, the parent's choice should be based on evaluation of the individual child's needs and having the desire to meet them. Parents still carrying around vendettas arising from their own childhood problems with school really do need to get over it—not only for their own mental health but also, and more crucially, so as not to let emotionality cloud their judgment regarding their child's educational needs. Not all schools are the same and even individual schools can change dramatically from generation to generation.

If the main motivator is disgruntlement over a school's management of a child's academic or behavioral problems, parents have many options. By working with teachers and other school personnel, parents can become part of a team approach to solve the problems (Crespi, 1997; Ryan et al., 1995). If the child needs more individual attention in a specific learning area than either the teacher or the parent can provide, after-school tutors can be enlisted. If a particular teacher/child matchup is not working out, larger schools may agree to transfer the student to a different classroom.

Parents can work through conflicts with teachers or suspected teacher inefficiencies by enlisting principals or other administrators as mediators. If general school policies need reforming, parents can work with the district administration. Getting involved with parent-teacher organizations and volunteering time at school are two ways of creating relationships with school personnel that can foster team efforts, as well as providing springboards for addressing school policies that affect the best interests of all students. If parents cannot find common ground with their public schools, they can always consider private schools, move to or apply to another district, or, if they have the resources, hire a full-time professional tutor. After evaluating all the alternatives, parents may decide that the best option for their child is home schooling—so long as the preceding relevant factors have been examined and the choice is not made simply by default.

What are the pluses and minuses of the computer age for children?

Children and Computers

Microcomputer technology has simplified tasks and facilitated information processing to an extent far beyond the fantasies of earlier generations. Computers touch our lives—and those of our children—daily. They have become so ingrained that computer literacy is arguably essential to building a successful life in Western culture (Neill, 1995). Concerned parents, however, may recall the pioneering "computer nerds" of their own youth—the brilliant but isolated, socially awkward stereotype featured in the *Revenge of the Nerds* movies. Are these parents' concerns founded? Probably not. As the following discussion describes, it is not the machine itself that can contribute to developmental problems but how the machine is used (Haughland & Wright, 1997).

How Computers Can Hinder. A major drawback of the computer is that it exposes children to a limited, very narrow range of experiences. Computer use also presents many of the same problems as television viewing. Sitting alone at a terminal does not supply the physical activity and social interaction necessary for healthy child development and growth. Software content itself can be problematic. Many arcade-style games focus predominantly on aggressive or downright violent activity, and such programs are associated with greater incidence of aggressive feelings, thoughts, and behaviors (Anderson & Dill, 2000; Funk et al., 2000). Program content is also often highly stimulating, raising questions about how generalizable such learning is to the real world, where so many of the problems of daily living that we must solve are mundane. Because all software is coded, it is limited in the variability of outcomes it can offer; closed-ended programs are neat and predictable, lacking the imperfections of real life and thus repeatedly presenting children with an unrealistic view of the world (Turner, 1992).

Drill and practice programs designed to develop math and reading skills do succeed, especially for children who are younger or are doing poorly (Lepper & Gurtner, 1989). These programs are less effective with younger learning disabled students, who get better results from a teacher's instruction aimed at their unique zones of proximal development (Babbitt & Miller, 1996; Wilson et al., 1996). Often even nondisabled children are less inclined to successfully work alone with a computer, perhaps needing peer prodding and instructor guidance beyond what is available in a computer-driven instructional environment. Moreover, when children spend extensive time with closed-ended programs such as drill and practice, their general creative effort may drop by as much as 50% (Haugland, 1992).

Developmental neuropsychologists express some concern regarding how computer use affects the younger child's developing brain (Healy, 1998). As you will recall from earlier chapters, brain development occurs by means of activities that foster complex interactions among motor, sensory, and cognitive processing. Outside distractions such as bombardment by chaotic computer-produced stimuli and choices may interfere with the normal processes of brain development, as well as detracting from development of selective attention (Mariani & Barkley, 1997). Software is not designed with such considerations in mind, and it is doubtful that computers will ever replace the actual experience of doing (Stoll, 1995). Thus developmental neurologists recommend that use of the computer be extremely limited if not avoided altogether until after age seven, at which time much of a child's crucial brain development will already have taken place (Healy, 1998).

Another caution concerns the concept of "computer addiction" (Shaffer et al., 2000). Excessive computer use is often a symptom of other problems in a person's life, as it provides escapism from the difficulties of daily living. Children need to address their developmental tasks, not seek escape from them.

How Computers Can Help. In spite of these drawbacks, appropriately invested computer time can actually enhance learning and development (Lepper & Gurtner, 1989). Word processing is a good example. The ability to go back, reorganize material, and change wordings promotes development of writing skills, since children are less concerned about making mistakes. Teaching children how to program computers has shown increases in creativity, problem-solving skills, and general concrete operational ability (Clements, 1991). And, contrary to visions parents might have of turning children into isolated "computer nerds," computer use actually tends to promote interaction among classmates as they consult with one another for joint problem-solving and show off their accomplishments (Weinstein, 1991).

Computer-assisted instruction programs are software designed to promote learning, most frequently in the areas of basic math and reading skills. The most effective programs are referred to as being "developmentally appropriate" (Haugland & Wright, 1997). Rather than using a drill and practice format, **developmentally appropriate software** is open-ended and exploratory. The child controls the direction taken by the program, making decisions and problem-solving, all the while using trial and error to get the program to produce his or her desired results. Developmentally appropriate software lets the experience fit a variety of learning styles. Participatory learning of this nature works hand in hand with Piaget's concept of concrete operational development, as the child practices a variety of strategies for making things happen (Papert, 1993). The effectiveness of developmentally appropriate software may be in part due to its allowing the child to make choices and to personalize learning, which taps into a child's intrinsic motivation (Lepper, 1985).

PAVING PATHWAYS ALONG MIDDLE CHILDHOOD COGNITIVE MILESTONES: CHOOSING SOFTWARE FOR CHILDREN

Suppose you wanted to find a new computer program for a particular group of children. What exactly would you look for? The following considerations may help you minimize possible drawbacks and maximize the benefits of children's use of computers (Haugland & Wright, 1997).

▶ *Age appropriateness.* Is the program developmentally appropriate for the particular children you have in mind?

▶ *Controls.* Does the child or the program control such procedures as setting the pace and the ability to escape or start over ?

▶ *Clear, simple instructions.* Are the instructions user-friendly, perhaps using pictures to illustrate explanations or instructions that are complex or are beyond the child's verbal abilities?

▶ *Expanding complexity.* Are there multiple levels of performance requirements, allowing the child to choose increasingly advanced options?

▶ *Can be used independently.* After initial instructions, will the child be able to use the program without extensive adult supervision and guidance?

▶ *Nonviolent and/or prosocial themes.* Does the program imply social values appropriate for the developing child?

▶ *Process-oriented.* Are the lessons being taught based on learning new processes such as problem-solving, rather than drilling and practicing rote information?

▶ *Reality-based.* Do themes played come close enough to the real world for children to be able to generalize learning to their own lives?

▶ *Technically sound.* In a nutshell, does the program actually work the way it is supposed to?

Gender Differences in Computer Use. By middle school, boys are spending much more time with computers than are girls (Miura, 1987). Yet kindergarten-age consumers show no gender differences in the amount of time devoted to computer-based activity (Bergin et al., 1993). What influences during middle childhood promote such a disparity? Some suspect cultural biases that attribute computer use to maleness, thus widening the gender gap in the same manner as appears to occur with other science- and math-related skills.

However, it is important to note that there are a greater number of computer games designed around themes attractive to boys, such as aggression and competition (Ogletree & Williams, 1990). Because software that emphasizes cooperative content over competitive content does indeed seem to increase girls' use of computer programs, creation of more such programs might sustain girls' interest as they grow older (Lepper, 1985).

Children and the Internet. The Internet has the capacity to connect children to a vast network of knowledge. Unfortunately, this network contains both good and bad information. Internet use can give children access to violent and sexual material as well as instructions for building a bomb or enticements for joining a cult. As a result of freedom of expression, much information floating around the Internet consists of outright falsehoods. Access to "chat rooms" and e-mail have provided child predators and other unsavory types with new opportunities for harassing children and arranging face-to-face encounters with unwitting victims.

Spending excessive time on the Internet has caused social problems for adults, especially among those who have proved themselves susceptible to other addictive behaviors (Young, 1998). A study of adults and children over age 10 looked at how some social and emotional factors measured up after 1 or 2 years of their being online. Participants had decreased their communication with family members, had fewer friends, and reported increases in feelings of depression and loneliness (Kraut et al., 1998). While it is still unclear whether similar phenomena are occurring in younger children or if excessive Internet use interferes with normal socialization activity, developmental neurologists have expressed some concerns over a sort of "glazed," detached look observed in some children who spend extensive amounts of time glued to the monitor (Healy, 1998).

PAVING PATHWAYS ALONG MIDDLE CHILDHOOD COGNITIVE MILESTONES: STRUCTURING CHILDREN'S INTERNET USE

Setting up rules for Internet use can help avoid many of the potential dangers (Benson & Fodemski, 1996; Hughes, 1998). Young children, not being able to sort out good and bad information, are most vulnerable and need a lot of guidance:

▶ Structure the amount of time as well as the time of day that the child spends on the Internet.

▶ Limit the particular services the child is allowed to access.

▶ Instruct children that they should never give out personal information such as name, address, or photographs over the Internet.

▶ Emphasize that not everything the child encounters on the Internet is true; in fact, people may represent themselves as someone they are not.

▶ Remind them that just as they should be cautious of strangers they meet elsewhere, they should never meet with strangers encountered through the Internet unless the meeting has been parent-arranged.

▶ Encourage children to tell you if something they have come across just doesn't seem right.

Some parents use **filtering software** as a means of protecting their children. Programs such as Surfwatch, NetView, and NetNanny are designed to restrict access to specific sites and materials. They can also be used to control the amount of time or time of day children spend on-line, as well as prevent children from sending out personal information.

As children mature they become better able to critically evaluate good versus bad information. Developing their ability to do so in fact requires exposure to a diverse collection of views. More and more high schools now offer access to the Internet as a means of obtaining and evaluating information. They often ensure that access is learning related by imposing certain structures (Murray, 1997). Students must have parental permission to perform searches. The purpose of each search must be explicitly stated. A computer "hall monitor" must be present during searches. Information from searches used in written works must be appropriately referenced. Most important, critiques of the specific Web sites used are required. How does information gleaned from the Internet measure up to reputable works, such as the empirical data and their applications presented in the "Tried . . . . and True" features of this textbook?

How does language ability change during middle childhood, and what language issues arise for bilingual children?

LANGUAGE

"Why did the man throw his alarm clock out the window?"
"Because he wanted to see time fly!"

Why do children laugh so uproariously at humor we adults might see as cute but otherwise somewhat bland? As children reach school age, the word associations and shifts in meaning involved with humor are just becoming available to them, and only by being capable of experiencing these processes can they understand the joke. Word-play humor is therefore a novel discovery. What is happening with the child's language ability that promotes such understanding?

Vocabulary

In spite of having concluded the fast-mapping stage of the preschool years, the school-age child's vocabulary continues to expand, typically doubling between the ages of 6 and 12 to about 30,000 words. During these years a child's qualitative understanding and management of words changes (Holzman, 1983; Markman, 1989). Take, for example, the word, "lollipop." Rather than focusing solely on its concrete, observable characteristics—such as being "red" or "sweet"—the school-age child will consider more abstract associations of the word, such as membership of "lollipop" in the categories "candy" or "found at the corner store." So although the child is learning fewer words, the utility of the words the child learns is increasing rapidly, including the dual meanings that contribute toward understanding word humor!

Grammar

The child's understanding and use of the rules of grammar also change qualitatively (Chomsky, 1969; de Villiers & de Villiers, 1978). At age 6, children have a simplified and limited understanding of **syntax**, or how words are organized into meaningful sentences and phrases. By age 12, they have developed an understanding of the concepts of passive voice ("The cookies were *baked by Mom*"), infinitives ("Jimmy wants *to go*"), and rules for pronoun use ("David and *I* are playing basketball"). Their increasing ability to comprehend the abstract associations between words also results in the use of comparatives ("Susan is *faster* than Sharon) and similes ("He came in from the rain *looking like a drowned rat*").

Reading and Writing

One of the most notable accomplishments of the school-age child's language abilities is learning to read and write. Studies of level of ability for these skills suggest some genetic influences, including demonstration of girls' superiority in the writing domain (Pajaras et al., 1999). However, environmental influences appear to be most responsible for any changes in ability that occur between age 7 and 12 (Wadsworth et al., 1999).

How to teach children to read is a matter of considerable debate (Goswami & Bryant, 1990). One side proposes that they learn more effectively by using the **whole language approach**. Children are taught to sight-read whole words as they occur in daily usage, thus teaching them to associate words with their meanings. The other side argues that the **phonics approach** is more effective. Children are taught such basic general concepts as how words can be sounded out by breaking them down into letters and syllables. Currently educators recognize the value of using techniques from both approaches during the process of teaching children to read (Bus & van IJzendoorn, 1999; Durkin, 1987).

Bilingualism

What if children speak two languages? How will this affect their language ability, and how are they most effectively educated (Hakuta, 1999)? Data regarding bilingualism and child development are difficult to sort out. There are many reasons children become bilingual: They may immigrate to an area where a different tongue is spoken, two languages may have been spoken in the home since birth, or a second language may be formally introduced to the child only after he or she enters the school system. Bilingualism is also tied to culture. Is an observed outcome the product of the child's growing up speaking a minority language, or has it occurred because of his or her different cultural experiences?

How different cultures react to bilingualism also varies. Bilingualism is built into some societies, as in Quebec, Canada. In a process called **immersion**, all school children are successfully instructed using both French and English throughout their education (Harley et al., 1987). Programs using immersion into the Spanish language have been found to actually increase English-language ability (Cunningham & Graham, 2000). However, in many countries such as the United States, all instruction is typically given in a single, primary language, with a variety of other languages taught as electives.

Many states in the United States take the view that students who speak a minority language should be educated by means of immersion in the language of the majority, if for no other reason than the logistical nightmare of trying to supply teachers for multiple languages. As might be expected, however, children instructed in languages they can only marginally understand tend to underachieve and drop out (United States Commission on Civil Rights, 1975). Yet if they do not find some way of becoming fluent in English, how successfully are they likely to integrate into moderate and higher socioeconomic levels of employment, given that such status is also usually driven by familiarity with the English language?

Most U.S. schools that provide bilingual education offer a transitional solution (Slavin, 1988). During their early years, children speaking minority languages receive classroom instruction in their own tongue, with a curriculum that includes English lessons. As children become more fluent, they are mainstreamed into the regular classroom. Some protest that since language is closely tied in with culture, training children into the language of the majority in this manner may also move them away from their cultural roots. This may in fact be the case, perhaps reflecting one of the inevitabilities of living in a society created by merging cultures. As educators, politicians, linguists, and developmentalists continue to argue the point, hopefully they will center on solutions that consider what is most adaptive for these children as they become members of society (Genesee, 1994).

Education aside, how does bilingualism affect the cognitive development of the child? Wouldn't you expect the burden of sorting out two languages to hinder the development of a child's language ability? At first it does (Merriman & Kutlesic, 1993; Umbel et al., 1992). But after children are able to recognize and separate out the different forms and functions of the two languages, their language skills eventually catch up with those of their monolingual peers (Cummins, 1991; Gathercole, 1997; Winsler et al., 1999). Some measures of bilingual children's cognitive abilities show them exceeding those of their monolingual peers (Cunningham & Graham, 2000). They are quicker to pick up the concept that the printed word represents the spoken word (Bialystok et al., 2000). They tend to become more aware of the intricacies of language, and may show benefits in overall concept formation and analytical reasoning (Bialystok, 1991). Some evidence suggests that they may develop better attentional control than do monolingual individuals (Bialystok, 1999).

SUMMARY

Piaget's Concrete Operations

Middle childhood brings the Piagetian period of concrete operational ability, moving away from the dominance of perception over reasoning. Because children can now mentally manipulate information, they are capable of skills such as reversibility and decentration.

Information Processing

Advances in information processing evolve around interaction between what the child wants to know and developing the skills necessary for absorbing it. Attention span increases as the child learns what to attend to and what to ignore. Memory becomes enhanced as children learn to use memorization strategies such as rehearsal, categorization, and imagery.

Intelligence, Learning, and Special Needs

The WISC-III, the most frequently used IQ test, is often used to identify students with special needs. However, many IQ tests do not accurately predict abilities for those of diverse cultures, since the materials and testing procedures reflect Western, Caucasian-American, middle-class exposures. The K-ABC is more culturally fair than the WISC-III, and is more informative about a particular child's information processing and its relationship to learning.

Numerous factors affect a child's learning and achievement levels. Traditional classroom settings are better at instructing basics such as math, reading, and writing, while open classroom settings are better for developing independent working ability and tolerance for diverse solutions and perspectives. Students who enjoy academic success are more likely to be high in need for achievement, intrinsically rather than extrinsically motivated, and/or have a mastery rather than helpless achievement orientation. Teachers who enhance achievement demonstrate a positive, supportive, confident attitude toward their students. Having peers who are high achievers and having opportunities to work with groups of peers are associated with learning and achievement, as also is a cultural emphasis on the importance of achievement and having authoritative parents.

Children suffering from mental retardation, autism, ADHD, and learning disabilities all benefit from early intervention. During middle childhood this is typically accomplished with personalized combinations of mainstreaming and special education services. While intellectually gifted children often benefit from mentorships and special summer and weekend programs for the gifted, the pullout programs characterizing most schools' approaches to the needs of the gifted may best be guided toward raising standards and challenging all students. Creatively gifted children are more difficult to identify as well as to teach.

Classrooms organized around the concept of "flexible predictability" provide all children with opportunities to stretch the wings of their creativity.

Home schooling as an educational experience does not appear to turn out students of significantly lesser or greater academic ability or personal adjustment, although students may experience some difficulties if transferring to traditional schooling. Critics are concerned about the more limited social exposure of home schooling, and how it may affect elements of cognitive and social development that depend upon exposures to multiple social stimuli. Supporters of home schooling recommend careful consideration of the many relevant factors and potential options before deciding if home schooling is a viable choice for a particular child and home situation.

A child's computer use can become problematic if it replaces physical activity, has violent content, or encourages unrealistic expectations of the world. However, computer-assisted instruction using developmentally appropriate software can enhance learning by means of its open, participatory, and personalized nature. The lower number of girls using computers can be increased by developing software more interesting to them, such as those employing themes of cooperation rather than competitiveness and aggression. The dangers of letting children surf the Internet can be mediated by providing appropriate instruction and using filtering software to restrict certain forms of access.

Language

Children double their vocabulary during middle childhood, develop more complex understandings of the words they know, learn and use more sophisticated forms of syntax, and apply all of the above as they learn to read. In the United States, programs for bilingual children typically instruct them in their own tongue while simultaneously instructing them in the English language until they are sufficiently fluent to learn in the English-speaking classroom.

◤ KEY TERMS

attention deficit hyperactivity disorder (ADHD)
autism
autistic savant
categorization
computer-assisted instruction
concrete operations
convergent thinking
decentration
developmentally appropriate software
divergent thinking

dyslexia
filtering software
full inclusion
helpless orientation
imagery
immersion
Kaufman Assessment Battery for Children (K-ABC)
learning disabilities
mainstreaming
mastery orientation
need for achievement

open classroom
phonics approach
rehearsal
reversibility
self-fulfilling prophecy
syntax
transitive inference
Wechsler Intelligence Scale for Children-III (WISC-III)
whole language approach

CONCEPT REVIEW

1. New cognitive manipulations such as _____ and _____ help concrete operational children employ increased _____ and _____ in their thinking. How quickly children develop their concrete reasoning capacity depends upon _____ and _____ .

2. Concrete operational thinking is limited in how it manages _____ and _____ reasoning.

3. School-age children's attending ability improves as neurons become _____ , personal _____ accumulate, and their _____ becomes larger. Children can be taught to use strategies such as _____ , _____ , and _____ as means of improving their recall memory.

4. The WISC-III is the intelligence test most often used to determine conditions such as _____ and _____ . The K-ABC focuses more on the _____ behind correct or incorrect responses to test questions. Children of diverse cultures often do not perform as well on intelligence tests because they are less familiar with _____ and the _____ , and their culture manages _____ differently.

5. Classrooms now typically use both traditional lecture/independent paperwork teaching strategies and _____ classroom strategies, which allow for more student-directed learning opportunities.

6. High-achieving students tend to be _____ motivated and work within a _____ orientation, while underachieving students tend to be _____ motivated and function from a _____ orientation. Teachers' attitudes can affect achievement level due to _____ .

7. Peers tend to draw a child's achievement level toward _____ achievement level. Working in groups of peers is important as children fill in each other's "blanks" within their _____ .

8. Children of some diverse cultures may be better achievers because of differing cultural _____ , as well as differing parental _____ . Parents of high achievers are _____ in their children's academic lives, tend to use an _____ parenting style, set high but attainable _____ and focus more on achieving _____ than personal _____ .

9. In terms of degree of impairment, most mentally retarded children are _____ . In concordance with Public Law 94–142, which re-

quires schools to develop _____ programs for students with special needs, such students typically spend part of their day in a resource room and when possible are _____ into the regular classroom.

10. Autistic individuals are often _____, but are most notable for their lack of _____ connectedness and _____ expressiveness and their _____ behaviors.

11. Children with ADHD are at a disadvantage in the classroom because of their impaired _____ and their _____ behavior. The condition occurs more among the _____ gender and may not include hyperactivity, especially among the _____ gender. The condition is typically best controlled by a combination of _____ and _____ interventions.

12. Children with specific learning disabilities are typically of _____ intelligence. Examples include _____ —a difficulty with accurately tracking visual stimuli while reading, _____ impairment, and written expression disorders involving the _____ of information between oral and written form.

13. Intellectually gifted children not only benefit from opportunities to use their advanced _____ skills and their self-motivational style called _____, but also from activities that address the potential for neglected _____ and _____ development. Strategies offered within the _____ classroom appear to get better overall results than does the more typical _____ program.

14. Creative intelligence is characterized more by _____ thinking, rather than the _____ thinking that characterizes analytical intelligence. Classroom activities that offer _____ provide both structure and opportunities for the creative student to pursue the uniqueness of his or her independent thinking style.

15. Home-schooled children do/do not academically perform as well as traditionally educated children. Home schooling runs the risk of not providing the developing child with sufficient opportunities for interpersonal and academic learning if their life exposures are not sufficiently _____ or _____-oriented.

16. Children's computer use should be limited because software programs are experientially _____ and _____ focused. Children benefit more from developmentally appropriate software because it is _____ and _____. Excessive or inappropriate Internet use can be controlled through use of _____ software and by establishing _____ for Internet use.

17. The school-age child's vocabulary expands both in size and in actual possibilities for word _____. The whole language approach for teaching children to read helps children _____ words and associate them with their _____, while the phonics approach teaches children how words can be _____.

18. Typically, bilingual children are at first schooled using the _____ language, and as they become sufficiently fluent spend more and more time in the _____ classroom. Bilingual children have shown some superiority over monolingual children in their _____ abilities.

1) reversibility; decentration; organization; flexibility; heredity; environmental exposures; 2) abstractions; scientific; 3) myelinated; experiences; knowledge base; rehearsal, categorization; imagery; 4) giftedness; learning disabilities; cognitive processes; English; test items; verbal interactions; 5) open; 6) intrinsically; master; extrinsically; helpless; self-fulfilling prophecy; 7) their own; zones of proximal development; 8) values; expectations; invested; authoritative; standards; learning goals; superiority; 9) educable; individualized education; mainstreamed; 10) mentally retarded; social; emotional; ritualistic; 11) attention span; hyperactive; male; female; medications; behavioral; 12) normal; dyslexia; math; transfer; 13) analytical; rage to master; social; emotional; regular; pullout; 14) divergent; convergent; flexible predictability; 15) do; diverse; socially; 16) limited; unrealistically; open-ended; exploratory; filtering; rules; 17) usage; memorize; meanings; sounded out; 18) home/native; English-speaking; cognitive

► RESOURCES FOR FURTHER READING

Benson, A. C., & Fodemski, L. M. (1996). *Connecting kids and the Internet: A handbook for librarians, teachers, & parents.* New York: Neal-Schuman.

Haugland, S. W., & Wright, J. L. (1997). *Young children and technology: A world of discovery.* Boston: Allyn & Bacon.

Hughes, D. R. (1998). *Kids online: Protecting your children in cyberspace.* Grand Rapids, MI: Revell.

Koetzsch, R. E. (1997). *The parents' guide to alternatives in education.* Boston: Shambhala.

Power-deFur, L. A., & Orelove, F. P. (1997). *Inclusive education: Practical implementation of the least restrictive environment.* Gaithersburg, MD: Aspen.

Rich, D. (1988). *MegaSkills: How families can help children succeed in school and beyond.* Boston: Houghton Mifflin.

Siegel, B. (1996). *The world of the autistic child: Understanding and treating autistic spectrum disorders.* New York: Oxford University Press.

Smith, C., & Strick, L. (1997). *Learning disabilities, A to Z: A parent's complete guide to learning disabilities from preschool to adulthood.* New York: Free Press.

Wade, T. E. (Ed.) (1991). *The home school manual: For parents who teach their own children.* Auburn, CA: Gazelle Publications.

Wadsworth, B. J. (1996). *Piaget's theory of cognitive and affective development,* 5th ed. New York: Longman.

Webb, J. T., Meckstroth, E. A., & Tolan, S. S. (1994). *Guiding the gifted child: A practical source for parents and teachers.* Scottsdale, AZ: Gifted Psychology Press.

Wender, P. (1987). *The hyperactive child, adolescent, and adult: Attention deficit disorder through the lifespan.* New York: Oxford University Press.

INFOTRAC COLLEGE EDITION

For additional readings, explore InfoTrac College Edition, your online library. Go to http://www.infotrac-college.com/wadsworth and use the passcode that came on the card with your book. Try these search terms: academic achievement and children, achievement motivation, attention deficit disorder, autism, bilingual education, cognition in children, cognition and culture, computers and children, creativity and children, culture and education, giftedness and children, home schooling, immersion programs, Internet and children, learning disabilities, mainstreaming in education, memory in children, mental retardation, whole-language approach

CHILD DEVELOPMENT CD-ROM

Go to the Wadsworth Child Development CD-ROM for further study of the concepts in this chapter. The CD-ROM also includes quizzes and additional activities to expand your learning experience.

REFERENCES

For a list of references for this chapter, see the Wadsworth Psych Study Center Web site at: http://www.wadsworth.com/product/0534348092s

CHAPTER 13

Middle Childhood Social and Emotional Development

FOCUS QUESTIONS

► How is personality development characterized during middle childhood?

► What is competence, and how do relationships influence its development?

► How does sexual abuse affect a child's adjustment, and how can it be prevented?

► What advances in development occur in the school-age child's experiencing and expression of emotions?

► How do school-age children express severe emotional conditions, and how can these be treated?

► How does moral reasoning change during middle childhood?

► What affects a school-age child's self-concept and self-esteem, and what can parents do to foster good self-esteem?

OUTLINE	

Personality Development
   Psychodynamic Influences
   Culturally Based Skill Building
   Competence
Relationships
   Relationships with Parents
   Family Constellations
   Paving Pathways: Easing the Effects of Divorce on Children
   Relationships with Peers
   Child Sexual Abuse
   Paving Pathways: Preventing Sexual Abuse

Emotions and Middle Childhood
   Normal Emotionality
   Excessive Emotional States
   Paving Pathways: Helping the Anxious Child
   Paving Pathways: Helping the Depressed Child
   Paving Pathways: Helping the Acting-Out Child
Moral Development
Self-Concept and Self-Esteem
   Self-Concept
   Self-Esteem
   Paving Pathways: Encouraging Good Self-Esteem

Frieda sat among her fellow students as they watched their school talent show. A new girl at their school walked onstage and falteringly presented a vocalized rendition of an unfamiliar song.

"She sure doesn't sing very well," Frieda whispered to Jeremy, the boy sitting next to her. "Who is she, anyway?"

"She's my cousin," Jeremy replied.

Embarrassed, Frieda wanted to correct her social blunder.

"Actually, she doesn't sing that bad," she backpedaled. "It's that silly song. I wonder why she picked it out?"

"Because I wrote it."

As is true for physical and cognitive advances, school-age children mold their increasingly complex social and emotional lives through skill building. They develop a sense of who they are as they delve into new fields such as writing and singing new songs. As they become more intuitively aware of their emotional states and continue to learn the rules of social interaction, they make considerable progress toward a more sophisticated integration of this knowledge and interpersonal style.

How is personality development characterized during middle childhood?

PERSONALITY DEVELOPMENT

While conversations with newly verbal three-year-olds are delightful for the fresh glimpses of personality they often reveal, interactions with school-age children open whole new realms. During middle childhood, children can better explain their reasoning and feelings even though both have become significantly more complex. We adults may find ourselves feeling vitally challenged as we adjust our interactions in order to foster newly emerging aspects of the school-age child's personality. Yet in spite of the advances and increased complexities, consistencies of temperament from earlier ages continue to be observed, especially the introversion-extroversion personality factor (Hagekull & Bohlin, 1998).

Psychodynamic Influences

Sandwiched between the energetic, loosely organized social life of young childhood and the hormone-driven social turbulence of adolescence, personality development during middle childhood is a time of relative calm—or so Sigmund Freud (1914/1959) saw it. While observing school-age children through his psychosexual filter, he noted that they exhibited fewer sexuality-related behaviors, such as masturbating or speaking about sex matters. He interpreted his observations as an indication that the highly sexually charged issues of the phallic stage had been resolved one way or another, and that children were proceeding into a nonsexual period he called the **latency stage**. He proposed that this nonsexual calm cleared the way for more objective processing as children approached and mastered the many new skills learned between the ages of 6 and 11.

Subsequent investigation has offered alternative conclusions for Freud's observations. During the Victorian era of sexual restrictiveness, children learned both by word and example that behaviors related to sexuality were considered socially unacceptable. By middle childhood we would expect the children of Freud's era to have integrated much of these cultural teachings. However, as is also the case when faced with the semirestrictive sexual attitudes in current Western cultures, children actually continue to pursue normal sex play and sex talk when disapproving adults are not around (Rosen & Hall, 1984). They also demonstrate their continuing sexual development through junior-league courtship rituals, rehearsing for future relationships. On any school playground you are likely to hear occasional repetitive chants such as "Dennis loves Mandy" or "Mandy has a boyfriend," and observe games such as "girls chase the boys" (Thorne, 1993).

Culturally Based Skill Building

Having discarded the sexual connotations supporting Freudian beliefs regarding the latency stage, Erikson (1985) focused instead on the skill mastery components of Freud's observations. Feats of learning and accomplishment are strikingly apparent during middle childhood. Children begin learning the survival skills of their particular culture, with improvements in Piagetian cognitive functioning increasing their effectiveness at gathering relevant social and ethnic knowledge (Ocampo et al., 1997). Western cultures teach children skills such as reading, writing, performing mathematical calculations, managing money, using computers, and negotiating streets and neighborhoods safely.

Both the herder and the software investigator are proceeding normally within the skill-building emphasis of middle childhood.

In less industrialized cultures, children of this age group are often not only indoctrinated into the world of adult survival skills but are also expected to contribute toward the subsistence of the community. In the Luo culture of East Africa, boys are given the responsibility of herding cattle during the day. Girls receive some training in herding so they can care for the animals in the event that the village goes to war, but they are largely trained in the domestic chores they are expected to perform such as meal preparation (Ocholla-Ayayo, 1980).

In the Afikpo village of Nigeria, boys spend middle childhood training and rehearsing to become members of the male secret societies that direct village functioning. They are encouraged to gather in same-age groups and practice dancing and mask-making, develop the practical skills for which they will be tested during initiation into adulthood, and form peer relationships that will follow them into their adult hierarchal organization. Afikpo girls, however, are likely to leave the village upon reaching adulthood, as they follow their husbands, on whom they are now dependent. Therefore during middle childhood they are fostered into strongly dependent relationships with their mothers and spend considerably less time developing an independent social structure among their peers (Ottenberg, 1989). In general, the values of the child's culture largely determine the degree of interdependence versus independence or orientation toward the collective versus the individual that will be incorporated during the child's self-development (Raeff, 1997).

Besides the cultural component, what impact does this period of learning and skill building have on a child's personality development? Erikson (1985) viewed the phase as a time of **industry versus inferiority**. A child who experiences successes will soar into a continuing pattern of industriousness, while a child who perceives his or her efforts as unsuccessful will droop under the weight of real or imagined inferiority. This testing of ability directs itself toward a specific goal: the development of a personal sense of competence.

What is competence, and how do relationships influence its development?

Competence

The Hawks and the Sea Stars are battling at the hoops. Karen, the Hawks' usually high-scoring forward, has met her match in the taller girls of the Sea Stars. Fortunately, her team's great defense has kept them within a few points in a low-scoring game. They chase back and forth across the court, neither team able to score during this final series, the clock running out. Finally Karen fakes to the outside, and as the player blocking her shot shadows left she turns right, hooks the ball over the taller girl's outstretched arm and watches it roll into the basket. The Hawks win! Her teammates go wild, squealing and dancing group-hug style. Their parents are on their feet clapping, cheering, exchanging a few high-fives. Time stands still as the girls jubilantly celebrate their moment in the sun.

Karen has just earned another charm to align along the linkage of her sense of competence. It will join other charms, equally contributing to her sense of competence but having arrived with less fanfare: the twinkle in her eye as she held up a successfully constructed beadwork project, the expression of wonder on her face when she arrived at the point of comprehending a difficult concept.

Developmentally, just what is competence? **Competence** can be defined as demonstrating a pattern of effective adaptation to the environment (Masten & Coatsworth, 1995). This definition can be applied broadly, describing competence as an individual's overall adjustment to current developmental tasks and his or her age, gender, and culture. But it is more useful to this discussion to look at competence as the ability to achieve or find success within specific domains. During middle childhood, children develop their sense of competence in four basic areas (Masten & Coatsworth, 1998):

► *Adjusting to school.* Adjustment to the school milieu is children's first real test of how well they, on their own, can fit in with social structures and expectations. School adjustment requires that they sort out intrinsic and extrinsic motivators, become comfortable expressing opinions, develop self-esteem, understand the norms of school social conduct, and develop the various social relationships necessary for successful adjustment (Wentzel, 1996).

► *Establishing peer relationships.* Developing good middle childhood peer relationships is both a task of competence and a strong predictor of competence later in life (Hartup, 1996).

► *Learning to play by the rules.* Rule-abiding as opposed to rule-breaking behavior during middle childhood often predicts both social competence over the next decade and the child's ability to establish academic competence (Maguin & Loeber, 1996; Masten et al., 1995).

► *Achieving academically.* The ability to perform academically affects children's perceptions of their competence, which in turn affect achievement levels (Greene & Miller, 1996).

What factors contribute to solid infusion of a sense of competence? A healthy self-concept and good self-esteem, construction of prosocial moral and value frameworks that the child can successfully apply, the ability to self-regulate, and relationships that foster all of the above are paramount to good social and emotional development during middle childhood. The remainder of this chapter demonstrates how all of these factors work together toward helping a child develop competence.

RELATIONSHIPS

B. J. wakes up each weekday morning to her mother's greeting and gentle prodding to get ready for school. She walks to school with neighborhood friends and while at school interacts with yet another group of children. She interrelates with teachers until after school, when she participates in mentoring from her gymnastics coach or Girl Scout leader, then goes to her sitter's home. She spends her evenings with her mother, sharing her daily triumphs and struggles. On weekends she visits with her father across town.

What roles do all of these relationship factors play in how she develops her sense of competence? Let's take a look at the roles of parents, family constellations, and peer influences.

Relationships with Parents

Even though parents spend about half as much time with their children during middle childhood as they did during the preschool years, their influence remains substantial (Hill & Stafford, 1980). During middle childhood, children benefit from being allowed to practice increasingly significant independent decision making. Nevertheless, parents still play the important roles of monitor and stopgap when the need for guidance becomes apparent (Maccoby, 1984). Children learn the rules of their society and culture—their road map for establishing competence in their world—by means of family interactions such as these (Schaffer, 1996). When parents are consistent and firm yet warm and sensitive as they interact with their children, lessons of competence are likely to be integrated and applied. In fact, when children have a good relationship with their parents, they are often capable of developing a healthy state of competence even in the face of extremely adverse living situations (Masten, 1994). Even high-risk urban African-American youths demonstrate greater personal resiliency when parents are highly involved and have high yet attainable expectations of them (Reynolds, 1998).

When parents use power-oriented or coercive methods of controlling child behavior, especially those accompanied by hostile expressiveness, children are less likely to either internalize the proposed standards of behavior or comply with them. Academic problems, poor peer relationships, befriending of deviant peers, and aggressive and disruptive behavior in the classroom—outcomes that represent the antithesis of competence—are all associated with this authoritarian style of parenting (Patterson et al., 1992).

Parents also teach competence by example. When children have strong relationships with parents who model effective coping with the ups and downs of daily living, they are likely to become competent copers as well (Kliewer et al., 1996). How parents react to their child's emotions affects competence at self-regulation. When mothers respond to their child's expression of unpleasant emotional experiences with problem-focused reactions, their children are found to demonstrate higher levels of social functioning and coping ability. When mothers minimize the situation, such as saying "it's not all that bad," their children demonstrate lower levels of social competence and higher levels of coping by means of avoidance (Eisenberg et al., 1996a).

A number of programs have attempted to address problematic parent-child relationships that affect the development of competence. Programs that focus on changing destructive patterns of interactions within families have succeeded in both promoting development of social competence and preventing antisocial behavior and delinquency (Reynolds, 1998; Yoshikawa, 1994).

Family Constellations

The traditional, intact, two-parent family is no longer the norm. Researchers predict that over one-half of the children who were born in the 1990s will experience divorcing parents, and thus at some point will be living in a family headed by a single parent (Furstenberg & Cherlin, 1991). As parents remarry, children experience another transition as they become part of a stepfamily. About one-half of children of divorce can expect to have stepfathers within four years of their parents' separation (Furstenberg, 1988).

There are some cultural differences among patterns of family constellation changes. African-American children are twice as likely as Caucasian-American children to experience parents divorcing, and are more likely to become single parents themselves during adolescence and young adulthood (Orbuch et al., 1999). African-American and Hispanic-American parents are also less likely to remarry after they separate; thus a greater number of their children live in single-parent homes (Cherlin, 1992).

Though trends are changing, most single-parent homes lack fathers. On the one hand, father-absent homes have been found to be more likely to have a greater atmosphere of warmth, a higher level of interaction with Mom, and more secure attachment between mother and child than is seen in traditional father-present homes. On the other hand, children of father-absent homes see themselves as less cognitively and physically competent than do children from father-present homes (Golumbok et al., 1997).

However, a review of the literature suggests that such effects are small and that the most important developmental factors affecting child adjustment are the stability and predictability of the caregivers, regardless of how many are present in the home. The review proposes that the concept of an "essential" mother—and more recently a form of "essential" father—may have emerged from gender-based differences in parent-child relationships in Western cultures. Thus strengthening the father-child bond rather than simply having a father present may reflect the child's genuine needs in this respect (Silverstein & Auerbach, 1999).

Considering the child's developmental need for dependability and stability, what effect do the changes inherent to divorce and remarriage have on development of competence? A number of studies have looked at the effects of divorce and remarriage on children's future personal adjustment (Hetherington & Stanley-Hagan, 1999; Neher & Short, 1998; Sandler et al., 2000). Many factors other than the divorce or remarriage itself appear to mediate how well children weather such transitions (Hetherington et al., 1998). Actually, in spite of the initial trauma immediately following divorce or remarriage, the vast majority of affected children develop into competent, well-adjusted individuals (Emery & Forehand, 1994).

A variety of individual differences among the children themselves are influential. Those with easy-going temperaments, higher levels of intelligence, social maturity, and fewer predivorce behavioral problems seem to come through the experience with less wear and tear (Block et al., 1986). A tendency to appraise events negatively increases the likelihood that a child will experience psychological symptoms after the divorce (Mazur et al., 1999; Sheets et al., 1996). Preschoolers may have more immediate as well as more lasting adjustment problems when parents divorce during this developmental period (Pagani et al., 1997; Zill et al., 1993). Remarriage, however, is more likely to have lasting negative effects on personal adjustment when the event occurs during the preadolescent years (Hetherington & Jodl, 1994; Pagani et al., 1998).

While boys are somewhat more strongly affected by divorce than are girls, current differences do not seem to be as great as had previously been observed. This may be because fathers have become more involved with their children postdivorce, and continuing contact with fathers appears to be more important to boys' future adjustment than girls' (Amato & Keith, 1991). Boys and girls do seem to differ some in their reactions to divorce. Boys are more likely to externalize their grief and frustration, becoming angry and acting out. Girls are more likely to internalize their distress, blame themselves for the breakup, and/or become depressed (Holroyd & Sheppard, 1997).

The absence of a parent due to either death or divorce is generally associated with poorer adjustment, but seems to be more often the case for children of divorced parents (Amato & Keith, 1991). Mere frequency of contact with noncustodial parents is not what seems to make the difference but rather the quality of the individual contacts. Adjustment appears to benefit when contact with the noncustodial parent involves low interparental conflict and competent, supportive, authoritative parenting (Amato, 1993).

New parental stresses related to having divorced can indirectly affect the child by interfering with effective parenting. Custodial mothers typically find their incomes reduced to as much as one-half of their previous levels (McLanahan & Sandefur, 1994). They also have the additional burden of trying to manage households on their own (Emery, 1994). The painful emotional distress caused by the divorce itself can interfere with the custodial parent's ability to be caring and supportive (Hetherington & Stanley-Hagan, 1995).

The behavior of divorcing parents frequently has an impact on their children's adjustment. Overt conflict between parents, whether they are divorced or still together, has a greater impact on a child's future adjustment than the phenomenon of divorce itself (Amato et al., 1995; Kitzmann, 2000). Adjustment problems following remarriage also hinge on the quality of the relationships among the members of the new family. Children seem to do well when the stepfamily climate is characterized by authoritative parenting, warmth, harmony, and cohesiveness (Hetherington et al., 1998).

PAVING PATHWAYS ALONG MIDDLE CHILDHOOD SOCIAL AND EMOTIONAL MILESTONES: EASING THE EFFECTS OF DIVORCE ON CHILDREN

Suppose you were in the process of divorcing. Given the preceding observations, what might you do to minimize the effect of changes in family constellation on your children? Following are some suggestions (Neuman, 1998):

► Maintain as much of your usual family routine as possible. Try not to change residences; but if you must, attempt to keep your children in the same school and near their old neighborhood. Avoid drastic changes in discipline.

► Since children often blame themselves for the breakup, assure them that they are not at fault.

► Let them talk about their losses and acknowledge their sadness, worries, anger, and other grieving experiences. Assure them that these feelings are normal.

► Find an avenue for dealing with your own emotional distress, and if your children observe your emotionality, assure them that you nevertheless will be all right.

► Reassure them that there will always be someone to take care of them, perhaps reminding them that a major part of the divorce proceeding involves making sure that they will be appropriately cared for.

► Try to arrange for the noncustodial parent to remain active in your children's lives.

► Do not use the children as pawns for expressing anger toward your ex-spouse. If conflict must be sorted out do so in private.

Relationships with Peers

As I was working on this chapter in May of 1998, my word processing efforts were temporarily interrupted by a horrifying radio broadcast announcement. In Springfield, Oregon, a 15-year-old boy hid several guns under his trenchcoat, walked into a crowded school cafeteria, and opened fire. Two students were killed and many others were wounded. Later, authorities found the boy's parents at home, also having been shot and killed. Subsequent questioning of the boy's peers revealed that he had been considered an oddball noted mainly for his preoccupation with bomb building, killing, and other forms of violence and had received the dubious honor of being voted "most likely to start World War III" (*Oregonian*, May 24, 1998). The results of this young man's psychopathology portray a tragic consequence of the failure to develop either satisfying peer relationships or social competence.

What is the relationship between peer friendships and development of competence during middle childhood? These two variables appear to be interdependent. Meta-analysis of the many studies on this topic shows that beginning in middle childhood and continuing on into adolescence, there is a resounding correlation between forming friendships and various forms of social competence (Newcomb et al., 1993). Furthermore, when children experience peer rejection over an extended period, previously competent performance in areas such as academic achievement may deteriorate (O'Neil et al., 1997). It is not yet clear whether success at friendships affects competence or whether competence levels determine the likelihood that certain kinds of friendships will be formed. In all likelihood, the two tendencies interact. Furthermore, particular aspects of friendships appear to have an impact on specific developmental outcomes (Hartup, 1996). Let's take a closer look at friendships from the standpoints of simply having friends, the identity of the friends, and the quality of particular friendships.

Having Friends. Many studies of children's friendships have centered on the behaviors observed as friends and nonfriends work together toward specific goals (Newcomb & Bagwell, 1995). When children are working together on a task, performing joint problem-solving, or working on collaborative storytelling, groups of friends accomplish their goals with a greater level of success than do groups of nonfriends (Azmitia & Montgomery, 1993; Hartup et al., 1995; Newcomb & Brady, 1982). The comradeship provided by the presence of friends also appears to aid the process of adjusting to the school milieu (Ladd et al., 1996).

Identity of Friends. Children tend to gravitate toward playmates they perceive as being similar to themselves, perhaps sharing common interests such as sports, computers, or performing arts. Some friendships form on the basis of specific personality characteristics. Boys tend to attract friends exhibiting a level of shyness equivalent to their own, while girls are more likely to form friendships with those who place similarly along the prosocial/antisocial continuum (Haselager et al., 1995). Over the course of a friendship, the members of a particular dyad tend to become more like one another, at least in terms of their particular dimension of similarity (Dishion et al., 1994). A common concern arises among parents and teachers alike when two "troublemakers" get together. Typically their friendship results in an increase of antisocial behavior (Dishion et al.,

1995). This process of attracting and being attracted to like children and selectively reinforcing one another's behaviors thus can have a significant impact on children's developmental direction (Hartup, 1996).

Friendship Quality. Good friends establish a healthy balance between closeness and individuality, providing support and companionship yet not smothering or coercing one another (Shulman, 1993). When children experience such friendships, they are more likely to demonstrate healthy academic achievement, school involvement, popularity, and personal reputation (Cauce, 1986). Their overall psychosocial adjustment and self-esteem seem to benefit as well (Buhrmester, 1990; Perry, 1987). Having quality friendships correlates negatively with difficulties in school, identity problems, and depression (Compas et al., 1986; Kurdek & Sinclair, 1988; Papini et al., 1990). Thus it appears that the quality of a child's friendships, rather than the existence of a friendship in and of itself, provides the major benefit regarding peer relationships and development of competence.

How does sexual abuse affect a child's adjustment, and how can it be prevented?

Child Sexual Abuse

Sexual abuse of children is one of the most destructive relationships to affect a child. It occurs in all ethnic, racial, and socioeconomic populations (Finkelhor, 1994; Roosa et al., 1999). Some surveys report that approximately one in four girls and one in six boys have been sexually abused by the time they reach age 18, but these figures are only estimates, since the vast majority of cases go unreported (Martin et al., 1993). A survey study involving over 2000 Caucasian-American, Mexican-American, Native-American, and African-American participants reported that about one-third of children, regardless of racial background, are sexually abused (Roosa et al., 1999). The prevalence of sexual abuse in the life histories of children with severe emotional disturbances is especially high (Sansonnet-Hayden et al., 1987). Most children who are sexually abused are victimized by men, but a number of children are sexually abused by women (Pryor, 1996; Saradjian & Hanks, 1996).

What developmental impact does sexual abuse have on children? The immediate symptoms vary widely in type and intensity (Deblinger & Heflin, 1996; Haugaard & Reppucci, 1988). Sexually abused children may develop emotional problems such as anxiety, sadness, anger, and shame. Behaviorally they may withdraw, become noncompliant, act out aggressively, exhibit inappropriate sexual behaviors, or even attempt suicide. They often develop cognitive patterns that center on self-blame and extreme distrust of others. Physical symptoms such as headaches, stomachaches, and extreme startle responses may appear. As sexually abused children progress into adulthood, their childhood baggage may follow along in the form of long-term severe mental health conditions such as certain personality disorders, posttraumatic stress disorder, and, under some of the most severe abuse conditions, multiple personality disorder (American Psychiatric Association, 1994; Morrissette, 1999). The vast majority of sex offenders were themselves offended against as children (Finkelhor, 1984).

The extreme nature of these mental health consequences stems from the severity of the violation of boundaries when adults sexually abuse a child. Children depend on adults to take care of them and protect them and internalize what they learn from them as a blueprint for caring for themselves. They develop self-understanding and both personal and interpersonal boundaries on the basis of how adults interact with them. The trauma and extreme boundary violation of child sexual abuse not only disrupts the development of healthy self/other boundaries but also represents major betrayal within relationships upon which they are developmentally dependent.

Thus, as might be expected, damage tends to be more extensive when the offender is a parent or stepparent. Conversely, the damage tends not to be as great if a nonoffending parent is supportive once the abuse is revealed (Conte & Schuerman, 1987). In addition to the issue of betrayal, the sources of developing dysfunctions include having become prematurely sexualized in a traumatic manner, the relative powerlessness of the child, and the stigma of being involved in such a relationship (Finkelhor & Browne, 1985). Treatment of child sexual abuse typically works toward diminishing the effects of these four underlying factors (Haugaard & Reppucci, 1988). Art and play therapy are found to be especially effective mediums for treating younger children who have been sexually abused (Johnston, 1997).

PAVING PATHWAYS ALONG MIDDLE CHILDHOOD SOCIAL AND EMOTIONAL MILESTONES: PREVENTING CHILD SEXUAL ABUSE

In years past, parents made token gestures at protecting children from sexual abuse with admonishments of "don't talk to strangers." Unfortunately, since most sexually abused children are victimized by parents, stepparents, relatives, or other adults with whom they have developed trusting relationships, this advice does not go far toward prevention (Alter-Reid et al., 1986).

Current efforts toward preventing child sexual abuse typically focus on providing presentations to school-age children. Long-term programs appear to be most effective, especially when they provide opportunity for children to become actively involved (Davis & Gidycz, 2000). Such programs educate children regarding what sexual abuse is, who could potentially offend, and what they can do to protect themselves. In the process, these programs also attempt to instill understanding of the following concepts (Conte et al., 1985; Finkelhor, 1986):

▶ Children have the right to control access to their bodies, and some parts of the body are private.
▶ There are many ways people touch one another. Some touching feels good, some bad, and some can be confusing.
▶ If they do not like the way an adult wants to touch them, they have the right to say no, resist, or run away if need be.

> ► Some secrets should not be kept, such as when an adult attempts to coerce a child into not telling anyone about "bad" touching.
> ► If inappropriate touching occurs, the child should tell a trusted adult, and keep telling until the abuse stops.

However, the most important element for both preventing or surviving child sexual abuse is the existence of a strong relationship with a supportive parent—someone the child can trust to listen to his or her complaints, put an end to any abuse or preliminary overtures, and provide a warm, caring, and safe environment (Kendall-Tackett et al., 1993).

EMOTIONS AND MIDDLE CHILDHOOD

What advances in development occur in the school-age child's experiencing and expression of emotions?

The school-age child experiences a vast complement of nuances and contradictions within emotional states. The school-age child is better than the preschooler at recognizing the emotions represented by the facial expressions of others, which contributes to his or her own emotional reacting (Gosselin & Simard, 1999). The most notable advance at this age is the child's development of a capacity for **emotional regulation** (Thompson, 1994). Can the child exert some control over whether or not an emotion occurs? Can the child purposely maintain desired emotional experiences or shorten the duration of undesirable ones? Can the child moderate the intensity of a feeling state? Emotionality affects a child's ability to control behavior, and behavioral control is clearly a necessary component for establishing competence (Cicchetti, 1996). During middle childhood, children become much better skilled at moderating their behavior when emotionally provoked, with girls succeeding to a greater extent than boys (Murphy et al., 1999; Underwood et al., 1999).

The ability to regulate emotions and level of emotional intensity is strongly tied to social functioning. For example, if Debbie feels extremely upset every time her playmates don't want to play the game she would prefer, her intense feelings are likely to interfere with her ability to negotiate a satisfactory common ground. If she typically resorts to tantrums in the face of conflict, she may also very well find herself without any friends with whom to negotiate. Measures of emotionality early in middle childhood predict not only the quality of current social status but also the social competence of children later in middle childhood (Eisenberg, Fabes et al., 1997). The Tried . . . . and True boxes on pages 396–397 take a closer look at the relationship between emotionality and social competence.

Individual differences in the ability to regulate emotions are influenced by inborn temperament (Rothbart & Bates, 1997). The temperamentally sensitive child is likely to have more difficulty taming the dragons within than the child inheriting a calmer temperament. Skill at shifting attention toward or away from specific stimuli plays a role, since management of emotions requires attending to or ignoring certain aspects of emotionally charged feelings or situations (Hinshaw, 1992). Children's observations of how their parents cope with emotions teaches them specific modes of self-regulation that they often emulate (Kliewer et al., 1996). During middle childhood, children also begin to experience varying levels of success in applying their advancing cognitive creativity. They may manage emotional situations by reminding themselves "next game, our team will cream them," or "just close your eyes, this will soon all be over" (Altshuler & Ruble, 1989).

Children of this age endeavor to mold their emotional responding according to perceived social rules and desired outcomes. Thus the emotionality we actually observe changes as they learn to hide or fake emotional expressions in order to appear to conform and/or try to get their way (Harris, 1989). Among these social requirements are perceptions regarding gender, one message being that boys are not supposed to cry or reveal vulnerability when they are upset (Bly, 1990).

Normal Emotionality

Several developments converge during middle childhood that contribute toward new routines of emotional experiencing. Let's take the example of Jake. During his preschool years he was constantly supervised. He was aware of certain expectations regarding his social behavior but was allowed considerable leeway. His relatively unsophisticated cognitive ability kept the world and his self-awareness fairly simple and clear-cut.

Upon reaching school-age Jake spends less time under direct, one-on-one supervision. He therefore faces more conflict or difficulties on his own, suffering the consequences of social blunders yet also able to take fuller credit for his successes. As was described in the previous chapter, the higher standards of expected performance and the increasing number of performance domains introduce new twists to Jake's experiences of stress and anxiety. His greater perceptiveness regarding the world and his own inner workings open up both contradictions and possibilities, requiring healthy emotional processing as Jake considers, reacts to, and reflects upon his choices.

Jake's understanding of his emotions is also becoming more advanced. When experiencing mixed feelings, he has developed a fuller understanding of how he or others can feel two emotions at the same time (Arsenio & Kramer, 1992). He also recognizes that his emotional reaction to a situation can be very different from that of one of his playmates (Gnepp & Klayman, 1992).

How do school-age children express severe emotional conditions, and how can these be treated?

Excessive Emotional States

Following the Springfield school shooting incident described earlier, public forums abounded. How could this have happened? These things didn't use to happen in schools. What is happening to kids these days? There were flurries of hypotheses: Kids aren't spanked enough. They're messed up because they've been spanked. There's too much violence on TV. Guns are too easy to get. School personnel aren't attentive enough. Parents aren't involved any more. Parents just don't care.

BOX 13.1   Negative emotions and social status

Eisenberg, N., Guthrie, I. K., Fabes, R. A., Reisner, M., Murphy, B. C., Holgren, R., Maszk, P., & Losoya, S. (1997). The relations of regulation and emotionality to resiliency and competent social functioning in elementary school children. *Child Development, 68,* 295–311.

HOW DOES A CHILD'S PERSONAL STYLE OF MANAGING emotions affect social competence? Nancy Eisenberg and her colleagues investigated this question by looking at the relationship between negative emotionality and social status. They examined 199 elementary school children, about half boys and half girls, in grades kindergarten through third grade. They gathered information about the children using several assessment measures.

The teachers provided information about the participants' emotionality by filling out measures using two different assessment methodologies. One required that teachers rate students using a seven-point Likert scale, indicating the degree to which they agreed or disagreed with a certain item. The teachers' choices for the emotionality scale ranged from "never" to "always," in response to items such as "When this child experiences anxiety, it is normally very strong."

The second emotionality assessment measure was a *Q-sort*. Q-sorts typically involve a set of cards with one item on each card. The rater is asked to arrange the cards in order according to which items seem most or least true. Q-sorts are useful for mitigating the tendency of some responders to simply rate items at all highest or lowest values, eliminating the nuances reflected by indication of degree. In this study the emotionality Q-sort contained items such as "Cries easily" and "Is calm and easy-going." The scores from the two measures were combined into a single emotionality score.

Social status was also determined by using two measures, one provided by the participants' teachers and another provided by classmates. The teachers responded to a popularity measure using a four-point scale containing items such as "This child finds it hard to make friends." The peer raters were given a list of classmates who were participants and were asked to assign each child on the list a single-number rating based on a five-point likability scale. A 5 meant "you play with the child a lot—that he or she is like a best friend"; a 1 meant "you do not play together because you do not want to." Each participant's peer ratings were averaged into a single score.

When emotional negativity and social status scores were compared, the teachers' emotionality ratings significantly correlated with both the teacher ratings of popularity and the student ratings of likability. As is usually the case for statistical analyses made up of correlations alone, the data do not tell us whether children are unpopular because of their negative emotionality or if their negative emotionality is a result of being unpopular. We might suspect that both are true.

Additional elements of this particular study looked at the variables that seem to mediate the relationship between emotionality and social competence. A child's ability to shift or sustain attention seems to play a major role. If children can find ways to distract themselves from their worries or move away from negative thinking by looking at their experiences in a more positive light, they may succeed in keeping their emotional reactivity from interfering with the development of social competence.

Tried

BOX 13.2   Cognitive therapy for school-age children

..... and True

"I'M JUST NOT ANY GOOD AT ANYTHING," 11-YEAR-OLD Rolanda sighed, sad and dejected-looking as she sat with her school counselor.

"Really?" Mr. Clark says. "That's hard for me to believe. I can think of several things you would be good for right here in this office."

He opened the office door and invited her to stand against it.

"See?" he said. "You're doing a great job of keeping the door open."

He continued to lead her around the room, setting up various simple roles Rolanda could easily fulfill. When Mr. Clark asked her to lean on a stack of papers so the breeze from the window could not blow them around, Rolanda suppressed a giggle. Mr. Clark smiled with her.

"Yes, this is silly, isn't it. But it's really not true that you aren't good at anything, is it?"

Negative emotionality is frequently driven or accompanied by negative thinking. Cognitive-behavioral strategies can help children look at how they evaluate their world, and how their evaluations affect their emotions. By teaching them how to gather information in a more accurate, "scientific" manner such as Mr. Clark showed Rolanda, therapists and counselors show them how they can ease negative emotionality by altering how they look at things (Wilde, 1996).

Rolanda's negative emotionality emerged because of her negative evaluation of herself after failing to be chosen for the Hummingbird Club, the top choir at her school. The cognitive distortion fueling her reaction is called *overgeneralization*. Because she did not succeed at one task, she has generalized that observation to mean that she is a failure at everything. Believing this, of course she feels sad and dejected!

Mr. Clark continues to work with Rolanda. He has her create a list of all the different things she can think of that she does well, including academic subjects, ways she helps out at home, special skills and activities, and getting along with friends. With a little encouragement she comes up with a list of seven competencies. He then has her list a few things she does not do well. As they look over the two lists he asks her, "So are you a failure, or are you a competent person?" He helps her conclude that she is neither. She is simply a person who does some things well and some things not so well, the same as everybody else. He moves on to show her the relationship between negative thinking and her emotions.

"Rolanda, when you find yourself thinking, 'I'm not any good at anything,' how do you feel?"

"It makes me feel really bad."

"Yes, I can imagine it would. If I thought I wasn't good at anything I would feel really bad, too. Suppose instead you said to yourself, 'I might not be good enough at singing to get into the Hummingbird Club, but I am good at double-dutch jump rope, fraction problems, and keeping secrets my friends tell me.' Then how do you feel?"

"Well, I still feel bad because I didn't get into the Hummingbird Club. But I don't feel as bad as I did when I thought I couldn't do anything."

"That's a great observation! And you know what? That's what makes *you* in charge of how good or bad you feel. Everybody feels a little badly when they fail at something. But you have the power to decide what you will say to yourself about it. If you tell yourself you are a failure, you will feel even worse. You might even give up and not try new things that you could actually do well! If you tell yourself it was only one thing and remind yourself of all the things you do well, sometimes you can make bad feelings go away completely."

Wilde, J. (1996). *Treating anger, anxiety, & depression in children and adolescents*. Washington, DC: Accelerated Development Press.

Most of us recall observing incidents during our own school years similar to this scene, in which troubled children are acting out frustrations that have become too great to bear.

Elizabeth Crews/Stock Boston

Actually, there have always been "broken" children (Heide, 1998). Their choices of how to act out their despair, however, have changed with the cultural norms. In decades past, a similarly disturbed youth might have latched onto a baseball bat, hatchet, or some other familiar item as he lashed out against the objects of his frustration. His behavior might still have been deadly, but the carnage would not have been so extensive or so horrific as to be the opening news story on two out of three major national networks.

While it is certainly true that child abuse can produce emotional difficulties as severe as this young man had demonstrated, mental illness develops more often from genetic influences than from inappropriate parenting practices (Bertelsen, 1979; Rutter et al., 1999b; Thapar & McGuffin, 1997). When does emotionality during middle childhood become significantly abnormal? Let's look at three areas of emotional difficulties: fears and anxiety, depression, and acting-out behavior.

Fears and Anxieties. While preschoolers' fears are more likely to stem from phenomena reminiscent of the "bogeyman," school-age children's fears reflect more of the realistic aspects of daily living (Muris et al., 2000; Weems et al., 2000). The most common normal fears for this age group include getting hurt or punished, school-related concerns such as test-taking and getting good grades, and socially based factors such as peer rejection, public humiliation, and the disapproval of adults (Greenspan, 1993; Reed et al., 1992). Twin studies suggest that susceptibility to fluctuations in anxiety is related to both nature and nurture in roughly equal proportions (Legrand et al., 1999).

As many as 20% of all children will at some point go through a period of excessive anxiety, and this percentage is rising (Beidel, 1991; Twenge, 2000). Most commonly when a child's anxiety goes beyond the norm it becomes evident in school attendance (Blagg, 1987; Elliott, 1999; Kearney, 2001). **School phobia** begins with vague complaints about school and expression of reluctance about attending, eventually progressing into refusal to go. It is even common in Japan, where cultural expectations strongly emphasize the importance of school (Kameguchi & Murphy-Shigematsu, 2001). No amount of persuasion, threats, punishments, or pressure from parents, teachers, and other officials reverses their refusal. Some children even say they want to attend and prepare to do so, but just can't make themselves go. When forced, they become extremely anxious and upset and may even have panic attacks. They may show a variety of bodily symptoms characteristic of anxiety disorders, such as headaches, stomachaches, nausea, dizziness, and sleep difficulties; and their behavior may progress into tantrums, acting-out, and depression (American Psychiatric Association, 1994). Refusing to go to school becomes more and more likely as they grow older, and if such children come from less actively involved home environments, the symptoms tend to be worse (Hansen et al., 1998).

Children suffering from school phobia differ from those who are truant (Blagg & Yule, 1984; Galloway, 1985). Truant children do not show the same anxious responding regarding school. And unlike parents of truant children, parents of children with school phobias are aware of their children's absence from school and know exactly where they are. The children themselves typically do not show the antisocial behavior often seen in truant children, who also are more likely to come from troubled home environments. School phobia can occur at younger ages, while truant behavior typically does not appear until age 11 or 12.

When school phobia first appears during middle school, the fears are often responses to accurately evaluated threats, such as excessive parental pressure, overcritical teachers, bullies, and/or rejection by peers. Boys and girls appear equally likely to suffer from school phobia, and there is some indication that it occurs more often among youngest or only children. Sometimes one of the parents also suffers from an anxiety or depressive disorder, and may reinforce clingy or dependent behavior. Genetic influences, especially inheritance of a shy temperament, have also been associated with child phobias (Beidel & Turner, 1998; Bernard & Joyce, 1984; Blagg, 1987; King & Ollendick, 1997; Pilkington & Piersel, 1991).

Cognitive therapists look at anxiety by examining how individuals evaluate the world around them (Beck, 1976; Ellis & Whitely, 1979). As anxious children evaluate the seriousness of a situation and the likelihood that they can cope, they often view situations as excessively threatening and their own resources as excessively limited. Thus their anxiety is in part fueled by low self-esteem, which encourages them to believe they need the constant approval or physical presence of a parent in order to be "safe" (Greiger & Boyd, 1983). By means of cognitive restructuring techniques, anxious children can learn to develop more realistic self-evaluations and world evaluations (Bernard & Joyce, 1984). Other strategies that have proved useful for children with school phobias are systematic desensitization and providing reinforcers for school attendance (Bernstein & Borchardt, 1991; Gordon & Young, 1976).

> ## PAVING PATHWAYS ALONG MIDDLE CHILDHOOD SOCIAL AND EMOTIONAL MILESTONES: HELPING THE ANXIOUS CHILD

Suppose you are a teacher and have a girl in your classroom who seems prone to excessive anxiety. You don't want to push her over the edge, but at the same time the learning process cannot occur without occasional constructive criticism and suggestions for improvements. How could you interact with this child in ways that would consider her oversensitivity and perhaps calm her fears? Following are some suggestions (McCarney et al., 1993):

▶ Encourage her to ask questions before and during assignments if there is anything she does not understand.

▶ Encourage her to check her work before turning it in.

▶ Provide her with tasks that can be self-checked so she does not need to endure as much correction by others.

▶ Make sure she has a number of opportunities for demonstrating those things she can do well and provide plenty of positive reinforcement when she does so.

▶ When possible, phrase feedback as additive rather than subtractive: "A better way to do that might be . . . " rather than "You aren't doing this right."

▶ Provide feedback early, before small problems become big ones.

▶ Avoid giving feedback in front of other children.

▶ Make sure constructive criticism is distributed equally among the students.

▶ Provide positive reinforcement for appropriate responses to constructive criticism.

▶ Rather than requiring immediate correction of missed items, develop a "new" assignment for the next day that incorporates what has yet to be learned.

▶ Allow her to try out new things in private before she will need to do them in front of others.

▶ Change those aspects of the environment that seem to contribute to stress or frustration, such as sitting next to someone who makes insensitive remarks.

▶ Reduce emphasis in the classroom on competitiveness and perfection.

Depression. Children normally experience episodes of sadness and frustration as they react to the ups and downs of daily living. When faced with setbacks, they may pout or withdraw for a while but after a brief period of mourning will bounce back for the next challenge. When children are clinically depressed, they have lost their "bounce." Instead of recovering from disappointments they continue in a downward spiral lasting two weeks or longer (American Psychiatric Association, 1994).

As many as 2% of all school-age children are clinically depressed, with some estimates going much higher. Unfortunately, depressive symptoms in children can easily be overlooked or misinterpreted, as they differ somewhat from those of depression in adults (Puura et al., 1998; Schacter & Romano, 1993). Clinically depressed children may show the usual extended periods of crying and sadness but alternatively may express their condition with acting-out, aggressive behavior, or temper tantrums. They may cling to parents and other caregivers or may withdraw from adults and friends alike. Sleep problems, "spacing out" or difficulty concentrating, loss of appetite, and weight loss are also common.

The development of childhood depression usually has its roots in heredity, yet interacts with psychosocial and other environmental factors (Kazdin, 1990). A twin study suggested that while both nature and nurture play roles, environmental influences are the more common source of depression during middle childhood (Eley et al., 1998). More often than adult depression, childhood depression tends to be accompanied by other disorders, especially conduct and oppositional disorders, anxiety disorders, and ADHD (Gotlib & Hammen, 1992; Thapar & McGuffin, 1997).

Whether occurring during adulthood or childhood, clinical depression is not to be ignored. Depressed children are not immune to considering and succeeding at suicide (Orbach, 1988). A variety of therapies have proven successful in alleviating symptoms of childhood depression (Bemporad & Lee, 1988). Sometimes just changing the environmental factors that contribute to feelings of frustration or deprivation can be enough to swing younger children back uphill. Various forms of counseling—especially those that include working with the parents—and some drug therapies have also been helpful.

PAVING PATHWAYS ALONG MIDDLE CHILDHOOD SOCIAL AND EMOTIONAL MILESTONES: HELPING THE DEPRESSED CHILD

Having a clinically depressed child is a frustrating if not terrifying experience for parents. While waiting for therapeutic efforts to take effect, parents are often concerned about how they should treat their child or what they can do that will help. Helpful interactions are those that acknowledge the presence of the disorder and its symptoms but continue to provide the warmth and structure of authoritative parenting. Following are some suggestions for parenting the depressed child (Fassler & Dumas, 1997; Oster & Montgomery, 1995):

► Treat the child the same as you always have. Continuing the usual family structure provides security.
► Express your caring for the child and find ways to indicate to the child that he or she is valued.

- ▶ Praise and compliment successes you observe even though they may be minor.
- ▶ When the child talks about thoughts and feelings, listen. Do not minimize or discount them as being "silly" or "no big deal."
- ▶ Acknowledge that the child is suffering. Clinical depression is excruciatingly painful. Let the child know that you are concerned about the pain he or she is experiencing.
- ▶ Share examples from your own life when things were not going well but turned out all right in the end. Children have not yet had enough life experience with disappointment to have learned the lesson that eventually "this, too, shall pass."
- ▶ Take all threats of suicide seriously.

Acting-Out Behavior. Acting-out behavior is a child's way of saying he or she is angry. It can range from simple misbehaviors, such as hiding older brother's favorite action figures, to more serious social misconduct: throwing major tantrums, hitting other children, or destroying property. All children engage in minor acting-out behaviors such as telling the occasional white lie or seeing if they can get away with taking something that is not theirs. However, when these behaviors are severe, form an ongoing pattern, or are continually done in ways that guarantee the perpetrator will get caught, it is more likely to be a symptom of a greater problem. When severe, these conditions may be assigned clinical diagnoses such as conduct disorder or oppositional defiant disorder (American Psychiatric Association, 1994).

This chapter and previous chapters described a number of conditions that may coincide with acting-out behavior. Most commonly the child is reacting to something happening in his or her world that feels intolerable. The source of difficulty may be within, as is the case with anxiety, depression, or certain learning disabilities. At other times the triggers are external, such as problems at school, changes in family constellations, frustrations produced by permissive or authoritarian parenting, physical abuse, or child sexual abuse. Taking control of acting-out behavior requires that the underlying cause be identified and addressed.

> ## PAVING PATHWAYS ALONG MIDDLE CHILDHOOD SOCIAL AND EMOTIONAL MILESTONES: HELPING THE ACTING-OUT CHILD

While the cause is in the process of being remedied, the acting-out behavior may continue. Suppose you are an after-school child care worker and one of the boys in your group has parents who are divorcing. As he acts out his anger and fear, he has been picking fights with some of the other boys his age. His parents are aware of the problem and they are getting family therapy during this time of adjustment. Meanwhile the fighting continues. What would you do? Successful interventions are those that reduce the likelihood of conflictual situations or excessive frustration. Here are some suggestions (McCarney et al., 1993):

▶ Arrange that the boy does not spend time around the children with whom he is likely to get into fights or with any children who might be egging him on.

▶ Attempt to pair him up in activities with children who are likely to be a good influence.

▶ Maintain maximum supervision over this child, decreasing it over time as he assumes more control over his behavior.

▶ When you hear conflict emerging, intervene early so it does not escalate into physical fighting.

▶ Encourage the child to tell you about problems that occur with other children at the center.

▶ Describe in terms the boy can understand other ways he might react when problems such as these occur.

▶ Structure more of his time so he has less opportunity to get into trouble.

▶ When starting a new activity, make sure he knows the rules and is matched up with children who are likely to be compatible.

▶ Avoid involving him in activities in which he is likely to become over-stimulated.

▶ Make sure that the child is allowed to voice his opinions freely regarding situations in which he is likely to become upset.

▶ As always, provide plenty of praise and compliments when he handles situations well.

MORAL DEVELOPMENT

How does moral reasoning change during middle childhood?

After the Springfield school shooting, public opinion rushed in to condemn the status of today's youth. What the sweeping judgments of critics did not seem to consider was the behavior of other adolescents who were on the scene. One young man, a member of the wrestling team, lay bleeding on the floor. He saw that his girlfriend had also been shot; the gunman was continuing to shoot students. He knew something needed to be done. He jumped up and rushed the gunman, knocking him to the ground. As he attempted to wrest the gun away he was shot a second time through the hand. Several other students pounced on the struggling pair, eventually taking control of the weapons and subduing the gunman.

Later, when media interviewers asked this young hero what was going through his mind as he threw himself toward the armed teenager, he jokingly replied, "Poor judgment?" (CNN, May 24, 1998). But most likely multiple categories of judgment rattled around as he considered his options. Why was his

On August 10, 1998, Jake Ryker received the Honor Medal with Crossed Palms for his bravery during the Springfield school shooting incident (*The Oregonian,* August 11, 1998). The award is Scouting's highest honor for bravery and has been given to only 126 other individuals in its 50-year history. Ironically, on this same day the Jonesboro school shooting perpetrators were sentenced for their actions. All three major national television networks provided heavy coverage of the sentencing of the shooters during the evening news. Neither of the evening national news broadcasts by the two major networks that I saw mentioned the award being given to the Springfield hero. What impact do you think this biased media coverage has on society's view of today's youth, and what are the role model effects such coverage may produce in youngsters?

Ken Lax/Photo Researchers

immediate impulse to jump the gunman, rather than run for cover? We cannot help but suspect that on some level moral judgments were making their presence known.

Moral judgments reflect personal beliefs about what is right or wrong, the contents of what we commonly call the conscience. Stage theorists make certain assumptions about how moral thinking is fueled. They believe that some forms of moral reasoning are better than others and that the more a child matures, the more advanced, or "better," the child's moral reasoning will become. The general populace appears to be in agreement with these assumptions. College students who have no knowledge of stage theory nevertheless acknowledge some forms of moral reasoning as being more mature or socially appropriate than others (Thomas, 1997).

The previous chapter described how school-age children are busily incorporating and developing a variety of new reasoning skills. They are also advancing in their ability to recognize the emotional aftermath of their moral choices, increasing the self-reinforcers of any pride or guilt that may result (Bybee, 1998; Eisenberg, 2000; Shorr & McClelland, 1998). These changes pave the way for increasingly sophisticated moral reasoning, as the children become more and more influenced by their conscience and less by how others might view their behavior (Leverato & Donati, 1999). One of their major transitions is moving away from egocentrism and edging toward **sociocentrism** (Biggs, 1976). As this process unfolds, they build their capacity for recognizing the existence of others' needs, values, perceptions, and inner processes and acknowledge that these factors may be very different from what they themselves may experience.

The ability to recognize the needs and perspectives of others is a primary component for socialized moral reasoning (Litvack-Miller et al., 1997). Moral reasoning hierarchies typically range from the very self-centered view of the toddler and preschooler to the more other-focused view of adult moral thinking (Eisenberg & Fabes, 1991). The progression also reflects a shift from the young child's biases toward concreteness to the more abstract reasoning capacity of the adolescent and adult (Carlo et al., 1996). When read stories with moral themes, younger children are found to be less able to identify "the moral of the story" than are children approaching adolescence (Narvaez, Gleason et al., 1999). Advances also parallel a child's improving capacity for taking multiple perspectives into account (Carpendale, 2000).

Lawrence Kohlberg was first to examine this process as a series of stages. By studying the reasoning strategies of men and boys, he came to the conclusion that moral maturity is a product of how extensively an individual incorporates the principles of justice, fairness, and the treating of all human beings with respect (Kohlberg, 1981, 1984). Carol Gilligan (1982) took issue with Kohlberg's conclusions, pointing out that his findings were restricted to moral judgments made by members of the male gender. She found that girls and women were more likely to base their moral conclusions on compassionate caring and feeling responsibility for the well-being of their fellow human beings (Heckman, 1995). Table 13.1 shows that although these two sets of principles differ throughout the five stages, both move from a self-centered to an other-centered world view (Gump et al., 2000). Moral reasoning progresses as a series of between-stage transitionings, then consolidating new sociocentric views into more advanced forms of moral decision making (Thoma & Rest, 1999).

Some individual differences affect the progress of prosocial thinking. As might be expected, children who practice self-reflection are more likely to engage in prosocial moral reasoning, while those who are more hedonistic in their thought processes tend to be more self-centered in their moral decision making. Girls tend to show more of this type of reflectiveness than do boys, and also seem less likely to pursue prosocial behavior as a means of gaining approval (Carlo et al., 1996). Children who enjoy secure attachment to their mothers tend to progress more quickly (Van Lange et al., 1997). Those who demonstrate more empathic responding are also more likely to be skilled at emotional regulation (Eisenberg, Fabes, Murphy et al., 1996). Differing cultural emphases on interdependence, collectivism, and interpersonal closeness can affect the extent to which children learn prosocial thinking (Knight et al., 1981).

The proof of the pudding, so to speak, is whether or not children apply their level of moral reasoning to their behavior. They do, and education can help: Children exposed to increasingly higher levels of moral reasoning and given direct instruction in how to perform moral decision making showed increased ability to apply moral thinking to their behavior (Grier & Firestone, 1998).

Thus we see how children adapt their moral thinking styles to fit the physical and social demands and constraints of their worlds. Yet healthy adjustment

TABLE 13.1

Moral hierarchies representing Kohlberg's principle of justice and Gilligan's principle of compassion. Adapted from R. M. Thomas. *An Integrated Theory of Moral Development,* Westport, CT: Greenwood Press. Copyright © 1997. Reproduced with permission.

Level	Principle of Justice	Principle of Compassion
I	Moral choices seek to avoid punishment. "Wrong" behaviors are those that result in being punished.	Feels no sympathy for those in need and feels no pleasure when others succeed. People should look out only for themselves.
II	Other people's needs are recognized, but only for bartering value: "You scratch my back and I'll scratch yours."	Feels sympathy at times for friends, relatives, or pets that are in need, but feels no desire or obligation to offer help.
III	Conforms to a perception of "good boy" or "good girl," hoping to obtain others' approval by doing what is considered proper or fair.	Feels some sympathy for acquaintances or friends in need, and feels some obligation to help them if urged to do so by authority figures.
IV	Bases moral choices on the rules of the social system and laws of social order, believing that people are morally obligated to obey laws.	Feels sympathy for friends, acquaintances, and pets in need, and also feels obligated to help them if it does not require much personal sacrifice.
V	Bases moral choices on rules and laws, but also recognizes that these are relative constructs that can be changed. Certain human rights, such as physical well-being and liberty, take priority over rules.	Feels deep sympathy and some obligation for friends and relatives in need, as well as joy for their triumphs. Also feels some sympathy for needy people who are not friends or relatives.
VI	Bases moral choices on principles of justice and fairness, believing that all individuals share the same rights and should be respected.	Feels deep sympathy for and obligation to help close friends and relatives, feels joy for their triumphs and for those of people who are not close, even strangers.

requires that children's thinking styles also fit how children perceive themselves: the self-concept.

What affects a school-age child's self-concept and self-esteem, and what can parents do to foster good self-esteem?

SELF-CONCEPT AND SELF-ESTEEM

How do self-concept and self-esteem fit together? Self-concept is the broader construct derived from our perceptions of our cognitions, emotions, and choices of behavior. Self-esteem is the piece of our self-concept tied more closely to self-worth, how we evaluate ourselves and how we feel about ourselves based on that evaluation (Hattie, 1992). Let's look at the middle childhood passage through these constructs individually.

Self-Concept

During middle childhood, children shift away from defining themselves primarily on the basis of externally supported observations such as physical characteristics, roles, and behaviors. They move toward more mentally conceptualized attributes such as psychological traits, ideologies, beliefs, and values (Damon & Hart, 1988). Their self-concept often interacts with what they experience as enjoyable, such as considering themselves to be achievement-oriented because they like school and vice versa (Strein, 1993).

Their developing perceptions of who they are also establish more of the groundwork for understanding the relative continuity of the self's characteristics. When school-age children observe themselves performing a certain behavior such as being helpful, they intuit that they are characterized by that particular trait (Harter, 1986). As they make such personal observations, they tend to view these traits as permanent, having not yet incorporated the understanding that traits, values, and beliefs are likely to undergo shifts and amendments during the course of the life span (Benenson & Dweck, 1986).

In school-age children's process of moving away from egocentrism and closer to sociocentrism, **social comparison** begins playing a major role in how they view themselves (Marsh et al., 1991). They observe what their peers are doing and consider how their own characteristics or abilities compare. Their observations of those around them also help school-age children develop a fuller understanding of what society expects from them (Markus & Nurius, 1984). Out of these observations and conceptualizations they begin differentiating between the **ideal self**—what they would prefer to be like—versus the **real self**—the actual characteristics they perceive themselves as possessing—and strive to behave as the ideal self would dictate (Maccoby, 1980).

Self-Esteem

The inflated self-esteem of the preschooler gives way to more accurate self-evaluation during middle childhood. At first, children make note of how well they can perform certain tasks or how the results of their efforts compare to those of other children. Gradually they pull together such observations into an overall impression of their self-worth (Harter, 1982). Thus children who have been blessed with innate abilities and/or easy-going temperaments may have a leg up in the process of developing good self-esteem. However, ability alone does not guarantee good self-evaluation. Children who perceive themselves as being skilled within the domains they consider to be most important tend to have the best self-esteem. Therefore at some point children also need to make the judgment that those aspects of themselves that stand out are of value (Harter, 1990).

Children of diverse cultures growing up in environments where their ethnicity is valued may actually have higher self-esteem than do children not having close ties to an ethnic group (Allen & Majidi-Ahi, 1989; Garbarino, 1985). Yet at the same time as they become integrated with the mainstream culture, they risk losing such ties, creating a difficult balancing act that can affect self-esteem (Jones, 1985). Alternatively, if barred from opportunities in the mainstream culture that promote feelings of competence, they may seek out destructive ways of succeeding within the subculture that embraces them, such as becoming involved with gang activities (Ogbu, 1986).

PAVING PATHWAYS ALONG MIDDLE CHILDHOOD SOCIAL AND EMOTIONAL MILESTONES: ENCOURAGING GOOD SELF-ESTEEM

A child's belief in his or her ability to succeed plays a dramatic role not only in skill development but also in development of overall competency (Skinner, 1995). What can be done to improve a child's chances?

Thomas is an active, athletically built fourth-grader. He is one of the star players on the soccer team and is admired and sought out on the playground by classmates because of his ability. The relative ease with which he earns "A's" on assignments puts him in favor with teachers as well. However, Thomas's popularity is not all it seems to be. While other students may look up to him, he associates only with the social elite and looks down on everyone else. He never misses an opportunity to comment on others' mistakes or inadequacies. He manipulates and interrupts during class discussions, occasionally monopolizing its flow. When teachers or classmates do not go along with his demands or intrusions, he pouts or pulls back into an angry withdrawal.

How would you describe the status of Thomas's self-esteem? He behaves like a child with low self-esteem. In spite of his apparent gifts and abilities, he is dependent upon putting down or controlling everyone else in order to perceive himself well. His friendships are organized around bolstering his low self-esteem, as he seeks acceptability through high-status associations.

Scott does not have Thomas's prowess at sports and academics, but he tries hard in class and earns satisfactory grades. Teachers enjoy having Scott in the classroom because of his positive, friendly attitude. He is willing to assist or support other students during their academic efforts and compliments students like Thomas when they do well. During play other children enjoy having him in their midst. He is a good team player, able to smooth over the rough spots in the give and take of play activity. His friendships and associations emerge from common interests rather than social status. Scott's behavior indicates that he most likely has good self-esteem. He feels no need to put others "in their place," become the center of attention, or establish high-status friendships in order to experience good self-evaluation. His self-assurance and feelings of worth already flow from within.

As was mentioned in Chapter 10, parents usually play the greatest role in a child's development of good self-esteem. The warm, supportive disciplinary style of the authoritative parent continues to win hands down in this respect. What specifically can parents do during the middle childhood flurry of skill building to enhance this desired outcome? Following is a description of how parents can point their children in the direction of feeling good about themselves and experiencing confidence in their abilities (Joseph, 1994):

▶ *Provide unconditional positive regard.* Carl Rogers (1951) introduced the concept of **unconditional positive regard**. This style of interpersonal interaction centers on treating others as valued regardless of their strengths, weaknesses, talents, abilities, mistakes, successes, or failures. One way parents accomplish this end is by participating in quality time with their children. When children receive at least 20 minutes of undivided one-on-one parental attention 3 or 4 times a week, they learn that their ideas and interests are valued. During times of discipline, parents indicate their child's value by remembering to criticize the behavior rather than the child, and not becoming rejecting when the child errs.

▶ *Set the child up to succeed.* The first step in directing children toward success is to become aware of their strengths, limitations, talents, temperament, and vulnerabilities. Having done so, parents can help their children set realistic goals. As they work toward their goals children benefit from receiving feedback that is productive—direct, specific, objective, accurate, and not derogatory.

▶ *Empower the child.* A child's sense of empowerment can be encouraged by requiring that he or she behave responsibly, be accountable for his or her actions, and take the initiative to follow through on commitments and responsibilities. Empowerment flounders when parents make excuses for children's irresponsibility, protect them from experiencing the normal consequences for their actions, and make all of their decisions for them.

▶ *Foster good social skills.* Effective social interaction requires learning to perform skills such as perspective-taking, communicating effectively, showing empathy, negotiating, and problem-solving. Chapter 10 described a number of strategies parents can use to promote emotional intelligence, an important foundation for learning social skills (see pages 308–309).

▶ *Help the child become self-reinforcing.* Children learn to reinforce themselves because they have received the benefit of others reinforcing them first. Parents can promote such learning by praising significant effort in addition to actual successes, making sure compliments reflect their efforts or accomplishments accurately. Drawing attention to the child's feelings of satisfaction after completing a task or performing a good deed directs the child toward important inner sources of self-reinforcement.

▶ *Encourage positive thinking.* When encountering unfortunate circumstances and episodes of frustration or failure, children benefit from learning to use self-talk that minimizes the negatives and maximizes the positives. In addition to walking children through real-life situations, parents can assist the learning process by reading stories about protagonists who use such techniques.

▶ *Teach delay of gratification.* By using a problem-solving mode, parents can help children work through the pros and cons of immediate versus delayed gratification in specific situations the child might encounter or with respect to goals they may want to achieve.

▶ *Model all of the above.* Children learn what they see. If the parent's behavior is different from what the parent is teaching, lessons taught may go for naught.

SUMMARY

Personality Development

Freud's observation of the latency stage as a time of nonsexual calm more likely reflects that school-age children have learned that sexuality is private. During middle childhood, children develop skills and personal attributes relevant to succeeding in their culture. Their subsequent experiences with success or failure result in feelings of industry or inferiority with respect to the goal of competence. They develop competence in the areas of adjusting to the school milieu, establishing peer relationships, learning to play by the rules, and achieving academically.

Relationships

Relationships with others affect competence. Children develop competence when parents model well-adjusted behavior and also allow increasing independence as their children attempt to apply social rules; that is, they practice authoritative parenting. When parents divorce and remarry there is an initial disruption to child adjustment, but most children eventually readjust and become competent individuals. The child's predivorce personality traits or personal adjustment, gender, new stresses emerging from the divorce situation, and parental management of conflict all affect a child's postdivorce adjustment. Quality of peer relationships rather than their number appears to affect competence.

Child sexual abuse is observed in many cultures and is relatively common, experienced by about one in four girls and one in six boys. The resulting cognitive, emotional, and psychosomatic symptoms interfere with healthy adjustment and may result in serious, long-term psychopathology. The degree of seriousness is determined by the amount of physical trauma, betrayal, and boundary violation reflected by the acts. Psychotherapeutic treatment of child sexual abuse victims addresses these factors, as well as issues of empowerment, premature sexualization, and stigma. Prevention programs aim toward teaching children they have the right to control their bodies, the difference between "good" and "bad" touching, and what to do if someone attempts or succeeds in victimizing them.

Emotions and Middle Childhood

During middle childhood, children develop a greater capacity for emotional regulation. Increasing cognitive ability and more varied independent life experiences result in more complex emotional states, as well as greater understanding of others' emotions. Anxiety, depression, and acting-out behaviors may reach clinical levels in some children. Cognitive and behavioral therapies, prescription drugs, and careful management by parents and other caregivers can help children overcome severe emotional conditions.

Moral Development

Moral reasoning progresses from being self-focused and concrete to other-focused and abstract, fueled during middle childhood by increasing sociocentrism and advancing cognitive abilities. Stage theorists suggest that moral reasoning advances along continuums based on certain moral principles, such as justice, fairness, compassionate caring, and feelings of responsibility for one's fellow human beings. Differences such as a tendency to practice personal reflectiveness, empathic ability, mother-child attachment, and cultural milieu affect a child's rate of advancement.

Self-Concept and Self-Esteem

During middle childhood, children's self-concepts become increasingly less behaviorally oriented and more abstract, incorporating psychological traits, beliefs, and values. Social comparison helps them establish and develop a working relationship between their real and ideal selves. Self-esteem becomes more realistic as children recognize their shortcomings yet learn to value their strengths. Parents can help children develop good self-esteem by providing unconditional positive regard, helping them set attainable goals, encouraging their sense of empowerment, fostering their social skills, helping them become self-reinforcing, encouraging positive thinking, teaching delay of gratification, and acting as a good role model of skills taught.

KEY TERMS

competence   latency stage   sociocentrism
emotional regulation   real self   unconditional positive regard
ideal self   school phobia
industry versus inferiority   social comparison

CONCEPT REVIEW

1. Freud's observations of the school-age child's _____ stage as being a time of _____ calm were more likely the result of school-age children having conformed to the influences of their _____ .

2. Erikson pointed out that during their psychosocial stage of _____ versus _____ school-age children learn the survival skills relevant to their society, which leads them toward developing a sense of _____ .

3. The four basic areas within which children establish competence are adjusting to _____ , establishing _____ relationships, learning to function within _____ , and _____ achievement.

4. Parents foster development of competence when they use the _____ rather than _____ parenting style and when they _____ competence.

5. Most children who experience their parents' divorcing and remarrying grow up to be _____ . Poor outcome is associated with oversensitive _____ , lower level of _____ , poorer _____ adjustment, _____ from excessive situational changes, how divorcing parents manage _____ , and/or a tendency to appraise events _____ .

6. Children meet greater success while working on group tasks when group members are _____ . Middle childhood friendships are most likely to occur among children with _____ traits. The positive impact of friendships depends more on _____ than _____ of friendships.

7. Children who are sexually abused are likely to develop _____ problems such as anxiety, sadness, anger, and shame; _____ difficulties such as withdrawal, acting-out, and suicide attempts; _____ patterns such as self-blame and extreme distrust; and _____ symptoms such as stomachaches and headaches.

8. Child abuse prevention programs teach children how to identify
   _____, who could _____, and how they can
   _____ themselves.

9. The school-age child has a greater capacity for demonstrating emotional
   _____. How well the child can do so is related to
   _____, _____ abilities, and how
   _____ cope with adversity.

10. Development of mental illness is generally affected more by
    _____ influences than _____ practices
    during childhood.

11. The most common form of anxiety disorder during middle childhood is
    _____. Teachers can help fearful children by using strategies
    that take into account their _____.

12. Children's clinical depressions are often overlooked because they include
    symptoms that differ from those of adults, such as _____ and
    _____ behavior; and often coexists with _____.
    Parents are most helpful to depressed children when interactions acknowl-
    edge the presence of _____ and continue to provide both
    _____ and _____.

13. Acting-out behaviors develop in reaction to either _____
    or _____ events that are experienced by the child as
    _____. Acting-out children can be helped by interventions
    that reduce the likelihood of encountering _____ situations
    or excessive _____.

14. Kohlberg's and Gilligan's moral reasoning hierarchies reflect how a child pro-
    gresses from a _____ to a _____ orientation,
    and shifts from using _____ reasoning to using more
    _____ reasoning.

15. Children's moral reasoning advances more quickly if they practice self-
    _____, enjoy secure _____, and/or have
    demonstrated a capacity for _____ responding.

16. School-age children typically base their self-concept on what they
    _____, how they _____, and social
    _____.

17. School-age children are more likely to develop good self-esteem if they see
    themselves as _____ within domains that are
    _____. Having close ties with an ethnic group has a
    _____ effect on a child's self-esteem.

18. Parents can direct children toward good self-esteem by means of
_____ positive regard, arranging opportunities for and
challenges in which the particular child can _____, helping
the child feel _____, teaching good _____
skills and how to be self- _____, and encouraging
_____ thinking and tolerance for delay of
_____ .

1) latency; nonsexual; society/culture; 2) industry; inferiority; competence; 3) school; peer; rules; academic; 4) authoritative; authoritarian; model; 5) well-adjusted; temperament; intelligence; predivorce; stress; conflict; negatively; 6) friends; similar; quality; quantity; 7) emotional; behavioral; cognitive; physical; 8) sexual abuse; offend; protect; 9) regulation; temperament; attending; parents; 10) genetic; parenting; 11) school phobia; oversensitivity; 12) temper tantrums; acting-out; other disorders; symptoms; warmth; structure; 13) internal; external; intolerable; conflictual; frustration; 14) self-centered; sociocentric; concrete; abstract; 15) reflection; attachments; empathic; 16) enjoy; behave; comparisons; 17) skilled; valued; positive; 18) unconditional; succeed; empowered; social; reinforcing; positive; gratification

RESOURCES FOR FURTHER READING

Coles, R. (1997). *The moral intelligence of children: How to raise a moral child.* New York: Plume.

Fassler, D. G., & Dumas, L. S. (1997). *"Help me, I'm sad": Recognizing, treating, and preventing childhood and adolescent depression.* New York: Viking.

Greenspan, S. I. (1993). *Playground politics: Understanding the emotional life of your school-age child.* New York: Addison-Wesley.

Joseph, J. M. (1994). *The resilient child: Preparing today's youth for tomorrow's world.* New York: Insight Books.

Juvonen, J., & Wentzel, K. R. (Eds.), (1996). *Social motivation: Understanding children's school adjustment.* New York: Cambridge University Press.

McCarney, S. B., Wunderlich, K. C., & Bauer, A. M. (1993). *The pre-referral intervention manual: The most common learning and behavior problems encountered in the educational environment,* 2nd ed. Columbia, MO: Hawthorne.

Miller, A. (1984). *Thou shalt not be aware: Society's betrayal of the child.* New York: Farrar, Straus, Giroux.

Neuman, M. G. (1998). *Helping your kids cope with divorce—the sandcastles way.* New York: Times Books.

Teolis, B. (1996). *Ready to use self-esteem and conflict-solving activities for grades 4–8.* West Nyack, NY: Center for Applied Research in Education.

INFOTRAC COLLEGE EDITION

For additional readings, explore InfoTrac College Edition, your online library. Go to http://www.infotrac-college.com/wadsworth and use the passcode that came on the card with your book. Try these search terms: acting out and children, child sexual abuse, children and depression, children and friendships, children and phobias, competence and children, divorce—children, moral development and children, remarriage and children, self-esteem and children, self-concept and children

CHILD DEVELOPMENT CD-ROM

Go to the Wadsworth Child Development CD-ROM for further study of the concepts in this chapter. The CD-ROM also includes quizzes and additional activities to expand your learning experience.

REFERENCES

For a list of references for this chapter, see the Wadsworth Psych Study Center Web site at: http://www.wadsworth.com/product/0534348092s

Adolescent Physical Development

FOCUS QUESTIONS

- ► How does onset of puberty affect an adolescent's overall development?

- ► What advances occur in brain and motor abilities during adolescence?

- ► Why do adolescents take unnecessary risks, and how can this tendency be minimized?

- ► What factors are at work as adolescents develop a view of sexuality?

- ► What are the consequences of the ways adolescents manage their sexuality?

- ► How can teen parents best adjust to their multiple tasks and roles?

- ► How do sleep and nutritional requirements relate to the adolescent growth spurt?

- ► How and why are eating disorders associated with adolescence?

- ► How effectively does the "War on Drugs" influence adolescent drug use?

OUTLINE

Body Growth
  Puberty
  Effects of Puberty
Brain Growth
Motor Development
Risk-Taking Behavior
  Paving Pathways: Reducing Risk-Taking Behavior
Sexuality
  Sexual Attitudes and Behaviors
  Pregnancy
  Life as a Teenage Parent
  Paving Pathways: Arranging Home Lives of Teenage Parents

Sexually Transmitted Diseases
Date Rape
Paving Pathways: Preventing Date Rape
Health Issues
Sleep
Nutrition
Eating Disorders
Paving Pathways: Preventing Eating Disorders
Smoking
Substance Use and Abuse
Paving Pathways: Treating and Preventing Drug Abuse

Thirteen-year-old Jessica and Brian had been dating for several weeks. Brian, a little on the shy side, had not yet even attempted to hold Jessica's hand. Jessica was beginning to become impatient.

One evening as they were walking home from the mall Jessica commented, "Isn't it interesting how men and women are just the right size and shape?"

"What do you mean?" asked Brian, a little confused.

"Like while we're standing, your arm is just the right length for reaching over and putting it around my shoulders."

"Really?" exclaimed Brian. "Let's stop in my Dad's shop on the way home. I want to get out a tape measure and see if you're right!"

Imagine what it would be like if your body made a number of sudden, strange transformations. Many a sci-fi flick has centered on ponderous scenarios involving werewolves, body snatchers, Jekyll and Hyde, and the like. A similar state of affairs is a confusing yet wondrous reality for the developing adolescent. Changes in hormonal activity and physical characteristics converge, creating not only new ways of experiencing the self but also whole new realms of behavioral possibilities (Brooks-Gunn & Reiter, 1990). As anatomy, physiology, and behavior simultaneously take on dramatically new characteristics, adolescence reveals its uniqueness as the only stage of human development coming even close to metamorphosis, a "mega-morphosis" so to speak (Giannetti & Sugarose, 1997).

BODY GROWTH

Throughout childhood the rate of growth of a child's height and weight slowly decreases. As Figure 14.1 shows, a blip in this tendency is the adolescent growth spurt. This sudden increase in growth rate typically lasts about three or four years. During the growth spurt, boys achieve their highest rate of growth at about age 14 and girls at about age 12 (Tanner, 1991). The actual age of this milestone may vary by two years in either direction.

The adolescent growth spurt begins with weight gain, often resulting in a mildly chubby appearance. This extra weight is quickly redistributed as adolescents shoot up in height. Height gain in middle childhood occurs chiefly through lengthening of limbs and during adolescence chiefly through lengthening of the trunk (Tanner, 1990).

During adolescence boys pull much further ahead of girls in height, remaining so through adulthood. Boys also undergo substantially more shoulder and muscle development than do girls. As compared to girls, they develop proportionally larger hearts and lungs and greater aerobic cardiovascular efficiency, which in combination with their greater muscle mass contributes to their superior physical strength. Adolescent girls show greater growth through their hips than do boys. Even at birth they possess wider pelvic openings, and this difference becomes more pronounced during adolescence as their bodies prepare for the possibility of reproduction (Tanner, 1990).

Until reaching adolescence boys and girls share similarly soft-looking facial features. As the skeletal and muscular advances of the adolescent growth spurt

FIGURE 14.1

Graph illustrating the adolescent growth spurt. Notice that on average the growth spurt occurs about two years earlier for girls than for boys. From Santrock, J. W. (1993). *Children*, 3rd ed., Madison, WI: Wm. C. Brown, p. 497. Reprinted by permission of McGraw-Hill Companies.

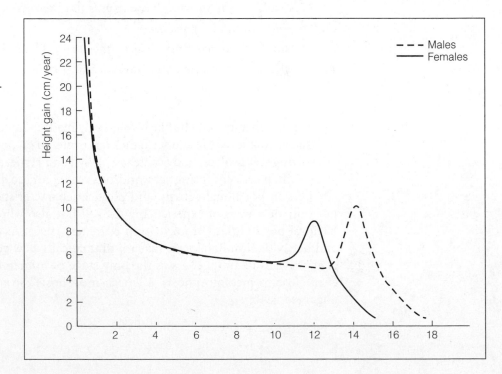

proceed, boys' faces become more defined and angular. As girls become young women, their facial definitions retain some of their soft appearance. The difference occurs because girls maintain a greater amount of subcutaneous fat than do boys, rounding out their features in spite of advancing skeletal and muscular growth (Burke & Hughes-Lawson, 1988; Cronk et al., 1983).

How does onset of puberty affect an adolescent's overall development?

Puberty

The sudden appearance of these growth patterns coincides with the hormonal changes that eventually lead to development of reproductive capacity. This phenomenal combination of structural growth, changes in body proportions, and maturing of sexual structures is called **puberty**. During puberty boys surge in the production of the hormone testosterone and girls in the production of estrogen.

Primary and Secondary Sex Characteristics. The resulting hormone-driven transformations are both directly and indirectly related to reproduction. Maturation of **primary sex characteristics** involves advancements of those structures directly related to producing a baby. Ovaries, fallopian tubes, the uterus, vagina, and skeletal birth canal structure become further developed in young women and the testes, penis, scrotum, seminal vesicles, and prostate gland become further developed in young men.

Michael Newman/PhotoEdit

Secondary sex characteristics simultaneously emerge. Both young men and young women sprout new body hair, especially in the pubic and underarm areas. They develop coarser and oilier skin and acne may become a problem. Their voices deepen as their larynxes lengthen and mature. While these changes occur in both genders, they appear in more robust form among young men.

Back in the sixties when I was coming of age, growing sideburns and/or moustaches was the style among my male cohorts. I remember noting that some of these attempts at fashion consisted of little more than uneven splotches of darkened peach fuzz and asking myself, "Am I supposed to be attracted by this?" My early confusion was a by-product of the phenomenon that some secondary sex characteristics, such as facial hair on young men, are often flaunted as billboards advertising sexual maturity. These characteristics are coveted by the developing adolescent, eager to display manhood or womanhood. For young women breast development is the secondary sex charac-

Young adolescents are especially concerned about body image, particularly regarding the emergence of their secondary sex characteristics.

teristic most enthusiastically tracked, often resulting in the use of "falsies" or "stuffing" as they attempt to hurry along the appearance of progress.

Menarche. **Menarche** is the milestone marking a girl's first evidence of the possibility of reproduction, heralded by the appearance of her first menstrual period. First menstrual periods are usually "dry runs," with ovulation often not occurring for another year or so. Full reproductive maturity will occur a few years later; in fact, a young woman's hips will not reach adult pelvic dimensions until six years after her first menstrual period (Lancaster, 1986). While adolescent girls may become pregnant before reaching full reproductive maturity, the immaturity of their reproductive structures poses a greater likelihood of miscarriage, low birth weight, and other complications (Golub, 1992).

The onset of menarche usually occurs around age 11 or 12, varying by about two years either way (Chumlea, 1982). Heredity appears to play a role in its timing. Mothers and daughters tend to be more similar than different in the age at which they begin menstruating (Damon et al., 1969). Puerto Rican, Mexican-American, and African-American girls tend to reach menarche earlier than Caucasian-American girls (Ten State Nutrition Survey, 1972; Westney et al., 1984). On the other hand, girls who have positive, harmonious family relationships tend to reach menarche earlier as well, suggesting one possible form of environmental influence (Ellis et al., 1999).

Over the last century, the age of onset of menarche has been dropping at the rate of about four months per decade (Petersen, 1979). Better nutrition, more advanced medical care, and other factors related to standard of living most likely contribute to the phenomenon. Consistent with such speculation are studies of girls' subcutaneous layers of fat. This layer of fat is necessary for storing the nutrients that will nourish a fetus and enrich breast milk. Girls who remain relatively lean are often slower to reach menarche (Garn, 1980).

Spermarche. **Spermarche** is the male counterpart of menarche, marked by a young man's first ejaculation of seminal fluid. It usually occurs as a result of masturbation or a "wet dream"—the popular name for nocturnal emissions that may or may not coincide with erotic dreaming. These early ejaculations, similar to early menstrual periods, are not yet evidence of full reproductive capacity. Viable sperm will be present in significant numbers in another year or so, and will increase in number over the next few years as the young man approaches full reproductive maturity (Muller et al., 1989; Thornburg & Aras, 1986).

Effects of Puberty

Onset of puberty is one of the few factors that concretely mark impending adulthood in Western cultures. What impact does this dramatic event have on adolescents? Compare the commentary of these two teenagers as they describe their pubescent passages (Martin, 1996, pg. 19):

Joe: "I was glad when I finally got taller and older. Being older you just get to do more, go out and stuff."

Nicole: "I didn't know what puberty meant. So am I supposed to be like a woman now? Or what? It seemed so awkward to be like a little girl with breasts, I couldn't have both, but I didn't want to be a woman, but like I didn't, it didn't feel right to me. It felt really awkward, but there wasn't anything to do about it."

Gender Differences. Boys and girls experience the onset of puberty differently. While they both have mixed feelings about it, feelings vary in degree and content (Brooks-Gunn, 1992). Ambivalence experienced by young men appears to surround their first ejaculation. As late as the 1970s most young men gleaned their repertoire of information or misinformation about ejaculation from friends, literature, or from the event itself. Correspondingly their first ejaculation often "scared the hell out of them" or led them to believe they were ill (Gaddis & Brooks-Gunn, 1985). They typically did not share the news of its occurrence with friends or parents.

Because young men are now more likely to learn about ejaculation from parents or educators, the first experience is much less aversive (Martin, 1996). In fact, spermarche is not anywhere near as memorable an event for boys as menarche is for girls (Zani, 1991). Nevertheless, boys still do not talk much about having reached that particular milestone, probably because its association with masturbation also associates it with cultural taboos.

The menstrual bleeding that occurs at menarche is a much more dramatic experience than first ejaculation. But as with spermarche, girls find it to be extremely aversive only when they have not been prepared to expect it. Otherwise they usually experience the event with a combination of excitement and apprehension. Unlike boys and their first ejaculation, girls usually share the news of their first period with close friends and female relatives. Girls are more likely to experience anxiety if they start menstruating in some non-normative situation, such as being away from home when it happens or being an early or late maturer (Gaddis & Brooks-Gunn, 1985; Martin, 1996).

Effect of Timing. The large time span over which a child can enter puberty has been associated with some developmental differences in personal adjustment. Boys who mature earlier seem to gain an advantage (Dubas et al., 1991; Simmons & Blyth, 1987). Because of their more mature appearance, adults treat them as if they were older, and greater adult expectations may act as a sort of self-fulfilling prophecy. Their physical superiority allows them to excel over the other children in athletics. And because they look older and more closely resemble the current socially desired stature for men, other children look up to them and often elect them to leadership roles. Thus early-maturing boys enjoy greater success in interacting with peers and develop a generally positive self-perspective. They also enjoy greater academic success during this time span, perhaps because of early brain maturation or because they receive greater attention and opportunities from teachers.

Being idealized and shoved to the forefront during the developmental years also has its downside (Martin, 1996). Early-maturing boys do not have to work to earn this acceptance, but later-maturing boys must prove themselves in order to define their social role and gain acceptance. They also have ample opportunity to work on coping skills while being excluded from the social elite, as well as dealing with being teased by peers for their childlike appearance. While the early maturers are being pushed prematurely into exhibiting a more adult-like stance, the later maturers have more opportunity to toy with identity possibilities and find a world view that works for them personally. Even during adolescence some late-maturing boys are already beginning to show the better personal adjustment expected from having worked through such experiences (Petersen & Crockett, 1985).

For adult men the consequences of having matured late or early are definitely mixed (Livson & Peskin, 1980; Martin, 1996). The early maturers were found as adults to be more self-controlled, responsible, and conformist, yet also more rigid and generally less satisfied with their lot in life. Those who matured later were found to be more impulsive and less likely to be leaders, yet were more flexible, independent, and in tune with their sense of identity. Even so, we must remember that differences based on maturational timing are found to be relatively slight in comparison with other factors affecting psychosocial development.

For girls the early advantage appears to go to those who mature later. While the early maturers enjoy the attention they may get as older boys take notice of their budding physiques, they are also uncomfortable with it and unsure of themselves (Clausen, 1975). Lacking the social maturity to know what to do with these attentions, they become prime candidates for being led astray, including involvement with activities such as drinking, smoking, and sexual activity (Caspi et al., 1993). Such partying behaviors may explain the lower academic achievement that sometimes characterizes early-maturing girls (Duncan et al., 1985). However, it is important to note that the early-maturing girls who do display these problems have typically shown some leanings toward such behavior before puberty, and the fact that earlier puberty is often found among children from stressful homes may also be playing a role (Caspi & Moffitt, 1991; Ellis & Garber, 2000).

Early-maturing girls also tend to have a greater propensity for obesity. Thus by the time the leaner, later-maturing girls have caught up, the early-maturing girls are comparatively shorter and more plump (Garn, 1980). In spite of the self-consciousness and dissatisfaction this may produce in early-maturing girls, by the time they become women they appear to be just as well adjusted as those who matured later (Stattin & Magnussen, 1990).

BRAIN GROWTH

What advances occur in brain and motor abilities during adolescence?

Fortunately, changes are taking place in the adolescent brain that bolster youngsters' decision-making ability as they manage their pubescent advances. Neural structures and functioning processes are fine-tuned over the next several years. Myelination of neurons continues through puberty (Jernigan et al., 1991). The most substantial brain growth during adolescence concerns strengthening of the glial cells bracing and nourishing the neurons (Yakovlev & Lecours, 1967). The number of interconnections between neurons continues to decrease, reflecting disintegration of redundant, unneeded, and inappropriate synapses (Feinberg, 1987). This shift in concentration of brain development energies appears to coincide with the emergence of formal operational reasoning, a Piagetian advance that is discussed in greater detail in Chapter 15 (Graber & Peterson, 1991).

MOTOR DEVELOPMENT

As structural and mental strength and efficiencies advance, the teenager's athletic skill, power, and physical endurance rapidly increase (Kemper & Verschurr, 1987). Because of their sudden changes in specific body proportions, especially in the interval between the lengthening of the trunk and the maturation of corresponding muscular support, adolescents often go through a clumsy, awkward stage. After about six months this discrepancy typically vanishes and coordination improves (Tanner, 1990).

While gross and fine motor skills improve for both genders, there are some gender differences regarding superiority in performing certain skills (Thomas & French, 1985). During adolescence boys' superiority at running speed and agility, jumping, and grip strength expands from slight to marked. Boys also become slightly better at tasks involving balance and gross eye-motor coordination. Girls tend to perform a little better than boys in the areas of fine eye-motor coordination and flexibility. Adolescents continue to benefit from regular physical exercise as they incorporate these advancing abilities. However, as was the case when they were younger, adolescents living in both rural or urban areas continue to engage in too little physical activity (Savage & Scott, 1998). Teenagers are more likely to engage in regular exercise and develop other good health habits if they have an understanding of the effect of their behavior on their health, place value on their physical health, and have parents who model good health habits (Jessor et al., 1998).

RISK-TAKING BEHAVIOR

Why do adolescents take unnecessary risks, and how can this tendency be minimized?

As active adolescents try out the new, improved versions of their bodies and spread their wings as a means of finding out who they are, risk-taking frequently follows. Normal adolescent risk-taking occurs for many reasons (Baumrind, 1987; Irwin & Millstein, 1992; Jessor, 1992; Kastner & Wyatt, 1997; Ponton, 1997; Siegler, 1997). Teenagers may engage in risky behavior in order to gain peer acceptance. Taking risks and coming out on top can have a fortifying effect on their self-esteem. Taking unnecessary risks also involves doing things parents would advise against, thus contributing toward feelings of independence. Younger adolescents, still bound in the sensations of the present, may not fully recognize the connection between immediate behavior and long-term consequences. For example, wanting to fit in with a group of peers who happen to be

Photofest

The prow-standing behavior of these two familiar characters from *The Titanic* illustrates the romanticizing of risk-taking often observed among adolescents.

smokers is much more salient than the prospect of emphysema or lung cancer during late adulthood.

Some research suggests that it is not so much unrealistic assessment as it is teenagers' choice to act in spite of the risk. Adolescents and adults do not appear to differ that much in their ability to realistically assess risk (Beyth-Marom et al., 1993). Adolescents and adults alike, however, appear to assess themselves as less vulnerable in a risky situation than they assess others to be (Quadrel et al., 1993). We also appear to be overconfident in what we know, which could further push us toward taking on unnecessary risk (Yates, 1992).

The amount of risk-taking pursued by adolescents varies widely. What accounts for the differences? Early or late maturation, male gender, recent major changes such as moving or parental divorce, low self-expectations, and being at odds with parents all are associated with greater amounts of risk-taking behavior (Byrnes et al., 1999; Slap & Jablow, 1994). Those with temperaments high in sensation-seeking tend to judge risky activities as less threatening than those who are low in sensation-seeking and are therefore more likely to take part in them (Zuckerman et al., 1978). For some adolescents risk-taking may represent self-destructive tendencies (Holinger & Luke, 1984). Many "accidental" deaths and even some homicides have actually involved risks knowingly taken by individuals who did not value their lives. Such individuals may give in to the thrills of risk-taking not so much because of suicidal tendencies but because their lives feel so tumultuous or hopeless that they do not feel they have that much to lose.

When adolescent risk-taking behavior becomes dramatically serious, therapists enlist the family structure as a means of helping adolescents gain better self-control (Kastner & Wyatt, 1997). Such family therapy attempts to develop greater family cohesiveness, enhance parental authority, reduce family conflict, and clarify and enforce appropriate boundaries for family members' behavior. Reducing environmental factors that contribute to risk-taking behavior, such as the adolescent's not having enough to do or hanging around with a risk-taking crowd, also increases the likelihood that risky behaviors will diminish to manageable proportions.

PAVING PATHWAYS ALONG ADOLESCENT PHYSICAL MILESTONES: REDUCING RISK-TAKING BEHAVIOR

How can parents reduce the chances that their adolescent will engage in dangerous behavior? The best preventive measure appears to be the firm, consistent limit-setting represented by the authoritative style of parenting (Slap & Jablow, 1994):

- ▶ Teens whose parents take an authoritative stance and are responsive to their questions, concerns, and feelings are less likely to engage in risky behavior (Baumrind, 1987).
- ▶ Maintaining an open, ongoing dialogue about risk-taking and typical risky behaviors not only is useful for educational purposes but also proactively provides an arena for discussion when risk-taking occurs or seems imminent (Kastner & Wyatt, 1997).
- ▶ Respecting the adolescent's developmental need for increasing freedoms reduces the likelihood of risk-taking. Resilient adolescents recognize and experience the fact that they are truly the only ones in control of themselves, and feel less need to prove this control by taking risks (Neighbors et al., 1993).
- ▶ Encouraging adolescents to be involved with extracurricular activities both keeps them off the streets and reduces the likelihood of their taking risks out of boredom, although some association has been found between involvement in athletics and use of drugs and alcohol (Eccles & Barber, in press; Ponton, 1997).
- ▶ Minor, developmentally appropriate risk-taking should be allowed. In addition to helping with feelings of independence and adequacy, it provides an opportunity for exercising and strengthening the conscience (Siegler, 1997).
- ▶ An absolute priority for preventing excessive adolescent risk-taking is the presence of a strong, cohesive, caring family structure (Arnett, 1995; Kastner & Wyatt, 1997).

What factors are at work as adolescents develop a view of sexuality?

SEXUALITY

Do you remember when you first discovered that you were a sexual being? Perhaps it was while you were dancing with someone. Or maybe it was while you were holding hands with your boyfriend or girlfriend. Watching a movie star or some other public idol may have tapped into your fantasies. Or perhaps a student sitting across the classroom whom you had been secretly admiring from afar suddenly turned and smiled at you. Regardless of the scenario, the end result was the same: a delightful new feeling of excitement and sensual pleasure— unplanned, primitively driven, and substantially detached from more sophisticated thought processes.

Sexual Attitudes and Behaviors

How do adolescents incorporate the newly discovered feelings of sexual responding into their lifestyles? Adolescent attitudes toward sexuality are shaped by culture (Holmberg, 1998; Smith, 1989). Western culture's attitude toward sexuality has changed dramatically over the last 40 years (Robinson et al., 1991). While sexual arousal and desires and sexual behavior were once expected to be repressed until after marriage, these standards have been replaced by more liberal social norms. The double standard whereby men's sexual activities enjoyed greater social acceptance than women's has relaxed some but has not disappeared. Currently, sexual intercourse without benefit of marriage is not judged so harshly if the two people are "in love," a position adopted by many teenagers (Dusek, 1991).

Unfortunately, typical teenagers—not to mention many adults—have difficulty distinguishing between being "in love" and being "in lust." They may conclude that normal sexual behavior consists of whatever they see on *Baywatch* or similar programming, which rarely models concepts such as monogamy, commitment, using contraception, or the natural physical and emotional consequences of ill-advised sexual behavior (Strasburger, 1989). Further complicating matters is the fact that children are arriving at sexual maturity much earlier than did those of previous generations. Still limited by concrete operational reasoning, early bloomers are unlikely to be able to generate enough alternative solutions for dealing with their evolving wellspring of sexual feelings and behavioral possibilities (Gordon, 1990). Thus they often base choices of sexual behavior on the present—desire, peer pressure, personal preferences—rather than on consideration of long-term consequences, of which there are many (Martin, 1996). About 40% of adolescents have experienced sexual intercourse by the time they are in the ninth grade (Centers for Disease Control and Prevention, 1995).

 Even when teenagers have received substantial sex education and know the potential consequences, many continue to engage in risky sexual practices. They have adult bodies with adult sexual needs, yet Western societies have lengthened the period of adolescence without establishing a manner for managing these needs. They experience an increase in libido and a need for emotional intimacy. They are passing through intense social changes as they shift dependencies away from parents, experience insecurities, and look to peers for both standards of behavior and sources of emotional support.

Everybody has a tendency to regress to previous levels of functioning while under stress, and teenagers may suffer lapses in judgment under the stress of managing their sexuality. Their increased self-consciousness can result in a form of grandiosity, leading to the oft-heard proclamation, "it won't happen to me" (Elkind, 1984; Hamburg, 1986; Petersen & Crockett, 1986). Interestingly, those teenage couples who are most inconsistent in their use of contraception are also those whose relationships experience lower levels of emotional, social, and intellectual intimacy (Davis & Bibace, 1999). The higher frequency of sexual activity reported among disadvantaged inner-city teens is hypothesized to be a result of poor educational resources, high unemployment, poverty, fatalistic attitudes, and a greater need to "prove" themselves than is the case with more socioeconomically advantaged teens (Chilman, 1986).

What are the consequences of the ways adolescents manage their sexuality?

Pregnancy

One piece of wreckage produced by this collision of maturational needs, developmental limitations, and social realities is teen pregnancy. The United States holds the dubious honor of having achieved by far the highest teen pregnancy rate of any industrialized nation, as Figure 14.2 shows (Alan Guttmacher Institute, 1994). Some blame this outcome on a "Puritan ethic" still prevalent among some U.S. subpopulations. Believing that discussing sexual matters with teenagers increases the likelihood of sexual activity, some parents, educators, and other influential adults avoid these important discussions. However, there is no evidence that talking about sex increases experimentation. The countries with the lowest incidence of pregnancy are actually those in which parents and educators speak openly with children about sexual matters at a relatively early age (Harris, 1996). Even when parents do share knowledge about sexual matters, a low congruence has been found between which topics parents and adolescents claim to have discussed, suggesting a need for multiple conversations (Jaccard et al., 1998).

Figure 14.2 also shows that about half of all U.S. teenage pregnancies end in miscarriage or abortion. The decision to obtain an abortion is associated with factors related to class, race, and socioeconomic status. Girls from two-parent homes are more likely to get an abortion than those from single-parent homes. Girls from affluent families or who do well in school are more likely to seek abortion than their less wealthy or lower-achieving counterparts. And more Caucasian-American girls choose to have abortions than do Hispanic-American or African-American girls (Hayes, 1987).

Although popular folklore suggests that the rate of teenage pregnancy is on the rise, it is actually much lower than it was 50 years ago. Several factors contribute to the illusion of an increase (Luker, 1996; McElroy & Moore, 1997). The number of teenagers in the United States has doubled in the last 50 years.

FIGURE 14.2

International figures of pregnancies, births, and abortions per 1000 women aged 19 and younger (1988 figures). Adapted from Alan Guttmacher Institute (1994), *Sex and America's Teenagers*, New York: Alan Guttmacher Institute.

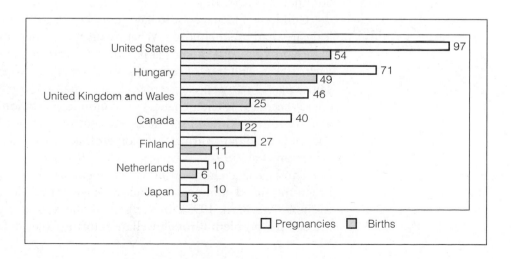

Simultaneously the economy has changed dramatically since the post–World War II era. In the 1950s if a girl became pregnant the father of her child was more likely to marry her, perhaps finish high school, and then find a job that would provide a living wage. Because today's economy does not so easily allow for these options, pregnant teenagers are more likely to become single parents, living with family or ending up in poverty and depending on welfare and other support agencies (Harris, 1997; Moore & Snyder, 1996). Thus those girls who do become pregnant not only are more visible to the public eye but also present more of a social problem.

Teenagers most at risk for becoming pregnant are girls who come from father-absent homes, live in poverty, or have been sexually abused. Often they have sisters or friends with sisters who are slightly older and have had babies. Diagnoses of conduct disorder and substance dependence are overrepresented among teenagers who have babies. The lives of teenagers who choose to give birth and raise their children are dramatically altered. Twenty years after becoming teenage mothers, only two-thirds of women have managed to complete school, stay off welfare, or noticeably improve their employment status. About half of them become pregnant again within two years. They are also likely to remain a single parent longer than nonteen single mothers (Corcoran, 1999; East & Jacobsen, 2001; Harris, 1996; Hotz et al., 1997; Musick, 1993; Zoccolillo et al., 1997).

Being the child of a teenage mother has been associated with a number of unfortunate outcomes. As was mentioned earlier, girls who become pregnant before their reproductive systems have completely matured are more likely to produce babies who are premature or low birth weight and consequently will have developmental problems. One longitudinal study found that 72% of babies born to teenage parents had been referred to special education by the time they reached the third grade (Egeland & Brunnquell, 1979). In general, the school performance and overall adjustment of children born to teenagers tend to be poorer than those who were born to adult parents (McElroy & Moore, 1997; Sommer et al., 2000).

Children of teenagers also have more health problems but receive less medical care than other children. What medical care they do receive is more likely to be paid for by others, such as parents or government programs (Wolfe & Perozek, 1997). Children of teenagers are more likely to be abused or neglected. Those placed in foster care remain longer than those of nonteen parents (Goerge & Lee, 1997). Their chances of economic, educational, or family success in young adulthood are substantially reduced, and they are three times as likely to end up behind bars during their adolescence or early twenties (Grogger, 1997; Haveman et al., 1997).

Thus teenage childbearing is detrimental for both mother and offspring. Programs aimed at improving their lot have not yet demonstrated much effectiveness (Maynard, 1995). In the United States, public policy efforts have addressed the problem through welfare reform (Coley & Chase-Lansdale, 1998).

Felicia Mendez/PhotoEdit

The responsibility of caring for an infant frequently interferes with pursuing the usual age-related pastimes that a teen parent might prefer.

Recent legislation aims at making it more difficult to be a dead-end welfare-dependent single mother by limiting cash benefits and requiring at least part-time employment, by requiring that biological fathers be identified and cooperate with welfare programs, and by requiring that minor mothers continue to live with their parents and complete their education (Leven-Epstein, 1996; United States House of Representatives, 1996).

Life as a Teenage Parent

So here we have one out of every ten teenage girls getting pregnant, about half of them giving birth, most of them keeping their babies, and the majority of these dyads spending at least the next few years living in the homes of the teenagers' parents (Hardy & Zabin, 1991). By my estimation, this suggests the existence of a very large number of U.S. households comprised of three such generations. Surprisingly, not much research investigates how to make these arrangements work when members of the middle generation are still being parented themselves.

We do know that when adolescent parents have strong, caring, dependable, supportive networks, they are not only more satisfied with their lives but also relate better to their children, are better parents, and are more likely to accomplish their own developmental goals (Unger & Wondersman, 1988). Coresidence with parents may work out better when the mother is a young teenager, as some studies suggest that older teenage mothers living at home experience more conflict, function less well as parents, and are slower to attain developmental goals (Coley and Chase-Lansdale, 1998; Speiker & Bensley, 1994). Babies tend to be more secure when grandmothers take primary responsibility for their care and are directive regarding their teen's mothering (Benn & Saltz, 1989). Interestingly, the presence and involvement of a grandfather plays an important role, increasing the child's compliance with maternal requests, decreasing the child's negative emotional expressiveness, and leading to greater perception of nurturance and support by the teen parent (Oyserman et al., 1993; Radin et al., 1991).

When there are substantial strains between teenage parents and their own parents, the ultimate losers are both the teens and their little ones (Brooks-Gunn & Chase-Lansdale, 1991). Teen parents living with families in which there is poor cohesion are more likely to abuse their children (McCullough & Scherman, 1998). Consider also the number of stressors created by the huge multiplicity of tasks teen parents face when, in addition to pursuing the usual adolescent developmental tasks, they now also must raise a child and build a life circumstance for supporting him or her.

How can teen parents best adjust to their multiple tasks and roles?

PAVING PATHWAYS ALONG ADOLESCENT PHYSICAL MILESTONES: ARRANGING HOME LIVES OF TEENAGE PARENTS

Setting up a three-generation living arrangement that considers everybody's rights and needs takes planning and organization. Following are some suggestions for creating a supportive, positive environment (Crockenberg, 1987; Mathes & Irby, 1993; Simpson, 1996):

▶ First, what are the priorities? Teen/baby dyads need physical security: shelter, food, medical care, and other basic necessities. They also need to establish some form of financial security, ensuring that basic necessities will continue to be available. The teenager needs to continue working on age-related tasks: establishing a personal identity and good self-esteem, becoming self-reliant, and setting up goals for the future that will support successful completion of these tasks.

▶ What are the parents'/grandparents' expectations? In spite of being parents themselves, teen parents are not yet adults. They still need parental guidance and support, and answer to the authority of their parents. How will responsibilities at home change and what will remain the same? What are the expectations regarding the teenager's continuing education? How will the teenager take responsibility for financially contributing toward this very expensive endeavor she or he has undertaken?

▶ Then there are the pragmatics of child care. In spite of their small size, infants take up a lot of space. Where will they sleep? Where will their equipment and supplies be stored? What level of cleanliness regarding picking up after the infant is acceptable? What happens with dirty diapers, burp rags, and other less pleasant entanglements of infant care?

▶ Teenagers typically do not recognize the reality of infant care as a 24-hour-a-day job until after they have experienced it. Developmentally they still subconsciously expect that Mom or Dad will be there to rescue them when things get rough, and usually they probably will be. However, the stakes have changed. The new grandparents cannot automatically be assumed to be willing and able to take on the roles of instant babysitter, midnight feeder, or crabby infant soother. The rules of play for how and when such help will occur need to be officially established.

▶ As the child begins moving around and getting into things, a style of discipline must be agreed upon. Parenting classes are an absolute must.

▶ What will the teen parent do to ensure that no child number two appears on the scene?

▶ Incorporate into any plan some means for the teen parent to have a little private space and private time. Any new parent needs these, but they are especially important for a parent who is still sorting out the meaning of life as a teenager.

Sexually Transmitted Diseases

Another consequence of earlier sexual maturation and later marriage is a longer spread of time over which young people may become infected by sexually transmitted diseases (STDs). STDs are currently most prevalent among teenagers and young adults: two-thirds of all new cases belong to these age groups (Ross, 1997). About 3 million teenagers a year contract sexually transmitted diseases (Eng & Butler, 1997). Although there is evidence that STD infection occurs more frequently among poor, inner-city African Americans, STDs are generally equal-opportunity host seekers, infecting individuals of all backgrounds and socioeconomic status (Centers for Disease Control and Prevention, 1996). Table 14.1 describes the most common STDs.

TABLE 14.1

A selection of sexually transmitted diseases, their typical symptoms, and their potential consequences

STD	Symptoms	Consequences
AIDS	None at first; as long as five years later problems related to immune system deficiencies attack the body.	Currently AIDS is fatal. It can be passed on to a developing fetus by either parent.
Gonorrhea	In men, a cloudy discharge from the penis, burning feeling during urination. In women, green or yellowish vaginal discharge; may go undetected.	Untreated, can lead to infertility, sterility, blood poisoning, arthritis, and inflammatory disease may develop.
Syphilis	Begins with painless chancre at infection site; progresses to a generalized skin rash.	Untreated, results in heart failure, blindness, mental disturbance, and possibly death. Can cause blindness and central nervous system defects in a developing fetus.
Genital Herpes	Small, red painful bumps on genitals that become open weepy sores; first outbreak may involve high fever, headache, and muscle aches.	Additional outbreaks likely; currently incurable. Can cause birth defects to a developing fetus if exposed.
Genital Warts	Warts growing on or near the vaginal area in women; on penis or scrotum in men.	Related to cancer of the cervix.
Chlamydia	In women, vaginal discharge accompanied by itching and burning; in men, discharge from the penis and painful urination.	Untreated, pelvic inflammatory disease, infertility, and sterility may occur in women; increasing inflammation and swelling of scrotal area may accur in men.

BOX 14.1   Abstinence versus safer-sex HIV-risk interventions

Tried......

Jemmott, J. B. III, Jemmott, L. S., & Fong, G. T. (1998). Abstinence and safer sex HIV risk-reduction interventions for African American adolescents. *Journal of the American Medical Association, 279*, 1529–1536.

TEENAGERS ARE CURRENTLY THE POPULATION CONSIDered most at risk for contracting the AIDS virus. As parents, educators, and health care professionals struggle to contain its frightening encroachment, substantial controversy swirls around the question of which type of intervention is most likely to discourage adolescents' risky practices. Many promote teaching adolescents "safersex" techniques, but others believe that encouraging abstinence is the only answer, some even going so far as to say that teaching children about sex encourages sexual behavior. Which of these perspectives are we to believe leads to the most effective strategy?

Drs. Jemmott, Jemmott, and Fong examined the effects of abstinence and safer-sex HIV risk-reduction interventions by evaluating a group of young inner-city African-American middle school children. Over 600 students, average age 11.8 years, participated in health education programs consisting of 8 one-hour presentations. They were randomly assigned to one of three programs:

- *The abstinence program.* The presentations given to the abstinence group acknowledged that condoms can reduce the risk of HIV, but emphasized abstinence as the more effective preventive measure. The program was designed to increase the participants' knowledge of HIV and other STDs, strengthen beliefs supporting abstinence, and increase self-efficacy and behavioral skills pertaining to resisting the pressure to have sexual intercourse.
- *The safer-sex program.* The presentations given to the safer-sex group pointed out that abstinence is the most effective way to avoid HIV infection, but emphasized the importance of using condoms when participants did choose to have sex. The program was designed to increase knowledge about HIV and the ability of condoms to reduce the risk of infection, address beliefs that condom use adversely affects sexual enjoyment, and increase self-efficacy and behavioral skills related to negotiating the use of condoms.
- *The control group program.* The control group participants received a health promotion intervention that was designed to be as enjoyable and useful as the other two programs but that did not focus on HIV. Presentations were designed to increase knowledge of and motivation to pursue healthful dietary practices, aerobic exercise, and breast and testicular self-examination, and to discourage cigarette smoking.

The children were interviewed before the intervention and during follow-up 3, 6, and 12 months after. These interviews took the form of questionnaires containing 5-point Likert-type items on which students rated their frequency of sexual activity and condom use, as well as their degree of agreement or disagreement with beliefs and attitudes regarding abstinence and condom use. Comparisons of the responses of the three groups revealed several significant findings. First, participants from both the abstinence group and the safer-sex group reported engaging in less sexual intercourse 3 months following the intervention than did the control group. However, 6 and 12 months after the presentations only the safer-sex group continued to indicate reduced sexual activity. Furthermore, only that group reported significantly more frequent condom use and less unprotected sex than did the control group. These effects were strongest among those students who were sexually active before the intervention.

This study suggests that both abstinence and safersex educational programs can have an immediate effect on frequency of adolescent sexual intercourse. It also dispels concerns that talking about sexual practices encourages sexual activity; on the contrary, in the long run talking about sex demonstrated superiority in terms of both reduced sexual activity and the practicing of safer sex. Although a combined abstinence/safer-sex approach seems prudent, it appears that an emphasis on safer sex may get longer-lasting results with sexually active teenagers.

... and True

BOX 14.2   Factors likely to promote safer sex practices among adolescents

"I need you, baby."
(*Five minutes later*) "You're so special, I can't stand it."
(*Three minutes later*) "C'mon, let's do it."
(*One minute later*) "It'll be real good, I promise."

INSERT SAFER-SEX CONSIDERATIONS HERE. GOOD LUCK! While most people are familiar with the term *safer sex,* waiting until the aforementioned moment to consider it from a practical standpoint is much too late, especially when you factor in the impulsiveness of youth. Exactly what goes into AIDS-preventive behavior programs that is likely to promote safer sexual practices among adolescents?

1. *Information.* Information that is useful for AIDS prevention tells teens what they need to know in order to avoid infection. While discussions of what a T cell is might make a fascinating biology class lecture, knowledge about how AIDS is spread and how that process can be interfered with is more relevant to their actual behavior. Upon successful completion of an AIDS-risk reduction program, participants should be able to answer questions such as:
   - By what means might I become infected?
   - Is my partner a member of a population at high risk for already being infected?
   - How do I use a condom?
   - Where can I get condoms, and how can I make sure I always have them on hand?
2. *Motivation.* Knowledge must be accompanied by the motivation to use it. Providing information about potential consequences—the numerical probabilities that AIDS will be contracted during unprotected sex,

testimonials from infected teens, discussions of personal goals that will be disrupted or forever changed after infection—all identify outcomes that teenagers will be motivated to avoid. They may also have mistaken beliefs or attitudes about using condoms that need to be corrected—such as that they "ruin" sensitivity, they're uncomfortable, you're not a "real man" or "real woman" if you use condoms, or your partner will be offended if you want to use them.

3. *Behavioral skills.* The successful progression of behavioral skills for AIDS-risk reduction includes the teen's acceptance of his or her own sexuality, getting the right information, bringing up and negotiating AIDS prevention with his or her partner, getting tested together with the partner and obtaining condoms, consistently applying preventive measures such as monogamy and condom use, and self- and partner-reinforcement for following through. Communication and assertiveness training techniques are often enlisted to help teens develop these skills.
4. *Self-efficacy.* Most importantly, teenagers need to believe in their ability to act in their own best interests regarding sexual encounters. Techniques such as role-playing, watching peer coping models, and sharing what they learn with friends and families help teenagers develop a sense of empowerment and reduce the likelihood that they will be swept away by last-minute seductions.

Fisher, J. D., & Fisher, W. A. (1992). Changing AIDS-risk behavior. *Psychological Bulletin, 111,* 455–473.

In addition to putting them at increased risk of becoming infected, adolescent reasoning styles and behaviors can compound treatment and containment once infection has occurred (Adimara et al., 1994; Moore et al., 1997). Adolescents are slower to recognize symptoms, and upon discovering infection are slower to seek treatment. Their compliance with treatment can be impaired by immature cognitive processes: forgetting to take medication, "forgetting" to take medication because they don't like the side effects, becoming confused by complex treatment regimens, or assuming that since symptoms have gone away they no longer need to take their medication. The prospect of needing to notify past sexual partners and adopt a lifestyle of protected sex or abstinence until an infection clears does not mesh at all with the social posturing and life priorities of adolescents; there is thus reduced likelihood that they will choose practices that prevent the spread of the disease.

Currently most adolescents are aware of what causes STDs and how they can be spread; they are especially aware concerning AIDS and HIV (Bowler et al., 1992). The problem is that knowledge alone does not appear to have much of an effect on their sexual practices (Richard & van der Pligt, 1991). Factual knowledge needs to be accompanied by personal processing and skill building designed to help adolescents apply what they know to daily living situations (Colon et al., 2000; Rosenthal et al., 1996). When parents use an authoritative parenting style, both discussing sexual matters and encouraging self-control rather than parent-control, adolescents are less likely to act out in a sexually irresponsible manner (Taris & Semin, 1998). A number of sex education programs have been developed in efforts to address the issues surrounding transmission of STDs by preventing risky sexual practices (Eng & Butler, 1997; Kim et al., 1997; Schenker et al., 1997). The Tried . . . . and True boxes on pages 432–433 take a closer look at such programs.

Date Rape

The ambiguous communicating and decision making that often characterize adolescent sexual behavior can lead to sexual activity that is undesired by one or both partners. One unfortunate potential result is **date rape**, which occurs when a partner—almost always a woman—is forced into unwanted sexual activity (Muehlenhard & Linton, 1987). Although some date rapes occur simply because the perpetrator is insensitively doing as he pleases, others are the result of poor communication and misguided expectations regarding sexuality (James et al., 2000). Either way, the consequences for victim and perpetrator alike can be devastating.

 In Western cultures the conventional flirting patterns prescribe that men pursue women for as much sexual contact as they can get and women tease and lead men on. At least this is how sexuality is often portrayed in the media. And in a whirlwind of passion, the two lovers are often shown giving in to their erotic impulses amid much female protestation and male pleading. Thus it is little wonder that some young men become confused about the validity of their para-mours' protests and find themselves being accused of rape.

> ## PAVING PATHWAYS ALONG ADOLESCENT PHYSICAL MILESTONES: PREVENTING DATE RAPE

Education and skill building can help adolescents protect themselves against the occurrence of date rape. Young men are best instructed to communicate be-forehand about what they and the objects of their desires are doing:

▶ Get an explicit "yes" before proceeding with any sexual contact.

▶ If the young woman changes her mind and says "no," stop for clarification.

▶ Always assume that "no" means "no," even if you think she is really saying "maybe."

▶ Do not presume that previous engagement in sexual intercourse is an on-going open invitation, even if you are married to the woman.

▶ Abstain from alcohol during first dates so you can depend on your ability to control impulses. Perpetrator alcohol use is a frequent correlate of date rape (Ageton, 1983).

Young women can be instructed to use a number of strategies that reduce the likelihood that date rape will occur:

▶ When meeting someone for the first time, do so in a public place.

▶ Do not use alcohol during dates until you know the young man well enough to trust him not to take advantage of you when your inhibitions are impaired.

▶ Decide how far you wish to go before initiating sexual activity, and com-municate this preference.

▶ Do away with false protestations and tell him exactly what you mean.

▶ If things get out of hand and he refuses to stop escalating, do not be afraid to do what is required to protect yourself.

▶ If all else fails, yell loudly, "What you're doing is rape and I'm calling 911." Responding in this manner has been found to stop most men's unwanted advances (Beal & Muehlenhard, 1987).

HEALTH ISSUES

Good physical health is a necessary precursor for normal adolescent develop-ment. Physical condition not only affects physical growth but also can affect psychosocial growth (Gortmaker et al., 1990; Gortmaker et al., 1993). Adoles-cents suffering from chronic illnesses may suffer delays in maturation, including onset of puberty (Seiffege-Krenke, 1998). Social and emotional development may be slowed due to increased school absences, the interference of pain and fatigue, development of fewer close peer relationships, and age-inappropriate dependence on parents resulting from the vulnerability created by illness (Cappelli et al., 1989; Connolly et al., 1987; Weitzman, 1986). Although most adolescents are spared the assault of chronic illness, more common health conditions also affect development. Following are discussions of adolescent needs for sleep and good nutrition, as well as the troublesome issues of eating disorders, smoking, and drug use and abuse.

How do sleep and nutritional requirements relate to the adolescent growth spurt?

Sleep

Although teenagers appear to give it little relevance, getting enough sleep is extremely important for the developing adolescent. Most growth hormone is released during the state of sleep. Teenagers need about 8 or 9 hours of sleep every night. Sleep requirements do not appear to diminish as adolescence proceeds. In fact, older adolescents show greater gains in performance levels after extended sleep periods than do preteens. They also seem to benefit from sleeping later in the morning than do adults or younger children. Some suggest that the circadian rhythm alters in concert with physiological changes during adolescence (Carskadon et al., 1993; Coren, 1996; Zammit, 1998). This difference in sleep needs has been observed in children as young as 11 or 12 (Sadeh et al., 2000). In response to the finding that a later high school starting time can result in better grades, a number of schools have set back the time of the first class in hopes of instructing students who are better rested and more alert (Wahlstrom, 1999).

Nutrition

As I watched my sons devour their way through their teen years, I occasionally speculated that there might be some truth to the adage regarding adolescent boys having hollow legs. In addition to extra sleep, the adolescent growth spurt requires massive nutritional support, especially for young men. While teenage girls need to consume about 2200 calories a day, younger teenage boys need about 2500 and older teenage boys about 3000. Adolescents engaged in athletics require even higher caloric intake. To support their substantial muscle growth, 10 to 15% of the calories consumed by adolescents should come from protein (National Academy of Sciences, 1989).

By adolescence, most youngsters already know they should eat a balanced diet. They may also be aware that for the sake of their future health they would best limit saturated fat and sodium, be sure to include fiber, and consume sufficient vitamins and minerals. And what they have not already picked up regarding what constitutes proper nutrition can be successfully taught through formal education (Chapman et al., 1997). However, even well-informed teenagers succumb to poor eating habits. Their reasons are many—the time crunch surrounding school, homework, extracurricular activities, hanging out with the crowd, part-time jobs, and increasing responsibilities at home (Slap & Jablow, 1994). As a result they may skip meals or just grab something that is handy, regardless of its nutritional value. After the big game or in the course of other adolescent social activities, the traditional ritual is often the pursuit of pizza, burgers, ice cream, and other fast foods high in fat and low in fiber or nutritional balance, which frequently replace the missed healthy meals. The unpalatable look of a school menu may encourage a teenager to forget about lunch or maybe check out the school vending machines instead. Eating differently from parents and more similarly to peers also reflects the normal breaking away and establishment of identity and autonomy that characterizes adolescence.

One instance of such independence is a sudden interest in vegetarianism. Unfortunately, the new eating regimen is typically embraced in the adolescent spirit of rejecting a norm as a means of exploring identity. Consequently, the new vegetarian will frequently reject meat and/or other animal products but place minimal emphasis on supplementing their diets with the substantial quantity of vegetables, legumes, and other whole grain products necessary for adequate vegetarian nutrition. The end result is often inadequate consumption of protein and other essential nutrients, leading to malnutrition and possibly stunted growth (Slap & Jablow, 1994; Tanner, 1987).

If teenagers pursue a vegan diet, which excludes both meat and dairy products, they are highly unlikely to be consuming sufficient zinc, iron, calcium, riboflavin, selenium, vitamin B6 or vitamin B12 unless they take vitamin and mineral supplements; sufficient amounts of selenium and vitamin B12 are particularly difficult if not impossible to consume without taking supplements. In addition to physical health consequences, psychological complications such as irritability, depression, anxiety, confusion, and memory loss can result when these two nutrients are not consumed in sufficient quantities. Thus nutritionists recommend that teenagers who become interested in a vegetarian lifestyle seek consultation with legitimate vegetarian organizations in order to ensure proper nutrition (American Dietetic Association, 1993; Freedman, 1998; Mertz, 1994).

Eating Disorders

How and why are eating disorders associated with adolescence?

Teenagers more commonly adopt unusual eating rituals to try to change the size and shape of their bodies (Rees & Trahms, 1989). Both African-American and Caucasian-American girls are found to base such dieting rituals on the amount of fat they perceive themselves as carrying, rather than whether or not they have demonstrated success at getting dates or establishing other social relationships (Halpern et al., 1999). Adolescent body concerns can become so excessive that the pursuit of the perfect physique can actually do harm. The normal pudginess at the beginning of the adolescent growth spurt often creates unwarranted body concerns, which can contribute to the initiation of unnecessary dieting patterns (Killen et al., 1992). Concerns about self-concept and self-worth, which are part

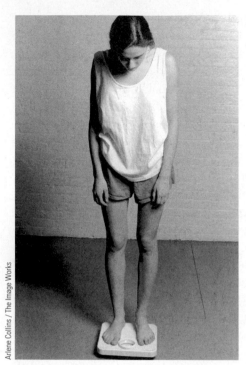

Arlene Collins / The Image Works

In spite of this anorexic girl's very thin physique, her thoughts as she scrutinizes the scale probably center on how she might lose even more weight.

and parcel of the adolescent experience, are also associated with development of eating disorders (Pryor & Wiederman, 1998). Thus it is typically upon the arrival of adolescence that clinicians begin seeing the symptoms of eating disorders; specifically, anorexia nervosa and bulimia.

Anorexia nervosa is an eating disorder characterized by dramatic undernourishment (American Psychiatric Association, 1994). Those suffering from anorexia seem as if they are trying to starve themselves to death. They eat as little as possible, and when they do eat something they often induce vomiting to get rid of it. They may use diet pills and diuretics to avoid calorie utilization. They may exercise as much as several hours a day, hoping to quickly burn off any calories that have found their way into their systems. Their perception of their bodies is severely distorted, as they see themselves as "fat" when they in fact look excessively thin; or expressing satisfaction with their appearance when others can see they are little more than skin over skeletons (Beumont et al., 1995).

Bulimia is a binge-purge cycle of eating. Bulimics eat a massive amount of food over a short period of time, stopping when the pain of stomach distension results in the sufferer inducing vomiting (American Psychiatric Association, 1994). Unlike those with anorexia, those who binge and purge are usually aware that their eating pattern is abnormal. They are in fact ashamed about it and make a point of trying to hide it from others. After a binge-purge cycle they often become depressed and self-critical.

In addition to underweight and emotional difficulties, eating disorders are associated with a variety of health problems (Treasure & Szmukler, 1995). These include fatigue and lack of energy, loss of menstruation in women, skin and bone problems, inability to sweat, circulation problems, gastrointestinal ailments, swelling in the face, hot flashes, rapid heartbeat, and breathlessness. Those who vomit regularly develop rotting teeth and ulcers of the esophagus. However, the most serious complication of anorexia is death, usually occurring as nocturnal cardiac arrest (Cooke et al., 1994). Even after these disorders are cured, some physical consequences, such as dental tooth wear, osteoporosis, and problems with reproduction and childbearing, can persist into adulthood (Brinch et al., 1988; Carmichael, 1990; Milosevic & Slade, 1989; Mitchell et al., 1991). Early onset of anorexia nervosa carries the risk of permanent short stature (Theander, 1996).

Causes of Eating Disorders. A resounding association has been demonstrated between development of eating disorders and Western culture's emphasis on excessive thinness, especially as represented in the media (Hamilton & Waller, 1992; McCarthy, 1990). Women in the media are almost always presented as stick-thin. Models, actors, dancers, and other entertainers often acquire eating disorders themselves in order to maintain such a physique. Barbie dolls have long been under attack because of the unrealistically voluptuous, thin-waisted model they present for little girls. Supposedly bending to public pressure, Barbie's manufacturers announced a change in her physique, but the new model was one that a woman could attain only by becoming anorectic and receiving breast implants—evidence that her manufacturers are still merely flirting with acknowledging the problem, and may even be taking another step backward. Word has it that they are once again reconsidering changes in her physique, reportedly finally moving toward realistically smaller breasts and larger hips.

Thus it is not surprising that young women are substantially more likely to develop eating disorders than are young men (Lucas et al., 1991; Touyz et al., 1993). While young men express greater satisfaction with their physiques as they go through the transformations of puberty, young women actually express greater dissatisfaction, as well as demonstrating a drop in self-esteem (Dorn et al., 1988; Gardner et al., 1999; Simmons & Blyth, 1987; Sinkkonen et al., 1998). The young woman's more substantial subcutaneous layer of fat may also predispose her for becoming overfat, and subsequently developing a preoccupation with weight gain (Mitchell & Truswell, 1987). Relationships found among onset of menarche, entering the world of opposite-sex socializing, and development of eating disorders illustrate the importance of social concerns as adolescent girls monitor their body image (Cauffman & Steinberg, 1996).

However, young men are not exempt from developing body image concerns, and may also adopt anorexic eating attitudes and behaviors (Nelson et al., 1999). Recently researchers have been investigating a phenomenon referred to as the "Adonis complex" (Pope et al., 2000). The supermale images portrayed by the media, the availability of anabolic steroids, and the unrealistic physiques now characterizing superhero toys have led many young men to accept an unrealistic standard to aim toward. Sense of self-esteem and masculinity enter into the mix, and some young men adopt obsessive and potentially destructive regimens of exercise, diet, and body-building drugs.

Why do some adolescents develop such difficulties while others do not? Several personality and environmental factors appear to be associated with children who develop eating disorders (Rastam et al., 1996; Sandbek, 1986). They tend to be excessively concerned about what others think about them. They have a poor self-image and poor self-esteem. They are perfectionistic, worrying a lot about being good enough. They are prone to emotions such as depression, guilt, helplessness, resentment, excessive anxiety, and unreasonable fears. They typically have experienced considerable stress in their lives, perhaps in the form of severe trauma (Vanderlinden & Vandereycken, 1997). They often feel they are losing control or are being excessively controlled by others. An estimated half of them are thought to have developed an avoidant personality style, which may interfere with their receiving social feedback that could help them feel better about themselves (Pryor & Wiederman, 1998).

How mothers handle their own dieting issues can affect young adolescent girls as well (Benedikt et al., 1998). Girls whose mothers provide straightforward, positive encouragement are more likely to eat a healthy diet and exercise reasonable amounts. Those whose mothers express dissatisfaction with their own bodies and engage in extreme weight loss behaviors themselves are more likely to pursue unhealthy weight-loss behaviors.

PAVING PATHWAYS ALONG ADOLESCENT PHYSICAL MILESTONES: PREVENTING EATING DISORDERS

What can parents do to help inoculate their children against developing eating disorders? Family relationships characterized by warmth, supportiveness, and reasonable levels of guidance—again, assets provided by the authoritative style of parenting—continue to play significant roles in encouraging healthy child development in this respect (Eisler, 1995; Waller et al., 1989). Based on the many factors associated with development of eating disorders, Slade's (1995) "Ten Commandments" for primary prevention offer this simplified, tongue-in-cheek advice (p. 390):

1. Do not physically abuse your child.
2. Do not sexually abuse your child.
3. Do not make a big issue about food or eating.
4. Do not make a big issue about weight or body shape.
5. Show your child love and affection without being overprotective or overcontrolling.
6. Do not set impossible or difficult standards for your child.
7. Do not insist on perfect behavior all the time.
8. Reward small attainments in the present rather than emphasizing major goals in the future.
9. Encourage independence in your child.
10. Encourage your child to be sociable and to mix with other children.

Children can also benefit from prevention programs presented in school systems (Carney, 1986; Crisp, 1988). These programs teach children the facts, concepts, and consequences of eating disorders; inform them of the normal body and eating processes; and attempt to counteract media influences. They also teach relevant skills and provide personal/experiential opportunities for young people to learn about themselves, filling voids that even many children who come from enriched environments have (Slade, 1995).

Smoking

The vast majority of smokers began smoking as adolescents (Institute of Medicine, 1994). In spite of the tobacco industry's fascinating display of denial in the face of a preponderance of evidence, nicotine is indeed an addictive substance. The number of drastic health conditions that have been associated with smoking continues to grow (United States Department of Health and Human Services, 1994). But by the time adolescents who smoke have established the healthy adult judgment that would deter them from such behavior, they are already hooked. Although the prevalence of adolescent smoking has significantly declined from what it was a couple of decades ago, we are now seeing a slight increase, especially among adolescent girls (Johnston et al., 1995a).

Why are some adolescents more inclined toward smoking than others? Some studies suggest that certain adolescents are genetically more susceptible, or perhaps may be responding to early addiction stemming from prenatal exposure to nicotine (Carmelli et al., 1992; Hughes, 1986; Kandel et al., 1994). But even identical twins are not necessarily both either smokers or nonsmokers. What other factors are involved? The decline of its prevalence since the seventies suggests that cultural tolerance plays a role in whether or not an adolescent chooses smoking as a pastime. Having peers who smoke is one of the better predictors of adolescent smoking (Chassin et al., 1998; United States Department of Health and Human Services, 1994).

Relationships with parents appear to be able to mediate the influence of peers. When parents do not smoke themselves, provide the high levels of support and guidance typical of authoritative parenting, and socialize their children with a stance that does not support smoking, children are more likely to choose against affiliating with peers who smoke (Melby et al., 1993). It is no surprise that adolescents who smoke are more likely to have parents who smoke. However, this connection appears to involve more than modeling or a perceived stamp of parental approval. When researchers also consider the factors of parental warmth and guidance, they find that parents who provide less warmth and guidance are both more likely to smoke and more likely to have adolescents who also choose to (Chassin et al., 1998; Kandel & Wu, 1995; Melby et al., 1993).

Adolescents are less likely to smoke when parents establish rules against the behavior (Kandel & Wu, 1995). When parents express anger about adolescent smoking and show approval when their adolescents choose not to, fewer adolescents smoke (Hansen et al., 1987). Unfortunately, other drugs currently available to adolescents present much more immediate dangers, and parents appear to divert the lion's share of their antisubstance-abuse interventions against these drugs (Chassin et al., 1998).

Substance Use and Abuse

How effectively does the "War on Drugs" influence adolescent drug use?

Over the last couple of decades the United States has poured substantial effort and resources into attempts to discourage adolescent drug use. Unfortunately, substance-abuse prevention programs have thus far been failing dismally (Meyer, 1996). As Figure 14.3 shows, a very large portion of the teenage population still chooses to use despite being aware of the risks, and their numbers are rising (Johnston et al., 1995b).

Children are experimenting with drugs at earlier and earlier ages. The extent of their use and abuse appears to differ among ethnic groups (Pilgrim et al., 1999; Sattler, 1998). Caucasian-American adolescents report more drug use

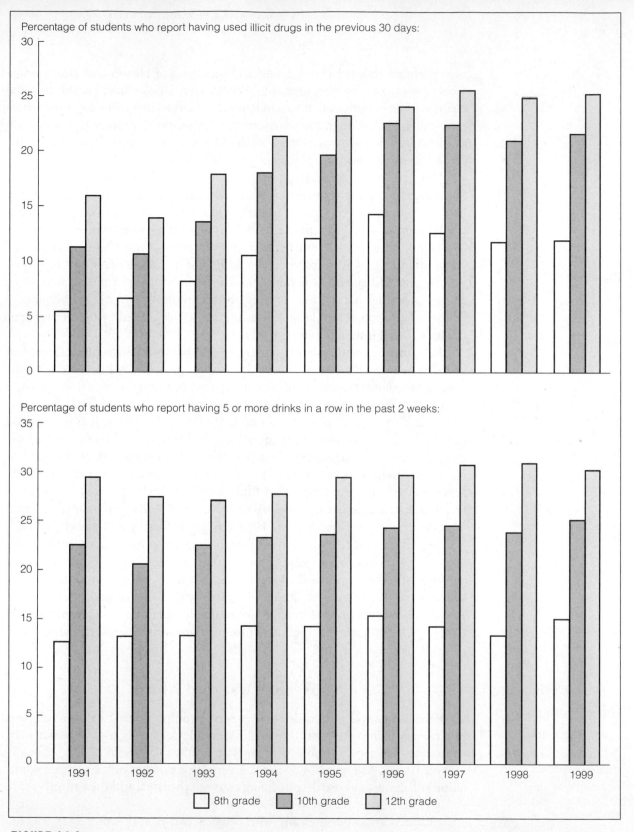

FIGURE 14.3

Percentage of 8th grade, 10th grade, and 12th grade students who have used alcohol or illicit drugs. Adapted from Federal Interagency Forum on Child and Family Statistics (1999). *America's children: Key national indicators of well-being.* Washington, DC: US Government Printing Office.

than do African-American, Asian-American, and Hispanic-American adolescents (Johnson et al., 1994; Wallace & Bachman, 1991). Native-American adolescents appear to abuse drugs—especially alcohol and inhalants—substantially more than do the other ethnic groups (Trimble, 1992; Young, 1992).

Adolescent involvement with drugs tends to run along a continuum that can be characterized as five stages (Nowinski, 1990):

- ► *Experimental stage.* First encounters with drugs are usually related to such factors as peer pressure, curiosity, and normal adolescent risk-taking.
- ► *Social stage.* Over time, drug use may become an expected activity within the adolescent's social circle. Or the adolescent may use drugs as a means of gaining access to a specific social circle.
- ► *Instrumental stage.* As users become familiar with how drugs affect them, they begin using for the purpose of experiencing these effects: getting "high" or feeling good, numbing depression or other unpleasant emotions, coping with stress, or loosening inhibitions.
- ► *Habitual stage.* Drug use becomes an integral part of the user's life. Users neglect relationships and previously enjoyed activities in order to pursue drugs. Users begin to experience some tolerance for drugs and need to take larger amounts or more powerful drugs to get the same effect.
- ► *Compulsive stage.* The user is addicted and will experience withdrawal without continual use. The user is now an addict, and getting the next fix is the adolescent's focus in life. School, friendships, and other aspects of living become of little or no concern.

Most adolescents who experiment with alcohol or marijuana do not become addicts. Genetic makeup, including having inherited a sensation-seeking temperament, appears to predispose some teenagers toward abusing drugs or becoming addicted (Anthonelli & Schucket, 1992; Pilgrim et al., 1999). Children and adolescents who are already suffering from psychological disorders also have a greater chance of becoming substance abusers (Morrison, 1991). While substance abuse is often linked with juvenile delinquency, its developmental path differs (Maggs & Hurrelmann, 1998). A number of other factors of personality and family background have been associated with a higher likelihood of drug abuse, as Table 14.2 shows (Kumpfer & Alvarado, 1995; Norman, 1996).

PAVING PATHWAYS ALONG ADOLESCENT PHYSICAL MILESTONES: TREATING AND PREVENTING DRUG ABUSE

Treatment programs for addicted adolescents have sprouted to meet the need. Such programs typically begin with an "intervention": a large number of people important in the teen's life confront the teen about the impact of his or her drug use and express their concern. Usually inpatient treatment is needed at first, as

TABLE 14.2

Risk factors associated with occurrence of adolescent substance abuse. Adapted from E. Norman (1995), Personal factors related to substance misuse: Risk abatement and/or resiliency enhancement? In T. P. Gullotta, G. R. Adams, & R. Montemayor (Eds.) *Substance misuse in adolescence.* Thousand Oaks, CA: Sage; and K. L. Kumpfer & R. Alvarado (1995), Strengthening families to prevent drug use in multiethnic youth. In G. Botvin, S. Schinke, & M. Orlandi (Eds.) *Drug abuse prevention with multiethnic youth.* Thousand Oaks, CA: Sage.

Individual Risk Factors (Norman et al., 1995)

Difficult child temperament (Brook et al., 1990):
- irritability, temper tantrums, withdrawal, frequent negative moods

Childhood emotional disorders (Shedler & Block, 1990)
- depression, anxiety

Childhood behavioral problems (Block et al., 1988)
- hyperactivity, poor impulse control, aggression, sensation-seeking, low harm avoidance, inability to delay gratification

Antisocial behavior (Kandel et al., 1986)
- theft, chronic fighting

School failure (Jessor & Jessor, 1977)

Having friends who use drugs (Brook et al., 1990)

Alienation from dominant societal values (Penning & Barnes, 1982)

Family-Related Risk Factors (Kumpfer & Alvarado, 1995)

Poor socialization practices (Kandel & Andrews, 1987):
- ineffective parental modeling of values and behaviors, little direct instruction in morals and behavioral skills

Poor supervision (Loeber & Stouthhammer-Loeber, 1986):
- failure to monitor child's activities, latchkey or sibling supervision situation, or overwhelmingly insufficient adult/child ratio

Permissive or authoritarian style of discipline (Barnes, 1990)
- lax, inconsistent, or harsh discipline

Poor quality of parent-child relationship (Brook et al., 1990)
- low parental warmth or attachment, low involvement or little time with child, maladaptive interactions

Excessive conflict and interpersonal violence (Kumpfer & Bayes, 1995)
- fighting among family members; physical, verbal, or sexual abuse

Family chaos (Wolin et al., 1979)
- little family structure or structure constantly changing, lack of family routines or rituals

Poor parental mental health (Conger & Rueter, 1995)
- parental depression, hostile or irrational behavior

Parent or sibling drug use (Brook et al., 1986)

the teen deals with symptoms of withdrawal and drug craving. The treatment regimen usually includes individual therapy, peer support groups, health education, and family therapy (Rickel & Becker-Lausen, 1996; Rosenberg et al., 1994). Unfortunately, only limited data are available to describe how well these programs work (Gilvarry, 2000). These data seem to indicate that more likely than not, treated teens will eventually fall off the wagon, just as many adult substance abusers do after treatment (Hubbard et al., 1989; Rickel & Becker-Lausen, 1996). However, those who are treated fare better than those who are not (Liddle, 1999; Morehouse & Tobler, 2000).

Thus at the time of this writing, neither prevention nor treatment programs seem to be making substantial headway against a problem that is dramatically detrimental to healthy child development. While it would be easy to become discouraged and declare the "War on Drugs" to be the Vietnam of the adolescent health world, researchers and practitioners alike continue to vigorously search for answers. As the research currently stands, programs appear to be more likely to have a lasting effect if they accomplish the following (Meyer, 1996; Shedler & Block, 1990):

- ▶ Provide teens with more than just information about drugs. Substance-abuse prevention programs work best when interventions are also aimed at reducing risk and promoting competencies.
- ▶ Focus on reducing susceptibility to abuse, rather than preventing use. It is probably impossible to completely prevent adolescents from experimenting, given the nature of this developmental stage. Instead, teenagers are more likely to benefit from learning how to anticipate problems and developing competencies that will help them avoid letting experimentation get out of hand.
- ▶ Explore alternative methods for adolescents to achieve whatever benefits they perceive drugs as providing for them. Eliminating drug use leaves a gap in their lives that must be filled with something else if they are to remain clean and sober. Help redirect them in ways that help them feel reinforced, such as being able to follow through on meaningful goals, becoming involved with other enjoyable activities, or developing more rewarding interpersonal relationships.
- ▶ Address the needs of both high-risk and normal-risk adolescents. High-risk teens seem to benefit most when community-level interventions are included, while programs focused on skills training and altering what adolescents perceive to be the social norm to get the best results with normal-risk teens.

As you can see from these observations, the realities of adolescent substance use require that programs, to be successful, cannot rely on simplistic generic answers but must use complex models that address the unique circumstances of each individual adolescent.

SUMMARY

Body Growth

Adolescents experience a growth spurt during which they not only approach their adult size but also develop gender-specific differences in physique. Hormonal changes and the onset of puberty result in both primary and secondary sexual characteristics. Although the spermarche of boys and the menarche of girls gives them the capacity for reproduction, their reproductive systems will not become fully mature for several more years.

Adolescents experience mixed feelings about the onset of puberty, with girls typically reacting more strongly to menarche than boys to spermarche. Timing of the onset of puberty can affect social and emotional development. Early maturation appears to benefit boys' experience of social acceptance, but the advantages become mixed as they reach adulthood. Early-maturing girls appear to experience some disadvantage as teenagers, but differences diminish when they are compared with later-maturing girls as adults.

Brain Growth

Brain growth proceeds with continuing increases in relevant synaptic connections, decreases in meaningless connections, and strengthening of the glial cells supporting and nourishing neurons.

Motor Development

Athletic skill and physical endurance and power increase for both genders. Boys' greater musculature gives them superiority in running speed, jumping, and other gross motor skills, while girls develop a slight superiority in eye-motor coordination and flexibility.

Risk-Taking Behavior

Normal adolescent risk-taking occurs as teenagers attempt to gain peer acceptance, fortify their self-esteem, and establish their independent identities. Greater risk-taking behavior occurs among adolescents who are male, going through major changes, or are experiencing social or emotional difficulties. Adolescents are less likely to engage in excessive risk-taking if they are parented authoritatively, experience parental acceptance and support of their emerging independence, and benefit from ongoing dialogues about risk-taking behaviors.

Sexuality

Adolescents' sexual attitudes and behaviors are shaped by their culture. The trend toward earlier physical maturation than previous generations combines with substantially looser cultural attitudes toward sexual behavior to contribute to poorly managed sexuality by many teens. Pregnancy is best prevented through open discussions of sexuality and the pragmatics of managing sexual behavior. The lives of teenagers who become parents will be shadowed by numerous social, emotional, economic, and educational disadvantages, which their children are also likely to experience.

Young teen parents benefit from living with their parents during their earliest years of childrearing. Older teenagers can also benefit from the emotional, social, and economic support of such an arrangement, as long as there are no excessive strains between them and their parents. A supportive environment sets priorities and establishes guidelines regarding the care of the child. Clarifying teenagers' parents' expectations regarding finishing education and setting realistic life goals also contribute to a cooperative, supportive three-generation living arrangement.

Adolescents are most effectively educated about STDs if they are also instructed as to how to apply their knowledge during situations that could lead to ill-advised sexual behavior. Date rape can be prevented by teaching adolescents to use certain dating-behavior precautions that counter common cultural fallacies regarding normal sexual behavior.

Health Issues

Teenagers' sleep patterns change in ways that promote growth. Nutritional needs expand in support of their growth spurts. But the adolescent lifestyle, attempts to be "different," and efforts to develop a certain physique can mitigate against healthy eating habits. Anorexia nervosa and bulimia make their first appearances during adolescence, more commonly among girls than boys. Correlates of eating-disordered behavior include cultural overemphasis on thinness and social and emotional factors such as low self-esteem, anxiety- and depression-related symptoms, overcontrolling parents, and physical or sexual abuse.

Tobacco use typically begins during adolescence, and occurs more often among children with certain genetic dispositions or who have peers or parents who smoke. Substance use is relatively common among teenagers in spite of their knowledge of the potential risks. Genetic predisposition and a number of individual and family characteristics correlate with progression to substance abuse. Substance-abuse programs for adolescents thus far show only limited long-term success. Treatments are more likely to be successful when they promote competencies, reduce susceptibility to abuse, explore alternative ways of feeling good, and address the differing characteristics of high- and low-risk teenagers.

KEY TERMS

anorexia nervosa
bulimia
date rape

menarche
primary sex characteristics
puberty

secondary sex characterstics
spermarche

CONCEPT REVIEW

1. During the adolescent _____ teenagers shoot up toward their adult height, beginning at about age _____ for boys and age _____ for girls. During this stage, boys develop even greater _____ than girls, supported by greater _____ and _____ growth. Girls grow more through their _____ than boys and establish a subcutaneous layer of _____.

2. During puberty, boys produce increased levels of _____ and girls produce increased levels of _____. These hormones contribute toward development of the _____ and _____ sex characteristics related to reproduction.

3. First menarche and spermarche typically do not include presence of _____ or _____; full reproductive maturity occurs after a few more _____. Age of onset of menarche is affected by factors such as _____ and _____. Emotionally, both boys and girls view these personal milestones with _____; and may find it to be aversive if not prepared by appropriate _____.

4. _____-maturing boys enjoy social favoritism over those who are _____-maturing; later-maturing boys may have greater opportunity for developing social _____ skills and exploring personal _____. Early-maturing girls are more likely to have difficulties related to _____ behaviors, low _____ performance, and weight _____.

5. In addition to _____ of neurons and a continuing _____ in the number of interconnections between them, brain growth during adolescence includes substantial strengthening of _____ cells.

6. Boys' motor skills pull further ahead of girls' in the areas of _____, _____, _____ strength, _____, and _____ eye-motor coordination.

Girls pull ahead in the areas of _____ eye-motor coordination and _____.

7. Some risk-taking during adolescence is considered _____.
    Excessive risk-taking is associated with early or late _____,
    _____ gender, low _____,
    _____ temperament, _____ tendencies,
    and/or drastic changes or problems at _____.

8. Excessive risk-taking is less likely to occur when the parenting style is
    _____, teenagers are involved with _____
    activities, and parents respect the teenagers' needs for increasing
    _____.

9. How a teenager views sexuality and appropriate sexual behavior is typically
    determined by _____ norms, _____ presentations, and maturation of _____ ability.

10. Speaking with children about sexual matters does/does not appear to be associated with greater incidence of sexual activity. Factors associated with likelihood that a teenage girl will become pregnant include _____
    home, history of _____ _____, and
    _____ dependence.

11. Children of teenage parents are more likely to show poor _____
    performance, have _____ problems, be _____
    or _____, and/or be less successful as _____.
    Living arrangements for teenage parents staying at home are most successful
    when parents/grandparents are _____ and when the living
    arrangement is formally organized around everybody's needs and rights.

12. About _____ of all new STD cases occur among teenagers
    and young adults. Adolescents are also at higher risk of compounding problems of treatment and containment due to immature _____
    and _____. Successful STD education programs include not
    only _____ about STDs but also instruction in
    _____ for dealing with relevant social situations.

13. Date rape often occurs because of poor _____ and misguided
    _____, which both can be successfully addressed through
    _____ and _____.

14. Teenagers need more/less sleep than they did when they were younger, and
    tend to sleep better when they go to bed and get up _____.
    They need substantially more nutritional intake in order to support their
    _____. Unusual eating and exercising regimens may occur
    due to issues of _____ exploration or _____
    concerns.

15. Two eating disorders that typically first emerge during adolescence are
_____ and _____. In addition to under-
weight, these disorders associated with numerous _____ and
_____ health problems, including fatality due to
_____.

16. Development of eating disorders has been associated with unrealistic
_____ expectations, low _____,
_____ issues at home, and having mothers who engage in
_____ behaviors.

17. Some adolescents are more likely to smoke because of _____
influences, or having _____ or _____ who
smoke. Adolescents whose parents establish _____ against
smoking and show _____ when they do and
_____ when they do not are less likely to smoke.

18. Extent and type of drug experimentation shows some variation among
_____ groups. Experimentation typically occurs due to
_____ pressure, _____, or normal adoles-
cent _____. Many factors are associated with abuse/addic-
tion, especially _____ and _____.

19. Successful adolescent drug treatment program interventions include those
that reduce _____, promote _____, focus
more on susceptibility to _____ rather than
_____, explore alternative life _____, and
address the differing needs of _____- and
_____-risk teenagers.

1) growth spurt; fourteen; twelve; physical strength; heart; lung; hips; fat; 2) testosterone; estrogen; primary; secondary; 3) ova; sperm; years; heredity; nutrition; ambivalence; education; 4) Early; later; coping; identity; partying; academic; gain; 5) myelination; decrease; glial; 6) running; jumping; grip; balance; gross; fine; flexibility; 7) normal; maturation; male; self-expectations; sensation-seeking; self-destructive; home; 8) authoritative; extracurricular; freedoms; 9) cultural; media; reasoning; 10) does not; father-absent; sexual abuse; substance; 11) school; health; neglected; abused; adults; supportive; 12) two-thirds; reasoning; behaviors; information; skills; 13) communication; expectations; education; skill building; 14) more; later; growth spurt; identity; body image; 15) anorexia nervosa; bulimia; emotional; physical; nocturnal cardiac arrest; 16) cultural; self-esteem; control; unhealthy weight loss; 17) genetic; peers; parents; rules; anger; approval; 18) ethnic; peer; curiosity; risk-taking; heredity; psychological disorders; 19) risk; competencies; abuse; use; reinforcers; high; normal

RESOURCES FOR FURTHER READING

Apostolides, M. (1998). *Inner hunger.* New York: W. W. Norton & Company.

Eng, T. R., & Butler, W. T. (1997). *The hidden epidemic: Confronting sexually transmitted diseases.* Washington, DC: National Academy Press.

Gullotta, T. P., Adams, G. R., & Montemayor, R. (1996). *Substance misuse in adolescence.* Thousand Oaks, CA: Sage.

Lang, P., & Lang, S. S. (1995). *Teen fathers.* New York: Franklin Watts.

Maynard, R. A. (Ed.) (1997). *Kids having kids: Economic costs and social consequences of teen pregnancy.* Washington, DC: The Urban Institute Press.

Ponton, L. E. (1997). *The romance of risk: Why teenagers do the things they do.* New York: Basic Books.

Seiffege-Krenke, I. (1998). *Adolescents' health: A developmental perspective.* Mahwah, NJ: Erlbaum.

Slap, G. B., & Jablow, M. M. (1994). *Teenage health care: The first comprehensive family guide for preteen to young adult years.* New York: Pocket Books.

Vallette, B. (1988). *A parents' guide to eating disorders: Prevention and Treatment of anorexia nervosa and bulimia.* New York: Avon Books.

INFOTRAC COLLEGE EDITION

For additional readings, explore InfoTrac College Edition, your online library. Go to http://www.infotrac-college.com/wadsworth and use the passcode that came on the card with your book. Try these search terms: anorexia and adolescents, bulimia and adolescents, date rape, drug abuse and adolescents, drug abuse treatment, growth spurt, menarche, pregnancy and teenagers, puberty and gender, puberty and timing, risk-taking and teenagers, sex education and teenagers, sexuality and teenagers, sleep and adolescents, smoking and adolescents, teenage parents, vegetarian diet

CHILD DEVELOPMENT CD-ROM

Go to the Wadsworth Child Development CD-ROM for further study of the concepts in this chapter. The CD-ROM also includes quizzes and additional activities to expand your learning experience.

REFERENCES

For a list of references for this chapter, see the Wadsworth Psych Study Center Web site at: http://www.wadsworth.com/product/0534348092s

CHAPTER 15

Adolescent Cognitive Development

FOCUS QUESTIONS

▶ What new reasoning abilities does the stage of formal operations bring?

▶ How can we help adolescents become better decision makers?

▶ What information-processing advances occur during adolescence?

▶ How do characteristics of secondary schools and advances in language and math abilities affect learning during adolescence?

▶ How do relationships with parents and peers affect success at school?

▶ What positive or negative effects do extracurricular activities and part-time jobs have on academic achievement?

▶ How can parents and society help adolescents succeed academically?

▶ How well do Western societies manage the transition from school to work?

▶ What factors do adolescents consider as they choose careers?

OUTLINE

Piaget's Formal Operational Reasoning
Hypothetical, Scientific, and Deductive Reasoning
Paving Pathways: Fostering Formal Operations
Egocentrism during Adolescence
The Fleeting Nature of Formal Operational Reasoning
Adolescent Decision Making
Paving Pathways: Teaching Decision Making to Adolescents
Information-Processing
Learning during Adolescence
Secondary Schools
Individual Academic Abilities

Parental Effects on Learning
Peer Effects on Learning
Extracurricular Activities
Part-Time Jobs
Paving Pathways: Helping Adolescents Succeed
Academically
Career Development
Transitioning from School to Work
Choosing a Career

"I think, therefore I know everything."—frustrated father's take on adolescent cognition

Most parents of teenagers have little difficulty identifying with this father's exasperation over adolescent reasoning processes: so close to adult reasoning, yet seemingly so far to go before effectively merging with worldly realities—with many an argument to follow in between!

The time span embracing puberty unveils changes in adolescent cognition that are qualitative, progressive, and internally directed (Moshman, 1998). Qualitatively, a variety of new thinking styles emerge that are rarely observed before age 11 (Case, 1998; Chandler & Boutilier, 1992). These new styles are progressive, producing an accurate or desired result more effectively than did the styles adolescents used when they were younger (King & Kitchener, 1994; Kitchener, 1986). We assume these changes are internally directed because children and adults alike come up with new ways of coordinating theories and evidence without ever having received direct instruction in doing so (Kuhn et al., 1995; Schauble, 1996). Also, changes such as these occur spontaneously among members of many unrelated cultures (Gelman & Williams, 1998; Karmiloff-Smith, 1992).

This chapter will examine these changes in adolescent cognitive processing as well as explore the school, work, and other day-to-day arenas within which teenagers practice their developing cognitive skills.

PIAGET'S FORMAL OPERATIONAL REASONING

What new reasoning abilities does the stage of formal operations bring?

Cognitive changes at adolescence launch children from the world of "what is" into the universe of "what if." **Formal operational reasoning** introduces thinking in terms of abstractions rather than relying upon concrete representations, as do younger children. By leaving behind these constraints, adolescents now have the capacity to integrate abstract concepts and coordinate a number of mental processes. In doing so they reason their way toward more advanced conclusions (Inhelder & Piaget, 1958; Piaget, 1972).

Hypothetical, Scientific, and Deductive Reasoning

The ability to consider abstract concepts contributes toward advances in how the adolescent generates and tests hypotheses. By using hypothetical reasoning they are moving beyond the confinement of personally observed cause and effect and are toying with ideas about things for which they have no direct knowledge. As they conjure up multiple hypotheses they can evaluate them by applying their more advanced **scientific reasoning**. As was described in Chapter 12, younger children reason scientifically by thinking up one or two reasons why something may have happened, testing their hypothesis(es), then giving up. Formal-operational adolescents are much more systematic in their scientific reasoning: They exhaustively test all conceived hypotheses, control certain variables to see if a change occurs, and systematically keep track of results.

As adolescents compare and contrast hypotheses, they are also demonstrating **combinatorial reasoning**—the ability to consider more than one relevant factor regarding the same problem. Combinatorial reasoning contributes, for example, to being able to use proportional logic (Falk & Wilkening, 1998). Suppose you present children with a bag to be filled with blue and red chips and tell them they will win a prize if they pick out a blue one. You let them select the actual number of red and blue chips to be placed in the bag, offering choices of several numerical combinations of the two colors. The younger child will choose the numerical combination containing the greatest number of blue chips. Beginning at around age 13 or so, children are more likely to additionally consider the number of red chips that might be drawn instead. By considering the number of both colors of chips they will make the choice that produces the combination that has the greater proportion of blue chips, thus increasing their probability of success.

Another positive by-product of thinking in the abstract is illustrated by the adolescent's ability to consider less concrete factors during problem-solving. In a task requiring participants to manipulate weights on a balancing apparatus and predict what will happen, younger children typically experiment with concrete factors such as the size and number of weights. Adolescents, on the other hand, will also consider spatial abstractions such as position, distance, and orientation of the weights (Amsel et al., 1996).

Researchers have noted some inconsistencies in how adolescents use their scientific reasoning. At times they fail to use strategies that their past performances give us reason to assume are familiar to them (Demetriou & Efklides, 1988; Flavell & Wohlwill, 1969). The cause is probably the fact that scientific reasoning is composed of multiple structures. They all contribute toward reasoning that assumes causality and looks for it experimentally but do not appear to all become fully functioning at once (Demetriou, Efklides, & Platsidou, 1993;

Adolescents can learn to generate scientific hypotheses and test them exhaustively because of their emerging formal operational reasoning ability.

Wayne H. Chasan/Image Bank

Klahr & Dunbar, 1988). When separating scientific reasoning into the components of combinatorial ability, hypothesis formation, experiment design, and the mapping of experimental results against the original hypothesis, researchers find that these processes develop separately but in an overlapping manner, seemingly spurring one another along as they do so (Demetriou, Efklides, Papadaki et al., 1993).

The crowning glory of new adolescent reasoning skills, however, is their improved capacity for deductive reasoning (Chapell & Overton, 1998; Inhelder & Piaget, 1958). **Deductive reasoning** is the process of drawing logical conclusions based on a set of givens, or premises, following patterns such as "if *a* then *b*" (Johnson-Laird, 1999):

Premise:
   "All students who get above a 3.5 GPA are placed in advanced science courses."

Logical Deductions:
   If *a* then *b:* "Susan gets above a 3.5 GPA (If *a*. . . .). She is therefore taking the advanced science courses (. . . . then *b*)."
   If not *b,* then not *a:* "Susan is not in advanced science courses (If not *b* . . .). She must not be getting above a 3.5 GPA (. . . . then not *a*)."

Over the course of adolescence, youngsters' ability to make logical inferences improves, at least when they are dealing with familiar territory (Klaczynski & Narasimham, 1998a; Markovits, 1993; Ward & Overton, 1990). In spite of these improvements there are no guarantees that all adolescents will successfully develop their deductive reasoning capacity. Even adult reasoning frequently displays leaps outside the bounds of logic (Evans & Over, 1996). Often, inferential errors made by adults and adolescents alike involve inappropriate manipulations of the "if *a* then *b*" premise, fueled in part by failure to consider possible alternative causes of an outcome. As adolescents become better able to generate alternative possible reasons, or multiple hypotheses, for an event's having occurred, they become less likely to make such errors (Evans, 1972; Markovits, 1993; Markovits & Vachon, 1990).

Constraints on the reasoner's information-processing also can interfere with successful deductive reasoning (Oaksford & Chater, 1993). Sometimes information is presented in ways that lead the reasoner astray, such as by implying "if and only if *a*, then *b*," which negates the possibility of alternative causes being at work (Markovits, 1993; Reyna, 1995). We also have some tendency to latch onto conclusions that are the most easily drawn or are most familiar, suggesting that those with rigid or narrow viewpoints or limited life exposures will be more susceptible to committing reasoning errors (Klaczynski & Gordon, 1996; Klaczynski & Narasimham, 1998b; Reyna & Brainerd, 1995).

PAVING PATHWAYS ALONG ADOLESCENT COGNITIVE MILESTONES: FOSTERING FORMAL OPERATIONS

From a developmental perspective, then, how can we encourage adolescents' growth in deductive reasoning and other reasoning skills?

- ► Provide adolescents with clear, accurate, and complete information.
- ► Help them explore a variety of positions and hypotheses rather than immediately discounting them in favor of personal prejudices.
- ► Ensure their exposure to a wide variety of environmental input.
- ► Be patient with the argumentativeness that, more often than not, will accompany this process.

When delivered in the form of authoritative parenting, these practices are associated with adolescents' superior performance in deductive reasoning (Chapell & Overton, 1998).

Egocentrism during Adolescence

What is the main impact of this improvement in reasoning ability on the adolescent's developing view of the self? Egocentrism moves onto an entirely new playing field—with the adolescent bounding onto center field as the star player! Adolescent egocentrism can easily be observed any time you drive through a neighborhood while middle school is letting out. Have you ever noticed how much more carefully you must proceed when passing groups of young adolescent pedestrians than when passing members of other age groups? In their self-absorbed state, some drift in and out of the street, perhaps not even looking to see if there is traffic; or if they do see a car coming, they assume it will stop. What is the impetus for such ill-advised behavior? To some extent it occurs because young adolescents are feeling their way along the fogged-up daze produced by the many changes occurring in their lives. Several mental processes unique to this developmental phase also contribute to self-absorbed behavioral choices, specifically "logic" and idealism, the personal myth, the invincibility fable, and the imaginary audience (Elkind, 1967; 1984; Inhelder & Piaget, 1958; Piaget, 1967).

Logic and Idealism. "I am a pedestrian; I have the right of way. It is logical that cars should stop." During their concrete operational lives, children observe absolute "rights" and "wrongs," around which all are expected to mold their behavior. Adolescents apply such perceptions within their newfound logic. Unfortunately, logic and the real world are two different things, with the world introducing other relevant variables besides what might be right or wrong. Adolescents can miss the fact that internally valid logic—even though it may be "right"—really isn't logical until it takes into account the realities and complexities of the world as it is, including the human frailties that might prevent a driver from seeing them or avoiding hitting them. Adolescents frequently band together behind idealistic causes, attempting to save the world with picketing, sit-ins, and other demonstrations of loyalty to "obviously" logical causes. The increase in altruistic feelings and behaviors observed during adolescence may be partially fueled by such egocentric and idealistic perceptions and dedication

Their blossoming ability to reason and draw conclusions on their own often results in adolescent idealism, drawing young people toward causes such as those supported by this "Earth First" rally.

AP/Wide World Photos

(Chou, 1998). Only after a number of serious collisions with reality do adolescents adapt their logic to include consideration of the world as it is, and choose their life battles and design their strategies in a manner more likely to get results.

The Personal Myth and Invincibility Fable. "Nobody would dare run me over. With my unique thinking and experiencing of the world, I'm too special and important to be lost." After having spent their entire lives depending on others to explain the world to them, adolescents' discovery that they can now draw logical conclusions on their own is pretty heady stuff. They create a **personal myth**, perceiving themselves as unique and destined for greatness. The personal myth provides impetus for their idealistic goals. They may fantasize about future endeavors such as personally finding a cure for AIDS, becoming one of the president's top advisors, making a billion dollars, or becoming a movie star. They are so special, in fact, that even if they were hit by a car it probably wouldn't do serious damage—thinking that represents the adolescent **invincibility fable**. One reason adolescents are more likely to take ill-advised risks is that they truly do not believe they personally could get pregnant, experience a drug overdose, or be killed while drag racing or drinking and driving. Even late in adolescence, teens continue to unrealistically calculate that they will experience more desirable and fewer undesirable events than will others (Klaczynski & Fauth, 1996).

The Imaginary Audience. "Of course that driver knows I'm going to cross the street now." Paradoxically, for all their self-declared independence, adolescents believe others are as absorbed in the unfolding of their life saga as they themselves have become. They carry along with them an **imaginary audience** that observes all they do, perhaps making its presence known as adolescents "hear" an inner narrative of their daily experiences. Within a crowded roomful of adolescents, each believes that he or she is the central focus. The predominant impact of the imaginary audience is extreme self-consciousness. Adolescents may spend hours preparing their physical appearance for an event, certain that they will be under so much public scrutiny that every hair out of place, clothing brand label, and facial blemish will be noticed and judged.

The personal myth, invincibility fable, and imaginary audience are most prominent during the middle school years, then slowly recede over the course of adolescence and young adulthood (Lapsley et al., 1988). The data adolescents collect while interacting with their worlds provide much of the reality testing that will eventually alter their self-perceptions. As they become more confident and secure with their increasing independence and sense of selfhood, they shed these artificial interpersonal attachments as having become no longer useful (Lapsley, 1990).

The Fleeting Nature of Formal Operational Reasoning

How often have you observed grown adults attempting to push unrealistically high ideals into practice? When an adult friend's point of view was challenged, did the adult react as if he or she were being personally attacked, rather than responding to the conflicting opinion as an intellectual exercise? Or maybe you've heard adult acquaintances draw conclusions on the basis of anecdotal evidence, such as "I watch a lot of TV and I'm not overweight, so I don't think there's a relationship between the two." You may also have encountered occasional adult circular reasoning: "We know that dams are responsible for flooding because flooding wouldn't happen if the dams weren't there"—a mere restatement of the theory rather than provision of any evidence to support it.

Regression into developmentally less-sophisticated styles of cognitive processing is fairly common among adults, especially when emotional undercurrents are at work. Effective use of formal operational reasoning must be learned. The brain's lack of an enclosed instruction manual may explain why most high school students continue to have significant difficulty with problems requiring formal operational reasoning (Bradmetz, 1999; Renner & Stafford, 1972). As many as 50% of college freshman are still functioning largely on a concrete operational level (Gray, 1979).

Fortunately, their lot is likely to improve over the next few years. They make their greatest improvement in formal operational reasoning between late adolescence and young adulthood (Klaczynski & Fauth, 1996). Its correct use appears to be learned by explicit instruction, rather than emerging on its own, and adolescents appear especially likely to use their newly learned reasoning strategies when a threat or some other strong motivator is present, such as trying to get a good grade (Klaczynski et al., 1997; Morris & Sloutsky, 1998). Not much additional improvement in scientific reasoning seems to take hold between earlier and late adulthood (Kuhn, 1993).

Some researchers argue that many individuals never truly master formal operational reasoning. Although it seems a person must possess at least an average level of analytical intelligence in order to develop formal operational reasoning (Inhelder, 1966), environmental variables appear to play a more significant role. Members of primitive cultures with less complex lifestyles have no need for formal operational reasoning and therefore do not pass standard Piagetian tests (Gellatly, 1987). Yet some show evidence of formal operational reasoning during activities crucial to their survival—such as developing hypotheses and making inferences while tracking and capturing prey (Tulkin & Konner, 1973).

A similar pattern occurs among adolescents. They develop formal operational reasoning as they are exposed to topics that require its use, which happens during their formal education (Artman & Cahan, 1993; Dasen, 1977). As with any new skill, practice improves performance (Marini & Case, 1994). Compared to their cohorts of the 1960s and 1970s, 1990s adolescents are better skilled at using formal operational reasoning, most likely because of its similarity to the intelligence test tasks that have become more predominant in adolescent education (Flieller, 1999).

We are also more likely to apply formal operations while working within familiar territory. When college students are given reasoning tasks in their major field of study, they demonstrate more formal operational reasoning than while addressing tasks in less familiar fields (De Lisi & Staudt, 1980). On the bright side, the ability to develop formal operational reasoning does not go away with age. Those from intellectually impoverished environments can develop this capacity later in life if given the appropriate exposures (Scribner, 1977).

Adolescent Decision Making

Adolescents in industrialized societies are entering a world that has become considerably more complex. The volume of information they must sort through has multiplied exponentially during the last half-century. Adults and adolescents alike frequently experience cognitive lapses produced by information overload (Bell, 1978). The information itself is constantly changing, requiring not only continual updating of personal knowledge but also an ability to evaluate the accuracy or utility of new information as it comes to light (Fletcher & Wooddell, 1981).

Promoting good personal decision-making ability during adolescence is an especially worthwhile endeavor. Consider the emphasis Western cultures place on liberty and freedom of choice and the degree of independent thinking required to make such choices. Stereotypical expectations and other social traditions having loosened their grip, adolescents face considerably more options as they seek out their preferred life roles. Adolescents face a number of demanding social situations that challenge their decision-making abilities—decisions about sexual behaviors, drugs, dropping out of school, and a variety of other potentially disastrous risk-taking circumstances. The adolescent faces all these against a backdrop of rapid physical, cognitive, and emotional changes; conflicting demands of school, parents, friends, and jobs; and formal operational and other cognitive abilities that they are still figuring out how to apply (Cassidy & Kurfman, 1977; Duryea, 1986; Nickerson et al., 1985; Zamansky-Shorin et al., 1988). Little wonder that older generations are often left clicking their tongues or shaking their heads in wonder as they observe adolescent decision making that just doesn't seem to add up!

Errors in Adolescent Decision Making. Actually, adolescents' errors in reasoning are fairly similar to the typical errors adults make (Baron & Brown, 1991; Beyth-Marom et al., 1991):

▶ *Insufficient search for options.* Sometimes decisions are made on impulse, with little thought given to alternative choices or potential consequences. Children are especially likely to sacrifice accuracy of choice in favor of speed, contributing not only to poorer decision making but also toward making considerably more impulsive decisions (Baron et al., 1986; Messer, 1976).

▶ *Single-minded decision making.* Sometimes while making decisions we drift into a sort of tunnel vision and consider only one relevant variable when in fact there are many (Montgomery, 1984; Tversky et al., 1988). Adolescents may easily fall into this error in trying to deal with the overload of conflicting information, interests, and demands. For example, an adolescent might decide to work additional hours in order to make car payments, ignoring her other valued goals, such as having enough time to complete her homework.

► *Persistence of irrational beliefs.* Have you ever noticed that some people will argue a point to the death, no matter how ridiculous their arguments may become? We often become personally invested in our ideas. In addition, re-arranging our knowledge bases to accommodate new information takes considerable effort. So once we do establish beliefs, we are somewhat resistant to altering them, often looking only for information that supports our biases and ignoring evidence against them. One result of these practices is the persistence of irrational beliefs (Baron, 1989; Kruglanski & Ajzen, 1983). In addition to the effect it can have on day-to-day living, habitual use of this thinking style is especially detrimental to an adolescent's formal education, which requires openness to counterevidence and criticism.

► *Misapplying probabilities.* The infamous capacity of statistics to be manipulated to prove almost anything is also a source of reasoning error. Consider parents who do not have their children vaccinated after hearing about potential serious side effects, yet do not take into account that the probability of serious consequences is much higher for children who are not vaccinated. When probabilities are low, we tend to assume that the undesired outcome won't happen to us. An adolescent boy might decide that the one-in-ten odds of contracting AIDS during unprotected sex with an infected individual makes such behavior safe enough for him, not considering that many instances of unprotected sex significantly increase the probability of his contracting AIDS.

► *Shortsightedness.* We tend to overvalue the immediate consequences of our decisions and undervalue the possible long-term consequences. Most certainly, U.S. government policy regarding the conflict between environmental and energy needs and the plight of the U.S. Social Security system are clear examples of decision making that address current problems but do not sufficiently weigh the probability or importance of some rather obvious long-term consequences. Teenagers are often similarly shortsighted, as illustrated by the student who chooses to stay up half the night to do homework then has considerable difficulty concentrating at school the next morning. Given the serious nature of some issues and limitations teenagers must sort through, the consequences of some instances of shortsightedness can be much more immediately drastic.

How can we help adolescents become better decision makers?

PAVING PATHWAYS ALONG ADOLESCENT COGNITIVE MILESTONES: TEACHING DECISION MAKING TO ADOLESCENTS

Can effective decision making be taught to adolescents? Most certainly! Their formal operational capacity for pursuing exhaustive searches for answers and considering and combining multiple lines of thought primes them for learning this skill. Adolescents adopt the particular problem-solving strategies that they learn by observing their cultural norms (Ellis, 1997). When adolescents take part in formal programs for teaching valid decision-making strategies, they not only demonstrate improved strategy use but also report they believe they are making better decisions (Beyth-Marom et al., 1991).

The quality of a decision is determined by the quality of the process used to make it. Effective decision-making processes consider the relevant goals, the options available, the potential outcomes of those options, and the relative probability that each potential outcome could come to pass (Baron, 1989; Laskey & Campbell, 1991). These processes both support and augment the backbone of healthy decision making: the adolescent's emerging comprehension that bad choices are more likely to result in bad outcomes, good choices are more likely to result in good outcomes, and the teenagers themselves are the ones who both make their behavioral choices and experience the resulting consequences (Rosemond, 1998).

Some decisions are simpler than others. Simple problem-solving consists of defining the problem, generating options for solving the problem, looking at the pros and cons of each option, then choosing the option with the most favorable and/or least unfavorable evaluation. Adolescents are more likely to use more advanced reasoning strategies when the situation is relevant to their own lives, rather than someone else's (Klaczynski, 1997). So let's look at a situation personally relevant to Matt.

Matt's biology class is organized around completion of group project assignments. One of Matt's group members, Dave, is really getting on his nerves. When they are working on an assignment, it seems to Matt that he and the other two group members are doing all the work while Dave just sits there, thumbing aimlessly through the textbook or staring out the window. In fact, if someone doesn't out-and-out tell him to do some busywork part of the assignment, he doesn't do anything at all. Yet he gets the same grade as the rest of the group. Matt decides to apply the problem-solving technique he learned in his health class:

1. *Define the problem.* In Matt's view the problem is that Dave isn't doing his fair share of the group work, so Matt and the other group members end up having to do more.

2. *Separate out the subproblems.* Subproblems are other difficulties that may be related to the main problem but do not need to be solved in order to take care of the main problem. Removing subproblems keeps them from interfering with selecting a solution. If necessary, the subproblems can always be addressed later. Matt can think of two subproblems:
   ► Dave hangs out with the "skaters." Matt hates "skaters."
   ► Matt doesn't believe the instructor gives them enough time to do a really good job on projects, even when Dave does help out.

3. *What might be causing this problem?* Hypothesizing potential causes can help with generating solutions. Why isn't Dave helping out? Matt can think of several possibilities:
   ► Dave's a slacker, and he's milking the situation for whatever it's worth.
   ► Dave is just plain stupid and couldn't help if he wanted to.
   ► Dave is shy and does not wish to impose himself.

- ▶ Dave knows that Matt doesn't like him and is afraid to say anything.
- ▶ Dave knows that Matt doesn't like him and is not helping out in order to get even.
- ▶ Dave isn't very good as a self-starter.

4. *Generate a list of potential solutions, and list the pros and cons of each solution.* Matt remembers that he is supposed to list every solution that goes through his head no matter how ridiculous it might sound, since we often act out on impulsive, ridiculous solutions just because we never stopped to think through the repercussions. Matt considers several solutions:
  - ▶ Beat Dave up after school.
    - Pro: Matt would feel good while beating him up, at least for the moment.
    - Con: He would probably get suspended. He would also probably feel badly about it afterwards.
  - ▶ See if the teacher will let them trade Dave for someone from some other group.
    - Pro: They would be rid of him.
    - Con: At the beginning of the year the teacher said group assignments were permanent except for extreme circumstances. Matt doesn't want to sound like a whiner. Besides, he doesn't think he could talk the other group members into such a move.
  - ▶ See if the teacher will divide the work into four standard parts that all groups follow.
    - Pro: Dave would have to take responsibility for one part.
    - Con: He still might not do his part and then their assignments would be late or incomplete.
  - ▶ Talk around him as if he isn't there until he takes the initiative.
    - Pro: Dave might figure out that they are waiting for him to contribute.
    - Con: Dave might not figure out why he is being shut out and do even less.
  - ▶ Ask him what his ideas are and what he would like to do at the beginning of each project.
    - Pro: Dave might be more likely to pull his weight if he gets to do something he wants to do.
    - Con: Dave might want to do things differently than Matt wants to do them.
  - ▶ Try to be friends with him.
    - Pro: Dave might try harder if he sees them as being friends.
    - Con: Since he really doesn't like Dave, it would feel hypocritical.

5. *Select the solution that has the most going for it and the least going against it.* Matt decides that of these six options, asking Dave what he would like to do would be the best solution. If it doesn't work out he can always try something else.

6. *Decide when to implement the plan and follow through.* Matt decides to try his new approach when they start on the next group assignment. In doing so he is surprised to find out that Dave does have some good ideas, and some are the same as Matt's. Dave continues to be a little slow to get involved and Matt decides he is probably shy. But as Matt and his group members make a ritual out of drawing him in at certain points, he contributes more and more to the group assignments.

Some decisions are more complex, requiring evaluation of more ambiguous factors such as the probability of an outcome happening or particular outcomes being more valued or more feared than others (Kleindorfer et al., 1993). Adolescents can be taught to use decision trees that take these considerations into account, creating and comparing mathematical values that indicate the best possible decision given the information at hand (Baron & Brown, 1991; Peel & Dansereau, 1998).

Suppose both Darren and Tom have asked Sheila to go to the winter prom. Darren is one of the most popular guys in school and she would really like to go with him, but he has frequently backed out of commitments at the last minute. Tom is okay and maybe a little boring, but very dependable. Sheila constructs a decision tree that reflects these factors. She decides upon the desirability or undesirability of four potential outcomes from her standpoint, using −10 as worst possible outcome and 10 as best possible outcome:

> She chooses Darren, he follows through: 10—a dream date
> She chooses Tom, he follows through: 5—an OK date, but at least she has one
> She chooses Darren, he backs out: −4—disappointing, but she still might be able to get Tom to go at the last minute
> She chooses Tom, he backs out: −6—even more disappointing, since Darren will most likely have found someone else to go with

Next, Sheila considers the probability of her potential dates following through. She figures that for Darren there is about a 40% chance and for Tom a 90% chance. She multiplies these values with those assigned to the potential outcomes:

Chooses Darren, he follows through:	$10 \times .40 = 4$
Chooses Tom, he follows through:	$5 \times .90 = 4.5$
Chooses Darren, he backs out:	$-4 \times .60 = -2.4$
Chooses Tom, he backs out:	$-6 \times .10 = -6$

What this exercise would look like as a decision tree is shown in Figure 15.1. The figures say that going with Tom results in both a higher positive value and lower negative value whether he shows up or not. Notice that if Sheila had not additionally considered the probabilities, choosing Darren would have looked like the best option because that option has a more positively valued desired

FIGURE 15.1

A decision tree. This style of decision making takes into account not only the differing possibilities but also the relative likelihood of potential outcomes, requiring the adolescent to consider multiple variables.

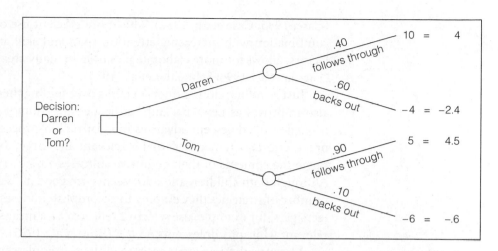

outcome and a less negatively valued undesired outcome. Similar combinations of priority-oriented values and relative probabilities can help adolescents explore and sort out a number of complex decisions facing them in today's world.

What information-processing advances occur during adolescence?

INFORMATION-PROCESSING

Before I became involved with disaster mental health work, my luggage-packing proficiency was fairly anemic. As I answered more and more urgent calls of "please come, come now!" I found myself fine-tuning my packing skills practically into an art form. I became increasingly better skilled at deciding what I needed to take and what I could leave behind. I discovered especially space-economical strategies for arranging the items that I always brought along, speeding up the packing process. I discovered techniques such as rolling clothes rather than folding them, which made room for additional items. As the packing process became more automatic, I not only became less likely to forget items but also benefited from the increased amount of time and energy I could devote to speculating upon what else would be especially useful for the particular disaster at hand.

Adolescent information-processing similarly advances along these factors of familiarity, practice, greater knowledge, and new skill attainment. For example, if you have watched a teenager play a board game with a younger child you may have observed teenage eye-rolling impatience during the waiting period preceding the younger child's "obvious" move. One quantitative change in adolescent cognitive ability is speed of processing (Anderson et al., 1997; Band et al., 2000; Keating & Bobbitt, 1978). The source of the above teenager's additional speed is not necessarily the use of more advanced reasoning strategies, but simply more extensive practice with the board game, resulting in quicker selection and application of already-known strategies (Kail, 1993). Quicker routine processing and automatic strategy utilization also free up space in working memory, thus creating a greater functional capacity for memory processes

(Case, 1985; Case et al., 1982). This more efficient use of working memory, in combination with increasing attention span and skill at attending to relevant factors, allows for more elaborate planning in many areas of an adolescent's life (Parrila et al., 1996; Schneider et al., 1984).

Just as rolling clothes offers benefits over folding them, adolescent memory also improves as new "packing" strategies are adopted. One interesting phenomenon of adolescent advances in information-processing is **selective memory**— efforts to remember what is relevant and forget the irrelevant as they arrange the contents of their cognitive suitcases (Bjork, 1970; Bray et al., 1983). Although both children and adolescents are good at "selective forgetting," the number of strategies they employ to accomplish it increases as they grow older; teenagers, for example, use selective rehearsal as a means of shutting out the irrelevant while preadolescents do not (Bray et al., 1985).

Memory also improves because of the way adolescents organize new material. Memory appears to manage information in "chunks," and we seem able to manipulate about seven chunks at any given time (Miller, 1956). Although the number we can handle does not appear to increase as we advance developmentally, the more knowledge we have tucked away in our memory stores, the more cognitive "glue" we can access for attaching additional material to these chunks. Thus as teenagers proceed through adolescence, their greater knowledge base increases their capacity for memory (Chi, 1978). As might be predicted, memory capacity is tightly related to the amount of formal schooling a person has received (Kail, 1990).

Yet the number of memory strategies we use appears to increase independently of formal instruction in their methods. For example, elaboration is a memory retrieval technique that improves recall by capitalizing upon construed relationships between items that an individual is trying to remember, such as by designing acronyms that act as cues for remembering lists of information or the visual imagery strategy described in Chapter 12 (see page 345) (Kail, 1990; Keniston & Flavell, 1979; Schneider & Pressley, 1989). When researchers teach elaboration techniques to both adolescents and school-age children, the younger children show increased performance in recalling word pairs but adolescents do not (Rohwer & Bean, 1973). This outcome may occur because adolescents are already effectively using such techniques. As Figure 15.2 shows, younger children seem to depend mainly on rehearsal as a memory strategy, while adolescents appear to apply rehearsal, elaboration, and other strategies as a matter of course (Beuhring & Kee, 1987a; 1987b).

Age also appears to play a role in determining whether the learning will transfer outside of the original learning situation. For example, after being instructed in the use of a novel memory-enhancing technique, the adolescents applied it to other tasks but the younger children did not (Pressley & Dennis-Rounds, 1980). Therefore both developmental and environmental variables appear to interplay as adolescents maximize their cognitive cargo capacity.

Remember how easily preschoolers develop false memories? Adolescents are not so readily led astray. Another advance of adolescent cognitive process-

FIGURE 15.2

Average number of memory strategy applications reported during paired-associate task by two age groups. While school-age children rely more heavily on rehearsal as a mnemonic device, adolescents more comfortably select from multiple mnemonic strategies. Adapted with permission from T. Beuhring & D. W. Kee (1987a) Developmental relationships among meta-memory elaborative strategy use, and associative memory. *Journal of Experimental Child Psychology, 44, 377–40;* and (1987b) Elaboration and associative memory development: The metamemory link. In M. A. McDaniel & M. Pressley (Eds.), *Imagery and related mnemonic processes: Theories and applications.* New York: Springer.

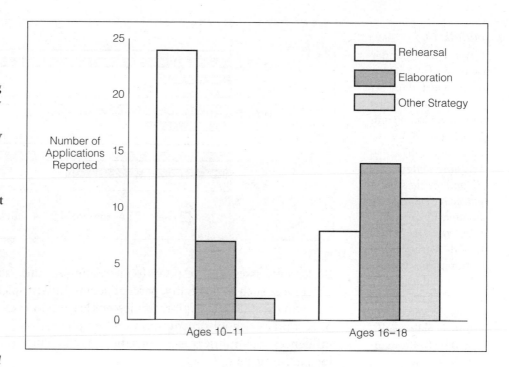

How do characteristics of secondary schools and advances in language and math abilities affect learning during adolescence?

ing is their greater skill at recognizing the source of a memory: actual event, imagined event, or an event relayed to them by someone else. So in addition to being larger in capacity and more elaborate, the adolescent's memory stores have become less vulnerable to inappropriate manipulations (Ackil & Zaragoza, 1998; Day et al., 1998).

LEARNING DURING ADOLESCENCE

Middle school and high school settings are the primary milieus for adolescents' development of cognitive skills as well as for their encounters with day-to-day learning. The lessons learned address not only academics but also the contexts of peer relationships and extracurricular activities. When asked what is the best thing about high school, the variations in teenagers' responses depend partly on their age. Figure 15.3 shows the differing fields of adolescent focus (Brown & Theobald, 1998). Peer relationships win out as the most outstanding feature of school regardless of the phase of adolescence. However, this emphasis is most lopsided early in high school, with academic learning regaining some attractiveness as graduation and transitioning to the real world loom large before them.

In addition to adapting to academic learning, students also negotiate transitions among their roles in home and work contexts, applying new learning as they go. Making adjustments as they move more freely and independently among multiple worlds with differing rules of play can at times be awkward, especially if unrealistic expectations flavor an adolescent's world view. How well

FIGURE 15.3
Grade level and differences in what adolescents report liking best about school. Adapted with permission from B. B. Brown & W. Theobald (1997), *Learning contexts beyond the classroom: Extracurricular activity, community organizations, and peer groups.* In 97th Yearbook of the National Society for the Study of Education, The adolescent years: Social influences and educational challenges, edited by K. Borman & B. Schneider.

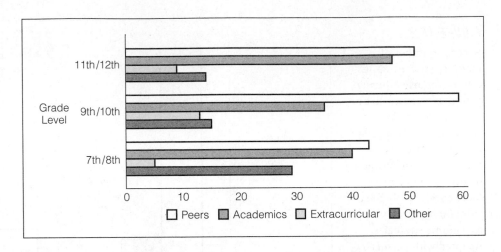

adolescents assess and respond to alternating settings is affected by individual differences such as flexibility, perceptiveness, and problem-solving ability. The following section will explore adolescent learning in reference to the elements of secondary school organization and emphases, academic abilities, parental influences, peer influences, involvement in extracurricular activities, and holding part-time jobs.

Secondary Schools

While communities at times blame the schools when students receive poor scholastic testing scores, school setting variables are not the strongest predictors of adolescent academic achievement. Family background—especially parents' educational level and socioeconomic status—and peer culture are the best predictors, with instruction quality ranking only below them (Mare, 1995; Newmann et al., 1996). What is high-quality instruction? The structure of the curriculum and the school setting appear to make the greatest contribution, rather than the particular teacher. Three main components contribute to quality instruction programs (Bliss et al., 1991; Lee et al., 1993; Newmann, 1998):

1. *Quality curriculum content.* The curriculum is solidly grounded in the knowledge base of the particular academic or technical discipline in such a way as to present an in-depth, integrated understanding of that knowledge base and its applicability, rather than presenting a disjointed factoid salad for students to chew then spew.

2. *Encouraging a mastery orientation.* The teacher, supported by adequate technical resources of the school, chooses activities that foster both the mastering of concepts and in-depth, applied understanding of them. Quality instruction is thus given an opportunity to engage students, which is essential for learning to take place. In fact, quality instruction, student engagement, and subject mastery seem to be inseparable, bolstering one another as the learning process proceeds (Newmann, 1992).

3. *Healthy learning atmosphere.* The school climate is characterized by high expectations of achievement for all students within an atmosphere of personal safety and orderly conduct. Civility and cooperation are expected among students and especially among staff. A collegial, supportive team spirit among teachers and administrators who are working together toward common goals goes far toward floating a successful program; nothing sinks the ship faster than a staff atmosphere of distrust, ego trips, and isolated self interest (Little, 1993; Talbert & McLaughlin, 1994).

Individual Academic Abilities

Language Skills. Adolescents continue to increase their capacities for vocabulary and grammar. Like any frequently used skill, these will continue to improve well into adulthood (Obler, 1989). One of the more notable changes in teenagers' use of language is their move away from the literal and greater use of abstraction in their verbiage. Sarcasm and slang that would go over the heads of most concrete operational children can become a conversational mainstay for adolescents (Spears, 1991; Winner, 1988). Another change concerns gender differences in language ability. Beginning with the utterance of their first words, girls as a group demonstrate more advanced language skills than do boys. While girls continue to maintain a slight advantage, this gap between the genders closes considerably during adolescence (Hyde & Linn, 1988; Marsh, 1989).

Keeping step with their more complex reasoning abilities are changes in adolescents' inner processing and experience of reading (Thomson, 1987). As concrete operational children read stories, they typically conjure up mental images, make sporadic short-term predictions about what might happen next, think how the story relates to their own experiences, and experience empathy when they recognize characters' feelings. Formal operational adolescents spend less time mulling over surface understandings and consider more abstract, alternative possibilities. What motive does this character's behavior suggest? How might this plot progress or the theme be played out? What might this passage symbolize?

Reading comprehension is aided by adolescents' more advanced information-processing skills. Individual differences in reading comprehension frequently reflect differences in strategy development. For example, when students who have read a passage are required to answer questions about it, the students who show poor comprehension have yet to develop successful strategies for seeking answers (Cataldo & Cornoldi, 1998). Historically, instruction to improve reading comprehension has been designed to encourage students to find the "main idea," but teaching them instead to connect newly read material to what they already know appears to result in better comprehension (Spires & Donley, 1998).

Mathematics Skills. Their more advanced cognitive abilities enable teenagers to tackle more complex mathematical manipulations and to now comprehend processes within calculus, trigonometry, and other advanced math and math-related sciences. Complex math skills require considerable attending, concentration, and manipulation of multiple variables—mental processing abilities that adolescents now have within their grasp.

During the high school years the oft-touted superiority of boys' math skills over girls' makes its first appearance. Over the last few decades research has revealed that this gender difference has been somewhat exaggerated. Meta-analysis of 100 studies measuring differences between girls' and boys' math performance has indicated a couple of tendencies (Hyde et al., 1990). During the elementary school years there are no consistent differences, although girls do demonstrate a slight superiority in computational skills. While boys pull out ahead during high school and college, their better performance is limited to the area of complex problem-solving, and mainly only among gifted students (Gallagher et al., 2000). Overall, differences are fairly modest.

However, aptitude at complex problem-solving is especially significant because it is the gateway to all math- or science-related fields. In the United States and other societies participating in the global technological revolution, men are dramatically overrepresented in these fields (Baringa, 1994; Betz & Fitzgerald, 1987). Why do boys pull ahead of girls when complex problem-solving becomes a major factor? While some have tried to associate this phenomenon with boys' better spatial skills, spatial ability has not held up as a good predictor of math performance (Benbow, 1988; Linn & Hyde, 1985). Others have investigated the differences from a sociological perspective. Male math superiority has become a cultural stereotype (Tiedemann, 2000). As early as age 12, female math students view their performance with less confidence than do boys even though their actual computation ability does not differ (Vermeer et al., 2000). To do well at math, women must buck this stereotype, but doing so raises anxieties that in turn interfere with the attending and concentration necessary for complex problem-solving. Being faced with this form of "stereotype threat" has in fact been associated with decreased math performance (Spencer et al., 1999).

Another interesting explanation of this gender difference that also considers the role of attending interference proposes a process of **self-objectification** (Fredrickson & Roberts, 1997; Tiggerman & Lynch, 2001). This line of thinking looks at how women in our culture are sexually objectified (more so than are men): Their sexual identity is treated as inanimate or separate from their personal individuality or human beinghood. Researchers revealed a concrete example of this cultural bias by examining the media's photographic depictions of men and women. They found that photo and film representations of men focused more on their faces, while those of women were much more likely to zero in on body parts or positioning related to their sexuality (Archer et al., 1983). As young women internalize these and other such cultural instructions, they learn to treat their bodily appearance as separate from their inner identity. As they self-objectify, they also learn to evaluate themselves more from a third-person perspective, focusing on identity concerns such as "how do I look" and "what do others see" rather than tapping into their inner, privileged, first-person perspective of "what am I capable of" or "what really interests me" (Fredrickson et al., 1997).

This division of attending due to self-objectification, especially in combination with stereotype threat, may disrupt or slow the concentration necessary for focusing on complex problems such as advanced math. One clever line of research had women try on either a swimsuit or a sweater, then take a math test. Those who tried on the sweater performed significantly better than those who tried on the swimsuit. When the study was replicated using both men and women, the men showed no such differences related to fitting room experience (Fredrickson et al., 1997). This phenomenon provides a provocative explanation for why girls may suddenly start falling behind in math at about the same time they are also beginning to have concerns about their body image.

Further evidence of possible cultural influences on girls' math performance is the fact that most women faculty in math- and science-related fields in the United States attended all-girl schools. In cultures abroad, women are much more likely to enter math-intensive scientific fields. For example, 3% of the physics professors in the United States are women, while in Hungary roughly 50% are (Baringa, 1994). Furthermore, female doctoral students in male-dominated programs in the United States have reported experiencing less faculty sensitivity and support than did doctoral students in gender-balanced programs; this difference was associated with significant drops in self-concept and career commitment during the course of their training (Ulku-Steiner et al., 2000).

Fortunately, the level of gender disparity observed in math performance has diminished considerably since the studies of the sixties and earlier. Most likely

The effect of gender stereotyping is one of the reasons why fewer girls than boys enroll in advanced math classes.

Gale Zucker/Stock Boston

this finding is related to the less-rigid gender stereotyping of more recent decades and to more encouragement of girls as they are shown the relevance of becoming proficient at advanced math skills. Parents who relate to their daughters that they view math and science as important to their daughters' futures appear to offset the negative influence of peer and cultural attitudes toward girls' academic choices (Olszewski-Kubilius & Yasumoto, 1995). As girls increasingly perceive themselves as welcome in math-related fields, this difference between the genders will most likely diminish further (Marsh, 1989).

Dropping Out. Progress in math, language arts, and other important fields of academic endeavor screeches to a premature grinding halt for almost 10% of all children. Each year over a million students drop out of school. The impact this choice will most likely have on their futures is substantial. They can expect to earn about $6000 less per year than high school graduates, whose financial advantage will multiply exponentially if they go on to higher education. Students who drop out are six times more likely to be unwed parents, three times more likely to be arrested, and twice as likely to be unemployed. Half the people living in jail cells and half the people living on welfare are school dropouts (Coley, 1995; Committee for Economic Development, 1987; McMillan & Kaufman, 1996; Schorr & Schorr, 1988).

Which teenagers are more likely to drop out of school? Boys are more likely than girls (Wagenaar, 1987; Denton & Hunter, 1991). More adolescents from single-parent homes than from two-parent homes drop out (Gilbert et al., 1993). Low socioeconomic status plays a role, most consistently for boys (Ensminger et al., 1996). Dropout rates are higher in rural areas (Gilbert et al., 1993). Those with ethnically diverse backgrounds are more likely to drop out; however, no differences based on ethnicity are found when socioeconomic status is taken into account (Wehlage & Rutter, 1986). Dropping out has been linked to excessive hours at part-time jobs (Greenberger & Steinberg, 1986).

From a psychological perspective, students who drop out tend to have lower self-esteem, less sense of control over their lives, and lower expectations of educational achievement and occupational level than students who finish their educations (Rumberger, 1987). Teenagers with learning disabilities are especially at risk, not only for dropping out of school but also for dropping out of life in general (Masi et al., 1998; Owings & Stocking, 1985; Zigmond, 1990). The Tried . . . . and True boxes on pages 474–475 elaborate on the unfortunate association between learning disabilities and suicide.

Why do teenagers choose to stay in school? The trend of high school graduations over the last half-century sheds some light on one major motivator. Between 1940 and 1990 the percentage of students completing a high school degree increased from 44% to 85% (Dorn, 1996). This increase coincided with the growing utility of a high school degree, as the labor market increasingly favored students with training in basic skills. This circumstance has not changed: Clearly, education continues to play a major role in an adolescent's future career opportunities.

Why do so many adolescents continue to drop out? Personal problems and detrimental family influences certainly play roles (West, 1991). However, many students no longer perceive a connection between school and career, as high school curricula have become less and less relevant to the working world (Dorn, 1996; Tanner et al., 1995). Students in general do not appear to view counselors, teachers, and other knowledgeable educational/vocational personnel as possible resources in planning for their futures; more often they consult with parents and peers when making educational and career decisions (Mau, 1995). It is unclear whether this is because vocational advice is unavailable during this critical time, the school personnel themselves being too overburdened with paperwork and other responsibilities to provide individual counseling, or because the students and their parents are unaware of their utility (Commission on Precollege Guidance and Counseling, 1987; Lee & Ekstrom, 1986). Hopefully as schools become more centered on facilitating the connection between school and the working world greater numbers of students will finish their educations.

How do relationships with parents and peers affect success at school?

Parental Effects on Learning

In spite of the increasing independence of thinking found among adolescents, their relationships with parents continue to pack a considerable wallop as they pursue their academic careers. Adolescents' perceptions of their math and language competencies are more strongly influenced by their parents' perceptions of these than they are by the actual grades they have earned (Frome & Eccles, 1998). Adolescents' academic performance continues to benefit when parents stay actively involved with its progress (Stevenson & Baker, 1987). Unfortunately, parents tend to involve themselves with their adolescents' school activity only about half as much as they did during the elementary school years (Steinberg et al., 1996). Interestingly, parents are more likely to stay involved with their daughters' education than with their sons' (Carter & Wojtkiewicz, 2000).

The usual effects of parenting styles also apply to adolescent academic achievement: Authoritative parenting is beneficial; permissive and authoritarian parenting are not. The most detrimental pattern is one that uses harsh discipline, inconsistently applied (Dornbusch et al., 1987). The harshly controlling authoritarian style has indeed been demonstrated as detrimental to adolescent academic achievement cross-culturally, even within cultures having substantially stricter standards of child behavior (Leung et al., 1998). The cooperative, interactive style of authoritative parents fosters high academic achievement and intellectual performance as they coach their children through academic problem-solving and other school-related tasks (Portes et al., 1998).

These results are explained in part by the fact that each of the three styles activates a different source of adolescent academic motivation. The authoritative style is associated with intrinsic motivation, the permissive or neglectful with amotivation, and the authoritarian with extrinsic motivation or amotivation (Leung & Kwan, 1998). Correspondingly, adolescents benefit from developing an inner, learning-based emphasis on their schoolwork, rather than an external,

BOX 15.1   Learning disabilities and adolescent suicide

Tried

McBride, H. E. A., & Siegel, L. S. (1997). Learning disabilities and adolescent suicide. *Journal of Learning Disabilities, 30,* 652–659.

CONSIDER THE LIFE CIRCUMSTANCE OF HAVING A LEARNing disability from the perspective of adolescents. School success is continually thrown before them as the primary route to success. They try their hardest to academically succeed, yet still struggle. If they are identified as learning disabled they endure jibes from peers because of the social stigma attached to spending time in the resource room—during a life phase when fitting in with peers is a major priority. If their disabilities are unidentified they are frequently chastised by instructors and parents for not trying hard enough. Because learning disabled adolescents frequently also have difficulties with problem-solving, social skills, and interpersonal relationships, their resources for dealing with the consequences of their disabilities may also be somewhat limited.

We might expect learning disabled students constantly faced with such impossible-seeming challenges to be particularly susceptible to emotional problems. In fact, a common set of impairments known as arithmetic/writing disability has been associated with a greater likelihood of depression. Could learning disabled teenagers also be especially susceptible to suicide? Hazel McBride and Linda Siegel (1997) explored this possibility in a study using four groups of participants, all selected from the same geographic area:

- Twenty-seven adolescents who had recently committed suicide and had left suicide notes. None of these adolescents were identified as having had learning disabilities or having been recipients of special education assistance.
- Twenty-eight learning disabled (LD) teenagers, so identified on the basis of scores received on the Wide Range Achievement Test and the Woodcock Reading Mastery Tests.

- Forty-one nonlearning disabled (non-LD) students.
- Ten older adults who had committed suicide and had left suicide notes.

The experimenters dictated a selection of the adolescent suicide notes to the LD and non-LD students, who transcribed them. The notes read to each particular student were selected on the basis of age similarity. Four raters who were blind to group membership rated the spelling accuracy on all original and reproduced notes, producing a score based on proportion of correctly versus incorrectly spelled words. They also judged handwriting quality by comparing the notes to samples from the Test of Written Language.

As expected, they found that the LD participants made significantly more spelling and handwriting errors than did the non-LD participants. The scores received by the original composers of the suicide notes were also significantly lower than the non-LD participants, and were comparable to the scores of the LD participants. The performance level of the older suicide completers, however, was more consistent with the performance of the non-LD adolescents.

These data suggest that a considerable number of adolescent suicides had learning disabilities. Since the notes of the older adult suicides did not contain similar errors, the writing deficiencies cannot be blamed on the extreme stress or emotional turmoil of the moment. We might ask if perhaps learning disabled adolescents are more likely to leave notes than nonlearning disabled suicide completers; however, other research has indicated that this is not the case. If learning disabilities are indeed an unrecognized risk factor for adolescent suicide, the importance of routine screening and providing intervention for adolescents once their disabilities are revealed becomes dramatically greater.

BOX 15.2   Supporting learning disabled adolescents

... and True

IN ADDITION TO DEPRESSION AND THE GREATER LIKELI-hood of dropping out, adolescents experience many adverse reactions to dealing with their learning disabilities. Their anxiety over whether or not they can succeed is not only unpleasant but also further interferes with attending and concentration. They may experience futility—why try at all? In their frustration they might act out against the adult world that has placed seemingly impossible demands upon them. Since misery loves miserable company they may also be drawn to make friends with other underachievers who on one hand can personally sympathize with their plight but on the other hand may draw the adolescent into ill-advised behaviors that produce further stressors.

What can parents do to provide support for their learning disabled adolescents (Slap & Jablow, 1994)?

- Evaluate the possibility of the presence of a learning disability as the first signs appear. While learning disabilities often reveal themselves during grade school, smart children may compensate for their deficits at that time. The greater demands placed on students during middle school and high school then overwhelm them, leaving parents and teachers bewildered over their poor performance. The earlier a learning disability is identified, the less opportunity adolescents will have for attributing their failures to being "stupid" or in some other way questioning their self-worth.

- Help teenagers figure out what kind of learning style works best for them. "Learning disability" is not synonymous with "can't learn"; most people with learning disabilities are of average intelligence. Their styles of learning simply differ from the norm.

- Teach them how to break tasks down into smaller and smaller parts until goals are more easily accomplished.

- Be flexible, willing to try new ways of approaching problems and alternative course studies.

- Remember that while being directive about children's homework times and school activity involvement may have been appropriate when they were in grade school, such a controlling approach will almost surely backfire when used on adolescents. Give them as much control as possible over what, how, and when they study, so long as the tasks are getting done. In doing so you are expressing confidence in their ability to manage themselves, thus bolstering their own confidence.

- Play up their strengths and downplay their weaknesses. Likewise provide encouragement and the reinforcement of compliments for their successes and minimize criticism. They already know when they are not succeeding and do not need you rubbing it in.

- Show as much concern for their feelings about the academic performance as you do about their report cards.

- Remain open-minded and positive about teenagers' future career and academic pathways. The presence of a learning disability does not mean that the student cannot pursue higher education, but you may want to be especially selective, choosing a school with resources available for those with disabilities. Assist learning disabled students as they pursue their post-high school pathways, speaking of "when" they go to college rather than "if"!

Slap, G. B., & Jablow, M. M. (1994). *Teenage health care: The first comprehensive family guide for preteen to young adult years.* New York: Pocket Books.

performance-based emphasis. When they perceive that getting the grade is the only important factor, they are more likely to worry about school, experience test anxiety, make less efficient use of information-seeking and advanced cognitive strategies, and cheat (Anderman et al., 1998; Butler, 1999; Chapell & Overton, 1998). Solid feelings of attachment toward parents have also been associated with motivation to succeed academically (Learner & Kruger, 1997).

Peer Effects on Learning

The particular peer group a student adopts is a tremendously powerful predictor of academic achievement (Brown et al., 1993; Wentzel & Caldwell, 1997), as Figure 15.4 shows. When examined both as an entire population and in terms of "crowd" affiliation (see Chapter 16, page 506), crowds can differ by as much as two full letter grades—a greater difference than the standard deviation found for the entire population! Unfortunately, scholastic indifference may be a requirement for membership within some peer groups (Steinberg, Dornbusch, & Brown, 1992). Gifted students may purposely underachieve if getting good

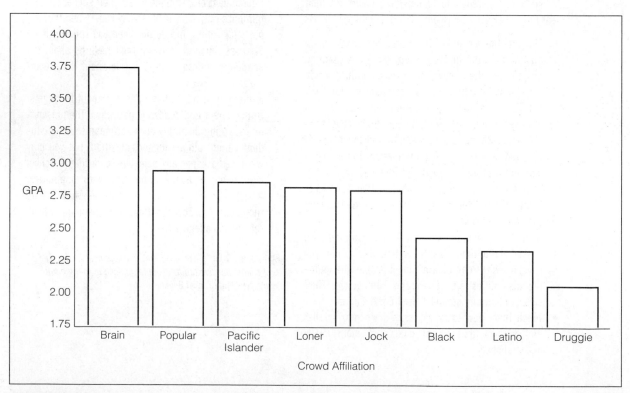

FIGURE 15.4

Grade point averages of those affiliated with various crowd types. While peers influence an adolescent's attitude toward academic achievement, the differences here could also reflect a tendency for adolescents to affiliate with those who share their attitude toward academic achievement. Adapted with permission from B. B. Brown, S. D. Lamborn, N. Mounts, and L. Steinberg, Parenting practices and peer group affiliation in adolescence. *Child Development, 64,* 467–482. Copyright © 1993 by Society for Research in Child Development.

grades runs them the risk of being ostracized by the lower-achieving peers with whom they affiliate—and affiliation can sometimes be mandated by ethnic background rather than chosen by the adolescent (Fordham & Ogbu, 1986).

In addition to the influence of peer group membership, the adolescent school culture in general seems to encourage thinking and behaving that would not be expected to foster academic achievement. Attractiveness rather than achievement level appears to be the main determinant of popularity, especially among younger teens (Boyatzis et al., 1998). High achievement may even work against popularity. In a line of research in which thousands of teens were interviewed, the following statistics came to light (Steinberg et al., 1996):

▶ Adolescents report that only 32% of their friends think getting good grades is important.

▶ Twenty percent say their friends make fun of those who try to do well.

▶ Over 50% say they never discuss schoolwork with friends.

▶ Only 20% regularly spend time studying with a friend.

Also influential is the status adolescents attribute to the various peer groups. Adolescents were asked which crowd they would like to join:

▶ Five times as many wanted to be with the "populars" or "jocks" as wanted to be with the "brains."

▶ Three times as many wanted to join the "partyers" or the "druggies" as wanted to join the "brains."

▶ One-half of the "brains" wished they were in a different crowd.

Hopefully these biases will change as the relevance of education becomes more effectively tied with students' future vocations—a topic explored later in this chapter.

What positive or negative effects do extracurricular activities and part-time jobs have on academic achievement?

Extracurricular Activities

Schools have sponsored activities outside of regular classroom instruction for centuries. Even ancient Greece, with its emphasis on didactic and Socratic instruction, supported extracurricular activities such as honor societies and speaking competitions (McKown, 1952). Currently about 70% of high school students participate in at least one extracurricular activity, a statistic that has remained amazingly stable over the last several decades (Brown et al., 1991; Dement, 1924). Girls tend to participate more than boys, and Caucasian students are more likely to become involved than African-American, Asian-American, or Hispanic students (Brown & Theobald, 1998). Athletic programs enjoy the greatest participation levels, with interest clubs and performing arts following in succession (Brown et al., 1991).

I recall attending a presentation at my children's neighborhood high school where the speaker encouraged us to get our children involved in extracurricular activities as a means of improving their grades. This speaker had most likely been influenced by the flurry of studies demonstrating that students who are involved in extracurricular activities also perform better academically. However,

FIGURE 15.5
Average number of extracurricular activities pursued by dropout and nondropout students. Students may feel encouraged to stay in school because they enjoy extracurricular involvement; but these data could also reflect a general lack of interest in school, including both classroom and extracurricular aspects. Adapted with permission from J. L. Mahoney and R. B. Cairns, Do extracurricular activities protect against early school dropout? *Developmental Psychology, 33,* 241–253. Copyright © 1997 by the American Psychological Association.

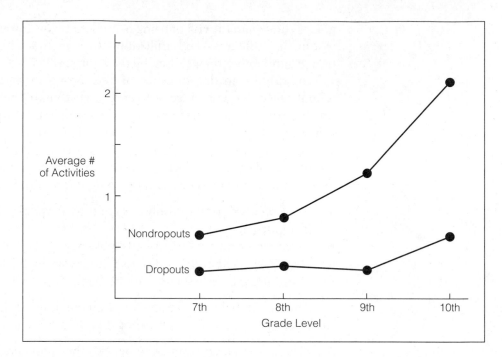

when studies control for academic performance before such participation, participation in extracurricular activities shows neither beneficial nor detrimental effects on academic variables. Apparently, the same attributes or factors that encourage students to achieve academically also influence participation in extracurricular activities (Feltz & Weiss, 1984; Marsh, 1992). Especially notable is that students who do participate have higher educational aspirations than do nonparticipants, suggesting that the presence of an achievement motivation may influence both behaviors (Snyder & Spreitzer, 1977).

Although it appears that encouraging my children to sign up for extracurricular activities probably didn't have any effect on their academic achievement, other beneficial forms of learning have been associated with such involvement. Participation appears to enhance students' self-esteem and self-confidence (Holland & Andre, 1987). And when activities include multiracial participation, interracial attitudes and behaviors show positive effects (Crain et al., 1982; Schofield, 1982). Studies of involvement in athletic activity suggest that participation may promote improved citizenship and help build leadership skills (Stevenson, 1975). In addition, when students at risk for dropping out become involved in extracurricular activities, they appear to have a greater chance of still being in school when their senior year rolls around, as Figure 15.5 shows (Mahoney & Cairns, 1997).

Part-Time Jobs

Most teenagers hold some form of part-time job. Some teenagers do so toward financing their college educations, others do so to earn money for extras, and still others do so from financial necessity. Having a little money jingling in their pockets that they have earned themselves does create money-management opportunities based on a personal, relevant perspective. However, parents and educators worry that jobs interfere with the interests of getting an education. They are concerned that work takes time away from studies and distracts teenagers from the importance of academic achievement. Having a job to rush off to can interfere with involvement in extracurricular activities and seeking help from teachers after hours (Bachman & Schulenberg, 1993; Mortimer & Johnson, 1998).

Experts viewing the relationship between academic achievement and part-time employment offer mixed perspectives. On one hand, if an adolescent enters a work culture made up of young coworkers who place a greater value on adventure, risk-taking, and having fun than working toward goals for the future, concerns about the work culture may be warranted (Coleman, 1961). In addition to monopolizing an adolescent's spare time, some jobs can use up energy that might better be directed toward pursuing educational goals (Greenberger & Steinberg, 1986). Teenagers who work especially long hours have shown a greater inclination toward delinquency and the use of alcohol, tobacco, and drugs (Steinberg & Dornbusch, 1991).

On the other hand, experts point out that holding a job can actually contribute toward important adolescent learning. While trying out various jobs, teenagers learn which aspects of the vocational world they do or do not enjoy, thus motivating them to seek further training or higher education as they develop vocational interests (Hormuth, 1984). Part-time work teaches transferable practices that everybody in the work world needs to learn, such as accepting responsibilities, following directions, following through, and interacting appropriately with superiors—practices that also contribute to academic success. And if work is interesting and challenging rather than mundane and monotonous, it can be invigorating rather than an energy drain (Marks, 1977).

Empirical evaluation of the relationship between adolescent employment and academic achievement has indicated a variety of conflicting positive and negative correlates (Bachman & Schulenberg, 1993; Greenberger & Steinberg, 1986; Mortimer & Johnson, 1998). One study sorted out some of the discrepancies by showing a curvilinear relationship between number of hours worked and academic achievement, suggesting that teenagers who work about 20 hours a week do better academically than those who work more or less than 20 hours (Schill et al., 1985). However, we must make note of the fact that most of these studies are cross-sectional. As such, they do not demonstrate whether working impairs academics or whether those who are academically deficient are inclined to turn to the workforce.

Longitudinal investigation suggests that the latter is true. Students who were already uninterested in school, had low educational expectations, and had no interest in extracurricular activities or the school milieu were later more likely found to be seeking the world of work instead (Steinberg, Fegley, & Dornbusch, 1993). A longitudinal study following the school and subsequent work histories of over a thousand adolescents found neither deleterious nor beneficial relationships with grades, times spent on homework, or pursuit of higher education

(Mortimer et al., 1996). Taken all together, observations suggest that, rather than having a job in and of itself, it is the quality of a work experience that will have the most influence on adolescent behavioral adjustment, vocational development, mental health, and relationships with peers and parents (Finch et al., 1997).

How can parents and society help adolescents succeed academically?

PAVING PATHWAYS ALONG ADOLESCENT COGNITIVE MILESTONES: HELPING ADOLESCENTS SUCCEED ACADEMICALLY

Educational background is one of the most crucial factors affecting an adolescent's future options. What can parents—and society at large—do to help adolescents succeed academically?

What Parents Can Do

As was stated earlier, the authoritative parenting and parental involvement that proved beneficial for younger children's school achievement continue to have positive effects on adolescent academic achievement. But what other specific steps might parents take that would be especially likely to affect school performance during adolescence? Following are some suggestions (Schneider & Coleman, 1993; Steinberg et al., 1996; Stevenson & Baker, 1987).

▶ *Foster a home atmosphere that promotes completion of schoolwork.* Parents should make sure their teenagers have a quiet, private space to work. If they cannot afford computers, encyclopedias, and other necessary resources, they can endeavor to arrange access to them elsewhere. They should communicate their interest and expectations of success at school, and let their word and behavior illustrate their respect for completing schoolwork as a main priority in the teen's life.

▶ *Broaden school involvement.* When parents are trying to be helpful they often do so by monitoring and assisting with homework and giving the occasional pep talk. Surprisingly, other kinds of parental involvement may relate even more strongly to academic success than direct assistance with schoolwork. Parents of the most successful students attend school programs and student performances, play roles in facilitating extracurricular activities, and attend teacher conferences and "back-to-school" nights. This level of involvement sends a strong message to students and school staff alike. When adolescents see their parents giving up so much of their valuable free time to participate in school activities, the importance of school and their parents' expectations for academic achievement are unmistakenly underscored. Staff often apply a sort of "halo effect" to students of dedicated parents, assuming that the students are especially likely to do well if given the time and attention. Staff also know that if they behave inappropriately, these parents will be among the first to complain to administrators!

► *Address problems by involving the school system.* When parents receive notice that their child is struggling at school, they may try to address academic difficulties by working with the child on their own. This is not necessarily the most effective strategy. First, parents do not have the same expertise as highly trained and experienced educators, especially considering the advanced nature of many high school courses. Second, at times the difficulty is the result of the system's having failed for the particular student rather than something the student can change by trying harder. When parents of successful students receive notices of deficiencies, they meet with the teacher involved and discuss the program and where the student's gaps in understanding may lie, and together teacher and parents come up with a plan that will help them all to help the student. By doing so, parents are modeling their faith in school personnel's ability to educate their children—which of course is their job!

► *Influence their choice of peer group.* The last thing parents of adolescents should ever expect to be able to do is choose their friends for them. Yet peer group choices have such a tremendous impact on adolescent academic achievement that any influence steering them toward nonproblematic friendships is welcome. Parents can influence their children's choice of peers by taking advantage of the three factors most likely to lead to individuals becoming friends: near proximity, similarity of beliefs and attitudes, and reciprocity of positive feelings (Byrne, 1971). What type of neighborhood have they chosen for raising their children? While more affluent neighborhoods tend to have better schools, playgrounds, and recreational opportunities for after school and weekends, another factor that appears to play an equally important role is the influence of living in a neighborhood where there are a number of authoritative parents (Steinberg et al., 1996). While a greater number of authoritative parents are found in affluent neighborhoods, there are also considerable numbers of authoritative parents in neighborhoods inhabited by those who are less well off.

Joining churches or other family-oriented community groups is another strategy for placing children in the proximity of peers of the parents' choosing. Parents can also encourage child participation in extracurricular activities—not only assisting with development of the child's individual interests but also putting them in contact with children who are similarly inclined toward pursuing healthy activities. And when children appear on the horizon who look like they might provide positive influences, parents can encourage reciprocity of feeling by "allowing" them to come over and suggesting them as someone to bring along during family activities.

What Society Can Do

Keeping students involved and interested in academic success does indeed take a village-full of effort. Yet American societies tend to be disjointed and disorganized in what they offer the developing adolescent. Following are some

Intern positions in the community can help create a strong connection between future careers and the education intended to prepare adolescents for entering them.

Bob Daemmrich /Stock Boston

suggestions for the direction that communities and their schools might take not only to help adolescents see the relevance of learning but also to help integrate them as productive fellow members (Brown & Theobald, 1998).

▶ *Reduce the duplication of effort that occurs among different community factions.* For example, both schools and community centers offer athletic programs, classes in the use of artistic mediums, and the like. Limited resources might be better allocated without such duplication.

▶ *Reconnect adolescents with the "real world."* This is already happening in some communities. At-risk youth have benefited from being enrolled in community service programs, which facilitate transition into responsible social roles (Taylor & Bressler, 2000; Zoerink et al., 1997). Some school programs such as health careers require internships and other exposures to health service delivery out in the community (Hamilton, 1990). Students in sociology and social science classes have benefited from being required to perform volunteer work at soup kitchens and other community service programs (Yates & Youniss, 1996).

▶ *Make participation in extracurricular activity more attainable.* Aim to engage all students rather than a select few. Many extracurricular activities have cutoffs affecting who can participate; for example, only the most athletically skilled may be allowed to play team sports, or a certain grade point average may be required for participation in intellectual groups. Other requirements can get in the way as well, such as needing to be enrolled in a French class in order to be a part of the French club. These practices are often unnecessarily restrictive. As much as possible, the sole criterion for participation should be the student's interest. If there is high interest, broaden the program so that all may participate, as commonly happens in European,

Australian, and other societies. As work in the classroom becomes more closely tied to what is happening outside the classroom, involvement in extracurricular activities will naturally broaden and will require adjustments of this nature (Schine, 1997).

▶ *Arrange extracurricular activities in a way that respects all peer crowds, as well as loosens up some of their exclusiveness.* Extracurricular activities tend to reward certain groups: athletic programs are sponsored for the "jocks," honor societies are created for the "brains." Involvement in extracurricular activities can reduce the dropout rate, yet the activities offered often cater to individuals who are not at risk. What about the "skaters"? Or the "loners"? Even the "druggies" have interests other than taking drugs. What sorts of innovative clubs might tap into their unique interests and abilities, as well as provide more exposure to and supervision by appropriate mentors? Developing programs that reach out to multiple peer groups provide the additional benefit of reducing some of the preoccupation with the prestige often associated with one group over another (Holland & Andre, 1995).

▶ *Increase communication and coordination between schools and community efforts.* When programs conflict, students have to make difficult choices, and may even decide not to become involved. Reducing the number of competing demands increases the variety of exposures an adolescent can pursue.

Yes, given how our society currently functions, these suggestions comprise a fairly tall order. Smaller communities more easily adapt to this level of coordination, having fewer factors to juggle. Larger communities might make the task more manageable by shifting more power to individual schools. Neighborhood schools are not only more sensitive to local concerns and resources than distant bureaucracies could be, but also are more effective in organizing instruction to suit the unique needs of their student populations (Elmore et al., 1996).

CAREER DEVELOPMENT

During my sixth-grade graduation ceremony each student was asked to tell the audience what his or her career goal might be. I remember the boys stating they wanted to be policemen, firemen, millionaires, and the like. The girls' responses were limited to teachers, nurses, and mommies until I announced over the microphone: "I would like to be an author." The response from the audience was along the lines of "Aw, isn't that cute," my career aspiration not being taken particularly seriously. I recall also receiving some ribbing from my peers in reaction to my nontraditional response.

Times have changed. While gender stereotyping still abounds, the views of parents and peers have loosened up some in regard to gender and career goals. And in terms of current political correctness, playing down a young girl's nonstereotypical career aspiration would now be considered a major faux pas! These and other cultural, economic, and institutional changes all influence how today's adolescents develop career aspirations and prepare themselves for entering the world of work.

Transitioning from School to Work

How well do Western societies manage the transition from school to work?

At least in the United States, the transition from school to the workforce is much less cut and dry than it had been for previous generations of adolescents (Aronwitz & Difazio, 1994). In decades past, graduating high schoolers typically either found a lower-rung job with room for advancement or went on to higher education and training, either option serving as starting points for specific career paths they would expect to follow for a lifetime. Thanks to the increasing technological and informational complexity permeating current Western societies, the working world is becoming dichotomized into two vocational options: pursuing the massive education and technical training necessary for the well-paying higher-status jobs or settling for dead-end, lower-paying employment involving service delivery or relatively unskilled manual labor (Mare, 1995). During the last 20 years, despite improvements in basic skill levels of graduates, the hourly wage for those with only a high school education has dropped almost by a quarter. Simultaneously the wages of those who hold college degrees, especially advanced degrees, have continued to rise (Mishel et al., 1997).

Even upon finishing a two-year or four-year program, graduates do not typically progress into an established career path (Green, 1995; Karabell, 1998). College educations are valuable for a number of personal growth purposes. They encourage critical thinking, inspire curiosity, and impart a fuller understanding of the world's complexities—all contributing to the learner's ability to find and apply solutions to the problems of the world, as well as to his or her own life. However, many programs that students might pursue no longer provide any guarantee that jobs will be waiting for them upon completion of their education. Their degrees must have some relevance to the working world.

Furthermore, as the number of college degrees have increased, society has not responded by creating enough jobs to make productive use of their training. Even when a graduate finds a job, today's rapid changes in technology and lowered sense of loyalty between firms and their employees create the likelihood of shorter-term periods of employment than in decades past. Thus regardless of their level of education adolescents and young adults alike commonly bounce around among a series of jobs and periods of training, developing skills and competencies as they go and perhaps making a number of career shifts throughout their lifetimes.

Given these changes, how well has U.S. society been facilitating transition to the working world? In the United States, the connection between school and work has become embarrassingly loose (Stevenson et al., 1998). In other countries such as Japan and Germany, the transition is tightly coordinated. Test scores and specific high school degrees directly funnel students into certain labor and educational tracks (Federal Ministry of Education and Science, 1992; Stevenson & Baker, 1992). In the United States, high schools differ so much among themselves in program content and achievement standards that their diplomas are almost meaningless to employers. Companies thus screen applicants themselves, using qualifying tests that are as diverse as high school assessment practices—further collapsing possibilities for coordination between high school experience and job readiness (Bishop, 1990). And as you might recall from your own college application experiences, institutions of higher education are becoming much more reliant upon college entrance examinations than high school GPAs as they consider applicants for admission.

The School-to-Work Act of 1994 aimed at creating closer ties between educational practices and employability (United States Department of Labor, Secretary's Commission on Achieving Necessary Skills, 1992). Unlike the so-called vocational tracks of previous decades, the School-to-Work Act supports programs that coordinate with local businesses and give students direct experiences in the workforce. This form of give-and-take is especially valuable for those students who do not go on to higher education. The ability to work in groups, take initiative, follow instructions, and be responsible are all attributes desired of such potential employees, yet those high school students who go directly into the workforce tend to lack these abilities (Stevenson et al., 1998). By coordinating efforts, schools and businesses can provide training and experiences that help students develop general work setting skills and thus increase their employability.

However, a pivotal factor for improving the transition between school and work remains the development of a meaningful public record of students' training and ability (Stevenson et al., 1998). Some form of consistency must be established before employers will perceive student records as relevant to their interests. Creating specialized programs to develop the unique talents or address the needs of students in a community is only worthwhile if programs eventually translate into their ability to get a job. Unfortunately, this has not been the historical trend. Furthermore, our society needs to reinstate a sense of value and honor to becoming a lab technician, secretary, or plumber so that individuals who are not inclined toward or interested in higher-status professions, big business, or management positions can feel comfortable pursuing these worthwhile vocations (Valdes, 1997).

Regarding students who do pursue higher education, colleges should take fuller responsibility for the influence they have over their students. Encouraging them to mold their entire education around "ivory tower" aspects of the college experience is appropriate for students who plan to move into the ivory tower. However, most students benefit from guidance that centers on how they will use their education in the outside world. With the assistance of the school career counseling center, students should be encouraged—if not required—to explore such options during the course of their education, rather than waiting to select a specific job as they approach graduation (Karabell, 1998). Such guidance requires more than imparting knowledge about available career paths; preferably students should be directed toward an adaptive long-term career trajectory that recognizes the likelihood of shifts in career focus over the course of a lifetime (Bidwell et al., 1998).

What factors do adolescents consider as they choose careers?

Choosing a Career

So how does the status of today's job market affect adolescents' choices of careers? As might be expected, most teens look forward to having careers that require higher education. As Figure 15.6 shows, interest in pursuing higher education has risen exactly as the wages students would expect to earn without that college degree have sunk. Unfortunately the financial cost of attaining these lofty goals has risen far more quickly than the rate of inflation, seemingly keeping the same percentage of aspirants out of school as in previous generations (Stevenson et al., 1998).

"What Do You Want to Be When You Grow Up?" We ask young children this question knowing full well that they have given the topic some thought. Children pass through phases of career aspiration (Super, 1980). During early and middle childhood they fantasize about possible careers, their options under consideration frequently revealed during games of make-believe. Career aspirations of younger children typically do not consider their actual capabilities and what a job might require of them. I recall hearing a feminist father complain that his bright 6-year-old daughter repeatedly insisted she would one day become a secretary in a lawyers' office, in spite of his encouragement to consider becoming a lawyer. I asked him what role he thought her mother might be playing in

FIGURE 15.6
Percentage of students who plan to attend college and percentage of those who actually attend. Adapted with permission from D. L. Stevenson, J. Kochanek, and B. Schneider (1998), *Making the transition from high school: Recent trends and policies.* In 97th Yearbook of the National Society for the Study of Education, The adolescent years: Social influences and educational challenges, edited by K. Borman & B. Schneider.

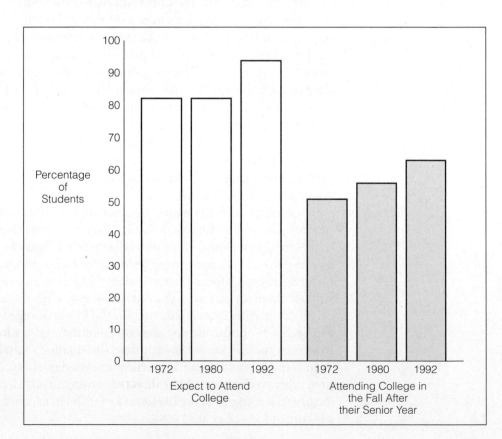

her career aspirations. "She's a legal secretary," he replied. This father had encountered a common influence in early childhood vocational fantasies: the profession of the same-gendered parent. Similarly visible career roles, especially those that sound exciting or high status, are also highly represented among young children's career fantasies.

Adolescents begin looking at career options from a more realistic perspective. Their ability to consider multiple relevant variables helps them evaluate their own interests and abilities and make tentative vocational choices reflecting what they believe they might enjoy. Their choices still tend to be somewhat overoptimistic, reflecting the influence of the personal myth. As they enter late adolescence and young adulthood, the same collisions with reality that diminish the personal myth help them narrow their career goals to those more likely to be accomplished. Often their career choices are influenced by what their parents do for a living, taking advantage of the knowledge and work setting connections available right at home (Grotevant & Cooper, 1998).

Gender Differences. Western cultures continue to be patriarchal, and adolescents' career choices continue to be influenced by the gender stereotypes represented within them. The vocational choices of adolescent boys demonstrate a clear bias toward high-powered, stereotypically male career paths (Sandberg et al., 1991). Although adolescent girls are showing more and more interest in entering male-dominated professions, they also worry about how their vocation will fit in with having a family and childrearing, a factor not so often considered by adolescent boys. In doing so, girls may pursue less challenging careers, erroneously believing that such choices will better accommodate motherhood. As successful role models for combining motherhood with scientific and other higher-ability careers become more visible and available, adolescent girls will hopefully cease imposing such limitations on their career aspirations (Cole & Zuckerman, 1987).

SUMMARY

Piaget's Formal Operational Reasoning

Formal operations introduce the abilities of considering abstract concepts, generating and exhaustively testing multiple hypotheses, and simultaneously juggling multiple variables. Improvements in deductive reasoning allow adolescents to apply logic more effectively. However, whether or not adolescents learn to use or apply formal operational skills is affected by level of education, culture, openness to varied perspectives, emotional state, topic familiarity, and practice. Discovery of their newfound independent reasoning ability contributes to a new egocentric phase, during which they perceive themselves as special, invincible, and under extreme public scrutiny.

The increasing independence and breadth of choices confronting adolescents necessitates that they capitalize upon their ability to learn formal decision-making and problem-solving techniques. Reasoning errors such as insufficiently searching for options, single-minded decision making, persisting in irrational beliefs, misapplying probabilities, and shortsightedness are common to adults and adolescents alike. Adolescents benefit from learning techniques that teach them to define and separate problems, generate and evaluate potential solutions, weigh desirability and probability of potential outcomes, and select and follow through on chosen solutions.

Information-Processing

Information-processing ability improves as adolescents work with increasingly more familiar material, experience opportunities to practice information-processing skills, build larger knowledge bases, and develop new information-processing skills. New skill attainment is affected both by direct instruction and developmental maturity.

Learning during Adolescence

Secondary schools provide the most effective education for adolescents when curricula are solidly grounded in appropriate knowledge bases, encourage a mastery orientation, and are presented within an atmosphere of high expectations for success, personal safety, and orderly conduct. Language ability is enhanced by ongoing improvements in grammar and vocabulary. Adolescents' experience of reading begins touching upon more abstract, hypothetical notions such as possible motives and symbolism. Reading comprehension is aided by teaching students to integrate what they read with what they already know. The ability to perform more complex mathematical manipulations is supported by adolescent improvements in attending and ability to consider multiple variables. Male students' better performance in complex problem-solving may be due to cultural expectations and the effect that bucking stereotypes may have on female students' attending ability. Adolescents drop out of school for numerous personal and social reasons, many stemming from lack of a perceived connection between school and their future lives.

Parental variables have the greatest effect on adolescent academic achievement, especially socioeconomic status, level of education, and use of the authoritative parenting style. Adolescent academic achievement benefits from continued parental involvement and solid feelings of attachment between parent and adolescent. The values and attitudes of the friendship groups with whom an adolescent decides to associate have a tremendous effect on academic success. The positive correlation between academic achievement and participation in extracurricular activities probably means that an achievement orientation influences both behaviors. Part-time jobs are a part of the "school of the world," imparting learning that can be applied to the academic world as well. The negative correlation sometimes found between hours at work and academic success most likely means that adolescents who are already uninterested in school choose to invest their energies in employment instead.

In addition to parenting authoritatively, parents can help teenagers succeed academically by providing a home environment that fosters school attendance and completion of homework, broadening their involvement with the school, addressing academic problems by involving the system, and endeavoring to influence their child's choice of peer group. Society can help by reducing the duplication of effort between school and other community resources, providing opportunities for adolescents to reconnect with the community, making participation in extracurricular activity more attainable and available for all student crowds, and increasing communication and coordination between schools and community efforts.

Career Development

The transition from school to work has become murkier because of increasing technology and job complexity; less effective coordination among high schools, colleges, and job markets; and the increasing fluidity of careers over the life span. Children's earliest career fantasies involve jobs that sound exciting or have high visibility. At adolescence, they begin assessing their interests and abilities realistically as they consider potential careers. Girls at times unnecessarily limit their aspirations as they stumble over the obstacle of how to coordinate a career with having a family.

KEY TERMS

combinatorial reasoning   imaginary audience   scientific reasoning
deductive reasoning   invincibility fable   selective memory
formal operational reasoning   personal myth   self-objectification

CONCEPT REVIEW

1. Changes in adolescent thinking skills are _____,
    _____, and _____ directed.

2. Formal operational reasoning is a product of the adolescent's greater capacity
    for considering _____ concepts and _____
    multiple mental processes. These abilities contribute to their scientific reasoning by means of both more advanced _____ testing and
    _____ reasoning.

3. Adolescents' deductive reasoning shows the most improvement when working with material that is _____, and they are less likely to make errors in logical deductions if they can think of _____ for why an event has occurred.

4. The presence of _____ beliefs, the _____ myth and _____ fable, and the _____ audience are all typical elements of adolescent egocentrism.

5. Formal operational reasoning improves most between _____ and _____. In addition to age, factors that appear to promote development of formal operational reasoning include direct _____, _____, sufficient level of _____, _____ relevance, and _____.

6. Adolescent decision making can be impaired by insufficiently searching for _____, _____ decision making, _____ persistence; misapplying _____, and _____. They are capable of learning effective decision-making processes that consider relevant _____, available _____, potential _____, and _____ that certain outcomes will occur.

7. Improvements in adolescent information-processing occur through greater _____ with mental processing, more _____ with it, a greater _____, and attainment of new cognitive _____.

8. Secondary schools are most effective in educating adolescents if they include a curriculum grounded in an integrated, solid _____ and real-world _____, a _____ orientation, and a healthy _____.

9. Adolescent reading comprehension is more likely to improve in concert with developing strategies for _____, rather than figuring out the _____.

10. During adolescence, boys show a slight advantage over girls in math skills related to _____. From a sociological perspective, girls may have difficulty with these skills through _____ threat or the division of attention that self-_____ causes.

11. Teenagers are more likely to drop out of school if their gender is _____, they are from _____ homes, have _____ socioeconomic status, live in a _____ area, and/or have difficulties with _____. They are less likely to drop out when they see the connection between school and _____.

12. The _____ parenting style has the greatest association with high adolescent academic achievement, most likely because of its greater association with _____ motivation. Peers influence academic achievement by means of _____ affiliation and general peer _____ regarding achievement.

13. Teenagers who are involved with extracurricular activities are <u>more/less</u> likely to do well academically, and a greater number of hours at a part-time job is associated with <u>greater/less</u> likelihood of academic success.

14. Parents can assist adolescent learning by fostering a _____ at home, broadening their own _____, addressing academic difficulties by involving the _____, and attempting to influence choice of _____.

15. Communities can help adolescents achieve academically by consolidating _____, reconnecting school with _____, increasing _____ of participation in programs, and increasing coordination between _____ and community efforts.

16. The transition from school to work has become more difficult for adolescents in the United States because of insufficient _____.

17. Adolescents' career choices are often influenced by _____ occupations, _____ issues, and _____ stereotypes.

1) qualitative; progressive; internally; 2) abstract, coordinating; hypothesis; combinatorial; 3) familiar; alternative explanations; 4) idealistic; personal; invincibility; imaginary; 5) late adolescence; adulthood; instruction; motivation; intelligence; cultural; practice; 6) options, single-minded; irrational belief; probabilities; short-sightedness; goals; options; outcomes; probabilities; 7) familiarity; practice; knowledge base; skills; 8) knowledge base; applications; mastery; learning atmosphere; 9) seeking answers; main idea; 10) complex problem-solving; stereotype; objectification; 11) male; single-parent; low; rural; self-esteem; career; 12) authoritative; intrinsic; crowd; attitudes; 13) more; less; 14) learning atmosphere; school involvement; school system; peer group; 15) program resources; community service; accessibility; school; 16) coordination; 17) parents'; cohort; gender

RESOURCES FOR FURTHER READING

Baron, J., & Brown, R. V. (Eds.) (1991). *Teaching decision-making to adolescents.* Hillsdale, NJ: Erlbaum.

Borman, K., & Schneider, B. (Eds.) (1998). *The adolescent years: Social influences and educational challenges.* Chicago: University of Chicago Press.

Mathews, J. (1998). *Class struggle: What's wrong (and right) with America's best public high schools.* New York: Times Books.

Rosemond, J. (1998). *Teen proofing: A revolutionary approach to fostering responsible decision making in your teenager.* Kansas City, MO: Andrews McMeel Publishing.

Steinberg, L., Brown, B., & Dornbusch, S. M. (1996). *Beyond the classroom: Why school reform has failed and what parents need to do.* New York: Simon and Schuster.

INFOTRAC COLLEGE EDITION

For additional readings, explore InfoTrac College Edition, your online library. Go to http://www.infotrac-college.com/wadsworth and use the passcode that came on the card with your book. Try these search terms: academic achievement and gender, career choice, cognition in adolescence, egocentrism, extracurricular activities, high school curriculum, working adolescents

CHILD DEVELOPMENT CD-ROM

Go to the Wadsworth Child Development CD-ROM for further study of the concepts in this chapter. The CD-ROM also includes quizzes and additional activities to expand your learning experience.

REFERENCES

For a list of references for this chapter, see the Wadsworth Psych Study Center Web site at: http://www.wadsworth.com/product/0534348092s

CHAPTER 16

Adolescent Social and Emotional Development

FOCUS QUESTIONS

► How do developmental and cultural factors interact as the adolescent seeks an independent identity?

► How does the adolescent's relationship with parents change?

► How do peers influence adolescent social and emotional adjustment?

► Is adolescent depression normal?

► Why is suicide more likely to occur during adolescence, and how can it be prevented?

► How are morals and values likely to change during adolescence?

► What factors lead to juvenile delinquency, and what can be done to reduce its prevalence?

► Which factors are likely to affect adolescent self-esteem?

► What are "rites of passage" and how do they affect identity formation?

O U T L I N E

Personality Development
    Psychodynamic Influences
    Erikson and the Search for Identity
    Gender and Identity Formation
    Ethnicity and Identity Formation
Relationships
    Relationships with Parents
    Paving Pathways: Parenting and Teenagers
    Relationships with Peers
Emotions
    Emotional Regulation
    Depression and Suicide
Development of Morals and Values

Juvenile Delinquency
    Development of Juvenile Delinquency
    Controversy Regarding Development of Juvenile Delinquency
    Paving Pathways: Preventing and Intervening in Juvenile Delinquency
Self-Esteem
Rites of Passage
    Characteristics of Rites of Passages
    Problems Evolving from the Absence of Rites of Passage
    New Passages
    Paving Pathways: Creating Rites of Passage
    Transitioning to the Passages of Adulthood

"Get out of my life! . . . but first could you take me and Cheryl to the mall?" —book title by Anthony E. Wolf

Such opposing agendas! Having the drive and desire to move forward into adult autonomy, yet still developmentally and pragmatically dependent upon parents. This balancing act is a prevailing characteristic of the social and emotional life of adolescents, who teeter back and forth between contradictory sets of needs while edging ever closer toward an equilibrium of more adultlike self and world perspectives.

How do developmental and cultural factors interact as the adolescent seeks an independent identity?

PERSONALITY DEVELOPMENT

Must an adolescent's adult personality always emerge by means of battling through such turmoil? Not necessarily. Early in the twentieth century Margaret Mead observed the course of development of girls in a Samoan society (Mead, 1961). The only differences she noted between prepubertal, pubertal, and postpubertal girls were their bodily changes. Given the adolescent behavior characteristic of Western cultures, how could this be? Mead explained that much of adolescent turmoil is created—or avoided—by culture. In Samoan culture there are no conflicting messages regarding sex: It is treated as natural and normal, and prescribes sensible yet relaxed standards for how it is pursued. Familial bonds and boundaries are looser and less intense. Societywide acceptance of specific moral standards and expectations regarding vocational roles erase the individual's need for making gut-wrenching life choices. The Samoan day-to-day pace is unhurried and lacks the economic and social crises that face adolescents living in more complex cultures.

Yet Mead also noticed a lack of deeper feelings and appreciation for individual personality differences in Samoan culture as compared to Western cultures. Is this a problem? Adolescents in Western cultures would answer this question with an emphatic "yes!" Clearly the answer is relative to an individual's culture. The following discussion of personality development centers on self-definition as a product of the individual's sorting through the many contradictory pressures and choices encountered while coming of age in current Western cultures.

Psychodynamic Influences

Freud (1920/1965) was one of the first to try to explore the contradictory dependencies and emotional storms observed in adolescents. During this final **genital stage,** as he called it, he believed the adolescent's press for independence is psychosexually driven, a product of coping with a resurgence of Oedipal leanings while now having a body that can actually follow through on sexual urges. He also believed that we establish such strong dependencies on our parents during childhood that we never truly attain the goal of genuine independence. Freud emphatically recommended that children receive sex education, preferably in the schools—a rather radical proposal, considering the Victorian age in which he lived. He hoped that such education would help children learn that sexual urges are natural and to be expected and would therefore lower the levels of psychosexually induced feelings of guilt and anxiety he was observing in adult neuroses (Freud, 1907/1959).

Freud's daughter, Anna, who was also a psychoanalyst, explored the turmoil of adolescence more extensively than did her father (Freud, 1958). Observing teenagers' tendency to reduce the amount of time spent around their parents and to express contempt for them, she hypothesized that certain practices serve as temporary shelters against their strong resurgence of Oedipal feelings. Adolescents develop the defense mechanism of *intellectualization* for protection as they begin to evaluate the meaning of all facets of life in an objective, emotionally detached manner. Noting the odd regimens that teenagers adopt, such as group-defined ways of dressing and behaving that change from cohort to cohort, Anna Freud suggested that these practices also provide a temporary haven during a time when identifying with parents has become obsolete but the adult identity is not yet complete.

Erikson and the Search for Identity

Adults often envy the innocence of childhood: the lack of worry over how to obtain necessities and the simplified view and acceptance of the self. As children enter adolescence, however, emerging formal operational abilities for abstraction and deeper reasoning open windows to life's uncertainties. The adolescent begins to absorb the harsh reality that one day he or she will be functioning as an independent individual. Who will this person be? How will this person fit in with the rest of the world? What must this person be like in order to survive and also experience happiness? While they ponder these questions they also need to make decisions that both directly and indirectly affect their futures—educationally, vocationally, and interpersonally.

I recall a Sunday afternoon during my high school years that had become monopolized by the need to address massive homework demands. As I attempted to master complex lesson concepts, my concentration was repeatedly interrupted by the antics of my younger siblings, who were frolicking back and forth through the dining room. I picked up my books and moved to my room. My "room" was actually a space against a wall between two areas blocked off for my sisters. As might be predicted, the cavorting made sweeps through those areas as well. Exasperated, I gathered up my books, put on my coat, and headed toward the front door. My mother ordered me to stay. Observing that there was no reason to stay—other than having been given a direct order to do so—I left.

I walked to a library a mile or so down the road and succeeded in completing my work. While sitting in the library I remember experiencing an unfamiliar, disorienting, transitional type of feeling. At the time I attributed it to the contrast between the peaceful calm of the library and the noisy chaos of home. But in retrospect I remember it also as a novel feeling of independent confidence. Having realized that certain needs affecting my future were not likely to be met by depending on home influences, I had summoned the strength and self-efficacy to seek out what I needed in spite of pressures to the contrary. The incident also marked the first recognition that pursuing my higher educational goals would require my moving away from home. I jumped through the hoops necessary for gaining admission and finances to attend an out-of-town university (and on the far side of that state, just for emphasis!). I sometimes contemplate whether the feelings of cozy comfort and peace I experience while mining the assets of the stacks are in some way tied to my rebellious teenage library exodus.

While disobeying parental dictates during the teen years looks like rebellion, in reality it represents something much more complex. An independently functioning identity cannot be formed without first breaking away from some of the family dependencies characteristic of childhood. In a manner similar to that of the oppositional 2-year-old individuating away from babyhood and toward childhood, teenagers learn to explore who they are and transition to the independence of adulthood by means that can be extremely irksome to their parents. Early in adolescence their behavior may resemble the pure oppositionalism of the 2-year-old, seemingly occurring for the sole purpose of being able to observe the effect. By late adolescence it is motivated more by the needs of self-exploration and pursuit of identity-bound goals than a desire to go against parental wishes. All adolescents must work through this individuation process, since they are the only ones who can search their souls for a life pattern that will work specifically for them (Caldwell, 1996; Grotevant & Cooper, 1986; Holmbeck & Leake, 1999; Larson et al., 1996).

Erikson emphasized the psychosocial challenge of adolescence as a time of **identity versus role confusion** (Erikson, 1968; Waterman, 1999). Specifically, teenagers work toward integrating pieces of self-understanding into a coherent, accurate, functioning, complete identity (Adams et al., 1992; Douvan, 1997). At first they find themselves torn between a variety of possibilities, experiencing multiple, conflicting facets of selfhood. Over time they identify with the roles, values, standards, behaviors, interests, and educational and career goals that feel most consistent with their inner experience and become less influenced by their external social domain (Harter, 1999; Markus & Nurius, 1986). The degree of importance they place on their identity and individuality will vary according to the values of their particular culture (Oerter, 1986; Schneider, 1998).

James Marcia describes the various stages of identity formation that teenagers pass through as they seek their equilibrium between self and society (Berzonsky, 1992; Marcia, 1980; Markstrom-Adams, 1992; Schwartz & Dunham, 2000):

► *Identify diffusion.* During **identity diffusion** adolescents have not yet begun processing their questions of independent identity, or if they have they are not yet making any lasting decisions about its status. Identity diffusion may continue indefinitely when adolescents abuse substances, as chemically induced mood states overpower the impetus of the task (Jones, 1992).

► *Foreclosure.* When in a state of **foreclosure,** adolescents have made premature commitments to identity without the necessary self-exploration. Foreclosure often occurs when authoritarian parents tell adolescents what they should be like or pressure them into career goals more reflective of the parents' desires. Interestingly, the opposite extreme of family structure, consisting of enmeshed relationships and avoidance of confrontation at all costs, can also contribute to identity foreclosure (Perosa et al., 1996). Serious illnesses such as cancer during adolescence are associated with a higher incidence of identity foreclosure, perhaps because the stressors of the illness overwhelm the stricken adolescent's ability to address developmental stressors (Madan-Swain et al., 2000). At times identity foreclosure results from overidentification with peers' identity decisions, as adolescents forestall this developmental task by just "going along with the crowd."

► *Moratorium.* During **moratorium** adolescents find themselves at a crossroads, experiencing the "identity crisis" of multiple conflicting inner influences and states of being. They seek out relevant information as they evaluate the possibilities, and depend less and less on the positions of parents and peers as they do so (Ungar, 2000). During this stage—and to a lesser extent during identity diffusion—adolescents experience lowered ego strength, an indication of the vulnerability they experience as they enter unfamiliar territory (Markstrom et al., 1997).

► *Identity achievement.* Having evaluated the inner processes driving their identity crisis and their options for resolving it, adolescents accomplish **identity achievement**. They commit themselves to various aspects of selfhood: ways of being, ways of behaving, and their preferred niches in society. In spite of the give-and-take with the environment preceding identity achievement, twin studies suggest that some aspects of the self-concept that adolescents eventually discover have genetic origins (Hur et al., 1998).

Gender and Identity Formation

The adolescent process of establishing a separate identity differs somewhat between the genders (Cosse, 1992). Boys establish themselves as men by drawing a clear line between themselves and their mothers, attempting to eradicate any remaining identification established during the dependencies of childhood. Girls, being of the same gender as their mothers, maintain their gender identification. Their individuation process is therefore less pronounced than it is for boys, and their identity formation focuses more on how to be a self in the context of relationships (Chodorow, 1978; Gilligan, 1990). Some controversy surrounds a suggestion that because of these differences, the timing of Erikson's proposed adolescent task of identity and the young adult task of establishing intimacy is in fact reversed for girls (Horst, 1995; Waterman, 1985).

Cultural definitions of masculinity and femininity continue to play substantial roles in how adolescents define the self. Early in adolescence, middle schoolers experience a burst of increased flexibility regarding male/female stereotypes. Feeling unceremoniously dumped into a school milieu differing vastly from elementary school, they pour much of their energies into learning the ropes of social expectations, including those regarding gender. During the process of middle school acculturation, issues related to social status and attracting the opposite sex come rushing to the forefront. Such issues increase the perceived relevance of gender, and thus rigid gender stereotyping reemerges (Alfieri et al., 1996; Eccles, 1987).

In reality, individuals of either gender may adopt varying levels of so-called masculine and feminine traits (Bem, 1981). Figure 16.1 illustrates four possible combinations of these varying collections of traits. At one time individuals were believed to be most well-adjusted if they fell into the **androgynous** quadrant,

FIGURE 16.1

Gender role types. While the androgynous gender role is more balanced, the assertive, self-reliant characteristics of the traditional masculine gender role are found to have the greatest association with good adjustment in Western cultures.

		Masculine Traits	
		Low	High
	Low	Undifferentiated	Traditional Masculine
Feminine Traits			
	High	Traditional Feminine	Androgynous

FIGURE 16.2

Level of voice expressed among adolescent girls. While girls who adopt the traditional feminine gender role are less likely to assert themselves in public arenas, they still seem able to express themselves assertively among themselves. Adapted with permission from Harter et al., Level of voice among female and male high school students: Relational context, support, and gender orientation, *Developmental Psychology, 34,* 892–901. Copyright © 1998 by the American Psychological Association.

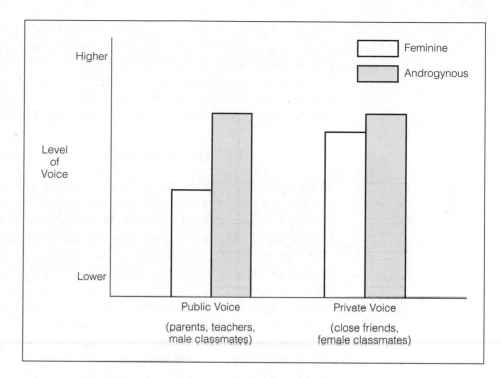

exhibiting both masculine and feminine stereotypical characteristics, but research does not support this belief (Taylor & Hall, 1982). Instead the strong, assertive, self-reliant attributes that Western cultures ascribe to masculinity appear to have the strongest association with good adjustment.

This state of affairs puts adolescent girls at a disadvantage: Society seems to prescribe a certain set of characteristics for womanhood, yet adoption of such a role may frustrate achievement of desired goals. Part of this disadvantage concerns what has been called "voice": the belief that expressing one's thoughts and opinions is acceptable (Gilligan, 1993). Some have argued that girls experience a loss of voice as they adopt feminine attributes such as being nice, polite, quiet, nurturing, and unassertive. In fact, girls who adopt traits ascribed to masculinity are found to experience less depression than those who adopt feminine traits (Obeidallah et al., 1996).

However, loss of voice does not appear to be limited to girls, nor to be associated predominantly with gender identity considerations (Harter et al., 1997). When comparing strength of voice in both adolescent boys and girls, researchers do not find differences based on gender alone, but do find an association between voice and level of perceived support for self-expression. As Figure 16.2 shows, girls adopting a more feminine stereotypical identity do not seem to lack voice while interacting in private relational contexts, but rather refrain from exercising it during more public interactions (Harter et al., 1998).

As compared to the study of adolescent girls, research regarding the relationship between stereotypical gender expectations and young men's gender identity formation is still a relatively new field of investigation. Yet in one sense, boys' voice may be encumbered with an even more profound cultural straitjacket than the one constraining girls. As boys adopt the prescribed nonemotionality of stereotypical masculinity, they lose voice with respect to the freedom to express feelings (Brody, L. R., 1993; Pollack, 1998). The fact that investigation into the personal impact of stereotypical gender expectations was first done on women's lives (and by women!) may in itself be evidence that society allows women greater license to admit feelings of vulnerability and express their disdain.

Ethnicity and Identity Formation

In Western societies, adolescents who are members of cultural or racial minorities have the additional task of sorting out their ethnic identity. Minority adolescents are more likely to identify themselves by their race or ethnicity largely because members of majority cultures tend to identify them as such (Goldberg, 1995; Tatum, 1997). Under these circumstances, establishing ethnic identity appears to be a necessity for healthy personal adjustment. This tendency is especially strong for African-American adolescents. Their choice of friends is influenced more by shared ethnic identity than by the shared attitudes toward academic performance or drug use that influence the peer choices of Asian-American and Caucasian-American adolescents (Hamm, 2000). Also, African-American adolescents with weak ethnic identities have been found to experience difficulty with fidelity in relationships, an association that is not found among Caucasian-American adolescents (Markstrom & Hunter, 1999). Exploring cultural roots and developing a strong racial identity has been found to contribute to adolescent self-esteem and resiliency; this association varies according to the individual's personal regard for his or her race or ethnicity, not according to public regard (Cross, 1991; Miller, 1999; Rowley et al., 1998; Tse, 1999).

The establishing of ethnic identity appears to follow the same path as other aspects of identity development, beginning with concerns about external perceptions and influences, sorting out conflicting roles, and eventually creating a personalized internal version of the ethnic self (Cross, 1991; Ying & Lee, 1999). The primacy placed on the identity task of establishing a capacity for autonomous, independently functioning behavior is more culturally relevant to mainstream Western society (Grotevant & Cooper, 1998). Many ethnic subcultures, especially those with Asian and Latin American roots, have greater expectations regarding adolescents' continuing duty to respect and assist their family of origin, regardless of the family's composition and socioeconomic background. Adolescents appear able to conform with these expectations and still develop adaptive levels of autonomy or independence (Fuligni et al., 1999).

RELATIONSHIPS

Between infancy and adolescence, parent/child relationships undergo considerable shifts in emphases. Infants spend almost all of their time with parents and primary caregivers. As children grow older they spend increasingly larger portions of their time with friends, classmates, or by themselves. During adolescence they whittle down the amount of time spent alone with adults—including their parents—to only about 7% of their waking hours, spending about a quarter of their time in solitude and increasing the amount of time spent with peers to over 50% (Csikszentmihalyi & Rathunde, 1993; Larson et al., 1996). These shifts reflect movement toward relationships that will foster the adolescent pursuit of identity formation and independence.

How does the adolescent's relationship with parents change?

Relationships with Parents

If you have watched nature films you have no doubt observed a variety of different species as they raise and care for their young. As their offspring grow older they live side by side, more or less peacefully. As the young approach maturity, however, parents and offspring show signs of not getting along. They become easily irritated with one another and the young eventually leave voluntarily or are run off. This is an adaptive outcome ethologically because it reduces the likelihood that inbreeding will occur and weaken the gene pool.

Some suggest that the parent/child conflicts of adolescence occur because human beings are similarly programmed (Steinberg, 1989). Observers other than Freud, such as philosophers, sociologists, cultural anthropologists, and behaviorists, have long noted the conflict and strife between the generations that typically first emerge at adolescence (Elder, 1980; Mead, 1978). As children become pubescent there are not only increases in quarreling and negative feelings toward parents but also decreases in the number of pleasant interactions, such as doing things together, making positive statements to one another, and reported feelings of closeness between parent and child (Montemayor, 1986; Montemayor et al., 1993). While these distancing tactics are often attributed to

The normal process of developing adolescent independence includes adolescents' identifying ways in which they differ from or are otherwise separate from their parents, which provides substantial fuel for conflict and arguments.

Billy E. Barnes/Stock Boston

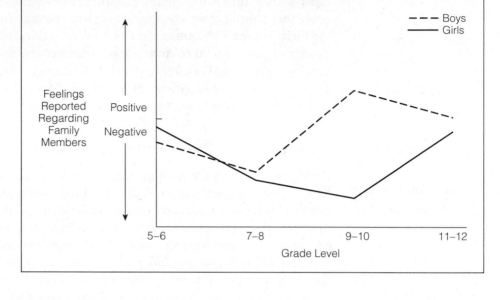

FIGURE 16.3

Feelings of adolescents toward family members. During the course of adolescence boys appear to recover positive feelings toward their parents more quickly than do girls. Adapted with permission from Larson et al., *Changes in adolescents' daily interactions with their families from ages 10 to 18: Disengagement and transformation. Developmental Psychology, 32,* 744–74. Copyright © 1996 by the American Psychological Association.

irritating adolescent behavior, the temperament of an adolescent's parents may actually play a greater role in determining the degree of conflict than the temperament of the adolescent (Galambos & Turner, 1999; Kawaguchi et al., 1998).

Even though exposed to vastly differing perspectives on authority and autonomy, adolescents across cultures show remarkably similar alterations in the degree of conflict and cohesion with their parents (Fuligni, 1998). Specifically, conflict increases, doing so more often between adolescents and their mothers, while cohesion decreases, doing so more often between adolescents and their fathers (Collins & Russell, 1991; Steinberg, 1990). This increase appears to reflect a rise in the degree of emotionality connected with conflict rather than an actual increase in the occurrence of conflicting agenda (Laursen et al., 1998). Conflict most typically centers on parents' attempts to regulate their adolescents' daily lives, such as how late they stay out, what they do with their friends, and whether they are following through on responsibilities (Smetana, 1988; Kastner & Wyatt, 1997).

As might be predicted, the normal adolescent pursuit of independence does not mesh well with these parental efforts. The escalation of conflict typically reaches its height during middle adolescence, then declines as the child passes through late adolescence, mirroring the progress of the adolescent's individuation process (Laursen & Collins, 1994). Some gender differences have been found, such as boys' recovering positive feelings toward parents and other family members earlier than do girls, as Figure 16.3 shows (Larson et al., 1996).

Yet parental influences are necessary for the growing adolescent, whose immaturity still requires the benefits of parental support, guidance, and monitoring (Ryan & Lynch, 1989). Adolescents themselves do not necessarily see conflict with their parents as evidence of something being amiss. In spite of the increase in turmoil, most adolescents rate their relationships with their parents as being positive (Hill & Holmbeck, 1986). Secure attachment to parents during adolescence is associated with more efficient stress management, such as coping by means of problem-solving and support-seeking (Greenberger & McLaughlin, 1998). Such attachment also has been found to have a positive relationship with various aspects of self-image, such as body image, vocational aspirations, and attitudes toward sexuality (O'Koon, 1997). Adolescents who do not experience secure attachment to their parents are more likely to develop depressive disorders (Armsden et al., 1990). When an excessively stressful family life interferes with attachment, adolescents show negative effects both emotionally and academically (Forehand et al., 1998). Poor attachment history can carry its legacy into late adolescence and early adulthood, resulting in preoccupation with intimate relations or avoidance of them altogether (Carnelley et al., 1994).

The attachment between adolescent and parent does not appear to require extreme emotional engagement. The less intense father-child emotional engagement observed throughout childhood actually appears to become adaptive at adolescence (Shulman & Klein, 1993). Fathers typically display a more realistic model of both closeness and separateness in relationships than do mothers. The fact that conflict typically increases more with mothers than with fathers during adolescence may reflect that fathers interfere less and show greater respect for age-appropriate independent behavior (Steinberg, 1987). Their emotional aloofness may even act as a motivator as adolescents develop their individuality and take personal responsibility for their life choices (Hauser et al., 1987). Level of intimacy with fathers appears to be a better predictor of adolescent adjustment than intimacy with mothers (LeCroy, 1988). In spite of their more distant style of relating, adolescents do not view their fathers as being less involved in their lives than their mothers on important issues such as discipline and academic problems (Shulman & Klein, 1993).

PAVING PATHWAYS ALONG ADOLESCENT SOCIAL AND EMOTIONAL MILESTONES: PARENTING AND TEENAGERS

The major obstacle to parenting teenagers is that interacting with them can become so unpleasant. Even the simplest requests can turn into major arguments. The experience can be so unrewarding that parents are tempted to react by becoming more coercive and demanding; or on the flip side of the coin give up and ignore unsocialized behavior. Either course of action is maladaptive and in fact is associated with increased adolescent deviant behavior, including substance use (Bell & Chapman, 1986; Patterson, 1986; Stice & Barrera, 1995). Having a father who demonstrates low self-restraint such as lack of patience and inappropriate expression of anger appears to be particularly detrimental for early-adolescent boys, who in subsequent years are found to have more difficulties regarding academics, peer relationships, risk-taking behavior, and overall personal adjustment, regardless of their mothers' level of self-restraint (D'Angelo et al., 1995).

Thus parenting teenagers requires a few tactical adjustments. The support and guidance provided by authoritative parenting during adolescence continues to be associated with the best results, including enhanced school performance, psychosocial competence, and lower incidence of problem behavior (Lamborn et al., 1991; Slicker, 1998; Weiss & Schwartz, 1996). Such positive effects of authoritative parenting continue to be observed cross-culturally (Leung et al., 1998). How the support and guidance are delivered, however, looks a little different from what is appropriate with younger children. Following are some suggestions for how parents can more effectively interact with their adolescents during this trying period (Caldwell, 1996; Kastner & Wyatt, 1997; Wolf, 1991).

- ► Be accepting of normal emotional distancing, such as reduced involvement in family activities and increased insistence on privacy. At the same time be careful not to become overaccepting of problematic distancing, such as the adolescent's never being at home or with family or refusing to speak with parents at all. Except under the circumstances of clinical depression, parental overinvolvement, or complete parent-child breakdown, teenagers eventually choose to bring their dilemmas to their parents—on their own terms, of course!

- ► Continue setting limits, but remain willing to take part in related discussions and negotiations in spite of their lengthier and more intense nature. When adolescents reach adulthood they may nevertheless make the same questionable choices you were hoping they would not. But meanwhile they will have matured and will have benefited from what your explanations during negotiations taught them.

- ► Increasingly negotiate additional privileges, allowing for as much freedom as the particular adolescent's competencies and past behavior suggest are advisable.

- ► If adolescents make poor choices that result in failures, let them fail. If you protect them or rescue them from the consequences of their choices, you will only prolong the period of time over which they must learn important life lessons. For example, spending a few years learning from the "school of the world" has readjusted many a reluctant young adult's view on the necessity of pursuing training or higher education in order to build a fulfilling and comfortable lifestyle.

- ► Maintain a family atmosphere in which disagreements and anger with one another are acceptable, as long as these are appropriately expressed and they do not lead to grudges or loss of love.

- ► Limit confrontation over little things that are not particularly important. Confrontation with an adolescent is such a tumultuous event that it is best saved for the problems that really matter.

- ► If you know you are going to have to veto something, do not immediately jump in and state absolute opposition. You can be sure that such an approach will lock the individuating teenager into his or her opposing position. State your concerns but commit yourself neither way. Over time, adolescents often encounter enough information to draw the same conclusion on their own. Or the whole idea may have only been a fleeting whim that the adolescent would have abandoned anyway. For example, while my daughter was attempting to choose a university she came to an arbitrary (at least in my view!) decision that she wanted to attend school in southern California. Such a plan would entail substantially more expense, would put her further away from home than I believed she was ready for, and would not have provided any greater benefit to her current educational goals than attending school in-state. I shared my concerns with her but did not rule anything out. As luck would have it she had an opportunity to go to southern California with another school-seeking friend and visit several campuses. The experience helped her realize exactly how far away from home she would be and what cultural adjustments such a move would entail. Upon returning home she announced that she was going to limit her search to within state and consider southern California for graduate school.

▶   Do not overreact to the inconsiderate behavior stemming from adolescent egocentrism. Remember not to take it personally: It is a product of their developmentally normal self-absorption, not necessarily a reflection of their attitude toward your feelings. Confront selfish behavior in ways that are brief, to the point, and using only limited emotional expressiveness. Long, angry admonishments tend to result in the intended message getting lost. Take heart: Much of their self-centeredness will be overcome in response to confrontation by their peers—one of the positive influences of the adolescent peer group.

Relationships with Peers

How do peers influence adolescent social and emotional adjustment?

As adolescents become more distant from parents and family, peer relationships become much more central to their personal development and day-to-day lives (Brown, 1989; Brown et al., 1993; Parker & Asher, 1994). Feeling that they fit in with their school's social milieu is associated with higher grades, spending more time on homework, greater motivation to achieve, and higher academic aspirations (Hagborg, 1998). When adolescents develop supportive friendships, they are more likely to feel good about themselves, have a positive attitude, and be successful in future relationships—including romantic ones (Hartup, 1993).

Teenagers seek greater emotional support from their friends and become more reciprocal in providing it (Hortacsu, 1989; Youniss & Haynie, 1992). Those who experience weak parental bonding can be buffered by having a relationship with a special "chum," as evidenced by a lower incidence of psychopathology (Bachar et al., 1997). The perceived attitudes of peers toward issues such as academic achievement and drug use can push adolescents' choices in either direction along those behavioral continua (Brown et al., 1986; Fordham & Ogbu, 1986; Jessor et al., 1995; Mounts & Steinberg, 1995). Thus how they form affiliations and with whom they identify play major roles in both adolescent identity formation and future personal adjustment (Bukowski et al., 1993).

Adolescents do vary in their susceptibility to peer influence (Berndt, 1979; Steinberg & Silverberg, 1986). Having been freshly cast into a sea of social uncertainty, younger adolescents tend to be more likely to cling to peer influences as they seek ways of fitting in (Brown et al., 1986). Another factor appears to be how adolescents are parented. Those who perceive their parents as authoritative are more likely to be influenced by their friends' high achievement orientation and less likely to be influenced by the lifestyles of drug-using friends (Mounts & Steinberg, 1995). Authoritative parenting is also associated with adolescents' peer selection practices, because they are more likely to choose friends who have the same values as their parents (Fletcher et al., 1995). Adolescents often choose their source for advice according to the particular issue at hand. They are more likely to seek out peers when making decisions about how to dress, which social events to attend, and which pastimes to pursue and are more likely to seek out parents' input regarding long-term circumstances such as educational and vocational goals (Sebald, 1986).

Crowds, Cliques, and Friendships. Adolescent affiliations come in several forms. The largest group affiliation is with "the crowd" (Brown, 1990; Brown et al., 1994; Steinberg et al., 1996). The crowd typically comprises teenagers having similar attitudes or interests, so identified with labels such as "jocks," "stoners," "skaters," "preppies" "geeks," or "brains" (Brown et al., 1993). The crowd is divided into a number of "cliques"—friendship groups with whom teenagers are most likely to spend their time; although cliques may include individuals affiliated with more than one crowd (Gavin & Furman, 1989; Urberg et al., 1995).

Adolescents develop particularly close relationships with one or two "best friends" and several other "good friends," with the status of "best" or "good" occasionally rotating among friendship group members (Berndt et al., 1989). Girls tend to be more connected with peer networks than are boys, and the affiliations of both male and female adolescents become more exclusive as adolescents grow older (Richards et al., 1998; Urberg et al., 1995).

Dating. Most adolescents begin dating between the ages of 12 and 16; by age 17, 90% have begun dating (Thornton, 1990). As with other interpersonal relationships, girls place much greater emphasis on the importance of this pastime than do boys (Cooper & Grotevant, 1987). About one-fifth of adolescents have been involved in a steady relationship by age 15, but about one-quarter still have not "gone steady" by the time they reach age 18 (Thornton, 1990). A history of having had a steady relationship during the teen years correlates positively with adolescent self-esteem (McDonald & McKinney, 1994). On the other hand, girls who casually date a number of young men tend to demonstrate greater decision-making self-sufficiency, as well as having parents who respect their ideas and independent choices (Cooper & Grotevant, 1987).

Early adolescent dating is influenced mainly by peer expectations, curiosity, and jostling for social status—the agenda of trying to fit in. Older adolescents are more interested in looking for someone who has similar values and interests and/or might make a good life partner (Roscoe et al., 1987). Either way, dating serves as an appropriate arena for adolescents to figure out the culture of romantic and opposite-sex relationships, learning that comes largely by way of experimentation. Not surprisingly, most teenage romances do not survive beyond high school, and those that do become significantly less satisfying (Shaver et al., 1985). Adolescents are much more likely to choose partners who will mesh pleasingly with their own life plans once they have a more completely developed sense of identity and have incorporated worldly realities into the idealism of their youth.

Excessive Social Influence.   When does the influence of others become excessive? The most extreme form of excessive social influence is practiced by cults (Singer & Lalich, 1995). Cults are groups organized around self-appointed leaders who state or imply that they have some special knowledge or life mission. The leader is typically charismatically gifted and uses his or her charisma to dominate and control. "Truth" within the cult centers on the beliefs and the desires of the leader, rather than on God or some other stable purpose or principle. The group presents itself to prospective members as innovative and exclusive, typically providing simplistic, instant answers to the problems of living.

Cults are especially attractive to adolescents (Miller et al., 1999). They provide relief from the angst of their primary developmental tasks. New cult members receive immediate acceptance by the group, eradicating any need for figuring out how to fit in. Cult dogma offers automatic identity in the form of the group identity. Cults may also offer such means for perceived autonomy as encouragement to move into a cult dormitory. The extreme agendas typically endorsed by cults are so far afield from mainstream beliefs that they are easily absorbed into the adolescent process of seeking identity by challenging the norms. Unfortunately, being adopted by a cult does not resolve issues of identity crisis, but rather creates a state identity foreclosure (see page 497). In addition to stunting psychosocial development, cults exert influence by disempowering and controlling their members, typically by using tactics that reduce members' feelings of self-efficacy and presenting the cult as the only escape from the trials of living (Sadock, 1985).

Most teenagers who become involved with cults are relatively normal children from normal families. Some join cults in reaction to depression occurring after losses, humiliations, or extreme disappointments in their lives or feeling pressured to grow up too quickly (Singer, 1992). Fortunately, exit counseling has proven successful in reclaiming about 90% of teenagers who have been lured into cult membership, and most who decide to go back after having received exit counseling eventually leave on their own anyway (Clark et al., 1993).

The same mechanisms of excessive social influence that lure adolescents into cults can also result in their unhealthy identification with almost any group or individual. Boyfriends and girlfriends may use psychological warfare similar to cult tactics as means of disempowering and controlling one another, dynamics that can become precursors to battering relationships. Many problem behaviors such as drug use, dropping out of school, delinquency, and sexual acting-out can occur when troubled teens cluster together and adopt group-defined attitudes and values, functioning together as one rather than asserting their independent identities (Beauvais et al., 1996; Oetting & Beauvais, 1987).

EMOTIONS

When the underpinnings of teenagers' emotional lives first received the speculative attention of psychologists, Hall proposed a "storm and stress" model (Hall, 1905). This ethological stance viewed adolescent emotionality as a tumultuous clash of conflicting impulses related to the evolution of the species, pitting selfishness against altruism and cruelty against sensitivity. Reworking the same idea, Anna Freud interpreted adolescent emotionality as a period of adjustment between the selfish id and altruistic superego functions (Freud, 1972).

What evidence do we have that supports or refutes these early beliefs? The hormonal changes of puberty have been demonstrated to have some effect on adolescent mood swings, but these effects are not large (Brooks-Gunn et al., 1994; Susman et al., 1987; 1997). There is also some evidence that adolescents are experiencing their emotions differently; for example, feelings of guilt emerge more frequently from conflict among internal thoughts and beliefs and less because of aggressive or otherwise inappropriate acts (Williams & Bybee, 1994).

Nevertheless, many believe that while adolescence may involve some emotionality, the storm and stress concept has been blown out of proportion (Arnett, 1999). Cross-cultural studies indicate that, in general, adolescents' attitudes toward themselves and their subjective well-being are fairly positive, and become more so as they progress through adolescence (Nottelmann, 1987; Offer, 1988). There is surprisingly limited study of adolescent stress and coping and emotionality in general, given the press it receives (Compas, 1998; Losoya et al., 1998). The Tried. . . . and True boxes on pages 510–511 take a closer look at storm, stress, and the adolescent in current Western cultures. Interestingly, a review of adolescent emotionality in less industrialized societies finds significantly less "storm and stress," supporting Mead's early notion that extreme presentations are related more to environmental influences (Schlegel & Barry, 1991).

Emotional Regulation

From their socialization experiences children learn certain "scripts" describing a peer's, parent's, or other adult's likely response to how they express their emotions (Wierzbicka & White, 1994). In doing so they are recognizing that emotion is not only an inner experience but also a source of interpersonal communication serving specific social purposes (Thompson, 1994). Boys and girls differ in emotional regulation, in part because they have observed differing responses to the emotional expressiveness of the two genders. Boys report regulating emotions, especially sadness, more than do girls, out of fear of not receiving support or being belittled for expressing them (Fuchs & Thelen, 1988;

Zeman & Shipman, 1997). As might be expected, different cultures teach different lessons regarding the acceptability of expressing negative emotions (Cole & Tamang, 1998).

Relatively limited attention has been given to developmental advances in emotional regulation during the teen years (Gnepp & Hess, 1986; Saarni, 1988). As is true for the lion's share of adolescent learning, much of their progress in emotional management occurs as they interact with peers. Their increases in emotional dependence and reciprocity with peers, combined with their expectation of nonsupportive reactions by parents, fuels greater interest in how their emotional displays affect others (Papini et al., 1990). Children appear to invest the greatest amount of energy in emotional regulation during the early teen years, a time when they are especially concerned about fitting in (Zeman & Shipman, 1997). In fact, one study demonstrated that adolescents may choose friends who experience equivalent levels of inner distress and then vary their inner experience in accordance with variations occurring with their peers (Hogue & Steinberg, 1995).

Is adolescent
depression normal?

Depression and Suicide

The normal moodiness of adolescence at times results in feelings of sadness or depression (Petersen et al., 1993). Incidence of depressed mood in children increases dramatically between the ages of 13 and 15 years, then levels off and declines by about age 18 (Radloff, 1991). Its prevalence and invasiveness characterizes it as a sort of adolescent "mood of choice," frequently coming along for the ride when other negative emotions such as guilt, fear, anger, contempt, and disgust occur (Watson & Kendall, 1989). Those who excessively dramatize their lives or engage in thinking patterns that make them less tolerant of frustration are likely to spend more of their adolescent experience in a depressed mood (Marcotte, 1996). Hispanic-American adolescents report experiencing more depressed moods than Caucasian-American, African-American, or Asian-American adolescents, regardless of socioeconomic status; and this statistic follows them into adulthood. However, it is not clear from these reports whether Hispanic-American individuals experience more depressed moods or require less mood disruption for them to report depressed mood (Guarnaccia et al., 1989; Siegel et al., 1998).

Clinical Depression. As is the case with younger children, depressed mood that is prolonged and combined with other symptoms paints a picture of clinical depression (American Psychiatric Association, 1994) (see Chapter 13). Estimates of the percentage of adolescents suffering from a major depressive disorder at any given point in time range between 0.4 and 8.3% (Birmaher et al., 1996). Among younger children, girls and boys are equally affected, but during adolescence twice as many girls as boys become clinically depressed—a statistic consistent with surveys of depression during adulthood (Fleming & Offord, 1990).

Although it was once suggested that the hormonal changes related to girls' earlier puberty explained this finding, such a hypothesis was not supported by

BOX 16.1   The relationship between negative events and unhappiness

Larson, R., & Ham, M. (1993). Stress and "storm and stress" in early adolescence: The relationship of negative events with dysphoric affect. *Developmental Psychology, 29,* 130–140.

HALL'S CONCEPTION OF YOUNG ADOLESCENTS AS BEING programmed to experience extreme emotionality is generally no longer accepted as a hard and fast inevitability. Just the same, we still observe a lot of emotionality in teenagers, as did Hall and the others who originally proposed such beliefs. Might there be some other explanation for these observations? Larson and Ham's study hypothesized that teenage emotionality is actually a result of stressors typically experienced during the teen years, rather than an emergence of built-in mechanisms.

The researchers compared the stressors teenagers encountered with their experience of negative feelings in order to see what sort of relationship might exist between the two. They did so by looking at 483 randomly selected fifth to ninth graders from a middle-class community. To get an idea of what stressors they might be experiencing, both the students and their parents filled out an inventory describing various events that had been encountered by the students over the last six months. As a means of tracking feelings, the students carried pagers for a week. The pagers beeped at various odd intervals, and students recorded what their feelings had been just before the beep according to three seven-point Likert-type scales: happy-unhappy, friendly-angry, and cheerful-irritable.

As the researchers suspected, the young adolescents did indeed experience a significantly greater number of negative life events than did the preteens. The level of negative feelings reported in reaction to a given event appeared to suggest that these events create greater day-to-day stress for the adolescents than they did for the preteens. Perhaps the older students were more aware of the possible ramifications of the negative events than were the younger ones. Also, they may have been experiencing the isolation and insecurity that can result from feeling more of a pull to manage their lives independently, rather than depending on parents to help them out.

However, this study does have its limitations. As was described in the discussion of cross-sectional research in Chapter 2, age and cohort are confounded. We do not know whether to attribute the difference between the two groups to their differing ages or to differing experiences in handling negative events. Also, since the data are correlational, we cannot say whether negative events lead to negative feelings, negative feelings lead to negative events, or some third unknown variable is contributing to both.

Tried

a study controlling for age of pubertal onset (Angold & Rutter, 1992). More relevant are the unrealistic standards for feminine appearance and sex role identification that girls most strongly encounter at this age, as well as the greater number of areas within which girls in America must develop a sense of competence (American Association of University Women, 1992; Wichstrom, 1999). Thus girls can experience more chronic strain and a lower sense of mastery than adolescent boys (Nolen-Hoeksema et al., 1999). Particularly relevant to the development of depression is girls' tendency to become progressively more likely to internalize blame for their woes; by contrast, boys externalize blame and thus are more likely to experience anger or develop acting-out behaviors instead (Leadbeater et al., 2000; Leung & Wong, 1998; Robins, 1991; Zahn-Waxler, 1993).

BOX 16.2   Helping adolescents manage stressful social situations

. . . . and True

REGARDLESS OF WHETHER NEGATIVE EVENTS CAUSE negative feelings or negative feelings cause negative events, what is clear from the Larson and Ham study is that adolescents report experiencing more stressful events than do younger children. Their newly developing formal operational ability no doubt contributes to increased awareness of the significance of the events. Add in their tendency to try to rely less on their parents as a resource for dealing with their lives and to rely more on themselves, and you have an understandably scary set of circumstances. How can we use these observations in ways that might help adolescents along?

One solution is helping them enhance their skills at dealing with critical situations as they arise. Thomas Brigham (1989) developed a program that respects and capitalizes upon adolescents' newly emerging cognitive strengths in ways that address their increased experiencing of stress. The program teaches adolescents the principles of behavior modification, such as positive and negative reinforcement, punishment, extinction, shaping, stimulus control, and modeling. The adolescents learn how these principles operate in their daily lives and how they can use them to their advantage as they manage stressful events.

For example, one high school student, Sarah, was upset by the constant trash talk she endured from another student at her school, Raphael. Any time he was standing around with a group of friends as she walked by, he called her names and his friends laughed. She responded by retaliating, making insulting comments about him in order to make her friends laugh at him. This only made matters worse.

As Sarah worked her way through the program, she recognized that to make behaviorism work for her she needed to decrease the number of positive reinforcers for trash-talk and increase positive reinforcement for more friendly behavior. First, she made a point of never being around while Raphael was with his friends so that there was no opportunity for the reinforcer of friends' laughter. If he insulted her on other occasions, she ignored him or pretended she had not heard his comments. Then she made a point of going up to him occasionally while he was alone and not trash-talking, instead delivering the reinforcer of saying "Hi, how are you doing?" Although at first he was so astonished he did not know how to respond, the procedure eventually extinguished his trash talk and increased the number of times he behaved neutrally or even pleasantly. As for Sarah, her general popularity increased, she received better grades, and her stress levels declined.

Brigham, T. A. (1989). *Managing everyday problems*. New York: Guilford.

A host of developmental, biological, cognitive, and socioemotional systems converge at adolescence that, unfortunately, can predispose adolescents toward developing a depressive self-organization (Cicchetti & Toth, 1998). The transition from elementary to middle school appears to be a crucial period for future adolescent adjustment (National Research Council, 1993). It represents a giant leap: No longer does a teacher hover over students to make sure that they are doing their assignments, are getting to where they need to be on time, or are not misbehaving. Individual attention and one-on-one guidance in general are much less prevalent. During a time when increasing independence is part of their primary developmental task, middle school students are often expected to spend less time in free discussion and more time sitting quietly and listening or working on assignments. They receive less support in the areas of developing academic competence, autonomy, and a sense of belonging at their new school, when these factors play a crucial developmental role in establishing their identities.

As these factors collide, overchallenged adolescents can develop problems of academic alienation, poor school performance, and even minor delinquency (Eccles et al., 1993; 1996). Depressive symptoms then arise from feelings of futility and poor self-evaluation (Cole, 1991). They may attempt to cope with their floundering sense of belonging by becoming involved in antisocial activities and substance abuse, which in turn further reduce feelings of self-worth (Rosenberg, 1986).

Depressed adolescents who attempt to cope by means of feeling-state moderation techniques experience some developmental stumbling blocks. Because they are still sorting out the differences between feeling states and personal identity, the rigid perspective that protects their emerging identities may prevent them from adopting the alternative ways of thinking that might alleviate their depressive symptoms. Adolescents also tend to have less faith in their ability to moderate their mood than they did when they were younger. Depressed adolescents are thus less likely to attempt to alter their depressed mood or to be successful when they do try (Garber et al., 1995). Nevertheless, cognitive-behavioral therapies, especially in a group format, appear to help reduce adolescent depression (Marcotte, 1997). Those who develop a problem-solving and/or help-seeking coping style when under stress are less susceptible to becoming depressed, suggesting a potential avenue for primary prevention (Lee & Larson, 1996).

Why is suicide more likely to occur during adolescence, and how can it be prevented?

Adolescent Suicide. The adolescent's focus on identity formation in the here-and-now takes a lot of energy away from the ongoing sense of identity that promotes having an investment in the future. Thus adolescents who become depressed are especially at risk for suicide (Chandler, 1994). The statistics regarding adolescent suicide are sobering. Between the ages of 13 and 19, 5 to 6% of adolescents attempt suicide, 12 to 15% report having come very close to attempting suicide, and over 50% report having occasional suicidal ideations (Gallup, 1994). Some studies find the incidence of reported adolescent suicidal attempts and ideations to be even higher (Harkavy-Friedman et al., 1987; Smith & Crawford, 1986).

The rate of teen suicide increased 200% between 1960 and 1988, while it rose only 17% for the general population. Suicide is the third leading cause of death for adolescents, coming in close behind homicide and accidents. While the elderly are most likely to complete a suicide, adolescents make the most attempts (National Center for Health Statistics, 1991). Boys are more likely to complete suicide than girls, usually because they tend to choose more lethal means such as guns or hanging. Girls are more likely to choose passive means such as taking an overdose of drugs or slitting their wrists, which provide time windows during which they might be rescued or change their minds and seek help (Berman & Jobes, 1991).

Which adolescents are most susceptible to suicidal behavior? Because of its epidemic nature, this topic has been heavily researched. Mood disorders such as depression are tightly connected with considering, attempting, and completing suicide (Flisher, 1999). Adolescents who have attempted in the past are at the greatest risk for attempting again (Garrison et al., 1991; Shaffer et al., 1988). Having a peer who attempts or completes suicide also increases incidences of attempts, a scary prospect given that 60% of all teenagers report personally knowing someone who has attempted suicide (Gallup, 1994; Ho et al., 2000; Lewinsohn, 1994). Suicide attempts by family members seem to have a similar effect (Brent et al., 1990). A history of physical or sexual abuse by parents, general family discord, and low family cohesiveness are associated with greater suicide risk (Deykin et al., 1985; Fremouw et al., 1993; van der Kolk et al., 1991). Substance abuse is another common correlate of suicidal behavior (Lester, 1992). The discovery that the incidence of adoptees' suicidal behavior is a closer match to that of the biological parents than to that of the adoptive parents—independent of familial psychiatric conditions—suggests a genetic component of suicidal behavior, perhaps related to impulse control (Kety, 1986).

Several factors produced by society at large have been associated with teen suicide. Some suggest that the increase in adolescent suicide over the last few decades is a product of the greater psychosocial stress of trying to launch into a more complex, limited, and overpopulated economy (Garrison, 1992; Hendlin, 1987). Media coverage of suicides, whether actual or fictional, seems to promote a sort of copycat effect (Davidson & Gould, 1989). The heavy metal music subculture with its fatalistic themes has been associated with higher incidence of suicidal ideation and attempts (Scheel & Westefeld, 1999; Stack et al., 1994). The erosion of practices related to an adolescent's culture of origin—be it Hopi, Micronesian, or rural southern African American—can contribute to a greater incidence of suicidal depression as the adolescent attempts to individuate without the ongoing security of early grounding (Brent & Moritz, 1996; Levy & Kunitz, 1987; Shaffer & Fisher, 1981).

Preventing Adolescent Suicide. Adolescents follow a typical path as they meander toward contemplation of suicide (Grosz et al., 1991; Rudd, 1990; Yang & Clum, 1994). They begin with some form of predisposition toward suicidal behavior, usually depression but possibly any other combination of risk factors. They experience an extreme stressor, most often some perceived failure or personal rejection. If they do not succeed at applying their problem-solving abilities or in seeking out pain-moderating social supports, their sense of despair and hopelessness points them toward one fatal solution.

Interrupting this fateful passage first requires recognition that the process is occurring. Teenagers throw out substantial clues that can be indicators of their suicidal intentions; these are listed in Table 16.1 (Capuzzi, 1994). Once identified, some suicidal youths need to be hospitalized during the 24- to 72-hour period of suicidal crisis, while others benefit from outpatient counseling

TABLE 16.1

Common behavioral cues preceding adolescent suicide attempts. Adapted with permission from Capuzzi, D. (1994). *Suicide prevention in the schools: Guidelines for middle and high school settings.* Alexandria, VA: American Counseling Association.

Unusual or sudden changes in social patterns

Declining school performance

Increase in risk-taking behaviors or sexual acting-out

Uncharacteristic interest in how others are feeling

Sudden increases or decreases in eating behaviors

Insomnia or always wanting to sleep

Preoccupation with death and/or violent themes

Decreased quality of thinking, logic, or concentration skills

Attempts to put aspects of their personal lives in order, or make amends

Statements of desire or intent to commit suicide

Indirect comments such as "you're going to be sorry for how you've treated me" or "someday I'll show everyone how serious this is to me"

Giving away of prized belongings

Sudden, unexplainable improvement after a period of depression

alone. Interventions used with suicidal teens are aimed at redirecting the factors that lead up to suicidal ideations, such as by increasing problem-solving skills, promoting a more successful social support system, and addressing predispositional factors leading to their vulnerability. Such interventions are intended to enable adolescents to develop protective factors more characteristic of those who are relatively more stress-resistant and adaptable, better able to handle the foibles of adolescent living (Pfeffer et al., 1993).

Outcome studies evaluating the success of such treatments have not been particularly encouraging (Pfeffer et al., 1994). Part of the problem is that the study participants are usually those who are the most severely troubled and therefore show more limited gains. The ethical inappropriateness of assigning a no-treatment control group and the lack of sufficient specificity and comparison regarding the particular interventions used may also contribute toward hiding true effects (Zimmerman, 1995). But if we examine the treatment outcome of specific cases, many teenagers have clearly benefited from these interventions (Berman & Jobes, 1991).

How are morals and values likely to change during adolescence?

DEVELOPMENT OF MORALS AND VALUES

Chapter 13 described how children adopt increasingly sophisticated strategies of moral reasoning as they mature, becoming more and more in sync with prosocial principles such as justice, fairness, and caring about fellow human beings (see pages 403–406). Adolescents' increased ability to understand and manipulate abstractions assists their progress toward becoming principled moral thinkers, and they apply such thinking ever more frequently and more readily over the course of adolescence (Narvaez, 1998). Toward the end of adolescence their morals tend to be more internally driven, and measuring up to their own moral standards is increasingly important to their self-esteem (Daniels, 1998).

However, the capacity for abstraction alone is not enough to guarantee that a child will progress to more advanced moral reasoning. Individual differences in adolescent moral reasoning have been associated with a number of factors. One of the most consistently reported research findings concerns the relationship between adolescents and their parents. The most advanced moral reasoning is found among children whose parents used disciplinary techniques involving reasoning, especially pointing out others' perspectives and the expected consequences of taking certain actions (Buck et al., 1981; Parikh, 1980). The process of such lessons actively teaches more advanced moral themes. Another contributing factor is the presence of a positive family atmosphere, exhibiting warmth, supportiveness, and intrafamily involvement (Speicher, 1992; Walker & Taylor, 1991). The level of moral reasoning used by the parents themselves thus plays a role. They not only teach it and model it, but are also more likely to choose the nonviolent and caring authoritative parenting style that is associated with more advanced moral development (Powers, 1988).

In addition to parenting, higher education appears to contribute to level of moral development (Colby & Kohlberg, 1987; Rest and Narvaez, 1991). Higher education facilitates an individual's ability to manage abstractions. But we must remember the obvious as well: Higher education is a teaching ground. In addition to training students for future careers, well-rounded college programs require exposure to whole new worlds of information and provide instruction in numerous strategies for exploring them, perhaps revamping the more limited moral learning experiences of childhood. One study found advanced moral reasoning to have an even greater association with adolescent and young adult educational level than with their parents' level of moral reasoning (Speicher, 1994).

As adolescents sort through and evaluate their experience of morality, they build sets of values. What constitutes right and wrong, appropriate or inappropriate behavior? To be sure, the culture within which children are reared has an effect on the type of values they will adopt (Narvaez, Getz, et al., 1999; Schwartz, 1990). Culture also affects how they believe violations of moral rules should be dealt with. For example, Indian adolescents are more likely than American adolescents to absolve moral transgressions if they were performed by young children or the perpetrator was under emotional duress (Bersoff & Miller, 1993).

Unfortunately for children in the United States, substantial conflict sparks between presentations of cultural values. While children are taught that being kind, empathic, and considerate of others is important, the self-focused values of materialism are also greatly emphasized (Schwartz & Bilsky, 1990). To make matters worse, an antithetical relationship appears to exist between the two stances: The more individuals value financial gain, the less efficient they are at having warm relationships with their fellow human beings (Richins & Dawson, 1992).

Children are more likely to lean toward prosocial values if they grow up in a nurturing family atmosphere (Kasser & Ryan, 1993; Kasser et al., 1995; Kohn, 1990). Homes that meet children's basic developmental needs free them from self-preoccupation, allowing for development of values that consider the needs, rights, and feelings of others. Cold, non-nurturing homes result in self-concerns and self-doubts, thrusting the yardstick of financial gain before them as a substitute means of perceiving self-worth. Parents who overvalue financial gain can have a similar influence as they put the all-mighty buck on a pedestal, over any other value-based considerations, including a child's self-expression, self-acceptance, quality of interpersonal relationships, and dedication to community.

Socioeconomic status affects cultivation of values in other ways (Kasser et al., 1995). Since lower socioeconomic status creates a greater family focus on financial considerations, meeting basic physical and security needs may interfere with developing the self-actualization that fuels higher-order values (Maslow, 1954). Parents' low-income jobs tend to require more conformity and less self-guided direction, creating another impediment to passing on values that require inner focusing (Kohn, 1977). Life in a low-income, high-risk neighborhood often is not conducive to adoption of prosocial values related to community connectedness. Some suggest that focusing on inner prosocial values may not even be adaptive in such a setting, where basic survival requires that so many externals be pursued or avoided (Burns et al., 1984). Unfortunately, learning some techniques of basic survival in high-risk settings can contribute toward the topic described in the next section: juvenile delinquency.

What factors lead to juvenile delinquency, and what can be done to reduce its prevalence?

JUVENILE DELINQUENCY

The number of crimes committed by adolescents over the last two decades has actually decreased (Sautter, 1994). However, an illusion of increased juvenile delinquency has evolved as the crimes they commit have become more serious. Over this same time span, the number of juveniles arrested for carrying handguns or committing murder has more than doubled (Children's Defense Fund, 1996). Gang activity, once limited to large inner cities, has infiltrated more of the general populace and thus increased the visibility of juvenile crime. The

The potential consequences of early delinquent behavior can have long-term legal results, even if the period of delinquency is short-lived.

problem does not necessarily end after adolescence. Over half of juvenile offenders go on to become chronic adult offenders (Blumstein et al., 1988).

Development of Juvenile Delinquency

A number of factors interplay as they lead down the road to eventual antisocial and criminal behavior (McWhirter et al., 1998). Antisocial children usually have received parenting that is harsh, lax, inconsistent, and/or characterized predominantly by negative interactions—as is typically seen in permissive and authoritarian homes (Baumrind, 1993). When verbally or physically violent behavior is the norm in family interactions, violent behavior is both modeled and reinforced as children learn to use it to counteract violence directed toward them. Chronic family stressors such as poverty, alcoholism, and marital problems also appear to contribute (Patterson et al., 1989). Ethnic minority parents living in poor communities as either unemployed or unskilled laborers are especially at risk for having antisocial children, probably due to lack of time, resources, or educational background for investing in effective parenting (Tolan & Guerra, 1994). However, it is important to note that a behaviorally or temperamentally difficult child can create a stressful home environment; not all stressors are parent-caused (Ge et al., 1998; Henry et al., 1996; Neiderhiser et al., 1999; Patterson et al., 1989; Raine et al., 1996).

Children apply what they learn at home as they attempt to function in other roles. At school their academic performance suffers from poor training in controlling impulses or using cognitive skills such as concentration, reasoning, and staying on task (Catalano & Hawkins, 1996). They have difficulty perceiving the social norms of their peers, often misinterpreting situations, behaving inappropriately, and eventually experiencing rejection by nondelinquent peers (Fraser, 1996). They often cluster with other troubled children who have learned to live by the same social guidelines, and encourage and reinforce one another's deviant behaviors (Beauvais et al., 1996). Other correlates with violent and delinquent behavior are early involvement with drugs and alcohol, easy access to weapons, and exposure to crime and violence in their neighborhoods or as portrayed in the media (Eron et al., 1994). High levels of angry feelings combined with poor impulse control, rather than angry feelings alone, appear to be the internal recipe for juvenile delinquent behavior (Colder & Stice, 1998). Some genetically determined factors may also be at work (Edelbrock et al., 1995; Pike et al., 1996).

Controversy Regarding Development of Juvenile Delinquency

Mounds of research have examined the developmental pathways of violent and antisocial behavior. The evidence piles up in support of the suspicion that not all children move toward delinquent lifestyles for the same reasons. In fact, the research raises controversy regarding some of the assumptions that have driven popular approaches to researching its underpinnings (Loeber & Stouthamer-Loeber, 1998).

One such assumption is that aggressive and violent tendencies emerge early and then tend to be stable over the life span. This notion has gained momentum because of the numerous studies producing strong correlational statistics between measurements of aggressive tendencies during early childhood, middle childhood, adolescence, and young adulthood (Farrington 1994; Haapasalo & Tremblay, 1994; Stattin & Magnusson, 1989). However, even relatively strong correlations account for only part of the variance in relationships between variables (see Chapter 2). In other words, among these same research populations there are substantial numbers of aggressors who desist from engaging in aggressive behavior at other times in their lives.

Some researchers have redirected their attention toward this apparent instability of aggressive behavior over the life span. For example, aggressive behavior is relatively normal among preschoolers but typically decreases as children move into middle childhood (Loeber & Hay, 1997). An increase in minor forms of aggression is commonly observed during adolescence and young adulthood (Loeber & Farrington, 1998). Many teenagers engage in delinquent behavior only during adolescence, not having done it during earlier childhood and desisting from such activity in young adulthood (Kingston & Price, 1995; Moffitt et al., 1996; Sampson & Laub, 1993). Yet others may not show any signs of antisocial or violent tendencies until reaching adulthood (Moffitt et al., 1996; Windle & Windle, 1995). Such variability in aggressive and antisocial behavior brings into question a mainstream belief that all delinquent behavior has its roots in early childhood (Lynam, 1996).

Development of juvenile delinquency has been studied as if it follows a single pathway when in reality there may be three developmental pathways differing in terms of the type of delinquent behavior (Loeber & Hay, 1994; Loeber et al., 1997; Patterson et al., 1991). Some children's early difficulties mainly involve conflict with authority, which progresses into behaviors such as running away, truancy, or ignoring curfews. Others make up the populations highlighted by the research on interpersonal violence, beginning their career in juvenile delinquency with bullying and annoying others, then progressing to more serious forms of aggression such as fighting, gang violence, assault, and rape. A third subgroup acts out in the form of more indirect personal aggression, first choosing behaviors such as frequent lying and shoplifting, then moving on to vandalism, fire setting, burglary, fraud, and serious theft.

Different pathways appear to be associated with different factors. Violent offending has demonstrated greater and differing connections with physiological processes than have crimes involving indirect personal aggression. Differing levels of certain hormones and neurotransmitters such as testosterone, serotonin, and cortisol have been associated with those committing violent crimes but not those committing crimes against property (Blackburn, 1993; McBurnett et al., 1996; Susman et al., 1997). Resting heart rate tends to be lower than average among violent offenders, while skin conductance is lower than average among nonviolent offenders (Buikhuisen et al., 1985; Raine et al., 1997). Certain early childhood temperament variables such as poor impulse control and excessive negative reactivity to stress are associated only with violent offenders (Henry et al., 1996). Family background also differs between the two groups. Violent offenders are more likely to have a history of maternal rejection or conflictual family atmosphere than are nonviolent offenders (Pulkkinen, 1983; Raine et al., 1994).

Gender differences in the developmental pathways of delinquent behavior also need closer scrutiny (Marcus, 1999; Pakiz et al., 1997). Some differences have begun to emerge as early as toddlerhood (Loeber & Hay, 1997). Since boys have been found to engage in a greater proportion of aggressive and delinquent acts, most research has focused on their experiences and behaviors. Yet, despite their smaller numbers, girls who demonstrate ADHD and/or antisocial behavior have been found to be substantially more likely to demonstrate antisocial behavior later in life than are boys with similar behavioral histories (Bird et al., 1993; Loeber & Keenan, 1994). They are also more likely than boys to become future offenders if they have been abused or neglected, or if they have deviant relatives (Mednick et al., 1987; Raine, 1993; Rivera & Widom, 1990). The genders also differ in age of onset. Girls' delinquent behavior is more likely to first appear during adolescence or adulthood, while boys' delinquent behavior typically begins earlier in childhood (Kratzer & Hodgins, 1996; McGee et al., 1992; Zoccolillo, 1993). Delinquent girls also are more likely than boys to have poor classroom and school attendance (Weist et al., 1998).

Given all of these individual differences, future research in the field of juvenile delinquency will benefit by employing greater specificity regarding its developmental pathways. Also, what factors lead up to aggressive children desisting from aggression? Do differences in type or level of provocation make a difference for some but not for others? Examining these issues, differing onset patterns, types of delinquent behavior, and gender differences will hopefully provide both greater understanding of individual differences and clearer direction for intervention in the development of juvenile delinquency.

PAVING PATHWAYS ALONG ADOLESCENT SOCIAL AND EMOTIONAL MILESTONES: PREVENTING AND INTERVENING IN JUVENILE DELINQUENCY

Thus far, the diversion of children off developmental pathways toward juvenile delinquency has been most successful when it addresses impairments in the vital life skills that ensure basic social competence (Wagner, 1996). Three main components appear to be most essential (McWhirter et al., 1998):

▶ Interpersonal communication skills, including assertiveness, resistance, and refusal
▶ Cognitive restructuring, focusing on building skills at problem-solving, decision making, self-management, self-control, and healthy self-talk
▶ Stress management skills, such as relaxation techniques, visual imagery, and positive self-talk

Successful programs are integrated in nature, addressing not only life skill needs but also educational and very basic unmet physical needs—factors certainly likely to distract a child from higher-order learning! Integrated service delivery to high-risk children includes activity at the individual, family, school, and community levels (Dryfoos, 1998). Children benefit individually from both early intervention and one-on-one attention. Youth empowerment is a key component, not only teaching children life skills but also getting them personally involved in solving the community problems they see around them (Adams, 1994). Parents benefit from parent effectiveness training, which in turn benefits their children (Gordon, 1989; McWhirter & Kahn, 1974). Parents in high-risk situations are more likely to get involved if programs are non-threatening, useful, and also help them access resources such as food, shelter, and medical care (Dryfoos, 1998).

On the school level, children become high-risk when they view themselves as having fallen hopelessly behind. The schools need to closely track and address the individual teen's deficits in academic competence to improve his or her achievement (United States Department of Education, Office of Research, 1994). School settings can also help by arranging for exposure to healthier peer influences, perhaps in the form of peer mediator, peer tutor, and "natural helper" peer facilitator programs (Corn & Moore, 1992; Lane & McWhirter, 1992; Tansy et al., 1996).

Community after-school programs such as the one illustrated here provide children with a safe alternative to gang involvement.

Gale Zucker/Stock Boston

Community efforts can play a tremendous role (Dryfoos, 1998). Such "safe haven" youth groups as Boys and Girls Clubs and the Urban League provide teenagers not only with safe, alternative gathering places but also with access to interactions with supportive, nonjudgmental adults. Providing food—especially the ever-popular pizza and hamburgers—seems to be an especially effective draw for the typically hungry teenager. Programs such as these are also in a position to provide hands-on instruction regarding skills in business and finance as participants work together on fund-raising efforts and other campaigns.

When are such programs more likely to fail (Dryfoos, 1998)? Sometimes failure is due to inadequate implementation by poorly trained facilitators. Interventions can fail because they are too brief, too limited in scope, too early in the child's development, or too late. Targeting middle school children seems to provide greater benefit than waiting until high school. However for some hardcore inner-city students, even middle school appears to be too late (Colyer et al., 1966; Webster, 1993).

 Programs also must be culturally sensitive. The well-known and expensive "McGruff" program has been attempting to take a bite out of crime for well over a decade. Unfortunately, the character may be too white middle-class for poor, ethnically diverse, high-risk children to be able to identify with him. As with the "D.A.R.E." drug-resistance program, little evidence has been found to support the effectiveness of the McGruff program in reducing target behaviors, although it appears that these government-sponsored programs may serve as arenas for improving relationships between citizens and police officers (Dryfoos, 1998; Ringwalt et al., 1994; United States Department of Justice, Bureau of Justice Assistance, 1993).

*Which factors are
likely to affect
adolescent self-
esteem?*

SELF-ESTEEM

How often do you see the average teenager pass a mirror, window, or other reflective surface without at least attempting to catch an admiring or critical glimpse of his or her appearance? Adolescent narcissistic self-preoccupation can easily be misinterpreted as an overdose of good self-evaluation. In reality, it more commonly represents the insecurities of their age. Adolescents are presented with a full plate of competency-based developmental tasks: transitioning to secondary school, achieving academically in a way that prepares them for higher education or the working world, successfully engaging in extracurricular activities, forming close friendships with people of both genders, and developing a cohesive sense of self (Masten & Coatsworth, 1998). Self-esteem flounders as they become increasingly aware of all they must accomplish and they evaluate how well they are doing so. The lowest point in this dip appears to be at about age 13, after which self-esteem begins to show improvements (Rosenberg, 1986).

Body image is especially important to an adolescent's self-esteem, particularly for girls (Harter, 1993; Kotanski & Gullone, 1998; Simmons & Blyth, 1987). Teenagers are anxious to look more like adults, and are concerned about how attractive their developing bodies have become and have yet to become. The emphasis placed on attractiveness by those around them contributes to these concerns. Attractive teenagers certainly have more friends than unattractive ones (Rutter, 1980). Even teachers tend to show more favoritism toward middle schoolers who are attractive (Lerner et al., 1990). The current unrealistic emphasis on thinness perpetrated by Western cultural standards pumps up anxieties even among those whose bodies match the cultural ideal, at times contributing to eating disorders (see Chapter 14).

In addition to body image concerns, the genders appear to differ in how experiences related to social behavioral adjustments affect their self-esteem. Boys are more likely to report higher levels of self-esteem after experiences such as successfully asserting themselves among their male friends. Girls report experiencing higher levels of self-esteem as a result of having been able to help their female friends, and report lower self-esteem when they do not feel that they have their friends' approval (Thorne & Michaelieu, 1996).

Faltering self-esteem also corresponds with school transitions, first as adolescents enter middle school and then as they enter high school. With each transition they are faced with new systems and higher standards, and establishing confidence in their ability to handle the tasks before them takes time (Eccles et al., 1993). Thus it is not surprising that when students only transition once, as when moving from an eight-year elementary school program to a four-year high school, self-esteem fares better (Simmons & Blyth, 1987).

The door appears to swing in both directions regarding their academic successes and self-esteem. Academic achievement contributes to self-esteem, but is also more likely to occur among students who have faith in their ability to achieve (Greene & Miller, 1996). Experiences in the working world can also become adolescent arenas for promoting feelings of self-worth. As they take advantage of opportunities for developing skills that represent success in the adult world, their sense of self-efficacy and self-confidence are enhanced (Mortimer & Finch, 1996).

What are "rites of passage" and how do they affect identity formation?

RITES OF PASSAGE

When my daughter was 16 I accompanied her on her trek in search of a driver's license. While holding up the wall at the DMV I observed a number of other parents and their teenage driving proteges, nervously rehearsing material out of the driver's manual or receiving last-minute instructions as they prepared to take the road test. As they emerged from the testing grounds victorious, newly qualified drivers would be met with cheers, hugs, expressions of pride, high-fives, and other demonstrative celebrations typically reserved for outstandingly meaningful events. There amidst the cluttered number-taking and bureaucratic pontificating, teenagers were being anointed with a new piece of independence—as well as adult responsibility.

When does a child become an adult in Western cultures? Is the title bestowed after achieving rights such as driving, voting, consuming alcohol, or being drafted into the armed forces? Or does adulthood occur at age 18, when the child reaches legal majority? Maybe adulthood is marked by graduation from high school. Or are children only considered to be adults if they can live independently and be self-supporting? And what about physical maturity? Does becoming able to reproduce signify adulthood? Is getting married sufficient for holding that status?

The term *adolescence* was first seriously addressed at the beginning of the 1900s, in part as an acknowledgment of the greater length and complexity of the childhood-adulthood transition during our evolving industrial era (Hall, 1905). Over the last half-century the transition has become even murkier as young people in their late teens and early twenties spend more time exploring who they are and lifetime possibilities before setting on their chosen paths (Arnett, 2000). In earlier ages the transition from childhood to adulthood was clearer. Often the shift would be punctuated by **rites of passage**: formal rituals, ceremonies, or other procedures that mark the passage from one social status to another (van Gennep, 1961). Rites of passage into young adulthood are very tightly connected with establishment of social identity.

Such rituals have been standard features of tribal societies for millennia (Campanelli, 1998). The ingrained significance that rites of passage hold within the human experience is evidenced by their having evolved independently in cultures all over the world: the vision quests of many Native American tribes, the Australian aboriginal walkabouts, the Japanese Shikoku pilgrimages, as well as a variety of initiation ceremonies practiced among African tribes to this day (Fried & Fried, 1980; Holm & Bowker, 1994; Mahdi et al., 1996). Most major religions also observe some ritual or requirement marking the passage from

During this rite of passage, adolescent males prove they are ready to be accepted into the status of manhood by standing and clutching their spear throwers for many hours.

James R. Holland/Stock Boston

childhood to adulthood: the Hindu *upanayana* and *tirandukuli,* the Judaic bar mitzvah and bat mitzvah, the Muslim first observance of *sawm,* the Confucian rite of capping and rite of coiffure, and the Christian confirmation (Holm & Bowker, 1994). And in the absence of formal rites, we appear to spontaneously project ceremonial importance onto bureaucratic rituals such as obtaining driver's licenses!

Characteristics of Rites of Passage

Rites of passage share common stages or component parts (Christopher, 1996; van Gennep, 1961). Youths are typically separated from familiar surroundings; boys may be taken to a special training ground in the forest or girls to a menstrual hut. In this novel setting a period of transitioning begins. Often tests of courage are involved, such as fasting, enduring pain, or spending long periods of time in isolation or in training. Initiates are educated regarding the ins and outs of their new social roles, expectations for adult behavior, and their new responsibilities and obligations. They may be allowed access to privileged knowledge and be trained in skills that are reserved for adults only. They develop new social relationships, bonding with co-initiates and establishing mentoring relationships with same-sex elders. At the end of the transitioning period they are reincorporated into their society. Other members of their society recognize and respect their new status, reinforcing the sense of power, autonomy, and selfhood initiated by the ritual.

Problems Evolving from the Absence of Rites of Passages

Children are assigned the task of growing up. Typically when we are given tasks, we expect their completion to be acknowledged, or at least to be able to tell ourselves that a goal has been accomplished. How do adolescents know they have completed the goal of establishing an adult identity? Western cultures currently do not have a standardized means of officially verifying "yes, he has achieved manhood," or "she is now a woman" (Grimes, 1995). Even after young adults become self-supporting members of society, how often do we hear older adults make reference to them with comments such as "he's just a kid"?

Consistent with our species' apparent urge to socially punctuate adult status and fueled by the adolescent pursuit of identity, teenagers in Western cultures appear to be creating their own rites of passage. Hazing, drinking games, and other forms of dare-taking all mimic the test of courage that so many traditional rites of passage impose as a condition of group acceptance. Sexual acting out and teen motherhood are common solutions for identity-confused young women, who abort their search for identity and substitute it with the premature roles of being so-and-so's lover or "mommy" (Dorr, 1996). Young men have found that gang activity can provide them with a sense of being initiated into an adult status. Gangs often set up initiation rites that mirror the component parts found in rites of passage throughout the world (Hill, 1992; Sanyika, 1996).

The absence of formal mentoring processes also deprives adolescents of important social influences. *The Rocket Boys* is an autobiography describing how a West Virginia coal miner's son—with the help of a supportive teacher—was able to explore his interest in rocket-building to the point of eventually becoming a trainer of astronauts. Another true story, *When Cuba Conquered Kentucky*, describes a group of extremely impoverished small-town youngsters who—after a strong mentor stepped in—progressed from practicing Harlem Globetrotter-type moves with a wadded up ball of rags to forming a team that won the state basketball high school championship. In addition to finding more success at meeting life goals, teenagers who develop important relationships with nonparental adults have a better self-concept; girls show less incidence of depression and boys show less delinquent behavior (Greenberger et al., 1998; Turner & Scherman, 1996).

At the very least, absence of a formal acknowledgment of adult status brings to pass a lingering sense of role uncertainty—not only for young men and women, but also for those who interact with them in their society.

New Passages

A wellspring of interest has bubbled up as many have begun reexamining the benefits initiation rites can provide for young people (Mahdi et al., 1996). Attempts at revitalizing the concept have taken many forms. Some advocate transitioning young people by getting them involved with community service. Organizations such as the Peace Corps, AmeriCorps, Up with People, and military services follow a sequence of physically relocating young adults and training them in skills related to becoming adult contributors to the good of society (Caras, 1996; Christopher, 1996; Colwell, 1996). Others explore the possibility of practicing individualized rites of passage, perhaps mimicking traditional rituals practiced by other cultures. For some, this approach reflects a return to the young adult's own cultural roots or religious heritage (Mahdi, 1987; Turner, 1996).

Some prefer to develop unique ceremonies of their own. Homegrown rites of passage are more likely to be effective if several key elements are present (Eckert, 1996). The initiate must sincerely desire to attain the rights and privileges associated with the rite. There must be firm standards designating the appropriateness for graduating to adult status that require training or preparation, just as becoming a physician requires the affirmation of having successfully completed training at a medical school. The characteristics of the chosen initiator are crucial: Does he or she practice the same ethics and values that will be taught? Does the initiator respect the rite as a marker of passage into a new social role, and enforce the humility of our ongoing incompleteness as we continue to progress through the course of human experience? The rite itself should evoke an unusual or out-of-the-ordinary state of consciousness, spiritual in nature; whether it comes in the form of feeling oneness with God, connectedness with nature or the human race, or even just team spirit. Accomplishment of such a state of consciousness produces a strong emotional marker of change, reinforcing the rite as a symbolic death/rebirth experience.

PAVING PATHWAYS ALONG ADOLESCENT SOCIAL AND EMOTIONAL MILESTONES: CREATING RITES OF PASSAGE

Suppose you wanted to create a rite of passage formally marking your own transition from adolescence to adulthood. What might you include? Following are some guidelines for designing an event reflecting the separation, transition, and reincorporation characteristic of rites of passage (Foster, 1990; Mumm, 1995).

▶ Establish the purpose of the ceremony. Why do you want to have it? Are there aspects of childhood you wish to formally leave behind? Do you sense the need to make adjustments or changes in your life, or perhaps realize the necessity of taking on new roles or responsibilities?

▶ Select an appropriate initiator. Since rites of passage accentuate movement into the greater society, choosing a nonfamily member or extended family member is preferable to choosing someone from the immediate family. Remember that the initiator and the initiate should share the ethics, values, and standards of adulthood adhered to during the rite and that the initiator should represent an elder of the adult society and preferably also be available to play the role of mentor.

▶ Decide who you would like to have present during the ceremony. As with a marriage ceremony, some prefer to invite everyone they know while others prefer gatherings that are private and intimate. Be sure to include those in your life whom you expect to play an important role in respecting your new adult status or assisting you as you apply it.

▶ Write your scripts and work with the initiator regarding what he or she will say. What do you wish to say? Consider giving thanks to parents and others who helped get you this far in your personal development, expressing commitment to adult responsibilities, and describing what you are planning to do with your life. A script written as a dialogue between the initiator and the initiate can effectively explain expected standards and provide opportunity for the initiate to personally respond.

▶ Consider symbols for transition. What forms of symbolism would have personal meaning for you? Is there a style of dress that would accomplish such an end? Is there an especially meaningful object of childhood that would represent what you are leaving behind, or objects representing adulthood that help you experience that status? There are also a number of symbolic actions that can help you experience the transition, such as making vows, chanting, lighting candles, filling or emptying containers, praying, kneeling, burying or smashing an object, using masks, dancing, or singing.

Transitioning to the Passages of Adulthood

The drive and energy of adolescence is both invigorating and explosive. *Litima* is one ancient society's name for this phenomenon, referring not only to urges toward independence and the seeking of high ideals but also as a potential source of ruthlessness and brutality (LaFontaine, 1958). Rites of passage provide positive receptacles for these natural forces, as well as helping to make sense out of the confusion and chaos permeating adult life in modern Western societies. Regardless of whether or not adolescents take part in formal rites, they will ferret out a port of entry into the passages of adulthood. And hopefully, society will be prepared to receive them!

SUMMARY

Personality Development

Culture moderates the degree of turmoil adolescents experience as they forge their adult personalities. Freud believed the turmoil preceding adult independence reflects coping with a resurgence of Oedipal feelings. Anna Freud suggested that the unique behavioral patterns common during adolescence actually serve the purpose of providing temporary havens from this inner conflict.

Identity formation requires independent adolescent self-exploration, often resulting in considerable oppositional or rebellious behavior. Erikson described adolescence as a time of identity versus role confusion, with adolescents sorting out multiple and conflicting facets of selfhood as they individuate. After passing through stages such as identity diffusion, foreclosure, moratorium, and identity achievement they eventually establish an independent self-concept. Cultural gender expectations affect their identity formation. Stereotypical male characteristics are associated with healthier adjustment; thus girls may experience a loss of public "voice" as they adjust to the nonassertive female stereotype. Correspondingly, boys are subjected to a loss of "voice" in the sense of freedom to express feelings.

Relationships

During adolescent individuation, relationships with parents become more conflictual, especially with mothers; and less close or cohesive, particularly with fathers. However, teenagers continue to benefit emotionally and cognitively from secure attachment to parents, even though this attachment may be more aloofly expressed. Likewise, authoritative parenting continues to be associated with the greatest benefits, although it is delivered differently during adolescence; it is characterized by acceptance of increased emotional distancing, becoming more interactive during limit setting, gradually allowing more privileges of independence, and being more flexible and explanatorily concise as adolescents explore their behavioral possibilities.

Peer relationships become more influential during adolescence, providing more emotional supportiveness than they do for younger children. Academic achievement, identity formation, and emotional adjustment are associated with an adolescent's choices of crowds, cliques, and individual friendships. Younger adolescents are more influenced by peers than are older ones, and girls place more importance on social relationships than do boys. Dating during adolescence provides a means of practicing couplehood, both personally and socially. Adolescents are especially susceptible to excessive social influence, as observed in cults and groups of adolescents who cluster on the basis of shared life struggles and problem behaviors.

Emotions

Increases in emotionality during adolescence are in part associated with hormonal changes and adjustment to more complex cognitive processing. Children invest the greatest amount of energy in regulation of emotional expressiveness during the early teen years. Adolescents commonly experience normal depressed moods as they sort out and react to developmental issues. Depression reaches clinical levels twice as often in adolescent girls as in boys. Adolescent clinical depression may be fueled in part by the teenager's not having adequate skills for addressing or coping with changes in academic and social expectations.

Adolescents attempt suicide more than any other age group. Suicide prevention programs are most likely to succeed when they help the teen develop more effective problem-solving and support-seeking skills and address predisposing factors such as societal stressors, substance abuse, family history, and past traumas.

Development of Morals and Values

Adolescents' advances in moral reasoning correspond with their greater understanding and ability to manipulate abstractions. Parenting style, home environment, and exposure to higher education also play roles in determining levels of moral reasoning attained.

Juvenile Delinquency

Although the rate of juvenile delinquency has not increased, the seriousness of crimes committed by adolescents has. Development of juvenile delinquency has been associated with heritability, family stressors, nonauthoritative parenting, peer rejection, drugs and alcohol use, and overexposure to weapons and crime. Different patterns of delinquent behavior appear to follow differing developmental pathways, and delinquent behavior is not as stable over the life span as has been historically implied. Although girls begin showing delinquent behavior later than boys, its appearance has greater implications regarding childhood stressors and likelihood of future offending. Successful treatment of juvenile delinquents includes teaching the basic life skills they often lack and helping them meet basic physical needs not being met elsewhere. Such treatment is best delivered on individual, family, school, and community levels.

Rites of Passage

"Adolescence" is in part an artifact of the need for more advanced job training created during the industrial era. In many cultures, rites of passage continue to mark movement from childhood to adulthood. Western cultures' lack of official rites of passage and uncertainty regarding when adolescence ends and adulthood begins can impede development of an adult identity. Adolescents may react by creating artificial "rites" such as hazing, taking dares, teen pregnancy, and gang involvement. Adolescents may experience a sense of movement into adulthood by becoming involved in community service activities, returning to "roots" and seeking out past cultural rites, or developing individualized rites of passage. Such rites involve a temporary physical separation from society as a mentor guides the initiate toward letting go of the things of childhood and moving into the behavioral expectations and goals of adulthood.

KEY TERMS

androgynous   identity achievement   moratorium
foreclosure   identity diffusion   rites of passage
genital stage   identity versus role confusion

CONCEPT REVIEW

1. Margaret Mead's studies of Samoan society suggest that adolescent emotional turmoil is more a product of _____ than _____. However, the psychodynamic perspective suggests that turmoil is created by a resurgence of _____ feelings, which is coped with by learning to use defense mechanisms such as _____.

2. Teenagers are at times rebellious in reaction to their need to overcome _____ and establish an autonomous _____. During this psychosocial stage of _____ versus _____, adolescents first are conflicted by the many _____ influences presenting possibilities, then eventually shift toward an _____ -based self-definition.

3. According to Markstrom, adolescent identity formation proceeds through the stages of _____ _____, and _____.

4. During middle adolescence teenagers experience a resurgence of gender _____, which can put girls to a disadvantage because the _____ stereotype has a greater association with _____. Stereotypical influences cause girls to experience loss of "voice" regarding expressing _____, and boys to experience loss of voice regarding expressing _____.

5. Minority-group adolescents are more likely to identify themselves by their _____ and doing so contributes toward _____. Conforming with cultural expectations of continuing interdependencies with families of origin does/does not appear to affect establishment of a healthy identity.

6. During identity formation, interactions with parents typically demonstrate an increase in _____ and negative _____, and a decrease in _____ interactions. Cross-culturally, among adolescents and parents _____ increases while _____ decreases. Nevertheless secure _____ with parents is associated with better adjustment, and teenagers do/do not view the conflict as abnormal.

7. The _____ style of parenting is still most effective for teenagers. During the teen years it is characterized by some changes, such as being accepting of normal _____, allowing greater license for negotiating _____ and _____, not intervening in minor _____, allowing appropriate expression of negative _____, limiting _____ and automatic _____, and avoiding overreactions to _____.

8. Adolescents are more likely to succeed academically and interpersonally when they feel that they fit in with their _____. Susceptibility to peer influences is associated more with _____ adolescence and varies according to style of _____ received.

9. Girls tend to be more concerned about _____ networks and _____ than are boys. Early dating trends are influenced more by concerns about _____, while older adolescents are more likely to be considering issues of _____.

10. Excessive social influence, such as that found in _____ and _____ relationships, is detrimental to adolescent development as it may result in identity _____.

11. Some believe that Hall's suggestion of adolescence being a time of _____ has been blown out of proportion. Teenage improvements in emotional regulation are fueled by concerns about how emotional regulation affects _____ relationships, and how they regulate their emotions will differ according to both _____ and _____ expectations.

12. Culturally, depression is reported more frequently among _____ -American teenagers; the _____ gender experiences more depression, most likely due to more demanding _____ expectations. Difficulties with depression during adolescence can be traced to many issues of _____ transition, as well as the _____ of belief systems that may work against them.

13. Suicide is the _____ leading cause of death for adolescents, and occurs more frequently among boys because they select more _____ methods. Interventions that can inoculate adolescents against suicide typically increase _____ skills, promote development of _____, and address the many _____ factors associated with adolescent suicide.

14. More advanced moral reasoning is aided by adolescents' greater ability to understand and manipulate _____, and is also associated with the _____ parenting style and pursuing _____. Values adopted have been found to reflect _____ teachings, _____ atmosphere, and _____ status.

15. Development of juvenile delinquency is associated with _____ and _____ parenting styles, chronic _____, _____, and _____ difficulties.

16. Research has pointed out that an individual's aggressive behavior frequently occurs at one _____ and not another, and that differing types of delinquency—conflict with _____, interpersonal _____, and _____ aggression—follow differing developmental pathways. Most research addresses delinquency among members of the _____ gender; juvenile delinquent behavior among those of _____ gender is more likely to continue into adulthood.

17. Interventions most likely to help delinquent teenagers are those that promote social _____, including improvements related to _____ skills, _____ restructuring, and _____ skills. Intervention is most effective if it incorporates efforts by _____, addresses _____ needs, and includes involvement in the _____.

18. Due to the many transitional issues of adolescence, such as _____ transitions, _____ behavioral adjustments, and _____ concerns, teenagers typically experience a temporary drop in _____.

19. Many _____ and _____ accentuate the beginning of adulthood with rites of passage, which are tightly connected to establishment of an adult _____. These rites usually teach expectations of new _____ and create new _____ with other adults, after which the young adult holds a new _____ within the societal group.

20. In Western cultures, absence of rites of passage is suspected of being responsible for teenagers' pursuing behaviors such as _____ -taking, _____ membership, and teen _____. Attempts at revitalizing the concept of rites of passage into young adulthood include transition by means of _____, returning to practices within an individual's _____, and developing _____ rites of passage.

1) environment; heredity; Oedipal; intellectualization; 2) dependencies; identity; identity; role confusion; external; internally; 3) identity diffusion; foreclosure; moratorium; identity achievement; 4) stereotyping; masculine; good adjustment; opinions; feelings; 5) ethnicity; good adjustment; does not; 6) quarreling; feelings; positive; conflict; cohesion; attachment; do not; 7) authoritative; emotional distancing; limit-setting; additional privileges; failures; feelings; confrontations; vetoes; egocentrism; 8) social milieu; early; parenting; 9) peer; dating; fitting in; mate selection; 10) cults; abusive; foreclosure; 11) storm and stress; peer; gender; cultural; 12) Hispanic; female; societal; school; rigidity; 13) third; lethal; problem-solving; support systems; pre-

dispositional; **14**) abstractions; authoritative; higher education; cultural; home; socioeconomic; **15**) permissive; authoritarian; family stressors; poverty; temperamental; **16**) age; authority; violence; indirect; male; female; **17**) competence; communication; cognitive; stress management; schools; parental; community; **18**) school; social; body image; self-esteem; **19**) cultures; religions; social identity; roles; social relationships; status; **20**) dare; gang; pregnancy; community service; cultural roots; personalized

RESOURCES FOR FURTHER READING

Adams, G. R., Gullota, T. P., & Montemayer, R. (Eds.) (1992). *Adolescent identity formation.* Newberry Park, CA: Sage.

Barnes, B. (1998). *Preparing your child for dating.* Grand Rapids, MI: Zondervan.

Dryfoos, J. G. (1998). *Safe passage: Making it through adolescence in a risky society.* New York: Oxford University Press.

Mahdi, L. C., Christopher, N. G., & Meade, M. (1996). *Crossroads: The quest for contemporary rites of passage.* Chicago: Open Court.

Pipher, M. (1994). *Reviving Ophelia: Saving the selves of adolescent girls.* New York: Ballantine Books.

Pollack, W. (1998). *Real boys: Rescuing our sons from the myths of boyhood.* New York: Random House.

INFOTRAC COLLEGE EDITION

For additional readings, explore InfoTrac College Edition, your online library. Go to http://www.infotrac-college.com/wadsworth and use the passcode that came on the card with your book. Try these search terms: body image and adolescents, conflict and adolescents, cults and adolescents, ethnicity and adolescence, gang intervention, delinquency, moral development and adolescents, self-esteem and adolescents, stress in adolescence

CHILD DEVELOPMENT CD-ROM

Go to the Wadsworth Child Development CD-ROM for further study of the concepts in this chapter. The CD-ROM also includes quizzes and additional activities to expand your learning experience.

REFERENCES

For a list of references for this chapter, see the Wadsworth Psych Study Center Web site at: http://www.wadsworth.com/product/0534348092s

GLOSSARY

AB search error—the tendency of the young infant, when shown an object in two different hiding places, to look for it only in the first hiding place observed

ABAB design—an experiment during which a study participant is repeatedly measured either with or without the presence of the experimental variable

accommodation—Piaget's concept of how children change old schemes or create new ones in order to take new knowledge into account

acquired immune deficiency syndrome (AIDS)—a fatal viral disease that destroys the immune system, typically passed on through sexual contact, intravenous drug use, or prenatal exposure

age of viability—the earliest point at which a fetus has a chance of surviving outside the womb, usually between the 22nd and 26th weeks of gestation

amniocentesis—the extracting of a small amount of amniotic fluid through a needle inserted in a pregnant woman's abdomen and examining of loose cells shed by the fetus for any genetic abnormalities

amniotic fluid—the prenatal fluid within which the baby floats

anal stage—Freud's proposed second stage of psychosexual development, during which infants spend their second to third year exercising their will by means of potty-training compliance or noncompliance

analytical intelligence—the ability to solve problems, acquire and retain knowledge, understand abstract concepts and relationships, and achieve academically

androgynous—exhibiting both male and female stereotypical personality characteristics

animistic thinking—the young child's tendency to attribute lifelike qualities to inanimate objects

anorexia nervosa—an eating disorder characterized by extremely reduced nutritional intake and severe weight loss, motivated by an unrealistic overwhelming fear of becoming fat

anoxia—the condition of a neonate receiving insufficient oxygen during the birth process

Apgar scale—a scale used to measure neonate physical condition immediately after birth

assimilation—Piaget's concept of how children take new knowledge and incorporate it into an existing scheme

attention deficit hyperactivity disorder (ADHD)—a neurologically based disability characterized by excessive distractibility, impulsiveness, disorganization, and motor activity

attribution of prosocial characteristics—telling the young child that his or her moral or altruistic behavior is tied to inner traits

attrition—loss of study participants during the course of experimentation

authoritarian parenting—a parenting style characterized by excessive control and demands for high performance and heavy reliance on criticism, punishment, and rigid enforcement of boundaries

authoritative parenting—a parenting style characterized by supportiveness and warmth; the setting and reinforcing of limits through reasoning, explaining, praise, and encouragement

autism—a developmental disorder characterized by severe impairments in social and emotional connectedness, often accompanied by mental retardation

autistic savant—an autistic individual who exhibits spontaneous gifted abilities often involving memory, mathematical calculations, or musical talent

autonomy versus shame and doubt—Erikson's proposed psychosocial conflict of the second and third years, its resolution dependent upon caregivers' support and guidance as the child flexes his or her sense of independent will

avoidant attachment—a classification of the Strange Situation technique, characterized by the infant's appearing indifferent to the presence or absence of the mother

Babinsky reflex—the tendency for neonates' toes to fan out when the bottoms of their feet are stroked

babbling—the infant's repetitive sounding of single syllables, such as "ba-ba-ba," without any intended meaning

basic trust versus mistrust—Erikson's proposed first psychosocial conflict of infancy, its resolution depending upon the quality of a mother's handling during feeding

between-subjects design—an experimental design that compares measurements of two or more groups of participants over time, rather than examining multiple measurements of the same participants

bioecological model—Bronfenbrenner's systems model of child development, which takes into account the interrelationships among individual developmental processes, the environment, cultural and social contexts, and continuities and changes in the culture over time

bipolar disorder—a potentially psychotic disorder characterized by periods of severe depression and/or manic "highs," believed to originate in part from hereditary influences

blastocyst—A fluid-filled sphere formed from differentiating cells as the zygote travels to the womb during the germinal stage of prenatal development

blind experimentation—experimentation during which observers measuring participants' progress do not know whether each is in the control group or the experimental group

bodily self—Allport's classification of an infant's first sense of independent self-concept, characterized by perception of bodily sensations

bonding—the tendency for parents to exhibit caring and affection toward their infants by looking into their eyes, speaking softly to them, and gently stroking their skin

brain growth spurt—the extensive growth of the brain during the first two years of life, expanding from 25% to 75% of its eventual adult weight

brainstem—the innermost, most primitive structures of the brain; associated with basic survival functions such as breathing and heartbeat

breech position—presentation of a fetus's feet or buttocks first during the birth process

bulimia—an eating disorder characterized by binge eating that is typically followed by induced vomiting

canalization—the tendency of some inherited traits to be limited to very few potential developmental outcomes

case study method—the developing of hypotheses by observing a single participant

castration anxiety—according to Freud, a young boy's fear that his father will castrate him as punishment for competing for his mother's affections

categorization—a memory strategy that enhances recall by organizing items into categories and memorizing them as groups

centration—according to Piaget, the tendency of the preschooler to focus on only one salient aspect of a situation and therefore neglect other relevant information

cephalocaudal—describing a growth pattern in which development begins at the head, and maturation works its way downward

cerebellum—the brain structure responsible for physical coordination and refined body movements

cerebral cortex—the outer, more advanced structure of the brain; associated with thought, volun-tary control, perception, and knowledge

cesarean delivery—a surgical procedure by which a baby is delivered through an incision made in the lower abdomen

child abuse—causing a child psychological, physical, or sexual harm

child neglect—failure of a caregiver to meet a child's basic emotional or physical needs

chorionic villus sampling—a process of extracting cells from the tissue surrounding a fetus so they can be examined for genetic abnormalities

chromosomes—strands of DNA found in our cells' nuclei, which contain genetic codes for development

circular reaction—according to Piaget, an infant's attempt to repeat an event perceived to have been self-caused

classical conditioning—learning that occurs when a previously neutral stimulus is paired with a meaningful stimulus so that the neutral stimulus produces the same response as the meaningful one

clinical case studies—studies that observe participants in artificial settings, usually using interviews or standardized tests

codominance—influence from both members of a gene pair in the expression of a phenotype

cohort—a collection of persons who share some statistical factor of interest to scientists; in developmental psychology, typically related to their generation or the era during which they have lived

combinatorial reasoning—the ability to consider multiple variables before drawing conclusions

competence—demonstration of a pattern of effective adaptation to the environment

computer-assisted instruction—instruction by computer programs designed to promote learning

conception—the fertilization of an ovum by a sperm resulting in a zygote

concrete operations—in Piagetian theory, exercises of a child's ability to perform mental operations on pieces of information, including the ability to conserve, occurring in the school-age period of cognitive development

confirmation bias—the tendency to notice only examples that confirm what the observer already believes to be true

confounded variables—the inability to separate out the effects of two or more such variables because of the experimental design

conscience—the collection of moral or societal values a person has adopted

conservation—the Piagetian concept of a child's ability to recognize that changing the shape or configuration of an object or collection of objects does not affect its size or quantity

control—in scientific method, arranging an experimental design so that extraneous variables can be accounted for

control group—the group in an experiment that is not assigned the experimental variable

convergent thinking—a thinking process that pulls together collections of information and draws an appropriate conclusion

cooing—sing-song sounds made by infants, usually while looking in someone's eyes

corpus callosum—the bundle of neurons connecting the left and right hemispheres of the brain

correlational studies—studies indicating that as one variable changes another is also likely to change, but not allowing specific predictions of causality to be made

creative intelligence—the ability to produce original works or find novel solutions to problems

crisis—according to Erikson's psychosocial theory, the turning point of a particular stage of development, during which we develop adaptive and maladaptive ways of addressing specific developmental tasks

cross-sectional experimental design—an experiment that measures a number of different age groups at a single point in time

date rape—the forcing of a dating partner into undesired sexual activity

decentration—in Piagetian theory, the school-age child's emerging ability to consider more than one manner of grouping or relating objects

deductive reasoning—the process of drawing logical conclusions from a set of givens or premises

defense mechanisms—strategies for coping with the anxiety resulting from conflict between the id's impulsiveness and the superego's moralism

deferred imitation—the ability of an infant to repeat an observed behavior when there has been a delay between the presentation of the behavior and the attempt to copy it

deoxyribonucleic acid (DNA)—long, double-stranded molecules that make up our chromosomes

dependent variable—the variable in an experimental design hypothesized to change under the influences of the independent variable

deprivation dwarfism—a childhood condition of stunted growth, occurring because lack of affection and emotional support interfere with normal production of growth hormone

depth perception—the ability of a viewer to judge the relative distance of objects

descriptive statistics—statistics that describe a population, such as percentages and averages

development quotient—in infant intelligence testing, the ratio score produced by comparing a child's chronological age and mental age as measured by developmental scales

developmental psychology—the study of how individuals change or remain the same over time, and the factors that relate to such change and continuity

developmentally appropriate software—open-ended, exploratory educational computer programs that allow children to pursue learning in an active, personalized manner

deviation intelligence quotient (DIQ)—an intelligence test score assigned by using a system of standard score tables, developed from standard deviations of age group performances

differentiation—the process by which, during prenatal development, individual cells take on the characteristics of the structures they will eventually become

difficult child—in studies of temperament, a child who is often irritable, is unpredictable in the timing of biological needs, and reacts strongly and disagreeably to changes in the environment

dishabituation—our tendency to take notice of an environmental stimulus if something about it has been altered

disorganized/disoriented attachment—a classification of the Strange Situation technique, characterized by the infant's ambivalent attitude toward mother and unpredictable crying spells

divergent thinking—a thinking process that involves expanding the range of possibilities applicable to a specific problem

dizygotic twins—fraternal twins, having developed from two zygotes and therefore not sharing identical DNA

dominance hierarchy—a set of relationships that establishes who will have the most or least influence within a group

dominant genes—genes that, when paired with differing genes, will most likely be expressed by the phenotype

double-blind experimentation—experimentation during which neither the study participants nor those observing their behavior know whether the participants are in the experimental group or control group

Down's syndrome—a developmental condition resulting from a chromosomal abnormality that involves mental retardation, characteristic facial and other physical features, and certain medical problems

dualism—the belief introduced by Descartes that the physical body and the mind or soul are separate entities

dyslexia—a learning disability characterized by a tendency to distort, substitute, or omit words while reading

easy child—in studies of temperament, a child who is generally happy, friendly, has regular biological rhythms, and adapts easily to new environments

ectoderm—the outer layer of cells of an embryo that will develop into the nervous system, skin, hair, nails, and sweat glands

ectopic pregnancy—the implanting of a zygote somewhere other than within the uterus, such as in an ovary or fallopian tube

ego—according to Freudian theory, the part of the psyche that deals with reality and mediates between the id and the superego

ego-ideal—what a person aspires to be; the ideal self

egocentrism—the preschooler's lack of consideration that others' experiencing, thoughts, and knowledge base are different from his or her own

Electra complex—according to psychoanalytic theory, the desire of the young girl to sexually possess her father as a means of vicariously experiencing possession of a penis

embryo—the term used to describe prenatal life between the third and ninth weeks after conception

embryonic disk—the collection of cells within the blastocyst that will eventually form the embryo

emotional intelligence—a form of practical intelligence related to the ability to recognize and manage one's own feelings and consider and appropriately respond to the feelings of others, as applied to successful real-world functioning

emotional regulation—an individual's ability to exert control over the occurrence, strength, or endurance of an emotion

empathic concern—a quality of children that influences their ability to recognize and react in a caring manner to the feelings and needs of others

endoderm—the inner layer of cells of an embryo that will develop into digestive organs, lungs, and other vital organs

epinephrine—a hormone released during stress, resulting in "fight-or-flight" physiological responses

equilibration—according to Piaget, the back-and-forth mental adjustments that are made among contrasting schemes and that shape children's cognitive development

ethology—the study of animal and human behavior within the context of evolution

event sampling—arranging to gather study data as target events occur, rather than over a set time period

experimental group—the group that is assigned the experimental variable

experimental variable—the variable under study in an experiment designed to test the researcher's hypothesis

experimenter bias—the tendency for experimenters' observations of study participants to be biased in favor of what experimenters expect or want to find

extinction—in behavioral learning theory, the cessation of a learned behavior after the connection between it and a stimulus has been disrupted

extraneous variable—any variable that is not the object of study in an experimental design but has the potential to affect the results

extrusion reflex—a reflex of the newborn such that the tongue sticks out when touched or pressed down

fast mapping—the young child's use of an organized mental grid of word categories as a means of quickly incorporating new vocabulary

fetal alcohol syndrome—a condition occurring in children whose mothers consumed alcohol during pregnancy, often causing mental retardation or learning disabilities and a characteristic pattern of facial abnormalities

fetoscopy—inserting a tiny lens and lighting mechanism into a pregnant woman's uterus in order to observe the fetus

fetus—the term used to describe prenatal life between the eighth week and the time of birth

filtering software—computer programs that allow parents to restrict a child's access to certain aspects of the Internet

fine motor skills—movement skills primarily using smaller muscles

fishing error—the obtaining of a significant-looking statistic by running so many statistical comparisons that such a statistic occurs by chance

foreclosure—the identity status of individuals who have committed themselves to certain social roles without first considering their personal identity or establishing identity achievement

formal operational reasoning—according to Piaget, the adolescent's ability to think in terms of abstractions and coordinate multiple factors and reasoning processes while testing hypotheses and drawing conclusions

fragile X syndrome—a break lo-cated on one or both of an individuals X chromosomes, resulting in characteristics such as mental retardation and certain mild physical abnormalities

full inclusion—the concept of having all disabled students participate in regular classrooms only

gender constancy—a young child's recognition that dressing or behaving differently will not change the person's gender assignment

gender identity—the sense of the self or others as being male or female

gender roles—culturally determined expectations regarding how the genders should look, behave, or participate in societal activity

gender schema—the young child's organization of all individuals as male or female

gender schema theory—the theory that a young child's development of gender-role expectations is influenced both by cognitive developmental ability and by observation and reinforcement of social norms

gender stability—the young child's recognition that gender assignment does not change over time

general adaptation syndrome—the body's hormonal reaction to prolonged stress, which if left unchecked eventually results in physical exhaustion and illness

generalizability—the ability to assume that experimental results apply to other individuals in the population represented by the participating sample

genes—segments of DNA within chromosomes that provide the blueprint for development of hereditary characteristics

genetic counseling—a process of evaluating couples regarding their risk of producing a genetically defective child and advising them of their reproductive options

genetic engineering—methods using artificial genetic manipulations to produce the desired genetically determined traits

genital stage—according to Freud, the psychosexual phase of adolescent development; characterized by the transformation of Oedipal feelings into adult sexuality and issues of reproduction

genotype—the combination of dominant and/or recessive genes within a gene pair

glia—cells that support and nourish neurons

goal-directed behavior—behavior coordinating actions for the purpose of achieving certain objectives

grasping reflex—the tendency of neonates to close their fingers around anything touching the palms of their hands

gross motor skills—movement skills accomplished mainly by using larger body muscles

habituation—our tendency to no longer notice stimuli that are constant or repetitive

helpless orientation—a learning attribution style characterized by perceiving failures as resulting from one's own lack of ability

herpes—a sexually-transmitted disease resulting in recurring genital sores that, if present during childbirth, can cause neonate brain damage or death

heterogenous genes—gene pairs that contain programming for differing variants of a gene characteristic

holophrase—the infant's tendency to use one word to express an entire thought, such as "deuce" meaning "I want juice"

homogenous genes—gene pairs that are identical in their programming for a gene characteristic

history—anything that might happen in a study participant's life between experimental measurements that has the potential to affect the results

hostile aggression—aggression occurring for the sole purpose of hurting the object of the aggressive act

hypothalamus—a brain structure regulating hunger, thirst, temperature, and other bodily functions

id—according to Freudian theory, the biological part of our personality, made up of instincts and impulses

ideal self—as opposed to the real self, the personal characteristics a person would prefer to possess

identification—in psychodynamic theory, the belief that a young child resolves the Oedipus or Electra conflict by identifying with the same-sex parent and in doing so adopts that parent's perceived gender characteristics

identity achievement—the identity status of individuals who have successfully explored personal identity issues and have committed themselves to specific identity-related roles and behaviors

identity diffusion—the identity status of adolescents who have not yet begun exploring and sorting out an independent identity

identity versus role confusion—the term Erikson uses to describe the adolescent task of establishing an independent identity

imagery—a memory strategy that enhances recall by imagining key elements to be memorized as part of a mental picture

imaginary audience—the adolescent's egocentric belief that he or she is the central focus of others' attention and concern

immersion—a school environment practice that requires student fluency in both a native and a second language

implantation—the initial attachment of the blastocyst to the wall of the uterus

imprinting—an inherited behavioral program that results in animals of some species bonding to whichever creature is present immediately following their birth

independent variable—the variable a scientist assigns or changes in an experimental design

induction—explaining to the young child how his or her actions affect others, especially their feelings

inductive reasoning—development of general rules based on observation of multiple examples

industry versus inferiority—according to Erikson, the psychosocial developmental stage of school-age children during which they determine their competence by their successes and failures

infantile amnesia—the normal inability to recall personal experiences that occurred during the first two years of life

inferential statistics—statistics showing relationships between experimental variables that allow you to make inferences regarding how they can be expected to vary

informed consent—an agreement of willing participation in an experiment after having been fully informed of the risks and possible benefits

initiative versus guilt—according to Erikson, the young child's psychosocial developmental task of establishing a healthy sense of conscience from others' reactions to their behaviors

instrumental aggression—aggressive behavior aimed at achieving an end other than hurting someone, such as obtaining a desired toy

intelligence quotient (IQ)—the ratio score formed by comparing a child's chronological age and mental age as measured on an intelligence test

interactional synchrony—a back and forth communication style between caregiver and infant that results in gratification of infant needs and promotes secure attachment

intermodal perception—the ability to integrate information received from multiple sensory systems

intervention effects—changes in study participants' behavior due to measurement or any other condition arising solely from being involved in an experiment

introspection—gaining knowledge by examining one's own thought processes and experiences

intuitive thought substage—according to Piaget, the 4- to 7-year-old's undiscriminating acceptance of pieces of knowledge as they are perceived or explained

invincibility fable—the adolescent's egocentric perception that he or she will not suffer harm or negative consequences from ill-advised behavior

invulnerable child—a type of child who grows up to be well-adjusted in spite of difficult or traumatic childhood experiences

irreversibility—according to Piaget, the inability of the preschooler to mentally return to the beginning of a problem that has been transformed by a series of problem-solving steps

karotype—a systematically arranged chart illustrating an individual's chromosomes

Kaufman Assessment Battery for Children (K-ABC)—an intelligence test that focuses on a child's mental processes leading up to conclusions drawn; considered to be more culture-fair than other IQ tests

Klinefelter's syndrome—a condition occurring in men inheriting one or more extra X chromosomes, displaying characteristics such as tallness, fat distribution more similar to that of women, impaired verbal intelligence, and sterility

kwashiorkor—a condition found in children consuming insufficient amounts of protein, resulting in the characteristic swelled bellies and other symptoms

Lamaze method—a form of natural childbirth involving a support person who coaches the mother as she uses breathing and relaxation techniques for pain management

language acquisition device—a concept, proposed by Chomsky, of an innate grammatical method for learning and using various language structures

latency stage—according to Freud, the school-age child's nonsexualized phase of psychosexual development

learning disabilities—the phenomenon of otherwise normal children experiencing excessive difficulties with specific learning areas, such as math or reading

Leboyer method—a method of adjusting the birthing environment in hopes of reducing the child's birth trauma, such as by giving a warm transitional bath and placing the baby on the mother's stomach after birth

level of significance—the strength of a statistical finding

locomotor skills—motor skills associated with moving from place to place

long-term memory—a relatively permanent form of memory storage

longitudinal experimental design—an experiment that measures the same cohort a number of times

lymph system—an organ system that plays a role in immunities and absorption of certain nutrients

mainstreaming—the practice of having students with disabilities spend part or all of their school day in a regular classroom

marasmus—a condition of severely undernourished children, resulting in wasting away of body tissue and a "skin and bones" appearance

mastery orientation—a learning attribution style characterized by perceiving failures as opportunities for further growth and mastery

matched designs—research designs that control for a certain variable by arranging for its equal representation in both the experimental and control groups

maturation—as an extraneous variable, changes that occur between experimental measurements as a result of natural growth processes

Maximally Discriminative Facial Movement Coding System (MAX)—a systematic rating technique for evaluating facial expressions as evidence of emotional states

meiosis—the process of cell division that produces sex cells, each containing only half of the parent cell's chromosomes

menarche—the onset of menstruation

mesoderm—the middle layer of cells of an embryo that will develop into muscles, connective tissues, the skeleton, and the circulatory system

meta-analysis—a method of combining a number of similar studies and analyzing the overall results

mitosis—the process of normal cell division, resulting in two identical cells

monozygotic twins—twins who are identical in their genetically determined characteristics, having developed from a single zygote

Montessori method—a method of teaching each whole, individual child, addressing multiple learning-based developmental needs and zones of proximal development rather than focusing only on academic readiness

moratorium—the identity status of adolescents as they sort out the multiple and conflicting facets of their inner identity, aiming toward resolving their identity crisis

Moro reflex—a neonate startle response during which neonates arch their backs, throw out their arms, then pull their arms tightly toward

their chests when they sense a loss of physical support

mosaicism—a condition occurring in women who inherit one or more extra X chromosomes, displaying characteristics such as mild developmental delays, tallness, and deficits in verbal intelligence

"motherese"—the simplified language and singsong tone of voice used by adults as they talk to infants

myelin sheath—a fatty coating surrounding neurons that aids the efficient transmission of electrical impulses

myopia—nearsightedness

natural selection—according to Darwin's evolutionary theory, changes in species occurring over time because the more adaptive heritable characteristics are being passed on to the next generation

naturalistic observational study—a study in which researchers gather data by observing study participants in their natural settings

nature versus nurture—the debate over how much of our development is determined by biology and how much by learning and experience

need for achievement—McClelland's concept of experiencing an intrinsic, independent desire to achieve and the willingness to pursue achievement

negative reinforcers—undesired stimuli that result in an increase in behavior aimed at eliminating them

neonate—the term used to refer to a newborn during the first month of life

neural tube—a hollow tube of cells formed by the folding over of the ectoderm and that will eventually become the brain and spinal cord

neurons—cells of the nervous system

neurotransmitters—substances released between neurons that result in the relay of information from one neuron to the next

niche-picking—the tendency of individuals to place themselves in environmental settings that both compliment and reinforce their inherited traits

nightmare—a bad dream; a sleep condition common to young children

nonorganic failure to thrive—cessation of infant growth due to insufficient affection and/or stimulation from the environment

norms—in measures of psychological assessment, average scores attained by test-takers of various ages or according to other consistent criteria

obese—weighing 20% or more over the expected weight for age, gender, and body build

object permanence—Piaget's belief that a young infant perceives an object as no longer existing if it is hidden from view

objectivity—the extent to which others would make the same observations

observational learning—learning that occurs by means of watching a role model perform a behavior

Oedipus complex—according to Freud, the desire of the young boy to replace his father and possess his mother's affections

open classroom—a less structured classroom format that allows the student to pursue personal areas of interest with hands-on learning

oral stage—Freud's proposed first stage of psychosexual development, during which infants spend their first year seeking pleasure by means of the mouth

organization—according to Piaget, combining and integrating available schemes into coherent bodies of knowledge

overextension—the tendency for a child to apply new words too broadly, such as by calling all furry four-legged animals "doggie"

overregularization—applying newly learned language rules where they do not belong, resulting in words such as "go-ed"

ovum—the sex cell produced by a woman, also known as an egg

participants—in an experimental design, representatives of the population described by the experimental hypothesis selected to participate in the experiment

penis envy—according to Freud, a young girl's recognition that she does not have a penis and her desire to own one

perception—the interpretation of information received through sensory relay systems

perception-bound thought—according to Piaget, the preschooler's tendency to focus only on the concrete, perceptual appearance of objects

perceptual learning—learning that promotes more efficient methods of perceiving, recognizing, and otherwise processing stimuli in our environments

permissive parenting—a parenting style that provides supportiveness and warmth but little structure and guidance

personal myth—the adolescent's egocentric perception that his or her new reasoning skills and emotional experiencing are evidence of being personally and uniquely special

phallic stage—according to Freud, the developmental stage of the 3- to 6-year-old; characterized by issues surrounding gender identification and development of the conscience

phenotype—the characteristics actually expressed by a gene pair

phonics approach—a method of teaching reading that focuses on teaching word skills, such as sounding words out by breaking them down into letters and syllables

pincer grasp—picking up an object with the thumb and forefinger

placebo effect—the tendency for study participants to show a particular effect if they believe it is likely to occur for them

placebo group—a form of control group, the members of which are assigned a noneffective treatment as a means of counterbalancing placebo effects in the experimental group

placenta—the organ lining the mother's womb that promotes the exchange of nutrients and waste between the mother and the embryo/fetus

plasticity—referring to the ability of a young child's brain to compensate for functions that

have been affected by damage to an area of the brain

polygenic—characteristics that are determined by more than one gene pair

positive reinforcer—any consequence that increases the occurrence of a behavior

practical intelligence—the ability to successfully apply knowledge to daily living, sometimes called "common sense"

practice effects—changes in study participants' responses due to previous exposure to experimental conditions and measurements

pragmatics—the conventions of using language effectively within a social context

predictive statistics—statistics showing relationships between experimental variables such that you can predict how they will vary

preformationism—an early belief that human beings begin as completely developed, tiny human figures within the man's sperm or the woman's ova

preoperational thought—according to Piaget, the 3- to 7-year-old's simultaneous ability to consider mental representations of reality and inability to perform cognitive operations on such material

preterm infants—infants born more than three weeks early and weighing less than 5½ lb

preverbal gestures—gestures made by the infant to express a thought or desire, such as pointing at a wanted toy

primary circular reaction—according to Piaget, infants' repetition of chance behaviors that they have observed as getting a certain result

primary sex characteristics—structures maturing at puberty that are directly related to producing a baby, such as maturation of an adolescent girl's ovaries and uterus and an adolescent boy's testes and seminal vesicles

private speech—according to Vygotsky, self-talk representing the child's attempts to improve task performance through self-coaching

proximal processes—enduring patterns of interactions between a child and another individual that facilitate child learning and growth

proximodistal—a growth pattern in which development begins at the center of the body and with maturation works its way outward

psychosexual theory—stages of growth proposed by Freud that suggest that personality emerges as a product of dealing with specific libidinal conflicts at specific ages

psychosocial theory—Erikson's belief that we progress through eight stages of development during which we sort out specific tasks of self-definition

puberty—maturational changes in an adolescent's body that result in his or her ability to reproduce

punishers—consequences that result in a decrease in the frequency of a behavior

qualitative change—modification of preexisting abilities or characteristics and the addition of ones that are completely novel to an individual

quantitative change—changes in an individual's abilities or characteristics involving factors such as size, number, speed, or frequency

random assignment—assigning study participants to an experimental design in such a way that all participants have a relatively equal chance of being assigned to the experimental or control group

random selection—selecting study participants in such a way that all members of the population under study have a relatively equal chance of being selected

range of reaction—the range of potential outcomes possible for a specific genetically determined tendency

real self—as opposed to the ideal self, the personal characteristics an individual perceives himself or herself as actually possessing

receptive language ability—the ability to understand what is being said, even though the listener might not be capable of using the language at a similarly advanced level

recessive genes—genes that, when paired with more dominant genes, will most likely not be expressed by the phenotype

rehearsal—a memory strategy used to enhance recall by repeating information over and over

reinforcer—any consequence that increases the frequency of a behavior

REM (rapid eye movement) sleep—the sleep period during which we typically dream; so named because the sleeper's eyes are usually darting around during this sleep period

resistant attachment—a classification of the Strange Situation technique, characterized by an infant's clinginess in a play situation, extreme distress if mother leaves, and difficulty being consoled even if she returns

respiratory distress syndrome—breathing difficulty that develops in neonates born more than six weeks early, usually a result of insufficient lung development

reversibility—in Piagetian theory, the school-age child's new ability to reverse mental operations

Rh factor—a blood protein that, if present in a first child and not in the mother, can result in maternal antibodies that prenatally destroy red blood cells of subsequent children

rites of passage—culturally prescribed rituals that mark passage from one social status to another

rooting reflex—the tendency of neonates to turn their heads toward any stroking or touching of their cheeks

rough-and-tumble play—a form of play that looks like aggression but is in fact good-natured rehearsals of the roles of aggressor and victim

rubella—"German measles," a disease found to cause birth defects if contracted by a pregnant mother

running narrative report—in observational studies, the practice of watching study participants and writing down all observed behaviors over a specific period of time

schemes—according to Piaget, cognitive structures that organize a child's body of knowledge and change qualitatively with age

schizophrenia—a potentially disabling psychotic disorder that is in part inherited

school phobia—fear of and/or refusal to attend school; panic attacks and other symptoms of anxiety occur if the child is forced to attend

scientific method—a systematic process of measuring observations that allows for maximum objectivity by controlling extraneous variables

scientific reasoning—generating a number of hypotheses then systematically and exhaustively testing them

secondary circular reaction—according to Piaget, the infant's recognition that his or her actions have an effect on the environment, replacing the perception of the environment solely as something that affects the infant

secondary sex characteristics—gender-related physical changes at puberty that are not directly related to producing a baby, such as an adolescent girl's body becoming more shapely and an adolescent boy's growing facial hair

secure attachment—a classification of the Strange Situation technique in which infants are comfortable with exploration away from mother, are distressed if mother leaves, but are easily consoled when she returns

selective attention—the ability to limit one's focus to relevant stimuli, rather than be distracted by all stimuli

selective memory—the ability to commit relevant material to memory and shut out irrelevant material

self-efficacy—an individual's belief that if he or she attempts a behavior, the desired outcome will occur

self-esteem—a person's evaluation of himself or herself as inherently good or bad

self-objectification—the process of dissociating the sexual aspects of one's identity due to conformance to societal influences and expectations

self-fulfilling prophecy—the tendency for children to perform at the level they perceive influential adults to be expecting of them

self-identity—Allport's classification of an infant's second year, noting the addition of continuity of self over time to the infant's self-concept

sensation—the physical stimulation of sensory relay systems

sensorimotor intelligence—according to Piaget, the intellectual processing that occurs during the first two years; characterized by interplay between the child and the environment

separation anxiety—an infant's tendency, beginning at around 6 months, to become upset if his or her preferred caregiver leaves the infant's presence

separation-individuation—according to Mahler, the infant's discovering and practicing separateness by means of independent exploration, using mother as a "base" to which he or she can return

sequential experimental design—an experiment that measures more than one cohort at more than one age during more than one time period

short-term memory—memory maintained for less than half a minute

sign—according to Piaget, a recognized convention—such as a word or number—used to represent a mental concept

single-participant experimental design—introducing an experimental variable to a single study participant and measuring its effect

sleep terrors—a sleep disturbance during which the sleeper appears to be awake and extremely aroused, is difficult to wake, and upon waking has no memory of the event

slow-to-warm-up child—in studies of temperament, a child who is generally mild-mannered, somewhat inactive, and slow to react and adjust to changes in the environment

small-for-date infants—full-term infants weighing less than 5½ lb

social comparison—a means of evaluating self-concept by comparing one's characteristics to those of others

social referencing—an infant's tendency to look to others' facial expressions for information when approaching an ambiguous situation

sociocentrism—a self/other orientation that recognizes and responds to the needs, values, and inner processes of others

sociocultural theory—Vygotsky's theory of how culture and interaction with more skilled members of society affect a child's development, especially specific ways of thinking

somnambulism—sleepwalking

sperm—the sex cell produced by a man

spermarche—the level of sexual maturity represented by a young man's first ejaculation

standard scores—test scores that have been converted so that each age group has equivalent means and standard deviations; most major intelligence test battery scores are standard scores

standardization—in an experimental design, procedures or conditions that ensure that all study participants within a group receive consistent treatment

statistical significance—the extent to which experimental results indicate that relationships found did or did not occur due to chance

stepping reflex—the tendency for newborn infants to make steplike motions when held in a standing position on a supportive surface

stimulus generalization—the tendency to respond to a neutral stimulus because of its similarity to a meaningful stimulus

Strange Situation—an assessment technique used by researchers to determine quality of infant attachment

stress—a physiological condition created when factors occur that lead us to feel pressured to act

stress buffer—a relationship with a trustworthy caregiver or other social support in a child's life; its mere existence minimizes the impact of stress or trauma on a child

structured observational study—a study in which participants are observed in a laboratory or some other artificial setting

sudden infant death syndrome (SIDS)—an infant sleep-wake disorder, during which sleeping infants expire after unexplainably ceasing to breathe

superego—according to Freudian theory, the moralistic part of the psyche, made up of the conscience and ego-ideal

Supermale syndrome—a condition occurring in men who inherit an extra Y chromosome, displaying characteristics such as tallness, and have some other minor physical differences but are otherwise physically and intellectually normal

symbiosis—according to Mahler, the young infant's experiencing mother and self as a single merged entity

symbol—according to Piaget, the mental representation of an abstract sensory experience

symbolic function substage—according to Piaget, the 3- to 4-year-old's advancing ability to use symbols, such as thoughts or speech, to represent experiences

synapse—the juncture between two neurons

syntax—the organization of words into meaningful phrases or sentences

syphilis—a sexually transmitted disease that, when present in the mother at birth, can result in neonate blindness and central nervous system impairments

tabula rasa—"blank slate"; Locke's belief that we are born with empty minds and that we can train into them anything we would like

telegraphic speech—the toddler's simplified, two-word sentences, such as "juice gone" or "ball mine"

temperament—inborn character traits that contribute to a person's personality development

teratogens—agents that, when present during pregnancy, are likely to cause birth defects

thalamus—a relay station in the brain between the cerebral cortex and the brain structures taking in sensory information

thalidomide—a drug that results in infant physical malformations when taken by pregnant mothers

theory of mind—our perception that others have thoughts and emotional processes

time-lag experimental design—an experiment that measures more than one cohort when participants are of a particular age

time of measurement—a consideration during experimentation regarding the extent to which current cultural or societal events may affect how study participants respond

toxoplasmosis—a parasitic infection that can be transmitted to a pregnant mother by raw meat or feces from an infected cat and that can result in birth defects

transductive reasoning—preschoolers' reasoning style of going from specific to specific without applying the internal consistency of logic

transitional object—a soft toy or other object an infant may use as a traveling companion while separate from mother

transitive inference—the ability to mentally compare abstractions and draw conclusions, a skill not seen during the period of concrete operations

true experimental design—an experimental design that allows for random assignment of participants to the experimental and control groups and enables the experimenters to manipulate assignment of the independent variable

Turner's syndrome—a condition occurring in women who inherit only a single fully formed X chromosome, displaying characteristics such as small stature, a shield-shaped chest, under-developed secondary sex characteristics, steril-ity, and mild cognitive deficits

type A behavior pattern—a hurried, competitive, achievement-oriented behavior style that is fueled by low self-esteem and hostility

ulnar grasp—the voluntary grasp of an object ac-complished by slamming all the fingers against the palm

ultrasound—a diagnostic technique that uses sound waves to create a visual image of a devel-oping fetus

umbilical cord—the structure attaching the baby to the placenta, allowing for the transfer of nu-trients and waste products

unconditional positive regard—Rogers's concept of treating others as valued regardless of their strengths, weaknesses, successes, or failures

underextension—the tendency for a child to un-derapply new words, such as using "juice" to mean only apple juice

uninvolved parenting—a parenting style charac-terized by an aloof attitude toward the child and little provision of structure or guidance

variable—in an experimental design, any factor that can vary within the findings

vicarious punishment—punishing effects that are learned by seeing a role model receive a pun-isher for a behavior

vicarious reinforcement—reinforcing effects that are learned by seeing a role model receive a re-inforcer for a behavior

Wechsler Intelligence Scale for Children—III (WISC-III)—one of the most widely used in-telligence tests for school-age children; pro-vides verbal, performance, and full IQ scores

whole language approach—a method of teaching reading by means of sight-reading and relating words to immediate experiencing

within-subject design—an experimental design that compares multiple measurements of the same group of participants

zone of proximal development—according to Vygotsky, a "space" between what a child al-ready knows and what a child is capable of learning if given guidance at that moment

zygote—a cell formed by the union of an ovum and sperm

NAME INDEX

Abel, E. L.,102, 104
Ablard, K. E., 352
Abroms, K. I., 87
Ackil, J. K., 467
Adams, G. R., 444, 497, 533
Adams, J. W., 345
Adams, M., 520
Adams, R. J., 140
Adamson, L. B., 176, 183
Adderly, B. D., 147, 155
Adimara, A. A., 434
Adolph, K. E. 15, 137, 155
Ageton, S. S., 435
Ahnert, L., 290
Ainsworth, M. D. S., 23, 193
Ajzen, I., 460
Alansky, J. A., 201
Alarcon, M., 359
Alberman, E. D., 97
Aldous, P., 83
Aldred, H. E., 95, 121
Alexander, J. M., 366
Alfieri, T., 498
Allgne, C. A., 235
Allen, L., 408
Allen, S. F., 339
Allen, V. L., 288
Allison, C., 225
Allport, G., 205
Aloise, P. A., 306
Alpert, B. S., 332
Altemeier III, W. A., 114
Alter-Reid, K., 393
Althaus, M., 87
Altshuler, J. L., 395
Alvarado, R. 443, 444
Alvesalo, L., 71
Alvy, K., 240, 298
Aman, C. J., 358
Amaro, H., 108
Amato, P. R., 389, 390
Ames, L. J., 264
Ampofo-Boateng, K., 238
Amsel, E., 454
Anand, K. J. S., 143
Anastasi, A. 169, 348
Anderman, E. M., 476
Anderson, C. A., 369
Anderson, D. R., 255, 269
Anderson, E. S., 273
Anderson, M., 465
Andersson, K., 200
Andre, T., 478, 483
Andrews, K., 444
Andrews, S. R., 171
Angle, J., 334
Angold, A., 510
Angst, J., 263, 287
Anthonelli, R. M., 443
Anthony, E. J., 207
Apgar, V., 111
Apostolides, M., 451
Aras, Z., 420
Archer, D., 470
Arievitch, I. M., 18

Armsden, G., 503
Arnett, J., 425
Arnett, J. J., 508, 523
Arnold, L. E., 358
Aronwitz, S., 484
Arsenio, W. F., 304, 395
Artalmittelmark, R., 102
Artman, L., 344, 459
Asaman, J. K., 278
Asendorpf, J. B., 205, 209
Asher, S. R., 505
Askan, N., 187
Aslin, R. N., 142, 175
Astington, J. W., 260, 261, 278
Auerback, C. F., 201, 389
Austin, R. J., 112
Ayasse, R. H., 241
Azmitia, M., 391

Babbitt, B. C., 369
Bachar, E., 207, 505
Bachman, J. G., 443, 479
Bagwell, C., 391
Bahrick, L. E., 146
Baillargeon, R., 140, 161
Bain, A., 16
Baird, P. A., 71
Bakeman, R., 263
Baker, D. L., 84
Baker, D. P., 473, 480, 484
Baker-Ward, L., 257
Baldwin, D. A., 204
Bales, J., 12
Ballif, F., 300
Bancroft, J., 71
Band, G. P. H., 465
Bandura, A. 2, 302, 313, 324
Banks, M. S., 139
Barbur, B. L., 425
Bard, C., 319
Barela, J. A., 137
Baringa, M., 470, 471
Barkin, L. B., 206
Barkley, R. A., 358, 370
Barlow, D. S., 54
Barnes, B., 533
Barnes, G. E., 444
Barnes, G. M., 444
Barnet, A. B., 175, 183
Barnet, R. J., 175, 183
Barnett, R. C., 286
Baron, J., 46, 461, 462, 464, 491
Baron-Cohen, S., 209
Barr, R. G., 142, 204
Barrera, M., 503
Barrett, D. E., 134
Barry, F. D., 245
Barry, H., III, 508
Bartlett, D., 111
Bartlett, F. C., 257
Baruch, C., 142
Baruch, G. K., 286
Baskett, L. M., 288
Bates, J. E., 394
Bauer, A. M., 414

Baumrind, D., 294, 295, 423, 425, 517
Bayes, J., 444
Bayley, N., 168
Beach, D. R., 345
Beal, C. R., 274, 284
Beal, G., 435
Bean, J. P., 466
Beardslee, W. R., 264
Beauvais, F., 508, 518
Beck, A. T., 399
Becker-Lausen, E., 445
Beckwith, L., 191
Beeghly, M., 70
Beidel, D., 398
Beidel, D. C., 399
Bell, D., 460
Bell, L. M., 234
Bell, M. A., 161
Bell, R. Q., 503
Bell, S. K., 329
Bellinger, D., 102, 107, 121
Belmaker, R. H., 74
Belsky, J., 174, 191, 192, 196, 198, 200, 201, 291
Bem, S., 283, 498
Bemporad, J. R., 401
Benasich, A. A., 171
Benbow, C. P., 220, 361, 470
Bendersky, M., 104
Bendersky, R., 439
Benenson, J. F., 187, 407
Benn, R., 429
Bennett, J. W., 87
Bennetto, L., 72
Benowitz, N. L., 105
Bensley, L., 429
Benson, A. C., 372, 380
Berenbaum, S. A., 224
Berezin, J., 198
Berezin, N., 110
Berg, K. M., 130
Berg, W. K., 130, 142
Bergamasco, N. H. P., 143
Berger, K. S., 218, 318
Bergin, D. A., 371
Berk, L., 99, 252, 255
Berman, A. L., 512, 514
Bernard, J., 68
Bernard, M. E., 399
Berndt, T. J., 506
Berninger, V. W., 346
Bernsaw, N. J., 131
Bernstein, G. A., 399
Bernstein, N., 136
Berry, G. L., 271, 278
Berry, J. W., 11
Bersoff, D. M., 516
Bertelsen, A., 81, 398
Bertenthal, B. I., 140
Berzonsky, M. D., 497
Best, D. L., 345
Best, J. B., 256
Betz, N. E., 470
Beuhring, T., 466, 467
Beumont, P. J. V., 438

Beyth-Marom, R., 424, 462, 460
Bialystok, E., 375
Bibace, R., 426
Biddle, S., 324
Bidwell, C., 485
Biggs, J. B., 404
Bigler, R. S., 286
Bilsky, W., 516
Binet, A., 167
Bing, E. D., 102
Birch, L. L., 132, 229, 231, 232
Bird, H. R., 519
Biringin, Z., 193
Birks, E., 134
Birmaher, B., 509
Bishop, D. V. M., 271
Bishop, J., 485
Bizzel, R. P., 267
Bjork, R. A., 466
Bjorklund, D., 55, 61
Black, J. E., 129, 130, 140
Black, M. M., 168, 183, 291
Blackburn, R., 519
Blagg, N., 399
Blampied, N. M., 54
Blass, E. M., 144
Bliss, J. R., 468
Block, D., 313
Block, J., 300, 444, 445
Block, J. H., 389
Bloom, F. E., 14, 130
Bloom, L. 174
Bloom, M., 68
Blos, P., 282
Blumstein, A., 517
Bly, L., 155
Bly, R., 137, 395
Blyth, D., 421, 439, 522
Bobbitt, B. L., 465
Boddy, J., 148
Bogardus, C., 135
Bohanon, J. N., III, 195
Bohlin, G., 384
Bono, M. A., 204
Bonnet, M., 226
Bonta, B. D., 239
Booth, A., 352
Borchardt, C. M., 399
Borke, H., 253
Borman, K., 491
Bornstein, M. C., 165
Bornstein, M. H., 140, 267, 320
Botino, P. J., 71
Botvin, G., 444
Bouchard, C., 330
Bouchard, T. J., Jr., 80, 82
Boukydis, C. F. Z., 203
Bourne, L. E., 256
Boutilier, R. G., 453
Bower, B., 220
Bower, G. H., 20, 22
Bowker, H., 523, 524
Bowlby, J., 23, 189, 193, 197
Bowler, S., 434
Boyatzis, C. J., 477

Boyd, J. D., 399
Brachfeld, S., 113
Bradley, R. H., 170, 171
Bradmetz, J., 459
Brady, J. E., 391
Bragg, B. W., 288
Brainerd, C. J., 256, 456
Brand, C. R., 80
Braswell, L., 359
Braungart, J. M., 187
Bray, N. W., 466
Brazelton, T. B., 121, 214
Brehm, M., 225
Brenner, V., 298
Brent, D., 513
Bressler, J., 482
Bretherton, I., 23, 189, 305
Breznitz, Z., 225
Bridges, L. J., 198
Brigham, T. A., 511
Brim, O. G., Jr., 5
Brinch, M., 438
Brody, J., 234
Brody, L. R., 234, 500
Bronfenbrenner, U., 9, 12, 13
Bronstein, P., 196
Brood, L. P., 313
Brook, J. S., 444
Brooks-Gunn, J., 171, 417, 421, 429,
    477, 505, 508
Broughton, J. M,. 306
Brown, B. B., 467, 476, 482, 491,
    506
Brown, J. R., 261
Brown, R. V., 460, 464, 491
Brown, W. T., 72
Browne, A., 393
Browne, J. E., 230
Bruch, H., 330
Bruck, M., 260
Bryant, D. P., 359
Bryant, P., 374
Buck, G. M., 131
Buck, L. Z., 515
Bucknam, R., 155
Buechler, E. J., 86
Bugental, D. B., 11, 239, 345
Buhrmester, D., 392
Buikhuisen, W., 519
Bukowski, W. M., 505
Burchinal, M. R., 198, 267
Burke, P. H., 419
Burns, A., 516
Burns, G. W., 71
Burt, S., 254
Burton, R. V., 150
Bus, A. G., 374
Bushnell, M. M., 47
Butler, R., 476
Butler, R. J., 228
Butler, W. T., 431, 434
Butterfield, E., 142, 165
Butterworth, G., 184
Butterworth, N. T., 313
Bybee, J., 404, 508
Byrne, D., 481
Byrnes, J. P., 424

Cahan, S., 459, 344
Cairns, R. B., 292, 321, 478
Caldwell, B. M., 170
Caldwell, E., 496, 504
Caldwell, K., 476
Caliendo, M. A., 327
Calkins, L., 278
Campanelli, P., 523

Campbell, D. T., 54
Campbell, F. A., 265
Campbell, S., 85
Campbell, V. N., 462
Campos, J. J., 23, 141, 202
Campos, L. A., 202
Canki, N., 71
Cantor, J. H., 20
Caplan, J. B., 301
Caplan, P. J., 301
Cappelli, M., 436
Capuzzi, D., 513, 514
Caras, Jr, E. H., 526
Carlo, G., 405
Carpendale, J. I. M., 405
Carlson, S. M., 260
Carmelli, D., 441
Carmichael, K. A., 438
Carnelley, K., 503
Carney, B., 440
Carpenter, M., 167
Carpenter, M. W., 102
Carr, M. N., 357
Carruth, B. R., 335
Carskadon, M. A., 130, 436
Carter, A. S., 193
Carter, R. S., 473
Carter-Saltzman, L., 220
Case, R., 6, 453, 459, 466
Caspi, A., 78, 422
Cassidy, E. W., 460
Cassidy, J., 191, 201
Castle, J., 170
Catalano, R. F., 517
Cataldo, M. G., 469
Catherwood, D., 140
Cauce, A. M., 392
Cauffman, E., 439
Ceci, S. J., 6, 12, 30, 258, 260, 344
Chandler, M., 453, 512
Chapell, M. S., 455, 456, 476
Chapman, M., 503
Chapman, P., 436
Chapman, R. S., 175
Chappell, P. A., 225
Chase-Lansdale, P. L., 428, 429
Chasnoff, I. J., 104
Chassin, L., 441
Chastain, G., 50
Chater, N., 456
Chavajay, P., 255
Cherkes-Julkowski, M., 116
Cherlin, A. J., 200, 388
Cherney, I. D., 284
Chess, S., 74–75, 78
Cheung, L. W. Y., 339
Chi, M. T. H., 344, 466
Chilman, C., 426
Chinsky, J. M., 345
Chiriboga, C. A., 104
Chiva, M., 142
Chodorow, N., 498
Choi, S., 177
Chomsky, N., 174, 374
Chou, K., 458
Christopher, N. G., 524, 526, 533
Chumlea, W. C., 420
Church, M. W., 104
Churchill, H., 110
Ciaccio, N., 25
Cicchetti, D., 70, 148, 313, 394, 511
Clark, B., 361
Clark, D., 507
Clark, E. V., 272
Clarke, R., 195
Clarke-Stewart, K. A., 195, 197

Clarkson, M. G., 141
Clarren, S., 105
Clausen, J. A., 422
Clements, D. H., 370
Clinton, H. R., 241
Clum, G. A., 513
Coatsworth, J. D., 386, 522
Coghill, G. E., 15
Cohen, J., 358
Cohen, L. H., 333
Cohen, R., 361
Cohen, R. L., 102
Cohen, S., 331
Cohen-Overbeck, T. E., 86
Cohler, B. J., 207
Cohn, D. A., 305
Cohn, J. F., 203
Colas, A., 178
Colborn, T., 106, 121
Colby, A., 515
Colder, C. R., 518
Cole, D. A., 512
Cole, J. R., 487
Cole, M., 9, 10, 30, 289
Cole, P., 509
Cole, R., 414
Coleman, J. G., 480
Coleman, J. S., 479
Coley, R. J. 479
Coley, R. L., 352, 428, 429, 472
Collins, W. A., 8, 334, 502
Colon, R. M., 434
Coltheart, V., 256
Columbo, J., 169, 184
Colwell, P., 526
Colyer, E., 521
Commons, M. L., 6
Compas, B., 508
Compas, B. E., 333, 392
Conger, R. D., 444
Conner, C. K., 328
Connolly, J., 436
Connolly, J. A., 249
Constanzo, P. R., 330
Conte, J. R., 393
Cook, T. D., 54
Cooke, R. A., 438
Coon, D., 129
Cooper, C., 496
Cooper, C. R., 487, 500, 506
Cooper, R. P., 175
Coopersmith, S., 23, 307, 313
Corcoran, J., 428
Coren, S., 220, 245, 436
Corkum, V., 48
Corn, K., 520
Cornoldi, C., 469
Corrigan, S. A., 332
Cosse, W. J., 498
Costabile, A., 321
Constigan, K. A., 75, 102
Cotton, P., 131
Courage, M. L., 140, 164
Courchesne, E., 71
Covington, M. V., 349
Cowan, P. A., 189
Cowart, B. J., 143
Cox, M. J., 196
Craik, F. I. M., 256
Crain, R. I., 478
Cramer, B. J., 121, 214
Cramer, P., 24, 300
Crandell, L. E., 263
Cratty, B. J., 319
Crawford, S., 512
Crawley, R. A., 164

Creasy, M. R., 97
Crespi, T. D., 368
Crisp, A. H., 440
Crittenden, P. M., 240
Crockenberg, S., 430
Crockenberg, S. B., 210
Crockett, L. J., 422, 426
Cronk, C. E., 419
Crook, C., 142
Cross, W., 500
Crum, J. F., 320
Csikszentmihalyi, M., 360, 362, 501
Cummins, J., 375
Cunningham, C. E., 298
Cunningham, T. H., 375
Cummings, E. M., 193
Cummings, M. E. 313
Curtiss, S., 175
Czeizel, A., 83

Dahlgren, S. O., 357
Dahlquist, L. M., 333
Damon, A., 420
Damon, W., 407
D'Angelo, L. L., 503
Daniels, D. H., 515
Daniels, H., 18, 30
Danish, S., 50
Dansereau, D. F., 464
Darlington, R., 264
Daro, D., 239
Darwin, C., 15, 24, 64–66, 360
Dasen, P. R., 459
Davalos, M., 147
David, H. P., 88
Davidson, L., 513
Davies, B., 286
Davis, B., 176
Davis, C. M., 229
Davis, M. J., 426
Davis, M. K., 393
Davis, S. M., 167
Dawber, T., 238
Dawson, G., 147
Dawson, S., 516
Day, K., 467
Day, N. L., 105
De Angelis, T., 292
Deater-Deckard, K., 195, 198
Deblinger, E., 392
DeCasper, A. J., 100, 142
Deci, E. L., 350
DeCrespigny, L., 85, 92
DeFries, J. C., 92
de Haan, M., 140
Delevati, N., 143
De Lisi, R., 459
Dement, A. L., 477
Dement, W. C., 130
Demetriou, A., 454, 455
Dempster, F. N., 256
DeMulder, E. K., 290
Dennis, M., 135
Dennis, W., 135
Dennis-Rounds, J., 466
Denton, M., 472
D'Entremont, B., 140
Descartes, R., 4, 16
DesRosiers, F., 205, 306
Deutsch, G., 220
de Villiers, J. G., 374
de Villiers, P. A., 374
de Vries, J. I. P., 98
DeVries, R., 250
de Winter, M., 366
De Wolff, M., 192, 200, 201

Deykin, E. Y., 513
Dhillon, B., 221
Diamond, A.,162
Dieden, B., 325, 339
Dieter, J. N. I., 147
Dietz, W. H., 335
DiFazio, W., 484
DiFranza, J. R., 131
Digeronimino, T. F., 100, 112
Digman, J. M., 287
Dill, K. E., 369
DiLorenzo, T. M., 324
DiPietro, J. A., 70, 75, 102, 324
Dishion, T. J., 391
Divitto, B., 113
Dixon, R. L., 108
Dixon, W. E., Jr., 179
Dlugokinski, E. L., 339
Dobber, M., 103
Dobbings, J., 131
Doh, H.-S., 288
Dollard, J., 22
Donate-Bartfield, D., 195
Donati, V., 404
Dondi, M., 142
Donley, J., 469
Donovan, W. L., 188
Dooling, M., 237
Dorn, L. D., 439
Dorn, M., 72
Dorn, S., 472, 473
Dornbusch, S. M., 367, 473, 476, 479, 491
Dorr, S. B., 525
Dougherty, T. M., 169
Douvan, E., 497
Dragoi, V., 22
Drake, C., 142
Drotar, D., 148
Drucker, R. R., 231
Dryfoos, J. G., 520, 521, 533
Dubas, J. S., 421
Duffy, R., 313
Dumanowski, J. D., 121
Dumas, L. S., 401, 414
Dunbar, K., 455
Dunham, R. N., 497
Duncan, P., 422
Dunn, J., 189, 261
Dunn, J. F., 352
Dupont, R. L., 301
Durand, F., 139
Durham, W., 65, 68
Durik, A. M., 110
Durkin, D., 374
Durkin, K., 300
Duryea, E. J., 460
Dusek, J. B., 426
Dweck, C. S., 350, 352, 407

Eacott, M. J., 164
East, P. L., 428
Eaton, W. O., 187
Ebstein, R. P., 74
Eccles, J. S., 320, 425, 473, 498, 512, 522
Eckert, H., 224
Eckert, H. M., 320
Eckert, R. P., 526
Edelbrock, C., 518
Edelman, M. W., 289
Edwards, M. E., 127, 155
Efklides, A., 454, 455
Eimas, P. D., 165
Eibl-Eibesfeldt, I., 321
Eiger, M. S., 133, 145, 155

Eisenberg, N., 23, 78, 197, 198, 298, 300, 304, 388, 394, 396, 404, 405
Eisenberger, R., 363
Eisler, I., 440
Ekman, P., 201
Ekstrom, R. B., 473
Eley, T. C., 401
Elder, G. H., 7, 43, 501
Elkind, D., 264, 426, 457
Elliott, J. G., 399
Ellis, A., 399
Ellis, B. J., 420, 422
Ellis, S., 461
Elmore, R. F., 483
Ellsworth, J., 264, 361
Emde, R. N., 189
Emery, R. E., 389
Emory, E. K., 147
Eng, T. R., 431, 434, 451
Engle, B., 121
Ensminger, M. E., 472
Epstein, C. J., 70
Epstein, L. H., 330, 331
Erickson, F. D., 11
Erikson, E., 24, 25, 30, 188, 281, 283, 384, 385, 495–497
Ernst, C., 263, 287
Eron, L. D., 518
Eronsen, M., 358
Erwin, C., 313
Espanschade, A., 224
Evans, G. W., 263
Evans, J. B. St T., 456
Evans, M. I., 85
Everly, G. S., 102
Ewart, C. K., 332
Eyer, D. E., 116
Ezzo, G., 155

Fabes, R. A., 298, 300, 394, 396, 405
Fagot, B. I., 207, 285, 291
Falbo, T., 288, 289
Falk, R., 454
Fantz, R. L., 140
Faraone, S. V., 358
Farrington, D. P., 518
Farris, M. P., 365
Fassler, D. G., 401, 414
Fauth, J. M., 458, 459
Fegley, S., 479
Feinberg, J., 423
Feingold, B., 358
Feinman, S., 205
Feldman, J. F., 169
Feldman, R., 116, 193
Feltz, D. L., 478
Fenson, L., 271
Ferber, R., 227, 245
Fergusson, D. M., 134, 234
Field, D., 250
Field, T., 23, 113, 147, 196, 292, 293
Fifer, J. W., 142
Fifer, W. P., 100
Finch, M. D., 480, 523
Fincham, F. D., 354, 355
Fine, G. A., 321
Finkelhor, D., 392, 393
Firestone, I. J., 405
Fisher, A. T., 11
Fisher, C. B., 50, 61
Fisher, D. M., 136
Fisher, E. P., 249
Fisher, J. D., 433
Fisher, P., 513
Fisher, W. A., 433
Fitzgerald, H. E., 165

Fitzgerald, L. F., 470
Fivush, R., 257
Flannagan, D., 348
Flavell, J. H., 209, 250, 255, 260, 261, 344, 345, 454, 466
Fleming, J., 509
Fletcher, B. H., 460
Fletcher, A. C., 506
Flieller, A., 459
Flisher, A. J., 513
Fodemski, L. M., 372, 380
Fonagy, P., 192
Fong, G. T., 432
Forgays, D. K., 332
Fordham, S., 477, 505
Forehand, R., 389, 503
Foster, S., 526
Fox, M., 83
Fox, N. A., 74, 147, 161, 196, 200
Fox, R. A., 298
Frank, G. C., 231
Frankel, E., 67
Frankenburg, W. K., 225
Franklin, R. D., 54
Franzosa, S. D., 367
Fraser, M. W., 518
Fredrickson, B. L., 470, 471
Freedman, M. R., 437
Freitas, A. L., 8
Fremouw, W., 513
French, K. E., 224, 225, 423
Freud, A., 495, 508
Freud, S., 7, 8, 12, 13, 23, 24–25, 187–188, 281–283, 384, 495
Freund, L. S., 72
Fried, M. H., 523
Fried, M. N., 523
Fried, P. A., 104
Friedman, B. J., 229
Friedman, M., 332
Friedman, R. C., 19, 364
Friedmann, T., 83
Friesen, W., 201
Frithe, U., 261
Frodi, A. M., 195
Frome, P. M., 473
Fryns, J. P., 71
Fuchs, D., 508
Fuligni, A. J., 500, 502
Funk, J. B., 369
Furman, W., 292, 506
Furstenberg, Jr., F. F., 388
Furrow, D., 273
Furth, H. G., 254

Gaddis, A., 421
Galaburda, A. M., 220
Galambos, N. L., 502
Gallagher, A., 360
Gallager, A. M., 470
Galloway, D., 399
Galper, A., 264
Garbarino, J., 408
Garber, J., 422, 512
Garber, M. D., 77
Garber, S. W., 77
Garcia-Coll, C. T., 113
Gardner, H., 19, 245, 360, 361
Gardner, L. I., 148, 235
Gardner, R. M., 439
Garn, S. M., 330, 420, 422
Garner, P. W., 300
Garrison, C. Z., 513
Garvey, C., 273, 320, 324
Gathercole, S. E., 164
Gathercole, V. C. M., 375

Gavin, L., 506
Ge, X., 517
Geary, D. C., 359
Gehring, W. J., 66, 92
Gellatly, A. R. H., 459
Gelles, R. J., 239
Gelman, R., 273, 289, 453
Gelman, S., 163, 250, 278, 343
Genesee, F., 375
Gentner, D., 272
Geschwind, N., 220
Gesell, A., 15, 135
Gettman, D., 278
Getz, I., 515
Gianetti, C. C., 417
Gibbons, J., 76
Gibson, E. J., 16, 23, 141, 146, 221
Gilbert, S., 472
Gidycz, C. A., 393
Giere, R. N., 34
Gilberg, C., 357
Gilles, J. J., 358
Gilligan, C., 405, 406, 498, 499
Gilvarry, E., 445
Girouard, P. C., 113
Glaser, D., 240
Gleason, T., 405
Gleason, T. R., 248
Glidden, L. M., 87
Gnepp, J., 395, 509
Goerge, R. M., 241, 428
Goin, R. P., 228
Goldberg, M., 500
Goldberg, S., 113, 116
Goldfarb, W., W., 190
Goldman, J. A., 232
Goldman, J. D. G., 284
Goldman, R. J., 284
Goldschmied, E., 214
Goldsmith, H. H., 78, 187, 201
Goldson, E., 14
Goldstein, H., 229
Goleman, D., 203, 265, 278
Golinkoff, R. M., 271
Golub, S., 420
Golumbok, S., 388
Goodenough, F. L., 7
Goodman, S. H., 147
Goossens, F. A., 196, 200
Gopnik, A., 164, 184, 261, 260
Goran, M., 330
Gordis, E. B., 240
Gordon, A. C. C., 261
Gordon, D., 399
Gordon, D. E., 426
Gordon, J., 147, 155
Gordon, T., 520
Gortmaker, S. L., 329, 435
Gosden, R. G., 83, 92
Gosselin, P., 394
Goswami, U., 374
Gotlib, I. H., 147, 401
Gottesman, I. I., 8, 81
Gottesman, J., 80
Gottlieb, G., 81, 82, 172
Goubet, N., 161
Goudas, M., 324
Gould, M., 513
Gould, S., 349
Graber, J. A., 423
Graham, C. R., 375
Gralinski, H. H., 305
Gralinski, J. H., 350
Gray, R. L., 459
Gray, S. W., 264
Green, A., 240

Green, P., 484
Greenberg, M. T., 313
Greenberger, E., 472, 479, 503, 525
Greene, B. A., 349, 386, 522
Greene, R. L., 260
Greenfield, P., 269
Greenfield, P. M., 348
Greenough, W. T., 14, 129, 130, 140
Greenspan, S. I., 323, 398, 414
Greiger, R. M., 399
Grier, L. K., 405
Grigorenko, E. L., 79
Grimes, R. L., 525
Grogger, J., 428
Grolnick, S. A., 206
Grolnick, W. S., 203, 206
Groome, L. J., 100
Groos, K., 321
Gross, A. L., 300
Gross, M. U. M., 360, 361
Gross, R. T., 121
Grossman, K., 194
Grosz, D. E., 513
Grotevant, H., 487, 496, 506
Grotevant, H. D., 500
Grusec, J. E., 305, 306
Grych, J. H., 195
Guarnaccia, P. J., 509
Guerra, N. G., 517
Guilford, J. P., 19, 362
Gullone, E., 522
Gullota, T. P., 444, 451, 533
Gump, L. S., 415
Gunnar, M. R., 143, 205
Gurtner, J., 369, 370
Gussow, J., 335
Guthrie, I. K., 78, 304, 396

Haapasalo, J., 518
Haddad, J., 112
Hadi, F., 333
Hagan, R., 291
Hagborg, W. J., 505
Hagekull, B., 204, 384
Hagerman, R. J., 72
Haggerty, R. J., 332
Hahn, C-S., 70
Haight, W. L., 289
Haith, M. M., 139, 142, 143, 169
Hakuta, K., 374
Hall, C. S., 23
Hall, E., 384
Hall, G. S., 508, 523
Hall, J., 499
Hall, N. W., 239, 241
Hallahan, D. P., 356
Haller, M. C., 353
Halpern, C. T., 437
Halpern, D. F., 113, 220
Halverson, Jr., C. F., 284
Ham, M., 510
Hamberger, L., 95, 98, 108, 121
Hamburg, J., 426
Hamilton, C. E., 196
Hamilton, K., 438
Hamilton, S. F., 482
Hamm, J. V., 500
Hammen, C. L., 401
Hamond, N. R., 257
Hanks, H., 392
Hans, S. L., 193
Hansen, C., 399
Hansen, D. J., 240
Hansen, W. B., 441
Happe, F. G. E., 261
Harasty, J., 178

Harden, D. G., 71
Harlow, H. F., 190, 192
Hardman, M. L., 353
Hardy, J. B., 429
Hardy-Brown, K., 178
Hardyck, C., 220
Harkavy-Friedman, J., 512
Harkness, S., 131
Harley, B., 375
Harley, K., 164
Harold, R. D., 320
Harrington, D., 239
Harris, I. B., 427
Harris, J. R., 7, 8, 30, 287
Harris, K. M., 428
Harris, M. J., 351
Harris, P. L., 261, 395
Harrist, A. W., 290
Hart, B., 263
Hart, C. H., 291, 292
Hart, D., 407
Harter, S., 23, 306, 407, 497, 499, 522
Hartup, W. W., 23, 386, 391, 392, 505
Harvey, E., 197, 198
Harvey, J. A., 104
Harwood, R. L., 192
Haselager, G. J. T., 391
Hasselhorn, M., 345
Hatano, G., 10
Hattie, J., 407
Haugaard, J. J., 392, 393
Haugland, S. W., 369, 370, 371, 380
Hausfather, A., 267
Haveman, R. H., 428
Hawkins, J. D., 517
Hay, D. F., 518, 519
Hayes, C., 427
Haynes, C. W., 121
Haynie, D., 482, 505
Hays, R., 362
Haywood, K. M., 319
Healy, A. F., 256
Healy, J. M., 173, 179, 220, 221, 222, 245, 370, 372
Heath, A. C., 74
Heath, S. B., 348
Hecht, B. F., 272
Heckman, S. J., 405
Hedges, L. V., 349
Heerman, J. A., 195
Heflin, A. H., 392
Heide, K. M., 398
Heller, R. F., 339
Heller, T. L., 298
Hendershot, G. E., 133
Henderson, A., 137
Henderson, V. L., 350
Hendlin, H., 513
Henker, B., 358
Henry, B., 517, 519
Hepper, P. G., 100
Herbert, T. B., 331
Herrnstein, R. J., 266, 278
Hersen, M., 54
Hess, D. L. R., 509
Hess, R. D., 352
Hetherington, E. M., 389, 390
Hewlett, B. S., 195, 291
Heyns, M., 105
Hickey, P. R., 143
Hifler, S. R., 221
Hilgard, E. R., 20, 22
Hill, B. A., 203
Hill, C. R., 387
Hill, J. P., 502
Hill, P., Jr., 525

Hill, R., 238
Hilton, S. C., 102
Hinde, R. A., 189, 200
Hines, M., 224
Hinshaw, S. P., 394
Hinsz, V. B., 11
Hirschfeld, L. A., 283
Hirsh-Pasek, K., 177
Hitch, G. H., 346
Hitchcock, P. J., 106
Ho, T., 513
Ho-Yen, D. O., 105
Hobson, R. P. 263, 356
Hock, H. S., 345
Hodgens, S., 519
Hodgson, D. M., 75, 102
Hoffman, L. W., 290
Hoffman, M. L., 210, 305
Hogue, A., 509
Hohmann, M., 278
Hohnen, B., 271
Hojat, M., 291
Hokada, A., 354, 355
Holbrook, D., 362
Holcomb, B., 197, 214, 290
Holgren, R., 396
Holinger, P., 424
Holland, A., 478, 483
Holley, F. B., 139
Holloway, S. D., 352
Holm, J., 523, 524
Holmbeck, G. H., 496, 502
Holroyd, R., 389
Holtzman, N. A., 83
Holzman, M., 373
Hong, K., 206
Hong, Y., 11
Hook, E. B., 71
Hopkins, B., 148
Hormuth, S. E., 479
Horn, T. S., 320
Horney, K., 282
Hornik, R., 205
Horst, E. A., 498
Hortacsu, N., 505
Hotz, V. J., 428
Householder, J., 104
Howard, R. W., 20
Howe, M. L., 164, 257, 345
Howes, C., 196, 264
Howlin, P., 357
Hoyseth, K. S., 105
Hubbard, R. L., 445
Hubbard, R. S., 363, 364
Hubel, D. H., 10
Hughes, C., 261
Hughes, D. R., 372, 380
Hughes, J. R., 441
Hughes-Lawson, C. A., 419
Hunter, A. A., 470
Hunter, C. L., 500
Hunter, F. T., 196
Hur, Y., 497
Hurrelmann, K., 443
Huston, A. C., 269
Hutcheson, J. J., 148
Huttenlocher, P. R., 129, 130, 149
Hyde, J. S., 469, 470

Inciardi, J. A., 104
Inhelder, B., 248, 250, 253, 454, 455, 457, 459
Irby, B. J., 430
Irvine, S. H., 11
Irwin, C. E., Jr., 423
Irwin, D. M., 47

Isaacson, R. L., 130
Isabella, R., 192
Israelashvili, R., 195
Izard, C. E., 201, 202

Jablow, M. M., 424, 437, 451, 475
Jaccard, J., 427
Jacklin, C. N., 178
Jackson, S., 214
Jacobsen, L. J., 428
Jacobsen, T., 298
Jacobson, J. L., 105
Jacobson, S. W., 107
James, W., 139
James, W. H., 434
Jang, K. L., 74
Janveau-Brennan, G., 254
Janos, P. M., 360
Jeans, P. C., 101
Jelalian, E., 331
Jemmott, J. B., 432
Jemmott, L. S., 432
Jencks, C., 11
Jenest, V., 245
Jenkins, E. C., 72
Jensen, A. R., 79, 348
Jernigan, T. L., 219, 422
Jessor, R., 423, 444, 505
Jessor, S. L., 444
Jobes, D. A., 512, 514
Jodl, K. M., 389
Johnson, C. C., 108
Johnson, H. H., 61
Johnson, M. H., 15, 139, 140, 141, 165
Johnson, M. K., 479
Johnson, M. O., 76
Johnson, T. R. B., 75, 102
Johnson-Laird, P. N., 253, 455
Johnston, C., 11
Johnston, L. D., 441, 443
Johnston, S. S. M., 393
Jones, G. V., 220
Jones, N. A., 147
Jones, P. J. H., 105
Jones, R. M., 497
Jones, S., 64
Jones, S. S., 271
Jordan, N. C., 359
Joseph, J. M., 8, 409, 414
Joseph, R., 130, 146
Joss, A. W. L., 105
Joyce, M. R., 399
Jung, C. G., 282
Jusczyk, P. W., 175
Juvonen, J., 414

Kaczynski, T., 360
Kagan, J., 5, 8, 73, 75–78, 85, 307
Kahana-Kalman, R., 162
Kahn, E. J., 330
Kahn, S. E., 520
Kail, R., 255, 345, 465, 466
Kaitz, M., 195
Kameguchi, K., 399
Kammerman, S. B., 198
Kandel, D. B., 441, 444
Kant, I., 16
Kanter, J., 105
Karabell, Z., 484, 485
Karen, R., 189
Karmiloff-Smith, A., 18, 175, 453
Karp, R., 229
Kasser, T., 516
Kastner, L. S., 423, 424, 425, 502, 504
Katz, V., L., 102

Kauffman, J. M., 356
Kaufman, A. S., 347, 348
Kaufman, F. R., 224
Kaufman, P., 472
Kaufmann, E., 110
Kawaguchi, M. C., 502
Kawakami, K., 142, 143
Kazdin, A. E., 401
Kearney, C. A., 399
Keating, D. P., 465
Kee, D. W., 466, 467
Keen, C. L., 101
Keenan, K., 519
Keith, B., 389
Kellogg, L., 175
Kellogg, R., 225
Kelly, K., 358
Kelman, M., 353
Kemper, H. C. G., 423
Kendall, P. C., 359, 509
Kendall-Tackett, K. A., 394
Kendrick, A. S., 232, 330
Keniston, A. H., 466
Kennel, J. H., 214
Kerns, K. A., 191
Kety, S., 513
Killen, J. D., 437
Killen, M., 306
Kim, N., 434
Kimchi, R., 18
Kimm, S. Y. S., 229
Kindermann, T. A., 9
King, K. L., 270
King, N. J., 399
King, P. M., 453
Kingston, L., 518
Kirsch, I., 39
Kitchener, K. S., 453
Kitchener, R. F., 254
Kitzmann, K. M., 390
Klaczynski, P. A., 455, 458, 459, 462
Klahr, D., 19, 455
Klaus, M. H., 214
Klaus, P. H., 214
Klaus, R. A., 264
Klayman, J., 395
Klein, M. M., 503
Klein, T. W., 351
Kleindorfer, P. R., 464
Klesges, R., 335
Klibanoff, R. F., 178
Kliewer, W., 333, 388, 395
Klin, A., 357
Klineberg, O., 201
Knight, G. P., 405
Koch, H. L., 288
Kochanek, J., 486
Kochanska, G., 5, 23, 193, 304
Koetzsch, R. E., 380
Kogan, N., 193
Kohlberg, L., 228, 405, 406, 515
Kohn, A., 516
Kolata, G. B., 330, 335
Kolb, B., 126
Kollins, S. H., 55
Kolominsky, Y., 106
Konner, M. J., 459
Kopp, C. B., 207, 210, 305
Koppitz, E. M., 225
Korbin, J. E., 239
Kornhaber, M., 195
Kornilova, K. A., 79
Kosofsky, B. E., 104
Kotanski, M., 522
Kramer, R., 395
Krantz, D., 331

Kratzer, L., 519
Kraut, R., 372
Kreppner, J. M., 235
Kroonenberg, P. M., 194
Krosnick, J. A., 47
Kruger, L. J., 476
Kruglanski, A. W., 461
Kugler, P. N., 136
Kuhl, P. K., 146, 175
Kuhn, D., 453, 459
Kumpfer, K. L., 443, 444
Kunitz, S. J., 513
Kupfersmid, J., 282
Kurdek, L. A., 392
Kurfman, D. G., 460
Kutlesic, V., 375
Kwan, K. S. F., 473

Labbok, M. H., 133
Lachelin, G. C. L., 97
Ladd, G. W., 23, 391
LaFontaine, J. S., 527
Lagattuta, K. H., 300
Lagercrantz, H., 109
LaGreca, A. M., 339
Laible, D. J., 290
Lalich, J., 507
Lamaze, F., 109
Lamb, M. E., 194, 195
Lamborn, S. D., 476, 504
Lampinen, J., 85
Lancaster, J., 420
Landrum, R. E., 50
Lane, P. S., 520
Lang, P., 451
Lang, S. S., 451
Lange, G., 345
Laosa, L. M., 37
Laplante, D. P., 140
Lapsley, D. K., 458
Larson, R., 510, 512
Larson, R. W., 496, 501, 502
Laskey, K. B., 462
Laub, J. H., 518
Laursen, B., 502
Lavigne, J. V., 227
Lazar, I., 264
Leach, P., 178
Leadbeater, B. J., 510
Leake, C., 496
Leaper, C., 195, 291
Learner, D. G., 476
Leavitt, L. A., 14
Leboyer, F., 110
Lecanuet, J.-P., 100
LeCroy, C. W., 503
Lecours, A. R., 422
LeCouteur, A., 358
Lederer, J. M., 356
Lee, B. J., 428
Lee, K. W., 401
Lee, M., 512
Lee, P. A., 500
Lee, S., 351
Lee, V., 468, 473
LeFrancois, G., 30
Legrand, L. N., 398
Leichtman, M. D., 258
Leinbach, M. D., 207
Lemery, K. S., 8, 281
Lepper, M. R., 350, 369, 370, 371
Leppert, P. C., 101
Lerner, R. A., 522
Lerner, R. M., 5, 12
Lesch, K. P., 74
Lester, B. M., 203

Lester, D., 513
Lester, G., 353
Lester, R., 108
Leung, K., 473, 504
Leung, P. W. L., 510
LeVay, S., 10
Leven-Epstein, J., 429
Leverato, M. C., 404
Levin, S. R., 255
Levine, S. C., 262
Levy, G. D., 283
Levy, J. E., 513
Levy, L. S., 245
Levy-Shiff, R., 70, 195
Lewinsohn, P. M., 513
Lewis, C., 292
Lewis, C. C., 267
Lewis, M., 50, 104, 169, 203
Lewkowicz, D. J., 142, 146
Li, S.-Y, 72
Libon, L. S., 286
Lichtenberger, E. O., 347
Lickliter, R., 146
Liddle, H. A., 445
Lieberman, A. F., 205
Lifshitz, F., 134, 135
Lillard, A., 249, 260
Limper, S. P., 200
Lindauer, B. K., 255
Lindzey, G., 23
Linn, M. C., 98, 469, 470
Linton, M. A., 434
Lipsett, L. P., 20
Litman, C., 210
Little, J. W., 469
Litvack-Miller, W., 405
Livson, N., 422
Llabre, M. M., 333
Locke, J., 7, 13, 16, 271
Lockhart, R. S., 256
Lockman, J. J., 136
Loeber, R., 386, 444, 518, 519
Loehlin, J. C., 8, 74, 79
Loftus, E. F., 260
Lorch, E., 255
Lorenz, K. Z., 81, 82
Losoya, S., 298, 396, 508
Lowrey, G. H., 219, 330
Lozoff, B., 101, 229, 328
Lubart, T. I., 363
Lubinski, D., 361
Lucas, A., 133
Lucas, A. R., 439
Ludman, M. D., 84
Luke, K., 424
Luker, K., 427
Luther, S. S., 207
Lynam, D. R., 518
Lynch, J. E., 470
Lynch, J. H., 502
Lynn, S. J., 257
Lyons-Ruth, K., 200
Lytton, H., 291, 301
Lyytinen, P., 162

Maccoby, E. E., 8, 9, 178, 255, 285, 294, 301, 387, 407
MacDonald, K., 291
MacKinnon-Lewis, C., 293
MacKintosh, N. J., 19, 30
Madan-Swain, A., 497
Maggs, J. L., 443
Magnussen, D., 45, 422, 518
Maguin, E., 386
Mahdi, L., 523
Mahdi, L. C., 525, 526, 533

Mahler, M. S., 205–206
Mahlmeister, L. R., 115
Mahoney, J. L., 321, 478
Maier, S., 331
Main, M., 193, 201
Majidi-Ahi, S., 408
Malinosky-Rummell, R., 240
Mandler, J. M., 161
Manginello, F. P., 100, 112
Manion, V., 366
Maratos, M., 273
Marcia, J. E., 497
Marcon, R. A., 267
Marcos, H., 195
Marcotte, D., 509
Marcovitch, S., 161
Marcus, D. E., 283
Marcus, G. F., 273
Marcus, R. F., 241, 519
Mare, R. D., 468, 484
Margolin, G., 240
Mariani, M., 370
Marini, Z., 459
Markman, E. M., 373
Markovits, H., 254, 455, 456
Marks, S., 479
Markstrom, C. A., 497, 500
Markstrom-Adams, C., 497
Markus, H. J., 407, 497
Marlier, L., 143
Marsh, H. W., 407, 469, 472, 478
Martin, C. L., 284
Martin, H. P., 240
Martin, J., 392
Martin, J. A., 294
Martin, J. C., 105
Martin, J. H., 97
Martin, K. A., 420, 421, 422, 426
Martin, M., 220
Martin, R. P., 102
Masi, G., 472
Mask, C., 261
Maslow, A. H., 516
Masten, A. S., 386, 387, 522
Maszk, P., 396
Matheny, A. P., 187, 238
Mathes, P. G., 430
Mathews, J., 491
Matias, R., 203
Matthews, K. A., 332
Matula, K., 183
Mau, W., 473
Maulik, D., 112
May, K. A., 115
Mayaux, M. J., 101
Mayer, J., 265, 266
Maynard, R. A., 428, 451
Mayringer, H., 261
Mazur, E., 389
McBride, H. E. A., 474
McBurnett, K., 519
McCarney, S. B., 400, 403, 414
McCarthy, G., 191
McCarthy, M., 438
McCartney, K., 79, 82
McCarty, M. E., 160
McCauley, E., 72
McClearn, G. E., 92
McClelland, D. C., 349
McClelland, J. L., 18
McClelland, S. E., 404
McClure, V. S., 113
McConkey, K. M., 257
McConnell, S. K., 97
McCoy, P. A., 131
McCrae, R. R., 74, 287

McCullough, M., 429
McCune, L., 162, 175
McCurdy, K., 239
McDaniel, M. A., 345, 467
McDonald, D. L., 506
McEachin, J. J., 357
McElroy, S. W., 427, 428
McEwen, B. J., 235
McGee, R., 519
McGrath, M. L., 228
McGraw, M. B., 135, 136
McGuffin, P., 398, 401
McGurk, H., 169
McInerney, V., 366
McKay, K., 255
McKenna, J. J., 131
McKinlay-Gardner, R. J., 71
McKinney, J. P., 506
McKown, H. C., 477
McLanahan, S., 389
McLaughlin, M. W., 469, 503
McLoyd, V. C., 12
McMillen, M. M., 472
McShane, J., 18, 30
McWhirter, J. J., 517, 520
Meacham, J., 12
Mead, M., 494–495, 501
Meade, M., 533
Mecksroth, E. A., 380
Mednick, S. A., 519
Mehrabian, A., 265
Meins, E., 290
Meints, K., 272
Melby, J. N., 441
Mellon, M. W., 228
Melton, G. B., 245
Meltzoff, A. N., 146, 163, 164, 165,
    166, 184, 210
Mendel, G., 66
Mendelsohn, A. L., 234
Mendelson, B. K., 329
Mendelson, M. J., 292
Merrill, M. A., 167
Merriman, W. E., 375
Mertz, W., 437
Messer, S. B., 460
Meyer, A. L., 441, 445
Meyerhoff, M. K., 170
Michaelieu, Q., 522
Michel, C., 106
Mill, J., 16
Mill, J. S., 16
Millar, G. T., 221
Millberger, S., 105
Miller, A., 240, 245, 414
Miller, D. B., 500
Miller, G. A., 466
Miller, J. G., 10, 516
Miller, L. B., 267
Miller, L. T., 255
Miller, N. B., 295
Miller, N. E., 22
Miller, P. H., 256, 278, 306
Miller, R. B., 386, 522
Miller, S., 44, 61
Miller, S. P., 369
Miller, T. W., 507
Miller-Jones, D., 347
Mills, K., 264
Mills, R., 305
Millstein, S. G., 423
Milosevic, A., 438
Mindell, E., 229
Mindell, J. A., 227, 229
Minty, B., 241
Miranda, S., 169

Mischel, W., 22
Mishel, L., 484
Mitchell, J. E., 438
Mitchell, P. B., 439
Miura, I. T., 371
Miyake, K., 194
Moawad, A. H., 112
Modell, B., 85
Modell, M., 85
Moffitt, T. E., 422, 518
Molfese, U. J., 263
Money, J., 235, 240
Montani, T. O., 359
Montemayor, R., 444, 501, 533
Montgomery, H., 460
Montgomery, R., 391
Montgomery, S. S., 401
Montour, K., 360
Moon, C., 100
Moore, C., 48
Moore, D., 520
Moore, K. A., 427, 428
Moore, K. L., 98, 103
Moore, M. K., 163, 164, 165
Moore, S., 434
Morales, M., 175, 198
Morehouse, E., 445
Morgan, J. L., 175
Morgan, K. J., 328
Morgan, S. B., 329
Morris, A. K., 344, 459
Morrison, M. A., 443
Morrissette, P. J., 392
Moritz, G., 513
Morris, P., 13
Morrongiello, B. A., 142, 238
Mortimer, J. T., 479, 480, 523
Morton, J., 140, 141
Morton, T. C., 350
Moses, C. J., 204
Moskowitz, D. S., 332
Moss, E., 290
Mounts, N. S., 476, 505, 506
Muehlenhard, C. L., 434, 435
Muir, D. H., 140
Muller, J., 420
Muller, U., 161
Mumm, S., 526
Munakata, Y., 161
Muris, P., 227, 398
Muro, M., 100
Murphy, B. C., 78, 394, 396, 405
Murphy, J., 234, 335, 340
Murphy, J. K., 332
Murphy-Shigematsu, M., 399
Murray, A. D., 147
Murray, B., 365, 366, 373
Murray, C., 266, 278
Murray, K. T., 193
Musick, J., 428
Myers, J. P., 121
Myers, N., 257

Nabuzoka, D., 321
Nair, P., 104
Nanez, J., 141
Narasimham, G., 455
Narvaez, D., 405, 515
Needham, A., 140
Needham, J., 3
Needleman, H. L., 102, 121
Neher, L. S., 389
Neiderhiser, J. M., 517
Neighbors, B., 425
Neill, M., 369

Neisser, U., 266, 348
Nelsen, J., 313
Nelson, C. A., 14, 130, 140
Nelson, H., 112
Nelson, K., 179, 278
Nelson, W. L., 439
Nettles, S. M., 321
Neuman, M. G., 390, 414
Neustaedter, R., 234
New, M. I., 224
Newall, A., 19
Newcomb, A. F., 391
Newmann, F. M., 468
Nicholls, J., 325
Nickerson, P. S., 460
Nicolaides, K. H., 85
Nilsson, L., 95, 98, 108, 121
Nolen-Hoeksema, S., 510
Nolte, J., 127
Norbeck, J. S., 102
Norman, E., 443, 444
Nottleman, E. D., 508
Novosad, C., 281
Nowinski, J., 443
Nurius, P. S., 407, 497

Oaksford, M., 456
Obeidallah, D. A., 499
Ober, C., 87
Obler, L. K., 469
Ocampo, K. A., 384
Ocholla-Ayayo, A. B. C., 385
O'Conner, S., 114
O'Connor, M. J., 169
O'Connor, T. G., 170
O'Doherty, N., 111
Oerter, R., 497
Oetting, E. R., 508
Offer, D., 508
Offit, P. A., 234
Offord, D., 509
Ogbu, J. U., 408, 477, 505
Ogletree, S. M., 371
O'Koon, J., 503
Olby, R., 66, 92
Olds, S. W., 96, 133, 145, 155
Ollendick, T. H., 399
Olson, D. R., 261
Olson, R. K., 271
Olszewski-Kubilius, P., 472
Omer, H., 102
O'Neil, R., 391
Oppenheim, J., 184
Orbach, I., 401
Orbuch, T. L., 388
Orelove, F. P., 356, 380
O'Reilley, T., 267, 320
Orenstein, P., 203
Orlandi, M., 444
Oski, F. A., 131
Oster, G. D., 401
O'Sullivan, J. T., 257
O'Sullivan, M., 110
Ottenbacher, K. J., 147
Ottenberg, S., 385
Over, D. E., 456
Overton, W. F., 161, 283, 454, 456,
    476
Owens-Stively, J., 227
Owings, J., 472
Oyserman, D., 429

Pagani, L., 389
Pajaras, F., 374
Pakiz, B., 519
Palmer, S. E., 18

Palumbo, F. M., 335
Papadaki, M., 455
Papalia, D. E., 96
Papert, S., 370
Papini, D. R., 392, 509
Parikh, B., 515
Paris, S. C., 255
Park, C., 333
Park, K. A., 293
Parke, R. D., 7, 23, 30, 291
Parker, J. G., 505
Parker, W. D., 352
Parmelee, A. H., 98, 100, 147
Parrila, R. K., 466
Pascalis, O., 140
Pasnak, R., 344
Passman, R. H., 195, 207
Patrick, J., 98, 99
Patterson, G. R., 387, 503, 517, 519
Pauen, S., 165
Paul, M., 106
Paul, R., 175
Pavlov, I., 20–21
Pederson, D. R., 201
Pedersen, F. A., 196
Peel, J. L., 464
Pegg, J., 175
Pehoski, C., 137
Peisner-Feinberg, E. S., 267
Pelham, W. E., Jr., 358
Pelligrini, A. D., 55, 61, 267, 321, 324
Penning, M., 444
Pennington, B. F., 72
Perkins, D. N., 362
Perlis, L., 254
Perlmutter, M., 257
Perner, J., 261
Perosa, L. M., 497
Perozek, M., 428
Perry, T. B., 392
Persaud, T. V. N., 103
Peskin, H., 422
Petersen, A. C., 420, 422, 423, 426,
    509
Peterson, C., 271
Petrill, S. A., 167
Petrinovich, L. F., 220
Pettit, G. S., 321
Pezdek, K., 270
Pfeffer, C. R., 514
Piaget, J., 12, 17–18, 55, 139, 140,
    156–163, 166, 248–255, 304,
    314, 342–344, 423, 453–454,
    455, 456, 457
Pick, A. D., 146
Pierce, J. W., 329
Pierce, S. H., 345
Piersel, W. C., 399
Piirto, J., 364
Pike, A., 518
Pilgrim, C., 441, 443
Pilkington, C. L., 399
Pillow, B. H., 261, 344
Pinel, J. P., 127, 155
Pipes, P. L., 229, 230, 245, 327, 328,
    340
Pipher, M., 533
Pipp, S., 207
Pirkle, J. L., 235
Plato, 3
Platsidou, M., 454
Pleck, E. H., 195, 197
Pleck, J. H., 195, 197
Pless, I. B., 326
Plomin, R., 9, 14, 54, 66, 79, 92, 178,
    348

Plumert, J. M., 199
Podrouzek, W., 273
Poehlman, E. T., 330
Poest, C. A., 224
Pogrebin, L. C., 283
Polak, A., 261
Polit, D. F., 289
Pollack, W., 500, 533
Ponton, L. E., 423, 425, 451
Pope, H. G., 439
Porcerelli, J. H., 24
Porges, S. W., 165
Porter, R. H., 143
Portes, P. R., 11, 348, 473
Posada, G., 192
Postman, L., 20
Potts, R., 334
Poulin-Dubois, D., 272
Power, T. G., 217, 300
Power-deFur, L. A., 356, 380
Powers, S. I., 515
Pratt, M. W., 291
Pressley, M., 345, 346, 466, 467
Provins, K. A., 220
Prudhomme-White, B., 204
Pursley, J. T., 87
Pryor, D. W., 392
Pryor, T., 438, 439
Pulkkinen, L., 519
Puura, K., 401

Quadrel, M,, 424
Queenan, J. T., 107
Quinn, P. C., 165

Radell, P. L., 172
Radin, N., 291, 429
Radke-Yarrow, M., 210, 295
Radloff, L. S., 509
Raeff, C., 385
Raine, A., 517, 519
Ramey, C. T., 101, 265, 352
Ramey, S. L., 352
Ramsay, D., 203
Ramundo, P., 358
Rastam, M., 439
Ratcliffe, S. G., 71
Ratey, J. J., 358
Rathunde, K., 501
Rauh, J. L., 317
Ray, B. D., 366
Rayner, R., 21
Reed, L. J., 398
Rees, J. M., 437
Reese, E., 164
Reese, H. W., 55, 257
Reeve, J., 351
Reid, D. K., 359
Reid, J. R., 239
Reis, H. T., 189
Reis, S. M., 361
Reisner, M., 396
Reiss, M. J., 83, 92
Reiter, E. O., 417
Renner, J. W., 459
Renzulli, J. S., 361
Repacholi, B. M., 205
Reppucci, N. D., 392, 393
Rest, J. R., 405, 515
Reyna, V. F., 456
Reynolds, A. J., 387, 388
Reynolds, C. R., 348
Reynolds, M., 300
Reznick, J. S., 76
Rich, D., 355, 380
Richard, R., 434

Richards, D. D., 262
Richards, J. E., 139
Richards, M., 85
Richards, M. H., 506
Richert, E. S., 360
Richins, M. L., 516
Richman, H. B., 366
Richmond, J. B., 264, 339
Rickel, A. U., 445
Rico, G. L., 365
Ridderinkhof, K. R., 256
Ridenour, M. V., 150
Ridley, M., 66
Rieder, C. L., 68, 92
Rifkin, J., 83
Rilling, M., 13
Ringwalt, C., 521
Risley, T., 263
Rivera, B., 519
Rizzo, G., 99
Roach, M. A., 48
Roberts, K., 165
Roberts, J. E., 271, 272
Roberts, T., 470
Robins, L. N., 510
Robins, R. W., 14, 15
Robinson, I., 425
Robinson, N. M., 360, 361
Robinson, S. R., 100
Rochat, P., 192
Roche, A. F., 135
Rock, A. M. L., 192
Rodgers, J. L., 263
Rodin, J., 330
Rogers, C., 409
Rogers, S. J., 357
Roghmann, K. J., 326, 332
Rogoff, B., 254, 255, 326, 332, 344, 351
Rohwer, W. D., Jr., 466
Romanini, C., 99
Romano, P. S., 86
Romney, D. M., 291, 301
Roodenburg, P. J., 98
Roosa, M. W., 392
Rosander, K., 139
Roscoe, B., 507
Rose, D. H., 226
Rose, M. R., 65, 92
Rose, S. A., 169
Rosemond, J., 462, 491
Rosen, R,, 384
Rosenberg, B. G., 288
Rosenberg, D. R., 445
Rosenberg, M., 512, 522
Rosendaul, S. A., 50
Rosenman, R., 332
Rosenthal, D. A., 434
Rosenthal, R., 351
Rosenthal, M. K., 7
Rosenzweig, M. R., 147, 164
Ross, L. M., 431
Rosso, P., 101
Rothbart, M. K., 255, 394
Rothbaum, F., 192, 194
Rothblatt, M., 83, 92
Rothman, B. K., 86
Rousseau, J., 7, 13
Rovee-Collier, C., 164
Rowe, D. C., 7, 8, 167
Rowley, S. J., 500
Rozin, P., 229, 231
Rubenstein, A. J., 140
Rubin, D. H., 108
Rubin, K. H., 78
Rubin, Z., 23

Ruble, D. N., 307, 395
Rudd, M. D., 513
Rueter, M. A., 444
Ruff, H. A., 255
Rumberger, R. W., 472
Runco, M. A., 363
Russell, A., 295
Russell, G., 502
Russell, J. A., 300
Rutter, M., 6, 9, 14, 54, 55, 80, 92, 189, 200, 357, 398, 510, 522
Rutter, R. A., 472
Ryalls, B. A., 284
Ryan, B. A., 368
Ryan, R., 502
Ryker, J., 404

Saarni, C., 509
Sadeh, A., 436
Sadock, V., 507
Sadovnick, A. C., 71
Sadowitz, P. D., 131
Saelins, B. E., 331
Sagi, A., 196
St. James-Roberts, I., 204
Salapatek, P., 139, 140
Sales, B. D., 50
Salovey, P., 265, 266, 331
Saltz, E., 429
Sameroff, A. J., 170, 346
Sampson, R. J., 518
Samson, L. F., 105
Samuda, J., 347, 348
Samuelson, L. K., 175
Sandbek, T., 439
Sandberg, D. E., 487
Sandefur, G., 389
Sandgrund, A., 240
Sandler, I. N., 389
Sandman, C. A., 100
Sanson, A., 78
Sansonnet-Hayden, H., 392
Santrock, J. W., 138, 226, 251, 319, 418
Sanua, V. D., 357
Sanyika, D., 525
Sapolsky, R., 281, 329
Saradjiam, J., 392
Sarid, M., 255
Satter, E., 232
Sattler, J. M., 259, 441
Saudino, K. J., 74, 187
Sautter, R. C., 516
Savage, B., 109, 121
Savage, M. P., 423
Scafidi, F., 147
Scarr, S., 79, 82, 197, 198
Schacter, D. L., 278
Schacter, J. E., 401
Schaefer, C. E., 227
Schaffer, H. R., 387
Schardein, J. L., 104
Schauble, L., 453
Scheel, K. R., 513
Scheingold, K., 164
Schenker, I. I., 434
Scherman, A., 429, 525
Schiari, R. C., 71
Schill, W. J., 479
Schine, J., 483
Schinke, S., 444
Schlegel, A., 508
Schmidt, W., 100
Schmitt, M. H., 133
Schmuck, P. A., 351, 366
Schmuck, R. A., 351, 366

Schmuckler, M. A., 161
Schneider, B., 480, 486, 491
Schneider, B. H., 497
Schneider, M. L., 102
Schneider, W., 466
Schnorr, T. M., 106
Schofield, J. W., 478
Scholnick, E. K., 278
Scholte, E. M., 240
Schore, A. N., 214
Schorr, D., 472
Schorr, L. B., 472
Schrag, S. G., 108
Schucket, M. A., 443
Schuerman, J. R., 393
Schulenberg, J., 479
Schuler, E., 104
Schwartz, B., 363
Schwartz, D., 101
Schwartz, J. C., 504
Schwartz, S. H., 497, 515, 516
Schwarz, N., 47
Schwebel, D. C., 238
Schweinhart, L. J., 264
Scott, L. B., 423
Scribner, S., 460
Seabrook, C., 87
Sears, R. R., 20
Sears, W., 131, 137, 155, 203
Sebald, H., 506
Segall, M. H., 10, 11
Seifer, R., 200
Seiffege-Krenke, I., 436, 451
Seligman, M. E., 266
Selye, H., 331
Semin, G. R., 434
Senechal, M., 272
Serjeant, G. R., 68
Serpell, R., 10
Shaffer, D., 513
Shaffer, D. R., 69, 126, 128
Shaffer, H. J., 370
Shaffer, H. R., 8
Shaffer, J. W., 72
Shantz, C. U., 301
Shapiro, L. E., 266, 307, 314
Shatz, M., 273
Shaver, P., 507
Shedler, J., 444, 445
Sheets, V., 389
Sheffield, J. B., 221
Shepard, A. C., 78
Sheppard, A., 389
Sherman, S., 72
Sherrod, K. B., 114
Shields, J., 80
Shiller, M., 200
Shiner, R. L., 78
Shipman, K., 509
Shore, B., 19, 364
Shorr, D. N., 404
Short, J. L., 389
Shulman, S., 392, 503
Sidis, W. J., 360
Siegal, A. U., 291
Siegal, B., 380
Siegal, C. S., 474
Siegal, L. J., 339
Siegel, A. C., 150
Siegel, J. M., 509
Siegler, A. L., 423, 425
Siegler, R. S., 262
Sigman, M., 169
Sigman, M. D., 98
Silbergeld, E. K., 234
Silverberg, S., 506

Silverman, L. K., 360, 361, 362
Silverstein, L. B., 201, 389
Simard, J., 394
Simion, F., 184
Simkin, D., 109, 121
Simon, H., 19
Simmons, R., 421, 439, 522
Simner, M. L., 210
Simonton, D. K., 360, 362
Simpson, C., 430
Simpson, J. L., 87
Sims, M., 285
Sinclaire, R. J., 392
Singer, D. G., 269, 301
Singer, J. L., 269, 301
Singer, L. T., 104
Singer, M. T., 507
Sinkkonen, J., 439
Siperstein, G., 142, 165
Skinner, B. F., 12, 22, 174
Skinner, E. A., 23, 408
Slade, A., 314
Slade, P., 438, 440
Slap, G. B., 424, 437, 451, 475
Slater, A., 139, 140, 164, 169
Slavin, R. E., 351, 375
Slicker, E. K., 504
Slobin, D. I., 273
Slotkin, D. A., 109
Sloutsky, V. M., 459
Smetana, J. G., 304, 305, 306, 502
Smith, A. E., 351
Smith, B. A., 144
Smith, C., 380
Smith, E. A., 425
Smith, E. R., 11
Smith, G., 70
Smith, K., 512
Smith, L., 358
Smith, L. B., 125, 155, 162, 175
Smith, P., 85
Smith, P. H., 179
Smith, P. K., 283, 321, 324
Smotherman, W. P., 100
Snadler, H. M., 114
Snidman, N., 76
Snow, C. E., 179, 271, 274
Snowling, M. J., 359
Snyder, E., 224
Snyder, E. E., 478
Snyder, N. O., 428
Soken, N. H., 146
Solman, M. A., 325
Solomon, J., 193, 201
Solso, R. L., 61
Solter, A., 203
Somer, E., 121
Sommer, K. S., 428
Sonn, C. C., 11
Southard, B., 318
Southard, M., 344
Sparrow, S. S., 167
Spears, R. A., 469
Speicher, B., 515
Speiker, S. J., 429
Spelke, E. S., 140, 146, 196
Spence, M. J., 100
Spencer, S. J., 470
Spiker, D., 121
Spires, H. A., 469
Spitz, M. R., 108
Spitz, R. A., 23, 190
Spizman, R. F., 77
Spreen, O., 127
Spreitzer, E. A., 478
Springer, S. P., 220

Sroufe, L. A., 200, 203
Stack, S., 513
Staddon, J. E. R., 22
Stafford, D. G., 459
Stafford, F. P., 387
Stang, H. J., 146
Stanley-Hagan, M. S., 389
Starfield, B., 326
Starr, R. H., Jr., 116
Stattin, H., 422, 518
Staudt, J., 459
Stein, Z. A., 101
Steinberg, L., 332, 351, 352, 439, 473, 476, 477, 479, 480, 481, 491, 500, 502, 505, 506, 509
Steinberg, L. D., 472
Steiner, J. E., 143
Stenberg, G., 23, 204
Stern, D. N., 201
Sternberg, R. J., 19, 79, 348, 360, 363, 364
Stetsenko, A., 18, 350
Stevens, J. H., 263
Stevenson, C. L., 478
Stevenson, D. L., 473, 480, 484, 485, 486
Stevenson, H. W., 351
Stevenson, J., 240, 271
Stevenson, P., 70
Stewart, L. H., 287, 288
Stice, E., 503, 518
Stietz, J. A., 225
Stifter, C. A., 203, 204
Stipek, D. J., 207, 208, 307, 350
Stocking, C., 472
Stoddard, J. J., 235
Stoll, C., 370
Stone, L., 245
Stormshak, E. A., 293
Story, M., 230
Stouthhammer-Loeber, M., 444, 518
Strasburger, V. C., 426
Strassberg, Z., 299, 301
Straughn, R., 83, 92
Strauss, C. C., 329
Strein, W., 407
Streri, A., 143
Strick, L., 380
Strickman, J., 102
Sturm, L., 148
Strutt, G. F., 344
Stucky-Ropp, R. C., 324
Sugarose, M., 417
Stunkard, A., 135
Suess, G. J., 196
Sulloway, F. J., 286, 287
Super, C. M., 131
Super, D., 486
Susman, E. J., 508, 519
Sutherland, D. H., 224
Sutherland, G. R., 71
Sutton, P. J., 226
Sutton-Smith, B., 288
Swanson, H. L., 346
Swanson, M. W., 104
Sweet, A. P., 350
Swisher, L., 334
Szmuckler, G., 438

Tabor, A., 86
Tager-Flusberg, H., 273
Talbert, J. E., 469
Tamang, B. L., 509
Tamis-LeMonda, C. S., 175
Tannenbaum, A. J., 360

Tanner, J., 473
Tanner, J. M., 125, 134, 218, 219, 233, 317, 318, 418, 423, 437
Tansy, M., 520
Tardif, T., 177
Taris, T. W., 434
Tarquinio, N., 165
Tatum, B., 500
Tavris, C., 301
Taylor, A., 191
Taylor, A. S., 482
Taylor, H. G., 113
Taylor, J. H., 306, 515
Taylor, M., 499
Tees, R. C., 174, 177
Teolis, B., 414
Tenney, Y. J., 164
Terman, L. M., 19, 167
Teti, D. M., 195
Thapar, A., 398, 401
Theander, S., 438
Thelen, E., 15, 16, 125, 136, 149, 155, 508
Theobald, W., 467, 477, 482
Thoma, S. J., 405
Thoman, E. B., 281
Thomas, A., 74–75, 78
Thomas, J. R., 224, 225, 423
Thompson, H., 135
Thompson, R., 404, 406
Thompson, R. A., 34, 200, 218, 290, 318, 394, 508
Thompson, S. K., 283
Thomson, J., 469
Thomson, J. A., 238
Thoreson, C. E., 332
Thornburg, H. D., 420
Thorndike, E. L., 20
Thorndike, R. L., 167, 262
Thorne, A., 522
Thorne, B., 384
Thornton, A., 506
Tiedemann, J., 470
Tiggerman, M., 470
Tilden, U. P., 102
Tindell, N., 225
Tinsley, B. J., 334
Tobler, N. S., 445
Tolan, P. H., 517
Tolan, S. S., 380
Tomasello, M., 65, 179
Torosian, M. H., 233
Toth, S. L., 511
Touyz, S. W., 439
Tower, R. B., 270
Townes, B., 206
Trahms, C. M., 229, 230, 245, 327, 328, 340, 437
Trainor, L. J., 192
Traverso, D. K., 270, 278
Treasure, D., 322
Treasure, J., 438
Trehub, S. E., 141, 192
Tremblay, R. E., 518
Triebenbacher, S. L., 206
Trimble, J. E., 443
Trnavsky, P., 198
Tronick, E. Z., 23, 140, 204
Trost, S. G., 324
Truswell, A. S., 439
Tryon, W. W., 50, 61
Tsang-Tong, H. Y., 161
Tse, L., 500
Tubman, J., 5
Tucker, K., 335, 340
Tucker, L., 139

Tulkin, S. R., 459
Turkenheimer, E., 8, 82
Turner, E., 526
Turner, J., 369
Turner, P. K., 502
Turner, S., 525
Turner, S. M., 399
Turvey, M. T., 136
Tversky, A., 460
Twenge, J. M., 398
Tzuriel, D., 196

Ulione, M. S., 236, 237
Ulku-Steiner, B., 471
Ulmer, D., 332
Umbel, V. M., 375
Underwood, M. K., 394
Ungar, M. T., 497
Unger, D., 429
Urberg, K. A., 506

Vachon, R., 456
Valdes, A., 485
Vallette, B., 451
Valsiner, J., 9, 10
van Balen, F., 70
Vandell, D. L., 195, 198
Vandereycken, W., 439
Vanderlinden, J., 439
van der Kolk, B., 513
van der Pligt, J., 434
van der Veer, R., 18
Van Galen, J. A., 365
van Gennep, A. 523, 524
van IJzendoorn, M. H., 192, 194, 196, 200, 201, 239, 374
Van Lange, P. A. M., 405
Van Theil, D. H., 108
Vaughn, B. E., 200, 210
Vaughn, V., 361
Ventegodt, S., 8
Verba, M., 366
Verhulst, F. C., 87
Vermeer, H. J., 470
Vernon, P. A., 255
Verp, M. S., 87
Verschueren, K., 290, 307
Verschurr, R., 423
Versluis-Den Bierman, H. J. M., 87
Vietze, P. M., 114
Volker, S., 192
Volkin, J. I., 332
von Hofsten, C., 139
Voorhees, J. J., 71
Vorhees, C. V., 107
Votoubek, W. L., 131
Vreeke, G. J., 8
Vurpillot, E., 221
Vygotsky, L. S., 10, 17, 18, 170, 254–255, 344

Waber, D. P., 72
Wachs, T. D., 12
Waddington, C. H., 81
Wade, T. E., 367, 380
Wadsworth, B. J., 17, 30, 248, 343, 380
Wadsworth, S. J., 374
Wagenaar, T. C., 472
Wagner, M. G., 70
Wagner, W. G., 520
Wahlsten, D., 14
Wahlstrom, K. L., 436
Waitzman, N. J., 86
Wakschlag, L. S., 193
Walk, R. D., 23, 141

Walker, A. S., 146
Walker, C. E., 339
Walker, E. F., 81
Walker, L. J., 306, 515
Walker-Andrews, A. S., 162
Wallace, J. M., 441
Wallace, M., 287, 289, 314
Wallach, M. A., 363
Wallender, J. L., 339
Waller, G., 438, 440
Walton, G. E., 140
Warburton, D., 71
Ward, N., 101
Ward, S. L., 455
Wardle, J., 329
Warren-Leubecker, A., 195
Wartes, J., 366
Waterman, A. S., 496, 498
Waters, E., 193, 203, 293
Watkinson, B., 104
Watson, A. C., 261
Watson, D., 509
Watson, F., 83
Watson, J. B., 7, 13, 14, 21–22, 165
Waxler, C. Z., 47
Waxman, S. R., 178
Webb, J. T., 380
Webb, W. B., 226
Webster, D., 521
Wechsler, D., 262, 347
Weems, C. F., 398
Wehlage, G. G., 472
Weiderman, M. W., 438, 439
Weidner, G., 332
Weikart, D., 264, 278
Weinfield, N. S., 192
Weinstein, C. S., 370
Weinstein, R. S., 351
Weiss, L., 359

Weiss, L. H., 504
Weist, M. D., 519
Weitzman, M., 436
Weitzman, Z. O., 271
Wellman, H. M., 209, 257, 260, 261
Wender, P., 358, 381
Wentzel, K. R., 352, 386, 414, 476
Werker, J. F., 174, 177
Werner, E. E., 102, 197
Wertsch, J. V., 11
Wessells, M. G., 16
West, L. L., 473
Westberg, K. L., 361
Westefeld, J. S., 513
Westney, O. E., 420
Westra, T., 148
Whalen, C.K., 358
Whishaw, I. Q., 126
White, B. L., 148, 208, 214
White, G., 508
Whitely, J. M., 399
Wichstrom, L., 510
Widom, C. S., 241, 519
Wierzbicka, A., 508
Wiesel, T. N., 10
Wilcox, T., 161
Wilde, J., 397
Wilkening, F., 454
Wilkinson, L., 55
Wilkinson, S., 360
Willatts, P. 160
Williams, C., 508
Williams, E. M., 453
Williams, E. R., 327
Williams, S. W., 371
Williams, W. M., 6
Willmore, J. H., 332
Wilson, M. N., 289
Wilson, R., 369

Wimmer, H., 261
Windle, M., 518
Windle, R. C., 518
Wing, R. R., 329, 331
Winick, M., 101
Winner, E., 272, 360, 361, 469
Winsler, A., 375
Wissmann, D. A., 334
Wohlwill, J. F., 454
Wojtkiewicz, R. A., 473
Wolf, A. E., 494, 504
Wolf, D. P., 314
Wolfe, B., 428
Wolfe, D. A., 239
Wolfner, G. D., 239
Wolin, S. J., 444
Wondersman, L., 429
Wong, M. M. T., 510
Woodall, K. C., 332
Wooddell, G., 460
Woods, N. S., 104
Woody, E. Z., 330
Woody-Ramsey, J., 256
Woollett, A., 195
Wordon, P. E., 291
Wright, C., 134
Wright, J. C., 269
Wright, J. L., 369, 370, 371, 380
Wright, L., 54
Wu, P., 441
Wunderlich, K. C., 414
Wyatt, J. F., 423, 424, 425, 502, 504
Wynbrandt, J., 84

Yakovlev, P. I., 422
Yang, B., 513
Yarrow, M. R., 47
Yates, J., 424
Yates, M., 482

Yelland, N., 284
Ying, Y. W., 500
Yingling, J. L., 147
Yirmiya, N., 193
Yoshikawa, H., 388
Yasumoto, J., 472
Young, K., 372
Young, R., 399
Young, S. W., 142
Young, T. J., 443
Youngblade, L. M., 196, 291
Younger, B. A., 165
Youniss, J., 482, 505
Yule, W., 399

Zabin, L. S., 429
Zack, P. M., 329
Zahn-Waxler, C., 23, 78, 306, 510
Zallen, D. T., 92
Zamansky-Shorin, M., 460
Zammit, G., 436
Zani, B., 421
Zaragoza, M. S., 467
Zaretsky, E., 197
Zaslow, M. J., 292
Zeanah, C. H., 189
Zelazo, P. D., 161, 304
Zeman, J., 509
Zeskind, P. S., 101
Zigler, E., 264
Zigler, E. F., 24, 239
Zigmond, N., 472
Zill, N., 270, 389
Zimmerman, J. K., 514
Zoccolillo, M., 428, 519
Zoerink, D. A., 482
Zuckerman, H., 487
Zuckerman, M., 424

SUBJECT INDEX

A

AB search error, 161, 535
ABAB design, 55, 535
Abortion
  attitude study, 43, 47
  of defective child, 88
Abstract thinking, 454
Accidents to preschoolers, 236, 238
Accommodation, 17, 535
Achievement
  need for, 349, 541
  parental influence, 352, 354
  peer influence, 351
  student attributes, 349–350
  traits, 355
Acquired immune deficiency syndrome (AIDS), 65, 106, 431–434, 535
Acting-out behavior, 402–403
Adonis complex, 439
Adoption, 87
Affection, lack of, the effect on children, 235
African skill-building, 385
Age
  as developmental variable, 43, 44, 46, 58
  of mother at conception, 100–101
  of viability, 98, 535
Aggression, 300–301
  hostile, 301, 539
  instrumental, 301, 540
  minimizing, 303
  modeling, 302
  rough-and-tumble play, 321, 324–326, 543
Aggressiveness study, 52–54
AIDS, 65, 106, 431–434, 535
"Albert and the White Rat" study, 21–22, 165
Alcohol use during pregnancy, 104–105
Amniocentesis, 86, 87, 535
Amniotic fluid, 96, 535
Anal stage, 188, 535
Analytical intelligence, 19, 535
Androgenous, 498–499, 535
Androgens, 224
Anemia in children, 131, 134
Anger management in preschoolers, 300–301
Animistic thinking, 252, 535
Anorexia nervosa, 438, 535
Anoxia, 112, 535
Anxieties and emotional development, 398–400
Apgar scale, 111, 535
Assimilation, 17, 535
Athletics. *See* Sports
Attachment, 211
  adolescent and parent, 502–503
  avoidant, 193, 535
  background, 189
  disorganized/disoriented, 194, 537
  fathers as attachment figures, 194–196
  importance of, 189–192
  influential conditions, 200–201
  measuring, 193–194
  to mothers, 289–290, 293
  nonparental caregivers, 196–200
  resistant, 194, 543
  secure, 192–193, 201, 543
  self-concept, 207–209, 306–309, 406–407, 411
  separation anxiety, 200, 543

Attention deficit hyperactivity disorder (ADHD), 357–359, 535
Attention span
  middle childhood, 344–345
  preschooler, 255–256
Attribution of prosocial characteristics, 305, 535
Attrition, 45, 535
Authoritarian parenting, 294, 297, 298, 535
Authoritative parenting, 294, 295, 296, 535
Autism, 356–357, 535
Autistic savant, 356, 535
Autonomy versus shame and doubt, 188, 535
Avoidant attachment, 193, 535

B

Babbling, 176, 177, 535
Babinski reflex, 111, 535
Bandura, Albert, 22, 302
Bandura's social learning theory, 165
Barbie dolls as cause of eating disorders, 438–439
Basic trust versus mistrust, 188, 535–536
Bayley Scales of Infant Development, 168
Bed-wetting, 228
Bent twigs and fallen fruit, 6–9
Between-subjects design, 45, 536
Bias
  confirmation, 284, 536
  experimenter, 38, 538
Bilingualism, 374–375
Binet, Alfred, Stanford-Binet Intelligence Scale, 167, 168, 262, 263
Bioecological model, 12, 536
Bipolar disorder, 81, 536
Birth order, 263, 286–289
Birth process, 108–110, 118
Bladder and bowel control, 138–139, 188
Blank slate concept of the mind, 7, 16–17
Blastocyst, 96, 536
Blind experimentation, 38, 39, 536
Bodily self, 205, 536
Body growth
  adolescents, 418–422, 446
  infants, 125–126, 151
  middle childhood, 316–318, 336
  preschoolers, 218, 241
Body image, 438–440, 522
Bold temperament, 75, 78
Bonding, 114, 116, 118, 190, 536
Bottle-feeding, 133–134
Bowel and bladder control, 138–139, 188
Bowlby, John, 189, 197
Boys and Girls Clubs, 521
Brain. *See also* Intelligence
  cellular make-up, 127–128, 151
  damage, 130
  development before birth, 98, 100
  development after birth, 219–223, 241
    activities for coordination of functions, 222–223
    effect of computers, 370
    effect of television, 334
    handedness, 220
    hemispheric specialization, 219–220
    in middle childhood, 318, 336
    perceptual advances, 221–223

    early experience and brain development, 172
  functions, 129–130
  growth during adolescence, 422–423, 446
  growth spurt, 129–130, 536
  hemispheres, 128, 219–220
  optimal environment for development, 173
  scans for information on brain development, 14
  structures, 128–129
Brainstem, 128, 536
Breast-feeding, 133–134
Breech position, 110, 536
Brigham, Thomas, 511
Bronfenbrenner, Urie, 12
Bulimia, 438, 536

C

Calming practices and emotional development, 203–204
Canalization, 81–82, 89, 536
Caregivers
  and infant attachment, 196–201
  safety tips, 237, 238
Career development for adolescents, 483–487, 489
Case study method, 54–55, 536
Castration anxiety, 282, 536
CAT scans, 14
Categorization, 345, 536
Centration, 250–251, 536
Cephalocaudal, 125, 126, 536
Cerebellum, 128, 129, 536
Cerebral cortex, 128, 536
Cerebrum, 129
Cesarean delivery, 110, 536
Change
  quantitative vs. qualitative, 5
  vs. constancy, 4–5
Child abuse
  defined, 238, 536
  statistics, 239
  study, 52–54
Child development studies, 33–34, 55
  alternative experimental designs, 52–55, 59
  developing and testing beliefs, 33–34
  ethics of experimentation, 49–52, 58
  experimental variables, 47–49
  measurement, 42–47, 58
  reporting research findings, 55, 59
  scientific method and experimental design, 34–42, 52–53, 58
Child neglect, 238, 536
Childbirth process, 108–110, 118
Choking on foods, 230
Chomsky, 174, 180–181
Chorionic villus sampling, 86, 87, 536
Chromosomes
  anatomy of, 66
  anomalies, 70–72, 89
  defined, 536
  X and Y, 71–72, 88
Circular reaction
  defined, 159, 536
  primary, 160, 163, 542
  secondary, 160–162, 163, 543
  tertiary, 162, 163
Classical conditioning, 20–22, 165, 536

Cliques in adolescent relationships, 506
Clinical case studies, 54–55, 536
Coding system for behaviors, 49
Codominance, 67–68, 536
Coevolution, 65
Coghill, G. E., 15
Cognitive development of adolescents, 453
　career development, 483–487, 489
　formal operational reasoning. *See* Piaget's formal
　　operational reasoning
　information-processing, 465–467, 488
　learning. *See* Learning during adolescence
Cognitive development of infants, 16–22, 27, 158
　infant learning, 164–167, 180
　intelligence, 167–174, 180
　language and communication, 174–179, 180–
　　181
　processing of information, 18–19, 163–164, 180
　sensorimotor intelligence, 158–163
Cognitive development of middle childhood, 16–
　22, 27, 342
　attention span, 344–345
　children with disabilities, 352–353, 356–360
　creatively gifted children, 362–365
　effect of computers, 369–373
　home schooling, 365–369
　information processing, 18–19, 344–346, 376
　intellectually gifted children, 360–362
　intelligence, 346–348, 376–377
　language, 373–375, 377
　learning and achieving, 349–352, 376–377
　memory, 345–346
　Piaget's concrete operations, 342–344, 376
Cognitive development of preschoolers, 16–22, 27,
　247–248
　emotional intelligence, 265–271
　information processing, 18–19, 255–262, 274–
　　275
　intelligence, 262–265, 275
　language development, 271–274, 275
　Piaget's preoperational thought, 248–254, 274,
　　542
　Vygotsky's sociocultural theory, 18, 254–255,
　　274, 544
Cohort, 43, 44–46, 58, 536
Combinatorial reasoning, 454, 536
Common sense, 20
Communication development. *See* Language and
　communication development
Community after-school programs, 521
Competence
　defined, 386, 536
　development of, 386–387, 410
　and self-concept, 207–209, 306–309, 406–407,
　　411
Complications of neonates, 118
　insufficient oxygen, 112
　low birth weight, 112
　premature, 112, 116–117
Computer-assisted instruction, 370, 536
Computers and cognitive development, 369–373
Conception, 68, 70, 536
Concrete operations, 342–344, 376, 536
Conditioning
　classical, 20–22, 165, 536
　operant, 22, 165
Confirmation bias, 284, 536
Confounded variables, 44, 536
Connectionist perspective of learning, 18–19
Conscience, 24, 537
Conscious states of infants, 130–131, 151
Conservation, 250, 251
Constancy vs. change in developmental study, 4–5
Continuity vs. discontinuity in developmental
　study, 5–6

Control
　defined, 537
　of the experimental situation, 35
　group, 36, 537
Convergent thinking, 362, 537
Conversation development, 273–274
Cooing, 176, 537
Coronary-prone personality, 332
Corpus callosum, 129, 220, 537
Correlational studies, 53–54, 537
Crack babies, 104
Creative intelligence, 19, 537
Creatively gifted children, 362–365
Crib death, 131
Crisis, 25, 537
Cross-sectional experimental design, 44, 46, 58,
　537
Crowds in adolescent relationships, 506
Crying and emotional development, 203–204
Cults and adolescents, 507–508
Cultural evolution, 65
Culture
　influence on education, 351–352
　influence on school performance, 471
　and relationship development, 289
　and skill-building, 384–385
　study of differences, 10–12
Culturally relative vs. developmentally universal,
　9–12
Cystic fibrosis, 84

D
Dangerous behavior by adolescents, 423–425,
　446
D.A.R.E. drug-resistance program, 521
Darwin, Charles, 15, 64–66, 360
Date rape, 434–435, 537
Dating for adolescents, 506–507
Day care
　and attachment, 196–200
　　evaluation of day care facilities, 198–199
　　influence of, 197–199
　　separation anxiety, 200, 543
　effect on intelligence, 263–264, 266–267, 275
Decentration, 343, 537
Decision making by adolescents, 460–465
Decision tree, 464–465
Deductive reasoning, 253–254, 455–456, 537
Defense mechanisms, 24, 537
Deferred imitation, 166, 537
Deoxyribonucleic acid (DNA), 66–67, 537
Dependent variable, 35, 537
Depression
　adolescent, 509–512
　and emotional development, 400–402
　and infant stimulation, 147–148
Deprivation dwarfism, 235, 240, 537
Depth perception, 141–142, 537
Descartes, René, 16
Descriptive statistics, 41–42, 537
Development quotient, 168, 537
Developmental psychology, 2–4, 26, 537
Developmental study, 4, 26
　constancy vs. change, 4–5
　continuity vs. discontinuity, 5–6
　developmentally universal vs. culturally relative,
　　9–12
　nature vs. nurture, 6–9
　quantitative vs. qualitative change, 5
　single vs. multiple causes of changes in children,
　　12–13
　study behaviors, 13–15
　study thoughts, 13–15
Developmental systems, 12
Developmental variables, 43–44, 46, 58

Developmentally appropriate software, 370, 537
Developmentally universal vs. culturally relative,
　9–12
Deviation intelligence quotient (DIQ), 168, 537
Diabetes, 84
Dieting and eating disorders, 437–440
Diets for middle childhood, 329–331
Differentiation, 96, 537
Difficult child, 75, 537
Disabilities
　attention deficit hyperactivity disorder (ADHD),
　　357–359, 535
　autism, 356–357, 535
　learning disabilities, 359–360, 376–377, 474–
　　475, 540
　mental retardation, 352–353, 356–360
Discontinuity vs. continuity, 5–6
Dishabituation, 164–165, 537
Disorganized/disoriented attachment, 194, 537
Divergent thinking, 362, 537
Divorce and remarriage, 388–390
Dizygotic or fraternal twins, 70, 89, 537
DNA, 66–67, 537
Dominance hierarchy, 321, 537
Dominant genes, 66, 537
Double-blind experimentation, 39, 537
Down's syndrome
　among babies of older mothers, 101
　chromosomal anomaly, 70–71
　behaviors of mothers, 48–49
　defined, 84, 537
Drawings by preschoolers, 225–226
Dropping out of school, 472–473
Drug use
　by adolescents, 441–445
　D.A.R.E. program, 521
　by mothers during pregnancy, 103–105, 108
Dualism, 16, 537
Dyslexia, 359, 537–538

E
Easy child, 75, 538
Eating
　behaviors and television, 334–336
　disorders in adolescents, 437–440
　habits of preschoolers, 229–233
Ectoderm, 97, 538
Ectopic pregnancy, 97, 538
Ego, 24, 538
Ego-ideal, 24, 538
Egocentric speech, 254
Egocentrism, 252–253, 456–458, 538
Elaboration, 466
Electra complex, 282, 538
Embryo
　defined, 538
　described, 97, 99
　transfer, 70
Embryonic disk, 96, 538
Embryonic stage of growth, 97
Emotional development, 23–25, 27, 201, 211–
　212
　anger and aggression, 300–301, 302–303
　emotional states, 202–203
　fears, 301, 304
　infant crying, 203–204
　Maximally Discriminative Facial Movement
　　Coding System (MAX), 202, 540
　moral development. *See* Moral development
　preschoolers, 300–304, 310
　responding to others, 204–205
　self-concept, 207–209, 306–309, 310, 406–407,
　　411
　self-esteem. *See* Self-esteem
　stability, 288

Emotional intelligence, 265–271
  characteristics, 266
  defined, 538
  development of, 307
Emotional quotient (EQ), 307–309, 311
Emotional regulation, 394, 508–509, 538
Emotional state of pregnant women, 102, 107–108
Emotionality, 394–395
  acting-out behavior, 402–403
  depression, 400–402
  development, 394–395, 411
  excessive, 395, 398–403
  fears and anxieties, 398–400
  negative, 396–397
  normal, 395
Emotions in adolescents, 508–514, 528–529
Emphatic concern, 78, 538
Empiricism. *See* Scientific method
Employment
  for adolescents, 478–480
  career choices, 486–487, 489
  transition from school to work, 484–485
Endoderm, 97, 538
Environmental hazards
  and a developing fetus, 106–107, 108
  lead poisoning, 234–235
  secondhand smoke, 235
Epinephrine, 331, 538
Equilibration, 159, 538
Erikson, Erik, 25, 188, 282–283, 384, 495–497
Ethics of experimentation, 49–52, 58
  informed consent, 51, 539–540
  protection from harm, 50–51
  the right to privacy, 52
  the right to truth, 52
Ethnicity and identity formation, 500
Ethology, 15, 538
Event sampling, 49, 538
Evolution, 64–66, 88
Exercise during pregnancy, 102
Experimental design, 34–35
  alternative designs, 52–53, 59
  controlling the effects of history, 36
  correlational designs, 53–54
  cross-sectional, 44, 46, 58, 537
  generalizability, 36–37, 539
  intervention effects, 40, 540
  longitudinal, 44, 45, 46, 58, 540
  objectivity, 38, 541
  placebo effect, 39, 542
  scientific method, 34–35, 58
  sequential, 46–47, 58, 543
  single-participant, 54–55, 543
  single-subject studies, 54–55
  standardization of procedures, 39, 544
  statistical analysis, 41–42
  time-lag, 44, 45–46, 58, 544
  true experimental design, 40–41, 545
  variables, 47–49
Experimental group, 36, 538
Experimental variable, 35, 538
Experimenter bias, 38, 538
Extinction, 22, 538
Extracurricular activities for adolescents, 477–478, 482–483
Extraneous variable, 35, 538
Extraversion, 287
Extrusion reflex, 132, 538

F
False memories, 257–260
Family constellations, 388–390
Fast mapping, 271–272, 538
Fathers

as attachment figures, 194–196
  contributions during pregnancy, 107–108
  relationships to preschoolers, 291–292
Fears, 301, 304, 398–400
Feeding of infants, 191
Fertilization, 68, 70
Fetal alcohol syndrome (FAS), 104–105, 538
Fetal stage of growth, 98–100
Fetoscopy, 85–86, 538
Fetus
  defined, 538
  environmental hazards, 106–107, 108
  stage of development, 98–100
  vulnerability to teratogens, 103
Filtering software, 373, 538
Fincham, 354–355
Fine motor skills, 137–138, 225, 538
Fishing error, 46, 538
Fong, 432
Foreclosure, 497, 538
Formal operational reasoning, 453–454, 538. *See also* Piaget's formal operational reasoning
Foster care, 240–241
Fragile X syndrome, 71, 72, 538
Freud, Anna, 495, 508
Freud, Sigmund
  emotional development, 23
  introspection, 13, 540
  personality development, 7, 8, 187–188, 281–282, 384, 410
  psychosexual influences, 495
  theory of psychosexual development, 24–25, 542
Friendships
  in adolescent relationships, 506
  and personality development, 391–392
Full inclusion, 356, 538
Fussy babies, soothing strategies, 144–145

G
Gender
  and aggression, 301
  body image, 522
  and computer use, 371
  constancy, 283, 538
  developmental differences, 126
  differences in middle childhood, 320
  identity, 283–286, 498–500
  roles, 283–286, 538
  schema, 283–284, 538
  schema theory, 284, 539
  stability, 283, 539
  stereotypes, 471–472, 483, 487
  and violence, 519
Gene therapy, 83
General adaptation syndrome, 331, 539
Generalizability, 36–37, 539
Genes, 64, 88–89
  defined, 66, 539
  dominant, 66, 537
  heterogenous, 66, 539
  homogenous, 66, 539
  influence on attributes and conditions, 72–81
    intelligence, 79–80
    physical appearance, 72–73
    psychological disorders, 80–81
    temperament, 73–79
  recessive, 66, 542
Genetic counseling, 83–88, 90
  defined, 539
  developmental defects, 84
  testing procedures, 85–88
Genetic engineering, 82–83, 89, 539
Genie's story, 175

Genital stage, 495, 539
Genotype, 66, 539
German measles during pregnancy, 105
Germinal stage of growth, 96–97
Gesell, Arnold, 15
Gifted children, 360–365
Gilligan, Carol, 405
Glia, 130, 539
Goal-directed behavior, 160, 539
Grammar development, 273, 374
Grasping reflex, 111, 539
Grasps
  pincer, 138, 542
  ulnar, 138, 545
Gross motor skills, 137, 138, 224–225, 242, 539
Growth of children, 125–126, 151, 218
Growth spurt
  brain, 129–130, 536
  physical, 418

H
Habituation, 164–165, 539
Ham, 510
Handedness, 217, 220
Handicaps. *See* Disabilities
Handwriting skills, 319, 374
Harlow, Harry, 190, 192
Head Start Project, 264–265
Health issues of middle childhood, 326–336, 337
Health needs of preschoolers, 242
  eating habits, 229–233
  nutrition, 228–229
  sleep, 226–229
Health problems of preschoolers, 242–243
  accidents and injuries, 238
  environmental exposures, 234–235
  illness, 233–234
  lead poisoning, 234–235
  maltreatment, 238–241
  secondhand smoke, 235
  stress, 235
Hearing development, 142
Height in body growth, 125–126, 218
Helplessness orientation, 350, 539
Hemophilia, 84
Herpes, 106, 539
Heterogenous genes, 66, 539
Hierarchal classification difficulty of preschoolers, 253
History, 36, 539
HIV. *See* AIDS
Hokada, 354–355
Holophrase, 177, 539
Home Observation for Measurement of the Environment (HOME) inventory, 170–171, 180
Home schooling, 365–369
Homogenous genes, 66, 539
Horizontal-vertical illusion, 10
Hostile aggression, 301, 539
Hot tubs and the developing fetus, 107
Huntington disease, 84
Hyaline membrane disease, 112
Hyperactivity, 358
Hypothalamus, 128–129, 539
Hypothetical reasoning, 454

I
Id, 24, 539
Ideal self, 407, 539
Idealism of adolescents, 457–458
Identification, 282, 539
Identity
  achievement, 497, 539
  diffusion, 497, 539
  and ethnicity, 500

and gender, 498–500
versus role confusion, 496–497, 539
Illness of preschoolers, 233–234
Illusion of horizontal and vertical lines, 10
Imagery, 345–346, 539
Imaginary audience, 458, 539
Imaginary friends, 249
Imitation, 165–167, 174
Immediate memory, 256
Immersion, 374–375, 539
Immunizations, 234
Implantation, 96, 539
Imprinting, 81, 539
In vitro fertilization, 70
Independent variable, 35, 539
Individuation process, 496
Induction, 305, 539
Inductive reasoning, 253, 539
Industry versus inferiority, 385, 539
Infantile amnesia, 164, 539
Inferential statistics, 41–42, 539
Information-processing
adolescent, 465–467, 488
history of approach, 18–19
infant, 163–164, 180
middle childhood, 344–346, 376
preschooler, 255–262, 274–275
Informed consent, 51, 539–540
Initiative versus guilt, 283, 540
Injuries to preschoolers, 236, 238
Instrumental aggression, 301, 540
Intellectualization, 495
Intelligence, 19–20
analytical, 19
common sense, 20
creative, 19, 537
development of, 167–174, 180
effect of birth order, 263
effect of day care and preschool, 263–265, 275
effect of home environment, 263
emotional, 265–271, 538
genetic influence, 79–80
gifted children, 360–362
individual differences, 262–265
middle childhood, 346–348, 376–377
practical, 19–20, 542
predicting individual differences, 169–171, 174
preschoolers, 262–265, 275
sensorimotor. *See* Sensorimotor intelligence
testing, 167–168, 262, 346–348
Intelligence quotient (IQ), 19, 168–171, 174, 346–348, 540
Interactional synchrony, 192–193, 540
Intermodal perception, 146, 540
Internet use and child development, 372–373
Internships for adolescents, 482
Intervention effects, 40, 540
Introspection, 13, 540
Introversion, 287
Intuitive thought substage, 249, 540
Invincibility fable, 458, 540
Invulnerable child, 207, 540
Irreversibility, 250, 540
Isolettes for preterm infants, 112–113

J
Japan
educational practices, 351, 363–364
preschool programs, 267–268
school phobia, 399–400
Jemmott, 432
Jobs
for adolescents, 478–480
career choices, 486–487, 489
transitions from school to work, 484–485

Jonesborough school shooting, 404
Jung, Carl, 282
Juvenile delinquency, 516–521, 529

K
Kaczynski, Ted, 360
Kant, Immanuel, 16
Karotype, 85, 540
Kaufman Assessment Battery for Children
(K-ABC), 347, 348, 540
Klinefelter's syndrome, 71, 540
Kohlberg, Lawrence, 405
Kwashiorkor, 134, 540

L
Lactose tolerance and natural selection, 65, 541
Lamaze method of childbirth, 109, 540
Language acquisition device, 174, 540
Language and communication development, 180–
181, 271, 275
acquiring language, 176–179
adolescents, 469
conversation, 273–274
grammar, 273, 374
middle childhood, 373–375, 377
preschoolers, 271–274, 275
theories, 174–176
vocabulary, 271–272, 373
Larson, 510
Latency stage, 384, 540
Lead
and the developing fetus, 106–107
poisoning, 234–235
Learning
adolescent. *See* Learning during adolescence
defined, 20
disabilities, 359–360, 376–377, 474–475, 540
by infants, 164–167, 180
observational, 22, 541
perceptual, 221–223, 541
Learning during adolescence, 467–468, 488–489
dropping out of school, 472–473
effects of peers, 476–477, 481
extracurricular activities, 477–478, 482–483
language skills, 469
learning disabilities, 474–475
mathematics, 469–472
parental involvement, 473, 476, 480–481
part-time jobs, 478–480
secondary schools, 468–469
society direction, 481–483
Leboyer method of childbirth, 110, 540
Level of significance, 42, 540
Locke, John, 7, 13, 16
Locomotor skills, 137, 540
Logic of adolescents, 457–458
Long-term memory, 256–257, 540
Longitudinal experimental design, 44, 45, 46, 58,
540
Low birth weight babies, 112
Lymph system, 218–219, 540

M
Mahler, Margaret, 205
Mainstreaming, 353–356, 540
Maltreatment, 238–241
causes of, 239
effects of, 239–241
interventions, 240–241
Manic-depressive disorder, 81
Marasmus, 134, 540
Marcia, James, 497
Mastery orientation, 350, 540
Matched designs, 326, 540
Maternal factors in prenatal development, 100–102

Mathematics skills of adolescents, 469–472
Maturation, 36, 46, 421–422, 540
Maximally Discriminative Facial Movement Cod-
ing System (MAX), 202, 540
McBride, Hazel, 474
McGruff program, 521
Mead, Margaret, 494–495
Measurement of child development, 42–47, 58
Medula, 129
Meiosis, 68, 69, 71, 540
Memory
adolescent information-processing, 465–467
cultural effect on skills, 10
effect of suggestions, 258
false, 257–260
immediate, 256
long-term, 256–257, 540
middle childhood, 345–346
selective memory, 466, 543
short-term, 256, 543
strawberry experiment, 34–41, 47
Menarche, 317, 419–420, 421, 439, 540
Mendel, Gregor, 66
Mental representation of sensorimotor intelligence,
162, 163
Mental retardation, 352–353, 356–360
Mercury and the developing fetus, 107
Mesoderm, 97, 540
Meta-analysis, 80, 540
Midbrain, 129
Mind, theory of, 209, 260–262, 544
Mitosis, 68, 69, 540
Monkey attachment experiment, 190, 192
Monozygotic or identical twins, 70, 89, 541
Montessori method, 268, 541
Moral development
adolescent, 515–516, 529
early childhood, 304–306, 310
middle childhood, 403–406, 411
Moral hierarchies, 405, 406
Moratorium, 497, 541
Moro reflex, 111, 541
Mosaicism, 71, 541
"Motherese," 175, 178, 273, 541
Motor development, 152, 242
adolescent, 423, 446
bladder and bowel control, 138–139, 188
fine motor skills, 137–138, 225, 538
gross motor skills, 137, 138, 224–225, 242, 539
handwriting skills, 319, 374
in middle childhood, 318–326, 336–337
theories, 135–136
Mountain scene perspective experiment, 252–253
MRI scans, 14
Multiple births, 68, 70
Muscular dystrophy, 84
Myelin sheath, 127–128, 129, 219, 541
Myopia, 334, 541

N
Natural childbirth, 109–110, 118
Natural selection, 65–66, 541
Naturalistic observational study, 47, 541
Nature vs. nurture controversy, 6–9, 541
Need for achievement, 349, 541
Negative reinforcement, 22, 541
Neonate
complications, 111, 118
insufficient oxygen, 112
low birth weight, 112
premature, 112–113, 116–117
defined, 111, 541
during birth, 109–110
Neural tube, 97, 541
Neurons, 127, 129, 130, 219, 541

Neurotransmitters, 128, 541
Newborn infants, characteristics of, 111, 118
Niche-picking, 82, 541
Nicotine and fetal difficulties, 105, 108
Nightmare, 227–228, 541
Nonorganic failure to thrive, 148, 541
Norms, 167, 541
Nurture vs. nature controversy, 6–9, 541
Nutrition
  adolescent requirements, 436
  during pregnancy, 101–102
  early childhood, 327–331
  infant, 131–135, 151–152
  preschoolers, 228–229

O
Obese, defined, 328–329, 541
Obesity
  infant, 135
  middle childhood, 328–331
  preschoolers, 231, 232
Object permanence, 160–161, 541
Objectivity, 38, 541
Observational learning, 22, 541
Oedipus complex, 282, 495, 541
Open classroom, 349, 541
Operant conditioning, 22, 165
Oral stage, 187–188, 541
Oregon school shooting, 390–391, 395, 398, 403–404
Organ system growth rates, 219
Organization, 159, 345, 541
"Others" concept, 209–210
Overextension, 177, 541
Overgeneralization, 397
Overregularization, 273, 541
Ovum, 68, 96–97, 541

P
Parenting
  depressed children, 401–402
  dimensions, 294
  effect on adolescent learning, 473, 476, 480–481
  influence on achievement levels of children, 352, 354
  permissive, 294, 295, 297, 541
  promoting self-esteem, 409–410
  punishers, 22, 298–300, 542
  readiness, 115
  relationships to adolescents, 501–505
  relationships to children, 387–388
  single, 428–430
  styles, 294–298
  support for learning disabled adolescents, 475
  teenage, 429–430
  uninvolved, 294, 295, 545
Participants, defined, 35, 541
Pavlov, Ivan Petrovich, 20–21
PCBs and the developing fetus, 107
Peers
  effect on adolescent learning, 476–477, 481
  influencing achievement levels, 351
  relationships with, 292–294, 390–392, 505–508
Penis envy, 282, 541
Perception, 139, 541. See also Sensory and perceptual development
Perception-bound thought, 250, 541
Perceptual learning, 221–223, 541
Permissive parenting, 294, 295, 297, 541
Personal myth, 458, 541–542
Personality development, 383–384, 410
  of adolescents, 494–500, 527–528
  building skills, 384–385
  child sexual abuse, 392–394

competence, 386–387, 410. See also
  Competence
  defined, 23–24
  emotions, 394–403, 411
  gender identity and gender roles, 283–286, 538
  in infants, 187–188, 210–211. See also Attachment
  moral development. See Moral development
  negative emotions and social status, 396–397
  peer, 390–392
  relationships, 387–394, 410–411, 505–508
  psychodynamic influences, 281–283, 384
  self-concept, 207–209, 306–309, 310, 406–407, 411
  self-esteem. See Self-esteem
  temperament, 73, 281, 309
PET scans, 14
Phallic stage, 282, 542
Phenotype, 67, 542
Phenylketonuria (PKU), 84, 87–88
Phonics approach, 374, 542
Physical development of adolescents, 417
  body growth, 418–422, 446
  brain growth, 422–423, 446
  eating disorders, 437–440
  health issues, 435–445, 447
  motor development, 423, 446
  nutritional needs, 436–437
  puberty, 419–422, 542
  risk-taking behavior, 423–425, 446
  sexuality, 425–435, 446–447
  sleep, 436
  smoking, 440–441
  substance abuse, 441–445
Physical development of infants, 15–16, 27, 124–125
  body growth, 125–126, 151
  brain development, 127–130, 151
  conscious states, 130–131, 151
  difficulties, 150–151, 153
  gender differences, 126
  motor development, 135–139
  nutrition, 131–135, 151–152
  sensory and perceptual, 139–146, 152
  stimulation, 113, 146–150
Physical development of middle childhood, 15–16, 27, 316
  body growth, 316–318, 336
  brain growth, 318, 336
  gender differences, 320
  health issues, 326–336, 337
  motivation for physical activities, 322–323
  motor development, 318–326, 336–337
  nutrition, 327–331
  obesity, 328–331
  organized play, 320–321
  rough-and-tumble play, 321, 324–326, 543
  sports, 320–321, 325
  stress, 331–333
  television, 334–336
Physical development of preschoolers, 15–16, 27, 217
  body growth, 218, 241
  brain development, 219–223, 241
  eating habits, 229–233
  health problems, 233–241, 242–243
  height and weight growth, 218
  motor development, 224–226, 242
  nutritional needs, 228–229
  sleep requirements, 226–229
Piaget, Jean
  concrete operations, 342–344, 376
  effects of reasoning, 12
  reasoning strategies of children, 17–18
  stage theory, 6

theory of learning by children, 349
  view of infant visual perception, 140
  view of learned social rules, 304
Piaget's formal operational reasoning, 453–454, 487–488
  adolescent decision making, 460–465
  combinatorial reasoning, 454, 536
  deductive reasoning, 455–456
  defined, 538
  egocentrism, 252–253, 456–458, 538
  fleeting nature of, 458–460
  hypothetical reasoning, 454
  scientific reasoning, 454–455, 543
Piaget's preoperational thought, 248, 274
  defined, 542
  intuitive thought substage, 249, 540
  limitations, 249–254
  symbolic function substage, 248–249, 544
Piaget's sensorimotor intelligence, 158–159, 163, 164, 179–180
  deferred imitation, 166, 537
  mental representation, 162, 163
  primary circular reactions, 160, 163, 542
  reflexes, 159–160, 163
  secondary circular reactions, 160–162, 163, 543
  tertiary circular reactions, 162, 163
Pincer grasp, 138, 542
Pituitary gland, 129
Placebo effect, 39, 542
Placebo group, 39, 542
Placenta, 96, 109, 542
Plasticity of the brain, 130, 542
Play. See also Motor development
  defined, 320
  ideas for coordination of brain functions, 222–223
  make-believe, 248–249
  organized, for middle childhood, 320–321
  rough-and-tumble, 321, 324–326, 543
  sports, 320–321, 325
Polycystic kidney disease, 84
Polygenic, 68, 542
Positive reinforcement, 22, 542
Potty training, 138–139, 188
Practical intelligence, 19–20, 542
Practice effects, 40, 542
Pragmatics, 273, 542
Predictive statistics, 542
Preformationism, 3, 542
Pregnancy in adolescents, 427–429
Prenatal education, 115
Prenatal environment, 100, 108, 117
  father's contributions, 107–108
  maternal factors, 100–102
  teratogens, 102–107, 544
Prenatal stages of growth, 95, 117
  embryonic, 97
  fetal, 98–100
  germinal, 96–97
Preoperational thought, 248–254, 274, 542
Preschools
  and intelligence, 263–264, 275
  Japanese programs, 267–268
Preterm infant, 112–113, 116–117, 542
Preverbal gestures, 176, 542
Primary circular reaction, 160, 163, 542
Primary sex characteristics, 419, 542
Privacy rights in experiments, 52
Private speech, 254–255, 542
Problem-solving strategies, 462–464
Project Head Start, 264–265
Proximal processes, 13, 542
Proximodistal, 125, 126, 542
Psychodynamic influences on personality development, 281–283, 384, 495

Psychological disorders and genetic influence, 80–81
Psychosexual development, 24–25
Psychosexual theory, 542
Psychosocial development, 25, 188
Psychosocial theory, 542
Puberty, 419–422, 542
Punishers, 22, 298–300, 542
Punishment, vicarious, 22, 545

Q
Q-sort emotionality assessment measure, 396
Qualitative change, 5, 542
Quantitative change, 5, 542

R
Radiation and the developing fetus, 106, 108
Rain Man portrayal of autistic savant, 356
Random assignment, 37, 542
Random selection, 37, 542
Range of reaction, 81–82, 542
Rape, date, 434–435
Rayner, 21
Reading
    adolescent comprehension, 469
    development of vision for, 221
    learning to read and write, 374
Real self, 407, 542
Reasoning, 253–254
Receptive language ability, 177, 542
Recessive genes, 66, 542
Reflexes of newborns and infants
    Babinski, 111, 535
    extrusion, 132, 538
    grasping, 111, 539
    Moro, 111, 541
    rooting, 111, 543
    stepping, 136, 544
    substage of sensorimotor activity, 159–160, 163
Rehearsal, 345, 543
Reinforcement
    negative, 22, 541
    positive, 22, 542
    vicarious, 22, 545
Reinforcers, 22, 543
Relationships, 309–310
    adolescent, 500–508, 528
    culture, 289
    effect of birth order, 286–289
    family constellations, 388–390
    father, 291–292
    mother, 289–290
    parental, 294–300, 387–388, 501–505
    peer, 292–294, 390–392, 505–508
REM (rapid eye movement) sleep, 130, 543
Remarriage and child development, 388–390
Resistant attachment, 194, 543
Respiratory distress syndrome, 112, 543
Reticular formation, 129
Reversibility, 343, 543
Rh factor, 107, 543
Rich, Dorothy, 355
Risk-taking behavior by adolescents, 423–425, 446
Rites of passage, 523–527, 529
    absence of, 525
    characteristics, 524
    defined, 523, 543
    design guidelines, 526–527
    new passages, 525–527
    transitions to adulthood, 527
Rooming-in with newborns, 114
Rooting reflex, 111, 543
Rough-and-tumble play, 321, 324–326, 543

Rousseau, Jean-Jacques, 7, 13
Rubella, 105, 543
Running narrative report, 48, 543

S
Safety tips for child care providers, 237, 238
Samoan society and personality development, 494–495
Sampling
    event, 49, 538
    for experiment participants, 37
    time, 49
Schemes, 17, 543
Schizophrenia, 80–81, 543
School. *See also* Learning during adolescence
    and delinquency, 520
    dropping out, 472–473
    home schooling, 365–369
    lunches, 327, 328
    phobia, 399–400, 543
    secondary schools for adolescents, 468–469
    shooting in Jonesboro, 404
    shooting in Springfield, Oregon, 390–391, 395, 398, 403–404
    truancy, 399
School-to-Work Act of 1994, 485
Schooling techniques, 349–352, 365–369
Schoolwide enrichment model (SEM), 361
Scientific method, 34–35, 52–53
    controlling the effects of history, 36
    defined, 34, 543
    experimental design, 34–35, 58
    generalizability, 36–37, 539
    goal, 35
    intervention effects, 40, 540
    objectivity, 38, 541
    placebo effect, 39, 542
    standardization of procedures, 39, 544
    statistical analysis, 41–42
    true experimental design, 40–41, 545
Scientific reasoning, 454–455, 543
Search for identity, 495–497
Secondary circular reaction, 160–162, 163, 543
Secondary sex characteristics, 419, 543
Secure attachment, 192–193, 201, 543
Selective attention, 255–256, 543
Selective memory, 466, 543
Self-concept, 207–209, 306–309, 310, 406–407, 411
Self-conceptualization, 205, 212
    concept of others, 209–210
    development of, 306–309, 310
    self-concept issue, 207–209
    self-control, 210
    separation-individuation, 205–206, 543
    transitional objects, 206–207, 544–545
Self-control development, 210
Self-efficacy, 324, 543
Self-esteem
    adolescent, 522–523
    defined, 543
    early childhood, 306–309, 310
    middle childhood, 406–410, 411
Self-fulfilling prophecy, 351, 543
Self-identity, 205, 543
Self-objectification, 470–471, 543
Sensation, 139, 543
Sensorimotor intelligence, 158–163
    defined, 543
    mental representation, 162, 163
    primary circular reactions, 160, 163, 542
    processing of information, 18–19, 163–164, 180
    reflexes, 159–160, 163
    secondary circular reactions, 160–162, 163, 543
    tertiary circular reactions, 162, 163

Sensory and perceptual development, 139, 152
    hearing, 142
    infant stimulation, 113, 146–150
    integration of information, 146
    smell, 143
    taste, 142–143
    touch, 143, 146
    vision, 139–142, 221
Separation anxiety, 200, 543
Separation-individuation, 205–206, 543
Sequential experimental design, 46–47, 58, 543
Sex, abstinence vs. safer-sex, 432–433
Sex cells, 68–70, 89
Sex characteristics, development of, 419, 542
Sexual abuse, effect on personality development, 392–394
Sexuality of adolescents, 425, 446–447
    attitudes and behaviors, 425–426
    pregnancy, 427–429
Sexuality-related behaviors, 384
Sexually transmitted diseases (STDs), 431–434
Shapiro, Lawrence, 307
Short-term memory, 256, 543
Shy temperament, 75–78
Sickle-cell anemia, 68, 84
Sidis, William James, 360
Siegel, Linda, 474
Sign, 248, 543
Single causes vs. multiple causes of changes in children, 12–13
Single-participant experimental design, 54–55, 543
Single teenage parents, 427–430
Skills
    in Africa, 385
    building of, 384–385
    fine motor, 137–138, 225, 538
    gross motor, 137, 138, 224–225, 242, 539
    handwriting, 319, 374
    locomotor, 137, 540
    memory, 10
    sports, 320–321, 325, 386–387
    survival, 385
Skinner, 12, 22, 174, 180
Sleep
    adolescent requirements, 436
    bed-wetting, 228
    disturbances, 227–228
    nightmares, 227–228, 541
    requirements, 226–229
    sleepwalking, 228
    terrors, 228, 544
Slow-to-warm-up child, 75, 544
Small-for-date babies, 112, 544
Smell sensory development, 143
Smoking
    in adolescents, 440–441
    during pregnancy, 105, 108
    effects on preschoolers, 235
Social comparison, 407, 544
Social development. *See* Emotional development; Personality development; Relationships
Social referencing, 204–205, 544
Sociocentrism, 404, 544
Sociocultural theory, 18, 254–255, 274, 544
Software
    developmentally appropriate, 370, 537
    filtering, 373, 538
Somnambulism, 228, 544
Soothing behavior and emotional development, 203–204
Spanking as punishment, 298–300
Speech
    egocentric, 254
    private, 254–255, 542
Sperm, 68, 108, 544

Spermarche, 420, 421, 544
Spina bifida, 84
Spinal cord, 129
Sports
    and development of skills, 320–321, 325, 386–387
    and nutritional requirements of adolescents, 436–437
Springfield, Oregon, school shooting, 390–391, 395, 398, 403–404
Stage theory, 6
Standard scores, 168, 544
Standardization, 39, 544
Stanford-Binet Intelligence Scale, 167, 168, 262, 263
Star Trek series intelligence example, 265
Statistical analysis of experiment data, 41–42
Statistically significant, 42, 544
Statistics
    descriptive, 41–42
    inferential, 41–42, 539
    predictive, 542
    significance, 544
Stepping reflex, 136, 544
Stereotyping, 471–472, 483, 487
Sternberg, Lawrence, 19
Stimulation for infants, 113, 146–150
Stimulus generalization, 21, 544
Strange Situation, 193–194, 198, 544
Strawberry memory experiment, 34–41, 47
Stress
    buffer, 333, 544
    coping with, 332–333
    defined, 331, 544
    middle childhood, 331–333
    preschoolers, 235
Stress-relieving techniques and emotional development, 203–204
Structured observational study, 47, 544
Student attributes for achievement, 349–350
Study behaviors, 13–14
Study thoughts, 13–14
Substance abuse by adolescents, 441–445, 521
Sudden infant death syndrome (SIDS), 131, 544
Suicide in adolescents, 512–514
Sulloway, Frank, 287–289
Superego, 24, 544
Supermale syndrome, 71, 544
Survival skill building, 385
Symbiosis, 205, 544
Symbol, 248, 544
Symbolic function substage, 248–249, 544
Synapse, 128, 129–130, 544
Syndromes
    AIDS, 65, 106, 431–434, 535
    Down's. *See* Down's syndrome
    fetal alcohol (FAS), 104–105, 538
    fragile X, 71, 72, 538
    general adaptation, 331, 539
    Klinefelter's, 71, 540
    respiratory distress, 112, 543
    SIDS, 131, 544
    supermale, 71, 544
    Trisomy-21. *See* Down's syndrome
    Turner's, 72, 545
Syntax, 374, 544
Syphilis, 106, 544

T
Tabula rasa, 7, 544
Taste development, 142–143
Tay-Sachs disease, 84

Teacher bias, 350–351
Telegraphic speech, 177, 544
Television
    and children's health, 334–336
    as an educational tool, 269–271, 275
    cause of risk-taking behaviors, 334
Temperament, 73–79
    boldness, 75, 78
    defined, 544
    effect of environment and parenting, 9
    and emotionality, 394–395
    emphatic concern, 78, 538
    and personality development, 281, 309
    shyness, 75–78
    study benefits, 78–79
    types, 74–75
Teratogens, 102–103
    defined, 102, 544
    environmental hazards, 106–107, 108
    fetal vulnerability, 103
    maternal drug use, 103–105, 108
    maternal illness, 105–106
Tertiary circular reactions, 162, 163
Testing
    effect of culture, 347–348
    genetic, 85–88
    intelligence, 167–168, 262, 346–348
Thalamus, 128, 129, 544
Thalidomide, 103, 544
Theory of mind, 209, 260–262, 544
Thymus gland experimental treatment example, 34
Time-lag experimental design, 44, 45–46, 58, 544
Time of measurement, 43–44, 46, 58, 544
Titanic romanticizing behavior, 424
Touch sensory development, 143, 146
Toxoplasmosis, 105, 544
Transductive reasoning, 253, 544
Transitional object, 206–207, 544–545
Transitions from school to work, 484–485
Transitive inference, 343, 545
Treasure, Darren, 322
Tried and true
    achievement style and traits, 354–355
    adolescent depression, 510–511
    aggressive behavior, 302–303
    bonding and adjustment, 190
    brain development, 172–173
    child development study, 56–57
    emotionality, 396–397
    false memory of preschoolers, 258–259
    infant feeding, 191
    learning disabled adolescents, 474–475
    motivation for physical activities, 322–323
    newborn rooming-in and parenting adequacy, 114
    patenting readiness and prenatal education, 115
    preventing injuries, 236
    safer sex practices, 432–433
    safety tips, 237
    shyness, 76–77
    taste and calming fussy babies, 144
    soothing a fussy baby, 145
Trimesters of child development, 98–100
Trisomy-21. *See* Down's syndrome
Truant children, 399
True experimental design, 40–41, 545
Truth in experiments, 52
Turner's syndrome, 72, 545
Twins
    conception of, 68–70
    depression studies, 401
    dizygotic or fraternal, 70, 89, 537

    language development, 271
    monozygotic or identical, 70, 89, 541
    as study subjects, 53–54, 187
Type A behavior pattern, 332, 545

U
Ulnar grasp, 138, 545
Ultrasound, 85–86, 545
Umbilical cord, 96, 109, 545
Unconditional positive regard, 409, 545
Underextension, 178, 545
Undernourishment in children, 134
Uninvolved parenting, 294, 295, 545
Urban League, 521

V
Values development, 515–516, 529
Variables
    confounded, 44, 536
    defined, 35, 545
    dependent, 35, 537
    developmental, 43, 44, 46, 58
    experimental, 35, 538
    extraneous, 35, 538
    independent, 35, 539
Vegetarianism in adolescents, 437
Vicarious punishment, 22, 545
Vicarious reinforcement, 22, 545
Violent offenders, 519
Vision
    depth perception, 141–142, 537
    development for reading, 221
    development of, 139–140
    visual cliff experiment, 141
    visual preferences, 140–141
Vocabulary development, 271–272, 373
Voice, 499
Vygotsky, Lev
    concrete operational reasoning strategies, **344**
    sociocultural theory, 18, 254–255, 274, **544**

W
Watson, John, 7, 13–14, 21
Wechsler Intelligence Scale for Children—III (WISC-III)
    defined, 545
    IQ testing, 347
    scoring system, 168
Wechsler Preschool and Primary Scale of Intelligence (WPPSI), 262
Weight in body growth, 125–126, 218
Weight management foe middle childhood, 329–331
Whole language approach, 374, 545
Within-subject design, 45, 545
World Health Organization (WHO), 197
World War II era perspectives of nurture vs. nature, 7
Writing skills, 319, 374

Z
Zone of proximal development, 18, 170, **171**, 545
Zygote, 68, 96–97, 99, 545